11.25

DISCARDED

Searching for the Invisible Man

Searching for the Invisible Man

Slaves and Plantation Life in Jamaica

Michael Craton
with the assistance of
Garry Greenland

Harvard University Press
Cambridge, Massachusetts
London, England
1978

*Planting canes in
August, under the
constant threat of the
driver's whip.*

Library of Congress Cataloging in Publication Data

Craton, Michael.
  Searching for the invisible man.

  1. Slavery in Jamaica.   2. Worthy Park, Jamaica.
3. Slavery in Jamaica—Biography.   I. Greenland, Garry,
joint author.   II. Title.
HT1096.C7   301.44'93'097292   76-48281
ISBN 0-674-79629-2

To the memory of my mother, Edith Craton

BERMUDA 1609

BAHAMAS 1647

CAICOS ISLANDS

TURKS ISLANDS 1678

Florida

Florida Straits

Windward passage

Dominican Republic

Haiti

Cuba

Yucatan Channel

Mexico

BRITISH HONDURAS 1783

CAYMAN ISLANDS 1660

JAMAICA 1655

C A R I B B E A N

S E A

Panama

Puerto Rico

VIRGIN ISLANDS 1666

BARBUDA 1628

ANTIGUA 1632

ST KITTS 1624

NEVIS 1628

MONTSERRAT 1632

Guadeloupe

LEEWARD ISLANDS

DOMINICA 1763

Martinique

ST LUCIA 1796

ST VINCENT 1763

WINDWARD ISLANDS

BARBADOS 1625

GRENADA 1763

TOBAGO 1815

TRINIDAD 1801

GUYANA 1796

N

SCALE: Miles

0   250

Preface

ALTHOUGH concentrating on one island, Jamaica, and even one plantation, Worthy Park, this book might well have been subtitled An Inquiry into the Nature of Slave Populations, the Lives of Individuals in Slave Society, and the Fate of their Descendants. Though long in the making, it still comes early in the waxing tide of scholarship comparing slave and plantation systems in the western hemisphere, and in its scope it is as yet unique.

The writing provided the excitements, as well as the problems and perils, of pioneering. Yet it was not started entirely from scratch, stemming in part from a book written with James Walvin, *A Jamaican Plantation: The History of Worthy Park, 1670-1970*, the research for which was begun in 1965. The present book is not a defense or even revision of *A Jamaican Plantation*, but, rather, a long-planned refinement and expansion of the social aspects of Worthy Park's history, for which there had been too little time for research and insufficient space in the original book. It constitutes, in sum, an attempt to go beyond the mere description of the plantations and their operation, to delve beneath the shallow contemporary accounts by plantocratic writers, and to discover the lives of the ordinary toilers who made the plantation system possible.

Statistical analysis of West Indian slave populations is by no means new. British West Indian slaves were registered from 1812 onward, and the gathered data were analyzed demographically as early as 1830. Yet, being limited to a period long after the British slave trade ended, these data were scarcely typical. Besides, with few exceptions, analysis was restricted to whole colony populations and used chiefly to demonstrate the alarming decrease in the total number of slaves. How much more valuable, it seemed, would be the records of separate plantations, especially if coming from an earlier period when the slave plantation system was at its height, and if the nominal lists were augmented by details of individuals and of daily life.

Ten years ago the records of Worthy Park Estate seemed uniquely rich and accessible in these respects. They included a dozen ledgers spanning the period from 1783 to 1839, with more than thirty slave lists giving ages, colors, continent of birth, jobs, information on parentage, children, health, and behavior, as well as innumerable details of day-to-day life. Since *A Jamaican Plantation* was published, sources possibly even richer have been uncovered, such as the Barham, Dawkins, Gale-Morant, and Tharp papers from Jamaica, the Newton papers from Barbados, and the Codrington papers from Antigua. But these are only beginning to be tapped, and the analysis of the Worthy Park material has several years' head start.

A resolute beginning was made in Chapter Six of *A Jamaican Plantation*, based on a whirlwind ten weeks' culling of the ledgers by James Walvin in 1968, adding to and revising the work undertaken on a single Worthy Park record book as early as 1914 by the conservative American slave historian Ulrich B. Phillips. Despite the witty disdain of one distinguished Caribbean historian for such cliometrics ("Tchoh man, that's slave work!"), the enterprise has been expanded at least tenfold since 1970. The chief credit for the laborious compilation of data in the present book belongs to Garry Greenland, history graduate of the University of Waterloo, who has been able to identify and provide biographical details for over 1,300 individual slaves. This was achieved by transferring all data from the thirty-four slave lists in the Worthy Park books and from the 1817-1832 Jamaican Register of Returns of Slaves, first onto file cards and then onto well over 10,000 computer cards. Much of the mass of information stored in this biographical bank has been recovered by hand and used in old-fashioned ways. But the tabulation of the stored material through computer programming has been almost entirely owing to the technical skills of Bill Ableson, originally of the Department of Statistics, University of Waterloo. Both of these technical assistants are to be thanked for the way they planned programs and ironed out the inevitable snarls and also for the cheerful manner in which they overcame the difficulties of working with a non-numerate historian who was often an ocean or half-continent away, and whose concept of the project was constantly expanding.

The demographic analysis of the Worthy Park population placed the historian in the exciting position of knowing more about certain characteristics of sets of individuals living in the distant past than anyone alive at that time. But the overall analysis of the slave population—essentially completed during a sabbatical leave in 1972-73—turned out to be only Part One of a three-part book. The individualization of the 1,300 slaves and discriminating use of other material in the Worthy Park ledgers and elsewhere allowed for the recovery of at least an outline of many forgotten lives. Hence the biographical section, Part Two, was added in 1973-74.

The more questions were answered, the more new ones were posed. Even when Worthy Park had been placed in its context, its population analyzed, and the lives of certain individuals reconstructed, the true nature of slavery and the inner lives of the members of slave society still did not stand fully revealed. In the West Indies the slaves were virtually mute. Deprived of literacy, they left no written accounts of their experiences or feelings. There was no equivalent of that mine of first-hand reminiscences gathered in the 1930s from the survivors of the last phase of slavery in the United States and used so brilliantly by Eugene Genovese in *Roll, Jordan, Roll.*

Professional historians must be hesitant to go beyond their traditional evidence; white historians can add few of the intuitions that inform the work of such black West Indian scholars as the poet-historian Edward Kamau Brathwaite. In addition, in the wake of the furor that greeted Robert Fogel's and Stanley Engerman's *Time on the Cross,* particular caution has to be exercised not to infer too much concerning the quality of life and slave psychology from purely statistical data.

The controversial work of Fogel and Engerman did suggest another fruitful possibility, however: that slavery can be better understood by comparing it with what came after emancipation. The fortunate preservation of Worthy Park's early wage records invited a study of the transition from slavery to free wage labor. In this part of the project another history graduate student from Waterloo, Eric Pickering, provided valuable help in research. The findings reinforced the growing certainty, based on more than twenty visits to Worthy Park, that the overwhelming characteristic of life and work around a sugar plantation was not change but continuity. Surely then, it was decided, much about slavery could be learned by investigating the lives, work, and life-styles of the successors—even the direct descendants—of the members of slave society. This led to the final and most fascinating phases of research, though it also presented very different and difficult problems of method and presentation.

Some of the most rewarding excursions undertaken in the course of research had reluctantly to be relegated from the present book. Among these was the stream of genealogical information that began with the engaging statement in a letter from George Weenink of Westland, New Zealand, arriving out of the blue in June 1972: "Though hardly a source of family pride I am a descendant of Elizabeth Price, one of the two illegitimate children of Rose Price." Similarly, much of the material on the later history of the Price family of Worthy Park generously provided by Colonel Robin Rose Price of Tetworth Hall, Ascot, has also had to be filed for future reference.

More directly relevant was material from Jamaica, especially Lluidas Vale, and here the debts to individuals are legion. Most of all is owed to George Clarke of Worthy Park, a true gentleman, who never stinted his help, however much he disagreed with the drift of the research. Gratitude must also be expressed to G. C. Pantry, the Registrar-General of Jamaica, and his family, for help in tracing the descendants of John Price Nash.

The presentation of genealogical material in Part Three departed even further than the biographies in Part Two from the cliometric style of Part One of the book. One more method of research was added when the oral tradition among ordinary countryfolk was tapped, in the quest for modern perceptions of slavery and insights into the lives of slaves. Invaluable here was the interviewing undertaken by Sharon Chacko, a history graduate of the University of the West Indies. Though town-bred, she demonstrated an instinctive flair for the work and established a rapport and sympathy beyond the scope of non-Jamaicans. However, this final phase would not have been possible without the generous cooperation of the people themselves, above all that of Isaac Brown, the most forthright of the Lluidas Vale informants.

Books such as this seem destined to be planned as monographs but to expand and take on a life of their own. Seldom can a simple historian have been led into so many cognate fields—economic, demographic, sociological, anthropological—where he began, and in most cases remained, an innocent abroad. The debts to specialists and others laboring in similar fields, who looked over sections or the whole of the work in progress, are numerous; but special thanks are due to Philip Curtin, Richard Dunn, Stanley Engerman, Barry Higman, Richard Sheridan, Arnold Sio, and James Walvin. Archivists and librarians have been unfailingly helpful; in particular, Clinton Black and his staff at the Archives of Jamaica went far beyond the bare requirements of their duties, as did the personnel of the Jamaican Island Record Office, the Institute of Jamaica, and the West India Committee.

The debt to my mother, to whom this book is dedicated, is still too painful to calculate, and too late to repay. In different ways, innumerable colleagues, students, and other friends have also provided help, advice, and inspiration. Special gratitude is owed to Heather Baker, Madeline Grant, Hugh MacKinnon, John New, Vittoria Sarno, John Stubbs, David Wright, and my brother David, who have served as sounding boards and tuning forks for what must often have been a tedious threnody. But above all, thanks must be expressed—at three books removed from my dissertation—to my doctoral supervisor, Herbert McCready, for his encouragement and his exemplary rigor. It was, indeed, a memory of a marginal comment of his made ten years ago that led to the substitution of "Searching for" in place of "Discovering" in the title of the present book. His untimely death in October 1975 was a severe blow.

In a sense all history writing is work in progress, never completed. As a bridge between *A Jamaican Plantation* and *Searching for the Invisible Man*, some of the arguments and findings have already been presented in papers and articles. Appreciation is due to the organizers of the Association of Caribbean Historians, to Enrique Florescano, Ann Pescatello, Stanley Engerman, and Eugene Genovese, and to the editors of the *Jamaica Journal*, the *Journal of Caribbean History*, *Historical Reflections/Réflexions Historiques*, and *Histoire Sociale/Social History* for what are made by this book mere interim and partial statements.

Even this volume, though as complete as it can be, can hardly claim to be definitive. Its imperfections are a compound of data that, although fuller than elsewhere, are still deficient and programs that were not fully realized because time and resources were not illimitable. However, it is hoped that, coming at a time when comparative studies of slavery, plantations, and plantation society are rapidly proliferating, and when the increasing use of statistics is being termed (mainly by its practitioners) a "cliometric revolution," *Searching for the Invisible Man* provides not only interesting new material but also new methods. Above all, its aim is to bring to the plantation slaves of the British Caribbean and their descendants something like the degree of visibility which similar studies have recently restored to the blacks of the United States.

It may perhaps be seen as an irony that this radical project (radical in the literal sense: concerned with roots as well as branches) has only been made possible through the resources and facilities of one of the "have" countries commonly said in "radical" quarters to be exploiting the "have-nots" of the Caribbean. It is hoped that in expressing sincere gratitude for two grants from the Canada Council and the generous use of the multimillion-dollar computer complex at the University of Waterloo that enabled an English Canadian, three true Canadians, and a Jamaican to complete this book, we are not held to be accomplices in yet one more subtle exploitationist trick.

One critic of *A Jamaican Plantation* asserted that the history of slavery could properly be written only by black persons, and right-thinking black persons at that. Others held that the study of a sugar estate should confine itself exclusively to the black population. In at least two respects this book is likely to dissatisfy even the less extreme of these critics. The Prologue which follows, describing Worthy Park and its history before and after 1838 and placing it in its context, of necessity looks at the estate as an economic unit—the "planter's eye" or "imperialist" view. Blinkered readers might perhaps skip straight to the statistical, demographic, and biographical substance that follows, though to their disadvantage. Even then, sections of all three parts will disappoint them. In line with the ideas of Frank Tannenbaum, Elsa Goveia, Eugene Genovese, and Edward Brathwaite, slave society is conceived as having consisted not solely of slaves but of all elements in polities in which slavery was the mode of production. Accordingly, more than a passing mention continues to be given to the members of the society of Worthy Park and Lluidas Vale who happened, and happen, to be white or of mixed race, as well as those of pure African descent.

M.C.

Waterloo, Ontario

Contents

Contents

Tables

Figures

Maps

Illustrations

Prologue / Worthy Park and Its Context, 1670-1975

NO one estate can properly serve as an example for all unless its degree of typicality is clearly established. For this reason, the geography and history of Worthy Park and its surrounding area must first be placed in the context of the sugar industry of Jamaica and the rest of the West Indies. In certain respects Worthy Park was clearly exceptional. Its continuation and success demonstrated not only the exceptional fertility of Lluidas Vale but also astute management and sheer good fortune. Situated as far inland as any sugar estate established in slavery days, it was not only more isolated than most but bound to be bigger than average in order to offset transportation costs by economies of scale.

The optimal size of any sugar estate in slavery days was constrained by the limitations of eighteenth-century technology, cane husbandry, and slave management. Conditions varied from colony to colony and time to time, but all estates aimed towards the optimum in order to maximize profits. In this respect Worthy Park was entirely typical. That the average West Indian and Jamaican estate was smaller and less efficient than Worthy Park was owing to the fact that few were as compelled by conditions to approach optimal size. Worthy Park was exceptional chiefly in that only by possessing almost optimal local conditions could it ever flourish, or in hard times even survive.

Comparison of sugar plantations in different places and at different times is greatly aided by the fact that sugar technology and cane husbandry, if not labor management as well, have always been remarkably standard, both before and after the changes brought by the Industrial Revolution. Technology was almost static from before the arrival of Columbus and the Spaniards in America until after the ending of slavery in the British Empire. The standard vertical three-roller mill is said to have been invented by a Sicilian, Pietro Speciale of Palermo, as early as 1449. Only minor improvements in milling were introduced in the eighteenth century, such as the *doubleuse* to double-back crushed cane for a second pressing. The use of wind and water as well as animal power was well known in the Mediterranean sugar industry at the time of Columbus, and no advance was made until the invention of the hori-

1

zontal mill and the introduction of steam power into the West Indies in the early nineteenth century—long delayed through lack of capital.[1]

Mills varied in efficiency up to 50 percent according to their power source. Water mills turned fastest, most continuously and reliably, and were cheapest to run once installed; wind power was cheap but capricious as the wind itself; animal power turned mills slowly and was relatively expensive, but efficient as to juice extraction. But planters had no more choice than they were given by the resources available. In dry Antigua, for example, there were no water mills, but nearly every plantation had a windmill, with at least one cattle mill to use when the northeast trade wind failed. In equally stream-less Barbados the trade wind was so reliable that some estates had three windmills, and altogether windmills outnumbered cattle mills ten to one. In Jamaica with its many streams, the most prosperous sugar plantations had water mills, with one or two cattle mills apiece for the peak of the crop season or periods of drought. After 1753 Worthy Park had a water mill, with an aqueduct that never failed to produce running water, and a single cattle mill. Neighboring Swansea and Thetford each had a windmill and two cattle mills.

Before the introduction of the vacuum pan and centrifuge in the nineteenth century, factory technology was almost as static as cane milling. A Cypriot, Sicilian, or Andalusian boilerman would have adapted immediately to the factory illustrated in Richard Ligon's splendid *History of Barbados* (1657), and it was the so-called "Barbados Method" which spread over Jamaica from the time of Governor Mody-ford (1664-1679) onwards. The pace of West Indian operations was rather more intensive than that of the Mediterranean, but the quality of product—mostly consisting of the sticky brown unrefined sugar called muscovado—was actually lower than that of the loaf sugar that trickled into northern Europe from the south during the later Middle Ages. Only in the production of rum from molasses—an incidental function though a profitable one—did West Indian producers differ greatly from those of Mediterranean, though here again the technology, firmly established in the British West Indies by about 1680, did not advance greatly until modern times.

It was not just technology that determined the optimal size of West Indian plantations throughout the slavery period, however, but also the tendency of sugarcane to rot once cut, cane juice to ferment once squeezed, and "unpotted" sugar to molder if not processed fast enough. A factory could be enlarged to boil, cure, and distill the product of up to three mills, but the number and capacity of the mills could not be increased beyond the amount of cane slaves could cut and transport in bullock carts within thirty-six hours. Consequently, the proximity of the canefields to the factory, and their fertility, were important determinants of efficiency, with further improvements in productivity only possible through fertilization, better cane varieties, and the control of disease and pests.

All this, of course, was predicted on the availability of an efficient work force; a large enough number of healthy slaves, and the ability to control them and work them hard. An efficient estate also needed sufficient cattle. Though cheap in terms of the value of human life, slaves represented a large capital investment and a high proportion of plantation running costs. Slave labor was regarded as indispensable, and although planters constantly complained of the dearness of slaves this never seems to have prevented them from recruiting more if other economic considerations demanded and allowed for expansion. In a world where planters tended to regard and treat their slaves as little better than cattle, it was fitting that in some small islands like Barbados where there was little spare land for grazing, it was the shortage of cattle rather than of slaves which helped to limit the size of plantations.

There were certain social, or socioeconomic, factors (for nothing in slave society was wholly divorced from economics) which greatly affected the nature of slave plantations and may have had some effect on plantation size. It was always recognized that slaves could weaken plantations by sickness or low productivity, or sabotage operations directly through rebellion or running away. Writers on plantation husbandry argued whether Africans, new to plantation agriculture and sometimes difficult to control, made better slaves than the Creoles—or island-born—who knew the skills, but also the dodges. It was also often debated whether slaves were healthier, worked harder, and were controlled more easily on small or large estates.

These problems were never clearly resolved. The connection between slave health and plantation size was probably something of a red herring. Slave efficiency was determined by other factors than the numbers employed together, and though large slave populations, particularly those with a high proportion of Africans, could get out of hand, small plantations often had so few whites on them that the forces of control were alarmingly weak. Two important points were, however, generally recognized. It was regarded as socially as well as economically unwise to allow the exigencies of the five-month fury of the sugar crop to lead to the building up of a slave population larger than could be kept from dangerous, and unprofitable, idleness in the intercrop period. Also, because a superfluity of laborers was regarded as bad husbandry and led to the weakening of control, as well as the fact that sugar monoculture determined that plantations tended to have their peak labor demands at the same time, there was practically no movement of slaves between estates.

As a result, slave populations tended towards a social cohesion that matched the economic integration of each plantation. Proprietors quite often owned two or more estates, sometimes contiguous, but this did not lead to social mobility any more than to the consolidation of economic resources. The Codrington estates in Antigua were a rare exception, in that they used Barbuda for the recruitment of new slaves as well as for stock and provisions.[2] A more telling example is provided

3

A Jamaican sugar estate of the Golden Age. The mill, distillery, and boiling house, even the slave hospital, were more substantial than the overseer's house on the hill, let alone the slave huts in the wood behind the factory. Old Montpelier Estate, St. James, from a print by James Hakewill, 1820.

by the Tharp plantations in Trelawny Parish, Jamaica, founded in the 1760s. Here there were no less than seven contiguous sugar plantations, under a degree of joint management but with at least six quite separate factories and seven separate slave populations varying remarkably little in size and composition. Only in the joint breeding of stock and growing of provisions on two other related holdings, and the shipping of sugar to the coast, was there a degree of economic consolidation and consequently some social mobility, as is shown in Table 1.[3]

A modern commentator, Ward Barrett, has estimated that in the eighteenth century it was not economic anywhere in the Caribbean for an estate based on a single factory to exceed 600 acres in canes. With average production standards of one ton per acre (allowing for fallow and the lower yields of cut cane regrown not replanted, called ratoons), this would have meant a top yield of 600 tons of sugar a year. Following the general average of one slave per ton of sugar produced, the total population would be no more than 600 slaves, male and female, young and old, healthy and sick. With the usual balance of one acre in pasture and provision land and one acre of woodland for each acre in canes, this indicated an economic maximum holding rather under 2,000 acres.[4]

As is shown later, Worthy Park came remarkably close to Barrett's optimal maxima before the end of slavery, though this was well above the average even for Jamaica with its plentiful land. On the smaller islands developed first, the maximum practical area, production, and population seem to have been considerably less, and the actual averages smaller still—even after the consolidation for efficiency which occurred in the second stage of the sugar industry's development. Richard S. Dunn recently made a very complete analysis of holdings in Barbados in 1680 which bears this out.[5] In an island only 106,000 acres in extent, with no less than 3,044 property holders and over 840 identifiable plantations,[6] only one planter had 1,000 acres, and the largest 64 planters averaged only 394 acres—many with their holdings split. Only 175 planters had more than 60 slaves. Yet nearly all the 400 or so planters with 50 acres or more and at least 20 slaves had invested in mills and boiling and curing houses.[7] Richard Ford depicted over 1,000 mills in his 1674 map of Barbados. This may have been cartographer's licence to a certain extent,[8] but clearly the island was intensively cultivated, with only the hilly northeast not growing sugar in almost contiguous cane-pieces. From their numbers, the slaves would seem to have been extremely hard-worked, though with the sugar plantations not long established and African importations running at a high level, a very large proportion of slaves would have been healthy young males. Like all small islands, Barbados had the advantage that no plantations were far from the coast, and the consequent ease of shipment, as well as the proximity of mills to fields and the preponderance of windmills, partially account for the comparatively low number of cattle as well as slaves.

With the loss of those outstanding market and production conditions which made Barbados in 1680 "the richest colony in English America"—high demand and good produce prices, cheap slaves and provisions, and easy communications—some further consolidation was inevitable on the principle of economies of scale. Yet Barbados plantations remained relatively small and intensively cultivated. Those of the Leeward Islands, where none of the islands was even as large as Barbados, followed a similar pattern, with a time lag of thirty to forty years, and initial small holdings being consolidated about the time of the first Anglo-French wars, but rarely exceeding 500 acres or 200 slaves.[9]

Neither Barbados nor the Leewards could compete on equal terms with Jamaica—with ten of its twenty-one parishes each larger than Barbados and its fertile acres exceeding those of all other British islands combined—once it was safely settled, capital was found, and the advantage in communications enjoyed by the islands to windward overcome.[10] Yet Jamaica was neither so intensively cultivated nor ever given so heavily to sugar monoculture as Barbados and the Leewards.

In the style familiar in the smaller islands, the earliest Jamaican sugar plantations were close to the coast, the seat of government, and the defense forces. They were also comparatively small. In 1671 Jamaica had 57 sugar plantations and by 1684 as many as 246; but since the total exportation of sugar only rose from 1,000 to 10,000 hogsheads a year during that period, the average plantation was no larger than those of Barbados.[11] In looking at the wills of 198 planters who died between 1674 and 1701, Richard Dunn discovered that the average holding of the 54 definitely identified as sugar planters was only 63 slaves,[12] though doubtless the acreages they had patented without development were relatively huge. Large inland plantations, such as Carey Helyar's Bybrook and Thomas Modyford's estate at Sixteen Mile Walk, were initially failures.[13] A more typical early Jamaican sugar plantation was that which "Lieutenant" Francis Price, probably one of the survivors of the Guanoboa Regiment of the "conquering" Cromwellian forces, developed in Guanaboa Vale, before moving fifteen miles inland to even more fertile Lluidas Vale and becoming the founder of Worthy Park in 1670. Price's original sugar operation boasted merely "4 coppers, 2 stills, 1 mill and millhouse, boiling house, dwelling house, 8 horses, 6 mules, 200 sugar potts, 8 hoggs," and about 50 slaves.[14]

Lluidas Vale, the Worthy Park valley, is a heart-shaped *polje*, or fertile dry valley in limestone country, some eight square miles in extent, situated about five miles to the east of the exact center of mountainous Jamaica. Remarkably level compared with the shaggy, craggy "cockpits" which fringe it, the valley is completely enclosed within the 1,250-foot contour. To leave it for the coast—twenty-eight miles to the south and thirty-two to the north—entails a climb to almost 2,000 feet in any direction. Although there are several large ponds that never dry

2. Lluidas Vale and
Worthy Park Estate, 1972

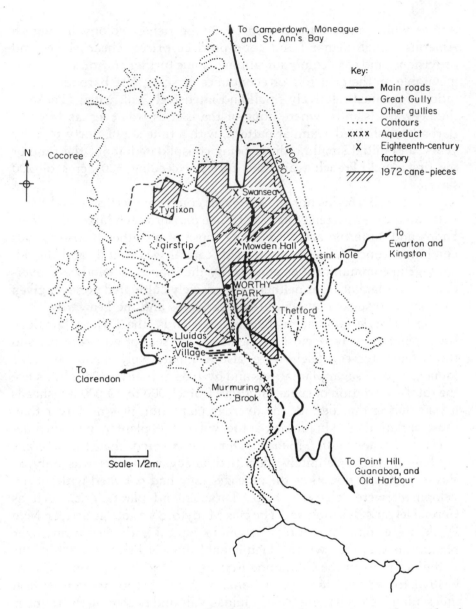

out, there is no permanent surface drainage. In common with much of the limestone interior of Jamaica, the landscape is veined with dry watercourses, leading to the Great Gully which carries off the rare floods by way of a sink hole to the Rio Cobre and the sea. The moderate damming effect of the sink hole has determined that erosion in Lluidas Vale is not severe and that the fertile alluvium around the gullies adds variety to the marl and clay soils characteristic of valleys in karst topography.[15]

Shielded by mountains, Lluidas Vale is spared the worst effects of hurricanes and northerly gales. The altitude guarantees a milder climate than that of the Jamaican lowlands, with an annual mean temperature of 73°, though with a rather greater seasonal and diurnal range. These conditions encourage a vigorous growth in sugarcane. The average

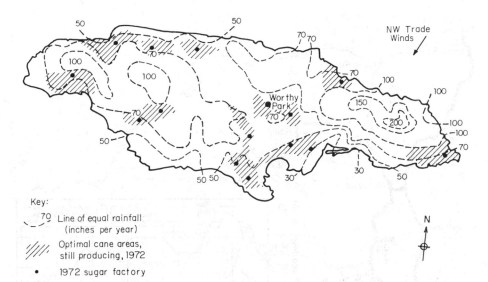

Key:

~~70~~ Line of equal rainfall
     (inches per year)

/// Optimal cane areas,
    still producing, 1972

• 1972 sugar factory

annual rainfall of Lluidas Vale also lies in the 60-70-inch range regarded as ideal for sugar growing. This precipitation, moreover, is particularly reliable—a characteristic related to the forested mountain slopes—so that planting, growing, and harvesting seasons have always been relatively predictable and rarely disrupted. Droughts do occur about once every eight years, but this is only half the frequency at which an irrigation system is regarded as economic.

The natural vegetation of Lluidas Vale before man came there was almost impenetrable tropical forest on the fertile lowland soils, where cane was later grown, shading to dense scrub on the steepest slopes. The least fertile third of the valley (still pasture rather than cane land) was originally saw-grass savanna, fingers of which thrust up into mountain glades. These were the conditions which confronted the first English settlers, who penetrated into Lluidas Vale a few years after the conquest of 1655 from the plantations they had taken over from the Spaniards at Guanaboa Vale. For the aboriginal Arawaks had barely reached the valley, and the few "Spanish" Maroons* who succeeded them had merely run cattle into the savannas and grown subsistence crops on the southern slopes—in an area still called Juan de Bolas after their most famous leader.

Long before development was feasible, the original English settlers were concerned to preempt the potential fertility which Lluidas Vale offered. Aided by a compliant government, no less than twenty individuals registered titles to parcels of the valley between 1665 and 1682. Francis Price was chief among these, with his "patent" for 840 prime acres around the bend of the Great Gully filed on March 13, 1670.[16] By means of sundry further patents, purchases, and encroachments, Price

---

*Maroons (from the Spanish *cimarrones*) were runaway slaves and their descendants, often interbred with Amerindian survivors. They were (and are) found in many West Indian islands, in the Guianas, and even within the present boundaries of the United States.

4. Worthy Park: Communications, 1670-1970s

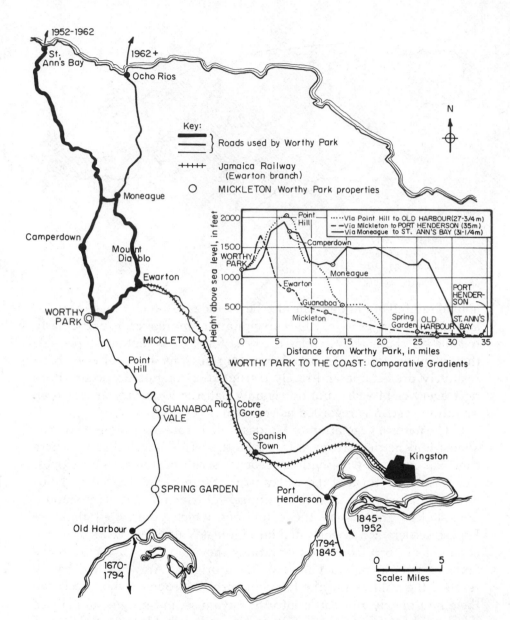

WORTHY PARK TO THE COAST: Comparative Gradients

managed to extend this holding to 1,774 acres (nearly three square miles) by the time of his death in 1689, making it, with Thetford and Swansea, one of the three largest of the five major holdings which by then covered and spilled out of Lluidas Vale (Tydixon and Murmuring Brook being the other two).[17] At least a third of Price's land—called "Worthly Park" on the original plan, though this may have been a misspelling—was later to prove excellent cane land. Yet the founder probably did no more than to set his few spare slaves to clear trees, plant provisions, and graze cattle at what was then called "Luidas Savanna." The time was not yet ripe for the opening up of the Jamaican interior for sugar production. For almost two generations after 1670 Lluidas remained much like the backwoods of the American mainland colonies, beyond the range of trade and easy communications, primitive, and vulnerable to attack—in this case from the proud and wily Maroons, who were not subverted until 1739.

Of the prime requirements for turning Jamaica into a sugar island even more successful than Barbados and the Leewards, the descendants of the self-styled conquerors possessed land in abundance by virtue of having turned themselves into a self-legislating aristocracy, or "plantocracy." Besides equating land with local power, and passing laws which for a time kept white servants as well as slaves firmly in subjection, the plantocratic Assembly quite blatantly authorized roads at public expense to serve their plantations. Lluidas Vale thus obtained its first road suitable for sugar wains in 1740—running to the south coast at Old Harbour by way of Guanaboa Vale—while Francis Price's grandson was a prominent member of the Jamaican Assembly. Water to power a mill and supply the factory came twelve years later, by means of a 2.5-mile aqueduct across neighboring holdings, authorized by another local enactment.

Even more important for the development of sugar plantations than land, roads, and the control of local legislation was the acquisition of a large, cheap labor force. A herd of unpaid laborers under absolute and permanent control—that is, slaves—was clearly preferable, on economic if not social and moral grounds, to the white servants the first settlers sought. Indentured servants were not only difficult to recruit but were also ambitiously restless and with a term fixed on their service, as well as being just as subject to mortality as slaves.

Besides this, once sugar production got fully under way in Jamaica there were never many more white men than were needed for senior and supervisory jobs on the plantations. One of the gradual social developments that occurred during the transition to sugar monoculture was the elevation in status of the white men employed from bondservants to managerial staff, albeit still under fairly binding contracts. "Staff" ranged from the overseer, through such master craftsmen as distillers and head boilermen, down to lowly field bookkeepers. Because of the social power lent them by their scarcity (rather than their color), even the lowliest plantation whites became members of an elite, irreversibly separated from the laborers, who were uniformly both slave and black.*

This important general socioeconomic change was exemplified in the early history of the Price estates. In 1680, a survey of St. John Parish

---

*Throughout this book, the word "colored" is used in the British West Indies' sense to apply to people of *mixed* African and European descent. In line with current United States' usage, the term "black" is preferred to "Negro" (the eighteenth-century word) for those of African descent.

Although West Indians sometimes used "mulatto" loosely, it is consistently used in this book in its technical, legal sense to mean only those with one white and one black parent. Similar precision is accorded the use of "quadroon" (one white, one mulatto parent), "mestee" or "octoroon" (one white, one quadroon parent), and "sambo" (one black, one colored parent). These distinctions are described more fully on page 235.

5. The Expansion of Jamaican Sugar Production: Jamaica around 1710

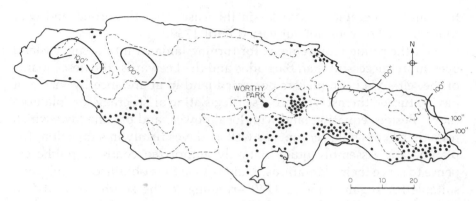

Sources: Adapted from Charles Leslie, *A New History of Jamaica* (London, 1740); Bryan Edwards, *The History, Civil and Commercial, of the British Colonies in the West Indies,* 2 vols. (London, 1793), I.

showed that Francis Price was the head of a community that consisted of one white woman and four children (presumably his own family), fifty-five adult and three child slaves, and seven "servants."[18] This was when Price's operations were concentrated on the embryonic sugar plantation at Guanaboa Vale. Fifty years later, when Worthy Park was fully producing sugar, there were still about as many whites on the plantation, but the number of slaves had quadrupled and the whites were no longer bondsmen but managerial and specialist staff. By 1750 the existence of white servants on Jamaican sugar estates was fairly exceptional.[19]

Both the acquisition of the slave labor force, which such a labor-intensive cultivation as sugar demanded, and the setting up of the relatively expensive "millwork, stillwork, and utensils" of a sugar and rum factory, required substantial sums of capital. This as much as anything slowed the development of the Jamaican sugar industry. To transform a farm to sugar production with the simplest factory took at least five years' profits from the growing of cocoa, tobacco, indigo, or ginger. Where the acreage had been used only for grazing cattle or growing provision crops, the process was even longer. Moreover, the outlay on slaves for sugar production required two or three times as much capital as the factory plant. Yet to a certain extent Jamaican capital was self-generating. Francis Price and his fellows transferred the profits from cattle herding, provision crops, and perhaps privateering, into low intensity export crop production, and from this into the first small sugar works close to the coast. Even Price's modest spread at Guanaboa Vale probably cost £1,200 to set up and may have run three years before a profit was turned. For Worthy Park, which could only be maintained on a far larger scale because of its greater distance inland, the initial cost was probably five times as high, with at least 50 percent of the outlay for slaves and 20 percent for the plant. The outlay for the building of the Worthy Park aqueduct of 1752 alone exceeded the entire cost of Francis Price's first small sugar venture at Guanaboa Vale, and was more than the cost of all the land he acquired in Lluidas Vale.

This scale of capital investment required heavy borrowing and good credit in London. Francis Price had already found this necessary as early as 1667. In order to develop his first sugar enterprise (and per-

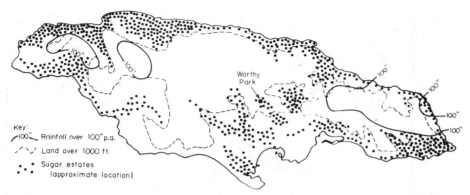

6. The Expansion of Jamaican Sugar Production: Jamaica around 1790

Sources: As for Map 5.

Note: For parish boundaries, see Map 7.

haps to facilitate joint speculations in undeveloped land as well), he had entered into a 50:50 partnership at Guanaboa Vale with William Beckford, scion of an important London merchant banking house and later lieutenant governor of Jamaica.[20] This followed a pattern fairly general throughout the British West Indies, whereby capital was acquired on a permanent system of credit in return for collateral, mortgage, or share of West Indian property, and the control of marketing by mortgagor or London-based partner.

This type of arrangement naturally depended on its profitability to planter and merchant accomplice alike. This in turn depended not only on good husbandry and management by the planter but also on the development of an extremely sophisticated and trustworthy system of credit machinery, on safe, rapid, and reliable communications, reasonable prices for supplies and slaves, and, above all, steady high prices for sugar and rum. The achievement of nearly all these conditions was aided by the fact that although the planters controlled the colonial legislatures, those in the metropolis interested in the "triangle trade" of supplies, slaves, and sugar and rum influenced the imperial government for at least seventy-five years to pass protective legislation and to authorize the naval defense of colonies, shipping routes, and slave-trading areas. Indeed, a whole politicoeconomic network was created while the sugar and slave trades were at their height. Fortunate families such as the Beckfords were merchants, bankers, shippers, planters, and politicians (imperial as well as colonial) too. For their part, the Price family offset the lack of a merchant branch by usually having at least one senior family member absent in England acting as a financial and political agent, while another—most notably, Charles Price, styled "The Patriot," Speaker of the Jamaican Assembly, 1745-1763—aimed to participate at the heart of Jamaican politics and reap its fruits. At the peak, around 1770, the Prices owned eleven estates in Jamaica apart from Worthy Park.[21]

Worthy Park and the two neighboring plantations in Lluidas Vale, Thetford and Swansea, began producing sugar for export between 1715 and 1720. This was part of a general expansion which saw Jamaican sugar exports double in the dozen years after the end of the War of the Spanish Succession and plantations proliferate into the fertile coastal

13

Figure 1. Comparative Sizes of Slave Populations of Four Jamaican Parishes, 1734-1833, Selected Years

Sources: Data for 1734-1760, Edward Long, *The History of Jamaica,* 3 vols. (London, 1774), II; 1787, Bryan Edwards, *The History, Civil and Commercial, of the British West Indies,* 2 vols. (London, 1793), I,229; G. W. Bridges, *Annals of Jamaica,* 2 vols. (London, 1828), II, 561-567; 1833, R. M. Martin, *The British Colonies: Their History, Extent, Condition and Resources,* 5 vols. (London, 1834), II, 188-191.

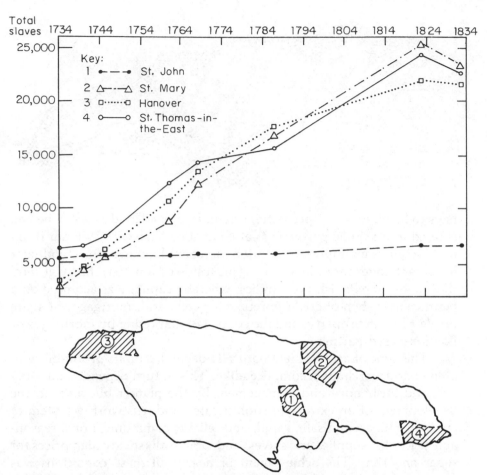

regions of north and west Jamaica.[22] It was only their great fertility and compactness which allowed the Lluidas Vale plantations to offset the great distance inland, and in keeping pace with the other new sugar operations they left the rest of St. John Parish and most of south central Jamaica well behind. In 1684 St. John's had been the third wealthiest of the fifteen Jamaican parishes, with sixteen sugar plantations.[23] This number had been increased to twenty-one by 1721, with a greatly increased total of slaves; but from 1721 both the number of plantations in the parish and its total slave population remained absolutely static to the end of slavery days.[24]

By 1730 Worthy Park was capable of producing 250 hogsheads (187 tons) of sugar a year, with its slave work force of about 200.[25] With 106 steers, 64 cows and calves, 90 mules, 17 horses, and numerous hogs and sheep, stock raising was still an important secondary function. With the building of the Old Harbour road, annual production reached a steady level of 275 hogsheads; but until 1789 the muscovado continued to be shipped to the coast in hessian bags containing one or two hundredweight, rather than in the unwieldy sixteen-hundredweight hogshead barrels.

The production of rum, which turned marginal operations into profitmakers and prosperous plantations into gold mines, became

increasingly important, particularly for inland estates to which it was
uneconomic to export the molasses from which rum was made. Between 1741 and 1744 Worthy Park was already producing an average
of thirty-five puncheons (3,850 gallons) of rum a year. By this time the
estate grossed about £ 6,000 a year, representing an annual profit of
perhaps £ 1,500,* or a return of between 10 and 15 percent on capital.[26]

The introduction of water power in the early 1750s gave Worthy
Park an edge over its neighbors[27] and helped the estate keep well ahead
of the Jamaican average, even during the great surge of expansion
which almost doubled the number of Jamaican sugar plantations and
more than doubled production, between 1755 and 1775. In 1759 one
writer claimed that Jamaica contained "450 sugar plantations, supposed
to produce one with another 89 hogsheads, containing 500 acres each,
is 225,000 acres on average of cane, pasture and woodland."[28] At that
time, Worthy Park was already producing about 300 hogsheads of
sugar and 80 puncheons of rum a year from 1,300 acres altogether, with
250 slaves and 200 cattle. During the following two decades production
was steadily raised to over 350 hogsheads and 125 puncheons in good
years. In the exceptional year of 1776 Worthy Park grossed well over
£ 10,000 from sugar products alone.[29]

At least as important as the building of the aqueduct was the acquisition of Spring Garden Pen near Old Harbour in 1776, which served,
with the original Price holding at Guanaboa Vale, as a second stopping
place on the long road to the coast. At Spring Garden, outgoing produce and incoming supplies could be stored to cut down on the number
of wains and wainmen needed, new slaves "seasoned," sick slaves sent
to recuperate, provisions grown, and cattle grazed and bred. About the
same time, the purchase of the mountain glades of Cocoree and Riverhead, suitable for "Negro provisions" and grazing, made Worthy Park
even more self-sufficient for food supplies and replacement cattle.[30]

The relative size of Worthy Park, its prosperity compared with the
rest of the parish, and the surge ahead of new areas which placed St.
John's a lowly sixteenth in slave population and twelfth in sugar production out of twenty parishes in 1768, are well illustrated in the pioneer
set of statistics published by Edward Long in his *History of Jamaica* in
1774, imperfect though the figures may be.[31] Long showed the twenty-
one sugar plantations of St. John producing an average of 105 hogsheads of sugar a year in 1768, remarkably close to the Jamaican average,
compared with 101 hogsheads for Middlesex County as a whole, 103 for
Surrey, and 109 for sugar-rich Cornwall. By interpolation, Long's figures indicated a slave population of about 144 for the average Jamaican
sugar estate.[32]

*Jamaica, like all British colonies, officially used English denominations of
pounds, shillings, and pence; but the local currency (styled "Currency") was discounted
from English money ("Sterling")—in Jamaica usually by a third. Throughout this book,
amounts in pounds, shillings, or pence should be taken to be Sterling values, unless
they are specifically indicated as Jamaican Currency.

7. Jamaica at the Time of
Edward Long and Bryan
Edwards, 1774-1793

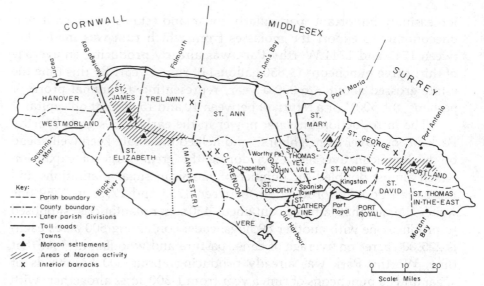

Source: Mainly Bryan Edwards,
*The History, Civil and Commercial,
of the British Colonies in the West
Indies,* 2 vols. (London, 1793), I, 246.

The period between 1775 and 1790 (particularly after the ending of
the American War of Independence in 1783) was one of moderate consolidation for Jamaican sugar estates, under the pressure of slowly tightening market conditions. In production and population Worthy Park
changed less than Jamaica as a whole, but in the later 1780s it actually
declined. This brought it closer to the Jamaican average. In 1793 when
Bryan Edwards described a model plantation, derived from "a survey
of the general run of sugar estates in Jamaica,"[33] he might almost have
had Worthy Park in mind in many respects.

In Edwards' model plantation, one-third of the land was in canes,
one-third in pasturage and provisions, and one-third in native woods.
Sugar production averaged 200 hogsheads a year, and, since Edwards
reckoned that estates generally needed 3 acres in canes for each 2
hogsheads of sugar produced, this meant 300 acres in canes out of a
total area of 900 acres. Edwards admitted, however, that the usual
Jamaican estate making 200 hogsheads of sugar a year considerably
exceeded this total acreage. This he attributed less to greedy engross-
ment (a common accusation) than to topographical reasons, such as the
prevalence of cockpits and wooded "waste" and the fact that it was
unusual to find 300 acres of flat fertile land all in one place. The slave
population of Edwards' estate was 250, and in addition there were
eighty steers and sixty mules. During the 1780s, Worthy Park averaged
about 260 acres annually in canes out of 456 acres of potential cane
land, producing an average of 260 hogsheads of sugar and 100 puncheons of rum. Some 75 acres were in provisions, and of the remainder
of the central block of 1,300 acres, 450 were said to be pasture. In the
previous few years, however, Worthy Park's undeveloped woodland,
mountain glades, and waste had been greatly increased by acquisitions,
which brought the total acreage to 3,000. The slave population in the
1780s, averaged 320, and there were about 200 steers and mules.[34]

Worthy Park, though very similar in pattern to Edwards' model

16

plantation, was slightly larger in every respect. Yet Edwards' estate, if "typical," was by no means an average one, according to figures which he produced himself. Because of the system of returns instituted for tax reasons a few years earlier, he was the first writer able to tabulate the number of slaves actually on Jamaican sugar plantations and thus enabled historians to tackle the difficult question of to what degree Jamaica was a sugar monoculture. Unfortunately there is still much room for doubt, since Edwards' criteria were little more precise than those of Edward Long, made nearly twenty years earlier.

Edwards tabulated that in 1789 there were 710 sugar plantations in Jamaica with 128,798 slaves on them, an average of 181.4 slaves each.[35] With Jamaica's sugar exports around 59,000 hogsheads a year this indicated an average production of only 83 hogsheads, or 124 if Edward Long's method of adding 50 percent for actual production is used. With a total island population of 250,000 slaves[36] (to which he added 30,000 whites, 10,000 free coloreds and blacks, and 1,400 Maroons), Edwards indicated that 51.5 percent of Jamaica's slave population lived on sugar estates,[37] at a time when sugar products constituted no less than 75 percent of the value of Jamaican exports.

A different calculation five years earlier had reckoned that Jamaica contained no less than 1,061 sugar estates.[38] This would serve not only to bring the average production down to fifty-five hogsheads of sugar for export and to place a higher proportion of the Jamaican slave population on sugar estates but also to make Worthy Park seem much less typical than it was in fact. The truth of the matter appears to be that both Bryan Edwards and Edward Long defined sugar estates as those predominantly devoted to sugar production, whereas the higher figure was for all estates growing some sugarcane. If calculations were limited to those estates like Worthy Park, Thetford, and Swansea, which were almost entirely given over to sugar production—with their own mills, factory, and means of transportation—the number of actual sugar estates would almost certainly be lower still and average production and population greater.

Another complicating factor is that many of the "other settlements" listed by Long and Edwards were in fact provision-growing "polinks" or grounds, cattle pens, or resting grounds, under the same ownership and economically linked with central sugar plantations. At different times, Guanaboa Vale, Spring Garden, Cocoree, Riverhead, and Mickleton—scattered over four parishes—were tied to Worthy Park as integral parts of the sugar-producing unit, with their slaves and cattle sometimes listed together. Thetford and Swansea estates included similar satellite holdings, and a painstaking and systematic analysis of the ownership of all Jamaican estates and the returns they sent in, such as that made later for the parishes of Trelawny and St. John, would almost certainly show that the Lluidas Vale pattern of linkage and enumeration was general.[39] This would mean not only that Worthy Park was a typically integrated Jamaican sugar estate but also that a higher proportion, perhaps 70 percent, of all Jamaican slaves were involved in some phase of sugar production, with perhaps 220 rather than 181 slaves in the average integrated unit.[40]

When Bryan Edwards produced the first of the many editions of his famous book in 1793, Worthy Park was only one of over 100 Jamaican estates producing 250 hogsheads or more of sugar a year with over 300 slaves. But by 1820 Worthy Park was one of a mere dozen with more than 500 slaves, and its production of 705 hogsheads of sugar in 1812 was one of the highest ever achieved by an old-style estate. This last great expansion at Worthy Park during the slavery period occurred between 1791 and 1795, as the result of large infusions of capital by the absentee owner, John Price of Penzance, and the personal management of his only son, Rose Price, who was to be sole owner between 1797 and 1835.

The collapse of the wider Price family empire—consisting of twelve plantations spread over 26,000 acres in eleven parishes—between the death of John Price's uncle Sir Charles Price in 1772 and the death of Sir Charles's son in 1789, was the most startling example of that general plantocratic decline which Bryan Edwards and others deplored, though at the same time exaggerated. For Worthy Park at least, dynastic accident decided that the estate should fall into single ownership, and careful management decreed that it should be shielded from the financial disaster faced by other Price lands. The complex juggling which led to multiple sales and transfers of mortgages actually aided the generation of the fresh capital and credit needed for the consolidation of the most favored and fortunate of the Price estates.[41]

Even in its expansion under Rose Price, Worthy Park remained more typical of Jamaican plantations than most modern accounts have indicated. Historians from L. J. Ragatz to Eric Williams and beyond, either taking at face value the complaints of beggary by planters arguing for the continuation of sugar protection, or eager to argue that the slave trade and slavery itself ended because plantations were no longer profitable, have written of a decline in the plantation economy long before it actually occurred and, when in fact plantations were still expanding. During the 1790s, under the stimulus of rapidly rising prices following the ending of competition from revolution-wracked St. Domingue (Haiti), Jamaican sugar plantations in general received their last large influx of investment during slavery days. Slave trade, slave population, and sugar production all reached their peaks during the years of the last French war (1793-1815), and at least one authority claimed (in 1856) that the number of Jamaican sugar estates reached its highest total (859 by his count) as late as 1804.[42] It was, however, a brittle and overoptimistic expansion, for the high sugar prices were artificial and temporary, and profits were eroded by inflated wartime costs. The estates which were to survive longest were those like Worthy Park

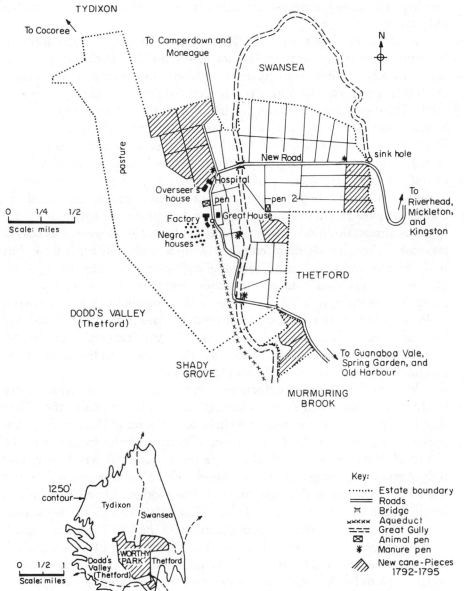

8. Worthy Park in 1795

Source: P.R.O., C.O. 441/4/4, No. 3.

Key:
- .... Estate boundary
- ═══ Roads
- ⋈ Bridge
- xxxxx Aqueduct
- =⁼= Great Gully
- ⊠ Animal pen
- ✳ Manure pen
- ▨ New cane-Pieces 1792-1795

which used new investment to consolidate and improve efficiency, as well as to expand.

In respect of the balance of lands, technology, cane husbandry, and slave management, the changes were not radical. Worthy Park's expansion was aimed to achieve optimal efficiency up to the limits imposed by topography, technology, and the problems of controlling the slaves. It was the goal of Rose Price, as of all dynamic planters, to produce as much as could be produced *regularly*, and then hope for a continuing favorable margin between costs and prices. Failing these conditions, any expansion was wasted and further changes impossible. Even if improvements in technology became available they could not be employed because the necessary capital was not attracted to nonprofitable areas.

Rose Price's chief concerns were to increase the sugarcane acreage, to improve yields, to keep the factory running each year as long as was economically feasible, and to improve communications to the coast. Within three years, nine new cane-pieces, totaling 161 acres, were created. This was done by transferring provision-growing from fertile lowland to within easy reach of the factory and by fertilizing marginal land with animal manure mixed with rotted canestalk trash, ashes, and factory effluent. Then the percentage of fallow land was drastically reduced by the introduction of new varieties of Tahiti cane, which allowed ratooning beyond the customary two years, up to sixth, eighth, or even further ratoons. Within a few years the total cane acreage was almost doubled, while the area replanted each year was barely increased. Average yields of cane per acre actually fell for a time, but with greatly increased cane tonnage and gradually improving cane quality, Worthy Park's sugar production rose from just under 300 hogsheads a year between 1776 and 1795 to 508 hogsheads a year between 1796 and 1815. At the same time rum output rose in proportion to over 200 puncheons (22,000 gallons) a year. Almost certainly this represented the upper limits of the factory's capabilities, with the crop period extended in many years to six months or more.[43]

Worthy Park's peak performance during slavery days was greatly facilitated by Rose Price's most lasting gift to Lluidas Vale, the "New Road" to Kingston by way of the shoulder of Mount Diablo, St. Thomas-ye-Vale, and the Rio Cobre gorge. Though 6 miles longer than the old road, the new one climbed a ridge more than 200 feet lower, had only 7 miles of steep gradients compared with 15, and no grades steeper than 1:12. Mickleton Pen just south of the modern Linstead, retained by the Prices despite the crash of the 1780s, served much the same purposes as Guanaboa Vale and Spring Garden on the Old Harbour route.[44]

Another result of Rose Price's close supervision of Worthy Park even after he returned to live in Cornwall—and one extremely relevant to the present book—was that he ordered the overseer to keep for the owner's perusal even more detailed accounts than those required by Jamaican law since 1783 to be forwarded to the parish vestries.

Thanks only partly to the inflation of the wartime years, Worthy Park's gross annual revenue for the twenty years after Rose Price returned to England in 1795 was probably no less than £20,000, and for years the absentee proprietor enjoyed a net income of at least £10,000 a year, almost all from Worthy Park. Yet Rose Price's optimization of his resources was not made without severe cost, in human as well as financial terms. To intensify production, Worthy Park needed an expanded labor force. By far the largest of Rose Price's expenditures was about £15,500 for the purchase of 225 new Africans between 1791 and 1793.[45] By this means the population of the estate was rapidly raised, from 338 in 1789 to 541 in 1793, and the field labor force almost dou-

bled. The immediate result was a wave of epidemic among the "unseasoned" newcomers that carried off no fewer than 115 during Rose
Price's residence in Jamaica. This is dealt with in much greater detail
later.

The Worthy Park death rate stabilized to a more normal 3.9 percent per year by 1795, and by dint of small annual purchases—preferably of seasoned Creole slaves—the population was kept more or less
constant until well after the ending of the Atlantic slave trade in 1808.
Around 1817, though, the acquisition of new slaves appears to have
become much more difficult and, as for Jamaica as a whole, the triennial slave registration returns initiated in that year disclosed an
alarming net decline in the total population. In the case of Worthy Park,
the number of slaves fell from 527 in 1817 to 431 in 1829.

In 1830, however, a last large acquisition of slaves was made when
about 100 were brought to Worthy Park from Arthur's Seat Estate in
neighboring Clarendon Parish. Although these were not unseasoned
Africans, their arrival had something of the same effect as the influx of
Africans forty years earlier, the death rate among old and new slaves
alike rising steeply for two or three years. Even then, the steady net
decline in the total population continued until the end of slavery and
apprenticeship.

Later on, in the chapter entitled "Economics, Employment, Social
Cohesion," the question of whether the comparative economic stability
brought to Worthy Park by Rose Price for a period of twenty years
after 1791 was associated with a degree of social stability is discussed.
Certainly what followed, the upsetting of economic equilibrium with
the ending of the last French war in 1815, was accompanied by social
dislocation, though whether the connection was causal has yet to be
seen. Economic stability could last only while moderately high profits
continued, and the Indian summer of Jamaican sugar came rapidly to
an end after the peak of 1805.

The development of the newly acquired colonies of Trinidad and
Guiana relegated Jamaica to a position of relative inferiority, much as
the sugar development of Jamaica a century earlier had led to a decline
in the relative importance of Barbados and the Leewards. Worthy Park,
with its annual production rarely over one hogshead per slave, or per
acre in canes, was—like Jamaica as a whole—extremely vulnerable to
competition from areas that expected to do at least twice as well.
Though the estate reached its own peak of production as late as 1812,
profits had already started an accelerated decline. Even the expansion
of production to the full capabilities of field, factory, and labor force
could not offset the effects of overproduction throughout the extended
British Empire and the gradual erosion of protection which increased
competition from foreign producers as well. The sugar price continued
to fall, and with it, in zigzags, Worthy Park's revenue. Moreover, the
expansion of the 1790s, predicated on continuing high produce prices,

had greatly increased the estate's interest charges on borrowed capital. Meanwhile other costs rose steadily because of the general inflationary trend. The loss of the cheapest possible labor force through emancipation between 1834 and 1838, coming as it did after a long period of declining slave productivity, was one more—though not quite the final—blow.[46]

The passing of slave registration laws after 1815 multiplied the data relating to slaves and estates, a factor that facilitates comparisons between Worthy Park and other Jamaican estates during the last two decades of slavery, when the entire system was approaching crisis. Tables 5, 6, and 7—derived for the most part from the invaluable lists published in the annual *Jamaica Almanack*—are aimed not only at placing Worthy Park in the general picture of Jamaican sugar but also at providing relevant details of particular areas. For this purpose the holdings and ownerships in Worthy Park's parish, St. John, are listed alongside those of Trelawny, a larger and more generally fertile parish devoted more exclusively to sugar, though developed latest of all Jamaican sugar areas. Broadly, these comparisons show that although Worthy Park (and the other chief Lluidas Vale estates) were fairly exceptional within their parish, they were far more typical of Jamaica as a whole, particularly those areas where geography determined that sugar predominate.

In the tables it is reasonable to presume that nine-tenths of all 418 Jamaican estates with more than 200 slaves in 1828, and possibly a third of the 617 with 100 or more, were sugar plantations with their own mills and factory. A close study of the contrasting details for St. John and Trelawny parishes suggests four further conclusions: that 150 slaves was the smallest number possible for a viable sugar operation in 1828; that those estates with less than 150 slaves where cattle outnumbered slaves were cattle pens; that the largest of the rest were coffee plantations; and that the remainder grew provisions and other crops. Examination of ownership patterns, including those straddling parish boundaries, bears out the degree to which the pattern followed by Worthy Park, Swansea, and Thetford was general. It is clear that for the most part it was these larger, integrated units, averaging at least 400 slaves, which remained strongest and survived longest as economic conditions deteriorated. In this sense, Worthy Park became *more* typical of existing Jamaican sugar estates as time went on and marginal operations folded.

Some indications of the overall decay of the system were already apparent during the Apprenticeship period of 1834-1838, a transitional phase during which the ex-slaves were constrained to continue working for their masters, but were paid wages for hours worked over 40½ per week. Throughout Jamaica there was a consistent fall of about 25 percent in the number of Apprentices compared with the number of slaves, owing mainly to the immediate freeing of children under six in 1834, as well as to manumissions and a continuing slight excess of deaths over births. However, closer analysis of numbers and ownership in the parishes suggests that perhaps a third of the sugar estates in Trelawny had either changed hands or ceased production altogether between 1828 and 1837. This implied a considerable redistribution of available labor forces at the very time when Jamaica was about to switch from compulsory slave to wage labor.

In St. John Parish the problem was, from the point of view of the planters, even more severe. It is clear from the estate returns that even some of those plantations which had large numbers of slaves had ceased sugar production as early as 1828. Moreover, the multiple redistribution of Apprentices in 1837 also suggests a pattern of wholesale dislocation well before full freedom occurred. Even Thetford (which made no Apprentice returns at all in 1837 because its ownership had reverted to the Crown) had already collapsed, and Swansea was probably in little better straits. This left Worthy Park not only isolated but surrounded by a very large number of unemployable ex-slaves in 1837.

The ex-slaves' point of view was, of course, very different. The collapsed estates had much land suitable for peasant-type squatters, especially on their undeveloped margins. At the same time, as is suggested by the preponderance of small parcels of slaves in St. John's, there was a great deal of land suitable for small freeholds such as ambitious ex-slaves could aspire to. Even a cursory look at the landholdings close to Lluidas Vale shows that there was ample room into which the ex-slaves could migrate once freed, whether they were forced to adopt subsistence farming because their former estate had ceased production or whether they made a voluntary choice to become peasants rather than "wage slaves."

The most suitable areas were to the south: the lovely climbing valleys of the Murmuring Brook and Roaring River, and the tumbled foothills and slopes of Juan de Bolas Mountain, steep but fertile and well watered. The dozen or more small estates into which the area was divided had all ceased to be viable as large-scale plantations. None of them had ever been really suitable for sugar or even cattle herding, and by 1838 those which had been optimistically converted to coffee were also fading. Most of the owners were absentees, barely able to afford an overseer to keep out squatters. But even those owners still resident in St. John Parish were losing interest. One of these was Samuel Queenborough of Juan de Bolas, who at the time of his death in 1815 was busily transferring most of his slaves to the sugar estates of Lloyd's and Aylmer's closer to the coast, while switching briefly and with little success to coffee growing.[47] The more realistic owners were soon ready to subdivide and capitalize by selling their lands piecemeal. In some cases the process of subdivision was already well under way because of overindulgent parents trying to make equal provision for all their children. Peter Douglas of Point Hill, for example, almost consigned his ten illegitimate children to the fate of Irish peasants by dividing among them equally at his death in 1821 a property that had never prospered as a unit.[48] Similarly, Dr. John Quier, on his death in the following year, started the process by which Shady Grove became first small holdings and then, by further subdivision, house lots, so that within three generations a strategically placed small estate had become a veritable village.[49]

The process of plantation decay, beginning soon after the end of the slave trade and accelerating towards the time of full freedom, meant that the slaves of Lluidas Vale would have fairly ready access to land—either with legal freehold tenure or by squatting—once they were freed. The availability of surrounding land did not, however, necessarily mean that Worthy Park and the two other chief Lluidas Vale estates were no longer typical of larger plantations throughout Jamaica on the eve of emancipation. The conditions in St. John Parish, as Edward Long and Bryan Edwards indicated earlier with their figures, almost certainly represented a situation close to the Jamaican average. It was only in parishes like Trelawny, where sugar monoculture had become almost absolute and owners and mortgagors jealously guarded their properties in the hope of renewed prosperity, or at least sales, that the ex-slaves had less than an average chance of escaping into an alternative existence.

With emancipation two important changes occurred, the one sudden and general, the other more gradual and limited. With only the brief transitional period of Apprenticeship, the labor system switched from the absolute constraints of slavery to the alleged freedom of wage payment. The ways in which this move affected the ex-slaves themselves—the manner and speed with which they became wage-earning peasants and villagers—is considered fully in later chapters. Such effects, however, were largely determined by the second change, the way that Worthy Park, as the sole survivor of five sugar plantations, gradually came to dominate Lluidas Vale and its surrounding area.

Technically, however, the agroindustrial system employed in Worthy Park's fields and factory underwent no great or sudden change. Indeed, Worthy Park, after a brief spurt of misplaced optimism in the 1840s, suffered from technical inertia for more than a century, chiefly through lack of capital. In this respect it differed from the majority of Jamaican estates only in not experiencing complete collapse.

Despite the yelps of the planters, all hopes for the Jamaican sugar industry were not lost as long as sugar prices did not fall permanently below the cost of production. For the majority of estates this fatal crossover point came between the slump of the late 1840s and the final removal of the protective sugar duties in 1854. In the struggle of the survivors to ensure that production costs stayed ahead of sugar prices, Worthy Park's owners were typical in being concerned both with raising productivity and with efforts to make wage labor at least as cheap and efficient as slave labor.

At least in theory, costs could be lowered by mechanization or by the type of consolidation practiced in Cuba and Brazil. Both, however, required more capital than Jamaica as a whole could generate. During the Free Trade era even British capital much preferred areas with large tracts of virgin land, where slavery continued into the 1880s. Worthy Park was exceptional in that the sons of Rose Price were able to raise some £ 50,000 of new capital in the 1840s, of which at least £ 30,000 was invested in mechanical improvements. By the introduction of steam power in the factory and railways and plows in the fields, George Price hoped to raise production to 700 tons of sugar a year by 1846 with no substantial increase in the labor force. In fact, miscalculation about the cost and difficulty of transporting and installing the new machinery and training the workers to use it meant that production in 1846 was no more than 303 hogsheads (227 tons), which would have been a poor yield in slavery days. With the plummeting of the sugar price from 49s. per hundredweight in 1840 to 23s.8d. in 1848, at a time when the cost of production was at least 23s. the Prices' improvements turned out to be visionary failures.[50]

Sugar prices did recover periodically during the second half of the nineteenth century, often running substantially above reduced costs of production. Yet the Price family found it financially impossible to continue as planters. Worthy Park was sold for the first time in 1863, to the Earl of Shrewsbury[51] on behalf of his two sons (named Talbot), for £ 8,500. This was as a result of the metropolitan West Indian Encumbered Estates Act of 1854, sponsored by W. E. Gladstone, whose habitual enthusiasm for financial reform was sharpened by the sympathy natural to one who was himself a member of a sugar-planting family.[52]

Predictably it was the Worthy Park work force which was to suffer most from the worldwide slump and the failure of the plans of Rose Price's sons. It is well known that emancipation was followed by the departure of many or most of the ex-slaves from the sugar plantations, and Worthy Park was no exception to the general trend. As mentioned earlier, there was a great deal of land available in the surrounding hills for the ex-slaves to live on and work, whether it was parts of decayed estates subdivided and sold, the margins of abandoned properties, or tracts of undeveloped Crown land. Within a short time of the ending of formal slavery, very few of the ex-slaves were living on Worthy Park land, and the surrounding hills were filling with an expanding population of peasants casually employed for wages. Most modern writers have assumed that such an existence was so much preferable to slave labor that the transition must have been entirely voluntary and refer to it as a flight from plantation labor.

Evidence presented in Part Three attempts to establish the scale, timing, and motivation of this "flight": whether it occurred immediately and as a direct result of the breaking of bonds in 1838, or whether it came rather later, more gradually, and for more complex reasons. Certainly, with the slump of the late 1840s, Worthy Park's owners—like all other Jamaican planters—came to regard the workers simply as a com-

9. Lluidas Vale Village, also known as Shady Grove, around 1850

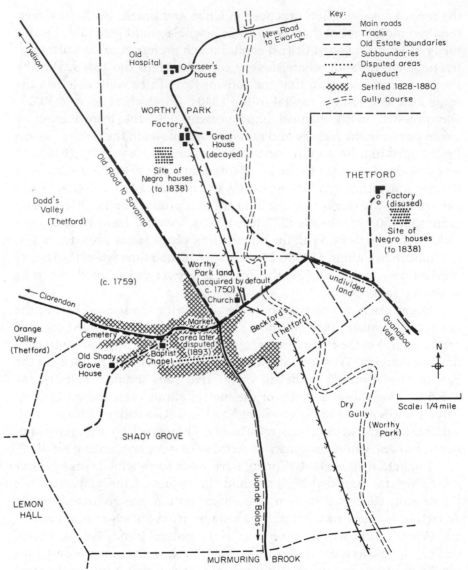

petitive labor pool, living outside the estate's boundaries, employed only when strictly required at rates that were second only to starving, and forced to fend entirely for themselves when not employed. This remained the standard policy until the day before yesterday, if not to the very present.

The symbol of the loss of the old cohesion and the increased impersonality of the Worthy Park labor force was the leveling and plowing under of the old "Negro Houses" behind the factory, so that absolutely no traces now remain.[53] The same was true of the other plantations then in Lluidas Vale. Today cattle graze where once five bustling villages thrived, almost African in their style. Within Worthy Park's old boundaries live only the owners, the privileged managerial staff, and a nucleus of permanent workers, including the descendants of the few East Indian "coolies" imported in the later nineteenth and early twentieth centuries.

26

The majority of the laborers of a greatly expanded Worthy Park Estate now live in Lluidas Vale Village, just outside the gates of the estate, which has grown from nothing to a population of over 2,000 since slavery ended. Worthy Park Estate has given the modern village a water supply, an Anglican church, and land for a police station, post office, public market, school, and government housing scheme (the last converted into a Youth Camp when the low cost housing proved too expensive and only two houses were bought). But these donations have merely served to emphasize the unfortunate dichotomy between village and estate, similar to that described (for Duckenfield in St. Thomas) by Edith Clarke in *My Mother who Fathered Me.*[54]

All villages at the edge of sugar estates are bound to be rubbed two ways; but the history of Lluidas Vale Village shows special reasons for friction. The first settlement grew at the natural site: where the ancient track from the south crossed the last shelf of the foothills, above the Great Gully. This was also the junction point between the three estates of Worthy Park, Thetford, and Shady Grove. The first free tenements sprang up on the Shady Grove land sold by Catherine Ann Smith, the granddaughter of Dr. John Quier, around 1828. Probably from this time, and certainly from the ending of slavery onwards, an unofficial market and sectarian religious services were regularly held at the junction of roads, and a large number of huts were built on what was technically Thetford land. All was relatively well until Worthy Park acquired Thetford in the 1880s, when the enlarged estate quickly asserted its right to all land north of the Clarendon road and on both sides of the old Shady Grove. One area of twenty-one acres remained in con-

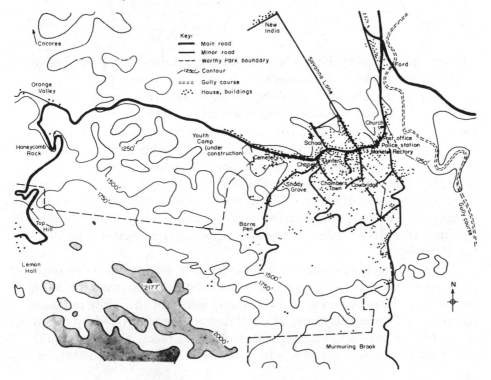

10. Lluidas Vale Village, also known as Shady Grove, 1972

11. Worthy Park Estate:
Consolidation, 1670-1955
(diagrammatic)

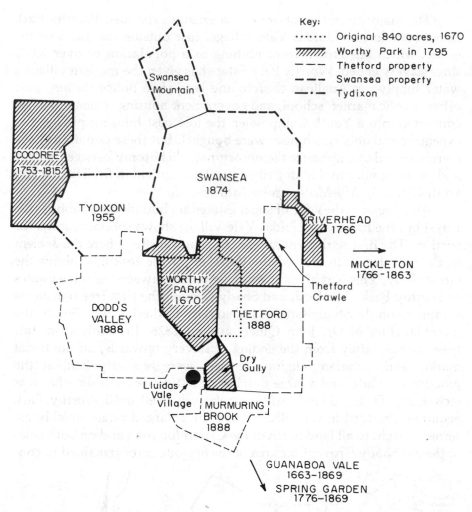

Key:
······ Original 840 acres, 1670
///// Worthy Park in 1795
--- Thetford property
-- Swansea property
-·- Tydixon

tention, with Worthy Park's famous overseer John Scarlett trying in vain in 1893 to evict as squatters all those living there.

Even today, Lluidas Vale Village is quite distinctly compartmentalized. Shady Grove remains a proud enclave of private land—sizable plots of "buy land" (bought, with clear title) worked as small holdings, smaller house lots of subdivided "family land" where the customary tenure is usually vague and complex, several sectarian chapels, and—fittingly—the village cemetery. Outside this independent sector are those symbols of authority, establishment, and respectability: police station, post office, public market, pound, school, church and parsonage, as well as those shops and houses whose tenants pay rent to Worthy Park Estate.

One other change occurred imperceptibly during the later nineteenth century, involving a mutation in the estate's management. With the coming of hard times after 1838, the majority of the white managerial staff fled the plantations. Their places were partly filled by a new generation of poor white immigrants to Jamaica (such as Henry Clarke of Westmorland, whose son was to purchase Worthy Park in 1918), but

28

also increasingly by that stratum of middle-class colored Jamaicans who still predominate in the middle managerial ranks of Jamaican enterprises. Almost absolute eighteenth-century racial barriers were broken down by this gradual change. Yet, significantly, the new recruits to the estates' managerial elites assumed and retained nearly all the socioeconomic characteristics of their white predecessors. The rewards were not measured in salaries (though the change from daily or weekly wages to monthly pay was regarded as important) so much as in relative security, free accommodation, an acre or two of land, and such subtle perquisites as the exercise of petty power. *Plus ça change.*

The period between 1846 and 1918 was the nadir of Worthy Park's economic history. Without further substantial capitalization, technology remained static or actually regressed. For example, the revolutionary vacuum pan introduced into other colonies as early as 1845, and even to Jamaica by 1860, did not reach Worthy Park until 1906; and once George Price's Boulton and Watt steam engine finally broke down, Worthy Park's cane was once again ground by the great waterwheel, until 1919.

The Talbot brothers retained Worthy Park for thirty-seven years, though only one of them ever visited the estate, and then briefly, in 1875. Although greatly enlarged in area, it was sold in 1899, for £300 less than Lord Shrewsbury had paid, to J. V. Calder, who was forced to treat it chiefly as a cattle ranch. Nineteen years later it was sold to the present owners, the Clarkes, Frederick L. Clarke purchasing the estate during the "bullish" period immediately after World War I, for £44,000.[55]

As to the consolidation of land, during the later nineteenth century Worthy Park sold off outlying nonsugar areas, while trebling the central acreage and spreading over almost the entire Vale of Lluidas. But this was a very different process from that which occurred in Cuba and Brazil or even that noticed earlier on the Tharp estates in Trelawny.[56] Guanaboa Vale, Spring Garden, and Mickleton were sold, partly because the system of resting pens was outdated by improved communications—first through the building of the New Road to Ewarton, and then by the extension of the Jamaica Railway into the interior—and partly because Worthy Park no longer had need of outside acreage for raising cattle and growing provisions. But the chief reason was to raise sorely needed cash. In return, the 3,575 acres of Swansea were purchased for £642 in 1874, and the 4,045 acres of Thetford and Murmuring Brook for £1,300 between 1881 and 1888, to bring Worthy Park close to its present 12,000 acres. However, as the meager prices paid suggest, Swansea and Thetford had long ceased to be viable sugar producers, and no more than a few of their very best cane-pieces were cropped until modern times.[57] Twentieth-century developments make the purchases of the 1870s and 1880s seem like far-sighted opportunism. It is probably more accurate to see them as a fortunate move with more

12. Worthy Park and
Lluidas Vale District: A
Sugar Estate and Its Sur-
rounding Peasantries, 1838-
1975

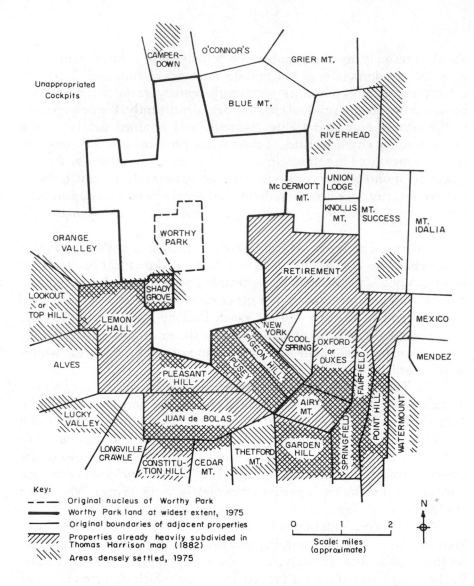

Key:

- - - Original nucleus of Worthy Park
───── Worthy Park land at widest extent, 1975
───── Original boundaries of adjacent properties
▨ Properties already heavily subdivided in Thomas Harrison map (1882)
▨ Areas densely settled, 1975

Scale: miles (approximate) 0 1 2

N

short-sighted and selfish aims—with little prospect of real development in view, to preempt encroaching competitors such as cattle graziers and squatters. In much the same way, in the seventeenth century, Francis Price and his generation had bought up huge inland acreages while they were available to favored plantocrats, for an annual quit rent of a half-penny per acre.

When Frederick Clarke bought Worthy Park in 1918 it was little more than a straggly cattle pen, producing sugar at an eighteenth-century level with early nineteenth-century methods. The subsequent realization of the estate's potential, along Cuban lines of mechanization and centralization, was made by astute management as well as through good fortune. The fortunate multiplication of the world sugar price in 1920 brought a dizzying influx of cash, but this was immediately reinvested in improvements in field, factory, and the motorized transportation of processed sugar to market. From 1933 on, a modest but increasing profit was made, averaging £8,203 a year down to 1940. Of

30

this total more than half was plowed back into the estate. An average of £3,036 was reinvested in the factory alone, as annual production was raised from 1,500 to 3,500 tons of sugar.[58]

There were, however, four extraneous influences which brought Worthy Park to its 1975 level of production, efficiency, and profit: the great expansion of the system of controls and quotas during World War II and the years of sugar shortage which followed it, the negotiation of the Commonwealth Sugar Agreements from 1951 on, the removal of Cuban competition from the United States and general world markets by the events of 1958-1962, and the inflation in sugar prices in line with all food commodities in the mid-1970s. Worthy Park's sugar production roughly doubled between 1940 and 1952, but thereafter rose even more rapidly to reach a steady level of around 17,000 tons a year by 1965. This increase was accompanied, and largely made possible, by a continuing policy of reinvestment. Expenditure on improvements in the factory, averaging a comparatively modest £3,670 a year between 1939 and 1945, totaled £259,000 between 1945 and 1965, and at the beginning of the 1970s was running at a level of £100,000 a year. Although one of the three smallest sugar estates still producing in Jamaica, Worthy Park was by then as close to optimization under modern conditions as it had been in the conditions which obtained at the end of the eighteenth century.

At a time when nearly every year saw another Jamaican estate face bankruptcy, close down its factory, or cease operations altogether, it might have been said that Worthy Park was as vulnerable in 1975 as it had been in 1812. The estate had already come close to maximizing cane production from its own lands. After the purchase in 1955 of Tydixon—last of the four other estates in Lluidas Vale to succumb to Worthy Park's expansion—cane acreage was eventually raised to 1,800, comprising almost all the flat fertile land within Worthy Park's boundaries. Even more important were increases in yield. Following intensive field research, the selection of plant varieties and methods of ratooning became much more scientific, and improvements were made in fertilization and disease control. Despite opposition from the unions some mechanization was introduced, in cultivation and in the loading and carrying of canes. All in all, the average tonnage yield of cane per acre (which was about 15 during the eighteenth century) was raised from 26.73 between 1940 and 1942, to 33.93 between 1953 and 1968. Meanwhile, because of improvements in sucrose content and the efficiency of milling, the number of tons of cane needed per ton of sugar was reduced to 7.74. Annual average produce of sugar from Worthy Park's canes, which had been 2.313 tons per acre between 1928 and 1939 and 3.238 between 1940 and 1952, accordingly rose to 4.608 tons per acre between 1953 and 1968. In the latter year Worthy Park was for the first time rated as the most efficient of Jamaican sugar estates, its record of producing 7.76 hundredweights per acre per month being said to be "comparable with the best cane growing areas in the world."[59]

Despite realizing the full potential of Worthy Park's sugar lands, this record amount accounted for less than half the factory's total production. The most important of all changes that occurred at Worthy Park in the twentieth century was that up to 65 percent of all the canes processed now came from independent farmers, working within a radius of twelve miles from Lluidas Vale. Beginning in 1937, and hugely extended by the increased demand and higher prices brought by World War II and subsequent events, this dual system of cane production produced something of a revolution in the underdeveloped areas to the west of Lluidas Vale. Yet indications were that this source too was running close to economic capacity. Although Worthy Park was obliged by law to accept all cane offered by its registered cane farmers, the high costs of fertilizing marginal lands, cutting the cane, and transporting it to the factory meant that in years of lower prices and lower sucrose content it proved extremely difficult to obtain sufficient farmers' canes, at the right times and with the right flow pattern.

The cost of transporting processed sugar to the coast had also become critical once more, despite great improvements since 1945 in motorized bulk carrying and the switch in choice of shipping port from the south to the north coast, where the conveyers constructed by a bauxite company at Ocho Rios were used after 1962. Jamaican roads did not permit the use of larger or speedier carriers, even if the capital had been readily available for their purchase. Besides, the cost of replacement vehicles mounted yearly far faster than the sugar price.

Similar constraints determined that the Worthy Park factory was also operating close to its economic capacity. Few factories of its comparatively modest size now operated profitably anywhere in the world. Quite apart from the difficulties of increasing the input of cane transported at reasonable cost was the perennial problem of capitalization. Hitherto, Worthy Park factory's remarkable advances in the modern period had been made entirely with capital generated by the estate itself. To raise production by another 50 percent might cost as much as £ 500,000, a sum that would require substantial borrowing. Worthy Park would then suffer the fate of most other Jamaican estates: the evaporation of profits in the payment of interest charges, brought about by the expansion of capital plant.

Of all the problems faced by Worthy Park's management that of labor remained the most severe. With each crop it became progressively more difficult to recruit sufficient cane-cutters or to keep them working exactly when and as long as they were needed. Although as recently as 1968 the number of workers employed in the crop period was more than three times that employed at the lowest point in the year, any labor shortage could no longer be attributed solely to the reluctance of laborers to accept work that was bound to be purely seasonal. In the recent past, Worthy Park had offered harvest workers only rotational employment in the out-of-crop season; but in 1971 for the first time all laborers who wished it were offered year-round work, and there was a labor shortage even out of crop. As the result of constant union negotiation at the national and estate levels, and almost annual local strikes, wages had risen steadily. But even at a scale once regarded by management as ruinous, they did not provide sufficient inducement to attract the laborers to the work offered.

The mechanization of cane-cutting seemed to provide solutions to more than one of Worthy Park's labor problems. The further increase in productivity (already raised by mechanical loading) would allow both higher wages and more nearly continuous employment. But there were snags. The labor unions tended to resist any change which cut down the number of their members employed. Cane-cutting machines were extremely expensive and presented the familiar problems of capitalization, maintenance, and replacement. Finally, it was said that a large proportion, perhaps a half, of Worthy Park's cane-pieces were not suitable for mechanical cutting by machines in their present state of development.

In sum, it seemed that Worthy Park as a sugar producer in 1975 was only capable of marginal extensions and improvements under current conditions. Moreover, even the present state of uneasy equilibrium was based on the existing scale of sugar prices and quotas. If the sugar price fell drastically, through the abrogation of the Commonwealth Sugar Agreement or the return of Cuban sugar into the general world market, Worthy Park would quickly follow the other Jamaican producers out of production.

In this case it was unlikely that Worthy Park, Ltd., as a private family concern, would suffer most. The estate was already heavily diversified, with cattle, citrus, and other minor crops utilizing almost the entire area not suitable for sugar and producing among them a revenue in excess of £100,000 a year. Citrus, in its way more chancy and less protected than sugar, was probably not capable of much expansion. But if sugar were to fail, the estate could well turn almost entirely to the production of beef and pedigree breeding stock. Selling 500 cattle a year out of a total herd of 1,500, Worthy Park was already one of the most efficient beef-producing operations in the world. To turn over the most fertile acreage—the sugar land—to cattle would mean a pause of up to three years, as new grassland was created and all heifers were retained for breeding. Thereafter, the estate's total revenue would never be so high as under sugar, but the percentage profit might be higher.

In the hypothetical circumstances outlined above, Lluidas Vale would have turned full circle, from 1980 back to 1680. By a reversion to a cattle pasture growing some minor crops, the long history of sugar, with its trials and tribulations, would be expunged. But the social cost would include the substitution of an economy employing nearly 1,000 laborers and 45 management staff, with one requiring perhaps 40 and 5 respectively. Such a change, in a country suffering from critical underemployment as well as rural land hunger, would certainly demand a political rather than a purely economic solution.

TABLE 1. Sugar Estate Consolidation, Jamaica Style: Tharp Plantations in Trelawny, 1817-1828

Plantation	Main function	Average slaves (1817/1828)	Cattle (1828)
Good Hope	Sugar	427	150
Covey	Sugar	457	146
Lansquinet	Sugar	374	174
Merry Wood	Sugar[a]	201	104
Pantre Pant	Sugar	341	195
Potosi	Sugar	285	160
Wales	Sugar	327	192
Top Hill	Provisions	69[b]	85
Windsor Pen	Cattle	223[b]	379
Total		2,704	1,585

Sources: 1817: *British Sessional Papers, Lords, Reports, 1831-2*, II, 249-262; 1828: *Jamaica Almanack, 1829.*

[a]Perhaps cane only.
[b]1828 only.

TABLE 2. Expansion of Jamaican Population by Parishes, 1734-1768, Selected Years

Parishes and counties	Area (thou. acres)[b]	1734		1740	
		Slaves	Cattle	Slaves	Cattle
St. John	62	5,242	2,561	5,875	2,837
St. Catherine	63	5,502	8,002	6,203	8,581
St. Dorothy	40	2,298	5,341	2,515	5,468
St. Thomas-ye-Vale	80	7,568	4,441	8,475	4,813
Clarendon	184	10,769	11,627	11,575	12,299
Vere	59	3,582	7,194	5,370	8,580
St. Mary	123	2,938	2,182	4,484	2,972
St. Ann	244	4,441	2,026	5,242	2,342
MIDDLESEX totals	855	42,340		49,739	
Kingston	4	3,811	483	4,534	607
St. Andrew	79	7,631	5,413	8,363	5,244
Port Royal	26	1,548	106	1,546	158
St. David	46	1,540	1,165	1,628	1,497
St. Thomas/East	132	6,176	5,488	6,618	5,256
Portland	14	640	125	775	178
St. George	90	1,085	1,485	969	1,024
SURREY totals	391	22,431		24,433	
St. Elizabeth[a]	387	7,046	9,184	6,641	9,695
Westmorland	172	9,081	6,915	11,155	8,921
Hanover	116	3,339	1,774	4,863	2,631
St. James	145	2,297	1,099	2,588	1,204
Trelawny	169				
CORNWALL totals	989	21,763		25,247	
JAMAICA totals	2,235	86,534		99,419	

Source: Edward Long, *The History of Jamaica*, 3 vols. (London, 1774).

[a]The huge parish of St. Elizabeth was split into Manchester (156,000 acres) and St. Elizabeth (214,000 acres) in 1824.
[b]Areas were added from R. M. Martin, *The British Colonies, Their History, Extent, Condition and Resources*, 5 vols. (London, 1834), though these were consistently understated. The true acreage of Jamaica is over 2,800,000.
[c]In his 1768 column Long gave the figures for Trelawny, which was not separated from St. James until 1770, but did not add them to the total since his figures for St. James were those preceding the separation.

34

1745		1761		1768		
Slaves	Cattle	Slaves	Cattle	Slaves	Cattle	Sugar estates
5,728	2,250	5,888	—	5,455	2,726	21
6,599	8,043	7,016	—	7,308	10,402	5
2,423	4,540	3,210	—	3,665	4,661	12
8,239	4,797	9,057	—	8,382	5,782	41
12,775	11,969	13,772	—	15,517	14,276	70
5,423	8,870	5,663	—	5,940	7,462	19
5,631	3,304	9,318	—	12,159	7,996	49
5,231	2,533	7,729	—	8,320	6,207	22
52,049		61,653		66,746	59,512	239
7,749	828	6,186	—	5,799	923	0
8,936	5,001	9,024	—	9,813	4,626	30
1,685	35	1,203	—	1,432	170	1
1,365	1,494	1,838	—	2,316	1,667	8
7,282	5,561	12,300	—	14,624	9,007	66
1,235	637	2,354	—	2,813	1,651	29
1,163	1,136	2,147	—	2,765	3,421	12
29,415				39,562	21,465	146
		35,052				
7,575	13,500	9,715	—	10,110	16,947	31
12,131	8,520	15,158	—	15,186	13,750	69
6,351	3,054	10,498	—	13,571	8,942	71
4,907	1,961	14,729	—	21,749	15,137	95
				[11,739	8,130	40]c
30,964		50,100		60,616	54,776	266
112,428		146,805		166,924	135,753	651

TABLE 3. Jamaica in 1768

Source: Edward Long, *History of Jamaica*, 3 vols. (1774).

[a]Trelawny figures, as in Table 2, are detached though not added into the Cornwall county totals. The separation of Trelawny from St. James did not occur until 1770.

[b]"Other settlements" are not specified but are understood to include coffee and other plantations, pens, and separate provision grounds.

[c]Not including rum and molasses.

Parishes and counties	Sugar estates	Sugar production (hhds.)	Other settlements[b]	Slaves	Cattle
St. John	21	2,200	50	5,435	2,726
St. Catherine	5	350	95	7,308	10,402
St. Dorothy	12	700	56	3,665	4,661
St. Thomas-ye-Vale	41	3,500	37	8,382	5,782
Clarendon	70	8,000	180	15,517	14,276
Vere	19	2,100	131	5,940	7,462
St. Mary	49	5,500	56	12,159	7,996
St. Ann	22	1,700	158	8,320	6,207
MIDDLESEX totals	239	24,050	763	66,746	59,512
Kingston	0	—	8	5,799	923
St. Andrew	30	2,600	122	9,813	4,626
Port Royal	1	60	11	1,432	170
St. David	8	550	35	2,316	1,667
St. Thomas/East	66	9,270	34	14,624	9,007
Portland	29	1,330	57	2,813	1,651
St. George	12	1,200	48	2,765	3,421
SURREY totals	146	15,010	315	39,562	21,465
St. Elizabeth	31	2,600	150	10,110	15,947
Westmorland	69	8,000	96	15,186	13,750
Hanover	71	7,500	35	13,571	8,942
St. James	55	3,080	36	10,010	7,007
Trelawny[a]	40	7,920	66	11,739	8,130
CORNWALL totals	266	29,100	383	60,616	54,776
JAMAICA totals	651	68,160	1,461	166,924	135,753

	Cattle mills	Water mills	Wind-mills	Sugar exports (hhds.)	Sugar exports value (Stg.)[c]	Sugar exports % of total	Whites
Other JAMAICA totals	369	235	442	45,026	61,871,000	61.0	17,949

Parishes and counties	Total slaves[a]	Sugar estates	Slaves on sugar estates	% of sugar estate slaves	Av. no. slaves per estate
St. John	5,880	21	3,713	63.1	177
St. Catherine	5,304	3	408	7.7	136
St. Dorothy	3,129	12	1,776	53.6	148
St. Thomas-ye-Vale	7,459	33	5,327	71.4	161
Clarendon	14,747	56	10,150	69.1	185
Vere	7,487	26	5,279	70.5	203
St. Mary	17,144	63	12,065	70.4	192
St. Ann	13,324	30	4,908	36.9	164
MIDDLESEX totals	74,474	244	43,626	58.6	138
Kingston	6,162	0	0	0	0
St. Andrew	9,613	24	3,540	36.9	147
Port Royal	2,229	3	358	16.1	119
St. David	2,881	12	1,890	65.6	157
St. Thomas/East	20,492	83	15,786	77.0	190
Portland	4,537	23	2,968	65.4	129
St. George	5,050	14	2,795	55.3	200
SURREY totals	50,964	159	27,337	53.5	172
St. Elizabeth	13,280	26	5,112	3.9	197
Westmorland	16,700	62	11,219	67.2	181
Hanover	17,612	69	13,330	75.7	190
St. James	18,546	67	12,482	67.4	186
Trelawny	19,318	83	15,692	81.2	189
CORNWALL totals	85,456	307	57,835	67.7	185
JAMAICA totals	210,894	710	128,798	61.1	181

TABLE 4. Jamaican Sugar Estates and Their Slaves, 1789

Source: Bryan Edwards, *The History. Civil and Commercial, of the British West Indies*, 2 vols. (London, 1793).

[a]From tax rolls.

Prologue

TABLE 5. Jamaican Slave Holdings and Sugar Estates, 1823-1834, Selected Years

Sources: Areas and slaves, 1833, R. M. Martin, *The British Colonies, Their History, Extent, Conditions and Resources,* 5 vols. (London, 1834), II, 188-191; slaves and proprietors, 1823, G. W. Bridges, *Annals of Jamaica,* 2 vols. (London, 1828), II, Appendix, 561-567; stock and slaves on estates, 1828, *Jamaica Almanack, 1829;* sugar estates, 1789, Bryan Edwards, *The History, Civil and Commercial, of the British West Indies,* 2 vols. (London, 1793), I, 219; sugar estates, 1804, 1834, Public Record Office, C. O. 137/330.

[a]Manchester was added to Middlesex when split off from St. Elizabeth in 1824, but is left with Cornwall here to aid comparison with earlier tables.

[b]Freeholders only.

[c]Without Kingston.

[d]In the columns for sugar estates in 1804 and 1834, the figures for St. Mary include those for St. George. The two parishes were for a time amalgamated and included in Middlesex. The totals for Middlesex and Surrey in 1804 and 1834 are therefore approximated.

Parishes and counties	Area (thou. acres)	Slaves		Animal stock (1828)	Proprietors (1823)
		1823	1833		
St. John	62	6,295	5,985	1,231	152
St. Catherine	63	7,357	7,507	4,703	282
St. Dorothy	40	4,759	5,142	3,173	105
St. Thomas-ye-Vale	80	12,050	10,733	3,025	223
Clarendon	184	17,608	16,156	6,549	167
Vere	59	7,759	8,002	3,373	63
St. Mary	123	25,402	23,544	17,208	439
St. Ann	244	24,761	24,821	20,674	476
MIDDLESEX totals[a]	855	105,991	101,890	59,936	1,907
Kingston	4	6,095	5,265	340	[168][b]
St. Andrew	79	15,316	13,545	1,831	326
Port Royal	26	6,407	5,965	271	184
St. David	46	7,704	7,417	1,761	100
St. Thomas/East	132	24,789	23,319	5,686	308
Portland	14	8,018	7,267	1,544	161
St. George	90	12,655	11,508	3,644	268
SURREY totals	391	80,984	74,286	15,077	1,347
Manchester[a]	170	17,416	19,304	7,708	223
St. Elizabeth	217	18,350	18,371	19,703	389
Westmorland	172	21,216	19,599	12,413	395
Hanover	116	22,250	21,826	8,374	370
St. James	145	24,130	22,019	6,498	572
Trelawny	169	26,795	25,337	18,203	419
CORNWALL totals	989	130,157	126,456	72,899	2,368
JAMAICA totals	2,235	317,132	302,632	147,912	5,622[c]

Estates in 1828 with slaves numbering						Sugar estates		
25+	50+	100+	200+	300+	400+	1789	1804	1834
20	14	7	2	3	2	21	23	11
27	14	12	5	1	0	3	11	5
11	10	5	4	3	1	12	18	11
30	30	29	10	2	0	33	46	23
38	34	37	18	5	2	56	62	40
9	3	12	11	3	2	26	29	29
42	26	45	27	16	2	63	95[d]	86[d]
85	85	56	16	1	2	30	41	30
262	216	203	93	34	11	244	c. 309	c. 227
—	—	—	—	—	—	0	24	14
41	36	33	7	4	0	24		
14	10	16	7	1	0	3	4	3
12	25	16	9	0	1	12	16	10
15	32	48	24	13	3	83	94	67
12	12	20	4	3	1	23	33	25
38	24	18	10	6	2	14	—[d]	—[d]
132	139	151	61	27	7	159	c. 187	c. 127
61	69	56	3	4	1	26	0	0
53	33	35	11	8	2		27	17
51	33	36	15	11	2	62	68	48
28	17	38	34	7	3	69	84	71
32	26	47	27	7	3	67	90	80
22	27	48	33	9	5	83	94	76
247	205	260	123	46	16	307	363	292
641	560	614	277	107	34	710	859	646

TABLE 6. St. John Parish: Estates with more than 25 Slaves or Apprentices, 1828 and 1837

Sources: Slaves and Cattle, 1828, *Jamaica Almanack, 1829;* Apprentices, 1837, *Jamaica Almanack, 1838.*

Notes: Blanks in columns indicate no returns made. St. John Parish, unlike Trelawny (Table 7), only listed taxable cattle, thus ignoring working steers, which were untaxed. Abbreviations: SD=St. Dorothy; STV=St. Thomas-ye-Vale; Cl=Clarendon.

[a]Operating sugar estate, 1828.
[b]Cattle pen.
[c]Recently defunct sugar operation, 1828.

St. John estates	Slaves (1828)	Cattle (1828)	Apprentices (1837)	Estates under same ownership in adjoining parishes	Slaves (1828)	Cattle (1828)
Worthy Park[a]	455		381	Spring Garden[b] (SD)	85	388
				Mickleton (STV)	74	
Swansea[a]	372		261	Hays[b] (SD)	33	14
Coffee Mountain	159		121			
Brown's Hall[b]	76	151	51			
Lloyd's & Aylmer's[a]	429	174	299			
Juan de Bolas	118		77			
Thetford[c]	301	16		Thetford Hall[b] (SD)	89	238
Fuller's Rest	16					
Cedar Mount[c]	179		139	Ann's Castle (SD)	13	
Garden Hill	90			Bannister[b] (SD)	215	83
Mendes	71			Blue Hole (SD)	232	
St. Faith's	10		77	Masters (SD)	197	12
				Whim[c] (SD)	313	63
Lemon Hall[c]	334	36	100			
Clifford's	144		109			
Longville Crawle	95					
Constitution Hill	33					
Watermount[a]	213	47	157			
Spring Vale[c]	208	6	135	Palmyra[c] (SD)	87	84
Belmont[c]	154		133	Burn's (Cl)	151	2
				Kellit's[a] (Cl)	464	77
				Mammy Gully[c] (Cl)	118	69
				St. Toolies[b] (Cl)	210	29

St. John estates	Slaves (1828)	Cattle (1828)	Appren-tices (1837)	Estates under same ownership in adjoining parishes	Slaves (1828)	Cattle (1828)
Mountain River[c]	125	15	99			
Retreat[c]	110	6	60			
Mount Idalia	98		73			
John Hoyes'	95					
Mount Pleasant I	95		81			
Harvey Bennett's	93	8				
Pleasant Hill	86	12	69			
Blue Mountain	70		68			
Retirement	64		48			
Tydixon Park[c]	62	131				
Spring Mount	57		46			
Mount Pleasant II	47		55			
Content I	41	1				
Fairfield	38		22			
Douglas Castle	35	4				
Envy Valley[b]	34	90	26			
Crawle	33	10	67			
Red Hills	32					
Mount Olive	30	6	60			
Robert Maxwell's	30					
Fair Prospect	30	1	68			
Friendship	29		22			
Content II[b]	29	40				
Shady Grove	29					
Barker's Valley	29					
Fruit Hill	28	8				
Content III	27	1	67			
Montpelier	26		14			
Dovecote Park[b]	25	100				
Elizabeth Valentine's	25					
Brown Wood			58			
Lemon Ridge			56			
Prospect			53			
St. Clair			44			
Gibraltar			32			
Look Out			30			

Prologue

TABLE 7. Trelawny Parish: Estates with more than 100 Slaves or Apprentices, 1817, 1828, and 1837

Sources: Slaves, 1817, *British Sessional Papers, Lords, Reports 1831-2,*II, 249-262; slaves and cattle, 1828, *Jamaica Almanack, 1829;* Apprentices, 1837, *Jamaica Almanack, 1838.*

Notes: Blanks in columns indicate no returns made. Abbreviations: SJ = St. James; CL = Clarendon; SA = St. Ann.

[a]Sold, transferred, or decayed, 1828-1837.
[b]Cattle pen.
[c]Not a sugar estate.
[d]Mixed sugar and cattle operation.

Trelawny estates	Slaves (1817)	Slaves (1828)	Cattle (1828)	Apprentices (1837)	Estates under same ownership in adjoining parishes	Slaves (1828)
Green Park	528	542	247	409	Spring Vale[b] (SJ)	187
Forest		196	141	202		
Arcadia[a]	314	319	243	220		
Cambridge	589	257	200	189		
Oxford		255	203	207		
Schawfield	107	190	168	187		
Piedmont[a,c]		160	12			
Garradu[d]	221	208	186	166	Arthur's Seat (Cl)	230
					Inverness (Cl)	46
Sportsman's Hall[a]	112	125	108	100		
Mount Carfax[c]		106	30	65		
Phoenix[d]	158	120	211	103		
Florence Hall[d]	245	231	246	156		
Gibraltar[c]	144	165	97	133		
Nightingale Grove[a]		160	103			
Hyde[d]	317	300	287	208	Retirement (SJ)	352
Swanswick[d]	292	263	241	193		
Long Pond	366	318	238	261		
Hampshire	327	306	210	245		
Mahogany Hall[b]		160	492	133		
Fontabelle	343	295	189			
Southfield[a]	235	180	102	331		
Duan Vale[a,b]		63	214			
Pembroke	257	314	206	208		
Greenside	256	222	176	182		
Maxfield	154	157	151	119		
Hopewell	228	239	183	184	Bellfield (SJ)	230
Biddeford	203	216	141	157	Harmony Hill (SJ)	31
					Retrieve (SJ)	103
Roslin Catle	188	184	132	139		
Manchester	140	209	157	151		
Brampton Bryan	247	279	202	207		
Bryan Castle[d]	155	166	194	195		
Chester		124	111	135		
Baron Hill[c]		124	92	98		
Grange	106	105	92	115		
Friendship	134	138	124	120		
Lottery	130	143	117	161		
Weston Favel[a,d]	312	297	239	208		

Trelawny estates	Slaves		Cattle (1828)	Apprentices (1837)	Estates under same ownership in adjoining parishes	Slaves (1828)	Cattle (1828)
	(1817)	(1828)					
Ulster Spring	108	160	121	133	Flamstead[b] (SA)	40	135
					Maida (SA)	61	41
Gale's Valley	244	246	179	189	Mount Hind-	176	
York	405	306	295	175	most (SJ)		
					Pens[b] (SJ)	45	203
Greenfield[a]		175	93				
Braco[d]	346	275	302	161			
Georgia	254	253	172	216			
Colchis[d]		144	175	120			
Unity	202	169	149	124			
Gray's Inn[a,c]		122	5				
Irving Tower		114	126	81			
Orange Valley	615	641	309	507	Hartfield[c] (SJ)	134	4
Hacton[b]		43	162	36	Iron Shore (SJ)	239	80
Golden Grove	314	306	186	221	Amity Hall[c] (SJ)	103	7
Kent	223	252	200	201			
Silver Grove[d]	131	112	137	72			
Spring[a]	122	148	136	148			
Lysworney[d]		100	120	119			
Steelfield	210	217	184	171			
Mount Pleasant[c]		106	60	64			
Linton Park	305	297	156	222			
Barnstaple[a]	186	185	132	121			
Holland	190	162	124	120			
Coffee Hall[a,c]		120	11				
Hampstead[a,d]	259	217	236	302			
Retreat[a]	143	196	185				
Dry Valley[a]	195	193	92				
Jock's Lodge[a,b]	136	138	257				
Water Valley[a]	275	297	120				
George's Valley	247	248	188	186	Phoenix Park[b] (SA)	73	342
Bunker's Hill[a]		238	136	142	Hazelymph (SJ)	288	59
Friendship		208	129	142			
Wakefield	151	118	118	98	York Valley (SA)	71	40
Claremont	104	126	126	88			
Peru[a]	147	178	133	125			
Kinloss	195	250	211	197			
Rose Hill[c]		10	2				
Stewart Castle	300	281	182	219			
Hyde Hall[d]	341	276	340	222			
Etingdon[d]	287	275	254	216			
Glamorgan[a]		95					

(continued)

Table 7 (*continued*)

Trelawny estates	Slaves (1817)	Slaves (1828)	Cattle (1828)	Apprentices (1837)	Estates under same ownership in adjoining parishes	Slaves (1828)
Bounty Hall[a]	275	157	79	108		
Tileston[a]	222	475	212	369		
Reserve[a]	212	180	154	131		
Keir[a]		100			Hampden (SJ)	255
Hague[a]	155	144	121	174		
Clifton[a]	124	140	109			
Orange Grove[a,b]	70	56	129	79		
Johnson Pen[a,b]		59	183	46		
Dundee	211	184	127	134		
Covey	451	464	146	353	Chippenham Park[b] (SA)	101
Good Hope	448	406	150	306		
Lansquinet	400	349	174	248	Hampton[c] (SJ)	144
Merry Wood	218	184	101	140	Green Pond (SJ)	120

TABLE 8. Worthy Park: Population and Sugar Production, 1783-1848

Note: Figures in boldface calculated rather than actually recorded.

[a]Worthy Park records.
[b]Jamaica Almanacks.
[c]Jamaica Archives.

	Worthy Park Slaves (various lists)				
	In working rolls[a]	"Given in" to St. John Vestry	St. John Vestry Returns[b]	Taxable[a]	Register of Returns of Slaves (1817-1822)[c]
1783	318				
84	331				
85	317				
86	307				
87	339				
88	343				
89	341				
1790	345				
91	377				
92	359				
93	541				
94	530				
95	483				
96	470				
97					
98					
99					
1800					
01					
02					
03					
04					
05					
06					
07					
08					
09					

Table 7 (*continued*)

Trelawny estates	Slaves (1817)	Slaves (1828)	Cattle (1828)	Apprentices (1837)	Estates under same ownership in adjoining parishes	Slaves (1828)	Cattle (1828)
Pantre Pant	358	325	195	215	Windsor	107	47
Potosi	306	264	160	196	Castle (SJ)		
Top Hill[c]		69	85	33			
Wales	355	299	192	217			
Windsor Pen[b]		223	379	148			
Lancaster	157	143	165	209	Mount Carmel (SA)	104	110
Maria Bueno[a,b]	178	140	268				
Vale Royal	289	274	141	211			
Stonehenge		174	119	120			
Belmont		227	167	157			
Ashley Hall		108	108	81			
Dromilly[a]	103	89					
Harmony Hall[a]	174	262		211			
Carrickfoyle[a,c]	98	95					

"Laborers" (1831-1834)	Apprentices listed in Jamaica Almanacks[b]	Worthy Park Slaves (various lists) Number purchased[a]	Mickleton Pen[a]	Spring Garden Pen[a]	Sugar production (hhds.)[a]
					270
		7			375
		5			245
					181
		25			172
					294
		4			334
		15			248
		15			267
		20			310
		92			375
		98	25		371
		3	33		306
			31		269
			31		468
			34		415
			34		499
			41		590
					435
					425
					505
					624
					673
					455
					500
					545
					460

(*continued*)

Table 8 (*continued*)

		Worthy Park Slaves (various lists)			
	In work-ing rolls[a]	"Given in" to St. John Vestry	St. John Vestry Returns[b]	Taxable[a]	Register of Returns of Slaves (1817-1822)[c]
1810		491			
11	509				
12	503				
13	511				
14	514				
15	514	518			
16	517	511			
17	527	526			529
18					
19					
1820		514			508
21	505	514			
22	494	499			
23	496	494			490
24	484	487			
25					
26		469			468
27		448			
28		397			
29					431
1830	461		522	503	
31			517	501	
32			494	478	491
33			483	469	
34			467	454	
35			417		
36					
37					
38					
39					
1840					
41					
42					
43					
44					
45					
46					
47					
48					

| "Laborers" (1831-1834) | Apprentices listed in Jamaica Almanacks[b] | Worthy Park Slaves (various lists) | | | |
		Number purchased[a]	Mickleton Pen[a]	Spring Garden Pen[a]	Sugar production (hhds.)[a]
					555
			33	74	456
			33	70	705
			33	70	570
			33	74	572
			31	75	475
			29	77	
				77	
					479
					533
					487
334			83	86	471
309					389
296					484
266					490
	260				427
	248				407
	234		65	19	370
					406
					342
					140
					263
					299
					232
					261
					309
					303
					267
					468

TABLE 9. Worthy Park Estate: Acreage, Production, Slave Population, Cattle, 1700-1850, Selected Years (rounded averages)

Source: Worthy Park records, Jamaica Archives, Spanish Town, Jamaica.

	Total acreage (thou.)	Cane acreage	Improved pasture (acres)	Other crops (acres)	Sugar production (tons)	Jamaican sugar (thou. tons)	Rum production (thou. gals.)	Slave population	Cattle
1700	1.8	0	200	50	0	7	0	50	75
1730	1.3	200	200	75	187	10	3	200	170
1740	1.3	250	200	75	200	14	4	250	180
1780	3.0	300	300	75	225	38	14	320	200
1790	3.0	350	430	75	250	47	17	345	200
1800	3.0	450	350	125	375	60	23	500	300
1810	3.0	450	350	125	410	63	25	500	300
1820	4.0	470	350	125	400	90	27	500	300
1830	4.0	480	350	100	350	69	23	461	300
1840	4.0	300	500	—	187	27	15	0	250
1850	4.0	250	550	—	150	30	12	0	150

TABLE 10. Jamaica, The Decline in Sugar Estates, 1804-1854, Selected Years

Sources: For 1804, 1834, and 1854, Public Record Office, C.O. 137/330; 1844, Jamaican Census; 1848, D. G. Hall, *Free Jamaica, 1838-1865: An Economic History* (New Haven, Yale University Press, 1959), p. 82.

Parish	1804	1834	1844	1848	1854
St. John	23	11	10	9	6
St. Catherine	11	5	5	5	3
St. Dorothy	18	11	10	10	5
St. Thomas- ye-Vale	46	23	24	23	12
Clarendon	62	40	41	23	17
Vere	29	29	29	27	17
St. Mary (with St. George and Metcalfe)	95	86	79	59	39
St. Ann	41	30	32	22	18
Kingston/St. Andrew	24	14	18	5	5
Port Royal	4	3	3	2	0
St. David	16	10	10	8	3
St. Thomas/East	94	67	61	54	21
Portland	33	25	24	13	3
Manchester	0	0	0	0	0
St. Elizabeth	27	17	20	12	12
Westmorland	68	48	48	46	34
Hanover	84	71	70	60	34
St. James	90	80	74	62	41
Trelawny	94	76	86	68	55
JAMAICA totals	859	646	644	508	330

TABLE 11. British West Indian and Cuban Sugar Production, 1815-1894, Selected Years (tons)

Source: British Sessional Papers, Commons, Reports, 1897, West India Royal Commission, as used by Eric Williams, *From Columbus to Castro; The History of the Caribbean, 1492-1969* (London, Deutsch, 1969), p. 366.

[a]Leewards include Antigua, St. Kitt's, Nevis, Montserrat, Tortola.

Colonies	1815	1828	1882	1894
Jamaica	79,660	72,198	32,638	19,993
Barbados	8,837	16,942	48,325	50,958
Leewards[a]	20,264	19,074	31,648	31,084
Trinidad	7,682	13,285	55,327	19,934
Guiana	16,520	40,115	124,102	102,502
Other British colonies	35,114	40,782	23,098	35,799
Total B.W.I.	168,077	202,396	315,138	260,211
Cuba	39,961	72,635	595,000	1,054,214

TABLE 12. The British West Indian Sugar Industry, 1897

Source: As for Table 11.

[a]Windwards include Dominica, Grenada, Tobago.
[b]Dashes indicate totals unknown.

Colonies	Cane acreage (thou. acres)	Sugar production (thou. tons p. a.)	Sugar workers (thou.)	Factories	Estates over 500 acres	Factories producing brown sugar	Steam mills
Jamaica	30	20	39	140	137	40	95
Barbados	74	51	47	440	23	432	99
Antigua	15	12	12	78	1	77	—[b]
St. Kitt's and Nevis	22	17	16	136	35	135	79
Montserrat	6	2	3	26	—[b]	26	12
Trinidad	34	47	14	56	—[b]	7	56
Guiana	67	103	90	64	57	2	64
Windwards[a]	4	2	3	44	15	37	20
Total	252	254	224	984	—[b]	756	—[b]

TABLE 13. Worthy Park Estate: Area, Production, Cattle, 1830-1970, by Decades (rounded averages)

Source: Worthy Park records.

	Total acreage (thou.)	Cane acreage	Improved pasture (acres)	Other crops (acres)	Sugar production (tons)	Jamaican sugar (thou. tons)	Rum production (thou. gals.)	Cattle
1830	4.0	480	350	100	350	69	23	300
1840	4.0	300	500	—	187	27	15	250
1850	4.0	250	550	—	150	30	12	150
1860	4.0	230	620	—	175	33	14	125
1870	4.8	300	550	—	230	25	18	125
1880	8.0	312	500	100	257	17	23	125
1890	10.0	426	600	120	234	17	40	200
1900	10.0	294	700	170	353	20	32	400
1910	10.0	368	750	350	255	20	40	540
1920	11.5	340	750	250	500	34	100	750
1930	11.5	819	400	100	1,700	65	250	250
1940	11.5	1,019	500	50	3,500	157	0	250
1950	11.5	1,200	1,000	100	7,500	400	0	500
1960	12.5	1,500	1,500	350	12,500	700	0	1,000
1970	12.2	1,550	1,600	450	17,000	400	0	1,800

Part One
The Slave Population at Large

Cane cutting in February, St. Kitts. The straggly fields and rather haphazard cutting gang suggests Worthy Park Estate in its early days.

1 / The Population before 1783

EXCEPT for a single list of slaves for the year 1730, tacked onto the will of Colonel Charles Price (1678-1730), Worthy Park's population is unrecorded before 1783, when the estate had already been in existence for 113 years. Naturally this book concentrates on the recorded period, but some background is necessary to lend perspective. In place of specific records, inferences about those who lived on the estate before 1783 must be made from the known facts of Worthy Park's economic development, in correlation with general descriptions of Jamaican slave society in its early and developing years. Yet this method can be positively advantageous. By going beyond the records which have survived, a wide view of slave society is possible than that circumscribed by the masters' lists. By delving back beyond the heavily recorded period it can also be seen that slave society in the plantations' early years was altogether cruder than that described in the majority of accounts—written when estates were well established and sophisticated enough to send in regular returns. In other words, it was the era of Hans Sloane rather than Thomas Roughley, Bryan Edwards, William Beckford, or even Edward Long.[1]

What then can be known of Worthy Park's earliest inhabitants, particularly the black slaves? How many were there: men, women and children? Where did they come from? What of their culture? How did they live, and work, and adapt?

When "Luidas Savanna" was simply an area of cattle pens, hog "crawles," and polinks (c. 1670-1710), there would have been no more than a handful of people living at Worthy Park. Compared with existence on a sugar plantation, their life would have been relatively healthy and free from constraint. Worthy Park's first population may well have included the most trusty of the Price's slaves, well-affected Creoles as well as lively Senegambians used to cattle husbandry from their native African savanna-lands. There were probably also some Amerindians or mestizos, seized from the Mosquito Coast of Honduras or inherited from the Spaniards—people of olive skin and long, lank hair, said to be "nought at working in the Fields or slavish work, and if chekt or drub'd . . . good for nothing, therefore . . . very gently treated, and well fed."[2]

With the clearing of trees and the beginning of sugar planting, the

53

quality of life for those working in Lluidas Vale inevitably deteriorated. Besides a few white servants to build, install, and run the factory, a herd of tractable blacks was needed, with no more skills than were called for in the West African agriculture of slashing, burning, and hoeing. These field and factory drudges would be controlled through the most reliable of the black drivers transferred from Guanaboa Vale. Within the second decade of the eighteenth century the population of Worthy Park soared through wholesale purchases, first to the minimum work force of about 150 needed to start a new sugar plantation, then to the 200 or more of a reasonably viable population. The notorious mortality of new Africans in the intensive agriculture of sugar cultivation suggests the purchase of well over 350 new slaves within the first ten years. In 1730 the population was 240, which increased steadily with Worthy Park's sugar production to 320 over the next fifty years. This later augmentation was not achieved by natural increase—for deaths probably exceeded births by about 2 percent per year—but by continuing purchases at the rate of about 3.5 percent, or 10 new Africans a year.

Worthy Park's 240 slaves in 1730 were carefully listed in seven categories, according to sex and value. First the 107 adult black males were divided into a group of 82 valued at £50 each, and one of 25—presumably the aged and diseased—valued at half as much. Similarly, 48 of the 75 adult black females were valued at £45 each, and the remaining 27 at £20. Additionally, there were 25 boys and 29 girls listed, all at £25 each. Finally, there were six Indians, valued at between £10 and £30 apiece, three with Spanish and three with Amerindian names: Augustin, Magdalin, Marea, Tabelon, Debako, and Edegoade.[3]

In the early years of the plantations slaves were not so carefully graded into gangs as they were later.[4] Yet since the first 45 adult male slaves alone were listed alphabetically, these may well have constituted a "First Gang" or prime field labor force, with the remaining 62 including—in random order—the body of "Lesser Negroes" employed in miscellaneous manual tasks, the specialist slaves, and the drivers. Except for the two grades of value, the roster of adult women showed no differentiation. Besides this, it is clear from their numbers that the list of boys and girls included all those called "pickaninnies" (from the Spanish *pequeños niños*); these were not only infants but also those aged 6 to 12 regarded as "fit to be put to clean the Paths, bring Fire-wood to the Kitchen &c. when a Boy Overseer with his Wand or White Rod, is set over them as Task-Master"—what was later called the "Pickney Gang."[5]

Projections have been made to show that in 1730 some 80 percent of Worthy Park's slaves were likely to have been born in Africa.[6] Since nearly all the boys and girls would have been Creoles, this meant that virtually all the adult black slaves were African- rather than Jamaican-born. Planters were at pains to mix Africans from different tribes, but this was more difficult in the early years when slaves were purchased in large groups and were often "ship-mates." The researches of Philip Curtin have shown that during the period of Worthy Park's establishment by far the most popular catchment area for Jamaican slaves was the Gold Coast—the slaves from which were usually called "Coromantines" after the chief shipping port. Between 1702 and 1775, more than a third of Jamaican slave imports came from the Gold Coast, though this was only one of seven areas tapped.[7]

Most Gold Coast slaves spoke one of the Akan languages, and the early preference for Coromantines seems borne out by the remarkably high proportion of slaves in Worthy Park's 1730 list who still bore Akan "day-names." Some 130 slaves were listed with African rather than European (or Amerindian) names, but of these no less than 63 carried one of the fourteen Akan names indicating on which day of the week they had been born. Among the pickaninnies the proportion was even more remarkable, 27 out of 54, probably because their parents had named them in the traditional way and there had not yet been time to assume or be labeled with a European name.

Coromantine slaves were thought to be hardy and resourceful, excellent workers once tamed, but tenacious of their culture and prone to rebellion.[8] After the dreadful slave revolt of 1760 led by Coromantines, lasting several months and leading to the deaths of 60 whites and 1,000 blacks, many Jamaican planters lost their enthusiasm for Gold Coast slaves and even tried to have their importation banned. Indeed, 1760 may have represented something of a watershed in Jamaican slavery, analogous in some of its effects to the so-called Indian Mutiny of 1857. After 1760 the plantations and their populations became increasingly well established and creolized (that is, adapted to the new environment, with their culture syncretized), but the planters were far more concerned about questions of standardization and control. Before 1760, plantation life was far more casual, and callous, but also more African in quality.

To Africans accustomed to subsistence farming, plantation agriculture was dislocatingly strange, if not unnatural. The planters' profit motive meant nothing to them, and their spirit probably resisted the forests' despoliation as much as the exploitation of themselves. Most slaves were driven harshly, roused from their huts by the conch shell long before dawn, and worked under the whip until after sundown. Dinner at midday lasted an hour, but if the slaves were allowed to leave the fields they were expected to carry loads as they went to avoid wasted labor.[9]

From the earliest days, the Jamaican slave laws made gestures towards the provision of minimal standards of food and clothing; but such clauses were almost impossible to implement, and most planters spent as little as possible on the upkeep of their slaves. Housing was rudimentary, though being constructed by the slaves themselves it was almost African in style. "The Negroes Houses are . . . at a distance from their Masters," wrote Hans Sloane, "And are small, oblong, thatch'd Huts, in which they have all their Moveables or Goods, which are generally a Mat to lie on, a Pot of Earth to boil their Victuals in, either Yams, Plantains, or Potatoes, with a little salt Mackaral, and a Calabash or two for Cups and Spoons."[10]

Most masters provided their slaves with only one simple suit of clothes each year, at Christmas: for the men "a little Canvas Jacket and Breeches," and for the women a plain smock and head kerchief. Contrary to most later illustrations of plantation life—which show slaves in their holiday best or working in European-style clothes—slaves in the early days worked almost naked in the fields and factories, "their Cloths serving them but a very small part of the year." Even the women wore little more than a breech cloth in the fields, "with their little ones ty'd to their Backs, in a Cloth on purpose, one leg on one side, and the other on the other. . . . The Mother when she suckles her young, having no Clothes to keep her Breasts from falling down, they hang very lank ever after, like those of Goats."[11]

The few respites from direct supervision must have been very precious to the slaves. Except during crop time, slaves were generally spared from the canefields and factories one and one-half days each weekend; but during this time they were set to cultivate the "Negro Grounds" which helped to make each Jamaican plantation almost self-sufficient for food. Slave diet therefore depended largely on the industry of the slaves themselves. At best it was unsuitable for hard manual labor, being heavy in carbohydrates and poor in proteins, though in these respects it was very similar to the normal diet of indigenous West Africans.[12] The very style of cultivation in the Negro Grounds provided a link with Africa that was never entirely broken, as well as with the independent peasant cultivation that was to come after emancipation.

Another obvious link with Africa was afforded by the slave celebrations at Christmas and Easter and on such weekend nights as were permitted by the masters. In the earliest days these were occasions for purely African dances, accompanied by music on African instruments, and African songs. Not surprisingly, the whites were hazy about what was going on, cloaking their ignorance in condescension, disparagement, or—where the powerful strangeness engendered fear—repression. Inventing a long-lived stereotype, many writers conceded that the blacks possessed rhythmic skills, though Europeans in general were ignorant of the wit, grace, and ritual significances of the songs and dances. Though Hans Sloane gave a careful account of African instruments, he claimed that all the songs were bawdy and all the dances lewd. He also reported that a certain type of trumpet (probably the cow-horn called the *abeng*) and a sonorous drum made out of tree-trunk were banned by the planters, since they were thought to be used in African warfare and might incite the slaves to rebellion.[13]

Ignorance and European pride led Sloane and others to claim that the Africans had no religion, though most such plantocratic writers' own accounts gave ample descriptions of animistic beliefs, under the label of "superstitions." For example, Sloane wrote:

The Negroes from some Countries think they return to their own Country when they die in *Jamaica* and therefore regard death but little, imagining they shall change their condition, by that means from servile to free, and so for this reason often cut their own throats. Whether they die thus, or naturally, their Country people make great lamentations, mournings and howlings, about them expiring, and at their Funeral throw in Rum and Victuals into their Graves, to serve them in the other world. Sometimes they bury it in Gourds, at other times spill it on the Graves.[14]

Naturally Sloane, a doctor, decried the ministrations of "Black Doctors" and nurses, and denied the efficacy of most "bush medicine." However, he gave careful descriptions of African methods and was forced to admit that some of them, for all he knew, might avail in some cases. As to the success experienced by black doctors in the use of "Jesuits' Bark" (quinine), Sloane was positively envious. Honesty also compelled the famous empiricist to describe many ways in which the black slaves, although unacculturated, still demonstrated qualities that were objectively admirable. When they had the chance they were extremely cleanly, bathing far more frequently than Europeans. Contrary to most opinion, they loved their children so much that masters risked the "melancholy decline" or even suicide of parents if children were taken away or sold separately. The African slaves, despite an alleged tendency to venery, were said by Sloane to be extremely scrupulous about marital, family, and kinship matters. "They have every one his Wife," he wrote, "and are very much concern'd if they prove adulterous, but in some measure satisfied if their Master punish the Man who does the supposed injury. . . . The care of the Masters and Overseers about their Wives, is what keeps their Plantations chiefly in good order, whence they ever buy Wives in proportion to their Men, lest the Men should wander to neighbouring Plantations, and neglect to serve them."[15]

The Price family estates never suffered from slave rebellions, though there were at least three serious uprisings in neighboring areas in 1678, 1686, and 1760.[16] One school of thought would attribute this to the effectiveness of the forces of control and the notorious savagery of the deterrents used by the masters. According to Sloane, the punishment for rebellion was public execution by being nailed to the ground and slowly burnt to death. For lesser insubordination, males slaves were said to have been castrated or their feet mutilated with an axe. Runaways were loaded with chains, and all slaves were encouraged by frequent whippings to work hard and obey. Obdurate blacks were said to have been first whipped raw and then to have had salt rubbed in their wounds or melted wax dripped into them.[17]

Yet Jamaican slave punishments were known to be more in the nature of drastic attempted cures than effective preventatives, and in the case of such slaves as the Coromantines they were notoriously counterproductive. Moreover, Worthy Park must have been among the most difficult of all Jamaican estates to control by physical means, being deep in the backwoods with only a few dozen whites within miles and the nearest military at least two days' march away. Equally plausible explanations for Worthy Park's lack of slave rebellions might include management that, though not weak, was at least judicious and social conditions that were increasingly self-controlling.

As Hans Sloane hinted, wise planters encouraged social cohesion within their plantations. Though cruelly worked and severely restricted in their movements outside the estate, the slaves were left much to their own devices in the Negro quarters. Some masters actively promoted the kind of family relationships with which the Africans were familiar and which made for a stable social group. Discriminating masters also made much use of the Africans' own natural leaders—so that privileged black drivers were said to become the worst of the slaves' domestic tyrants. For example, Sir Charles Price, "The Patriot" (who managed Worthy Park in the 1750s and 1760s), was famous for freeing a particularly faithful slave each year, thereafter using him as an agent. One Coromantine whom Price freed and gave authority to was said to have been instrumental in preventing the spread of the 1760 rebellion to the Price plantations—not only informing on dissidents but also persuading his fellow Coromantines not to rebel.[18]

Coromantines were exceptionally resistant to assimilation, but even they were gradually submerged, acculturated, creolized.* As time went on, the imprint and memories of Africa faded or became more generalized, as the proportion of Creoles in the population insensibly increased and the trickle of new recruits was taken indiscriminately from tribes as different from each other as Lapps from Basques or Greeks. In time, moreover, the pattern of kinship as well as hierarchy within the plantation became less dependent upon Africa than upon the plantation itself. The plantation became all that the members of its unique society had in common, for all its deficiencies, the only home they knew.

Were detailed records as deficient for the entire period of slavery as they are for the earlier phases, these conclusions would remain almost entirely hypothetical. An opportunity, however, can now be taken to see how well they square with the very large accumulation of data available for Worthy Park in the period 1783-1838.

---

*Throughout this book "assimilation" is used to mean complete absorption into the dominant culture. "Acculturation" is used in the Merriam-Webster Dictionary sense of "a process of intercultural borrowing between diverse peoples resulting in new and diverse patterns." "Creolization" is used for acculturation of the Caribbean type.

Day of Birth	Akan day-names	1730 (all slaves)	1730 (boys and girls)	1783-1838 (all slaves)
Monday	Cudjoe (male)	4	1	7
	Juba (female)	3	1	4
Tuesday	Cubbena (male)	3	2	1
	Beneba (female)	2	0	6
Wednesday	Quaco (male)	4	1	0
	Cuba (female)	5	2	8
Thursday	Quao or Quaw (male)	3	3	2
	Abba or Yabba (female)	11	6	7
Friday	Cuffee (male)	5	4	6
	Phibba (female)	6	2	9
Saturday	Quamina (male)	2	1	4
	Mimba (female)	5	2	1
Sunday	Quashee (male)	4	1	7
	Quasheba (female)	6	1	4
Total with Akan day-names		63	27	66
Total of slave population		240	54	1,377

Table 14. Worthy Park: Akan Day-Names, 1730 and 1783-1838

Source: Worthy Park records.

2 / Demographic Patterns, 1783-1838

DEMOGRAPHIC statistics are cold and impersonal in themselves, but when comprehensive they can suggest whole new insights into the quality of life. Moreover, detailed statistics spread over fifty-six years as in the case of Worthy Park allow for a dynamic presentation of plantation life that bears the same relation to the normal static description as movie does to snapshot.

This first of four chapters spanning the last half-century of formal slavery concentrates on the demographic outlines of Worthy Park's slave population, the changing patterns of total numbers, the age cohorts and average numbers, the proportion of males to females, Africans to Creoles, colored slaves to blacks. Even more than the three chapters that follow, this chapter deals chiefly with figures and their formal analysis. But not much imagination is needed to add, as color and flesh, the human dimensions.

A large number of people were crammed closely together in Worthy Park, but in an unusual, unnatural way. In numbers it was the population of a largish village; but it had few of the demographic characteristics of normal villages, in Africa, Europe, or elsewhere. It was an artificial village, created for a special purpose, and subject to imbalances and changes unknown outside the plantation colonies. There was an unnaturally high proportion of adults, yet hardly ever an equal number of men and women in the same age ranges. Children were always proportionately few. Moreover, the plantation society was a microcosmic melting pot, its members divided by race, by place of birth, and, consequently, by culture. Only in the last decades of slavery did these characteristics begin to fade, consequences of the ending of the slave trade, the hardening of racial lines, and the insensibly tightening embrace of the Creole environment.

In the statistical presentation which follows, the forms of the tables and graphs are more or less self-explanatory.* The so-called "population pyramids," the most important component of this section, perhaps

---

*Discussion of the statistical raw material and its deficiencies—particularly of inconsistent categories and sequential gaps, and the uses made of correlation and projection—is relegated to Appendix A.

require a little more explanation for the general reader. These diagrams, produced in their original form by the graphic printer of an IBM computer fed simply the sex, birth date, and continent of birth of each slave, show, laterally, the percentage of the total population represented by each cohort of five years. The proportions of the sexes in each cohort are shown by delineating males on the left of a vertical line, females on the right. The proportion of Africans in each cohort and sex group is shown by darker shading.

In line with normal demographic practice, five-year age cohorts were used, despite the rather limited sizes of the annual samples. In some years, ten-year cohorts might have proved more graphic, but the smaller interval was kept for the sake of consistency. Originally, "over 60" was to have been the oldest category, but so many slaves were found in that bracket that the pyramids became top-heavy, and "over 70" was chosen instead.

At first, pyramids were printed out for each of the twenty-seven years for which reasonably complete data existed, though the sequence lost clarity through the unevenness of the material. Some thought was given to clumping the pyramid data into groups of four to seven years, in order to smooth out deficiencies in the annual data by increasing the size of the samples and thus to show a more significant dynamic progression. The clumped years which suggested themselves were: the earliest recorded years before reorganization (1787-1792); the years of Rose Price's reorganization (1793-1796); the period immediately after the abolition of the slave trade (1811-1817); the critical years of the amelioration period (1821-1824); the last five years of full slavery (1830-1834); the Apprenticeship years (1835-1838). However, it was realized that since a population pyramid is of its nature a static census of a population, averages derived from several years would have very limited validity, and single years were, in the end, preferred.

The years chosen were those for which data were adequate, at five-year intervals as far as possible: 1790, 1794, 1813, 1818, 1823, 1828, 1833, 1838. A serious gap between 1794 and 1812 remained, though this could be filled in by projections at least as valid as that confidently extrapolated for the single year 1730 in the analytical conclusion of this chapter.

What patterns emerge from these tables, graphs, and pyramids, and what do they indicate? An immediate reaction is that, as far as the diagrams are concerned, the word "pyramid" is a misnomer in the case of a typical slave population. A perfectly stable and closed population is illustratable by a perfectly symmetrical pyramid; yet the same technique used to illustrate a slave population produces a diagram looking more like a lopsided Christmas tree. The "bulge"—or widespread lower branches—in the middle age ranges is, of course, the result of the need for a large labor force, the preference for those in the 15-25 age group, and the facility with which they could be recruited by means of the slave trade. The puny "trunk" which gives the slave population

(continued on p. 72)

Figure 2. Worthy Park: Population Pyramid I, 1790, and Data

Note: Males on left, females on right.

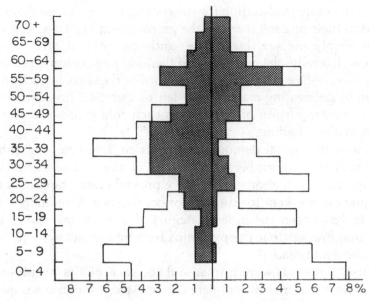

Cohort	Ages	Africans M	Africans F	% Total Africans of all	% African M of all	% African F of all	Creoles M	Creoles F	Total M	Total F	All M and F	% Cohort of all	% M of all	% F of all
1	0-4	0	0	0	0	0	11	19	11	19	30	12.55	4.60	7.95
2	5-9	2	1	1.26	0.84	0.42	13	13	15	14	29	12.13	6.28	5.86
	0-9	2	1	1.26	0.84	0.42	24	32	26	33	59	24.69	10.88	13.81
3	10-14	2	0	0.84	0.84	0	9	6	11	6	17	7.11	4.60	2.51
4	15-19	1	1	0.84	0.42	0.42	8	11	9	12	21	8.79	3.77	5.02
	10-19	3	1	1.67	1.26	0.42	17	17	20	18	38	15.90	8.37	7.53
5	20-24	2	1	1.26	0.84	0.42	3	4	5	5	10	4.18	2.09	2.09
6	25-29	2	6	3.35	0.84	2.51	2	8	4	14	18	7.53	1.67	5.86
	20-29	4	7	4.60	1.67	2.93	5	12	9	19	28	11.71	3.77	7.95
7	30-34	8	5	5.44	3.35	2.09	2	5	10	10	20	8.37	4.18	4.18
8	35-39	8	1	3.77	3.35	0.42	8	6	16	7	23	9.62	6.69	2.93
	30-39	16	6	9.21	6.70	2.51	10	11	26	17	43	17.99	10.88	7.11
9	40-44	8	2	4.18	3.35	0.84	2	0	10	2	12	5.02	4.18	0.84
10	45-49	5	4	3.77	2.09	1.67	3	2	8	6	14	5.86	3.35	2.51
	40-49	13	6	7.95	5.44	2.51	5	2	18	8	26	10.88	7.53	3.35
11	50-54	3	4	2.93	1.26	1.67	0	0	3	4	7	2.93	1.26	1.67
12	55-59	7	10	7.11	2.93	4.18	0	3	7	13	20	8.37	2.93	5.44
	50-59	10	14	10.04	4.18	5.86	0	3	10	17	27	11.30	4.18	7.11
13	60-64	3	5	3.35	1.26	2.09	0	1	3	6	9	3.77	1.26	2.51
14	65-69	2	3	2.09	0.84	1.26	0	0	2	3	5	2.09	0.84	1.26
	60-69	5	8	5.44	2.09	3.35	0	1	5	9	14	5.86	2.09	3.77
15	70+	1	3	1.67	0.42	1.26	0	0	1	3	4	1.67	0.42	1.26
	70+	1	3	1.67	0.42	1.26	0	0	1	3	4	1.67	0.42	1.26
Total		54	46	41.84	22.59	19.25	61	78	115	124		100.00		
Grand total		100					139		239		239			

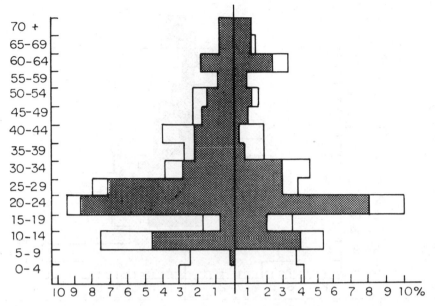

Figure 3. Worthy Park:
Population Pyramid II,
1794, and Data

Cohort	Ages	Africans M	F	% Total Africans of all	% African M of all	% African F of all	Creoles M	F	Total M	F	All M and F	% Cohort of all	% M of all	% F of all
1	0-4	0	0	0	0	0	15	19	15	19	34	7.54	3.33	4.21
2	4-9	1	0	0.22	0.22	0	11	16	12	16	28	6.21	2.66	3.55
	0-9	1	0	0.22	0.22	0	26	35	27	35	62	13.75	5.99	7.76
3	10-14	21	17	8.43	4.66	3.77	14	12	35	29	64	14.19	7.76	6.43
4	15-19	3	8	2.44	0.67	1.77	7	8	10	16	26	5.76	2.22	3.55
	10-19	24	25	10.86	5.32	5.54	21	20	45	45	90	19.95	9.98	9.98
5	20-24	40	36	16.85	8.87	7.98	7	8	47	44	91	20.18	10.42	9.76
6	25-29	31	13	9.76	6.87	2.88	3	3	34	16	50	11.09	7.54	3.55
	20-29	71	49	26.61	15.74	10.86	10	11	81	60	141	31.26	17.96	13.30
7	30-34	13	13	5.76	2.88	2.88	4	7	17	20	37	8.20	3.77	4.43
8	35-39	10	3	2.88	2.22	0.67	2	4	12	7	19	4.21	2.66	1.55
	30-39	23	16	8.65	5.10	3.55	6	11	29	27	56	12.42	6.43	5.99
9	40-44	10	2	2.66	2.22	0.44	8	6	18	8	26	5.76	3.99	1.77
10	45-49	8	3	2.44	1.77	0.67	2	0	10	3	13	2.88	2.22	0.67
	40-49	18	5	5.10	3.99	1.11	10	6	28	11	39	8.65	6.21	2.44
11	50-54	7	5	2.66	1.55	1.11	3	2	10	7	17	3.77	2.22	1.55
12	55-59	3	3	1.33	0.67	0.67	0	0	3	3	6	1.33	0.67	0.67
	50-59	10	8	3.99	2.22	1.77	3	2	13	10	23	5.10	2.88	2.22
13	60-64	8	11	4.21	1.77	2.44	0	3	8	14	22	4.88	1.77	3.10
14	65-69	3	5	1.77	0.67	1.11	0	1	3	6	9	2.00	0.67	1.33
	60-69	11	16	5.99	2.44	3.55	0	4	11	20	31	6.87	2.44	4.43
15	70+	3	6	2.00	0.67	1.33	0	0	3	6	9	2.00	0.67	1.33
	70+	3	6	2.00	0.67	1.33	0	0	3	6	9	2.00	0.67	1.33
Total		161	125	63.41	35.70	27.72	76	89	237	214		100.00		
Grand total		286					165		451		451			

Figure 4. Worthy Park:
Population Pyramid III,
1813, and Data

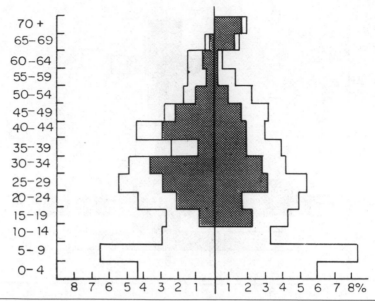

Cohort	Ages	Africans M	Africans F	% Total Africans of all	% African M of all	% African F of all	Creoles M	Creoles F	Total M	Total F	All M and F	% Cohort of all	% M of all	% F of all
1	0-4	0	0	0	0	0	21	27	21	27	48	10.21	4.47	5.74
2	4-9	0	0	0	0	0	31	39	31	39	70	14.89	6.60	8.29
	0-9	0	0	0	0	0	52	66	52	66	118	25.11	11.06	14.05
3	10-14	0	1	0.21	0	0.21	14	14	14	15	29	6.17	2.98	3.19
4	15-19	4	10	2.98	0.85	2.13	9	11	13	21	34	7.23	2.77	4.46
	10-19	4	11	3.19	0.85	2.34	23	25	27	36	63	13.40	5.74	7.66
5	20-24	12	7	4.04	2.56	1.47	8	16	20	23	43	9.15	4.26	4.89
6	25-29	14	14	5.96	2.98	2.98	11	10	25	24	49	10.43	5.32	5.11
	20-29	26	21	10.00	5.53	4.47	19	26	45	47	92	19.58	9.57	10.01
7	30-34	17	13	6.38	3.62	2.76	6	7	23	20	43	9.15	4.89	4.26
8	35-39	4	9	2.77	0.85	1.91	7	10	11	19	30	6.38	2.34	4.04
	30-39	21	22	9.15	4.47	4.68	13	17	34	39	73	15.53	7.23	8.30
9	40-44	14	9	4.89	2.98	1.91	7	5	21	14	35	7.45	4.47	2.98
10	45-49	10	8	3.83	2.13	1.70	3	7	13	15	28	5.96	2.77	3.19
	40-49	24	17	8.72	5.11	3.61	10	12	34	29	63	13.41	7.23	6.18
11	50-54	5	4	1.91	1.06	0.85	3	6	8	10	18	3.83	1.70	2.13
12	55-59	2	2	0.85	0.43	0.43	5	6	7	8	15	3.19	1.49	1.70
	50-59	7	6	2.77	1.49	1.28	8	12	15	18	33	7.02	3.19	3.83
13	60-64	3	2	1.06	0.64	0.42	4	1	7	3	10	2.13	1.49	0.64
14	65-69	1	5	1.28	0.21	1.06	1	2	2	7	9	1.91	0.42	1.49
	60-69	4	7	2.34	0.85	1.49	5	3	9	10	19	4.04	1.91	2.13
15	70+	0	8	1.70	0	1.70	0	1	0	9	9	1.91	0	1.91
	70+	0	8	1.70	0	1.70	0	1	0	9	9	1.91	0	1.91
Total		86	92	37.87	18.30	19.57	130	162	216	254		100.00		
Grand total		178					292		470		470			

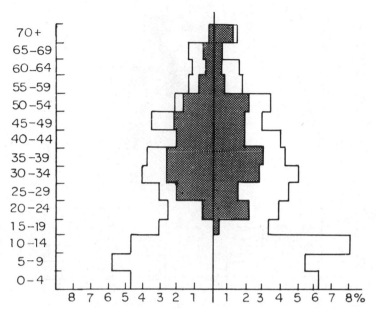

Figure 5. Worthy Park:
Population Pyramid IV,
1818, and Data

Cohort	Ages	Afri-cans M	F	% Total Afri-cans of all	% Afri-can M of all	% Afri-can F of all	Creoles M	F	Total M	F	All M and F	% Cohort of all	% M of all	% F of all
1	0-4	0	0	0	0	0	23	38	23	38	61	12.55	4.73	7.82
2	5-9	0	0	0	0	0	30	26	30	26	56	11.56	6.17	5.35
	0-9	0	0	0	0	0	53	64	53	64	117	24.07	10.91	13.16
3	10-14	0	0	0	0	0	22	37	22	37	59	12.14	4.53	7.61
4	15-19	0	1	0.21	0	0.21	16	14	16	15	31	6.38	3.29	3.09
	10-19	0	1	0.21	0	0.21	38	51	38	52	90	18.52	7.82	10.70
5	20-24	3	9	2.47	0.62	1.85	10	9	13	18	31	6.38	2.67	3.71
6	25-29	11	7	3.71	2.26	1.44	7	14	18	21	39	8.02	3.70	4.32
	20-29	14	16	6.17	2.88	3.29	17	23	31	39	70	14.40	6.38	8.02
7	30-34	14	13	5.55	2.88	2.67	8	9	22	22	44	9.05	4.53	4.52
8	35-39	13	14	5.55	2.67	2.88	5	6	18	20	38	7.82	3.70	4.12
	30-39	27	27	11.11	5.56	5.56	13	15	40	44	82	16.87	8.23	8.64
9	40-44	4	9	2.67	0.82	1.85	6	9	10	18	28	5.76	2.06	3.70
10	45-49	12	9	4.32	2.47	1.85	6	5	18	14	32	6.58	3.70	2.88
	40-49	16	18	7.00	3.29	3.70	12	14	28	32	60	12.35	5.76	6.59
11	50-54	9	9	3.70	1.85	1.85	2	7	11	16	27	5.56	2.26	3.30
12	55-59	4	3	1.44	0.82	0.62	3	6	7	9	16	3.29	0.62	1.85
	50-59	13	12	5.14	2.67	2.47	5	13	18	25	43	8.85	3.70	5.15
13	60-64	1	2	0.62	0.21	0.41	2	5	3	7	10	2.06	3.70	1.44
14	65-69	2	1	0.62	0.41	0.21	4	—	6	1	7	1.44	1.23	0.21
	60-69	3	3	1.23	0.62	0.62	6	5	9	8	17	3.50	1.85	1.65
15	70+	0	6	1.23	0	1.23	0	1	0	7	7	1.44	0	1.44
	70+	0	6	1.23	0	1.23	0	1	0	7	7	1.44	0	1.44
Total		73	83	32.10	15.02	17.08	144	186	217	269		100.00		
Grand total		156					230		486		486			

Figure 6. Worthy Park:
Population Pyramid V,
1823, and Data

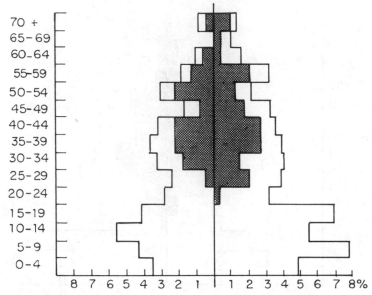

Cohort	Ages	Africans M	Africans F	% Total Africans of all	% African M of all	% African F of all	Creoles M	Creoles F	Total M	Total F	All M and F	% Cohort of all	% M of all	% F of all
1	0-4	0	0	0.	0	0	19	22	19	22	41	8.42	3.90	4.52
2	5-9	0	0	0	0	0	21	38	21	38	59	12.11	4.31	7.80
	0-9	0	0	0	0	0	40	60	40	60	100	20.54	8.21	12.33
3	10-14	0	0	0	0	0	28	25	28	25	53	10.88	5.75	5.13
4	15-19	0	0	0	0	0	21	34	21	34	55	11.29	4.31	6.98
	10-19	0	0	0	0	0	49	59	49	59	108	22.18	10.07	12.11
5	20-24	0	1	0.21	0	0.21	15	14	15	15	30	6.16	3.08	3.08
6	25-29	2	10	2.46	0.41	2.05	9	9	11	19	30	6.16	2.26	3.90
	20-29	2	11	2.67	0.41	2.26	24	23	26	34	60	12.32	5.34	6.98
7	30-34	10	7	3.49	2.05	1.43	7	13	17	20	37	7.60	3.49	4.11
8	35-39	12	11	4.72	2.46	2.26	7	10	19	21	40	8.21	3.90	4.31
	30-39	22	18	8.21	4.52	3.69	14	23	36	41	77	15.81	7.39	8.42
9	40-44	12	11	4.72	2.46	2.26	4	7	16	18	34	6.98	3.29	3.69
10	45-49	4	8	2.46	0.82	1.64	4	9	8	17	25	5.13	1.64	3.49
	40-49	16	19	7.19	3.29	3.90	8	16	24	35	59	12.11	4.93	7.18
11	50-54	12	6	3.69	2.46	1.23	4	5	16	11	27	5.54	3.29	2.25
12	55-59	7	8	3.08	1.43	1.64	3	7	10	15	25	5.13	2.05	3.08
	50-59	19	14	6.78	3.90	2.88	7	12	26	26	52	10.68	5.34	5.34
13	60-64	3	2	1.03	0.62	0.41	3	6	6	8	14	2.87	1.23	1.64
14	65-69	0	2	0.41	0	0.41	0	3	0	5	5	1.03	0	1.03
	60-69	3	4	1.43	0.62	0.82	3	9	6	13	19	3.90	1.23	2.67
15	70+	2	5	1.43	0.41	1.03	3	2	5	7	12	2.46	1.03	1.43
	70+	2	5	1.43	0.41	1.03	3	2	5	7	12	2.46	1.03	1.43
Total		64	71	27.72	13.14	14.58	148	204	212	275		100.00		
Grand total		135					352		487		487			

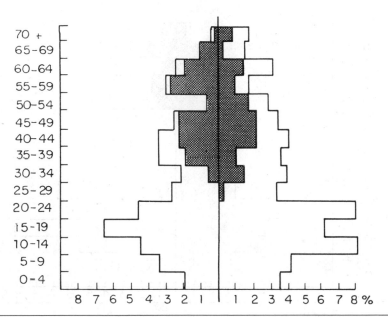

Figure 7. Worthy Park: Population Pyramid VI, 1828, and Data

Cohort	Ages	Africans M	F	% Total Africans of all	% African M of all	% African F of all	Creoles M	F	Total M	F	All M and F	% Cohort of all	% M of all	% F of all
1	0-4	0	0	0	0	0	11	14	11	14	25	6.36	2.80	3.56
2	5-9	0	0	0	0	0	11	16	11	16	27	6.87	2.80	4.07
	0-9	0	0	0	0	0	22	30	22	30	52	13.23	5.60	7.63
3	10-14	0	0	0	0	0	14	31	14	31	45	11.45	3.56	7.89
4	15-19	0	0	0	0	0	24	23	24	23	47	11.96	6.11	5.85
	10-19	0	0	0	0	0	38	54	38	54	92	23.41	9.67	13.74
5	20-24	0	0	0	0	0	17	30	17	30	47	11.96	4.33	7.63
6	25-29	0	1	0.25	0	0.25	10	12	10	13	23	5.85	2.54	3.31
	20-29	0	1	0.25	0	0.25	27	42	27	43	70	17.81	6.87	10.94
7	30-34	2	6	2.04	0.51	1.53	6	9	8	15	23	5.85	2.04	3.81
8	35-39	7	4	2.80	1.78	1.02	6	10	13	14	27	6.87	3.31	3.56
	30-39	9	10	4.83	2.29	2.54	12	19	21	29	50	12.72	5.35	7.37
9	40-44	8	9	4.33	2.04	2.29	5	6	13	15	28	7.12	3.31	3.82
10	45-49	8	9	4.33	2.04	2.29	1	5	9	14	23	5.85	2.29	3.56
	40-49	16	18	8.66	4.07	4.58	6	11	22	29	51	12.98	5.60	7.38
11	50-54	2	7	2.29	0.51	1.78	4	8	6	15	21	5.34	1.53	3.81
12	55-59	10	4	3.56	2.54	1.02	1	2	11	6	17	4.33	2.80	1.53
	50-59	12	11	5.85	3.05	2.80	5	10	17	21	38	9.67	4.33	5.34
13	60-64	7	6	3.31	1.78	1.53	2	7	9	13	22	5.60	2.29	3.31
14	65-69	3	1	1.02	0.25	0.78	1	5	4	6	10	2.54	1.02	1.53
	60-69	10	7	4.33	2.03	2.31	3	12	13	19	32	8.14	3.31	4.84
15	70+	0	4	1.02	0	1.02	1	3	1	7	8	2.04	0.25	1.78
	70+	0	4	1.02	0	1.02	1	3	1	7	8	2.04	0.25	1.78
Total		47	51	24.94	11.96	12.97	114	181	161	232		100.00		
Grand total		98					295		393		393			

Figure 8. Worthy Park:
Population Pyramid VII,
1833, and Data

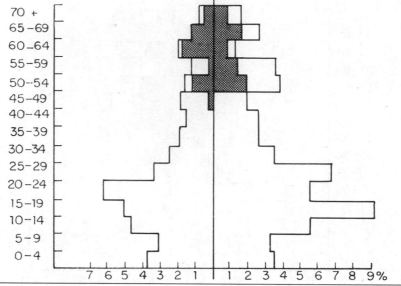

Cohort	Ages	Africans M	Africans F	% Total Africans of all	% African M of all	% African F of all	Creoles M	Creoles F	Total M	Total F	All M and F	% Cohort of all	% M of all	% F of all
1	0-4	0	0	0	0	0	11	10	11	10	21	7.00	3.67	3.33
2	5-9	0	0	0	0	0	10	10	10	10	20	6.67	3.33	3.33
	0-9	0	0	0	0	0	21	20	21	20	41	13.67	7.00	6.67
3	10-14	0	0	0	0	0	15	17	15	17	32	10.67	5.00	5.67
4	15-19	0	0	0	0	0	16	28	16	28	44	14.67	5.33	9.33
	10-19	0	0	0	0	0	31	45	31	45	76	25.33	10.33	15.00
5	20-24	0	0	0	0	0	19	16	19	16	35	11.67	6.33	5.33
6	25-29	0	0	0	0	0	11	19	11	19	30	10.00	3.67	6.33
	20-29	0	0	0	0	0	30	35	30	35	65	21.67	10.00	11.67
7	30-34	0	0	0	0	0	8	9	8	9	17	5.67	2.67	3.00
8	35-39	0	0	0	0	0	5	8	5	8	13	4.33	1.67	2.67
	30-39	0	0	0	0	0	13	17	13	17	30	10.00	4.33	5.67
9	40-44	0	0	0	0	0	5	8	5	8	13	4.33	1.67	2.67
10	45-49	1	0	1.33	0.33	0	5	7	6	7	13	4.33	2.00	2.33
	40-49	1	0	0.33	0.33	0	10	15	11	15	26	8.66	3.67	5.00
11	50-54	4	6	3.33	1.33	2.00	1	6	5	12	17	5.67	1.67	4.00
12	55-59	1	4	1.67	0.33	1.33	3	6	4	10	14	4.67	1.33	3.33
	50-59	5	10	3.00	1.67	3.33	4	12	9	22	31	10.33	3.00	4.00
13	60-64	6	2	2.67	2.00	0.67	1	2	7	4	11	3.67	2.33	1.33
14	65-69	4	5	3.00	1.33	1.67	0	3	4	8	12	4.00	1.33	2.67
	60-69	10	7	5.67	3.33	2.33	1	5	11	12	23	7.67	3.67	4.00
15	70 +	2	2	1.33	0.67	0.67	1	3	3	5	8	2.67	1.00	1.67
	70 +	2	2	1.33	0.67	0.67	1	3	3	5	8	2.67	1.00	1.67
Total		18	19	12.33	6.00	6.33	111	152	129	171		100.00		
Grand total		37					263		300		300			

68

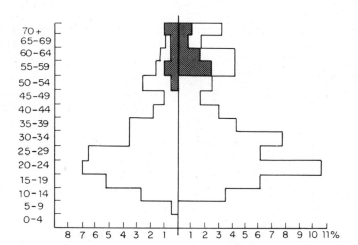

Figure 9. Worthy Park: Population Pyramid VIII, 1838, and Data

Cohort	Ages	Africans M	Africans F	% Total Africans of all	% African M of all	% African F of all	Creoles M	Creoles F	Total M	Total F	All M and F	% Cohort of all	% M of all	% F of all
1	0-4	0	0	0	0	0	0	0	0	0	0	0	0	0
2	5-9	0	0	0	0	0	1	0	1	0	1	0.44	0.44	0
	0-9	0	0	0	0	0	1	0	1	0	1	0.44	0.44	0
3	10-14	0	0	0	0	0	7	8	7	8	15	6.58	3.07	3.51
4	15-19	0	0	0	0	0	12	14	12	14	26	11.40	5.26	6.14
	10-19	0	0	0	0	0	19	22	19	22	41	17.99	8.33	9.65
5	20-24	0	0	0	0	0	16	25	16	25	41	17.98	7.02	10.96
6	25-29	0	0	0	0	0	15	14	15	14	29	12.72	6.58	6.14
	20-29	0	0	0	0	0	31	39	31	39	70	30.70	13.60	17.10
7	30-34	0	0	0	0	0	8	18	8	18	26	11.40	3.51	7.89
8	35-39	0	0	0	0	0	8	10	8	10	18	7.89	3.51	4.39
	30-39	0	0	0	0	0	16	28	16	28	44	19.30	7.02	12.28
9	40-44	0	0	0	0	0	4	7	4	7	11	4.82	1.75	3.07
10	45-49	0	0	0	0	0	2	5	2	5	7	3.07	0.88	2.19
	40-49	0	0	0	0	0	6	12	6	12	18	7.89	2.63	5.26
11	50-54	1	0	1.44	0.44	0	5	7	6	7	13	5.70	2.63	3.07
12	55-59	2	6	3.51	0.88	2.63	1	4	3	10	13	5.70	1.32	4.39
	50-59	3	6	3.95	1.32	2.63	6	11	9	17	26	11.40	3.95	7.46
13	60-64	1	4	2.19	0.44	1.75	2	6	3	10	13	5.70	1.32	4.39
14	65-69	1	2	1.32	0.44	0.88	1	1	2	3	5	2.19	0.88	1.32
	60-69	2	6	3.51	0.88	2.63	3	7	5	13	18	7.89	2.19	5.71
15	70+	2	3	2.19	0.88	1.32	0	5	2	8	10	4.39	0.88	3.51
	70+	2	3	2.19	0.88	1.32	0	5	2	8	10	4.39	0.88	3.51
Total		7	15	9.65	3.07	6.58	82	124	89	139				
Grand total		22					206		228		228	100.00		

Figure 10. Worthy Park: Percentages of Africans, 1784-1838

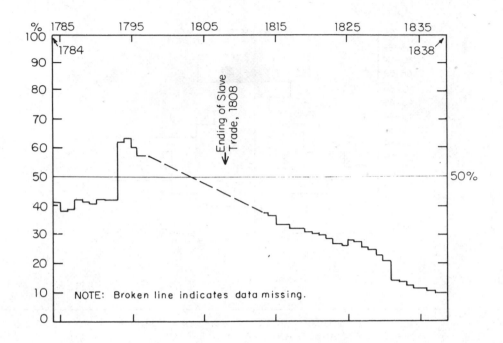

Figure 11. Worthy Park: Percentages of Males, 1784-1838

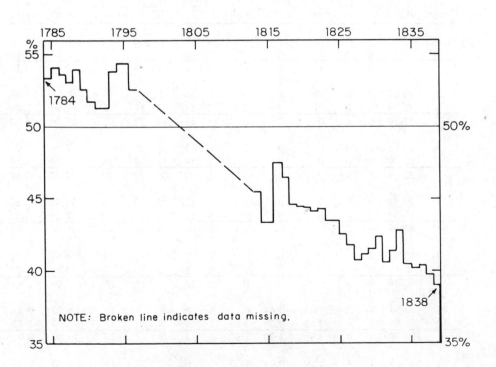

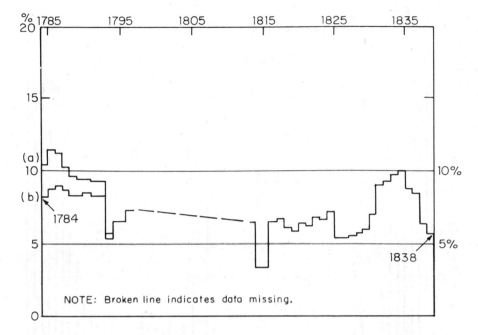

Figure 12. Worthy Park: Percentages of Coloreds, 1784-1838

Note: (a) = percentage of colored whose color is known; (b) = percentage of colored of total population.

NOTE: Broken line indicates data missing.

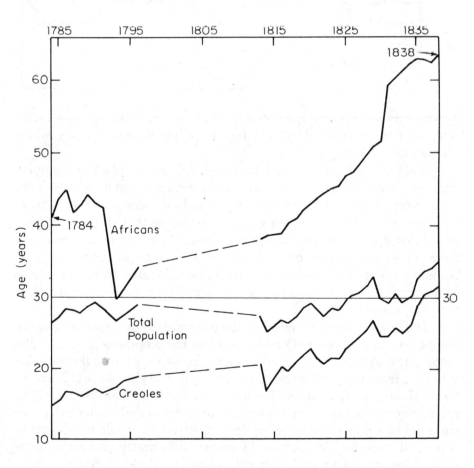

Figure 13. Worthy Park: Average Ages, Africans, Creoles, Total Population, 1784-1838

Figure 14. Worthy Park: Differential between Average Age of Females and Average Age of Males, 1784-1838

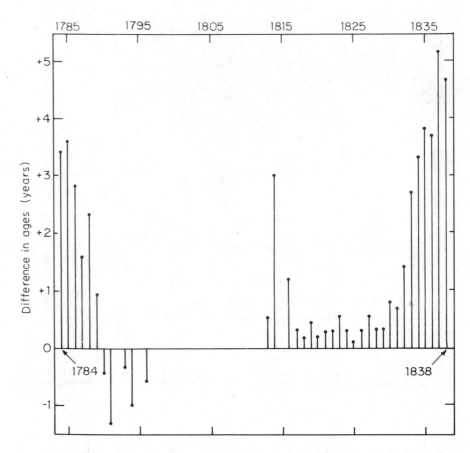

pyramid its top-heavy appearance is owing to the relatively low birth-rate, showing that far more entered the population as young adults than as newly born.

Whether the birthrate, or infant-survival rate, implied in the pyramids was also absolutely low, and what factors affected it, is considered in the next chapter. But it should be pointed out now that the "Christmas tree" effect is not in itself evidence to prove that slaveowners believed that it was "cheaper to buy than breed." Given the existence of a slave trade, the proportion of adults in a slave population would be bound to exceed the number who could be generated from those bred from infancy. This is an arithmetical invariable: not even rabbitlike breeding could upset it.

The slightly lopsided effect in the pyramids is the result of the imbalance of the sexes initially resulting from the preponderance of males among the Africans imported. Evidence varies as to whether this stemmed from the preference of planters (contrary to the statement of Hans Sloane quoted earlier) for more male than female workers, the preference of traders for male slaves who commanded higher prices, or from the fact that an excess of males was offered for sale by the caboceers and kings of West Africa. However, it is pretty certain that the slave ships carried about 60 percent males.[1] It would therefore be reasonable to expect males to predominate among the African-born in any

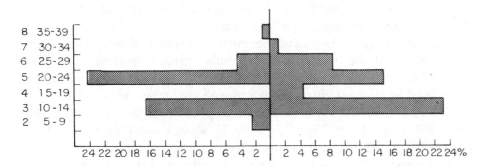

Cohort	Ages	Males	Females	Total	% males of all	% females of all	% in cohort
15	70+	0	0	0	0	0	0
14	65-69	0	0	0	0	0	0
13	60 64	0	0	0	0	0	0
12	55-59	0	0	0	0	0	0
11	50-54	0	0	0	0	0	0
10	45 49	0	0	0	0	0	0
9	40-44	0	0	0	0	0	0
8	35-39	1	0	1	1.15	0	1.15
7	30-34	0	1	1	0	1.15	1.15
6	25-29	4	7	11	4.60	8.05	12.64
5	20-24	21	13	34	24.14	14.94	39.08
4	15-19	0	4	4	0	4.60	4.60
3	10-14	14	20	34	16.09	23.00	39.08
2	5-9	2	0	2	2.30	0	2.30
1	0-4	0	0	0	0	0	0
Total		42	45	87	48.28	51.72	100.00

plantation population. It would also follow that a plantation with close to 60 percent males in its population would be likely to be close in time to its foundation or at least to have recently received an overwhelming influx of new Africans. As long as care is taken over the credibility of the data, these predictable effects are very noticeable in the Worthy Park figures.

Because it was not recorded until much later which slaves were Africans and which Creoles, it is not possible to know this information with certainty for about a fifth of the Worthy Park slaves in the earliest years of the records. The proportions of the sexes, however, can be ascertained with complete accuracy throughout, and these alone suggest significant trends. Although the Worthy Park sugar plantation population had already been in existence some sixty years, males still made up more than 53 percent of the population when the records began. This had fallen to little over 51 percent by 1791, but it soared to 54 percent in 1794. This sudden 3 percent shift implied the influx of no less than 200 newcomers among whom the proportion of males was 60 percent. As we know, Rose Price in fact purchased 225 new Africans in 1792 and 1793 alone.[2] Put another way, to achieve an upward shift of 3 percent in a population increased from 340 to 565 would imply that 132 of the 225 newcomers were males, or 58.7 percent.

Turning to the dynamics of the entire population illustrated by the pyramids, it will be noticed that the bulge greatly intensified in the 1790s with the influx of new African adults. But with time it not only diminished (at first rapidly and then more slowly) but also shifted upwards as it did so. This was particularly apparent in the first pyramids after 1808, since the ending of the Atlantic slave trade then meant that the chances of adding new adults were suddenly curtailed. However, some new recruits were still obtainable locally, and the fact that these newcomers were almost invariably Creoles in the young adult age range explains why the bulge continued to the end of slavery, despite the great decline in the number of Africans. This was especially noticeable after 1830 when the last large batch of new slaves was acquired from Arthur's Seat Estate.

Looking separately at the proportions of the African-born places the above changes even more clearly in perspective. After the influx of the 1790s the Africans constituted as much as 60 percent of the population, having made up approximately 40 percent during the previous decade. The proportion had already fallen by more than 5 percent within two years of the Africans' arrival, as a result of the savage seasoning process, but presumably it declined more gradually thereafter until 1808. After the ending of the slave trade, however, the Africans decreased quite rapidly in numbers and proportion, from just under 30 percent in 1821 to under 10 percent in 1838 (with a sudden drop of 6 percent in 1830), while at the same time moving upwards in the pyramids. This "ageing and wasting" effect was intensified by the fact that any children born, to Africans as to Creoles, would, of course, be listed as Creoles. This was the chief reason for the interesting disparity in the average ages of Africans and Creoles illustrated in Figure 13. By 1838, thirty years after the ending of the slave trade it would have been improbable to find any Africans in the lowest six cohorts, and in fact even in the over-45 ranges they had fallen to 35 percent of the total. In 1813 they had represented 55 percent of this group, though only 37 percent of the population overall.

The age and creolization trends apparent at Worthy Park for the last years of slavery are well in line with those for the rest of Jamaica for 1827-1829, illustrated before the Parliamentary Commission of 1831-32 in one of the earliest experiments in demographic analysis.[3] A less predictable effect that emerged from the Worthy Park data was that the proportion of males in the recorded population fell much further than for Jamaica as a whole, or even for the twelve sample estates analyzed in the 1832 Parliamentary Papers. From the graph, the number of males at Worthy Park would seem to have reached the 50 percent level to be expected in a stable population beguilingly close to the ending of the slave trade. But thereafter it fell to around 45 percent in the 1820s, and to just below 40 percent by 1838.

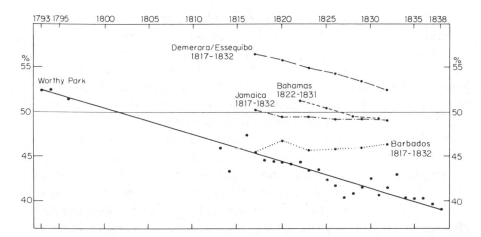

Figure 16. Worthy Park: Percentages of Males in Population, 1793-1838, compared with Whole Colony Populations during Registration Period, 1817-1832

This situation, which among other things meant that the field labor force consisted of up to two-thirds women, was clearly abnormal. The most obvious reason for it was the disparity in the mortality of the sexes, suggested in Figure 14 and dealt with more fully in the next chapter. Slave women throughout the plantation colonies, it seems, lived on the average at least 5 percent longer than slave men, a tendency that accelerated between 1808 and 1838. Neither at Worthy Park nor throughout the West Indies in general was the trend towards an excess of females exacerbated by manumissions, for almost everywhere the number of females manumitted outnumbered males by a ratio of 3:2. However at Worthy Park there was probably a special reason why the proportion of slave men declined so steeply: more men than women were transferred out of the work force in the reorganization that preceded emancipation. During this reorganization, the population actually recorded fell to 300 while totals of almost 500 were still being given in to the parish vestry.

As to the data on the colored population of Worthy Park, the evidence is even more puzzling. In any population in which miscegenation occurred at all, the statistician would expect the proportion of those listed as of mixed blood to have increased exponentially. Miscegenation was demonstrably common at Worthy Park, as on most Jamaican estates; yet the percentage of colored slaves recorded declined, from as much as 10 percent in the 1780s to an average of 7.4 percent in the 1830s. This was not solely owing to the African influx, or to manumission, for the total number of coloreds listed also declined perceptibly, even when the manumissions of colored slaves are taken into account.

Several explanations of this unexpected trend suggest themselves. It could have resulted from a quirk in the records, that as many coloreds fell back into the mass of blacks as emerged, because the offspring of Samboes and Negroes as well as the dark children of any two coloreds were listed as Negroes. Despite the suggestion of Edward Long and other writers that almost as many shades of color were recognized in Jamaica as in the Spanish colonies, it seems that the more complex varia-

75

tions were increasingly judged by eye rather than genetics and that the definition of black gradually widened as time went on.

Another reason for the apparent decline in the number of colored slaves could have been that mortality among coloreds was just as high as among black slaves. No more able than the blacks to increase their numbers naturally, they lacked the blacks' opportunities of recruitment from outside. Yet the failure of colored slaves to increase exponentially may also provide evidence both that the colored females chose not to procreate with persons darker than themselves (colored males, of course, had little choice) and that racial lines tightened up in slavery's last days. The number of whites at Worthy Park continued more or less static, but they seem to have procreated ever more discriminately, choosing as mates only the lightest colored female slaves, or even miscegenating less after 1800. These possibilities, which are completely consonant with the nonstatistical evidence, are considered more fully later.

The use of average ages of total populations is a dangerous business, greatly inferior to the breakdowns by cohorts and classes and the use of age statistics in assessing social health and calculating life expectancy that are studied in subsequent chapters. A low average could be the result either of high mortality during the working years and early deaths among adults or of high fertility and excellent health and survival rates among the very young; and the reverse could be true in each respect in the case of a high average age. Moreover, good health at both ends of the scale tends to have an identical effect to bad health at both ends, in reducing averages to a mean. However, average ages can be used here to illustrate and corroborate known developments in Worthy Park's history and trends in the accumulation of data.

The average age of the slaves rose steadily over the first seven years of the record by about a year in all, but then plummeted almost three years during the two years of the largest influx, from 29.21 to 26.67. The climb back in average age almost as steeply to 29.19 within the following three years was almost entirely the result of the horrifying mortality of the Africans.

The somewhat ambivalent data for the years 1813-1816 show an average considerably lower than for the 1780s, which may have been the result of the involuntary reliance on breeding rather than buying that came with the recent ending of the slave trade, while the survivors of the great African influx were still not too aged to bear children. Thereafter, the average age seems to have risen steadily, to over 28 by the 1820s, and to over 30 in the 1830s, marking an increase of over three years over a period of fourteen years. This ageing effect is to be expected in a population in which the survivors of a suspended system of imported recruits have passed the age of childbearing before their Creole successors have become demographically self-sustaining.

The soaring rise in the average age during the Apprenticeship period is even easier to explain. A population without youngsters to succeed it will age by a year each year if no one dies or leaves. The Worthy Park Apprentices of 1835, losing the children under six who were immediately freed, were 2.7 years older on the average than the Worthy Park slaves of 1834. That their average age rose only 1.9 years rather than 3 years in the following three years simply meant that the average age of those who died exceeded the average age of the total.

Of the material deployed and the methods used in this chapter, the most important and useful is undoubtedly the population pyramid. A basic pyramid can be drawn for any slave population for which the ages of all members are known. Almost invariably in these cases it would be possible to divide the pyramid into male and female sides, since sexes can be determined from any list of names. To have material with which able to delineate the Africans and Creoles, as was common after 1817, would be a bonus.

The main contention here is that once a pyramid is constructed for the population of a slave plantation, even if it is for a single year not one of a series, it is possible to assume the stage of development of the plantation from which it is derived. Within limits, the same holds true of whole colony populations. Clearly, when the proportion of the African-born is seen to have approached 100 percent this would mean a population at an early stage of development. But even where African births are not known, a pronounced bulge in the lower-middle age ranges, with more than 50 percent of the population aged between 15 and 30, would also indicate a "young" plantation, or colony—or at least one in which there had been massive recent expansion. This would also be true of populations in which the proportion of males was closer to 60 than to 50 percent. Conversely, a pyramid that disclosed a high proportion of Creoles, or females, or in which the bulge was minimal, would imply a plantation or colony long established, and "mature."

A series of population pyramids—such as the eight for Worthy Park displayed in this chapter—allows for a fairly precise morphological history of the plantation or colony treated. With care, a series of pyramids based on firm data can also be used to project information into areas where it is lacking. The data tabulated for Worthy Park in the period 1783-1838 are thus used here tentatively to reconstruct the demographic pattern of the plantation's population in 1730, for which little more than names are known—making an extreme contrast with the more truly pyramidical shape derived from modern Jamaican data.

A concluding axiom about the population pyramid in general: the closer it pertains to a true pyramidical shape, the closer the population represented is to a demographically stable state. The question of how far a demographically stable population is also bound to be socially and psychologically stable, and to what extent it is affected by other conditions, is discussed in the chapter entitled "Economics, Employment, Social Cohesion."

Figure 17. Worthy Park: Projected Population Pyramid, 1730

Note: The broken line indicates a theoretical "perfect" pyramid, with a normal birthrate, evenly equal sex ratios, and steady natural attrition.

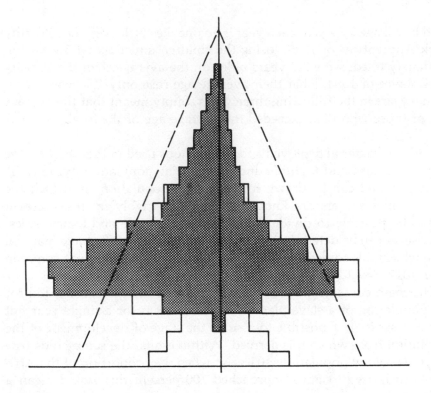

Figure 18. Jamaica: Population Pyramid, 1943

Source: G. W. Roberts, *The Population of Jamaica* (Cambridge, Cambridge University Press, 1957), p. 159.

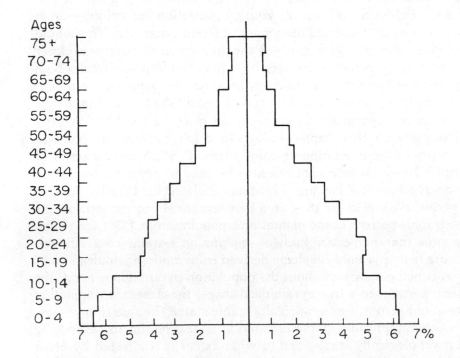

	Maximum number of slaves recorded	Slaves for whom ages known	Slaves for whom African/Creole origin known	Slaves for whom all data known for age pyramids
1784	331	229	237	183
1785	315	223	224	177
1786	299	220	215	174
1787	334	260	252	210
1788	343	272	260	222
1789	340	280	263	230
1790	342	289	269	239
1791	377	322	303	271
1793	541	503	471	443
1794	530	516	461	451
1796	466	452	407	401
1813	491	489	470	470
1814	458	458	448	448
1816	507	507	502	502
1817	535	535	530	530
1818	488	488	486	486
1819	500	500	498	498
1820	497	497	496	496
1821	505	506	503	503
1822	513	513	511	511
1823	489	489	487	487
1824	502	501	498	498
1825	423	422	422	422
1826	420	419	420	419
1827	407	406	406	406
1828	394	393	393	393
1829	386	385	385	385
1830	417	416	417	416
1831	332	331	332	331
1832	309	308	309	308
1833	301	300	301	300
1834	293	292	293	292
1835	261	259	260	259
1836	258	256	257	256
1837	247	245	244	243
1838	231	229	229	228

Table 15. Worthy Park: Total Population and Tabulated Data, for Years Tabulated, 1784-1838

Source: Worthy Park records.

Table 16. Worthy Park: Totals and Percentages of Africans and Creoles, with Percentages of Males and Females in Each, 1784-1838

Source: Worthy Park records.

	Total slaves (for whom A/C origin known)	Africans % of total in previous column	Africans		Creoles			Total population tabulated	A/C origin unknown
			% of males	% of females	% of total	% of males	% of females		
1784	183	42.1	50.7	49.3	57.9	50.9	49.1	229	46
1785	177	38.5	51.5	48.5	61.5	51.4	48.6	223	46
1786	174	39.1	51.5	48.5	60.9	50.0	50.0	220	46
1787	210	42.9	54.4	45.6	57.1	45.8	54.2	260	50
1788	222	41.0	55.0	45.0	59.0	48.9	51.1	272	50
1789	230	40.4	54.8	45.2	59.6	45.3	54.7	280	50
1790	239	41.8	54.0	46.0	58.2	43.9	56.1	289	50
1791	271	42.1	53.5	46.5	57.9	43.3	56.7	322	51
1793	443	62.8	55.4	44.6	37.2	47.3	52.7	503	60
1794	451	63.4	56.3	43.7	36.6	46.1	53.9	516	65
1796	401	57.8	54.7	45.3	42.2	47.3	52.7	452	51
1813	470	37.9	48.3	51.7	62.1	44.5	55.5	489	19
1814	448	37.0	45.8	54.2	63.0	41.8	58.2	458	10
1816	502	33.7	50.0	50.0	66.3	46.1	53.9	507	5
1817	530	32.6	49.4	50.6	67.4	44.4	55.6	535	5
1818	486	32.1	46.8	53.2	67.9	43.6	56.4	488	2
1819	498	31.3	46.8	53.2	68.7	43.6	56.4	500	2
1820	496	30.9	47.1	52.9	69.1	43.2	56.8	497	1
1821	502	29.9	48.0	52.0	70.1	42.6	57.4	505	3
1822	510	28.6	48.0	52.0	71.4	43.1	56.9	512	2
1823	487	27.7	47.4	52.6	72.3	42.1	57.9	489	2
1824	498	26.5	48.5	51.5	73.5	41.8	58.2	501	3
1825	422	28.4	45.8	54.2	71.6	41.1	58.9	422	0
1826	419	27.2	44.7	55.3	72.8	40.7	59.3	419	0
1827	406	25.6	45.2	54.8	74.4	39.1	60.9	406	0
1828	393	24.9	48.0	52.0	75.1	38.6	61.4	393	0
1829	385	23.6	48.4	51.6	76.4	39.5	60.5	385	0
1830	416	20.4	51.8	48.2	79.6	40.2	59.8	416	0
1831	331	14.2	48.9	51.1	85.8	39.4	60.6	331	0
1832	308	14.0	51.2	48.8	86.0	41.6	58.4	308	0
1833	300	12.3	48.7	51.3	87.7	42.2	57.8	300	0
1834	292	11.0	40.6	59.4	89.0	40.4	59.6	292	0
1835	259	11.2	37.9	62.1	88.8	40.4	59.6	259	0
1836	256	10.6	40.7	59.3	89.5	40.2	59.8	256	0
1837	243	9.4	34.8	69.2	90.6	40.3	59.5	245	2
1838	228	9.6	31.8	68.2	89.4	39.0	61.0	229	1

	Slaves for whom all data known (as used in pyramids)	Males	% of males	Slaves for whom sexes known	Males	% of males	% of females
1784	183	93	50.8	331	176	53.2	46.8
1785	177	91	51.4	315	170	54.0	46.0
1786	174	87	50.0	299	160	53.5	46.5
1787	210	104	49.5	334	177	53.0	47.0
1788	222	114	51.4	343	185	53.9	46.1
1789	230	113	49.1	340	179	52.6	47.4
1790	239	115	48.1	342	177	51.8	48.2
1791	271	129	47.6	377	193	51.2	48.8
1793	443	232	52.4	541	291	53.8	46.2
1794	451	237	52.5	530	287	54.2	45.8
1796	401	207	51.6	466	245	52.6	47.4
1813	470	216	46.0	491	224	45.6	54.4
1814	448	194	43.3	458	198	43.2	56.8
1816	502	238	47.4	507	241	47.5	52.5
1817	530	244	46.0	535	248	46.4	53.6
1818	486	217	44.7	488	218	44.7	55.3
1819	498	222	44.6	500	223	44.6	53.4
1820	496	220	44.4	497	221	44.5	55.5
1821	503	222	44.1	506	223	44.1	55.9
1822	511	227	44.4	513	227	44.2	55.8
1823	487	212	43.5	489	212	43.4	56.6
1824	498	217	43.6	502	218	43.4	56.6
1825	422	179	42.4	423	180	42.6	57.4
1826	419	175	41.8	420	176	41.9	58.1
1827	406	165	40.6	407	166	40.8	59.2
1828	393	161	41.0	394	162	41.1	38.9
1829	385	160	41.6	386	161	41.7	58.3
1830	416	177	42.5	417	177	42.4	57.6
1831	331	133	40.8	332	135	40.7	59.3
1832	308	128	41.6	309	128	41.4	58.6
1833	300	129	43.0	301	129	42.9	57.1
1834	292	118	40.4	298	118	40.3	59.7
1835	259	104	40.2	261	103	40.2	59.8
1836	256	103	40.2	258	104	40.3	59.7
1837	243	97	39.9	247	98	39.7	60.3
1838	228	89	39.0	231	90	39.0	61.0

Table 17. Worthy Park: Total and Percentages of Males and Females, 1784-1838

Source: Worthy Park records.

Table 18. Worthy Park:
Totals and Percentages of
Coloreds, 1784-1838

Source: Worthy Park records.

	Total population recorded	Color unknown	Negroes	Mulattoes	Samboes	Quadroons	Mestees	Known coloreds manumitted	Total colored	% of colored of total population	% o of who k
1784	331	75	229	19	3	5	0	0	27	8.2	
1785	315	73	214	19	3	6	0	0	28	8.9	
1786	299	60	212	18	3	6	0	0	27	9.0	
1787	334	51	254	20	3	6	0	1	29	8.7	
1788	343	54	261	19	3	6	0	0	28	8.2	
1789	340	49	263	20	2	6	0	0	28	8.2	
1790	342	39	274	21	2	6	0	0	29	8.5	
1791	377	43	303	23	2	6	0	0	31	8.2	
1793	541	23	488	22	3	5	0	0	30	5.5	
1794	530	5	490	24	4	7	0	4	35	6.6	
1796	466	19	415	24	3	5	0	0	32	6.9	
1813	491	3	457	20	5	6	0	0	31	6.3	
1814	458	4	439	7	2	5	1	0	15	3.3	
1816	507	3	471	20	3	8	2	1	33	6.5	
1817	535	13	487	21	4	8	2	2	35	6.5	
1818	488	6	453	78	5	6	0	0	29	5.9	
1819	500	11	460	18	5	6	0	0	29	5.8	
1820	497	7	459	17	6	8	0	0	31	6.2	
1821	506	7	468	17	6	8	0	0	31	6.1	
1822	513	3	475	20	6	8	1	0	35	6.8	
1823	489	0	456	17	6	10	0	0	33	6.7	
1824	502	6	461	18	6	11	0	5	35	7.0	
1825	423	4	397	16	2	4	0	0	22	5.2	
1826	420	3	395	15	2	5	0	0	22	5.2	
1827	407	3	382	15	2	5	0	0	22	5.4	
1828	394	2	370	15	2	5	0	0	22	5.6	
1829	386	2	361	16	2	5	0	0	23	6.0	
1830	417	2	386	18	7	4	0	0	29	7.0	
1831	332	2	300	18	7	5	0	0	30	9.0	
1832	309	2	279	18	7	3	0	0	28	9.1	
1833	301	3	269	18	7	4	0	0	29	9.6	
1834	293	4	260	18	7	4	0	3	29	9.9	
1835	261	1	237	13	7	3	0	0	23	8.8	
1836	258	3	233	12	7	3	0	0	22	8.5	
1837	247	9	223	8	6	1	0	2	15	6.1	
1838	231	7	211	7	6	0	0	0	13	5.6	

	Age-known sample	Average age total population	Male/female age-known sample	Average age		African/Creole age-known sample	Average age	
				Males	Females		Africans	Creoles
1784	229	26.53	229	25.0	28.4	183	40.8	15.0
1785	223	27.25	223	25.6	29.3	177	43.9	15.7
1786	220	28.48	220	27.2	30.0	174	44.9	17.0
1787	260	28.33	260	27.6	29.2	210	41.9	17.0
1788	272	27.95	272	26.9	29.2	222	43.0	16.1
1789	280	28.74	280	28.3	29.2	230	44.1	16.8
1790	289	29.21	289	29.4	29.0	239	43.3	17.4
1791	322	28.44	322	29.1	27.8	271	42.3	16.6
1793	503	26.67	503	26.8	26.5	443	29.9	17.8
1794	516	27.62	516	28.1	27.1	451	31.1	18.3
1796	452	29.19	452	29.5	28.9	401	34.3	19.1
1813	489	27.65	489	27.3	27.9	470	38.0	20.8
1814	458	25.48	458	23.8	26.8	448	38.5	17.3
1816	507	26.92	507	26.3	27.5	502	39.1	20.4
1817	535	26.47	535	26.3	26.6	530	40.4	19.8
1818	488	26.59	488	26.5	26.7	486	40.9	19.9
1819	500	26.83	500	26.6	27.0	498	41.9	20.0
1820	497	27.23	497	27.1	27.3	496	42.9	20.2
1821	506	27.97	506	27.8	28.1	503	43.7	21.1
1822	513	27.69	513	27.5	27.8	511	44.0	21.1
1823	489	28.35	489	28.0	28.6	487	45.0	21.9
1824	501	28.21	501	28.0	28.3	498	45.7	21.8
1825	422	29.85	422	29.8	29.8	422	46.9	23.0
1826	419	29.73	419	29.6	29.9	419	47.3	23.2
1827	406	29.58	406	29.2	29.8	406	48.3	23.1
1828	393	30.37	393	30.2	30.5	393	49.7	24.0
1829	385	30.89	385	30.1	31.4	385	51.1	24.6
1830	416	30.01	416	29.3	30.5	416	51.8	24.4
1831	331	29.56	331	28.6	30.3	331	59.6	24.6
1832	308	30.60	308	29.8	31.2	308	60.0	25.8
1833	300	29.54	300	28.0	30.7	300	61.5	25.0
1834	292	30.15	292	28.2	31.5	292	62.4	26.2
1835	259	32.91	259	30.6	34.4	259	63.2	29.1
1836	256	34.09	256	31.9	35.6	256	62.9	30.7
1837	245	34.04	245	30.9	36.1	243	62.6	30.8
1838	229	34.75	229	31.8	36.6	228	63.5	31.6

Table 19. Worthy Park: Average Ages, Total Population, Males, Females, Africans, Creoles, 1784-1838

Source: Worthy Park records.

Table 20. Total Slave Populations and Slaves Manumitted, by Sexes; Worthy Park compared with Whole Colony Populations, 1817-1835

Sources: For Jamaica, Barbados, Demerara/Essequibo, Bahamas, *British Sessional Papers, Commons, Reports, 1831-2*, XX; for Worthy Park, Worthy Park records.

	Total slaves	% males	Freed males (3 yrs.)	Freed females	% freed males
			Jamaica		
1817	346,150	50.07	366	650	36.02
1820	342,392	49.66	371	550	40.28
1823	336,253	49.54	346	611	36.15
1826	331,119	49.14	362	755	32.41
1829	322,421	49.08			
Total			1,445	2,566	36.03
			Barbados		
1817	77,493	45.62	108	142	43.20
1820	78,345	46.87	131	166	43.81
1823	78,816	45.88	126	196	39.13
1826	80,551	45.93	212	458	31.18
1829	81,902	46.02			
Total			577	962	37.99
			Demerara/Essequibo		
1817	77,867	56.68	36		—
1820	77,376	55.86	72		—
1823	74,977	54.98	132		—
1826	71,382	54.30	100	154	39.37
1829	69,467	53.47	187	272	40.74
1832	65,558	52.42			
Total			953		—
			Bahamas		
1822	10,808	51.16	35	49	37.23
1825	9,264	50.41	52	66	44.07
1828	9,268	49.72	190		—
1831	9,705	49.22			
Total			392		—
			Worthy Park		
1817	529	46.40	2	0	100.00
1820	508	44.50	1	1	50.00
1823	496	43.40	3	2	60.00
1826	468	41.90	0	0	—
1829	431	41.70	0	0	—
1832	372	41.40	9	11	45.00
1835	260	40.20			
Total			15	14	48.39

3 / Mortality, Fertility, Life Expectancy, 1783-1838

FOR the planters, the necessity of maintaining a viable population, with at least an equilibrium between births and deaths, became increasingly vital towards the end of slavery. A population which increased naturally was always more economic than one in which numbers could only be maintained by buying new slaves, as long as the cost of new recruits exceeded the cost of raising infants to the years of productive work.[1] The fact that West Indian planters continued to import new Africans as long as they could was not evidence of a preference for buying rather than breeding so much as the fact that buying was made necessary by the excess of deaths over births.

As plantation profits declined, however, it became increasingly important to buy as few new slaves as possible. Accordingly, from the 1780s the general economic well-being of the plantations was encouraged by local amelioration laws, which aimed to increase the number of births and to improve the chances of survival for Creole youngsters. Some owners went beyond the legal requirements to provide inducements and better conditions for mothers. Long before the ending of the slave trade efforts were being made, though with mainly economic motives, to make the trend less necessary. With the outlawing of the trade in 1808, however, the economic desideratum became a demographic necessity. Slaves would have to be encouraged to increase naturally or else the black laboring population would gradually age and decline towards extinction.

What then can be adduced from the records of the chances of the Jamaican slaves becoming demographically viable and of the effectiveness of ameliorating policies? All the evidence supports the view that the "natural decrease" (excess of deaths over births) of the Jamaican slaves had already eased by 1783, from a net annual loss of over 30 per thousand around 1730, to well under 20 per thousand. Figures for Worthy Park and other estates suggest a continuing decline, under normal circumstances, to around 5 per thousand per year.[2] The following tables indicate that the Worthy Park population could not reproduce itself naturally while slavery lasted. This is consonant with the indications from the general Jamaican figures for the registration period revealed by R. G. Amyot and T. F. Buxton in 1831, which shocked large sections of the English public.[3] However, the Worthy Park figures extend over a far wider time range than those provided by the Colonial Slave Registrar for 1817-1832 and are broken down by age cohorts as well as by sexes and the African/Creole ratios. This allows for a much more dynamic and detailed analysis than was possible in the preemancipation period. The general picture is pessimistic, and amelioration is shown to have been specifically ineffectual. But sufficient evidence is brought forward to show that estimates of life expectancy by previous commentators have been understated and to explain why it was that the Jamaican slave population became self-sustaining so soon after emancipation.

Again the tables are more or less self-explanatory. Here figures were clumped together in groups of years to improve the size of the samples and to relate summaries to known periods of Worthy Park's development. Crude numbers of deaths and births were ascertainable for most years, but in making further refinements greater selectivity was necessary, though estimates were avoided as much as possible.

The Worthy Park material allowed for the tabulation not only of crude death and birth rates but also of mortality and fertility breakdowns by sexes and African/Creole ratios over a long period. For the period 1817-1832 these findings could be corroborated by the data obtainable from the Register of Returns of Slaves in the Jamaica Archives. However, by providing ages at death for many slaves the Worthy Park data went further than the registration returns, making possible a table of mortality by age cohorts without which any estimates of life expectancy would have been impossible. Thanks to the thoroughness of the Worthy Park bookkeeping it was likewise possible to break down slave fertility into more categories than has hitherto been done for any slave population. The identification of mothers and their ages allowed the calculation not only of the fertility of females in general and of African against Creole women but also of the fertility of those specifically within the childbearing age range (15-49) and the age specific birthrate.

Much hinged, however, on the very real problems of accurately calculating infant mortality. It has long been established that infant mortality figures were generally understated because of those who were born and died within the intercensal periods. However, at Worthy Park, where records were as complete as anywhere, the indicated infant mortality was even lower than on the twelve Jamaican estates selected for illustration by the Registrar of Slave Returns in 1831.[4] This accords with the statement of Worthy Park's doctor, John Quier, that infant mortality on the estates was not excessive,[5] but the figures still require careful scrutiny.

The intercensal period during slave registration was three years, and estimates based on study of the registration returns have claimed infant mortality figures as high as 40 percent over the first six years, or even 25 percent within the first two weeks.[6] However, at the estate level the intercensal period, based on the returns to parish vestries, was six months from 1787 and a mere three months from 1817. Moreover, at Worthy Park and some other estates the ages of many of the very youngest infants were given in fractions of years, and there were also many cases where both the exact birth and death dates of those who died as infants were entered.

Preliminary study of the Worthy Park figures suggested an average annual death rate over the first five years of about 40 per thousand, or an overall loss of 20 percent in the first five years. This indicated a yearly breakdown, shown in Table 21, which seems too low for credibility.

Just as there was a great differential between the first and second five-year life periods and between the first five years of life overall and the first year, there was a similar differential within the first year itself, with the highest mortality within the first few weeks or even days of life. It was chiefly in this area that the records misled, since a fair number of the infants who were born and died within the shortest intercensal period were clearly not recorded, at Worthy Park as elsewhere. From careful calculations it seems that as many as 50 percent of the children who died before reaching the age of five may have gone unrecorded at Worthy Park, virtually all of them within the first year or even weeks of life. This indicated an annual average death rate of about 52 per thousand over the first five years, and a breakdown by years as shown in Table 22.

These figures are comparable with those given in Table 25 for the twelve selected Jamaican estates in the period 1817-1829, but are still much more moderate than estimates given by previous authorities.[7] However, to the record of infant mortality among the live-born should be added the lamentable number of stillbirths, miscarriages, and abortions, which may well have brought the number of unsuccessful pregnancies at Worthy Park close to 200 per thousand.

Some light is shed on these sad aspects of motherhood at Worthy Park by the information on births and miscarriages obtained by Rose Price from all the slave women on the estate in May 1795. Worthy Park's owner-manager discovered that of the 240 females then in the population (of whom approximately 128 would have been in the fertile age range and 174, or 72.5 percent, would have reached or passed through the childbearing years),[8] 89, or 37.1 percent, had given birth, 352 times in all. However, live births only totaled 275, indicating the alarming rate of one miscarriage for every 4.6 births. Moreover, besides the 77 miscarriages, 116 of the offspring were dead by 1795, leaving only 159 still living. No less than 70 mothers had lost one or more children by miscarriage or early death, and of the remainder 15 had borne and raised a single child, 3, two children, and one solitary mother, three.

The onus of bearing most of the children fell on a comparatively small proportion of the women. Yet under the general conditions it was something of a triumph actually to bear six live children, let alone raise them successfully in order to be excused manual labor under the law of 1787. In 1795 no less than seventeen women at Worthy Park claimed to have given birth to six or more live children, but only three mothers were excused work in that year for having six still living, and no more than eight mothers in any subsequent year.[9]

Any understatement of infant mortality clearly would affect overall mortality figures, and if in fact Worthy Park's infant deaths were understated by 50 percent in the records, the overall mortality figures in Table 23 should be increased accordingly by about 8 percent in each case.[10] By the same token, the ignoring of some of the infants who were born and died within the intercensal periods would affect fertility figures to an even greater degree. A 50 percent understatement of the number of live births would raise the overall fertility figures given in Table 26 by a similar percentage. However, since the nonenumerated died as well as being born they cancel themselves out and do not affect the calculations on natural increase and decrease given in Table 42.

In Table 26 the figures for 1800-1811, for which the Worthy Park records are missing, are almost entirely the result of estimations and projections, though a fair number of births for those years were extrapolated from later data. Good records exist for the period 1783-1796, but since they are deficient concerning ages and whether the slaves were Africans or Creoles, considerable uncertainty remains. In the table known information was balanced against known information even where both were clearly deficient (for example, known births to African mothers against known totals of Africans), on the assumption that such similarly based deficiencies might balance each other out.

Table 27 uses projected estimates to fill out all the deficiencies in the fertility data for 1783-1796. The resulting figures show some differences, but the overall trends and patterns disclosed are remarkably similar to those shown in Table 26, lending even more credibility to the general conclusions on slave fertility made later in the chapter.

Despite the availability of most of the necessary data, it is virtually impossible to construct a completely plausible life table for such a population as that of Worthy Park's slaves. With a maximum of abut 540 the census sample is really too small, and increasing the sample by aggregating different years presents difficulties because of substantial changes in the population from time to time. This is particularly true of population changes by purchase rather than birth during the period of the slave trade. With a considerable inflow of unseasoned slaves mainly in the age range 15-25, life expectancy figures would all be distorted, particularly those for the earlier cohorts and for all Creoles.

However, a discriminating choice of a sequence of years does allow for the construction of an abbreviated average life table (Table 30) that can serve to make valid comparisons and contrasts not only with that for the population of the twelve selected Jamaican estates for 1831 (Table 32) but also with the only slave life table previously constructed,

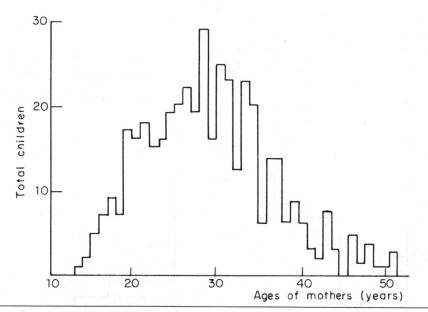

Figure 19. Worthy Park: Ages of Mothers at Birth of Children Wherever Mothers' Ages Known, 1784-1838, and Data

Mother's age	Births at each age	Total in cohort	% in cohort of total	Mother's age	Births at each age	Total in cohort	% in cohort of total
9	1	1	0.23	30	25		
10	—			31	24		
11	—			32	12		
12	—			33	23		
13	1			34	20	104	24.25
14	2	3	0.70	35	6		
15	5			36	14		
16	7			37	14		
17	9			38	6		
18	7			39	9	49	11.42
19	17	45	10.49	40	6		
20	16			41	3		
21	18			42	2		
22	15			43	8		
23	16			44	3	22	5.13
24	19	84	19.58	45	—		
25	20			46	5		
26	22			47	1		
27	19			48	4		
28	29			49	1	11	2.56
29	16	106	24.71	50	1		
				51	3	4	0.93
				Total		429	100.00

that made in 1952 by George W. Roberts for the whole population of Demerara/Essequibo between 1817 and 1832 (Table 33).[11]

For Worthy Park only the complete sequence of thirteen surviving annual lists for the period 1784-1813 was chosen to suggest, in Table 30, the life table characteristics of an "average" Jamaican slave population at the height of the plantation system. Over this span the effects of the

Figure 20. Female Age Specific Birthrates for Worthy Park, 1784-1838, compared with Jamaica and Puerto Rico, 1946, and Data

Sources: Worthy Park records; G. W. Roberts, *The Population of Jamaica* (Cambridge, Cambridge University Press, 1957), p. 150.

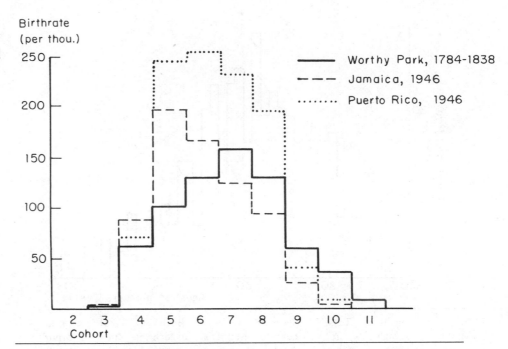

Cohort	Ages	% Mothers in each cohort	Annual average children born per cohort (total 11.37 p.a.)	% of females of total in each cohort	Annual average females in cohort (total 222.15)	Birthrate by females per cohort
2	5-9	0.23	0.026	10.60	22.38	0.12
3	10-14	0.70	0.080	8.41	17.76	0.45
4	15-19	10.49	1.119	8.77	18.52	60.44
5	20-24	19.58	2.226	10.46	22.09	100.80
6	25-29	24.71	2.810	10.32	21.79	128.93
7	30-34	24.25	2.757	8.27	17.46	157.90
8	35-39	11.42	1.299	4.80	10.14	128.12
9	40-44	5.13	0.583	4.48	9.46	61.66
10	45-49	2.56	0.291	3.75	7.92	36.76
11	50-54	0.93	0.106	5.99	12.65	8.36

abnormal influx of new Africans in the 1790s were offset by the characteristics of a mature old estate shown in the data for 1784-1792, and by the demographic leveling that had occurred over the long unrecorded period between 1796 and 1811, and before the effects of the ending of the slave trade in 1808 had seriously begun to show. The period 1815-1838, for which the records were fullest, was reluctantly rejected because of the significant demographic distortions that occurred after about 1815 because of the drying up of African replacements.

The ageing and wasting effect during the registration period seriously compromises both the study of the twelve Jamaican estates of 1817-1829 and that of the Demerara/Essequibo population. In the latter case, the credibility of the overall table is also shaken by Roberts' introduction of an infant mortality figure admittedly derived from the worst known period of epidemic, more than fifty years after the end of slavery (1890-1892), on the assumption that figures during the slavery period

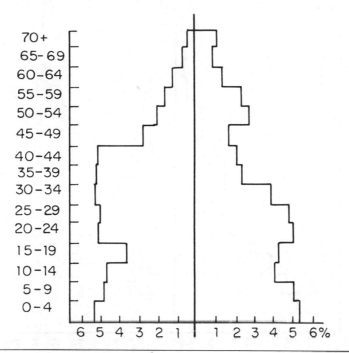

Figure 21. Worthy Park: Average Population Pyramid, 1784-1813, and Data

Cohort	Ages	Totals in cohorts	Males	Females	% in cohort of total	% of males in cohort of total	% of females in cohort of total
1	0-4	488	241	247	10.76	5.31	5.45
2	5-9	447	215	232	9.86	4.74	5.12
3	10-14	392	208	184	8.64	4.59	4.05
4	15-19	350	158	192	7.72	3.48	4.24
5	20-24	459	230	229	10.12	5.07	5.05
6	25-29	451	225	226	9.95	4.96	4.99
7	30-34	417	236	181	9.20	5.20	4.00
8	35-39	335	230	105	7.39	5.07	2.32
9	40-44	325	227	98	7.17	5.01	2.16
10	45-49	205	123	82	4.52	2.71	1.81
11	50-54	220	89	131	4.85	1.96	2.89
12	55-59	181	68	113	3.99	1.50	2.49
13	60-64	126	50	76	2.77	1.10	1.67
14	65-69	69	27	42	1.52	0.60	0.92
15	70+	70	11	59	1.54	0.24	1.30
Total		4,535	2,338	2,197	100.00	51.55	48.45

must have been at least as bad as the worst later period. In addition, the problem of averaging out the characteristics of the Worthy Park population over a time span that saw significant fluctuations and the importation of many adult Africans is more than matched in the Demerara/Essequibo case by the dangers of generalizing a population that included slaves in widely different sized groups and in many occupations other than sugar plantation work.

Despite the artificiality of singling out for statistical purposes any one element in a mixed population, and the problem of even smaller samples, life tables for the Creole-born at Worthy Park for 1790-1833

91

Figure 22. Worthy Park: Average Population Pyramid, Creole-Born, 1790-1833, and Data

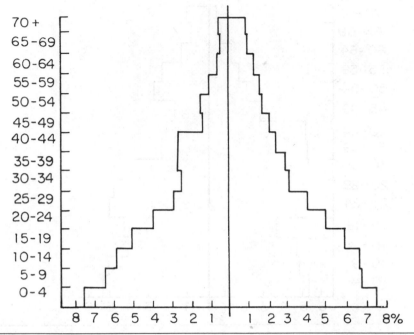

Cohort	Ages	Totals in cohorts	Males	Females	% in cohort of total	% of males in cohort	% of females in cohort
1	0-4	339	169	170	15.22	7.59	7.63
2	5-9	299	147	152	13.43	6.60	6.83
3	10-14	284	133	151	12.75	5.97	6.78
4	15-19	247	114	133	11.09	5.12	5.97
5	20-24	200	89	111	8.98	4.00	4.98
6	25-29	156	64	92	7.00	2.87	4.13
7	30-34	125	55	70	5.61	2.47	3.14
8	35-39	124	57	67	5.57	2.56	3.01
9	40-44	113	57	56	5.07	2.56	2.51
10	45-49	80	31	49	3.59	1.39	2.20
11	50-54	75	33	42	3.37	1.48	1.89
12	55-59	66	25	41	2.96	1.12	1.84
13	60-64	48	17	31	2.16	0.76	1.40
14	65-69	36	12	24	1.62	0.54	1.08
15	70+	35	13	22	1.58	0.59	0.99
Total		2,227	1,016	1,211	100.00	45.62	54.38

(Table 34) and for the twelve selected Jamaican estates for 1817-1829 (Table 32) are also included. These provide another, perhaps superior, basis for comparison with other areas, such as England during the same period (Table 35). However, it should not be forgotten that the populations of English towns also included a sizable proportion of adult migrants, as well as the "Native-born."

For a complete assessment of the material deployed in this chapter and to gain a sense of perspective, four exercises must be carried out. The Worthy Park mortality, fertility, and life expectancy data, while being properly differentiated, must be related to comparable data from the same area at a later period and from different areas and populations. The birthrates must be specifically related to the death rates. The data relating to Africans and Creoles, males and females, and slaves of different ages, must be compared and contrasted with each other. Finally, changes in the patterns over the course of time must be taken into account and explained where possible.

In certain respects the demographic condition of the Worthy Park population (and with it, comparable plantation populations) was neither so critical as that of some other societies, nor so gloomy as is generally made out in most descriptions of slavery. The overall figures for mortality were by no means disastrous in themselves and might be matched in many societies usually regarded as viable, such as, for example, the entire population of Italy over the period 1760-1860.[12] Only among new Africans and during epidemics were the death rates at an intolerable level. In a 1974 survey account of West Indian slavery it was argued that "at least one in ten slaves shipped died on the Middle Passage, representing a mortality rate in annual terms as high as 20 percent. As many as a third of the remainder perished in the seasoning process over the next three years . . . an annual rate as high as 12 percent. Yet the eventual survivors of this brutal process of transfer and aclimatisation could look forward to a life that probably averaged 30 years in 1730 and 40 years a century later."[13]

More detailed research at Worthy Park suggests only minor qualifications to the general statement. The high death rate during the seasoning process was well borne out by the disastrous mortality among the new Africans imported in the 1790s. The highest indicated rate for Africans was 80 rather than 120 per thousand (or twice rather than treble the average rate), but this was spread over five years rather than three and included old as well as new Africans. There were also an unfortunate gap in the records for the crucial years 1794 and 1795 and clearly some undercounting of those who died between arrival and the subsequent census.

Africans who survived the seasoning process seem to have been at least as durable as Creoles. Moreover, the influx of newcomers seems to have led to increases in the mortality of resident Creoles as well. The newcomers need not even have been Africans, as appears from the two-year surge in mortality after the import of new Creole slaves in 1830. This, and other short-term increases in the death rate, might well be attributed to one of the periodic waves of epidemic with which Jamaica in general was afflicted in the 1820s and 1830s. But again these were very likely expedited by the breakdown of the plantation system and the breakup and dispersal of plantation populations.[14]

As to life expectancy, the general situation suggested in 1974 remains generally true, but the picture is now much clearer in detail, particularly once African and Creole slaves are distinguished. West Indian patterns are also found to be consonant with world wide trends. For example, the slow but steady improvement in the demographic health of West Indian slaves was apparently matched in West Africa, where, somewhat surprisingly, the drain of the Atlantic slave trade was more than compensated for by an accelerating population increase. This in turn was comparable to the great increase in Europe during the Age of the Industrial Revolution, though Africa and the West Indies seem to have lagged rather behind.

Blacks in the West Indies as in Africa, whether slave or free, did not commonly live to a great age in the eighteenth or early nineteenth centuries. The tables show that the biblical standard of four score years and ten was much more the normal limit of a natural life than the average expectation it was already becoming in Western Europe. Yet, once they reached the end of their hazardous first year, Creole slaves probably always had an average life expectancy of over thirty years, and by the end of slavery this was not far short of forty years.

These expectations, though somewhat below those in Europe at that time were very likely similar to those to be found in West Africa. It was chiefly the process of transfer and immunization which increased mortality and lowered life expectancy figures. This effect was not peculiar to Africans, though, being typical of all newcomers to the West Indies. Figures obtained by the pioneer actuaries Alexander M. Tulloch and Henry Marshall showed that the death rate for European soldiers stationed in Jamaica was four times as high as that for black soldiers recruited locally. The Europeans' death rate from fevers was ten times as high as the blacks'.[15]

Mortality and life expectancy rates on slave plantations—particularly once they were well established as at Worthy Park during the period covered—were not disastrously worse than those for "free" Jamaica during the later nineteenth century, and in some respects were not worse than those in English industrial towns. Except for the early working years, the rates for Worthy Park's Creoles compare favorably with those for Jamaica as a whole as late as 1881—though it should be pointed out that by modern standards, even in the Third World, late nineteenth-century Jamaican conditions were fairly disgraceful. An interesting comparison is also made with three of sixteen English areas studied for the purpose of a parliamentary inquiry in 1832.[16] Demographic conditions on slave plantations were greatly inferior to those found in the healthy rural county of Essex but were closer to those discovered in London, and in some age ranges superior to those in Leeds and other industrial towns. Were they available, comparative figures from the previous century, when London and the early industrial towns notoriously sucked life from the rural areas, would doubtless place the plantations in an even less gloomy light.

Infant mortality among slaves has tended to be particularly overstated in the past. After the most rigorous calculations, the proportions of slave children born live who died in their first and second years are seen to be noticeably lower than in Jamaica as a whole in 1881, with the annual figures for the years from two to five roughly similar. Though

English birthrates were much higher, infant mortality rates throughout England seem to have been higher than on slave plantations, particularly in cities like Leeds and Bradford, where more than half of those born between 1813 and 1830 failed to survive their first five years.

Death rates for Jamaican slave plantations rose perceptibly in the last few years of slavery, reversing a general downward trend—largely because of high mortality among males and the surviving Africans. But it was never mortality alone which made the demographic situation disastrous; rather, it was a permanently low, and now further sagging, birthrate. Mortality at Worthy Park averaged less than 35 per thousand a year over the last twenty-five years of slavery; but for only one period covered by the Worthy Park records did the crude birthrate of the plantation's population seemingly rise above 30 per thousand. The average for forty-six years over the entire period 1783-1834 was no more than 23.16 per thousand, with the rate well below 20 per thousand in the earliest and latest years.

The Worthy Park fertility figures, which for the Registration period (1817-1829) were even lower by 5 per thousand than the average of 26.6 per thousand for other Jamaican plantations, make somber reading when compared with later Jamaican figures, even taking into account the steady modern decline.

The fragmentary information gathered by Rose Price for 1795 suggested that the complete eradication of stillbirths, miscarriages, and abortions would have raised the average from 23.2 to 28.5 percent.[17] But even this impossible ideal (to which Rose Price's generous inducements never brought Worthy Park close) would not have solved the overall problem. The population of Worthy Park, or any plantation, would not have increased naturally unless the crude live birthrate could have been raised above the crude death rate. The reason for the almost continuous failure of the Worthy Park slave population to sustain itself can be seen by relating the two.

In order to be demographically healthy and self-sustaining through an adequate birthrate, it is obviously helpful for a population to have a reasonable balance between the sexes, a well-balanced distribution of ages, and to be well integrated. In contrast, the Worthy Park population was characterized at different times by serious disproportions between the sexes and by distorted age patterns, as well as being divided between African and Creole slaves.

Some accounts of slavery attribute the failure of the slaves to increase naturally to the excess of males imported, a disproportion sometimes presumed to have been retained in the population. It is certainly true that at Worthy Park in the early years of the recorded period when there was a slight excess of males the crude birthrate was low and also that the crude birthrate did increase during the period when females first outnumbered males. Yet the trend was not sustained. Women lived on the average at least 5 percent longer than men, which led to a quite rapid increase in the proportion of women after 1808. For a time the disproportion kept up the crude birthrate, but during the later Registration period the birthrate, however measured, fell away rapidly so that it was finally at its lowest point when females were in the greatest majority.

Even more potent factors appear to have been the proportion of Africans in the population and the relative ages of the male and female slaves. Despite the fact that most African females were in the fertile age range when first bought, their average actual fertility was no more than half that of Creole females in the same age range. One reason seems to have been that there was an extremely high incidence of sterility among African females in the West Indies. The census made by Rose Price in 1795, at a time when Africans were at their most numerous, suggested that the birthrate among the women who actually had children was relatively healthy, but that a very high proportion of females—probably more than half—never gave birth at all. This suggestion appears to be corroborated by fragmentary data from other estate populations in the earlier period.[18] But it is by no means certain that a high level of sterility was peculiar to Africans. At Worthy Park there was a perceptible increase in overall fertility once the sex ratio was equalized and the number of African women began to decline; yet the birthrate made its steepest plunge as the proportion of females rose towards 60 percent and the number of African females in the fertile age range fell towards zero. Since this was also the period when the largest number of women were excused work for having six live children, the disparity between fertile and infertile women may have been at least as great then as in 1795. This, however, is an important question that requires further exploration.

The ever gloomier fertility situation at Worthy Park is at least partly explicable by the ageing and wasting effect already noticed in the plantation's population after the ending of the slave trade. All the surviving African women, and a high proportion of the Creoles, had passed out of the fertile age range by the last decade of slavery (for it was in the upper cohorts that the disproportion between male and female life expectancy was most marked). But since the proportion of women in the fertile age range actually increased towards the end of slavery, the accelerated decline in fertility then is extremely difficult to explain on purely demographic grounds.

What compounds the mystery of the declining birthrate is the fact (illustrated by Figure 19) that slave women at Worthy Park apparently reached their peak of fecundity at a later period—some five years—than women in modern West Indian populations. This might have counteracted the steadily increasing average age in slavery's last days, unless it was a characteristic general to all slave populations at that period. Certainly, the ages of menarche and peak fecundity have become progressively earlier over the last 150 years in most other populations studied throughout the world. Further study may well show that black slave women and Africans alike were slower to sexual maturity than modern women, despite the accusations of promiscuity and precocity leveled at them by contemporary writers.

The absolutely low birthrate indicated at all ages is more significant than the late peak of fecundity and late age of menopause suggested by Figure 19. This was despite ameliorating measures which included greater care during confinement, time off for nursing mothers, permanent relief from manual labor for mothers of six living children, better food and clothing allotments, and rewards, including money, for each successful birth.

By the end of the slavery period there were sufficient trends in the general demography of Jamaica to suggest reasons why the swing to natural increase occurred so soon after emancipation.[19] By 1834 the birthrate among Creole mothers for Jamaica as a whole had perceptibly surpassed the Creole death rate; this trend is marginally apparent in the data from twelve selected Jamaican estates for 1817-1829 presented to the British Parliament in 1832. Yet if this condition of demographic equilibrium was becoming true for Jamaica as a whole (as for such long-established sugar colonies as Barbados or for nonplantation colonies like the Bahamas and Bermuda), it was certainly not the norm for active Jamaican sugar plantations. At Worthy Park the population was only self-sustaining for six out of the fifty-six years studied, and the net decrease accelerated to such an alarming degree during the 1830s that it would be possible to make a projection suggesting (however implausibly) the total disappearance of the population by about 1870. Even the figures presented to Parliament in 1831 by R. G. Amyot and T. F. Buxton remain equivocal. The last triennium (1826-1829) of the four disclosed the worst figures rather than the best. Separating active sugar estates from inactive estates, cattle pens, and coffee plantations and carrying the data forward from 1829 to the end of the Registration period in 1832, would almost certainly show a reversal of the apparent trend towards a natural increase.

Clearly there remained something intrinsic to slave plantations such as Worthy Park that made the achievement of demographic equilibrium almost impossible, let alone a permanent excess of births over deaths. The reasons for high mortality on slave plantations are not far to seek, but the causes of low fertility—the chief reason for the sad demographic equation—have always proved more of an enigma. This chapter therefore ends with some tentative conclusions about different factors likely to have affected the general fertility of plantation slaves.

One plausible explanation of low fertility might be sought in the biological and psychological effects of dislocation, stress, and overcrowding. Clinical studies would probably show low fertility for all people separated from their homeland, their accustomed environment and culture, or placed in a situation tantamount to captivity. The example of prison and concentration camps suggest that people herded uncomfortably together in captivity become disinterested in sexual coupling, impotent, or practically sterile. Moreover, slave mothers could hardly be expected to share their captors' enthusiasm for raising children solely for slave labor. Even without the intentionally induced abortions of which the planters accused their female slaves, the dislocating stress of the transatlantic passage and plantation life and work would have led to low rates of ovulation and conception, if not also of sexual intercourse. This is one area at least in which the famous and controversial concentration camp analogy of Stanley Elkins could usefully be reexamined.[20]

On the other hand, ingenious recent research has led to a suggestion that in one respect the low rate of fertility among West Indian slaves might be a natural carry-over from Africa.[21] Even those slave women who bore many offspring rarely had children at intervals of less than thirty months. This has led to a speculation that the wide spacing between births, rather than a result of low fertility brought on by other causes, was socially determined and therefore a cause of low birthrate in itself. European travelers in West Africa and experts on West Indian slave management alike commented on the tendency towards extended periods of lactation among black women. At least one planter claimed that the habit of slave mothers to defer weaning as long as possible was a tactic to frustrate their owners' desire for infant replacements.[22] But Thomas Winterbottom, who published an account of his travels in Sierra Leone in 1803, testified that even in West Africa there was a potent taboo against sexual intercourse during the lactation period.[23]

A third clue to low slave fertility might reside in the common accusation of promiscuity leveled at the slaves by plantocratic writers in the last years of plantation slavery.[24] The accusation, albeit a notorious example of the double standard applied to the blacks by the fornicating whites, may have reflected the fact that slave intercourse was by then dislocated to the point of sexual anarchy. The nuclear family which Hans Sloane suggested was common in the earlier period, and which after slavery ended was to become gradually more common under the influence of Christianity and middle-class norms, may almost have disappeared through discouragement and deculturation. Along with it may also have gone much of the great love and concern for children which Sloane witnessed among the African slaves. Slave women now tended to form unifocal families—the matrifocal and matrilineal effects of which may still be traced in Jamaica—with sequential mates. Even at a biological level, such promiscuity is known to lower fertility levels. To the degree that they forced, or allowed, their female slaves to "prostitute" themselves in this manner, the masters may have been responsible for lowering the level of fertility towards that found among true prostitutes.

A more tenuous possibility, suggested by a well-known genetic effect, is that declines in the fertility of plantation slave populations were the result of inbreeding. Such a closed society as the normal slave population was bound to produce an involuted kinship, and this may have been exacerbated by the increasing habit of sequential mating leading to the accidental breakdown of traditional incest taboos. Within a few generations virtually all the members of the population were likely to be close cousins, with a predictable decline in general fertility, and perhaps vigor too. One way of restoring genetic variety and vigor was by infusions of fresh African blood, and the importations of 1792-93 may have accounted for the temporary rise in fertility levels at Worthy Park around 1813-1817. Another means was the miscegenation between the plantation's female slaves and white males, though from evidence already cited it appears that the colored slaves did not contribute much to the general fertility and were probably no more fertile than the majority in any case. Certainly there was a concurrence between the final calamitous decline in the Worthy Park birthrate and both the severing of the African link and the apparent decrease in the rate of miscegenation.

Another, and more commonly recognized explanation would look to the effects of hard work and poor diet, if not also overt cruelty. Such factors would doubtless all have affected fertility and sterility as well as mortality levels. Yet the planters recognized this, and the whole drift of the amelioration program after 1787 was to outlaw cruelty towards women in the childbearing ages, to provide them with better than average medical treatment, food and clothing, and to spare them work harder than necessary. Certain conditions, however, fell increasingly out of the wisest planters' control towards the end of slavery. Among these were the economic conditions which determined that slaves had to work harder in order that their owners could continue to make a profit, and the demographic facts which decreed that more and more women would be drafted into the laboring gangs. These two developments (which are considered more fully in a subsequent chapter) would surely have a deleterious effect upon general fertility levels.

Finally, it is clear that disease as much as anything affected fertility and sterility as well as determining mortality levels on slave plantations. Many endemic diseases such as syphilis, yaws, and elephantiasis, and epidemic diseases such as smallpox, measles, and scarlet fever, obviously increased the incidence of miscarriages and stillbirths, as well as reducing the ability or willingness to procreate. In addition, debilitating afflictions such as diet deficiency and intestinal parasites had imponderable effects upon sexual intercourse and reproduction. Disease as a cause of death and debility, and the questions of the type and efficacy of slave medicine at Worthy Park, are treated more fully in the chapter which follows.

TABLE 21. Hypothetical Death Rate for Worthy Park, Years One through Five, First Calculation, 1784–1838

Year of life	Annual death rate per thou.	Total dead each year of 10,000 in first year	Survivors of 10,000 at each year end
One	80	800	9,200
Two	40	368	8,832
Three	35	309	8,523
Four	32	273	8,250
Five	30	248	8,002

Source: Worthy Park records.

TABLE 22. Death Rate for Worthy Park, Years One through Five, Revised Calculation, 1784–1838

Year of life	Annual death rate per thou.	Total dead each year of 10,000 in first year	Survivors of 10,000 at each year end
One	150	1,500	8,500
Two	40	340	8,160
Three	35	286	7,874
Four	32	252	7,622
Five	30	229	7,393

Source: Worthy Park records.

	Total population	Maximum recorded	Males	Females	Africans known	Creoles known
1783	318					
1784	316	331	176	155	104	133
1785	313	315	170	145	90	134
1786	307	299	160	139	88	127
1787	339	334	177	157	114	138
1788	338	343	185	158	113	147
1789	339	340	179	161	110	153
1790	345	342	177	163	118	151
1791	357	377	193	184	135	168
1792	359					
1793	450	541	291	250	297	174
1794	528	530	287	243	294	167
1795	483					
1796	470	466	245	221	237	170
1811	505					
1812	503					
1813	511	491	224	267	178	292
1814	514	458	198	260	166	282
1815	514					
1816	527	507	241	266	170	332
1817	527	535	248	287	170	360
1818		488	218	270	156	330
1819		500	223	277	156	342
1820		497	221	276	153	343
1821	505	506	223	283	151	352
1822	494	513	227	286	146	365
1823	496	489	212	277	135	352
1824	484	502	218	284	132	366
1825		423	180	243	120	302
1826		420	176	244	114	305
1827		407	166	241	104	302
1828		394	162	231	98	295
1829		386	161	225	91	294
1830	522	417	177	240	83	332
1831	517	332	133	197	47	285
1832	494	309	128	181	43	266
1833	483	301	129	172	37	264
1834	467	293	118	175	32	261
1835		261	105	156	29	231
1836		258	104	154	27	230
1837		247	98	149	23	221
1838		231	90	141	22	207

TABLE 23. Worthy Park: Slave Mortality from Worthy Park Records, 1783-1838

Source: Worthy Park records.

Note: Reliable death data missing for 1786 and 1838 (as well as for 1797-1810).

Table 23 (*continued*)

	A/C unknown	Computed annual deaths	Recorded annual deaths	Male deaths known	Female deaths known	African deaths	African male deaths	Creole deaths	Creole male deaths	A/C deaths unknown
1783		11	7	3	3	1	1		—	6
1784	94	18	6	3	3	2	2	3	1	1
1785	91	4	4	3	1	—	—	3	3	1
1786	84	—	—	—						
1787	82	7	3	2	1	2	1	1	1	0
1788	83	12	13	10	3	5	4	3	2	5
1789	77	16	13	6	7	3	2	5	2	5
1790	73	6	5	2	3	1	—	3	1	1
1791	67	18	8	2	6	3	—	3	1	2
1792		14	14	6	8	5	3	7	2	2
1793	70	26	18	8	10	9	4	7	3	2
1794	69	56	54	38	16	39	27	8	5	7
1795		19	19	8	11	9	3	6	3	4
1796	59	22	23	13	10	19	11	1	—	3
1811			10	6	4	—	—	5	4	5
1812			15	5	10	4	1	7	4	4
1813	21		10	5	5	3	2	3	2	4
1814	10		13	7	6	2	—	9	6	2
1815			18	6	12	6	2	9	2	3
1816	5		9	6	3	2	1	6	4	1
1817	5		36	17	19	9	7	26	9	1
1818	2		2	2	—		0	2	2	0
1819	2		14	7	7	4	2	9	5	1
1820	1		13	5	8	4	—	9	5	0
1821	3		24	13	11	7	5	17	8	—
1822	2	17	20	14	6	8	4	12	10	0
1823	2	8	8	3	5	5	2	3	1	0
1824	4	18	19	10	9	6	5	11	5	2
1825	1		12	8	4	6	4	6	4	0
1826	1		12	11	10	11	4	10	7	0
1827	1		11	1	10	6	0	5	1	0
1828	1		16	6	10	7	3	9	3	0
1829	1		16	6	10	8	3	8	3	0
1830	—	23	28	12	16	6	3	22	9	0
1831	—	21	25	9	16	5	1	20	8	0
1832	—	16	14	4	10	6	4	8	0	0
1833	—	7	18	4	5	5	5	13	8	0
1834	—	7	8	4	4	3	2	5	2	0
1835	1		5	1	4	2	0	3	1	0
1836	1		13	7	6	4	3	9	4	0
1837	3		11	6	5	1	1	10	5	0
1838	2		2	—	2	1	0	1	0	0

Crude annual mortality (percent)	Average annual mortality, clumped yrs. (percent)	Male mortality of all males (percent)	Female mortality of all females (percent)	African mortality of all Africans (percent)	Creole mortality of all Creoles (percent)
39.5					
54.4	34.3	17.3	13.3	10.3	22.5
12.6					
20.6					
37.9					
47.1	35.1	24.1	24.2	23.7	19.8
17.4					
47.7					
39.0		79.6	52.7	81.2	44.0
48.1					
105.6	61.3				
39.3					
48.9		53.1	45.2	80.2	5.9
19.8					
29.8					
19.6	30.8	30.8	20.9	14.5	20.9
25.3					
35.0					
17.0		47.0	39.8	32.4	46.2
67.3					
4.1					
28.0	19.5	21.1	18.2	17.2	19.7
26.2					
47.4					
39.0					
16.1	35.2	45.5	27.4	46.1	30.0
37.8					
28.4					
50.0					
27.0	37.4	37.9	37.1	72.1	25.4
40.6					
41.5					
53.6					
48.4					
32.4	38.3	55.6	52.8	102.5	48.3
37.3					
17.1					
19.2					
50.4	37.9	45.6	32.7	88.6	32.3
44.5					

TABLE 24. Worthy Park: Slave Mortality from Registration Returns, 1817-1832

Source: Jamaica Archives, Register of Returns of Slaves, 1817-1832.

	Total population	Males	Females	Africans	Creoles	Median population (3 yrs.)	Males	Females	Africans	Creoles
1817	527	241	286	169	358	} 517	232	285	159	358
1820	508	223	285	149	359	} 501	217	283	139	362
1823	494	214	280	130	364	} 481	204	277	122	359
1826	468	195	273	115	354	} 449	189	260	102	347
1829	430	184	246	89	341	} 401	170	231	80	321
1832	372	156	216	71	301					

TABLE 25. Mortality on Twelve Sample Estates and on Worthy Park, with Triennial Totals and Average Percentages, 1817-1829

Sources: British Sessional Papers, Commons, Reports, 1831-2, XX, 565-577; Jamaica Archives, Register of Returns of Slaves, 1817-1832.

	Total population	Males	Males (percent)	Females	Africans	Creoles	African Males	African Females
1817	5,089	2,503	49.2	2,586	1,764	3,325	894	870
1820	5,067	2,483	49.2	2,584	1,597	3,470	806	791
1823	5,007	2,452	49.2	2,553	1,435	3,572	720	715
1826	4,916	2,392	48.6	2,534	1,235	3,681	607	715
1829	4,739	2,272	47.9	2,467	1,021	3,718	483	538

	Mortality					African		Creole	
	Crude	Male	Female	African	Creole	Male	Female	Male	Female
1817-1820	27.37	28.08	26.69	34.52	23.91	35.29	33.73	24.35	23.38
1820-1823	29.18	30.81	27.65	34.96	26.70	35.39	34.53	28.76	24.78
1823-1826	33.86	36.33	31.46	51.36	28.12	55.80	43.22	29.01	27.30
1826-1829	34.18	39.45	29.19	61.17	25.68	73.39	49.74	29.10	22.49
1817-1829	31.54	33.93	28.90	44.12	26.46	49.42	39.77	28.25	24.63
Worthy Park									
1817-1829	33.85	36.21	31.95	46.51	28.55	48.52	44.71	33.35	24.31

Total deaths (3 yrs.)	Males	Females	Africans	Creoles	Crude mortality, % of 3 yrs.	Male mortality, % of total population	Male mortality, % of all males	Female mortality, % of total population	Female mortality, % of all females	African mortality, % of all Africans	Creole mortality, % of all Creoles
51	24	27	15	36	32.9	15.5	34.5	17.4	31.6	31.5	33.5
50	29	21	19	31	33.3	19.3	44.6	13.9	25.0	45.6	28.5
47	27	20	16	31	32.6	18.7	44.1	13.9	24.1	43.7	29.0
47	13	34	22	25	34.9	9.6	23.0	26.0	43.6	71.9	24.0
69	30	39	17	52	57.3	24.9	58.9	32.4	56.3	70.9	54.0

Creole		Total deaths (3 yrs.)			African		Creole	
Males	Females		Males	Females	Males	Females	Males	Females
1,609	1,716	} 417	211	206	90	83	121	123
1,678	1,792	} 440	227	213	81	77	146	136
1,731	1,841	} 504	263	241	111	87	152	154
1,785	1,896	} 494	276	218	120	88	156	130
1,789	1,929							

TABLE 26. Worthy Park:
Slave Fertility from Worthy
Park Records, 1783-1834

Source: Worthy Park records.

Note: Estimated figures are
given in boldface.

	Births given in (1783-1796)	Recorded births	Cumulative totals	African mothers known	Creole mothers known	A/C mothers unknown	Official total popu-lation	Recorded popula-tion
1783	2	1		1		1	318	
1784	10	8	18	2	6	2	331	331
1785	5	6		1	3	2	317	315
1786							307	299
1787	10	11		3	6	2	339	334
1788	9	8		2	2	5	343	343
1789	7	7	44	2	4	1	341	340
1790		7		0	7	—	345	342
1791	8	10		2	4	4	377	377
1792	13	10		2	7	4	359	
1793	6	6		2	2	2	541	541
1794	8	8	48	2	3	3	530	530
1795	13	12		4	6	3	483	
1796	8	7		3	4	1	470	466
1800		9		5	4	—		
1801		5		3	2	—		
1802		6	56	4	2	—		
1803		4		2	2	—		
1804		3		2	1	—		
1805		15		6	9	—		
1806		7		0	7	—		
1807		11	86	4	7	—		
1808		17		9	7	—		
1809		15		7	7	1		
1810		7		3	4	—		
1811		17	37	6	11	—	505	
1812		20		6	13	1	503	
1813		18		4	14	—	511	491
1814		15		6	9	—	514	456
1815		19	88	8	11	—	514	
1816		22		6	16	—	527	507
1817		14		4	10	—	527	535
1818		11		3	8	—		488
1819		10	28	2	8	—		500
1820		7		1	6	—		497
1821		18		2	16	—	505	506
1822		10	45	2	8	—	512	513
1823		10		1	9	—	496	489
1824		7		2	3	—	502	502
1825		5		—	5	—		423
1826		11		1	9	1		420
1827		8	35	—	8	—		407
1828		2		—	2	—		394
1829		9		1	6	2		386
1830		6		—	6	—	522	417
1831		3	24	—	3	—	517	332
1832		10		—	10	—	494	309
1833		5		—	5	—	483	301
1834		1		—	1	—	467	292

Cumulative average population	Crude birthrate clumped yrs. (percent)	Females	Cumulative averages	Birthrate by females (percent)	Fertile females (ages known)	Calculated fertile females (1784-1796)	Cumulative averages	Birthrate by fertile females (percent)	African population
322	18.6	155	155	38.7	62	92	73	82.2	104
		145			44	64			90
		139			45	62			88
		157			59	75			114
		158			57	86			113
349	25.2	161	165	53.3	65	79	82	107.3	110
		165			70	82			118
		184			77	89			135
		250			132	144			297
477	20.1	243	221	43.4	139	143	126	76.2	294
		221			128	134			237
500	22.4		250	44.8			143	78.3	
500	28.7		255	56.2			143	100.2	
504	36.7		257	72.0			141	131.2	
		267			142				178
		260			133		137	128.5	166
519	33.9		270	65.2					
		266			134				170
		287			138				170
		270			133				156
495	18.9	277	274	34.1	134		133	70.2	156
		276			133				133
		283			134				151
504	22.3	286	283	39.8	141				146
		277			145		144	78.1	135
		284			152				132
		243			126				120
		244			130				114
402	17.4	241	237	29.5	131		127	55.1	104
		232			126				98
		225			121				91
		240			132				85
		197			100				47
340	17.6	181	198	30.3	102		107	56.1	43
		172			95				37
		175			102				32

Table 26. (*continued*)

Year	Cumulative averages	Crude African birthrate (percent)	African females	Cumulative averages	Birthrate by African females (percent)	Fertile African females	Cumulative averages	Birthr... fer... Afr... fem... (per...
1783								
1784	93	14.3	54	48	27.7	27	17	78
1785			48			12		
1786			46			12		
1787			52			20		
1788			51			20		
1789	118	15.3	50	54	33.3	20	21	85
1790			55			21		
1791			63			26		
1792								
1793			134			80		
1794	256	10.2	130	117	22.2	82	74	35
1795								
1796			109			73		
1800								
1801								
1802	250	26.6		123	54.0		86	77
1803								
1804								
1805								
1806								
1807	225	26.4		113	52.6		81	73
1808								
1809								
1810								
1811	197	30.5		99	60.6		74	81
1812			92			70		
1813			90			73		
1814	171	32.7		88	63.6		68	82
1815			85			65		
1816			86			65		
1817			83			65		
1818	148	13.5	83	82	24.4	62	61	32
1819			81			57		
1820			79			55		
1821			76			55		
1822	141	12.4	71	74	23.6		51	34
1823			71			48		
1824			68			46		
1825			65			41		
1826			63			40		
1827	105	3.8	57	57	7.0	36	35	1
1828			51			31		
1829			47			25		
1830			41			21		
1831	53	0.0	24	26	0.0	2	6	0
1832			21			1		
1833			19			—		
1834			19			—		

Creole population	Cumulative averages	Crude Creole birthrate (percent)	Creole females	Cumulative averages	Birthrate by Creole females (percent)	Fertile Creole averages	Cumulative averages	Birthrate by fertile Creole females
133	133	22.6	65	65	46.2	24	24	125.0
134			64			22		
127			63			23		
138			75			28		
147			76			26		
153	151	30.5	83	83	55.4	33	32	143.8
151			85			36		
168			95			37		
174			95			37		
167	169	26.0	90	91	48.4	38	38	115.8
170			90			42		
	240	19.1		119	38.3		46	99.1
	225	37.3		117	71.8		45	186.7
	312	38.5		168	71.4		64	187.5
292			162			67		
282			164			58		
	317	37.9		176	66.2		66	181.8
332			179			68		
360			200			72		
330			186			67		
342	338	21.7	193	191	38.4	71	71	103.3
343			195			76		
352			202			80		
365	359	25.1	208	207	43.5	83	91	98.9
352			204			96		
366			213			104		
302			178			85		
305			181			90		
302	300	20.0	184	180	33.3	95		65.2
295			181			95		
294			178			96		
332			199			111		
285	287	20.1	173	171	35.1	98	101	59.4
266			160			101		
264			153			95		
261			156			102		

TABLE 27. Worthy Park: Slave Fertility, 1783-1796, Projected Estimates

Source: Worthy Park records.

	Births given in	Recorded births	Cumulative totals	African mothers known	Creole mothers known	A/C mothers unknown	Calculated African mothers	Annual average
1783	2	1		1	—	1		
1784	10	8	18	2	6	2	6	2.0
1785	5	6		1	3	2		
1786								
1787	10	11		3	6	2		
1788	9	8		2	2	5		
1789	7	7	44	2	4	1	12	2.4
1790		7		—	7	—		
1791	8	10		2	4	4		
1792	13	10		2	7	4		
1793	6	6		2	2	2		
1794	8	8	48	2	3	3	18	3.6
1795	13	12		4	6	3		
1796	8	7		3	4	1		

	Calculated Creole females	Calculated fertile Creole females	Crude birthrate (percent)	Birthrate by females (percent)	Birthrate by fertile females (percent)	Crude birthrate of Africans (percent)	Crude birthrate of Creoles (percent)	Birth by Af. females (per...)
1783	89	43	18.6	38.7	82.2	15.5	20.7	30
1784								
1785								
1786								
1787								
1788								
1789	100	30	25.2	53.3	107.3	16.3	31.7	36
1790								
1791								
1792								
1793								
1794								
1795	97	43	20.1	43.4	76.2	13.0	30.0	29
1796								

TABLE 28. Worthy Park: Slave Fertility from Registration Returns, 1817-1832

Source: Jamaica Archives, Register of Returns of Slaves, 1817-1832.

	Total population	Males	Females	Africans	Creoles	Median population (3 yrs.)	Males	Females
1817	527	241	286	169	358	517	232	285
1820	508	223	285	149	359	501	217	283
1823	494	214	280	130	364	481	204	277
1826	468	195	273	115	354	449	189	260
1829	430	184	246	89	341	401	170	231
1832	372	156	216	71	301			

Calculated Creole mothers	Annual averages	Total population	Females	Calculated fertile females	Calculated Africans Total	Calculated Creoles total	Calculated African females	Calculated fertile African females
12	4.0	322	155	73	129	193	66	30
32	6.4	349	163	82	147	202	65	32
30	6.0	477	221	126	277	200	124	83

Birthrate by fertile African females (percent)	Birthrate by Creole females (percent)	Birthrate by fertile Creole females (percent)
66.7	44.9	93.0
75.0	64.0	128.0
43.4	61.9	140.0

Africans	Creoles	Births (inc. recorded born and died)	Males	Females	Total fertile females (ages 15-45)	% of fertile females of all females	Median fertile females	Crude birthrate (00/00)	Birthrate, fertile females
159	358	43	15	28	125	43	130	27.7	110.2
139	362	39	19	20	113	40	124	25.9	104.8
122	359	25	11	14	136	48	125	17.3	66.6
102	347	21	9	12	114	41	113	15.6	61.9
80	321	24	12	12	111	42	105	20.0	76.2

TABLE 29. Fertility on Twelve Sample Estates and on Worthy Park, with Triennial Totals and Average Percentages, 1817-1829

Sources: British Sessional Papers, Commons, Reports, 1831-2, XX, 565-577; Jamaica Archives, Register of Returns of Slaves, 1817-1832.

	Total population	Females	Total born (3 yrs.)	Males born	Females born	Children to African mothers	Children to Creole mothers
1817	5,089	2,586					
			421	204	217	112	309
1820	5,067	2,584					
			398	211	187	79	311
1823	5,007	2,553					
			417	208	209	48	369
1826	4,916	2,524					
			350	173	177	30	320
1829	4,739	2,467					
1817-1829			1,586	796	790	269	1,309
Worthy Park 1817-1829			128	54	74	22	106

TABLE 30. Worthy Park: Abbreviated Life Table, 1784-1813

Source: Worthy Park records.

[a]Twenty-one added for underrecording.
[b]Increased by 50% from 42 for underrecording.

Cohort	Ages	Numbers in each cohort	% of total in each cohort	Recorded deaths in each cohort[a]	% of dead in each cohort
1	0-4	488[a]	10.76	63[b]	14.26
2	5-9	447	9.86	24	5.43
3	10-14	392	8.64	17	3.85
4	15-19	350	7.72	13	2.94
5	20-24	459	10.12	55	12.44
6	25-29	451	9.95	28	6.33
7	30-34	417	9.20	28	6.33
8	35-39	335	7.39	26	5.88
9	40-44	325	7.17	33	7.47
10	45-49	205	4.52	27	6.11
11	50-54	220	4.85	21	4.75
12	55-59	181	3.99	17	3.85
13	60-64	126	2.77	19	4.30
14	65-69	69	1.52	26	5.88
15	70+	70	1.54	45	10.18
Totals		4,535	100.00	442	100.00

Crude fertility (percent)	Fertility by females (percent)	Crude African fertility (percent)	African fertility by African females (percent)	Crude Creole fertility (percent)	Creole fertility by Creole females (percent)	Worthy Park crude fertility (percent)
27.63	54.28	22.22	44.98	30.41	58.72	27.72
26.34	51.66	17.37	34.51	29.44	57.08	25.95
28.02	54.65	12.45	23.85	33.91	65.85	17.32
24.17	46.64	8.87	17.15	28.83	55.78	15.59
26.90	52.32	16.10	31.84	30.98	59.70	22.32
22.32	40.10	14.21	26.96	25.24	43.51	

Dead each year per thou. (av. mortality 39.37)[a]	Annual death rate (per thou.)	Probability of dying in cohort period	Dead in each cohort period of 10,000 at year 0	Survivors at end of each cohort period	Expectation of life at beginning of each cohort period (yrs.)
5.61	52.14	0.2607	2,607	7,393	25.5
2.14	21.70	.1085	802	6,591	28.6
1.52	17.59	.0879	579	6,012	26.8
1.16	15.03	.0752	452	5,560	24.1
4.90	48.42	.2421	1,346	4,214	20.9
2.49	25.03	.1252	528	3,686	21.8
2.49	27.07	.1354	499	3,187	19.5
2.31	31.26	.1563	498	2,689	17.2
2.94	41.00	.2050	551	2,138	14.9
2.41	53.32	.2666	570	1,568	13.1
1.87	38.56	.1928	302	1,266	12.0
1.52	38.10	.1905	241	1,025	9.2
1.69	61.01	.3050	313	712	5.8
2.31	151.97	.7594	541	171	2.3
4.01	260.39	1.0000	171	0	2.5

39.37

TABLE 31. Jamaica: Average Mortality by Age Cohorts on Twelve Sample Estates, in Percentages, 1817-1829, with Average Totals in Each Cohort from Slave Registration Returns

Source: British Sessional Papers, Commons, Reports, 1831-2, XX, 565-577.

Mortality	Under 6	6-11	12-17	18-23	24-29	30-35	36-41	42-47	48-53
1817-1820									
Crude	48.5	17.4	15.0	10.8	13.0	17.2	27.1	22.8	36.5
Male	49.3	19.3	14.6	12.3	13.4	14.7	39.5	20.9	55.6
Female	47.8	15.4	15.3	9.4	12.5	19.8	19.5	24.9	18.0
African	—	—	—	6.2	33.6	14.4	23.6	27.1	42.6
Creole	48.5	17.4	15.0	11.5	7.8	20.6	19.9	16.2	26.8
1820-1823									
Crude	61.7	16.3	11.8	16.1	18.3	18.4	19.7	24.2	32.3
Male	66.3	20.7	10.0	20.6	22.0	19.4	18.3	29.0	42.1
Female	57.4	12.1	13.7	11.5	15.1	17.2	18.7	19.4	22.1
African	—	—	—	—	14.9	19.6	17.0	28.1	39.0
Creole	61.7	16.3	11.8	16.6	19.9	17.2	21.0	18.3	19.5
1823-1826									
Crude	59.6	17.7	12.1	16.0	12.8	17.4	23.0	30.7	39.6
Male	57.7	18.6	12.6	11.7	15.8	13.3	25.9	37.9	45.8
Female	61.6	16.8	11.6	20.6	10.1	20.8	20.0	24.2	33.3
African	—	—	—	—	6.7	18.2	28.7	38.5	44.4
Creole	59.6	17.7	12.1	16.0	13.6	16.9	15.9	16.2	32.5
1826-1829									
Crude	48.3	12.5	14.9	16.4	23.1	18.6	28.7	27.7	51.5
Male	54.4	15.0	11.5	19.0	26.0	23.0	30.2	40.9	64.1
Female	41.7	10.2	18.0	13.6	20.0	15.0	27.0	17.2	40.5
African	—	—	—	—	—	23.1	41.5	34.4	65.3
Creole	48.3	12.5	14.9	16.4	23.1	16.4	17.3	16.4	33.3
1817-1829									
Crude	54.4	16.0	13.5	14.7	17.0	20.4	24.6	28.4	37.5
Male	56.6	18.4	12.4	15.9	17.2	19.1	28.0	38.6	46.2
Female	52.3	13.7	14.7	13.5	14.9	21.5	21.6	20.6	29.4
Average numbers in cohorts									
Males	327	267	249	220	217	257	253	177	166
Females	333	280	250	216	224	248	282	231	176
Total	660	547	499	436	441	503	535	408	342

114

Age	Crude death rate (per thou.)	Probability of dying in age interval	Total dead in each age interval (of 10,000 at age 0)	Survivors at end of each age interval (of 10,000)	Expectation of life at beginning of each age interval (yrs.)
0-5	54.4	0.3264	3,264	6,736	28.7
6-11	16.0	.0960	647	6,089	35.1
12-17	13.5	.0810	493	5,596	32.5
18-23	14.7	.0882	494	5,102	29.1
24-29	17.0	.1020	520	4,582	25.7
30-35	20.4	.1224	561	4,021	22.3
36-41	24.6	.1476	593	3,428	18.9
42-47	28.4	.1704	584	2,844	15.7
48-53	37.5	.2256	642	2,202	12.3
54 +	—	1.0000	2,202	0	9.0

TABLE 32. Jamaica: Abbreviated Life Table for Population of Twelve Selected Estates, 1817-1829

Source: British Sessional Papers, Commons, Reports, 1831-2, XX, 565-517.

Age	Probability of dying in age interval	Survivors to beginning of each age interval	Number dying in each age interval	Life table population in each age interval	Life table population at base age of each cohort and over	Expectation of life at beginning of each age interval (yrs.)
0-6	0.4000	10,000	4,000	40,000	227,674	22.8
6-12	.1182	6,000	709	33,873	187,674	31.3
12-18	.1036	5,291	548	30,102	153,801	29.1
18-24	.1119	4,743	531	26,865	123,699	26.1
24-30	.1121	4,212	472	23,856	96,834	23.0
30-36	.1573	3,740	589	20,673	72,978	19.5
36-42	.1901	3,151	599	17,109	52,305	16.6
42-48	.2680	2,552	684	13,260	35,196	13.8
48-54	.3200	1,868	597	9,417	21,936	11.7
54-60	.3950	1,271	502	6,120	12,519	9.8
60-66	.4650	769	358	3,540	6,399	8.3
66-72	.5400	411	222	1,800	2,859	7.0
72-78	.6550	189	124	762	1,059	5.6
78-84	.7700	65	50	240	297	4.6
84-90	.8850	15	13	51	57	0
90-96	1.0000	2	2	6	0	0

TABLE 33. Demerara/Essequibo: Abbreviated Life Table for Whole Population, 1817-1832, from Slave Registration Data

Source: George W. Roberts, "A Life Table for a West Indian Slave Population," Population Studies, 5 (March 1952), 238-243.

TABLE 34. Worthy Park: Abbreviated Life Table, Creole-Born, 1790-1833

Source: Worthy Park records.

Cohort	Ages	% of total in each cohort	% of dead in each cohort	Dead each year per thou. (av. mortality 30.650)	Annual death rate (per thou.)	Dead in each cohort period of 10,000 in first year of life	Survivors at end of each cohort period	Expectation of life at beginning of each cohort period (yrs.)
1	0-4	15.22	30.00	9.195	60.41	3,021	6,979	27.3
2	5-9	13.43	12.59	3.859	28.73	1,003	5,976	33.0
3	10-14	12.75	7.78	2.385	18.71	559	5,417	33.1
4	15-19	11.09	6.30	1.931	17.41	472	4,945	31.3
5	20-24	8.98	8.52	2.611	29.08	719	4,226	29.0
6	25-29	7.00	5.19	1.591	22.73	480	3,746	28.5
7	30-34	5.61	2.96	0.907	16.17	332	3,414	26.8
8	35-39	5.57	2.22	0.680	12.21	209	3,205	24.2
9	40-44	5.07	4.44	1.361	26.84	430	2,775	20.6
10	45-49	3.59	3.33	1.021	28.44	395	2,379	18.4
11	50-54	3.37	2.22	0.680	20.18	240	2,139	16.1
12	55-59	2.96	2.22	0.680	22.97	246	1,903	12.6
13	60-64	2.16	2.22	0.680	31.48	300	1,603	8.9
14	65-69	1.62	5.19	1.591	98.21	787	816	5.1
15	70+	1.58	4.82	1.477	93.48	816	0	2.5
Total		100.00	100.00	30.650				

TABLE 35. Comparison of Approximate Average Annual Death Rates (per thousand), by One-Year, Five-Year, and Ten-Year Cohorts: Worthy Park, Jamaica, Guiana, England, 1784-1951, Selected Years

Sources: Col. 1, 2, Worthy Park records; col. 3, *British Sessional Papers, Commons, Reports, 1831-2,* XX, 565-577; cols. 4, 5, and 6, G. W. Roberts, *The Population of Jamaica* (Cambridge, Cambridge University Press, 1957), p. 150; the last three columns, *British Sessional Papers, Commons, Accounts and Papers, 1831-2,* XLV; the proportions of those who died in years 1, 2, and 3-5, Manchester burial figures in the same source, which suggest a ratio of 9:5:6 (9:5:2:2:2); Worthy Park records.

Age group	Worthy Park, total (1784-1813)	Worthy Park, Creoles (1790-1833)	Twelve Jamaican estates (1817-1829)	Demerara/ Essequibo (1817-1829)	Jamaica (1881)	Jamaica (1951)	London (1813-1830)	Leeds (1813-1830)	Essex (1813-1830)
0-1	150	173	160	250	178	72	171	239	144
1-2	40	46	45	80	53	24	95	132	80
2-4	33	38	33	38	26	6	38	53	32
5-9	22	29	22	26	9	2	12	18	12
10-14	18	19	14	22	6	2	6	10	10
15-19	15	17	15	20	6	3	8	14	12
20-29	37	26	16	23	11	4	14	17	15
30-39	29	14	22	33	15	5	18	19	14
40-49	47	27	29	51	22	8	24	23	16
50-59	38	22	39	73	32	14	31	31	21
60-69	106	64	83	98	52	26	46	44	34

Age	Worthy Park, total (1784-1813)	Worthy Park Creoles (1790-1833)	Twelve Jamaican estates (1817-1829)	Demerara/ Essequibo (1817-1829)	London (1813-1830)	Leeds (1813-1830)	Essex (1813-1830)
0	25.5	27.3	28.7	22.8	30.3	22.0	33.9
5	28.6	33.0	34.5	30.6	42.4	39.0	44.6
10	26.8	33.1	33.0	30.0	40.2	37.6	42.7
15	24.1	31.3	30.4	27.9	36.3	34.5	39.4
20	20.9	29.0	27.5	24.5	32.6	31.9	36.8
25	21.8	28.5	25.0	21.4	**29.6**	**29.5**	**34.6**
30	19.5	26.8	22.3	19.5	26.7	27.1	32.4
35	17.2	24.2	19.5	17.0	**23.8**	24.5	29.5
40	14.9	20.6	17.2	14.6	21.4	22.2	26.8
45	13.1	18.4	14.0	12.6	**18.8**	19.5	**23.8**
50	12.0	16.1	11.3	10.9	16.5	17.4	21.0
55	9.2	12.6	9.1	9.5	**14.1**	14.7	**17.8**
60	5.8	8.9	**6.0**	8.4	11.5	12.6	15.2
65	2.3	5.1	**4.4**	7.1	**9.3**	10.5	**12.6**
70	2.5	2.5	**2.5**	6.0	7.9	8.7	10.4

TABLE 36. Comparison of Approximate Life Expectancies in Years, at Birth and Five-Year Intervals: Worthy Park, Jamaica, Guiana, England, 1784-1833, Selected Years

Sources: Cols. 1, 2, Worthy Park records; col. 3, *British Sessional Papers, Commons, Reports, 1831-2, XX,* 565-577; col. 4, G. W. Roberts, *The Population of Jamaica* (Cambridge, Cambridge University Press, 1957), p. 150; cols. 5, 6, 7, *British Sessional Papers, Commons, Accounts and Papers, 1831-2, XLV.*

Note: Figures in boldface are interpolated projections.

Period	Birthrate (per thou.)	Period	Birthrate (per thou.)
1844-1861	34.0*	1911-1915	37.9
1861-1871	35.5*	1916-1920	36.4
1871-1881	36.5*	1921-1925	36.5
1881-1885	37.4	1926-1930	36.4
1886-1890	36.9	1931-1935	33.4
1891-1895	38.4	1936-1940	32.1
1896-1900	38.8	1941-1945	31.8
1901-1905	39.2	1946-1950	31.8
1906-1910	38.3		

TABLE 37. Jamaica: Crude Birthrates, 1844-1950

Source: Derived mainly from G. W. Roberts, *The Population of Jamaica* (Cambridge, Cambridge University Press, 1957). However, Roberts' figures for 1844-1881 are questionable. They appear to be based solely on a projection upwards from the generally down-curving figures for 1881-1951. The asterisked figures are based on a more realistic projection between a peak of about 39 between 1896 and 1905 and the general Jamaican figure of about 32 at the end of slavery.

Period	Crude annual death rate (per thou.)	Crude annual birthrate (per thou.)	Crude annual increase/ decrease (per thou.)	Actual population changes[a]
1783-1785	34.3	18.6	−15.7	318-317
1787-1792	35.1	25.7	− 9.4	339-359
1793-1796	61.3	18.8	−42.5	541-470
1811-1817	30.8	34.7	+ 3.9	505-535
1818-1820	19.5	18.9	− 0.6	488-497
1821-1824	35.2	22.3	−12.9	506-502
1825-1829	37.4	17.4	−20.0	423-386
1830-1834	38.3	17.6	−20.7	522-467

TABLE 38. Worthy Park: Annual Rates of Natural Increase/Decrease, 1783-1834

Source: Worthy Park records.

[a]Includes sales, purchases, transfers, etc.

TABLE 39. Worthy Park: Comparison of Fertile Female Birthrates with Proportions of Fertile Females, 1783-1833

Source: Worthy Park records.

Period	% of females 15-49 of total females	% of females 15-49 of total population	Annual birthrate by total females 15-49 (per thou.)
1783-1785	51.96	23.45	82.2
1787-1791	47.25	22.46	107.3
1792-1796	56.36	25.90	76.2
1813-1817	48.61	26.34	128.5
1818-1820	47.75	26.46	70.2
1821-1824	48.49	27.25	78.1
1825-1829	52.56	30.91	55.1
1830-1833	54.06	31.51	56.1

4 / Death, Disease, Medicine, 1783-1838

EVEN while condemning the institution of slavery, many modern writers on the subject have echoed the early apologists of slavery in assuming that the health of plantation slaves can be positively correlated with the number of doctors and the amount of medicine used.[1] The motives of the slaveowners are usually acknowledged to have been economic calculation rather than disinterested philanthropy, but the facts that there were more so-called doctors in Jamaica in 1800 than in 1900, that nearly all plantations had their own practitioners, and that medicines featured largely in any list of imported plantation supplies are taken as evidence that slaves were relatively well cared for. Without such care, it is assumed, slave health conditions would have been far worse, perhaps even as bad as those in the notorious graveyard of the West African coast.[2]

More careful research, however, revises—even reverses—these views. Ignorance of the etiology of tropical diseases placed them largely beyond human control, a situation that was compounded by treatments based upon a purblind ignorance of human physiology and an irrelevant pharmacopoeia.[3] Even at Worthy Park which was serviced for fifty-five years by a doctor famous for his efficiency, slave medicine was a mixed blessing indeed.

Under the Jamaican Consolidated Slave Law of 1792, not only were overseers to hand in to the vestries annual lists of births and deaths on their plantations at a penalty of £50 for noncompliance but every plantation doctor was also "on oath, to give-in an account of slaves dying, with, to the best of his judgement, the causes thereof, under penalty of £100 for each neglect."[4] Thus, for at least those estates for which records have survived, there exist cause-of-death diagnoses up to the standards attained by eighteenth-century plantation doctors. In addition, at Worthy Park and some other estates the slave ledgers included, rather less systematically, comments on the health of slaves whose efficiency was impaired and lists of medicines used.

Table 40 shows all the causes of death ascribed in the Worthy Park records between 1792 and 1838, involving 401 slaves. Wherever possible, the slave doctor's diagnoses have been translated into modern

Newcomers were especially susceptible to West Indian diseases, not just Africans but also whites like "Johnny Newcome" in the popular series of satirical prints.

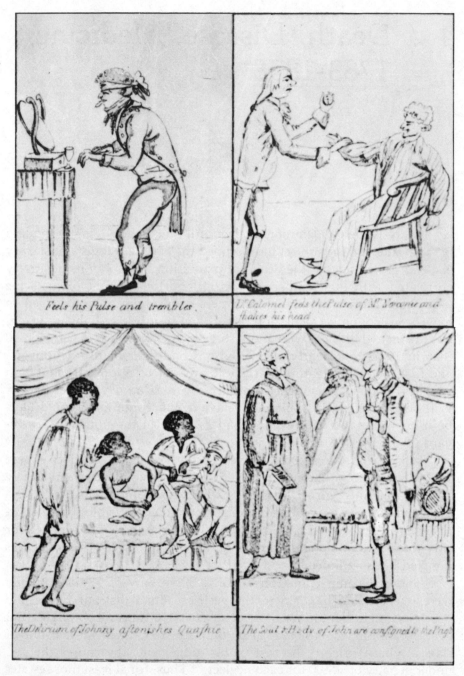

Feels his Pulse and trembles.

Dr Calomel feels the Pulse of Mr Newcome and shakes his head

The Delirium of Johnny astonishes Quashie

The Soul & Body of John are consigned to the Deep

terms and grouped into classes along the lines of the World Health Organization categories. Further on, the significance of the diagnoses given in the "Condition" columns of the Worthy Park slave ledgers is also discussed, but the Condition listings are so much less systematic and conclusive—so much less final—than Causes of Death, that they cannot easily be tabulated.

The 401 specific causes of death from Worthy Park represent perhaps the largest sample it is now possible to recover from a single Jamaican estate. However, any such single source needs careful preliminary evaluation before its general value is established. The two chief deficiencies of the data are that they are not complete and that they are derived from a population which changed considerably during the forty-six years covered, particularly in the gradual increase in the proportion of Creole and thus fully "seasoned" slaves. It is likely that between 1792 and 1838 some 1,100 slaves actually died at Worthy Park, so that causes of death are specifically unknown for almost two-thirds. However, the nature of the records determine that these causes of death can be regarded as virtually a random sample, scattered evenly over the entire period and over the whole range of the population.

Causes-of-death data are deficient for the two periods of exceptional mortality: following the large influx of new Africans in the 1790s, and the arrival of more than 100 new Creoles in 1830. This may have led to a slight understatement of the deaths by fever and flux. Yet these periods of exceptional mortality occurred in only about four of the forty-six years covered. Were all causes of death in those years specifically known and recorded, this would surely have led to a severe distortion of the overall situation. Moreover, only a minority of Jamaican estates had comparable influxes of population in slavery's last years.

Another area of slight doubt was the degree to which causes of infant death were underrepresented. As has already been established, infant mortality itself was commonly understated by plantation records, though not quite to the degree that some writers believe.[5] At Worthy Park, the number of those who were born and died during the intercensal periods and thus went unrecorded was probably no more than one in five overall. During the period 1792-1838 just over 30 percent of those born on the estate died in their first five years. Only about 20 percent of the known causes of death related to deaths in this age range. But since about a third of Worthy Park's slaves were African-born and never were infants at Worthy Park it seems likely that causes of infant death were not underrepresented at all.

It is a commonplace of plantation studies that new African slaves suffered far higher mortality rates and died from different diseases than seasoned Creoles. Yet it should be remembered that by the beginning of the period covered an established plantation of 500 slaves would, on the average, receive only two or three new Africans a year, and that from the ending of the British slave trade in 1808 the flow dried up altogether. Accordingly, for Jamaica as a whole, and for the most long-established estates, the proportion of Africans in the slave population declined from only about 50 percent in 1792, to no more than 10 percent in 1838. The Worthy Park figures were 42.1 percent in 1784, soaring to 63.4 percent in 1794, and then declining gradually to 37.9 percent in 1813 and 9.6 percent in 1838.[6] By and large therefore, it can be accepted that the causes of death at Worthy Park for the last half century of slavery were more or less random and representative.

Worthy Park was a typical Jamaican sugar plantation in most respects, though somewhat larger, further inland, and consequently even more self-contained than the average. How then did its pattern of death and disease compare with other types of settlement and other areas? Although comparable vital statistics were not obtainable, it has at least proved possible to compare the Worthy Park causes-of-death figures for 1792-1838 with the cause-of-death data from British Guiana, 1829-1832, and with figures for the total population of heavily urbanized St. Catherine Parish between 1774 and 1778, including free whites, coloreds, and blacks as well as slaves.[7]

In fact, when looking for comparisons with the Worthy Park causes of death, it was the data from St. Catherine—a lowland area with some sugar plantations but heavily dominated by Spanish Town, the Jamaican capital—which were first employed.[8] The contrasts between a tightly knit but closed and rural population of slaves, and a largely urbanized and geographically mobile population including all races and classes, were immediately apparent. This was particularly so in the far greater incidence of death by "fever" and the far smaller number of deaths by old age in Spanish Town and its environs. A tragically high proportion of those who died from fever in Spanish Town were members of the white army garrison who, during their period of acclimatization, suffered from one of the highest mortality rates in the world.[9] Urban slaves, on the average, did not suffer such severe mortality as newly arrived whites.[10] Though a surprisingly high proportion of urban slaves were Africans, a majority were employed as domestics. Rather better food and working conditions than on plantations were offset by a vulnerability induced by slum crowding, poor sanitation, nearby swamps, and the chances of reinfection by transients, particularly in respect of epidemics. For the total population, the mortality rates in tropical towns were probably twice the average for whole colonies, and higher than for any plantations, but the death rate of urban slaves came somewhere between that of the best and worst of rural populations.[11]

Though largely explicable, the very great differences between the causes of death at Worthy Park and at St. Catherine left the question of the typicality of Worthy Park as a sugar plantation up in the air. The discovery of the remarkable correlation between Worthy Park's figures and those for a larger sample drawn from sugar plantations in British Guiana, a thousand miles distant and in a rather later period, was therefore very exciting. Many contemporary writers spoke of sugar plantations as if they were standard in every respect and noted contrasts between different types of settlement and locations within the Caribbean. Some analysis has recently been made of differences in overall mortality figures.[12] But here for the first time was statistical evidence by specific causes of death. Moreover, from this it was clear that there were health characteristics common and peculiar to sugar plantations wherever they were found within the Caribbean region. These contrasted to a marked degree with West Indian towns, and probably differed to a lesser but significant degree from smaller, less intensively cultivated plantations growing staples other than sugar, in hillier areas—for which similar work remains to be undertaken.

In drawing up both cause-of-death tables there were many difficulties of classification. Too many of the alleged explanations of death from Worthy Park ledgers were nonspecific or downright evasive. What, for example, is learned from "accident"? And what can be made of "at hospital in Kingston," "suddenly," "in the night," or "a vindication of God"? In a dismaying number of cases the doctor was describing, and presumably had been treating, symptoms rather than actual diseases. "Convulsions" and gastro-intestinal complications were particularly difficult to identify, but even the common diagnoses of "flux," "fever," "ulcers," and "dropsy" proved troublesome. At first sight there seemed to be a remarkably high number of different causes of death. However, discriminating reclassification—first along W.H.O. lines and then, less scientifically, into the categories used for the British Guiana slaves—elicited a much clearer picture.

Despite the depredations of epidemics (not all of which were killers) and the decimation of the seasoning process among new slaves, the chief single cause of death on sugar plantations was still old age—or at least debility among elderly adults. That over a fifth of the slaves lived long enough to die of what were regarded as natural causes surely runs counter to the impression given by *average* survival rates, which suggest life expectancy at birth of less than thirty years for Creoles, and for new Africans an average expectation of no more than a dozen years after arrival.

Epidemics of measles, smallpox, and yellow fever carried off numbers of plantation slaves in some years, but the dreaded "fluxes" struck more regularly and killed even more overall. Known by their symptoms either as the "white" or "bloody" flux, these were nearly all varieties of bacillary dysentery, particularly infection by protozoa *shigella shigae*. Bacillary dysentery could kill quickly by dehydration and poisoning by bacterial toxins. Amoebic dysentery was probably less common and, where fatal, was not always identified as a flux, killing more slowly by chronic infection and secondary ulcerations in intestines, liver, or lungs.

Plantation deaths from "inflammation" and "mortification" were rather less common than might be expected. On the other hand, intestinal and subcutaneous parasites were extremely common, and it was not the most evident types, such as the nauseating tape and guinea worms, which were necessarily the most dangerous. The tiny hookworm in particular was a far more serious and widespread cause of ill-health, debility, and death than was recognized by contemporary doctors. The larvae of these creatures were picked up by bare feet, causing what was known as ground itch between the toes. Shedding their skin and burrowing, the larvae traveled through the bloodstream to the lymph glands or lungs, where they caused a cough. Migrating to the mouth, they were ingested, finding a home in the intestines, where they came to maturity. Still only about a centimeter long, hookworms, if undisturbed, could live in their host for seven or even ten years. Females in season laid thousands of eggs a day which, deposited in feces, restarted the cycle.

Where colonies of over 500 hookworms developed, ancyclostomiasis, or hookworm disease, resulted. This was characterized by symptoms often regarded as separate diseases: fluxlike emissions, fluid retention (dropsy), convulsions, and the mysterious craving to eat strange substances, particularly clay ("dirt eating").[13] Besides this, nonfatal ancyclostomiasis could stunt growth and delay puberty and cause chronic anaemia, which brought on the fatigue, dullness, and apathy which were often regarded as natural African traits.

Dysentery and intestinal parasites were promoted by unhygienic overcrowding, especially where drinking water, earth closets, and cooking facilities were in close proximity, and lack of washing water made personal cleanliness difficult. Worthy Park, with good running water from an aqueduct, was rather more fortunate in these respects than some estates and most of the crowded "yards" of the Jamaican towns. This may have been why the recorded cases of tetanus, or lockjaw, in infants—normally contracted through umbilical infection in unhygienic conditions, and invariably fatal—were fewer at Worthy Park than elsewhere. Another reason, though, might have been that the Worthy Park doctor was less ready than other plantation doctors to diagnose lockjaw as a cause of death.[14]

At least two fevers which were later recognized as tropical scourges, the food- and water-borne typhoid, and the louse, flea, and mite-borne typhus, were also encouraged by unhygienic conditions such as were found in West Indian plantations and towns. Unfortunately, certain identification of these fevers in the West Indies during slavery days is now impossible. However, if they did occur, typhoid was probably more common in the towns than on rural plantations, and of the three main types of typhus that most likely to have occurred on plantations was scrub typhus, carried by ticks and chiggers and characterized by dropsy-causing myocarditis. Cholera was apparently not known in the West Indies until after British slavery ended, though there were disastrous outbreaks then. Diptheria, if it existed, was not recognized during slavery days.

Of the endemic fevers detectable in the records, malaria (ague) and dengue were widespread, but the chief killer was probably yellow fever. This disease, so-called for the jaundicing that followed from liver infection, was technically endemic, but went through epidemic phases as different strains of virus went the rounds. Doctors correctly associated fevers with marshes, but erroneously attributed infection to miasmas rising from them at night, rather than to the *anopheles* and *aedes aegypti* mosquitoes that bred in them and carried the viruses. Slaves did what they could to repel mosquitoes by sleeping with permanently smoking fires nearby, but this was to reduce the nuisance rather than through a perception of danger. It was the immunization process of the passage of time rather than any preventive measures which brought about the gradual decline in deaths from fevers. Many slaves were already less likely to suffer from certain types of disease notoriously fatal to Europeans in the tropics. Most types of malaria and yellow fever were African in origin, and African slaves at least had built-in immunities. Sleeping sickness (trypanosomiasis), however, was only known among the African-born, since the infection was carried by the tsetse fly, which never migrated from Central Africa to the West Indies.

Rather more common killers than fever on plantations, even among acclimatized slaves, were the many varieties of pulmonary infection imported from Europe. In these cases, resistance was low through lack of immunization, but was also sapped by overcrowding, overwork, and deficient diet. Influenza could kill directly, but even the common cold could accelerate into fatal pneumonia, or a cough or "catarrh" degenerate into galloping consumption. Whooping cough, though not common, could be fatal to slave children. Diet and vitamin deficiencies also contributed to the high incidence of dropsy, a diagnosis applied to any swelling thought to be caused by an excess of one of the bodily fluids.

Dropsies were at least as common among the whites as among the blacks in Jamaica, with liver, heart, and urinary conditions often exacerbated by excessive drinking. Though some writers deplored the intemperance of town slaves, few slaves anywhere had opportunities for such overindulgence. This probably also explains why they so rarely suffered from the gout, or the mysterious "dry belly-ache" so common among Jamaican whites—now known to have been lead poisoning owing to drinking rum distilled in vessels made of lead and drunk from pewter pots.

Some dropsies and ulcers among slaves were symptoms of horrifying diseases originally imported from Africa which remained endemic among blacks, though whites were seemingly immune: elephantiasis, coco bays (alias Arabian leprosy), scrofula, true leprosy, and yaws. Of these, yaws, a highly contagious but nonvenereal variant of syphilis, was especially virulent. Often contracted in childhood, it was characterized first by raspberrylike eruptions, then by scarring and ulceration, and, in the prolonged tertiary stages, by excruciating "bone-ache" and damage to cartilages, spleen, and brain. Many sufferers died of old age or general debility rather than yaws itself, but the disease progressively sapped energy and will, as well as making the victims pathetically unsightly. On some Jamaican estates about a sixth of the slaves suffered seriously from yaws at any one time, and there was a separate "yaws hothouse," or isolation hospital, where the worst cases withered away.[15] At Worthy Park, however, the disease was rather less serious, and a second hothouse was not considered necessary.

From the death diagnoses, true venereal disease seems to have been relatively uncommon at Worthy Park and elsewhere, though the effects of yaws were often indistinguishable from those of syphilis, and gonorrhea may have been so common as to be considered unworthy of notice.[16] Certain other diseases which afflict modern society, such as heart disease, stomach ulcers, and cancers, were noticeably rare on slave plantations, either because the slaves did not have the opportunities to contract them, or did not live long enough to develop the symptoms. With the possible exception of the single slave "shot while stealing," no deaths recorded at Worthy Park were directly attributable to the slave condition. Deaths by accident were no more common than one would expect in any industrial situation with minimal safeguards; and suicides (of whom only three were certainly recorded) were probably no more common than in the British Army during National Service, or among undergraduates at a modern university.

The data derived from the Condition listings at Worthy Park are not only more fragmentary and capricious than those for Causes of Death, but for several reasons they also seriously understate the low level of general health on the plantation. Even for the years for which full records survive, the health of individual slaves was only noted if their condition incapacitated them. For example, there is no reference at all in the Worthy Park records to eye diseases, though it is unlikely that the plantation was entirely free from forms of opthalmia common among slaves elsewhere. Short-term or nonfatal illnesses such as colds and malaria were rarely recorded either. Cases of measles and smallpox which did not kill, however, sometimes were; for, though the immunization theory was not yet developed, it was already recognized that these diseases rarely recurred.

Many other diseases were too common for diagnosis, not diagnosed in their early stages, or not recognized at all. From the incidence of death from yaws, coco bays, scrofula, and dropsy, it seems likely that at least a third of the slaves suffered from diseases of the skin and tissues at some time during their lives, and perhaps half from serious internal disorders. In most cases these diseases were incurable and progressive, though not invariably fatal in themselves. If the debilitating effects of deficient diet and parasites less crippling than hookworm are included, nearly all slaves were subject to tropical ailments which lowered their efficiency, their fertility, and enjoyment of life.

In sum, though seasoned slaves on established sugar plantations were not more subject to fatality than most persons in the tropics, and much less so than the unacclimatized, the general level of their health was dismally low.

Masters and doctors alike were disposed by their "interest" and ignorance to minimize slave ailments. Owners and overseers were determined to keep all but the dying at work and to trim the costs of medical treatment. To their eyes, a successful doctor was one who satisfied these requirements. Paid a per capita fee, plantation doctors were positively rewarded for cursory treatment and encouraged to ignore failure and simulate success. Faced by a level of general health that condemned the plantation system by which they lived, or was beyond their care or ken, doctors tended to disguise the inadequacy of their treatments and the ignorance of their diagnoses with accusation of malingering, self-inflicted injury, and "natural" unhealthiness stemming from the slaves' racial origins. In this they perpetuated the malign ignorance of Dr. Thomas Trapham, who in 1679 attributed the high incidence of yaws among blacks to the alleged fact that they were an "animal people," subject to an "unhappy jumble of the rational with the brutal Nature,"[17] or even the distasteful fatalism of a slave trader in 1694 who wrote: "What the small-pox spar'd, the flux swept off to our great regret, after all our pains and care to give their messes in due order and season, keeping their lodgings as clean and sweet as possible, and enduring so much misery and stench so long among a parcel of creatures nastier than swine; and after all our expectations to be defeated by their mortality."[18]

The medical profession, like all self-legislating and self-perpetuating "misteries," has always been a conservatizing force. What particularly bedeviled eighteenth- and nineteenth-century medicine were the persistence of the fallacy of the the four "humors" in the teeth of the clinical evidence and the tradition that devalued surgery in favor of "physic." When Dr. Trapham wrote his *Discourse on the State of Health in . . . Jamaica* in 1679, belief in humoral theory was still absolute. Every human ailment, from hookworm to cancer, was said to be due to an excess of one of the four vital fluids which flowed from liver to heart: melancholy, phlegm, blood, choler—the counterparts of earth, water, air, and fire. The sole purpose of medicine, it was held, was to keep the elements in balance, the chief methods being bloodletting, "salivation," blistering, and purging. Physicians were neither willing nor able to use the surgeon's knife, save in emergencies such as amputations.

Besides this, doctors continued to make indiscriminate use of at least two dangerous specifics: mercury and opium. The first, beloved of alchemists as "quicksilver," had some success with "the pox," but produced crippling side effects which until recent times were thought to be symptoms of the disease it purported to cure.[19] The second quelled pain but was demoralizingly addictive, inducing withdrawal symptoms after very little use. That both mercurials and opiates were relatively expensive may have been positively beneficial to such dependent patients as slaves. The herbal remedies preferred for cheapness' sake were, where ineffectual, generally harmless. It might be argued that in the absence of antiseptics and anesthetics the reluctance of doctors to operate was also to the slaves' advantage.[20]

What medical progress was made during the slavery period was not owing to any revolution in theory or dramatic new methods (save inoculation for smallpox) but to a slightly more empirical attitude, a greater attention to the individual patient, and the first glimmerings of a belief in cleanliness, rest, and restorative diet. In these respects, the pioneers were the Englishman Thomas Sydenham (1624-1689) and Dutch clinicians such as Hermann Boerhaave of Leyden (1668-1738).[21] Hans Sloane, a disciple of Sydenham, displayed a comparatively open mind and a willingness to experiment (honestly recording failures as well as successes) in the descriptions he published of the many cases he treated during his brief stay in Jamaica (1688-89).[22] But neither Sloane nor his eighteenth-century successors made any systematic discoveries concerning causes or cures. At best they simply learned, through bitter experience, that a West Indian doctor was more likely to succeed the less he applied the "scientific" humoral theory and the pharmacy he had learned in the European schools.

This gradual awareness can be well illustrated by the career of Dr. John Quier, graduate of Leyden and London and Worthy Park's doctor from 1767 to 1822, from six published letters written to a former colleague during Quier's first years in Jamaica,[23] and from his later practice. From the letters it seems that Quier was not obsessed by humoral theory, but still placed too great an emphasis upon bodily fluids and the efficacy of cleansing the blood. From the description of some of his early treatments it seems that his patients might have stood a better chance with no treatment at all. For the eye disease he called "the dry opthalmies," for example, he specified a copious bleeding, "antiphlo-gistic" purges, a "cooling regimen" with niter, and blistering behind the ears and on the side of the neck, as well as the "emollient poultices" which alone might have brought any relief.

What caused Dr. Quier most concern were smallpox and measles, serious outbreaks of which occurred in Lluidas Vale during his first few years there. He has been given credit for advances in the prevention and diagnosis of these diseases—almost certainly exaggerated.[24] Although distinguishing clearly between smallpox and measles, he attributed quite distinct afflictions such as dysentery, dry bellyache, and even tetanus as "secondary manifestations" of them. Only in being able to diagnose whooping cough was Dr. Quier farther advanced than the Persian medical authority Rhazes (A.D. 860-932) who, while being the earliest correctly to identify smallpox and measles, was apparently not aware of any other endemic diseases.[25]

At least John Quier differed from the majority of his fellow slave-doctors in learning somewhat from his failures. At first he believed that excessive heat made the blood "putrescent," and he tended to let blood by venesection at the onset of any fever. He also administered savage purgatives such as the mercuric calomel, niter, or jalap in almost all cases of serious illness. When in some measles cases these led not to a salutary salivation and gentle evacuation but to bloody vomiting and diarrhea, he bled the patients more, applying blisters to the thighs. If the internal spasms and pains became too severe, he administered— literally almost as a last resort—heroic doses, up to four grains a day, of opium.

Although he never admitted that it was the medicine rather than the disease which was killing his patients, John Quier soon realized that excessive purging and bleeding weakened them and gradually relented. Ironically, strong "medicine" became reserved for those unfortunates whom the well-intentioned doctor regarded as strong enough to stand them. In the cases of the very old or young, the seriously undernourished and "naturally" debilitated, nature was allowed to take its course, and some patients clearly gained a fortuitous reprieve. In the eighteenth century it was medicine as often as death itself which acted as a great leveler.

As to inoculation for smallpox, John Quier was certainly no innovator. The technique of inoculation had been introduced into England from Turkey by Lady Mary Wortley Montagu as early as 1717, and there is some evidence that some form of "variolation," or intentional inoculative infection with the disease, was known in West Africa.[26] Quier himself acknowledged that he used the method developed by Thomas, Baron Dimsdale, consultant to Catherine the Great—infecting those who had not yet had the disease through a scratch on the arm, with matter drawn from smallpox pustules. Although effective in most individual cases, inducing only a mild form of the disease, it did not avert or check the general spread of smallpox and could lead to serious cases and death. There is no evidence that John Quier or any slave-doctor in Jamaica adopted the much more satisfactory system of vaccination by cowpox matter introduced by Edward Jenner, even when it gained widespread acceptance in England after 1800.

John Quier's method was to wait until a smallpox outbreak threatened, and then to inoculate large numbers of slaves together. In 1768 he treated over 700 slaves, receiving a flat fee of 6/8d. a head. As with his treatments, Quier's methods were almost indiscriminate at first. Yet experience and empirical observation taught him that it was pointless to inoculate those who already had the disease and dangerous to infect the young, the old, the weakly, those far gone in pregnancy, and anyone he classified as having "putrid blood." By excercising such discrimination Quier diminished his income at first; but as his reputation for success grew, the call upon his services increased.

Success for all West Indian doctors came with moderation and common sense. A wise and humane doctor, such as John Quier clearly became, was one who realized that since his medication could rarely cure, and no doctor could—or ought to—persuade planters to improve slave conditions in general, he should concentrate on ameliorating symptoms and, by providing care, cleanliness, fresh air, and decent food, encourage any natural tendency towards a cure, as well as the will to survive. Harsh medicine was simply for the peace of mind of those who paid, and for those patients strong enough to take it who believed in it.

Thus, while he continued to pay lip service to the crude, irrelevant, and harmful mysteries of his craft such as bleeding, blistering, and purging, John Quier more often came to prescribe strengthening diets, emollients, cooling lotions, and analgesics such as the opiate laudanum. It was also during his regime that the slave "hothouse" still standing at Worthy Park was built, which was, as on many Jamaican properties, one of the most substantial buildings erected. For women in childbirth, John Quier recommended that they be allowed to "lie in" at least two weeks. Observing that the blacks who worked in the stillhouse (distillery) were the fattest on the estate, he recommended that infants be drafted there to fatten up. Although Dr. Quier disapproved of the African customs of swaddling newborn infants and suckling children into their second year,[27] there is at least one scrap of evidence that he came to place as much credence in "African" medicine as in his own received pharmacy. Noticing that his black slave "doctoress" assistant was in the habit of bathing the swollen feet of yaws sufferers in urine he did not tell her to desist, and honesty compelled him to admit that the patients came to no further harm.

To modern eyes, the wisest section of Dr. John Quier's letters from Jamaica concerns a regimen for maintaining general health in a tropical climate. It could serve as a model in most respects even today: choose a dry, healthy location; practice temperance, drinking a little wine but selecting a diet more vegetable than animal, including fresh fruit; rise early, take a moderate amount of exercise, and avoid the nighttime damp; bathe frequently, and change clothing according to the time of day and season; maintain a cheerful disposition. Unfortunately, however, these excellent suggestions (which John Quier probably followed himself, for he lived to 83) were absolutely irrelevant to the lives of slaves. As Hans Sloane had found long before, they were also almost reversed by the habits of most of the Jamaican whites.

From the Worthy Park evidence for 1792-1838 it is clear that the level of health on slave plantations was low. Yet the situation should not be exaggerated. Disease alone did not account for the continuing natural decrease in the population, which was also influenced by purely demographic characteristics.[28] If sugar plantations, with their large cramped populations and intensive agriculture, were less healthy than mountain pens and coffee plantations, estates like Worthy Park in spacious highland areas were healthier than those in the swampy lowlands of St. Catherine, St. Thomas-in-the-East, St. Mary, or St. James; and all were far less disease-ridden than the ships on the transatlantic crossing and the barracoons of the African coast.[29] Besides this, the health situation which the Worthy Park records for 1792-1838 disclosed was almost certainly better than that which obtained in the plantation's earlier days—though the improvement, like that in the population's demographic balance, was largely beyond the understanding or control of planters, doctors, and amelioration laws.

The "triangle trade" of trade goods, slaves, and sugar made the West Indies a crossroads for the diseases of Europe, Africa, and tropical America. Until immunities built up (a process of years), newcomers infected with, and were infected by, unfamiliar strains of virus, germ, and parasite. This well-documented but unexplained phenomenon led to the death of perhaps half of all African slaves between the time of their original seizure and the conclusion of the seasoning process on a West Indian plantation four years later. It likewise killed almost as high a ratio of all whites newly arriving in the sugar islands, and an even higher proportion of white crewmen on the slave ships, or white soldiers cramped and ill-fed in barracks in the West Indies and West Africa.[30]

Because of the fallacies of humoral theory, medical treatment for diseases was totally inadequate: never curative, at best palliative or innocuous, at worst positively baneful. The greatest improvement came fortuitously, with the process of creolization. The increasingly closed nature of the plantation population made it a closed disease environment, rather less subject to attack from passing epidemics than towns or villages.

What remained, however, was serious enough: the general debility from ailments associated with unhygienic conditions, poor diet, and overwork. Here, it might be argued, "amelioration" legislation such as was passed in all British West Indian colonies from about 1787, and particularly after 1823, should have improved health conditions by regulating the workload and establishing standards of food, clothing, and medical care.[31] Yet these regulations were minimal, reflecting standards rather than improving them, often a form of window-dressing. Medical treatment was effectively beyond the control of legislation. Besides this, towards the very end of slavery the effects of any improvements were offset by the decline in plantation profits, which made masters inclined to work their slaves harder and spend less on their upkeep and care. If towards the end of formal slavery slaves were able to grow more food, to expand their homes, and to improve their clothing, it was mainly through their own efforts. It might also be argued that there was an ironic virtue in necessity, since the decline in expenditure on slave medicine may have been actually beneficial to health.

TABLE 40. Worthy Park: Incidence of Causes of Death Noted, 1792-1838, Assigned by World Health Organization Categories

Sources: Manual of the International Statistical Classification of Diseases, Injuries and Causes of Death, based on the Recommendations of the Eighth Revision Conference, 1965, and Adopted by the Nineteenth World Health Assembly, 2 vols. (Geneva, World Health Organization, 1967); Worthy Park records.

Worthy Park diagnoses	Number of incidences	Modern (W.H.O.) diagnoses (where different)	W.H.O. categories	
Dysentery	10	Bacillary dysentery	I	004
Flux	25	Diarrhoeal disease		009
Phthisis, consumption	15	Tuberculosis		011
Coco bays	2	Leprosy (Arabian)		030
Whooping cough, croup	4			
Locked jaw	2	Tetanus		037
Measles	5			
Smallpox	2			
Diseased brain, water on the brain	2	Encephalitis		062
Yaws	24			102
Dirt eating	9 ⎰	⎱ Helminthiasis		127
Worms, worm fever	14 ⎰	⎱ Internal parasites		129
Fever	26			
Palsy	3	Cerebral palsy	VI	343
Fits, convulsions, epilepsy	7	Epilepsy		345
Complaint in spine	1	Spinal chord disease		349
Apoplexy, stroke	2		VII	436
Elephantiasis	1			457
Violent cold, cough, catarrh	11	Acute common cold	VIII	460
Influenza	2			470
Pneumonia	1			480
Asthma	4			493
Pleurisy	10			511
Abcess in lungs	2			513
Rupture	3	Hernia	IX	551
Suppression of menses	2	Menstrual disorder	X	626
Childbed	7			644
Puny from birth, at birth, still born	18		XI	677
Ulcers, ulceration	14	Chronic skin ulcers	XIII	707
Spasms	1	Nervous system	XVI	780
Dropsy, "cold, bloated & dropsical"	38	Cardiovascular, lymphatic		782
Lung trouble, sore throat	3	Respiratory system		783
Stomach complaint	1	Upper gastro-intestinal		784
Bloated, swelled & bloated, inflammation of bowels	4	Lower gastro-intestinal		785
Swelled leg, sore foot	4	Limbs & joints		787
Old Age, decline, weakness, infirmity, invalid (where old)	89	Senility		794
Suddenly, in the night, sudden, act of god, vindication of God	7	Sudden death (unknown cause)		795
Diseased many years, infirmity, invalid (not aged), sick some time, worthless, at hospital in Kingston	7	Other sicknesses, unspecified		796
Accident	14		XVII	880
At poison, suicide by poison	3	Suicide		950
Shot while stealing	1	Legal intervention		970
Suffocation	1			994
Total	401			

Cause of death	Worthy Park slaves (1792-1838)	British Guiana slaves (1829-1832)	St. Catherine Parish (1774-1778)
Old age, debility	22.2	19.1	3.6
Dysentery, flux	8.7	12.0	9.3
Dropsy	9.5	9.2	3.4
Pulmonary diseases	11.4	9.2	5.7
Fevers (inc. measles, smallpox)	9.2	8.1	39.9
Yaws, ulcers	9.5	6.1	6.1
Inflammations, etc.	2.0	4.4	3.8
Gastrointestinal	6.0	4.3	3.8
Accidents	4.3	4.2	1.6
Leprosy	0.5	3.8	0
Convulsions	3.8	3.7	6.3
Lockjaw	0.5	2.6	0.8
Syphilis	0	1.0	1.1
Others & unknown	12.4	12.3	14.6
	100.0	100.0	100.0

TABLE 41. Percentage Causes of Death: Worthy Park, 1792-1838; British Guiana, 1829-1832; St. Catherine Parish (Spanish Town), 1774-1778

Sources: Basic categories and British Guiana percentages, G. W. Roberts, *The Population of Jamaica* (Cambridge, Cambridge University Press, 1957), p. 175. St. Catherine causes of death from Jamaica, Island Record Office, St. Catherine's Copy Register, Causes of Deaths, vol. I; Worthy Park percentages calculated from Worthy Park records.

5 / Economics, Employment, Social Cohesion, 1783-1838

TO claim that the character of slave society was determined entirely by the mode of production would overstate the case. The demographic and health factors already studied, as well as cultural and racial influences, played important independent roles in shaping slave society. Yet the population of slaves and their managers owed its very existence to the economic needs of a capitalist master class, and subsequent social development—including hierarchy, the interrelation between classes and races, social mobility, and assimilation—was obviously influenced by the demands and changing needs of the "factory-in-a-field" of the sugar plantation system.

This concluding statistical chapter of Part One therefore estimates the effects of economic factors upon Worthy Park's slave society, always bearing in mind that by their very nature the surviving records are slanted towards an economic determinist interpretation. It should also be remembered that the data derive exclusively from the last half-century of formal slavery, pointing up both the contrast with earlier days and those changes and conflicts which made the period 1783-1838 critical in West Indian history.

Worthy Park's owners, particularly the optimizing Rose Price, were more interested in production and prices than in the health of slaves, or rather, were interested in the welfare and organization of the slaves only as those related to costs and productivity. Consequently, there was a great deal in the Worthy Park records concerning the production of sugar and rum and the flow of supplies for the estate and its workers, though nearly all the ledgers dealing with costs and profits have, unfortunately, disappeared. Raw material is patchy, but it is possible to elicit enough data to draw up tables aligning Worthy Park's production of sugar and rum against the total number of slaves and those in the various components of the labor force and thus arrive at figures for productivity. Materials on the prices obtained for sugar and paid for supplies and slave replacements have to be derived largely from other sources; nevertheless, a reasonably reliable estimate of Worthy Park's profits can still be made. This too can be related to the number of slaves, to make some estimate of the profitability of their

*First Gang cane-holing.
Despite the summer heat
the artist has decently
depicted the laboring slaves
in their full issue clothing.*

labor. Subsequently, the social effects of the exploitation of the slaves' labor, particularly in times of economic decline, can also be estimated.

The following tables and graphs present, at least from the capitalist's eye view, the essential economic background to the slave society of Worthy Park between 1783 and 1838. Production followed the slightly zigzag path common throughout the sugar industry, usually in step with Jamaican production, since in most cases the fluctuations were due to islandwide climatic variations. Gross revenue, determined by a notoriously fluctuating London sugar price as well as by the amount and quality produced, varied more subtly.[1] As for all sugar producers, the best years for Worthy Park's owners were those in which the estate's sugar and rum production were higher than usual, at a time when sugar prices were relatively good because competitors had done less well. The most outstanding year was 1812, the year of Worthy Park's record production, which was not an especially productive year for Jamaica as a whole, and when the London price remained high.

Once Rose Price's improvements had taken effect, Worthy Park was expected to produce at least 500 hogsheads of sugar a year. Despite the cost of capital improvements, particularly the buying of slaves, and the inflation of the cost of supplies, freight, and insurance, the record wartime sugar prices brought Worthy Park's owner a princely level of profit. In 1848, one of Rose Price's sons referred nostalgically to a period when Worthy Park had brought his father £13,000 a year clear profit,[2] a sum that certainly seems from modern calculations the average level of profit over the whole period of the last French wars, 1793-1815.

Even by making the most generous estimates of the costs of slave upkeep (including the evaluation as a gift of the owners the goods and provisions the slaves acquired by their own efforts, as well as the "rental" of the houses and grounds they occupied and worked—though not, of course, the slaves' purchase price), there is no way that figures for the "return" to the slaves for the product of their labor can be brought close to the figure of 90 percent worked out for the slaves of the nineteenth-century American South by Fogel and Engerman.[3] Unless there is a serious flaw in the Worthy Park calculations, each of Rose Price's field hands brought him in annual profit almost the price of a slave replacement, between 1800 and 1815.

After 1808, however, new Africans were unobtainable, and sugar prices and profits began to fall drastically with the ending of the war in 1815. Though still making more than his predecessors, Rose Price found it increasingly difficult to maintain the life-style to which he had accustomed himself. Productivity per field slave was gradually increased, but it was a losing battle against falling profits. Even more irksome to Worthy Park's ledger-conscious owner must have been the calculation of the cost of nonproductive slaves, while amelioration laws and general inflation steadily increased the cost of all slaves' upkeep.

While in the 1780s Worthy Park had produced at least the £10 a

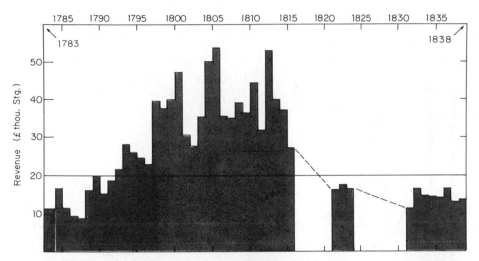

Figure 23. Worthy Park:
Gross Revenue, Sugar and
Rum, 1783-1838

Sources: Worthy Park records;
London sugar prices from Michael
Craton and James Walvin, *A Jamai-
can Plantation: The History of
Worthy Park, 1670-1970* (London,
W. H. Allen, and Toronto, Univer-
sity of Toronto Press, 1970), pp. 167,
189; Bryan Edwards, *The History,
Civil and Commercial, of the British
West Indies*, 2 vols. (London, 1793),
II, 267; L. J. Ragatz, *Statistics for the
Study of British Caribbean Economic
History, 1763-1833* (London, 1927).
Jamaican sugar production from *A
Jamaican Plantation*, p. 188; Noel
Deerr, *The History of Sugar*, 2 vols.
(London, Chapman & Hall, 1949-
50).

Note: Broken line indicates data
deficient.

year per slave which Bryan Edwards gave as a rule-of-thumb for
efficient operations[4] and up to three times that amount in the mid-war
years, by the 1830s income fell in some years well below half of Edwards' sum, despite inflation. By this time many planters had foolishly
convinced themselves that slave labor was no longer profitable. Accountancy (brought forward by emancipators to show that slavery was
inefficient as well as immoral, as well as by planters attempting to
prove that it was not grossly exploitative) seemed to prove that slaves
could neither live long enough nor be sufficiently productive to justify
their initial and upkeep costs. The flaws in the argument—that the only
true costs were for upkeep and that slave labor, whether economic or
not, was indispensable in the absence of alternatives—were brutally
brought home to the planters after 1838.[5]

The chief material deployed in this section, however, concerns the
employment of slaves, for which the Worthy Park ledgers are a veritable gold mine. By individualization and computer processing, correlation has been possible between employment and those categories already considered in other contexts: sex, age, color, African and Creole
birth. Fresh analysis of manumissions, runaways, and individuals'
names has also been undertaken.

These latter categories suggested themselves naturally from the
records, but the socioeconomic matrix used in computer programming,
on which the final evaluation of the mass of data tabulated depends,
was partly derived from the layout in the Worthy Park ledgers and
partly from certain assumptions. It therefore requires some explanation.

The Worthy Park slaves were first placed in employment categories in 1787, but during his three years' residence in Jamaica (1791-1794)
Rose Price methodically reorganized both work force and records along
the lines of the latest treatises on plantation husbandry. For example, it
was in 1793 that the all-important field workers, previously divided
simply into a main force of adults and a children's gang, were first
separated into four gangs, carefully graded according to age, strength,

Figure 24. Worthy Park: Productivity of Field Laborers, Sugar and Revenue, 1785-1838, Selected Years

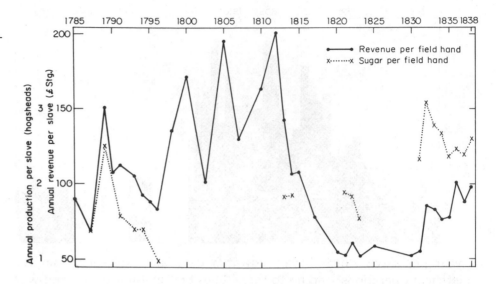

Figure 25. Worthy Park: Annual Profit per Slave, 1785-1835, Five-Year Intervals

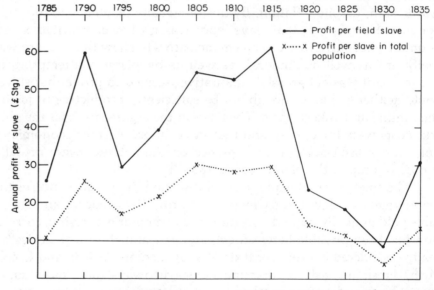

and function—a system that was essentially continued until emancipation more than forty years later.

Efficiency was Rose Price's obsessive theme. In the lists prepared for Price's eyes, very few slaves were accounted unemployed or unemployable. However, this led to a very high number of different classes of employment. Moreover, the bookkeepers whom Rose Price hired after he became an absentee were not so efficient as their employer or so permanently employed that the system's uniformity continued unblemished. Categories, or more often simply their labels, changed from time to time, according to minor changes in methods or the passage of laws such as the Emancipation Act of 1833, which decreed that slaves should be redesignated "apprentices," gangs "classes," and drivers "superintendents."

With much care it was, nonetheless, possible to reduce the Worthy

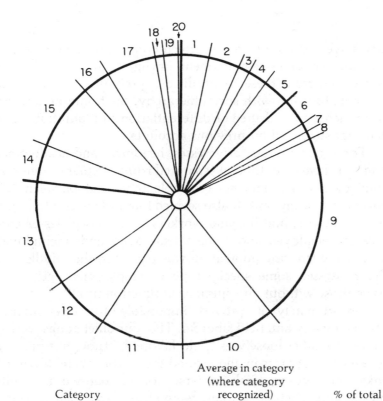

Figure 26. The Worthy Park Slave Work Force: Computer Matrix Employment Categories, with Approximate Totals and Percentages in Each, 1787-1838, and Data

Category	Average in category (where category recognized)	% of total
Slave elite		
1 Heads and drivers	13	2.91
Lower elite		
2 Domestics	17	3.81
3 Hospital	5	1.12
4 Factory craftsmen	10	2.24
5 Other craftsmen	14	3.14
Laborers		
6 Factory laborers	7	1.57
7 Stock workers	10	2.24
8 Nonfactory, nonfield	4	0.90
9 First Gang	94	21.08
10 Second Gang	47	10.54
11 Third Gang	42	9.42
12 Fourth Gang	28	6.28
13 Field laborers, misc. or unspec.	52	11.66
Unproductive		
14 Watchmen	18	4.04
15 Misc. unemployed (incl. sick)	32	7.17
16 Aged	16	3.59
17 Young (under six years)	24	5.38
18 Women with six children	4	0.90
19 Runaways	8	1.79
20 Manumitted	1	0.22
Total	446	100.00

Park slave population into fourteen consistent categories of employment and six of nonemployment (including manumissions and runaways) and from these to produce a preliminary matrix combining economic function with social hierarchy. Such minute analysis allows for a much greater degree of differentiation in plantation slave society than that suggested by previous accounts.

For a start, drivers, driveresses, headmen, and headwomen clearly formed a slave elite, though separated from the plantations's whites by a gulf even wider and less crossable than that between NCOs and officers in an army unit. It also seemed fair and natural to regard craftsmen, domestics, and hospital workers as a kind of lesser elite and to place the employed above the unemployed and unemployable. The mass of the laboring population was placed in the middle, with those who possessed some special type of employment generally placed above those without any specialized function at all.

Unfortunately it proved impossible to differentialte clearly between factory and field laborers. The four chief gangs were generally referred to rather loosely as "field laborers," though in most years the more menial laborers in and around the factory were drawn from their ranks: mill-feeders, trash-carriers, stokers, pan-women, gutter-girls, and cleaners. Factory workers were clearly specified as such in only four of the lists, since the distinction between a true field laborer and a factory menial was obviously not always easily made, and slaves were sometimes switched.

The method used in arriving at the basic socioeconomic categories at Worthy Park is best illustrated by showing first the entire population in one year (1793), using the estate's classifications but dividing them into the five broad classes: whites, slave elite, lower elite and specialists, laborers, nonproductive. Just as the relative value and importance of each white member of the population are suggested by the salary paid, so those of each slave are indicated by his or her approximate replacement cost and by the clothing and other issues made out of the estate's commissary, as shown in Table 44.

Of the patterns apparent in the employment tables perhaps the most surprising is the great and increasing reliance on women as laborers. That women were bound to work in large numbers in the fields was owing mainly to the monopolization by the men of the elite jobs of drivers, headmen, and craftsmen and of the specialized occupations of boilers, potters, distillers, stockmen, wainmen, and watchmen. These categories were, overall, 92.4 percent male.[6] Jobs that were specifically reserved for women, around the houses and hospital, were far less numerous. Accordingly, more women than men worked in the fields even in the period when men outnumbered women overall. As the overall percentage of women rose from 46 to 60 percent, their numbers in the fields increased almost proportionately: from around 58 percent of the "field" labor force in the 1790s, to over 65 percent throughout the 1830s.

	1 Heads and drivers	2 Domestics	3 Hospital	4 Factory craftsmen	5 Other craftsmen	6 Factory laborers	7 Stock workers	8 Non-factory, non-field	9 First Gang	10 Second Gang	11 Third Gang	12 Fourth Gang	13 Misc. field/unspec.	14 Watchmen	15 Misc. unemployed	16 Aged	17 Young	18 Women with six children	19 Runaways	20 Manumitted
Heads and drivers	188	3	2	3	12	0	9	0	11	0	2	1	10	12	3	5	0	0	2	0
Domestics	2	231	8	1	11	0	10	3	6	14	10	3	7	5	1	13	1	1	1	5
Hospital	2	6	43	0	1	0	0	0	5	3	1	2	2	1	9	15	0	0	0	0
Factory craftsmen	6	0	1	132	1	3	4	1	13	0	0	0	19	0	0	0	0	0	2	0
Other craftsmen	18	3	0	3	242	0	2	0	4	0	0	0	6	4	0	1	0	0	2	1
Factory laborers	0	0	0	2	0	3	0	0	11	0	0	0	0	0	0	0	0	0	0	0
Stock workers	13	4	1	1	3	0	70	1	32	14	1	1	20	5	1	1	0	0	8	0
Non-factory, nonfield	0	1	2	0	1	0	1	3	0	1	0	0	1	0	1	3	0	0	0	0
First Gang	15	6	14	12	4	12	42	3	1013	50	0	27	96	18	1	13	0	9	22	0
Second Gang	1	6	4	3	4	0	5	1	119	932	2	17	20	10	1	4	0	2	11	0
Third Gang	4	10	0	5	3	0	6	1	5	111	196	1	28	0	1	0	0	0	6	0
Fourth Gang	3	19	4	1	4	0	0	0	12	12	74	273	33	0	16	6	1	0	3	1
Misc. field/unspec.	10	29	5	26	5	4	37	0	266	71	69	42	384	15	3	11	2	1	15	0
Watchmen	4	1	0	2	0	0	2	1	2	0	0	0	4	307	8	11	0	0	5	0
Misc. unemployed	1	4	6	1	0	0	0	0	0	1	39	55	2	0	275	8	45	0	0	17
Aged	2	5	4	0	1	0	1	2	1	1	0	5	10	2	15	176	0	1	0	0
Young	2	10	0	0	1	0	3	0	0	0	18	58	82	0	13	1	365	0	2	5
Women with 6 children	0	0	1	0	0	0	0	0	0	0	0	2	1	0	3	4	0	59	0	0
Runaways	3	3	1	2	4	0	3	0	27	9	0	1	25	9	2	3	0	0	105	0
Manumitted	0	0	0	0	0	0	0	0	0	0	0	0	0	0	0	0	0	0	0	0

Clearly women were normally expected to perform the arduous tasks of digging and cutting, as well as the lesser jobs of weeding and carrying that books of slave husbandry advised as most suitable for their limited strength. It was significant that easily the best results recorded at Worthy Park during the eighteenth century—a production equivalent to 2.51 hogsheads of sugar per field hand—occurred in a year (1789) when 24 male cane-cutters were hired to augment a dangerously unbalanced field force, of which three-quarters were women.

However, as time went on, the women, along with the entire field force, were worked harder. Even though total production started to decline after 1812, production per field hand increased steadily until the 1830s, reaching its peak in 1832. Some of this increase was due to better agronomy and factory efficiency; but such improvements had mostly occurred before 1800, and their effect—to raise productivity by about 50 percent—had peaked in the 1820s. From then on sugar production per field hand was raised a further 50 percent, to average 2.28 hogsheads per field hand throughout the 1830s. At the same time, the proportion of women in the field force was as high as it had ever been.

The effect of this overworking of women on the fertility of the population has already been suggested. The effect on the general quality

Figure 27. Worthy Park: Individuals' Movements between Employment Categories, Total Entries for 22 Years out of 52, 1787-1838

Source: Race and Slavery in the Western Hemisphere: Quantitative Studies, edited by Stanley L. Engerman and Eugene D. Genovese (copyright (c) 1975 by The Center for Advanced Study in the Behavioral Sciences, Stanford, California), p. 278. Reprinted by permission of Princeton University Press.

Note: Left triangle = upward mobility; right triangle (italic) = downward mobility; diagonal (boldface) = stationary.

(continued on page 116)

Planting canes. Though
showing apprentices rather
than slaves, the methods
and tools used and the portraits of the laboring blacks
are notably authentic.

Figure 28. Worthy Park: Women in the Field Labor Force, with Totals and Percentages, 1784-1838, and Data

Note: Gaps in the graph and dashes in the table indicate data missing in the records.

[a]Twenty-four male field slaves were hired in 1789.

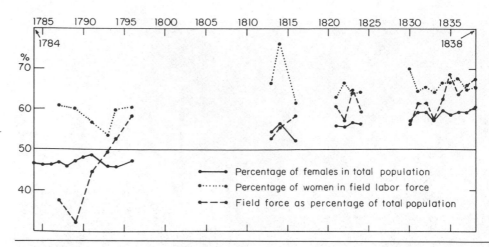

	Total population	Total females	Total field force	Field women	% of females in total population	% of field force in total population	% of women in field force	% of field women in total female population
1784	331	155	—	—	46.8	—	—	—
1785	317	147	—	—	46.4	—	—	—
1786	301	140	—	—	46.5	—	—	—
1787	334	157	126	77	47.0	37.7	61.1	49.1
1788	343	158	—	—	46.1	—	—	—
1789	341	161	133[a]	81	47.2	32.3	60.1	50.4
1790	342	165	—	—	48.2	—	—	—
1791	377	184	169	96	48.8	44.8	56.9	52.2
1793	541	249	267	145	46.0	49.3	53.9	58.2
1794	530	244	280	167	46.0	52.9	60.0	68.4
1796	469	222	274	166	47.3	58.4	60.6	74.8
1813	490	268	255	170	54.7	53.0	66.7	63.4
1814	458	260	254	193	56.8	55.4	76.1	74.2
1816	507	265	296	182	52.3	58.5	61.5	68.7
1821	504	282	308	194	56.0	60.9	63.0	68.8
1822	512	286	290	193	55.9	57.1	66.6	67.4
1823	489	278	317	203	56.9	64.8	64.0	73.0
1824	502	284	298	191	56.6	59.4	64.2	67.3
1830	414	237	233	163	57.2	56.3	70.1	68.8
1831	333	197	204	132	59.2	61.4	64.7	67.0
1832	311	184	191	125	59.2	61.4	65.4	67.9
1833	301	172	174	112	57.1	57.7	64.4	65.1
1834	293	175	184	123	59.7	62.7	66.8	77.4
1835	263	155	181	120	58.9	68.8	66.9	77.4
1836	260	154	165	112	59.2	63.9	67.9	72.7
1837	251	149	166	108	59.4	66.2	65.0	72.5
1838	233	142	157	103	60.9	67.5	65.6	72.5

of life can only be guessed at. It was indeed a curious society, as well as an inefficient agricultural economy, in which women for the most part were the laborers and men the specialist workers. The allocation of work in slave plantations may be the origin of the Jamaican tradition of hardworking peasant women, as well as a contributing factor in the development of matriarchy. There may have been African parallels, however, so that once again the social effects in determining general roles for men and women cannot be attributed solely to the slavery system with any certainty.

With care, equally significant patterns can be traced from the relative employment of African and Creole slaves. Despite attempts by the management to spread new arrivals in large numbers over the whole range of employment, Africans were destined mainly for the field gangs. Those Africans in positions of comparative authority and responsibility were generally mature survivors. The situation, testified to by some early writers, in which Africans were said to be valued for special skills in stock raising, metal and woodworking—and when, indeed, opportunities to exercise these skills were still open—was long past when the Worthy Park records start. Elderly Africans, with an authority that derived as much from Africa as from the mandate of the estate, still made the most effective drivers. But craftsmen, being trained on the estate and from an early age, tended increasingly to be Creoles, if not also colored.

More field slaves was the perennial demand on any long-established sugar plantation, particularly such "improving" estates as Worthy Park in the 1790s. It may have been this demand, and the abundance of more specialized slaves, which contributed to the increase in the ratio of slaves from the equatorial forests and further south—Biafrans, Congoes, Angolans—in the later years of the slave trade. The herdsmen, craftsmen, and more skilled agriculturalists from further north were less needed and cost more than the slaves the planters thought they could afford.[7]

When Rose Price purchased over 200 new Africans in the 1790s, nearly all Congoes, they could not be drafted directly into the canefields. Immediately on arrival, almost as many were set to odd jobs in the Great House garden and the most menial tasks around the factory as were placed in the actual field gangs. A majority were kept in a separate gang, totaling 83 in 1793, partly for training and partly for the process of acclimatization and immunization. Such seasoning was said to take three years, and, sure enough, as "pen Negroes" being gradually inured to the full burden of field labor, these Africans remained as a distinct group until 1796. Disease took a savage toll of all Africans, but the survivors, male as well as female, increasingly worked in the fields. The proportion of all Africans at Worthy Park who were true field laborers, as low as 37 percent in 1791, was 64 percent in 1796 and as high as 68 percent in 1816. In the peak year, 1794, almost 60 percent of all the adult field force was African-born and represented three-quarters of all male field workers.

With the ending of the African traffic, the picture changed inexorably. Africans remained in the field gangs at least in the proportion their numbers represented in the total population until 1823. But as the surviving Africans aged and became watchmen or superannuated unemployed, or died, they were superseded by Creoles. One of the most

Figure 29. Worthy Park: Africans in the Field Labor Force, with Totals and Percentages, 1784-1838, and Data

Note: Gaps in the graph and dashes in the table indicate data missing in the records.

[a]Eighty-three Africans not allocated jobs in 1793.
[b]Twenty-four male field slaves hired in 1789, but their country of birth unknown.
[c]Including pen Negroes.

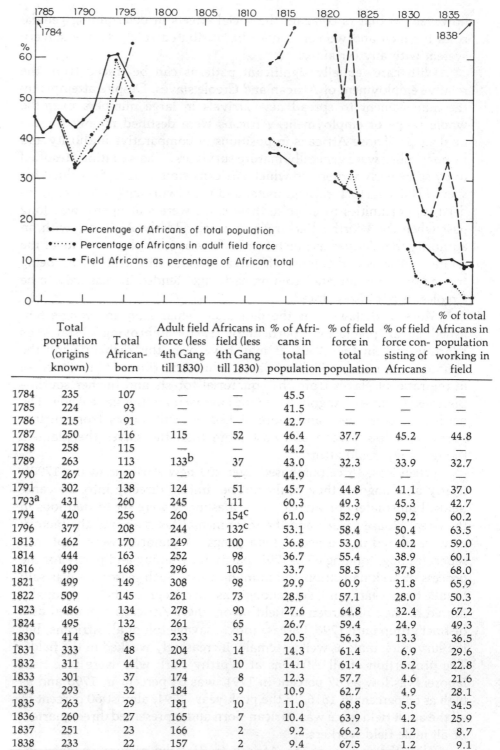

	Total population (origins known)	Total African-born	Adult field force (less 4th Gang till 1830)	Africans in field (less 4th Gang till 1830)	% of Africans in total population	% of field force in total population	% of field force consisting of Africans	% of total Africans in population working in field
1784	235	107	—	—	45.5	—	—	—
1785	224	93	—	—	41.5	—	—	—
1786	215	91	—	—	42.7	—	—	—
1787	250	116	115	52	46.4	37.7	45.2	44.8
1788	258	115	—	—	44.2	—	—	—
1789	263	113	133[b]	37	43.0	32.3	33.9	32.7
1790	267	120	—	—	44.9	—	—	—
1791	302	138	124	51	45.7	44.8	41.1	37.0
1793[a]	431	260	245	111	60.3	49.3	45.3	42.7
1794	420	256	260	154[c]	61.0	52.9	59.2	60.2
1796	377	208	244	132[c]	53.1	58.4	50.4	63.5
1813	462	170	249	100	36.8	53.0	40.2	59.0
1814	444	163	252	98	36.7	55.4	38.9	60.1
1816	499	168	296	105	33.7	58.5	37.8	68.0
1821	499	149	308	98	29.9	60.9	31.8	65.9
1822	509	145	261	73	28.5	57.1	28.0	50.3
1823	486	134	278	90	27.6	64.8	32.4	67.2
1824	495	132	261	65	26.7	59.4	24.9	49.3
1830	414	85	233	31	20.5	56.3	13.3	36.5
1831	333	48	204	14	14.3	61.4	6.9	29.6
1832	311	44	191	10	14.1	61.4	5.2	22.8
1833	301	37	174	8	12.3	57.7	4.6	21.6
1834	293	32	184	9	10.9	62.7	4.9	28.1
1835	263	29	181	10	11.0	68.8	5.5	34.5
1836	260	27	165	7	10.4	63.9	4.2	25.9
1837	251	23	166	2	9.2	66.2	1.2	8.7
1838	233	22	157	2	9.4	67.5	1.2	9.1

important effects of abolition in 1808 was that for the first time slaves born in the Caribbean really predominated in the field gangs. The implications of a change from a situation in which Creoles could expect a better job than their parents to one in which their lot might well be worse cannot be overstressed. When to this was added demands for higher productivity during slavery's last decades, social tension was almost bound to occur. In 1834, when 95 percent of the field force was Creole, production per capita was about twice what it had been in 1794, when over 59 percent were African-born.

Age patterns detectable in different employment categories followed trends which could be expected when it is recognized that Worthy Park's population, after a dip in the 1790s, aged steadily in general and if it is presumed that positions of responsibility as well as those which did not require physical strength went to the senior members. Thus drivers and headmen averaged 54.7 in 1793 when the average age of the whole population was 26.7, and 47.9 in 1796 when it was 29.4, rising again to 52.0 in 1835 when the overall average age was 32.8. Craftsmen too tended to achieve their positions with maturity, averaging 37.1, 39.1, and 35.7 in the years quoted.

These trends were doubtless largely accidental. Far more calculated was the system of gangs graded by age and physical capability, and the relegation of gangmen and gangwomen to certain distinct categories of employment once they were elderly or infirm. With an efficiency that Bryan Edwards or Thomas Roughley would have approved, Worthy Park's Fourth Gang in 1796 averaged 9.5 years of age, the Third Gang, 15.5, with the Second and First Gangs almost equal at 31.6 and 31.8. Over the entire period the Fourth Gang's average age was greater, because in later years it included elderly recruits to its squad of grass-cutting and dung-carrying youngsters. The Second Gang's average age was lower because the first two gangs were more regularly graded by age. The average ages of the four gangs over the whole period, in ascending order of size and importance, were 22.0 (based on 510 entries), 12.5 (773), 22.1 (866), and 32.4 (1,590). The average age for the entire field labor force, including the Vagabond Gang, pen Negroes, and those not specified as being in gangs, was 25.4. The average age for watchmen was 52.6, and for hospital workers, mainly elderly "nurses," 56.7. Indeed, one in each category was still being employed at 79.

With a population in which the colored comprised less than 10 percent of the total, dramatic patterns affecting those of mixed blood might not be expected. Yet it is immediately apparent that an overwhelming majority of the colored members of Worthy Park's population were found around the central compound, either as domestics or craftsmen. In 1796, for example, coloreds made up 60 percent of domestics and 25 percent of craftsmen, when they comprised only 6.6 percent of the population overall. Over the whole period, 50 percent of domestics were colored, and 15 percent of craftsmen, though the coloreds made up only about 8 percent of the entire population. At the same time, coloreds accounted for less than 2.5 percent of the field gangs, which amounted to considerably more than half the total population.

The implications of these figures are highly significant. The whites

(continued on page 152)   149

Cutting and carrying canes under the supervision of a white field bookkeeper and black slave driver.

kept their mistresses close to hand; but in turn masters and mistresses ensured that their offspring would fill their mothers' shoes (or bed) if girls, or gain a craftsman's post if boys. Certainly they would be spared field labor if possible. Miscegenation was not only the most obvious route to a relatively easy life but also, in a few cases, to manumission. Except in full slavery's last year, 1834, when 11 blacks were manumitted, it was colored slaves who were manumitted in every case but one where colors were known.

Those who wished to share the privileges of the whites had to become—or ensure that their children became—more like them, in culture as well as color. Thus was the system of white superiority perpetuated. It is debatable, however, whether the no-man's land of hopeless aspiration occupied by the coloreds, even when freed, was really preferable to the community, albeit degraded, of the unequivocally black.[8]

What do the tables of occupational mobility add to the patterns discernible in the separate job tables? Mainly it is corroboration. For example, the grading by age apparent in Table 50 and the differential slave prices quoted in Table 44 reinforce at least one intermediate conclusion: that the estate's evaluation of slaves was based not on such abstract qualities as ambition, fidelity, or long service but on usefulness. A driver or driveress could revert to watchman or nurse when the years of strength and maximum use were past. Thomas Roughley, in his unctuous manner, stressed the importance of having "confidential" watchmen,[9] and doubtless men and women who had once exercised authority retained respect among their fellows even as watchmen and nurses. Seniority and survival in themselves command respect within beleaguered social groups, beyond the ken and beneath the notice of economic masters. Yet the estate itself did nothing to preserve dignity once authority was no longer required. When it came to placing a monetary value on a slave, there was no comparison between what an able driver, driveress, and senior craftsman, or even an ordinary healthy gang laborer, on the one hand, and what an elderly watchman or nurse on the other, could command. The most pathetic of the 577 slaves on the 1793 list were also, in a sense, the most heroic: the only two who had survived long enough to be listed as superannuated—provided with less than a quarter of the cloth issued to members of the elite, and their bodies valued at a derisory £5 and £10.

By and large, however, the keynote of the mobility data (Figure 27 and Table 48) is not mobility but its lack. Except for automatic movements of limited significance, such as from gang to gang and from working to nonworking categories, a remarkably high proportion of Worthy Park's slaves stayed in their initial occupations. Slave society, from the point of view of economic function, seems to have been essentially static, and intentionally so.

The manumission data (Table 49) discloses little that has not already been discussed in relation to miscegenation. The greatest flurry of manumission came right at the end of slavery, with slaves and Apprentices mostly paying for their own freedom as it became legally possible for masters to acknowledge that their servants, far from being absolute chattels, owned money as well as property. No less than 17 slaves were unconditionally freed on August 1, 1834, and 5 Apprentices subsequently "bought up" their apprenticeship, one even paying £32 for the relief only five months before "full freedom" came to all.

The pattern disclosed by the data on runaways in Tables 47 and 49 is more complex and cannot be clearly resolved without reference to the individual biographies given later. The first impression is that the number of runaways was always substantial and increased greatly after 1812, averaging 3.2 a year in the years fully recorded between 1783 and 1797 and 9.7 between 1811 and 1834. In fact, only 51 of Worthy Park's 1,377 recorded slaves were involved altogether—some 3.7 percent. The annual figures were rather exaggerated by repeated offenders and by those few runaways who sustained their freedom long enough to be recorded in consecutive years.

Three exceptional slaves, Jack, Bob, and Mingo, were listed continuously as runaways from 1812 to 1830 and never returned to Worthy Park. Like the few other runaways whose return or recovery was not recorded, they may have perished in the woods soon after their flight, rather than performing the miracle of finding a haven in the heavily scrutinized small communities of free blacks in the towns. Their names were kept in the records not so much in the expectation that they would be found alive but so that the estate could be recompensed according to law once their dead bodies were found. In the great majority of cases, slaves came back or were brought back to Worthy Park after absences that did not exceed a month or two on the average. Punishment was almost certainly by lashes (the number laid down by law after 1792, but never recorded at Worthy Park) and a term in the Vagabond Gang.

Male runaways outnumbered females 3:1, probably not so much because they were fleeter of foot, hardier, and more ambitious, but because their occupations provided greater chances of escape. What is more surprising is that Africans outnumbered Creoles among runaways down to 1830. Though Africans might have been able to sustain themselves more competently in the Jamaican wilds, the Maroons had been allied with the whites to track down all runaways since 1739. In addition, it was doubly difficult for unacculturated Africans to remain undetected in the towns. The preponderance of Africans among the runaways is evidence, perhaps, not only of the continuing disaffection of Africans but also of the greater acceptance by the Creoles of their servitude, at least in the earlier period. It may even by argued that the reversal of the African/Creole ratio among the runaways after 1830 was as much an indication of that "reversal of acceptance," of which

(continued on page 156)   153

Feeding canes to a windmill. The demands of Worthy Park's water-powered machinery would have been more voracious.

154

some historians write,[10] as of the declining number of Africans and the increasing opportunities for runaways to remain undetected. Rather more speculative are what conclusions may be drawn from the fact that several of Worthy Park's persistent runaways had degrading names: Villain, Trash, Whore, Strumpet.[11]

The names of slaves are a fascinating subject for speculation and provide perhaps the best proof of acculturation or creolization. The names listed in plantation records were those by which the estate chose to call the slaves; but it is unlikely that bookkeepers forced slaves to reject their own familiar names as long as they were relatively easy to pronounce, or to accept alternatives. This was certainly true in 1730, when the estate allowed children to be called by African names, despite a great deal of duplication.[12] The gradual, and almost certainly voluntary, shift in the types of names—from a majority of African names to an increasing number of single English names, and to the first Christian names with surnames—provides a telling index of the decline of African influences and the increasing influence of Creole, Christian, and status norms.

From the earliest days English names seem to have carried more prestige than African names and to have been related to status. In 1730 only 22 of Worthy Park's 82 senior male slaves, or 27 percent, were listed with African names, though a very high proportion were African-born. Among the remainder of the population in 1730 the proportion of African names was 68 percent. By 1784 less than a third of Worthy Park's slaves still carried African names in the rolls, though almost half had been born in Africa. Some originally listed with African names changed later, particularly children once they started work. By 1838 not one member of Worthy Park's population had an African name, though 42 or the 219 still carried only one name, 20 were African-born, and 10 had carried African names when younger.

One reason for the decline in African names was that gradually the plantation environment became the chief influence which even the African slaves held in common. Increasingly, Worthy Park's slave recruits came from parts of West Africa widely different in culture and language. The decline in the dominance of Coromantine slaves and their culture indicated by the decrease in the use of Akan day-names, from 26.3 percent of the population in 1730 to 4.8 percent between 1783 and 1838, has been noted earlier.[13] By 1800 Congo slaves at Worthy Park alone outnumbered those from the Gold Coast, but they were never as dominant as the Coromantines had been.

An ethnologist studying the sixty-nine different African names found at Worthy Park might be able to suggest the geographical range from which the estate's Africans were drawn, despite the bookkeepers' tendency to anglicize names they found phonetically difficult or for which there were obvious English equivalents.[14] The wide catchment area from which the Africans were drawn in the later period is partly indicated by the distinguishing names such as Ebo Katy, Congo Tom, Coromantu Cubba, Chamba Lettice, Moco Sukey, and Bonny Yabba carried by 17 of the plantation's slaves after 1783.[15] Despite the notorious inaccuracy of the planters' African labels, these names suggest that the slaves in question were born in places as far apart, and as different, as London and Moscow, Stockholm and Palermo.

The more or less intentional mingling of Africans from different tribes and linguistic groups produced a melting pot effect, in which names were chosen from a variety that was increasingly syncretic. At the same time, English was the plantation lingua franca, with the "pidgin" of the African coast gradually changing into modern Jamaican Creole.[16] By the second and third generations, the slaves' African origins were completely generalized, and more and more Africans would have tended to have English names chosen for them by parents or bookkeepers.

Single English slave names were of five main kinds. Most common were simple Christian names, often in their diminutive or nickname forms. Of these some were obviously easy transitions from African equivalents, such as Joe (for Cudjoe), Jack (Quaco), Sam (Sambo), Abby (Abba), Bina (Cubbena), Phoebe (Phibba). Unlike English children, however, a large number of slaves acquired grandiose names from classical antiquity or biblical names, though some of these may have had African roots too. For example, Venus, like Bina, may have been derived from Cubbena, Cato may have come from the Yoruba word *keta*, Hercules (or Herakles) from the Mende *heke* (large wild animal), and Hagar from the Mende *haga* (lazy).[17] Some slaves were known by place names, such as London, Dublin, Kingston, or by the names of famous personages, such as Pitt, Grenville, Nelson. Others were known by nicknames describing alleged qualities or characteristics, originally accorded seriously, or with satirical or even degrading intent: Beauty, Carefree, Monkey, Villain, Strumpet. To a significant degree, all these single slave names were distressingly similar to those of the estate's cattle, so that it is almost possible to confuse one list with another in the Worthy Park ledgers.[18]

In the last two decades of slavery, however, an important cultural change occurred. An accelerating number of slaves acquired surnames, so that a majority entered freedom in 1838 with two names, like those who were already free. Some merely added a surname to their existing single name (if it were Christian), but the majority changed their first name at the same time as they acquired their second, signalizing a complete change of name, if not also persona.

The incidence of instant renaming was clearly part of the process of Christianization by baptism encouraged by the later Amelioration Acts. The earliest cases of slave baptisms at Worthy Park were two in 1809 and eight in 1811.[19] But the numbers of slaves baptized by the parish minister on his periodic circuits of the plantations increased rapidly as a result of the 1816 Act which offered ministers a per capita

157

Ladling sugar in the humid hell of a boiling house.

fee of 2s.6d. for each slave baptized, registered, and certificated, and the further encouragements included in the 1823 Act.[20] From the St. John Parish Register it seems that sometimes dozens of Worthy Park slaves were baptized together, or up to 50 slaves from different estates. By 1838 three-quarters of Worthy Park's population had surnames.

Parish clergy were likely to have encouraged baptism through the desire to augment their incomes, but to a large degree the christening process must have remained a matter of choice, because it was not universal. Although there is an unfortunate gap in the St. John's Register from 1835 to 1838, the adoption of surnames seems to have been invariably associated with baptism in church. But like most of the activities associated with the established Anglican church, it was a process much more of a social than religious significance. At the very least it represented a differentiation, almost certainly voluntary, from the mere cattle which the estate tended to regard so similarly to slaves.

Which slaves made this important acculturizing step first, and to what degree were surnames true patronymics? Without exception, the first slaves with surnames were senior men with a degree of responsibility.[21] But the custom spread rapidly through the ranks of the males, to women, and down to the newly born children. Many of the earliest of the baptized were craftsmen, but none of the surnames chosen derived from occupations (as was common in Europe). Instead, they were taken from practically every white man who ever came in contact with Worthy Park. This might be direct evidence of miscegenation—for many of those first acquiring surnames were colored slaves—were it not for the fact that by 1838 seven-eighths of those with surnames were unequivocally pure-blood blacks.

A more likely possibility is that at first names were chosen more or less randomly, with the most popular names bieng those of whites such as owners, overseers, and senior bookkeepers, who carried most prestige. From about 1825, however, it seems that children were normally given their father's adopted surname, in line with English custom. Certainly, they did not often have the same surname as their mothers, though mothers frequently had several children sharing a surname. This pattern, indicative of the infrequency of formal marriages but the prevalence of serial monogamy—and common in modern Jamaica—would have been a useful guide in filling in the sadly lacking details of marital cohabitation, family nucleation, and patrilineal descent, had it occurred earlier. As it is there are only a few cases in the 1830s, not many more than the paltry hints from the earlier lists in such names as Counsellor's Cuba, Washer's Juba, Young Caesar, Jacky's Sambo.

All in all, most slaves entered freedom with names that belonged to the Europeanized society which existed outside the plantations during slavery days and which they expected now to join. In this they were deluded. However, to call any European name, whether first name or surname, a "slave name" and reject it, as is a common custom today, is surely also a mistake. True slave names were often African, or little more than nicknames, and nearly all had disappeared by 1838. Freed slaves, by and large, had the names they chose for themselves as creolized West Indians. If these are slave names, the "slavery" does not relate to what came to an end with emancipation. To reject them in favor of African names would be retrograde, amounting to a rejection not so much of formal slavery as of postemancipation Creole society and the whole process of creolization.

In summary, what conclusions does this mass of socioeconomic tabulation justify? Broadly speaking, the Worthy Park population was one socially graded on a scale of economic values, and socially static. Race divided the workers from their managers, but the division had at least as much an economic as a social basis. Demographically, any slave society in which deaths normally exceeded births was bound to be peculiar, in having to rely on importations to keep up numbers. The social structure was also complicated by a type of miscegenation limited to white males and black or colored women.

Yet did these characteristics indicate that the plantation's population was more open than closed? Does the evidence not argue rather for a great and increasing degree of self-containment and social cohesion?

Figure 30. Worthy Park: Slave Name Patterns, 1730-1838, Selected Years, and Data

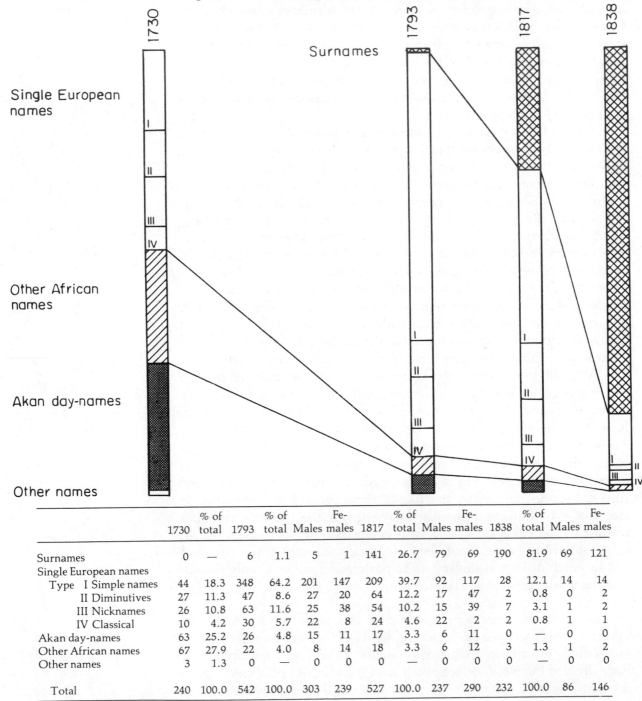

	1730	% of total	1793	% of total	Males	Fe-males	1817	% of total	Males	Fe-males	1838	% of total	Males	Fe-males
Surnames	0	—	6	1.1	5	1	141	26.7	79	69	190	81.9	69	121
Single European names														
Type I Simple names	44	18.3	348	64.2	201	147	209	39.7	92	117	28	12.1	14	14
II Diminutives	27	11.3	47	8.6	27	20	64	12.2	17	47	2	0.8	0	2
III Nicknames	26	10.8	63	11.6	25	38	54	10.2	15	39	7	3.1	1	2
IV Classical	10	4.2	30	5.7	22	8	24	4.6	22	2	2	0.8	1	1
Akan day-names	63	25.2	26	4.8	15	11	17	3.3	6	11	0	—	0	0
Other African names	67	27.9	22	4.0	8	14	18	3.3	6	12	3	1.3	1	2
Other names	3	1.3	0	—	0	0	0	—	0	0	0	—	0	0
Total	240	100.0	542	100.0	303	239	527	100.0	237	290	232	100.0	86	146

160

And if so, how did these conditions relate to the degrees of alienation, tension, and revolt by which the success of a society can be gauged?

Ignoring for the moment the plantation's whites, and with the important other exception of the supplementation of births by adult importations—at first of new Africans and then after 1808 by a trickle of local, mostly Creole, slaves—the Worthy Park population was not subject to the same types of fluctuations and influences as a normal open population. In the period between 1783 and 1838, the records at Worthy Park disclose only 6 slaves being sold off, 40 manumitted (more than half after August 1, 1834), 13 transferred, 8 transported or sentenced to life imprisonment, and perhaps 10 who ran away permanently. This represented a rate of "nondeath decreases" of less than 2 percent a year, compared with a death rate of some 4 percent. Against this can be balanced the birthrate of around 2 percent per year, and a rate of "nonbirth increases" averaging about 4 percent, to produce a population not only in equilibrium but also relatively closed.

Much evidence also points to a high degree of self-containment for Worthy Park and of social cohesion for its slaves, and little seriously challenges this interpretation. Over the entire period there are records of only 7 slaves being hired out, and after the 1790s it was not found necessary to bring in squads of "jobbing" slaves, or even the occasional hired craftsman. Worthy Park's population was thus denied even a form of social interchange that was fairly common in other parts of Jamaica, especially towards the end of slavery. Save that perhaps 2 in 100 slaves, as wainmen or cattle drovers, had legitimate reason regularly to roam far from Worthy Park, that one in 27 of the plantation's slaves ran away at least once in their life, and that a few others were carried to the Slave Court at Point Hill for other misdemeanors towards the end of slavery, most slaves' longest journeys would be the couple of miles to the provision grounds at the Cocoree.

The working of the provision grounds or "polinks" of Cocoree by the slave families on Saturday afternoons and Sundays was very important in providing an escape from the herd conditions of the working gangs, providing the slaves with some sense of independence, self-sufficiency, even ownership. It was the training for emancipation in the slave provision grounds, with its accompanying aspirations, that led Sidney Mintz to characterize the Jamaican plantation slave as a proto-peasant.[22] Unfortunately, no evidence remains from Worthy Park of the production of surplus provisions and stock for sale by the slaves in local markets, so brilliantly deduced by Mintz and Douglas Hall in a 1960 article. Indeed, the isolated nature of Lluidas Vale makes unlikely such a developed system as that traced closer to Kingston and Spanish Town.[23]

Nothing in the Worthy Park records tells precisely how the slaves worked at weekends in the Cocoree. The description given by William Beckford in 1790, however, seems convincingly close:

They generally make choice of such sorts of land for their grounds as are encompassed by lofty mountains; and I think that they commonly prefer the sides of hills, which are covered with loose stones, to the bottoms upon which they are not so abundant. Some will have a mixture of both, and will cultivate the plantain-tree upon the flat, and their provisions upon the rising ground; and some will pursue a contrary method; for the choice as well of change of situation. . . .

They prepare their land, and put in their crops on the [days] that are given to them, and they bring home their provisions at night; and if their grounds be at a considerable distance from the plantation, as they often are to the amount of five or seven miles, or more, the journey backwards and forwards makes this rather a day of labour and fatigue, than of enjoyment and rest; but if, on the contrary, they be within any tolerable reach, it may be said to partake of both.

The negroes, when working in their grounds, exhibit a picture of which it will be difficult to give a minute description. They scatter themselves over the face, and form themselves into distinct parties at the bottom of the mountains; and being consequently much divided, their general exertions can only be observed from a distance.

If the land be hilly, it is generally broken by rocks, or encumbered by stones; the first they cannot displace, but the last they gently remove as they proceed in their work, and thus make a bed for the deposit of the plantain-sucker and the coco, or of the corn and yam.

Upon these occasions they move, with all their family, into the place of cultivation; the children of different ages are loaded with baskets, which are burdened in proportion to their strength and age; and it is pleasing to observe under what considerable weights they will bear themselves up, without either murmur or fatigue. The infants are flung at the backs of the mothers, and very little incommode them in their walks or labour."[24]

Yet even the working of provision grounds under very little supervision did not amount to much geographical mobility. The majority of the Worthy Park slaves never left the confines of Lluidas Vale from the day they arrived there, either by birth or as newly purchased adults. Those who were not called on to work the provision grounds were restricted to the even smaller compass of the Worthy Park fields and slave quarters. It was a society almost as constricted as those in the forests of Africa and the deepest rural parts of England. At the same time, however, it was molded by influences common to all similar groups in the West Indies: the "European" plantation system, the memories of a generalized Africa, and the rising tide of the Creole environment.

In such a closed society, a sense of kinship, far from fading as many critics of slavery have asserted, must have been sustained and even grown stronger. How did this relate to the nature and development of family among the slaves? And, if family was the rule rather than the exception in slave society, was it of the strictly nuclear type—with man, woman, and their children cohabiting—or the looser bonds of those types of extended family common in Africa, and in Europe before the seventeenth century?

Whether the plantation system encouraged or destroyed the nuclear family among the slaves must remain controversial. Even if the evidence points towards the latter case, this does not necessarily mean that plantation societies were consequently less cohesive, or that some form of family did not remain common. The early writers Richard Ligon and Hans Sloane testified that planters tried to maintain a balance of sexes among new slaves and that wise masters encouraged marital relations among their slaves; but neither wrote of formal weddings or even permanent liaisons.[25] Nearly all later writers spoke of both the slaves' "promiscuity" and "polygamy." In articles written in 1973 and 1975, Barry Higman argued that the nuclear family was quite common in Jamaican and other West Indian slave societies.[26] But his evidence dated from the last years of slavery, when the influence of the churches and ameliorating laws may have been at work. Moreover, Higman's Jamaican evidence related simply to cohabitation where children were present, where the children belonged to the mother but not certainly to the father. It is not clear that the pattern he traced was very much different from the pattern of serial monogamy, technical illegitimacy, and matriarchy which is still the norm in Jamaica—and said by some writers to be legacies of slavery.[27]

The modern system of matriarchy cold not have been entirely rooted in West African polygyny; though this made children naturally cleave to their mother, and sometimes even involved matrilineage, it left the father as the focus of power. The slave system, on the other hand, devalued the paternal role of slave males. One example was the slave law which decreed that children would take the status of mothers, not fathers.[28] Designed to ensure that all children of slaves should remain slaves and to prevent the custom of miscegenation providing too easy a road to freedom for colored offspring of white fathers, it also had the effect of ensuring that slaves generally stayed with their mothers, and where they were born. This was also encouraged by the amelioration law which, while decreeing that slave families should not be split up, particularly insisted that slave children not be separated from their mothers.[29]

Although aiding social cohesion, both laws may have jeopardized the development of European-type nuclear families, as well as confusing the researcher into slave marital patterns. The first law recognized only those links between slave children and their mothers. Plantations were also ordered to identify mothers, both to investigate fertility and to discover the mothers of six living children, though they were not required to list fathers as well.[30] Accordingly, it is now virtually impossible to trace slave patrilineage. This, however, does not necessarily mean that fathers were unimportant at the private, family level or that even nuclear families were uncommon. On the other hand, it could be argued that the second law, rather than recognizing the disruptive

(continued on page 166)

Stokers in a trash yard. At the height of the crop the boiling house would operate throughout the night.

165

tendencies of slavery and achieving an improvement in family life, actually retarded it. Without laws either to encourage formal slave marriage or to forbid the breakup of slave families there was nothing to prevent planters encouraging marital cohabitation and the nuclear family if these were thought to be good husbandry. Once such laws were passed, however, masters who might wish to sell their slaves were more or less forced to discourage the creation of stable families.

In fact, the Worthy Park evidence shows both that children were not shipped off at all, with or without their mothers, and that the link between mothers and children was extremely strong. The small size of the social group and the fact that very few males left or came into the population meant that sexual relationships, if not formalized or permanent, must have been very well known. Besides, the African prejudice against cousin marriage must have encouraged a scrupulous regard for sexual relationships in a society where opportunities for exogamy were severely limited. The presence of a privileged and peripatetic group of white males contributed to sexual anarchy (if also the genetic pool); but, as has been shown earlier, this applied to only a small and select segment of the plantation's females. Towards the end of slavery even this type of miscegenation decreased.

Although it is dangerous here to argue from lack of evidence, there does not seem to have been even that limited degree of sexual interchange among the slaves of the different Lluidas Vale estates that some writers allege for other areas.[31] Opportunities for such genetic outbreeding should have increased as slavery relaxed, but either the social controls were not loosened before 1834, or evidence of such a development has been lost. At the same time, the status aspiration to European middle-class norms might argue for an increase rather than a decrease in the incidence of stable marital unions and nuclear families. However, though there are records in the St. John Parish Register of hundreds of slave baptisms in Lluidas Vale between 1811 and 1835, there is not one example of a slave wedding.[32]

In sum, it seems almost certain that while on slave plantations such as Worthy Park the "modern" type of stable nuclear family was not always, or ever, the rule, family life of some kind was the common experience, and the resulting network of kinship a dominant characteristic. It was a reconstituted system of kinship, almost accidental in origin and almost unrecognized by the master class. It developed because heterogeneous Africans were brought and bound together, and remained in a closed social unit for generations. In time, kinship became one of the most cohesive bonds within each plantation, and the masters were the unwitting and undeserving beneficiaries of this development. So ignorant were the planters of the ties of family and kinship within their plantations that they predicted that thousands whom they had formerly succoured—such as the old, the sick, the very young—would be destitute when the slaves were freed, forming a pathetic floating army of the needy in each colony. In fact, no such burden fell upon the parish and colony authorities. Families looked after their own, as well as staying for the most part locationally rooted.

Looking back, it seems that many a slave plantation population, after four or five generations must have been virtually one huge extended family. As is suggested in Part Three, elements of this close web of kinship can still be traced in the villages close to ancient plantations—such as Lluidas Vale Village—which almost entirely consist of the descendants of earlier closed and cohesive slave populations.

If the slave population was remarkably cohesive and self-contained, were these qualities shared by the plantation whites who formed the 2 percent master class in slave society? For whites below the rank of planter—overseers, bookkeepers, and the few white craftsmen—plantation life was crude and isolated, and owners did their utmost to treat their white employees like the indentured servants of an earlier period. But these conditions never led plantation whites to identify with the blacks as fellow victims or often to tie them emotionally or physically to particular locations. Though nominally bound by contracts which specified that they could not marry or move without permission, and subject to punishment without legal redress, whites in Jamaica were sufficiently scarce to be able to rely on their employers' need of them.

Whites were needed by individual planters to police the slaves and to save money by fulfilling the "deficiency" quota; they were needed by the plantocracy in general as voters and militiamen. Lesser whites therefore jealously guarded the three qualities which differentiated them from the slaves: their color, their nominal authority, and a mobility that was at least potentially open-ended. This they did by insisting on the absolute rigidity of the distinction between whites and nonwhites even where the latter were not slaves, by exercising authority that was arbitrary and brutal if not tyrannical, and by a restlessness which made them shift almost pathologically from estate to estate. Between 1783 and 1796 alone, there were eighty-five whites employed at Worthy Park, but never more than ten at any one time. Even the overseer changed five times in the thirteen years, though this may have been rather exceptional.

With such a turnaround of managerial staff it must have been almost as difficult for slaves to personalize any hatreds they felt for the system and their masters in general as it was for the whites to individualize the slaves—let alone identify with them. Views on both sides were inevitably generalized, so that the optimistic slave view of the power and attractions of the master society was probably as dangerously inaccurate as the pessimistic view of the black held by most plantation whites.

Alienation and delusion were common to both races. It seems at least arguable that the lesser whites were actually more alienated from the system than the slaves themselves, and more deluded. Slaves did not suffer from the illusion of choice, and over generations familiarity

167

breeds acceptance. It is only human to acquire an attachment for the only home you, and perhaps generations of your forebears, have known, however harsh the life has been there. The slaves' life-styles, at least in the cantonments and grounds, were largely, and increasingly, what they made of them themselves. Slaves, despite being legally chattels, came to possess money and own property and even tenements in all but law. Slave settlements on plantations, moreover, became almost sacred as the burial places of kinfolk.

In these feelings of belonging the slaves may have demonstrated an instinctive bond with their usually absent owners, who felt for their lands—and even their slaves—that type of affection which springs from legalized possession, not to mention a steady stream of profit. Perhaps Matthew Gregory "Monk" Lewis was not a myopic romantic or dissembler in depicting the positive joy with which, as an absentee owner, he was greeted by his Jamaican slaves in 1817.[33] Absence, as well as the largesse which visiting absentees traditionally distributed, doubtless aided the slaves' fondness. Yet, somewhat paradoxically, the slaves seem to have felt more respect for the true masters of their fate—their owners—than for their daily taskmasters.

However, when all is said and done, there remained in many respects closer links between plantation slaves and plantation whites than between either and any outgroup. These relationships, at the very least symbiotic, have led modern commentators to include whites with slaves in the same West Indian "slave society." To contemporary outsiders, the plantation whites were not only tied to the slaves, they were little different from the Creole blacks save in color and the degree of freedom. Though the whites never saw themselves as natives, their food, clothing, language, and customs made them more West Indian than English—Creoles in the purest, Spanish sense.

As time went on, Jamaican whites saw themselves as less rather than more integrated, became more rather than less racist. But these attitudes could be interpreted as responses to being increasingly locked within the system. Ambition sustained them, but as economic conditions deteriorated their chances grew slimmer of progressing the traditional route from craftsman to bookkeeper, bookkeeper to overseer, overseer to attorney, attorney to planter. At the same time they were coming under increasing competitive pressure, not only from the freedmen but from the Creole slaves themselves, who were more frequently filling the craftsmen's posts on the plantations. At Worthy Park, for example, the head boilerman in the 1790s was white, but by 1813 this all-important job had been given to a trusty slave. As late as 1820, however, there were still both black and white carpenters.

Despite its anarchic and degraded form, sex was something of a bridge and solvent. However, miscegenation was tainted by privilege, not dignified by love. Besides being of the artificial kind—white males coupling with black and colored women, never the reverse—sex was rooted in lust and unacknowledged on the one side, connived at through social ambition on the other. It led to sexual deprivation in black men (if not white women, too), reducing the chances of stable liaisons and normal family life even further, with permanently damaging effects.

The irony that plantation whites, though casually concupiscent themselves, accused the blacks of promiscuity, has been pointed out before. It could also be noted that because of their disaffection and greater opportunities, whites "ran away" from the plantations far more often than the slaves. No doubt all in plantation society (save the owners and attorneys, who in any case were not forced to live on plantations) would have forsaken the plantation system given equal opportunities and alternatives. Certainly, the incidence of slaves running away, and the necessity of drastic punishments such as transportation to another colony and hard labor for life for persistent offenders, offer the best evidence for the degree of disaffection with the plantation system among the slaves at Worthy Park. In the last analysis, however, it may seem a matter of opinion as to whether a tendency for up to 4 percent of a population detained but not forcibly restrained to go absent without leave in any one year constitutes evidence of *relative* disaffection, or the reverse.

There was a notable increase in the frequency of running away after the ending of the slave trade. But even this could be attributed to several apparently contradictory causes: the weakening of control (even an erosion of will on the part of the masters), greater ease in maintaining freedom, an increase in the attractions of freedom, an increased harshness in the treatment of slaves. With less obvious consequences of disaffection such as low productivity and low standards of health, a causal connection is likewise almost impossible to prove, while alternative reasons can be suggested. The three recorded cases of suicide at Worthy Park might be better evidence, though the ledgers naturally do not speculate on motivation. As to the most overt of the forms of slave resistance, armed rebellion, Worthy Park was directly spared throughout its history, both in the early days when African-led slave rebellions occurred nearby or in the last years of slavery when, in western Jamaica, revolt was led by the apparently most assimilated of slaves.

Yet, if there was in fact little mobility within the Worthy Park slave population, or out of it, little evidence of serious resistance, and much of cohesion and self-containment, do these characteristics imply stagnancy and the irreversible acceptance of the system? In conclusion, it is maintained that the evidence points strongly to a countervailing view in two crucial respects. These were the social effects of general economic changes and of the acceleration of the creolization process which followed from the ending of the slave trade—in particular, the shift in the ratio of sexes and the gradual disappearance of the African-born.

Table 42 shows that Worthy Park's production declined noticeably after 1812, like that of Jamaica as a whole after 1805. This general de-

(continued on page 172)

*Loading sugar hogsheads.
Once at the coast the huge
barrels might need man-
handling through surf to
coastal "droguers," as at
Old Harbour, Jamaica.*

cline is usually attributed to a response to the fall in sugar prices at a time of high and rising costs, and the consequent effect on profit levels. Yet, closer analysis shows that solutions had been attempted, which in turn were unsuccessful.

In the face of falling produce prices, two courses might have recommended themselves: economies of scale—producing more with the same work force—or producing the same amount with a smaller number of workers. Since overproduction was thought to be the cause of the decline in prices, it was generally preferable not to increase production unless costs could be greatly reduced. But trimming the work force implied the substitution of "free wage labor" for slavery, a solution which the planters in general were very slow to advocate. Instead, at the local level, attempts were made to maximize production through raised productivity, both by improvements in field and factory and by driving the work force harder. This policy was followed by Rose Price at Worthy Park.

Maximization under established conditions, however, could not continue to hold under the burdens of a containing decline in the sugar price and the increasing frailty of the slave work force. Total production at Worthy Park reached its peak in 1812, and profits were probably at their highest as late as 1815. But after 1815 the profit level rapidly fell, and in the very last years of slavery even the production per field hand began to decline again. The only logical course which remained, though it is not certain that is was apparent to very many planters, was to combine both general solutions: to introduce new technical methods to multiply production, while at the same time abolishing slavery so that as many workers as needed could be employed when needed, without the expense of maintaining them out of season or maintaining the nonproductive at all.

By the 1830s the capabilities of the work force (throughout Jamaica as at Worthy Park), with its inevitably high average age and high proportion of women, had reached its limits of productivity, and the recovery of high profit levels under the existing system began to seem impossible. Moreover, the occurrence of rebellions at the very end of slavery (in Barbados and Guiana as in Jamaica) suggests that perhaps all four possible reasons for increased tension and alienation mentioned earlier coexisted and were not contradictory after all. With declining profits and the efforts to raise productivity, the slaves were doubtless being pushed harshly at a time when they were neither strong enough nor willing enough to respond as intended. Creole slaves with no options but field work felt cheated of the chances of internal promotion, at a time when some of their fellow slaves were being worked less hard because of the collapse of estates, and the number of freed slaves was soaring yearly. In addition, the collapse of estates and the defection of many planters—moving to other areas, forsaking planting altogether, or advocating the radical solution of free wage labor—left the remaining planters weakened, and therefore desperate. When to this general socioeconomic climate was added the emancipation campaign (gradually gaining in power from 1815), in which the opponents of slavery on humanitarian and economic grounds joined forces, those who did not resign themselves to slavery's alternative resorted to the paranoia of a "siege mentality."[34]

Among the effects of the decline of the sugar plantation system was the opening up of an even wider gap between the races. The overreaction of the Jamaican whites to the slave uprising of 1831 was merely the culmination of a gradual breakdown in established relationships. For example, the demographic evidence from Worthy Park clearly suggests that the incidence of true miscegenation significantly declined towards the end of slavery. Throughout Jamaica and the rest of the West Indies the number of colored children of white fathers probably decreased greatly, even though the total of the colored population rose steadily because of the interbreeding of colored with colored, colored with black.

This regression to the serological norm reflected, on the one hand, a growing sense of integration and pride among the blacks, as well as a growing independence on the part of black women realizing the declining value of preferring mates of a lighter color then themselves. On the part of the whites it reflected a growing antipathy, based on fear and a general weakening of their position—which included a declining power to command the sexual attentions of black and colored female slaves. Paternal love, it might be argued, could only come from strength and self-assurance. Weakness bred hatred, or at least social discord.

Worthy Park's condition in the last years of slavery was not so critical as that of most Jamaican estates. The slaves did not rebel, sugar production and even profits continued, if at lower levels. Yet women dangerously outnumbered men, and the combined productivity of the work force remained too low. Even the politically reactionary Rose Price, having seen his once-expected annual income of £13,000 dwindle to a memory, became resigned to emancipation before it happened. In 1832, while many planters were still defending slavery to the last ditch, he wrote a vigorous pamphlet simply pleading—successfully as it turned out—for the continuation of some kind of enforced labor, as well as massive compensation for the slaveowners.[35]

Relating, as always, solely to his own interest of maximum returns, Rose Price had as little notion of the true causes of the situation as of the viability of alternative solutions. Yet it can be maintained that the causes, if not the solutions, were to be found in the records which Worthy Park's owner ordered his overseer to keep. The evidence to be found there is strong enough still to demonstrate that in the wider context of Jamaica as a whole, and even the entire British West Indies, the whole process of creolization speeded by the ending of the slave trade—particularly the equalization of the sex ratio and the decline in the number of Africans—determined the quality of life as much as did the decline in plantation prosperity, or even the ending of slavery itself.

173

TABLE 42. Worthy Park: Annual Production, Productivity, Revenue, Profits, 1783-1838

Sources: Worthy Park records; London sugar prices from Michael Craton and James Walvin,

A Jamaican Plantation: The History of Worthy Park, 1670-1970 (London, W. H. Allen, and Toronto, University of Toronto Press, 1970), pp. 167, 189; Bryan Edwards, *The History, Civil and Commercial, of the West Indies,* 2 vols. (London, 1793), II, 267; L. J. Ragatz, *Statistics for the Study of British Caribbean Economic History, 1763-1833* (London, 1927; Jamaican sugar production from *A Jamaican Plantation,* p. 188; Noel Deerr, *The History of Sugar,* 2 vols. (London, Chapman & Hall, 1949-50).

Note: Blank spaces = not calculable.

[a]Exclusive of duty.

	Total slave population	Field labor force	Sugar produced (hhds.)	Rum produced (puncheons)	Jamaican sugar production (thou. tons)	% of Worthy Park sugar of Jamaica total
1783	318	—	270	—	—	—
1784	316	—	375	—	—	—
1785	313	—	245	—	—	—
1786	307	—	181	—	—	—
1787	339	126	172	—	—	—
1788	338	—	294	—	58.7	0.38
1789	339	133	334	—	59.4	.42
1790	345	—	248	85	55.6	.34
1791	357	169	267	—	60.0	.34
1792	359	—	310	124	54.6	.48
1793	450	267	375	145	51.6	.55
1794	528	280	371	162	64.2	.43
1795	483	274	306	142	62.8	.37
1796	470	—	269	—	64.0	.31
1797	—	—	468	—	51.6	.68
1798	—	—	415	—	64.2	.48
1799	—	—	499	—	73.2	.51
1800	—	—	590	—	70.1	.63
1801	—	—	435	—	90.2	.36
1802	—	—	425	—	92.3	.34
1803	—	—	505	—	76.2	.50
1804	—	—	624	—	74.9	.63
1805	—	—	673	—	99.6	.51
1806	—	—	455	—	97.1	.35
1807	—	—	500	—	89.8	.42
1808	—	—	545	—	77.8	.53
1809	—	—	460	—	76.0	.45
1810	—	—	555	—	73.7	.57
1811	505	—	456	198	87.9	.39
1812	503	—	705	—	62.1	.85
1813	511	255	570	—	66.5	.65
1814	514	254	572	—	72.4	.59
1815	514	—	475	—	79.6	.45
1816	527	296	—	—	69.9	—
1817	527	—	—	—	85.9	—
1818	—	—	—	—	82.7	—
1819	—	—	—	—	80.7	—
1820	—	—	—	—	88.5	—
1821	505	308	479	204	84.0	.43
1822	494	290	533	250	70.7	.51
1823	496	317	487	188	70.9	.51
1824	484	298	—	—	72.6	—
1825	—	—	—	—	55.8	—
1826	469	—	—	—	75.0	—
1827	448	—	—	—	65.6	—
1828	—	—	—	—	68.2	—
1829	—	—	—	—	69.3	—
1830	522	233	555	—	69.0	.60
1831	517	204	471	—	69.8	.51
1832	494	191	589	—	71.6	.60
1833	483	174	484	—	67.9	.53
1834	467	184	490	—	62.8	.59
1835	417	181	427	—	57.4	.55
1836	—	165	407	—	52.7	.58
1837	—	166	370	—	45.2	.61
1838	—	157	406	—	52.7	.58

London average sugar price (shillings per cwt.)[a]	Total revenue [£1000 Stg.]	Profit, five-year intervals [£1000 Stg.]	Sugar per field slave (hhds.)	Sugar per slave of total (hhds.)	Profit per field slave, five-year intervals (£ Stg.)	Profit per slave in whole population, five-year intervals (£ Stg.)
45	12.05			0.849		
44	16.55			1.19		
45	11.03	3.18		0.783	26.5	10.1
50	9.05			.590		
50	8.60		1.37	.507		
55	16.17			.871		
60	20.04		2.51	.990		
65	16.12	8.98		.716	59.8	26.0
70	18.69		1.58	.720		
70	21.70			.863		
75	28.13		1.40	.833		
70	25.97		1.40	.703		
80	24.48	8.15		.634	29.6	17.0
85	22.87		0.982	.572		
85	39.78					
90	37.35					
85	39.92					
80	47.20	10.85			39.5	21.7
70	30.45					
65	27.63					
70	35.35					
80	49.92					
80	53.84	15.05			54.7	30.1
78	35.49					
70	35.00					
72	39.24					
79	36.34					
80	44.40	14.00				
70	31.92				52.8	28.0
75	52.98			.903		
70	39.90		1.84	1.40		
65	37.18		1.86	1.11		
57	27.09	15.25		1.11		
49				0.924	61.0	29.7
45						
42						
38						
37		7.05			23.5	14.1
34	16.27		1.88	.949		
33	17.59		1.84	1.08		
34	16.56		1.54	0.982		
32						
39		5.45			18.2	11.5
33						
32						
32						
27						
26	14.43	2.05			8.8	3.9
24	11.30		2.31	.911		
28	16.51		3.08	1.19		
30	14.52		2.78	1.00		
29	14.21		2.66	1.05		
33	14.09	5.60	2.36	1.02	30.9	13.4
41	16.69		2.48			
35	12.95		2.29			
34	13.80		2.59			

TABLE 43. Worthy Park: Annual Revenue, Costs, Profits, 1785-1835, Five-Year Intervals

Sources: As for Table 42.

[a]Exclusive of duty.

	Sugar production (hhds.)	Average London sugar price (shillings per cwt.)[a]	Gross revenue inc. rum (£ Stg.)	Sugar charges (freight, insurance, commission)	Provisions, supplies	Salaries
1785	200	45	9,000	1,125	3,000	650
1790	275	65	17,875	2,250	3,000	650
1795	300	80	24,000	6,600	5,100	750
1800	500	80	40,000	15,000	9,000	1,650
1805	600	80	48,000	18,200	9,000	2,750
1810	500	75	37,500	12,000	7,500	2,000
1815	500	60	30,000	6,000	6,000	1,750
1820	500	37	17,500	2,200	4,500	1,500
1825	450	35	15,750	2,000	4,500	1,500
1830	475	26	11,350	1,400	4,500	1,000
1835	450	35	15,750	2,000	4,500	1,250

TABLE 44. The Population of Worthy Park, with Employment Categories, Salaries, Valuations, Issues, 1793

Source: Race and Slavery in the Western Hemisphere: Quantitative Studies, edited by Stanley L. Engerman and Eugene D. Genovese (copyright (c) 1975 by The Center for Advanced Study in the Behavioral Sciences, Stanford, California), pp. 276 and 277. Reprinted by permission of Princeton University Press.

[a]As in Fig. 26.
[b]The whites' salaries listed here were taken from the Worthy Park ledgers, but the slave valuations were collated from material on other estates, particularly Green Park in Trelawny, found in the Institute of Jamaica, Kingston.
[c]The tenant and his wife were supported by the estate, probably rent-free, simply so that they could be registered as Worthy Park residents, and thus save taxation under the Jamaican Deficiency Law which penalized failures to keep up a certain quota of whites on each estate. Similarly, the doctor, John Quier, was placed on Worthy Park's list, though he served other estates as well.

Whites (12)

Employment	Number	(£ Jamaica Currency)[b]
Owner (normally absent)	1	
Overseer & wife	2	200
Head bookkeeper	1	100
Under bookkeepers	3	50-80
Head boilerman	1	150
Head distiller	1	100
Doctor (not resident)	1	6s.8d. per slave
Tenant & wife[c]	2	0

Slave Elite (21)

Computer matrix category[a]	Employment	Number	Osnaburg cloth (yds.)	Baize cloth (yds.)	Check cl (yds.)
1	Drivers & driveresses	7	10-12	3	3
1	Head housekeepers[d]	2	10	3	0
1	Head cooper	1	10	3	3
1	Head potter	1	7	2½	3
1	Second boilerman	1	7	2½	3
1	Head mason	1	10	3	3
1	Head sawyer	1	10	3	3
1	Head carpenter	1	10	3	3
1	Head blacksmith	1	10	3	3
1	Head cattleman	1	10	3	3
1	Head muleman	1	10	3	3
1	Head home wainsman	1	7	2½	3
1	Head road wainsman	1	10	3	3
1	Head watchman	1	10	3	3

Lower Elite & Specialists (95)

	Employment	Number			
2	Waiting boys	2	7	2½	3
2	Groom	1	7	3	3
2	Seamstresses	2	10	3	0
2	Washerwomen	2	10	3	0

New slaves	Interest	Total costs	Profit	Capitalization	Profit as % of capital
300	750	5,825	3,175	30,000	10.6
1,500	1,500	8,900	8,975	30,000	29.9
1,500	1,500	15,850	8,150	40,000	20.4
1,500	2,000	29,150	10,850	45,000	24.1
1,000	2,000	32,950	15,050	45,000	33.4
0	2,000	23,500	14,000	48,000	29.2
0	2,000	14,750	15,250	48,000	31.7
0	2,250	10,450	7,050	48,000	14.7
0	2,300	10,400	5,450	48,000	11.3
0	2,400	9,300	2,050	48,000	4.3
0	2,400	10,150	5,600	48,000	11.7

Slave Elite (21)

Hats	Caps	Knives	Coats	Blankets	Value (£ Currency)
1	0	1	1	0	120-150
1	0	0	0	0	60-80
1	0	1	0	0	140
1	0	1	0	0	140
1	0	1	0	0	180
1	0	1	0	0	170
1	0	1	0	0	150
1	0	1	0	0	140
1	0	1	1	0	180
1	0	1	0	0	120
1	0	1	0	0	120
1	0	1	0	0	150
1	0	1	0	0	150
1	0	1	0	0	80

Lower Elite & Specialists (95)

Hats	Caps	Knives	Coats	Blankets	Value (£ Currency)
1	0	0	0	0	60-80
1	1	1	0	0	80
1	1	0	0	0	50-60
1	1	0	0	0	50-60

[d] When the owner was in residence, the Great House domestic staff numbered as many as 25; when he was absent, as few as 2. In the owner's absence an attorney, resident in Kingston and managing perhaps half a dozen estates, was locally responsible for Worthy Park. Such a man, paid on commission, might make as much as £ 5,000 a year.

[e] Pen Negroes received a coat if female, a "frock" (i.e., smock) if male.

[f] Each of the sick slaves listed as "Yaws Negroes" received a coat, a frock, and a blanket. Mothers who had borne children within the year received 5 yds. "Daccas" cloth, 5 yds. flannel, 2 extra yds. osnaburg, and a "dollar" (probably 5 shillings). Those females who were pregnant at issue time each received 5 yds. Daccas.

TABLE 44. (continued)   Lower Elite & Specialists (95)

Computer matrix category[a]	Employment		Osnaburg cloth (yds.)	Baize cloth (yds.)	Check (yd
2	Cook	1	10	3	
3	Midwife	1	7	3	
3	Hothouse nurses	2	7	3	
3	Black doctor	1	12	3	
4	Coopers	6	10	3	
4	Boilers	9	7	3	
4	Distillers	4	7	3	
4	Potters	2	7	3	
4	Sugar guards	2	10	3	
5	Carpenters	9	7-10	3	
5	Sawyers	3	10	3	
5	Masons	2	10	3	
5	Under blacksmith	1	7	3	
7	Home wainsmen	6	7	2½	
7	Road wainsmen	7	10	3	
7	Mulemen	14	7	2½	
7	Hog tenders	3	7	2½	
7	Poultry tenders	2	7	2½	
8	New Negro tenders	3	7	2½	
7	Cattlemen & boys	8	5-10	2-3	
8	Ratcatchers	2	7	2½	

Laboring Gangs (364)

9	Great or First Gang	147	7	2½	
10	Second Gang	67	7	2½	
11	Third Gang	68	5-6	2	
12	Grass or Weeding Gang	21	3-5	2	
13	Vagabond Gang	13	5-7	2½	
13	Pen Negroes[e]	48	7	0	

Marginal or Nonproductive (97)

14	Watchmen	25	7	3	
16	Grass gatherers	7	7	2½	
15-16	Hopeless invalids[f]	18	5-7	2½	
16	Child watchers	3	5	2	
16	Pad menders	2	5	2	
16	Superannuated	2	2½	2	
17	Infants	37	2-4	1- 2½	
15	Women with six children	3	10	3	

Lower Elite & Specialists (95)

Hats	Caps	Knives	Coats	Blankets	Value (£ Currency)
1	1	1	0	0	50
1	1	1	0	0	150
1	1	0	0	0	90
1	1	1	1	0	140
1	1	1	0	0	120-140
1	1	1	0	0	110-140
1	1	1	0	0	100-140
1	1	1	0	0	120
1	1	1	0	0	50
1	1	1	0	0	100-120
1	1	1	0	0	100
1	1	1	0	0	120
1	1	1	0	0	120
1	1	1	0	0	90
1	1	1	0	0	90-120
1	1	1	0	0	90-110
1	1	1	0	0	80
1	1	1	0	0	50-60
1	1	1	0	0	50-80
1	1	1	0	0	80-120
1	1	1	0	0	80-100

Laboring Gangs (364)

Hats	Caps	Knives	Coats	Blankets	Value
1	1	1	0	0	50-125
1	1	1	0	0	50-100
1	1	0	0	0	50-80
1	1	0	0	0	50-60
1	1	0	0	0	50-100
1	1	1	1	1	50-100

Marginal or Nonproductive (97)

Hats	Caps	Knives	Coats	Blankets	Value
1	1	1	0	0	30-70
1	1	1	0	0	60
0	1	1	1	1	5
1	1	1	0	0	50
1	1	1	0	0	80
0	0	0	0	0	5-10
0	0	0	0	0	10-60
1	1	1	0	0	50-80

179

TABLE 45. Worthy Park: Numbers of Slaves in Each Employment Category, by Years Computerized, 1787-1838

Source: Worthy Park records.

Notes: Dashes indicate categories not used in that year. Employment categories as in Fig. 26.

	Total population, as computerized	Category unknown	1 Heads and drivers	2 Domestics	3 Hospital	4 Factory craftsmen	5 Other craftsmen	6 Factory laborers	7 Stock workers	8 Nonfactory, nonfield
1787	334	71	13	6	2	2	14	—	5	—
1789	341	12	20	17	4	16	13	—	22	1
1791	377	31	22	24	9	3	20	—	3	—
1793	541	89	7	58	—	10	22	—	9	—
1794	547	3	19	23	9	14	18	12	44	11
1796	469	4	19	15	9	11	17	5	33	4
1813	484	2	19	21	10	16	19	—	12	1
1814	453	2	10	5	4	13	—	5	32	1
1816	506	6	18	14	3	12	22	—	3	—
1821	504	7	14	15	8	12	24	—	2	—
1822	512	6	16	25	8	14	21	—	8	—
1823	489	0	15	18	4	11	19	—	3	—
1824	502	10	12	15	5	10	19	—	8	—
1830	414	1	13	16	6	12	15	—	9	—
1831	333	6	13	16	2	7	9	—	3	—
1832	311	4	11	16	3	7	10	—	3	—
1833	301	5	11	15	3	7	10	—	4	—
1834	293	2	11	15	3	7	10	—	3	—
1835	261	3	12	11	2	7	8	—	2	—
1836	260	0	7	15	4	8	11	—	9	—
1837	251	1	5	7	3	7	9	—	2	—
1838	184	0	6	7	2	6	8	—	2	—

TABLE 46. Worthy Park: Total Entries in Employment Categories, by Sex, African/Creole Birth, Color, for Years Computerized, 1784-1838

Source: Worthy Park records.

[a]As in Fig. 26.

	Category[a]	Males	Females	Africans	Creoles	A/C unknown	Black	Colored	Color unknown
1	Heads and drivers	234	63	91	191	15	253	38	6
2	Domestics	120	256	37	317	22	182	183	11
3	Hospital	14	90	54	42	8	97	6	1
4	Factory craftsmen	214	0	72	126	16	189	22	3
5	Other craftsmen	318	0	91	213	14	255	63	0
6	Factory laborers	22	0	22	0	0	22	0	0
7	Stock workers	205	16	76	102	43	212	5	4
8	Nonfactory, nonfield	7	11	16	2	0	16	2	0
9	First Gang	456	1146	541	1010	51	1579	18	5
10	Second Gang	313	557	146	713	11	839	26	5
11	Third Gang	360	413	114	650	9	728	39	6
12	Fourth Gang	173	343	93	415	8	481	25	10
13	Misc. field/unspec.	462	702	517	538	109	1108	19	37
14	Watchmen	413	11	286	71	67	405	8	11
15	Misc. unemployed	191	369	79	470	11	494	49	17
16	Aged	60	241	185	79	37	281	11	9
17	Young	293	360	7	638	8	452	99	102
18	Women with six children	0	75	19	53	3	75	0	0
19	Runaways	200	52	129	86	37	215	4	33
20	Manumitted	18	17	0	35	0	12	17	6

10	11	12	13	14	15	16	17	18	19	20
								Women		
Second	Third	Fourth	Misc. field		Misc.			with chil-	Runa-	Manu-
Gang	Gang	Gang	unspec.	Watchmen	unempl.	Aged	Young	dren	ways	mitted
—	—	11	117	4	1	22	48	0	18	0
—	—	—	108	26	8	25	58	1	9	1
—	—	45	126	24	—	20	41	0	7	0
46	71	22	6	27	—	17	33	0	1	0
63	66	20	73	30	18	18	36	3	4	5
49	61	30	46	22	—	16	34	2	4	0
—	—	—	249	25	85	2	2	4	17	0
48	44	2	160	26	16	2	72	—	11	0
43	51	—	17	25	17	—	73	5	12	0
25	34	—	152	14	62	2	8	6	20	0
53	54	29	6	20	68	7	6	7	14	0
59	49	39	5	18	53	13	4	7	7	0
84	52	37	5	18	57	25	6	8	6	5
67	38	41	2	17	35	32	3	5	16	0
57	39	38	16	15	20	28	2	4	4	0
55	39	32	16	17	16	23	2	5	3	0
51	38	29	13	17	28	17	2	5	3	0
46	34	37	13	15	4	15	1	5	1	17
41	32	39	13	13	—	14	0	3	4	1
28	17	35	3	14	18	1	0	3	4	0
30	28	11	2	8	37	0	0	0	4	2
2	2	10	2	6	36	0	0	0	3	0

TABLE 47. Worthy Park: Total Slaves in Employment Categories, by Sex, African/Creole Birth, Color, 1787-1835, Selected Years

Source: Worthy Park records.

Note: Blank spaces indicate categories not used in that year.

[a]As in Fig. 26.

1787

	Category[a]	Male	Female	African	Creole	A/C unknown	Black	Colored	Color unknown
1	Heads and drivers	12	1	10	3	0	10	1	2
2	Domestics	1	5	1	4	1	3	2	1
3	Hospital	0	2	2	0	0	2	0	0
4	Factory craftsmen	2	0	0	0	2	0	0	2
5	Other craftsmen	14	0	6	7	1	11	3	0
6	Factory laborers								
7	Stock workers	4	1	0	3	2	5	0	0
8	Nonfactory, nonfield								
9	First Gang								
10	Second Gang								
11	Third Gang								
12	Fourth Gang	0	11	1	7	3	10	0	1
13	Misc. field/ unspec.	50	67	53	32	32	107	1	9
14	Watchmen	4	0	2	0	2	4	0	0
15	Misc. unemployed	0	1	1	0	0	1	0	0
16	Aged	1	21	14	3	5	17	0	5
17	Young	19	29	0	47	1	27	8	13
18	Women with six children								
19	Runaways	11	7	6	4	8	11	0	7
20	Manumitted								
	Category unknown	59	12	18	28	25	46	14	11

1793

	Category[a]	Male	Female	African	Creole	A/C unknown	Black	Colored	Color unknown
1	Heads and drivers	6	1	6	0	1	7	0	0
2	Domestics	24	34	14	35	9	39	13	6
3	Hospital								
4	Factory craftsmen	10	0	3	5	2	8	2	0
5	Other craftsmen	22	0	9	9	4	18	4	0
6	Factory laborers								
7	Stock workers	9	0	4	2	3	8	0	1
8	Nonfactory, nonfield								
9	First Gang	60	63	72	29	22	121	0	2
10	Second Gang	16	30	36	7	3	46	0	0
11	Third Gang	33	38	41	27	3	69	0	2
12	Fourth Gang	10	12	0	22	0	21	0	1
13	Misc. field/ unspec.	4	2	2	1	3	5	1	0
14	Watchmen	27	0	15	1	11	24	1	2
15	Misc. unemployed								
16	Aged	3	14	12	0	5	16	1	0
17	Young	14	19	0	33	0	21	7	5
18	Women with six children								
19	Runaways	1	0	0	0	1	0	0	1
20	Manumitted								
	Category unknown	52	37	83	3	3	85	1	3

1796

Male	Female	African	Creole	A/C unknown	Black	Colored	Color unknown
17	2	11	5	3	18	1	0
4	11	3	11	1	6	9	0
0	9	7	0	2	8	0	1
11	0	5	4	2	10	1	0
17	0	5	10	2	11	6	0
5	0	5	0	0	5	0	0
31	2	12	9	12	33	0	0
3	1	4	0	0	4	0	0
26	62	48	25	15	84	1	3
12	37	36	9	4	49	0	0
32	29	33	26	2	60	1	0
12	18	1	28	1	25	4	1
27	19	42	3	1	45	0	1
22	0	16	1	5	21	0	1
6	10	10	0	6	15	1	0
16	18	0	34	0	17	8	9
0	2	0	1	1	2	0	0
3	1	2	1	1	4	0	0
3	1	0	3	1	1	0	3

1813

Male	Female	African	Creole	A/C unknown	Black	Colored	Color unknown
16	3	2	16	1	18	1	0
8	13	2	18	1	11	10	0
2	8	4	4	2	9	1	0
16	0	10	6	0	14	2	0
19	0	5	14	0	13	6	0
9	3	5	6	1	12	0	0
0	1	1	0	0	1	0	0
0	7	6	1	0	7	0	0
86	162	102	137	9	245	2	1
19	6	17	5	3	25	0	0
34	51	10	74	1	77	8	0
0	2	1	1	0	2	0	0
0	2	0	2	0	2	0	0
0	4	1	3	0	4	0	0
15	3	12	5	1	17	1	0
0	2	0	0	2	0	0	2

TABLE 47. (continued)

1821

	Category[a]	Male	Female	African	Creole	A/C unknown	Black	Colored	Color unknown
1	Heads and drivers	12	2	2	12	0	12	2	0
2	Domestics	1	14	1	13	1	8	7	0
3	Hospital	0	9	7	2	0	8	1	0
4	Factory craftsmen	12	0	5	7	0	10	2	0
5	Other craftsmen	24	0	6	18	0	20	4	0
6	Factory laborers								
7	Stock workers	2	0	2	0	0	2	0	0
8	Nonfactory, nonfield								
9	First Gang	25	74	61	38	0	99	0	0
10	Second Gang	7	18	0	25	0	25	0	0
11	Third Gang	16	18	0	34	0	34	0	0
12	Fourth Gang								
13	Misc. field/ unspec.	69	83	37	113	2	141	8	3
14	Watchmen	14	0	10	4	0	14	0	0
15	Misc. unemployed	19	43	3	59	0	52	6	4
16	Aged	0	2	2	0	0	2	0	0
17	Young	1	7	0	8	0	7	1	0
18	Women with six children	0	6	2	4	0	6	0	0
19	Runaways	19	1	11	9	0	20	0	0
20	Manumitted Category unknown	2	6	2	6	0	8	0	0

1831

	Category[a]	Male	Female	African	Creole	A/C unknown	Black	Colored	Color unknown
1	Heads and drivers	8	5	1	12	0	10	3	0
2	Domestics	5	11	0	16	0	5	11	0
3	Hospital	1	1	1	1	0	2	0	0
4	Factory craftsmen	7	0	1	6	0	7	0	0
5	Other craftsmen	9	0	2	7	0	8	1	0
6	Factory laborers								
7	Stock workers	2	1	0	3	0	3	0	0
8	Nonfactory, nonfield								
9	First Gang	6	48	3	51	0	52	2	0
10	Second Gang	24	33	1	56	0	55	2	0
11	Third Gang	15	24	0	39	0	34	5	0
12	Fourth Gang	14	24	8	30	0	37	1	0
13	Misc. field/ unspec.	14	2	2	14	0	16	0	0
14	Watchmen	15	0	11	4	0	14	1	0
15	Misc. unemployed	6	13	0	19	0	15	3	1
16	Aged	7	21	16	12	0	27	1	0
17	Young	0	3	0	3	0	3	0	0
18	Women with six children	0	4	1	3	0	4	0	0
19	Runaways	2	2	0	4	0	4	0	0
20	Manumitted Category unknown	0	5	0	5	0	4	0	1

				A/C			Color
Male	Female	African	Creole	unknown	Black	Colored	unknown
7	5	1	11	0	10	2	0
3	8	0	11	0	3	8	0
1	1	0	2	0	2	0	0
7	0	1	6	0	7	0	0
8	0	0	8	0	6	2	0
2	0	0	2	0	2	0	0
12	45	0	57	0	56	1	0
13	28	1	40	0	39	2	0
12	20	0	32	0	27	5	0
12	27	8	31	0	37	2	0
12	1	1	12	0	13	0	0
13	0	7	5	0	1	1	0
1	13	8	6	0	14	0	0
1	0	0	1	0	1	0	0
0	5	1	4	0	5	0	0
1	0	0	0	1	0	0	1
1	0	0	1	0	0	0	1
0	3	0	3	0	3	0	0

1835

TABLE 48. Worthy Park: Employment Mobility; Individuals' Category Changes, for 22 out of 52 Years, 1787-1838

Source: Worthy Park records.

Number of category changes	Number of individuals
0	499
1	222
2	216
3	153
4	107
5	75
6	33
7	25
8	18
9	7
10	5
11	1
12	2
13	1
14 or more	0
Total	1,364

TABLE 49. Worthy Park: Incidence of Runaway and Manumitted Slaves, 1784-1838

Source: Worthy Park records.

Note: Dashes indicate no records survive.

	Runaways						Manumitted	
	African		Creole		A/C unknown		Creole	
	Males	Females	Males	Females	Males	Females	Males	Females
1784	1	0	0	0	1	0	0	0
1785	1	0	0	0	1	0	0	0
1786	2	1	2	0	1	0	0	0
1787	5	2	1	1	2	1	0	0
1788	1	0	0	0	0	0	0	0
1789	1	1	1	0	2	0	0	0
1790	1	0	0	1	0	0	0	0
1791	1	0	0	0	1	0	0	0
1792	—	—	—	—	—	—	—	—
1793	1	0	0	0	0	0	0	0
1794	3	2	0	0	0	0	2	2
1795	—	—	—	—	—	—	—	—
1796	2	1	2	0	1	0	0	0
1797-1811	—	—	—	—	—	—	—	—
1812	6	1	6	0	0	0	0	0
1813	10	2	5	0	0	1	0	0
1814	7	0	4	0	0	0	0	0
1815	4	1	3	0	0	0	0	0
1816	4	2	3	3	0	0	1	0
1817	5	0	3	1	0	0	2	0
1818	3	0	1	0	0	0	0	0
1819	4	0	1	0	0	0	0	0
1820	4	2	1	0	0	0	1	1
1821	10	1	9	0	0	0	0	0
1822	7	3	4	0	0	0	0	0
1823	4	1	2	0	0	0	0	0
1824	4	1	1	0	0	0	3	2
1825-1829	—	—	—	—	—	—	—	—
1830	3	1	9	3	0	0	0	0
1831	0	0	2	2	0	0	0	0
1832	0	0	1	2	0	0	0	0
1833	1	0	0	2	0	0	0	0
1834	—	—	—	—	—	—	9	11
1835	—	—	—	—	—	—	0	0
1836	—	—	—	—	—	—	0	0
1837	—	—	—	—	—	—	0	2
1838	—	—	—	—	—	—	0	0

	Category[a]	1793	1821	1834	Separate years, 1787-1838
1	Heads and drivers	54.7	47.6	51.3	47.3
2	Domestics	35.5	41.0	35.6	33.6
3	Hospital	—	74.1	48.0	56.7
4	Factory craftsmen	37.1	38.5	34.7	35.3
5	Other craftsmen	39.7	35.0	37.5	36.4
6	Factory laborers	—	—	—	34.3
7	Stock workers	35.9	37.5	35.0	32.7
8	Nonfactory, nonfield	—	—	—	43.9
9	First Gang	30.0	36.8	31.9	32.3
10	Second Gang	31.0	17.0	22.6	22.1
11	Third Gang	13.2	13.0	15.4	12.5
12	Fourth Gang	5.8	—	23.8	22.0
13	Misc. field/unspec.	39.0	24.1	35.3	28.7
14	Watchmen	47.8	59.8	56.8	52.6
15	Misc. unemployed	10.0	8.8	8.5	18.8
16	Aged	57.7	64.5	70.8	53.2
17	Young	2.1	4.9	3.0	3.3
18	Women with six children	—	49.3	45.2	47.3
19	Runaways	—	38.0	—	36.7
20	Manumitted	—	—	2.4	7.1
	All categories	26.7	28.0	30.2	28.9

TABLE 50. Worthy Park: Average Ages of Slaves in Employment Categories, 1787-1838, Selected Years and Overall

Source: Worthy Park records.

Note: Dashes indicate categories not used in those years.

[a]As in Fig. 26.

Part Two

Individuals in Slave Society, Selected Biographies

Introduction

ONE of the chief dangers of statistical demography lies in assuming that there is such a person as the Average Man. Valuable though general statistics such as those treated earlier can be, particularly once they are broken down into the smallest possible categories, they are no substitute for the study of individual cases. By an illusionary trick, the individual is sometimes hidden more effectively by statistics than by absolute lack of knowledge. Slaves were no more average than free men, and the additional fact that they wrote even less about their individual experiences should not lead to depersonalization of them any more than of the masses of the free.

The alleged existence of an average family with a fractional number of children is a well-known layman's joke which is doubtless unfair to sophisticated demographers. Yet it is remarkable how often even in academic circles statistics which have little relevance when applied individually are used as proof of group characteristics. For example, the sad fact that approximately one-third of all new slaves died within three years of arriving in the plantations has led one commentator to talk of "five to seven years of useful work" as the norm for all slaves.[1] He might as well have taken into his calculations the even more somber circumstance that probably half of all blacks rounded up in Africa perished before they reached the New World and asserted "three to four years," instead. In individual cases no such averages apply. For many the realities were far grimmer than the worst average expectation. For the eventual survivors of seizure, transfer, and acclimatization, expectations were little worse for slaves than for other inhabitants of the plantation colonies.

Similar pitfalls lurk in the way of assessing most other aspects of slave life. One other example has already been touched on—the fertility of slave women. Pitifully few slaves did, or could, have children, but since as many as a third of the Worthy Park slave women may have had no children at all it could be argued that the fertility of the remainder was quite up to modern Latin American averages. Other examples need further exploration. The incidences of disease, miscegenation, and running away were apparently considerable; but to what degree were the statistics skewed, respectively, by a comparatively few chronically unhealthy individuals, a small class of already miscegenous domestics, a handful of persistent recidivists? Even more subtle: what was the interrelation between such factors as childbearing, health, status, and disaffection? Only the study of individuals can shed much light in these respects.

Yet we must not forget the extent of what we can never know. Even more than the ill-educated local whites, the slaves remained virtually mute. Innumerable absentee planters and visitors wrote about the West Indies, pretending to describe but usually defending or condemning the institution of slavery. In the crevices of their polemics we merely begin to glimpse the slaves as they actually were. We can never know with certainty what the slaves thought, what they felt, even what they *sounded* like.

What snippets remain of the testimony of the blacks themselves are all the more invaluable. Consider, for instance, Oloudah Equiano's reminiscence of the terror and bewilderment of capture and transportation, the momentary relief when in the sugar islands he met compatriots still speaking languages he understood, the sojourn at the well of loneliness once he was settled on an alien soil: "I was now exceedingly miserable, and thought myself worse off than any of the rest of my companions, for they could talk to each other, but I had no person to speak to that I could understand, In this state I was constantly grieving and pining and wishing for death."[2]

In these conditions the slave was not only open to the acculturating effects of the English language but, as Eugene Genovese has recently suggested so brilliantly in *Roll, Jordan, Roll*, was also peculiarly receptive to the solace and catharsis of religion, be it African or Christian.[3] The frequent references of plantocratic writers to *obeah*, *myal*, and *voodoo* take on a new dimension, just as the perspective of the slaves' spiritual life suddenly expands when one reads of the slave Job ben Solomon unrolling his sheepskin to perform his duty to Allah or gathering with his fellow Fulani to discuss the Koran. A similar flash of awareness occurs when, through the medium of a missionary describing the trial of the rebellious Jamaican slaves of 1831, one suddenly hears the authentic voice of the slave leader Samuel Sharp testifying that he believed that it was only the evil intransigence of the Jamaica whites which denied the blacks the word of God and the bounty of the English king.[4]

The testimonies of Equiano the Methodist barber settled in London, ben Solomon the repatriated Moslem, and Sharp the Creole revolutionary were exceptional and random, and may mislead. How different may have been the experience of the mass of slaves who never gave testimony or left any evidence behind? From Lluidas Vale, for example, there is no evidence of missionary activity or of rebellion, there are no records of slave marriages, no remaining slave artifacts, no archeological remains save for the shell of the old hothouse. The argument from absence can be fallacious, but it is surely not so when it is highly likely that what is missing *would* have been recorded, or survived in part, had it ever existed. It is not reasonable, then, to presume that the general atmosphere of Lluidas Vale was one of backwoods isolation, of backwardness in respect of old traditions, and of relative integration?

Certainly there seems to have been a contrast during the period studied in detail between the central interior of Jamaica and the western and northwestern parishes such as Westmorland, St. James, and Trelawny, with their contiguous sugar plantations, elaborate buildings including stone-built slave quarters, burgeoning towns, network of Baptist churches, and relatively sophisticated, ambitious, and quite frequently roaming slaves. Lluidas Vale was locked in by its hills, and two days distant from the nearest town. At Swansea and Thetford, as at Worthy Park, there may have been a contrast between the substantial buildings of the central compounds and the rickety huts of the slave cantonments. Yet, being so far from the trappings of "polite society," the Lluidas whites lived relatively closer to their slaves than elsewhere, in every respect. Many strained to escape, but where save in such an ambiance was the classic slave society likely to be found, rigidly stratified by function, class, and color shade, and in certain senses including the whites as well as the black and colored slaves?

Much can be inferred, but how difficult is certainty when the direct evidence is so meager. The largest question remaining to be answered is whether such an environment as that of the Lluidas Vale plantations was more likely to preserve the African culture than to act as a crucible for creolization. In other terms: in such an obviously closed society, which was likely to be the most dominant influence—Africa, Europe, or the tropical surroundings? Would that so much more direct evidence existed of kinship, folklore, dialect, beliefs, rituals, medicine, music, festivities, and of when and how they changed. The best that can be done today is to extrapolate backwards from the fading oral tradition. This is attempted towards the end of the book, but with decidedly parlous and rather surprising results.

If the evidence for the private lives, the thoughts and beliefs, the world view, of the members of slave society remains obscure, much evidence does remain of plantation life-styles in the record books. Above all, the records allow for individualization: the illustration in the case of a slave community of the commonplace that all societies consist not of "average" persons holding generalized views but of individuals, clearly or subtly different from each other.

The slaves and white members of slave society, then, can be made more visible by studying selected individuals than by reconstructing the Average Man, as long as the principles of selection are sound. Out of over 1,300 candidates at Worthy Park only 34 persons have been chosen here for individual study, and these were by no means selected at random. Eighteen were males, 16 females; 23 black, 8 colored, and 3 white; 21 Creoles, 10 Africans, and 3 British-born—proportions that in no way distort the general pattern. Most concern was shown to discover individuals who among them covered the whole spectrum of activities at Worthy Park, and to choose mainly those about whom much was known. As a result there may be a heavier emphasis upon hardy survivors than upon those who died soon or disappeared quickly from the records. Also, individuals from the last period of slavery, for which the records are fullest, may predominate. There has been, however, absolutely no conspiracy to choose individuals who suggest a Panglossian (or optimistic) rather than a Hobbesian view of slave society (with slaves' lives seen as "nasty, brutish, and short").

Besides the comparatively long-lived, two slaves whose lives at Worthy Park were measured only in months are used to illustrate the appalling number who did not survive long. For each craftsman there are as many ordinary laborers. For each individual who rose up the occupational scale there is at least one who declined in status, and more who stayed much on a level. To set against the notable accommodators to the system, there are those who resisted by withdrawing their labor, running away, or engaging in crime.

Delving into the records of individuals also offers the advantage, not possible through statistics alone, of uncovering some evidence of family kinship. Although fathers are never identified in the records, they can sometimes be guessed. Mothers on the other hand are listed more often than not, and thus it is possible to trace matrilineal lines, even patterns, of kinship. In the many cases of miscegenation traced, whole webs of relationship reappear. By tracing such kinship this biographical approach to Worthy Park's population by no means stops short at the 34 individuals chosen. All in all, some 290 of Worthy Park's slaves and whites are tangentially mentioned[5]—covering just about every major variant in what turns out to be a tightly knit but much more complex society than hitherto thought.

As to ascertainable facts about individuals, all details are given and none invented. The temptation to combine details from different individuals was rigorously resisted. Some license is shown, however, in reconstructing lives where detail is missing, from information obtained elsewhere, including outside the Worthy Park records. For example, when describing the lives of carpenter, blacksmith, and doctor, innumerable references about work methods, tools, materials, and medicines have been garnered from Worthy Park's worksheets, invoices, inventories, and lists of issues, and these woven into the bare biographical details. In a few places such materials have been gathered from the records of similar Jamaican estates, including the daily work schedules at Braco, details of medical treatment from Harmony Hall, and the valuations placed on slaves at Retreat Estate—all, as it happens, in Trelawny parish. In a very few cases, such as those of the two short-lived Africans, Duke and Clarissa, scanty details have been fleshed out from authentic knowledge obtained from relevant outside authorities.

One last word about the layout of the biographies. The following pages chopped into thirty-four sections, with biographies in arbitrary sequence by date of birth or alphabetical order, could be as disjointed as a dictionary. Instead, to aid digestion, the thirty-four biographies are distributed in six chapters, loosely differentiated to avoid distorting the diversity and overall integration of the population. The lives of six Africans (styled *bunga-men* in the Jamaican Creole language) are given first, with Africans in general placed before the Creole-born, and ordinary Creoles before members of the slave elite. The study of patterns of miscegenation and resistance seem both to cohere and contrast quite naturally, so these are grouped together after the studies of more ordinary slaves. The biographies of three *backra* (as white men were called in Jamaican Creole) are given last, as a reversal of the precedence usually given to such men and as an indication of the slight doubt that remains about how closely plantation whites were actually integrated into slave society.

From an ever-widening catchment area by methods increasingly illicit, Africans were captured, shackled, and driven to the coast by other Africans.

6 / Bunga-Men: Six Africans

MANY·of the new Africans acquired by Worthy Park in the 1790s were styled "Congoes"; that is, they came from somewhere in that huge catchment area of equatorial forest drained by the Congo River, between Cape Lopez in the north and the Angolan highlands in the south. Hunters and shifting agriculturalists for the most part, Congoes were the least suitable plantation slaves. Yet their very numbers and cheapness made them desirable in areas of high density and low efficiency such as Brazil, or in the British plantations at a time of declining profits and economies of scale. By 1790, four out of every ten slaves carried by British traders were Congoes or Angolas.[1] The brief lives of two of them are treated first in this chapter devoted to Africans.

Duke (1773-1794) and Clarissa, alias Prattle (1779-1796)

The two slaves named Duke and Clarissa by their first white masters were seized when little more than children, perhaps hundreds of miles in the interior, haltered and herded by forced march and canoe to one of the settlements on the coast—noncolonized Cabinda or Loango, or Portuguese Luanda.[2] There they would have seen ocean, sailing ships, and white men for the first time, objects of terrible legend. Ignorant as yet of their fate, like Oloudah Equiano they would only have known that once the birdlike ships took flight the white men would return but the blacks would not.[3]

The slaves were sold by the caboceers, to the traders, after a "palaver" which fixed their price in trade goods: iron bars, cloth, knives, guns, and rum, worth perhaps £20 a head. Once their wooden halters were replaced by leg irons on a running chain, they were ferried on shipboard, about 400 crammed into a vessel of 200 tons displacement. One morning (at dawn, both to catch the offshore breeze and in an effort to diminish alarm), the slaver would set out on the transatlantic voyage, the infamous Middle Passage—the extreme, and in many cases ultimate, horror of the slaves' lives.

Being far south of the Equator, the slaving captain would normally have made first for the sweltering Portuguese island of Saõ Tomé, to take on food, water, and wood. This would have been followed by a sluggish thousand miles voyage, westward along the Equator to clear the bulge of West Africa, before beating laboriously northwards into the latitudes of the northeast Trades. From there the run down to the West Indies might be quite rapid; but even when the Lesser Antilles were cleared, Jamaica was still another thousand miles to leeward. Altogether, the Middle Passage probably took six months, and the death of a quarter of the Congoes, from smallpox, pneumonia, dysentery, or suicide, would not have been unusual.[4]

Clarissa and Duke were carried in different vessels, probably the *Benjamin* and the *Ann Delicia*, commissioned by the "Portuguese" (Sephardic) Jew Alexandre Lindo of Kingston and his partners. As soon as slaveships entered Kingston Harbour, the traders placed advertisements in the biweekly *Royal Gazette*, such as the following:

> Kingston April 24, 1793
> FOR SALE
> On Wednesday the 8th of May next
> 323 Choice, Young, Healthy CONGO
> NEGROES
> Imported in the ship BENJAMIN Captain Thmas
> Mullineux, from ANGOLA
> LINDO & LAKE[5]

Rose Price, having paid £83 Jamaican Currency apiece for 85 partially seasoned young slaves late in 1792, was looking for cheaper additional recruits. Clarissa was among 43 Congoes purchased for £60 Currency each in May 1793, and Duke one of 63 bought for £57 Currency each two months later. These details can be traced in the deeds of sale recorded in the Island Record Office at Spanish Town.[6]

For the slaves, the bewildering horror of the Middle Passage was succeeded by the depersonalizing regimentation of the estate. Once they reached Worthy Park their chains were struck off, but they were branded on the shoulder with the "LP" (Lluidas Plantation) mark—similar, if smaller, to that still used on Worthy Park's cattle.[7] They were also given arbitrary slave names and taught to obey rudimentary commands in English. Normally, new African slaves, arriving in ones and twos, would be lodged in the huts of seasoned compatriots, who would be expected to act as monitors and train them in plantation ways.[8] But the Congoes of 1792-93 were so numerous that they were kept together as a separate "Mountain Gang," and sent three miles up into the almost African wilderness of the Cocoree Valley under the supervision of 17 ageing or ailing watchmen, at least one of whom was a Congo.[9] At Cocoree, the new Congoes were set to work transforming the bush into the "New Negro Provision Grounds"—clearing and planting in a manner with which they were familiar from Africa, before being trained in the strange tasks of cultivating cane. Significantly, the

The Middle Passage. Few slaves resisted violently; most entered the state of psychic shock, flat apathy, and depression that the Portuguese called banzo. *A lithograph from a rare photograph of slaves rescued by the anti-slavery squadron, about 1850.*

first tool they were issued was a hoe, the second a cutlass, the third a knife.

On arrival, the new Africans were distinguished by their nakedness, but almost immediately they were supplied with the clothing required by Jamaican law—crude, ready-made clothes run up by Creole seamstresses rather than the cloth yardage issued to seasoned slaves. The new men received an osnaburg linen work suit or frock (smock) and trousers and a second frock of woolen baize, the women an osnaburg skirt and blouse. A little later, all newcomers were issued imported felt hats and caps to keep off sun and rain and blanketing as proof against the chill, misty nights of inland Jamaica.[10]

Until their own provision grounds were bearing, the Congoes were provided with a wide variety of food, much of it strange to them. The several hundredweights of yams, plantains, and guinea corn purchased by Worthy Park in 1792 from other estates would have provided familiar fare; but the Congoes would have needed instruction in the preparation of the rice, peas, split peas, and corn flour also issued them. Stranger yet were the salt mashed herrings—often tainted—which provided their sole protein ration, unless they were able to trap agouti or iguana in the Cocoree underbrush. Moreover, as the French war deepened, supplies of imported herrings dried up.

As to housing, the Congoes may have been expected to fashion shelters, African-style, for themselves, but were more likely crammed together into barracks crudely constructed of wattle, daub, and palmetto thatch by Worthy Park's carpenters. Although Rose Price—as a careful manager rather than a humanitarian—did what he could not to starve, overwork, or cruelly abuse his new slaves, ignorance of diet, psychology, and the causes or prevention of epidemic disease savagely curtailed their lives. Thanks to the presence of a doctor familiar with the latest methods, John Quier, all of Worthy Park's new slaves were inoculated against smallpox. But they still died in distressing numbers—from African diseases like yaws, leprosy, and dysentery exacerbated by close contact and poor hygiene, from European afflictions such as pneumonia and tuberculosis, to which they had even less immunity than Creole slaves, and from West Indian afflictions like yellow fever and dengue transmitted by mosquitoes and parasites, to which they had no immunity whatsoever. The worst of all killers were amoebic and bacillary dysentery, the white and bloody fluxes, "beginning with . . . pain in the head, back, shivering, vomiting, fever etc."[11] and leading to almost certain death within a week.

Besides being cool and damp at night, and covered in long grass and dense bush that harbored myriad insects, the Cocoree was made even less healthy by a shortage of water. With no running streams and precious few standing ponds, the Congoes' valley provided no good drinking water and little to spare for the frequent washing and bathing to which the new slaves were accustomed in Africa. In such an ill-drained limestone area, the casual latrine arrangements were also dangerously insanitary. Lluidas Vale itself, once the Congoes were transferred there, was little better.

Of the 90 semiacclimatized Africans bought in 1792, four-fifths survived more than five years at Worthy Park, and 20 for no less than forty years. Yet, of Clarissa's and Duke's two coffles bought straight off the boats, more than half were dead within four years. Their miseries in this period can only be imagined. At least 2 Congoes, Fox and Boston, took a voluntary way out by eating poison.[12] Duke, aged 20, died of the flux on April 24, 1794. Shortly afterwards an alarmed Rose Price took most of the surviving Africans from the Cocoree and sent then twenty-five miles to the lowland, and well-watered, pen at Spring Garden, "for a change of air."[13] Clarissa lived long enough to return to

Worthy Park, to be employed on plantation work in the Second Gang, and to acquire a second name—or nickname—Prattle. But, as with so many of Worthy Park's Congoes, the hope that she was seasoned was premature. She too succumbed to the flux, on August 10, 1796, after three years and three months in Jamaica. She was only 17.

RAVEFACE (1768-1838+)

Although the curiously named Raveface was also one of the new Africans purchased by Rose Price, her fate was very different from that of Clarissa, Duke, and the many others who died before they were seasoned to Jamaican plantation life. Aged only 24 when she arrived at Worthy Park, Raveface was still among the older slaves in the parcel of 90 partly acclimatized Africans with names beginning with R, bought from Sir William Daggers in 1792.[14] That these new recruits were healthy youngsters who had already survived the crucial first months in the new environment—probably in some seasoning pen in the foothills—accounted for the comparatively high price of £83 Currency paid for each of them.

Rose Price was able to shuffle his first large purchase of new Africans almost immediately into Worthy Park working gangs. By 1793 nearly all the large group aged between 10 and 13 were listed in the Third Gang, those aged between 14 and 22 in the Second Gang, and those in Raveface's over-23 age range in the "Big" or First Gang. For at least two years they were mainly employed not in cane cultivation but in the simpler and even more toilsome labors of expanding and improving Worthy Park's fields and increasing the estate's efficiency—clearing and leveling new cane-pieces, carting, splitting, grading, and tamping stones for new internal roads, and constructing the important New Road into the Vale of St. Thomas, cut through forested mountain land.[15]

Among the healthiest of the surviving slaves, Raveface was retained in the First Gang once it concentrated again on planting and reaping cane from Worthy Park's expanded acreage. For over thirty years she was one of the roughly 100 women and 50 men chiefly responsible for raising the estate's sugar production from an average of 300 hogsheads a year in the 1790s to a peak of 700 in 1812. The only substantial break in the annual routine of planting, banking, molding, weeding, cutting, and carrying cane came in 1822, when Raveface was relegated to the Grass Gang, listed as infirm. Yet Raveface was still regarded as a valuable, faithful, and reliable slave. In 1831 she was made Fourth (or Pickney) Gang driveress, a position she held throughout the turbulent months leading to the first emancipation act and for much of the Apprenticeship period. In selecting her for this job, Worthy Park's overseer was doubtless following the advice of Thomas Roughley, the expert on slave management. In the *Jamaica Planter's Guide* (1823), Roughley unctuously described the Children's Gang as a kind of school for life:

The owner and overseer . . . should act the part of a parent, fosterer, and protector, looking on them as the future prop and support of the property. How pleasing, how gratifying, how replete with humanity it is to see a swarm of healthy, active, cheerful, pliant, straight, handsome creole negro boys and girls going to, and returning from the puerile field work allotted to them, clean and free from disease and blemish. . . . Negro children, after they pass five or six years of age, if free from the yaws, or other scrophula, and are healthy, should be taken from the nurse in the negro houses, and put under the tuition of the driveress, who has the conducting of the Weeding gang. It is an unquestionable evil to leave them there after they come to that age, as they imbibe, by remaining there, a tendency to idle, pernicious habits. . . .

An experienced negro women in all manner of field work, should be selected to superintend, instruct, and govern this gang of pupils, armed with a pliant, serviceable twig, more to create dread, than inflict chastisement. I Should prefer a women who had been the mother of, and reared a number of healthy children of her own, to a sterile creature, whose mind often partakes of the disposition of her body; who is stern without command, fractious and severe, with an indifference to impart instruction.

Each child should be provided with a light small hoe, with a proportionate handle to it well fixed. These little implements should always be ground for them, when out of order, by a carpenter or cooper, and kept wedged; they should be furnished with a small knife, and a small basket each, calculated to carry dung. They should be accustomed, in planting time, with those baskets to attend the great gang, and throw dung before them in the cane-holes, which they can do expertly; and by this they will be taught to observe the mode of planting, and putting the cane in the ground.[16]

It is remarkable that Worthy Park's management chose an African rather than a Creole to superintend the gang of children in the very last days of slavery. Raveface, it seems, never became a Christian. Certainly, she was never baptized and was one of the 14 Africans and 28 Creoles (the average age of whom was 42.3 years) who entered freedom with only their single slave name.[17]

By 1837, when she was 69, Raveface was beyond useful work and was at last regarded as a superannuated invalid. She survived, however, at least until full freedom was declared on August 1, 1838, absolving the estate from the responsibility of caring for her till she died. Presumably, in her last years she was looked after by one of her surviving children or grandchildren. By the standards of the other Africans, Raveface was quite fertile. She seems to have been pregnant on arrival at Worthy Park[18] and within nine years, between the ages of 24 and 35, bore four children. She had at least five grandchildren, and many of her descendants are probably still living today, though difficult to trace.

It is significant that all of Raveface's traceable relatives also lived out their lives as field workers, with only temporary exceptions, even after slavery ended. She founded a family, but not one notable for occupational mobility. Rachael, who was a sickly child, was probably employed in feeding cane to the mill, for she was killed on March 27, 1813, by falling into the machinery. Rachael's daughter, Molly, at first called a mulatto, began work as a domestic (1822), but then spent at least the last nine years of slavery working in the fields, where she was listed, implausibly, as a sambo (1830-1838). In 1842 she was still employed, as a cane-carrier. Of Raveface's other children, Sophia spent all her working life in the fields, before expiring of general debility on April 2, 1832, as a member of the Second Gang. George Marshall (Jacob) was in the Great Gang by the age of 16, and for the last years of slavery was a wagoner. In 1842 he was employed at Worthy Park as a plowman, and in February 1846 was listed as a fence-maker. Except for less than a year in the Great House (1822), William Defell (Cupid) followed a similar course, being employed as a home wainman in 1842.

GAMESOME (1774-1838 +)

The starkly simple biography of the second long-lived Congo, Gamesome, can stand as typical of the fate of most surviving Africans: inescapably tied to a life of field labor, varied by little more than the seasonal round, and by the dictates of age and usefulness.

Arriving at Worthy Park in 1793 at the age of 19, in Rose Price's second batch of new Congoes, Gamesome spent at least three years in the Cocoree Mountain Gang, at Spring Garden, and in training at Worthy Park. But around 1797, at the age of 23, she was allocated to the Great Gang. Thomas Roughley described this gang as an "admirable effective force, composed of the flower of all the field battalions, drafted and recruited from all the other gangs, as they come of an age to endure severe labour. . . . They are the very essence of an estate, its support in all weathers and necessities; the proprietor's glory, the overseer's favourite."[19]

The Great Gang—which at Worthy Park contained up to 185 workers—would have been subdivided into several working groups with separate drivers, including one group to perform the hardest manual labor in mills, boiling-house, distillery, and factory yard. The strongest laborers were also needed occasionally to work on the public roads, to cut and haul stone for the lime kilns on Mount Diablo, and to cut and carry wood. However, these tasks were generally allocated to the male slaves, leaving the women laborers to concentrate on true field tasks within the narrowest confines of the estate. As to the field laborers, even in crop time different subdivisions of the Great Gang would be differently employed. But within each group the emphasis was upon simple, monotonous, regimented, easily supervised tasks.

For all field workers the annual routine consisted basically of at least six months of planting and nurturing the cane, and up to six

From ship to plantation. This early eighteenth-century print symbolically illustrates the splitting of slave cargoes and of a black husband from his wife.

months of harvesting. Within one gang three months from August onwards might be spent in hoeing the stiff clay soils, digging the holes or trenches with heavier mattocks, and planting the cane shoots in a mulch of ox-dung, compost, and factory wastes. On an estate with heavy soils such as those in Lluidas Vale, this was regarded as the period of the most onerous work, particularly since it was the rainy season. The following three months might be comparatively easier, spent in banking and molding with hoes the growing shoots of plant canes, redigging drainage trenches with mattocks, cleaning the gullies and margins of the cane-pieces with bills, weeding the plants and ratoons with hoes and cutlasses, and trashing (removing superfluous leaves from) the growing canestalks with cutlasses and bare hands. Beginning in January and carrying on until June or even later, the whole of the Great Gang would be mobilized for harvesting—rhythmically chopping, topping, and trashing the thick stalks, carrying them to the cane-piece intervals and piling them, loading them on the field wains, and feeding them into the mills.

Inexorably the field laborers were conditioned by enforced drudgery to the rigid system and cycle of the sugarcane—so different from the harsh but voluntary life, the seasonless year, of the equatorial African forest. As years were varied only by incidents of drought, flood, and, much less frequently, hurricane, so each day was much like every other. Roused from the Negro houses before dawn by the hooting

204

of conch shells and cracking of whips, the slaves were herded to the fields as the sun began to burn off the mists, around 6:00 A.M. Working in double rows, they were rarely out of sight of the so-called field bookkeeper and never of the whip-wielding black driver. Being more of a threat and symbol of authority than actual goad, the whip was rarely laid on back or legs, and the slaves were encouraged to sing "animating, inoffensive" songs as they toiled.[20] But they were provided with few incentives to work harder than they needed to, and were not even allotted specific daily tasks for fear they would work themselves into dangerous idleness in the afternoons. Consequently the level of their performance —and what was expected of them—tended to decline.

Jamaican laws had standardized the slaves' working conditions since the time of Hans Sloane but had not improved them very much. At nine o'clock field slaves were served a hot breakfast prepared by the field cooks, before working on till a dinner break just after midday. At Worthy Park the slaves were allowed to return to their own cantonment, where they prepared their main meal from the ground provisions they grew themselves and the salt provisions regularly issued by the estate. Within two hours, while the sun was still almost vertical, they were back at work in the fields, kept there often until it was completely dark. In cool or rainy weather (especially when digging cane holes) field slaves were issued rum. During heavy showers they were allowed to take cover under the shelters used by the cooks, and if the rain was exceptionally heavy were even sent back to their huts. Rainwater, particularly on the unprotected scalp, was regarded as one of the most dangerous causes of disease.

Each week slaves were given Sunday to work provision grounds, and, out of crop period, most of Saturday too. But since these excursions into the Plantation Garden or the Cocoree were supervised by the drivers, they were scarcely holidays. Normally there were three holidays a year, at Christmas, "Pickney Christmas" (Easter), and "Crop-Over" (usually early August), at which times there would be traditional music and dancing, gluttonous feasting, and even jollity. At Worthy Park, as on some other estates, the overseer may have allowed, or been forced to turn a blind eye to, the celebration of a secret yam festival, sacred to most Africans.[21]

Gamesome spent about a quarter-century in the Worthy Park Great Gang. Her service in the fields was broken only by the intervals when she was relegated to lighter tasks while bearing children, and by the single brief interlude in 1818 when she ran away from the estate, like most runaways to be recaptured and returned in chains before she had gone very far. In 1824, at the age of 50, she was moved permanently into the Second Gang—employed in such auxiliary tasks as tending the nursery canes, weeding, hoeing, trashing, cleaning gutters, and carrying dry trash to feed the factory fires. Only four years later, worn out, Gamesome was listed as infirm and employed in the Grass Gang. Here she lingered until all slaves were freed in 1838, helping with

205

the lightest plantation tasks—cutting and carrying "hogmeat" and cattle feed, collecting manure and making compost, planting and tending corn, and looking after the small stock: sheep, hogs, and fowls.

Like Raveface, Gamesome entered her second new world, the life of nominal freedom, in old age, with only her single slave name. She was hardly any longer an African, but certainly not a Europeanized Creole. Unlike Raveface she did not found a family, surviving all three of her children. Jeannett, born in 1807, died obscurely in 1823. Blossom, born on July 14, 1812, never rose above the Second Gang, and died, of unexplained causes, on November 29, 1837. Princess, born on February 16, 1817, progressed even less far, perishing as a member of the Third Gang, on June 29, 1833, from "dirt-eating."

REGISTER, LATER CHARLES GRANT (1781-1836)

The life of Register illustrates that while surviving male Africans had a marginally better chance of occupational mobility and assimilation than females their lives too were often dogged with disease and ended miserably in middle age.

Register was barely 10 years old when carried out of Africa. He was first employed at Worthy Park in 1793 at age 12, in the Third Gang of adolescent trainees. At this time nearly half of the Third Gang were "shipmates"—that is, had come to Jamaica in the same slave cargo—a link that was said to be more binding even than common tribal origin.[22] It was usually the owner's policy to mix tribes as much as possible. Thus, especially with those seized as children, it was natural, as memories of Africa faded, to regard life as having properly begun only when experiences were first jointly shared, when the jangling African dialects were subsumed into a synthetic Jamaican Creole.

Like nearly all Africans, Register was destined for mere laboring; but though listed for years as a field worker he was seasonally assigned to the factory as a boiler. Although all those working in the boiling-house might aspire to become under head or even head boiler—the most important and prestigious slaves on any sugar estate—most of them toiled out their lives in the factory on menial tasks.[23] These consisted of setting and stoking the fires at their critical levels, adding lime to the boiling juice, skimming the bubbling crust, ladling successively from receiver to clarifier to copper to tayche—the last and hottest of the evaporating vessels—and then frantically emptying the tayche into coolers at the moment ordained for striking, and finally scooping, or "potting," the granulated sludge into the huge hogsheads for the draining process called "curing."[24]

Boiling-house work was strenuous, hellishly hot, and unhealthy. At Worthy Park, Africans were almost invariably chosen for this work, on the assumption that they would be more used to the heat and humidity, if not the cloying stench.[25] Although protected from wind and rain, factory workers sometimes worked eighteen hours a day and often collapsed from heat exhaustion, even though given extra rations of salt and frequent sustainers of rum. The end of each crop season must have come as a sweet relief, when the factory workers were transferred to such tasks as trimming trash or collecting cords of wood for the factory fires.

Unlike the Africans so far studied, Register became sufficiently assimilated to assume a Christian name. In 1816, the first year he was listed as a factory worker, he took the surname of one of the estate's white managerial staff, being baptized, either then or later, on one of the periodic pastoral visits by the rector of St. John's.[26] As Charles Grant, Register may have found some solace in Christianity for the hardship and pain of his transitory life, but the symbolic acceptance of the master culture would have had little practical value. One of the requirements for promotion to a supervisory post was quite remarkable strength, as well as acceptance and endurance. Register was, like the majority, unlucky. By 1822, aged 41, he was listed as diseased.

The nature of Register's debilitating illness was not specified, but likely it was an African legacy, yaws, complicated by the arthritic bone ache and gouty bloat brought on by cruel working conditions. By 1830, when the number of Africans used to factory work was declining fast, Register was back as a boiler, but now listed as lame. In 1836 he was labeled weakly again and once more relegated to a watchman's role. This time he did not survive, expiring on August 15, 1836, aged 55.

Rebus (1781-1838+)

Sixth of the ten Africans chosen for biography, Rebus was a shipmate of both Register and Raveface, though his career showed several notable points of difference.

Although they came in a single cargo, the slaves of 1792 who were given names beginning with R were not certainly all Congoes like those purchased by Rose Price in 1793. Despite the similarity of their names, the comparative unity of their employment suggests that they may have been a heterogeneous parcel gathered in from various points on the African coast—perhaps on one of those common voyages coasting northwards after a first landfall in Angola. Because he became a stock worker, Rebus may have come from the more northerly latitudes of West Africa, where the Negroes were familiar with domestic stock animals. At least one-third of all Worthy Park's slave pen workers were Africans—possibly Hausa, Fulani (Fulbe), or Mandingoes (Mande).[27]

Arriving at Worthy Park at the age of 11 or 12, Rebus spent at least three years in the Third Gang; but by the time he was old enough for the Great Gang he was listed as muleman, an occupation he held for about twenty-five years. Mulemen were valued specialists, who worked, tended, and even bred the animals which played an important part in the operation of a well-managed estate. Mules were comparatively nimble and were preferred for many tasks to the stronger but slower steers, though their breeding presented problems and they were notoriously difficult to handle. There were penkeepers in Jamaica who specialized in breeding mules for sale, but an economic planter kept donkey stallions and brood mares to breed his own. This seems to have been one of Rose Price's innovations at Worthy Park in the 1790s, during which period a mule pen for 100 animals was built at Rocky Point. At the same time a separate muleteer gang of up to 15 was formed, under a head muleman, and of this gang Rebus was one of the earliest and longest-serving members.[28]

Mules hauled the carts which carried cane from the fields, miscellaneous supplies, and even single sugar hogsheads or rum puncheons. They acted as pannier animals in roadless areas, carrying provisions, wood, and grass. They also often powered the two animal mills in the factory yard, and occasionally were harnessed to plow the lighter soils. Consequently, the life of a muleman like Rebus would have been much less monotonous, as well as more skilled, than that of plain field workers. As others toiled in the canefields, he would either drive mule carts between fields and mills or tend the animals driving the cattle mills in two-hour shifts—with frequent excursions for feed and water. Out of crop, he might be employed attending the plowmen, making and mending tackle, and tending the breeding stock. Often he would be sent into the hills, glades, and provision grounds for wood, fodder, and supplies, though it would be extremely rarely, and under tight control, that he would be sent out of the estate to Spring Garden or Port Henderson with sugar, rum, and molasses for shipment and to bring back supplies.

Mulemen spent most of their lives close to the beasts they worked, though less herded than the majority of their fellow slaves. It was a comparatively healthy life, and until the age of 50 Rebus does not seem to have suffered any major illness. In 1832, however, he was listed as weakly and until the end of slavery was assigned to the role of watchman—probably living in a little hut at Rocky Point to overlook the mule pen, night and day, throughout the year. Rebus outlived Register, and like Raveface entered freedom in 1838 with only a single slave name. Thereafter the records were mute, though Rebus—now christened—many have been one of the few elderly watchmen still employed by Worthy Park in the 1840s.

7 / Conformists: Ten Ordinary Slaves

THE great majority of slaves born on the plantation, and many of the Africans who survived to middle or old age, lived undistinguished lives in conformity with the plantation's rules. Few ever left the locality and fewer rebelled. Most worked quietly, if not industriously, in a limited range of jobs throughout their lives. Exceptional slaves demonstrated qualities that brought them into the small circle of the slave elite. Yet even this limited social mobility, with its small rewards of privilege and perquisite, was circumscribed by the needs of the plantation, the elite slave's usefulness, and his or her fidelity to the system and its code.

Of ten ordinary slaves selected for biography, two Creoles have been chosen first, to illustrate in subtly different versions almost the full extent of occupational and social mobility open to plantation slaves. Unfortunately, research into their lives also demonstrates the frustrations in trying to trace extended kinship patterns for males, even when they were members of the slave elite.

MANUEL, LATER ROBERT BLYTHE (1800-1846+) AND PARK, LATER CHARLES GORDON (1806-1846+)

Manuel was the sixth surviving child of the prolific black Creole slave Sarah, later Sarah Price (1763-1832),[1] a veritable slave matriarch, whose known family connections are illustrated here, to be linked up in Part Three with the "family tree" of one of her modern descendants, Isaac Brown. Because Sarah had already managed to raise five children, Manuel's birth was the occasion of her becoming one of the few Worthy Park slaves excused manual labor under the Jamaican Law of 1787. Transferred permanently from the Great Gang to the Negro houses, Sarah was able to spend more time than normal in bringing up Manuel and her other children. That she was grateful to the ambiguous magnanimity of the Jamaican system and that the tenor of her children's training was complete assimilation are suggested by the facts that Sarah had already had one mulatto child, Dick Richard, and was one of the first of Worthy Park's slaves to be baptized, in December 1813.[2]

Manuel was obviously regarded as a likely lad. In 1816, the year that he assumed the name Robert Blythe, he was taken out of the Second Gang and set to work in the overseer's house. Almost uniquely he was given, and seems to have seized, chances of acquiring a variety of useful skills—and of ingratiating himself with his white masters. Throughout the 1820s he was employed chiefly as a carpenter, under the tutelage of his brother, Dick Richard, head carpenter from 1822 to 1838. Manuel also gained much experience in the factory. In 1830, at the early age of 30, he was appointed to the all-important position of head boiler. In the last three years of Apprenticeship (1836-1838), Robert Blythe was the only male at Worthy Park listed as superintendent,[3] and during this time he would have been as crucially responsible for the estate's total apprentice work force as he had been for all of Worthy Park's sugar production between 1830 and 1836. He relinquished this supervisory role after emancipation, though he continued working as a carpenter at Worthy Park until at least 1846.

Manuel's eventual successor was a slave six years younger, the well-named, since evidently worthy, Park. Born within a year of the slave trade's ending, Park enjoyed few obvious advantages. He was the first child of the teen-aged Amelia (1788-1833), who had been brought to Worthy Park from Spring Garden as an infant, along with her sickly sister, Maxie (1787-1790), and their African mother, Juliet (1758-1826), purchased in 1784. "Spring Garden Amelia" went on to give birth at least five more times between 1807 and 1822; but since she was not fortunate enough to raise all six children, she was never excused field labor. Perhaps for this reason, she became disaffected, running away for well over a year in 1831. She was also diseased, perishing from extensive ulceration (yaws?) on July 15, 1833, aged 45.

Despite his mother's later misfortunes, Park—like Manuel—may have benefited from some kind of family environment, with the added advantage that as an eldest child he gained early a sense of responsibility. He too was recognized for certain qualities while in the Second Gang, and was transferred at the age of 15 to work and be trained in the Worthy Park Great House. In Park's case, however, there seems to have been no opportunity to train him in craftsmen's skills, and for the last decade of slavery he was returned to work as a trusty, energetic, and healthy field laborer. As soon as the slaves were freed he took over the supervisory job of Robert Blythe (who was perhaps too closely associated with slavery's pains and penalties) at the age of 32, remaining as field headman or driver at least until 1846. Unlike Manuel, Park did not acquire a Christian name until the age of 30, in 1836.

In choosing first Manuel and then Park as black supervisors, Worthy Park's owner and overseer were doubtless bearing in mind the qualities outlined in 1823 by Thomas Roughley:

> The most important personage in the slave-population of an estate is the head driver. He is seen carrying with him the emblems of his work and dignity, a polished staff or wand, with prongy crooks on

it to lean on, and a short-handled, tangible whip; his office combining within itself a power, derived principally from the overseer, of directing all conditions of slaves, relative to the precise work he wishes each gang or mechanic to undergo or execute. . . . He should, in any judgement, be an athletic man; sound and hardy in constitution; of well-earned and reputed good character; of an age, and, if possible, an appearance to carry respect; perhaps about thirty-five years old; clean in his person and apparel; if possible a native or Creole of the island, long used to field work, and marked for his sobriety, readiness, and putting his work well out of his hands. His civility should be predominant, his patience apparent, his mode of inflicting punishment mild. He should be respectful to white people; suffering no freedoms from those under him, by conversation or trifling private conduct. It is rare indeed, to find this manner of perfection in a negro; but if you may obtain a combination of most of these virtues; and as to petty vices, always inherent in some measure in human nature, they must be looked over, when not too full of evil.[4]

In order to encourage such a rare Jamaican "Uncle Tom," a politic planter ensured that he should receive every material advantage fitting to his limited station, and turned a blind eye to the exercise of certain prerogatives beyond the bounds of work that in some respects even exceeded the planter's own. Headmen were invariably given the largest issues of clothing (including, at Worthy Park, a broadcloth topcoat), food, and rum, on the tacit understanding that they alone of the slaves maintained some sort of household. Their houses were usually more substantial than those of ordinary slaves, containing several rooms, wooden furniture, and crockery, and often being set in a sizable garden plot.

The notion that slaves, being themselves chattels, could not own property was most obviously fictional in the case of slave drivers. Even planters admitted this.[5] Yet few planters were honest enough to admit that their headmen had slaves to work for them too, both around their yards and in their provision grounds. This practice grew out of the pretext of training newcomers, but even after the ending of the slave trade dried up the flow of recruits the headmen seem to have retained the power to command, and the means to induce, less fortunate slaves.[6] Altogether it was evident that certain elite slaves could quite easily in 1838 move into a minor landowning, employer's role that was simply an extension of practices already initiated informally. It would be remarkable if Robert Blythe and Charles Gordon had not acquired considerable wealth as well as prestige as slaves, and as ex-slaves they were probably among the first to become petty proprietors in Lluidas Vale.

In slavery days it was commonly remarked that certain privileged slaves also practiced polygyny in African style, exercising a kind of preemptive right over nubile black women not already set aside for the plantation's whites.[7] Barry Higman has traced this tendency in the records of Montpelier Estate, St. James Parish;[8] but unfortunately it is impossible to recognize the pattern with any certainty, let alone quantify, in most estate records, including those of Worthy Park. Fathers' names are rarely ascertainable, and mothers seem to have chosen their children's surnames almost as arbitrarily as their "Christian" names. In any case it is likely that the polygyny of privileged males was doomed when the end of formal slavery cut directly into the power of the headmen. After slavery ended, formal marriages, monogamous families, and children bearing their fathers' surnames did gradually become more common. Yet they never became general, and even today casual relationships, technical illegitimacy, and children brought up by mothers or grandmothers in fatherless homes are the rule in rural Jamaica. It is also still common for long-established headmen on sugar estates to be the reputed father of innumerable children.[9]

All in all it is unlikely that the life-style of Charles Gordon after 1838 differed substantially from that of Robert Blythe before slavery ended. Although direct lines of descent have proved impossible to trace, both probably founded dynasties, albeit almost anonymous, in Lluidas Vale.

DUNCAN, LATER JOHN VINNICOMBE (1775–1838 +)

Duncan was a long-lived Creole whose career was as varied as that of Manuel, but who, probably for health reasons, never rose to the status of the slave elite. Born in the first year of the American War of Independence, like all very young slaves he began work in the Pickney Gang at the age of 6. By the time he was 16 he had progressed to the Second Gang, but was variously employed as muleman and waiting boy around the Great House rather than as an ordinary field laborer.

This was the period when the young Rose Price and his tutor-companion from Oxford and the Grand Tour, the Reverend John Vinnicombe, were in residence at Worthy Park and living in the planter's traditional high style.[10] Between 1792 and 1795, there were no less than 30 domestics in Rose Price's household, with up to 25 more slaves engaged in clearing a park and garden round the rather modest Great House.[11] This was an establishment similar to, but even grander than, that described by Edward Long in 1774 as typical for resident Jamaican planters: "1 Butler; 1 Coachman; 1 postilion; 1 helper; 1 cook; 1 assistant cook; 2 footmen or waiting-men; 1 key or store-keeper; 1 waiting-maid; 3 house-cleaners; 3 washer-women; 4 seamstresses. In addition, if there were any white children, each child had a nurse and each nurse her assistant boy or girl."[12]

Duncan would have been chosen as waiting boy because he was of good appearance and cleanly and demonstrated qualities of quickness and fidelity. His duties would seldom take him into the house itself (largely a feminine preserve), but would include odd jobs and errands, help with the cleaning of plate, harness, and guns, and the grooming of horses. He would also have waited upon the master and his friends

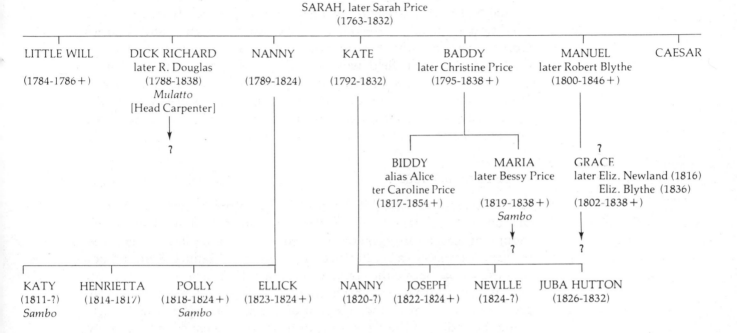

Figure 31. A Slave Matriarch: The Family of Sarah Price, 1763-c.1900

when they went out shooting for duck or baldpate pigeon, or into town in the coach-and-four. Occasionally he may have worn livery, and his normal clothing and food were rather better than those of ordinary slaves.

After they had worked as domestics, few slaves returned to field work, and Duncan was not exception to the rule. When the establishment of the Great House was reduced in number on Rose Price's return to England, Duncan was set to work as a sawyer, spending the twenty-five years of his maximum strength in the strenuous tasks of felling timber, sawing planks, boards, and beams, and making lathes and fencing. In 1821, however, he was seriously ruptured, and after being listed for two years as tradesman—jack-of-all-trades around the central compound—he was relegated once more to work in the Great House stable, at the age of 48. Here his role was keeping the tackle ready for the occasional visits of the attorney and against the increasingly hypothetical return of Rose Price.

It was in 1824, shortly after his return to the Great House, that Duncan was christened, significantly choosing the name of the Cornish clergyman whom he had served more than a quarter-century before.[13] Between 1830 and 1832 this black John Vinnicombe was still called a domestic, but his days of even limited usefulness around the house were numbered. In 1833, at the age of 58, he was made a watchman, listed by 1837 as weakly. By the last year of Apprenticeship, even the light though unending duties of guarding the houses and fields against thieves and animal pests were too much for Duncan, and he was last recorded in the apprentice records as unemployed and moribund.

Even more than most of the slaves of 1838, Duncan/John Vinnicombe had neither strength nor prestige to gain much from the novel condition of nominal freedom. Unlike Robert Blythe and Charles Gordon, he had neither kin nor many descendants, as far as the records disclosed. A female field worker and a cattleman surnamed Vinnicombe were employed at Worthy Park in 1842 and 1843, Joanna and James, and these may have been Duncan's children;[14] since that time the somewhat exotic surname seems to have disappeared from Lluidas Vale and Jamaica as a whole.

KENT (1807-1838+)

Not all slaves could exhibit the qualities or enjoy the good fortune of Manuel and Park, and Kent was even less fortunate than Duncan. Although at least a third-generation Creole whose grandmother enjoyed the same privileges as Sarah Price, the mother of Manuel, Kent did not promise to rise above the status of ordinary field worker. In general, like all blacks born after 1800 his chances were poor. Creoles were now greatly in the majority and competition for specialist jobs was keener, while the ending of the slave trade in the year of Kent's birth abruptly cut off the potential supply of African field laborers. Yet Kent was also unlucky. When only 24 he lost a leg in an accident and was condemned to a role constricted by his limited usefulness, to which even freedom did not offer any improvement.

Kent was the oldest child of the long-lived field slave Belinda (1758-1832), doctor's midwife in 1791, who was later excused work for having borne and bred six children. Entering the field labor force as soon as he was 6, Kent demonstrated his health and usefulness by rapid promotion. He was already listed in the Third Gang by the time he was 7, in the Second Gang by the age of 15, and in the Great Gang well before 1830, when he was 23. Then in 1831 disaster struck. After an accident with a field wain Kent's right leg was amputated. At first he was employed as a muleman, but even tending the animals and sitting in the cane cart proved too much for a one-legged man. After only a year he was relegated to the role of watchman.

Kent was a watchman throughout the period of Apprenticeship. Theoretically he performed a useful function for the estate, particularly in that restless period between full slavery and ostensible freedom; but his effectiveness was clearly curtailed by his lack of physical mobility. Set to live in a hut on the edge of the fields or provision grounds, his was an isolated and tedious life. Expected to be vigilant twenty-four hours a day, seven days a week, he and his pack of mongrels were employed in catching cane-piece rats, "freebooting hogs" from the slaves' pigsties, and also the slaves who came from neighboring estates or Worthy Park itself to steal cane or provisions—on the principle expressed in the old proverb, "Massa grass, massa horse, massa self."[15]

Watchmen were expected to patrol and mend boundary fences, and at Worthy Park they were also set to make rope, baskets, and pads for mules. They were armed with a cutlass, provided with candles and flints, issued with different provisions at different times from the other slaves, and even granted a regular rum allowance.

Potentially the separation of the watchmen from the other slaves allowed for a certain freedom in their lives, but only if the overseer were not vigilant and the watchmen were young, fit, and energetic enough to benefit from the lack of supervision. Thomas Roughley particularly cautioned against an unreliable head watchman. "If such a person is not looked after," he wrote in 1823, "he spends the greater part of his time gadding about; working a distant ground of his own; harbouring runaway slaves, whom he cheaply hires to perform some work for him; or perhaps takes an effective mule off the estate, to carry some provisions with dispatch to market. This is a bad example to the slave population, who are ever prone to catch infection of this kind."[16]

To guard against such slackness, Roughley recommended that head watchmen be compelled to visit and check on the station of each subordinate watchman at least once a day, to report daily at breakfast time to the overseer for orders, bringing with him the ratcatchers with evidence of their catch, and to patrol the entire boundary of the estate once or twice a week.

Even if at Worthy Park the overseer exercised less of the zeal and percipience enjoined by Thomas Roughley, the liberty enjoyed by the head watchman would obviously not have extended to a one-legged underwatchman. It was, indeed, the common practice to employ as watchmen only those men too old, feeble, or disabled either to labor or to take advantage of the absence of supervision—slaves who would have been expendable if not protected by Jamaican slave law. On most estates watchmen were commonly valued at a quarter the price of healthy field slaves. Even the head watchmen at Worthy Park was regarded as worth half as much as an ordinary tradesman.

A wily head watchman who had worked his own grounds and clandestinely made money would have moved more comfortably than most slaves into the condition of full freedom in 1838—if he were not too old. For Kent, however, the inability to escape vigilance, to move around, or work land while a slave, gave him no opportunities to prepare for the practicalities of an independent life. Although still only in his 30s he was not employed by the estate after 1838, when the number of watchmen was cut to a bare minimum. Thus for at least one slave the cutting off of the provisions and clothing which his owner had been forced by law to provide, followed perhaps by expulsion from his hut on the estate, may have meant that emancipation was nothing short

Authentic slave portraits are rare indeed. These hitherto unpublished sketches unflinchingly depict slaves in their humdrum daily lives.

of a personal disaster. As to what actually happened to Kent after 1838 —whether, for example, he had managed to build up a family which could help him survive—the records, unfortunately, are silent.

LITTLE ABBA, ALIAS YABBA (1749-1829), AND WHANICA, LATER LUSTY ANN SERVICE (1774-1838+)

The lives of two female slaves, Little Abba an African, Whanica a Creole, demonstrate how skilfully the estate managed to squeeze out useful work while their slaves were in decline through age or sickness.

Abba, whose Akan name suggests that she was born somewhere in the region of modern Ghana on the fifth day of the week, had been brought to Worthy Park around 1770, one of the steady trickle of recruits needed to keep up numbers in the face of natural decrease. By the time the surviving records begin she was recorded as a field slave, but already lame in her thigh. When the work force was carefully "ganged" by Rose Price in 1793, she was allocated to the Second Gang as bandy legged—an indication that as a child, either in Africa or Jamaica, she had suffered from rickets, caused by vitamin D deficiency.

By the time she reached her 60s, Abba was no longer capable of field work, and between 1813 and 1814 she was listed as "nurse . . . attending on the children." In 1816, apparently on her last legs, she was

again employed as a children's nurse, though weakly. These duties entailed minding and feeding the infants (either in the fields or back in the Negro houses) from the time their mothers were sent back to work until they entered the Pickney Gang, at the age of 6.

Only in 1823, when she was 74, was Abba listed as a superannuated invalid. In fact she lived on for a further six years, to be for a long time the estate's oldest inhabitant. During this very last period, Worthy Park was still responsible by law for supplying Abba with adequate food and clothing, though the amounts issued were cut to a minimum—approximately a third of those given to nursing mothers. From the records it seems likely that Abba, like so many African slave women, had no children who survived her.

Whanica—whose African-sounding name may in fact have been a corruption of Juanita—was also not born at Worthy Park, though seemingly she was a Creole.[17] She was purchased by John Price of Penzance in March 1787 at the age of 13, in a parcel of 30 slaves costing £ 67 Currency apiece.[18] Between 1787 and 1791 Whanica was listed simply as a field girl, but by Rose Price's reclassification she was placed in the Second Gang in 1793. One of the healthiest of Worthy Park's slaves, she toiled in the Great Gang from 1796 until at least 1825, though frequently excused work for a few weeks while bearing children: Foster in 1803, Hector in 1805, Fidelia in 1808, Yorky in 1814, and Pussy in 1821 (born when Whanica was 47).

Whanica, however, did not gain a remission from toil by successfully raising the arbitrary number of children decreed by law. She was eventually relieved of field labor sometime before 1830 only because of declining strength. Like Abba she was appointed nurse, but working in the hospital (or hothouse, as it was called) rather than as a mere attendant of children. Apparently she was one of those elderly females, without any proper training and whose death would not be regarded as a serious blow to the estate, who were employed to feed and clean the sick and carry out the simple medication prescribed by the white doctor on his periodic visits. Whanica seems to have made a success of her hospital job, for between 1832 and 1836 she was accorded the superior honorific of doctoress.

The period after the deaths of the far-famed Dr. John Quier and of his black doctor assistant, William Morris,[19] was probably one in which Worthy Park suffered from a succession of less efficient and humane practitioners, and the ministrations of even an unqualified doctoress were vital. Thomas Roughley, though he called the black practitioners "a most fearful fraternity" who could "promote and establish an infinite number of disorders," admitted that they might also "do a great deal of good." Obsessed by the planter's fear of being poisoned or sabotaged by his slaves, he recommended that dangerous drugs should be kept out of the hands of the black doctors, and that they be limited to "a few doses of glauber salts, sulpher, rhubarb, castor oil, camphorated spirits, bitters and plaisters to dress sores and make blisters of, with two or three lancets, a pair of scissors, and spatula."[20]

Fearful of "black arts," Roughley also deplored many of the unregenerate African practices of midwives and nurses, though in view of the primitive nature of contemporary European pharmacopoeia, and such medical practices as leeching, cupping, blistering, and vomiting, it is quite likely that African and Creole "bush medicine" was medically preferable—not to mention actually preferred by the patients themselves.

Whether Whanica relied chiefly upon the medical wisdom of Africa or Europe, it may be significant that it was during her years as doctoress that she was baptized, acquiring on February 1, 1835, the splendidly appropriate name of Lusty Ann Service.[21] Advancing age or illness, however, made her eventually unsuitable for hothouse work, and in 1836, aged 52, she was turned out into the fields once more—now employed not in mixing and dispensing medicines but as a field cook. It was in this capacity that she, along with the other adult slaves, was freed on August 1, 1838.

AMELIA, LATER AMELIA PARKER (1784-1838+), AND ELSEY (1784-1831)

Had all female slaves been as healthy and fertile as Amelia and Elsey, twin sisters, and their mother, Betty Madge, planters would have been justified in believing that it was "cheaper to breed than to buy," the slave trade might have ended long before it did, and the years between 1807 and 1838 would not have seen a distressing net decline in the slave population. Daughters of a slave who herself produced at least six children, Amelia and Elsey bore six children each, nine of whom grew up to be adults, and seven outlived slavery itself.

Unfortunately the suspicions that such slaves as Amelia, Elsey, and Betty Madge were regarded simply as valuable breeding stock, and that a large number of children implied neither a strong sense of family nor much social mobility, are suggested by the facts that mothers and children shared eight different surnames, and that all but one lived out their working lives as field laborers.

The birth on July 16, 1784, of Amelia and Elsey to Betty Madge, probably herself a Creole, is one of the earliest records in the surviving Worthy Park slave books. Only one other child of Betty Madge is traceable in the records, Sukey (1781-1830); but in 1789 the mother was listed as unemployed, "having many young children." Later she was officially recorded as being excused work for having six children living, and in 1793 Rose Price noted that she was "to go among those free."

Amelia, who was also called Big Amelia or Betty's Amelia before being christened Amelia Parker in 1838, went with her twin steadily through the sucessive field gangs: to the Pickney or Grass Gang in 1790, the Third Gang in 1793, the Second Gang around 1800, and into the Great Gang by 1815. Her six children, all of whom survived, were born between 1805 and 1818 while she was between the ages of 21 and 34. Presumably as each was born—or, rather, survived the critical first few weeks—Amelia was given the special reward of six yards of Dacca cloth and a dollar decreed by Rose Price. With the birth of Floss in 1818 she emulated her mother in being excused all manual labor.

Amelia's usefulness to the estate, however, was by no means ended. From 1830 until 1836 she was listed as midwife, presumably chosen for her notable success in bearing and bringing up her own children. As in Africa, midwives were highly respected members of the community. For obvious reasons they were also regarded as of crucial importance to the estate. Yet their methods were a mystery, particularly to the planters. Successes added to their popular authority, while the blacks tended to be fatalistic as to their failures. The planters, on the other hand, ungenerously attributed successes to luck, while at the same time using midwives as scapegoats for infant mortality.

African though her methods probably were, Amelia possessed no magic touch. For reasons quite beyond her control, the last years of slavery saw little improvement in infant mortality and an actual decline in the plantation birthrate. Yet it was probably ill-health rather than lack of success which brought Amelia's job as a midwife to an end. In 1837 and 1838 she was listed as an unemployed invalid, though only 53 to 54 years old.

Figure 32. "Breeding
Slaves": The Families of
Betty Madge, Amelia, and
Elsey, c.1740-c.1890
Note: f = field worker

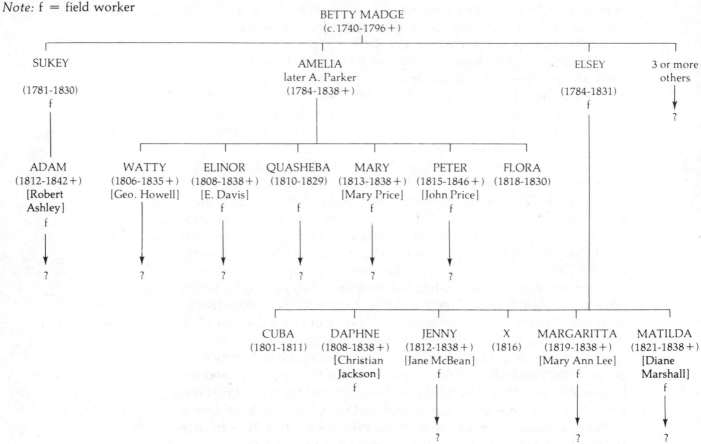

Elsey was as fertile as her twin sister, but far less lucky in her health and that of her children. She had her first child, Cuba, at the age of 17, five years before Amelia's Watty was born; but the little girl was subject to fits and died at the age of 10. Between the ages of 17 and 37 Elsey bore six children in all, but since never more than· four were alive at any one time she did not come close to being excused manual labor. Accordingly she spent the bulk of her working life in the field gangs, though unable to maintain her place in the Great Gang for more than a dozen years. Like so many slaves, Elsey suffered from progressive ulceration. Around 1825 she was demoted to the Second Gang and, in 1831, the last year of her life, was only fit to attend to the fowl house. She died on December 21, 1831, ostensibly of influenza, but also listed as diseased—at the age of 47.

Two years before Elsey died no less than nine of the ten surviving children of Betty Madge's twins were working as field laborers. The facts that none were colored, and that eight of the ten were females, were not irrelevant. The one exception to the pattern was Amelia's eldest child, Watty, who, though he progressed through each of the field gangs, had become a cooper by 1830, and in 1835 was actually able to buy up his apprenticeship.

DOROTHY (1729-1823) AND COUNSELLOR'S CUBA (1729-1796 +)

Two female slaves, Dorothy and Counsellor's Cuba, were chiefly distinguished by living to great age. Dorothy, an African, lived to be 94, the oldest slave of whom there is record at Worthy Park. Cuba, born in the same year, did not live nearly so long; she was a Creole, whose birth at Worthy Park, shortly after sugar production started, is the earliest that can be definitely corroborated from the records.

It is not known when Dorothy was brought to Jamaica and Lluidas Vale, but it was almost certainly before the Seven Years' War (1756-1763). When her occupation was first listed in the surviving Worthy Park plantation books, in 1787-1789, she was described as a field laborer, but already elderly and weakly. Thereafter she was variously employed as field cook and nurse—feeding one of the gangs and looking after the infants carried by their mothers to the field. In 1793, when all the estate's colored domestics were concentrated in the Great House to care for Rose Price, Dorothy was drafted to help out in the bookkeepers' house. In the following year, after disease had decimated the labor force, however, she was back in the fields, employed cutting grass and "pulling hogmeat" (collecting green fodder for the hogs) in the Fourth Gang. Already she was too old for even these lightest of all gang tasks, and in 1796 at the age of 67 she once more became field cook, to the Third Gang. When heard of again in 1813 Dorothy was employed once more as nurse, though between 1814 and 1816—already by far the oldest Worthy Park slave—she was unemployed. Remarkably, she lived on a further seven years, until November 18, 1823. Yet almost incredibly, in 1821 and 1822, at an age when even today most women would need full-time geriatric nursing care, she was herself officially employed as nurse. Dorothy's record is scarcely less notable than that of Henry Byndloss, a slave on neighboring Swansea Estate, who was baptized at Thetford on December 5, 1811, and said to be 105 years old.[22]

When Dorothy came to Worthy Park, Counsellor's Cuba had already grown to adult life upon the estate. Described as a Creole 65 years old in 1794, she was almost certainly one of the two girls called Cubba (presumably because they were born on a Wednesday) listed in the will of Colonel Charles Price in 1730, and daughter of the senior male slave called Counsellor, also listed there.[23] That Counsellor's Cuba was one of only a handful of slaves identified by father rather than by mother implies either a high value attached to continuity in the estate or some special distinction in her father—perhaps borne out by his very name.[24]

Counsellor's Cuba was one of the first generation to whom Worthy Park was their whole life—who did not experience a life straddled between Africa and Jamaica. Nearly all the slaves among whom she was brought up had been in the gangs which had first cleared the estate for sugar cane, erected and started the first mill and factory, and pioneered the painful long route to the coast. Yet it was the slaves like herself who were born on the estate once it was already established who were most tied to it and to plantation life. Cuba's memories and the landmarks in the history of Worthy Park in its eighteenth-century heyday were coincident. To such a long-lived slave, her coming of age, falling in love, the birth and growth of her children, the death of family and friends, would have been marked by such events as the hurricanes of 1744, 1780, 1784, the famine and unrest accompanying the wars of 1739-1748, 1756-1763, and 1775-1783, the building of the great aqueduct and water wheel in the 1750s, the rebuilding of the Great House, the opening up of the Cocoree, and the construction of new roads.[25] Cuba was too young to have remembered Colonel Charles Price, the son of Worthy Park's founder. But she must often have seen the two famous Sir Charles Prices, father and son, both speakers of the Jamaican Assembly, who managed and partly owned the estate. Although the politicking of these grandees was beyond the ken of ordinary slaves, the showy trappings of their power were not. Above all it was sure to be known that Sir Charles Price the elder was in the habit each year on his birthday of freeing the slave who had most distinguished himself by hard work and fidelity. In such ways were the "right kind" of Creole slaves bred.[26]

When first heard of in Worthy Park's plantation books, Cuba was a seamstress. Between February 1784 and January 1785 alone, she was issued 114 yards of osnaburg to make coats, frocks, and trousers for new Negroes, and 58¼ yards of blanketing to make 39 kneeling pads. In particular, on June 16, 1784, she was given 12 yards of osnaburg to make trousers for the four new Africans, Falmouth, Homer, Sam, and Phillip, and 16½ yards to make 6 frocks, and on July 16 she was given 5¼ yards to make a single frock for Dutchess.

A valued slave, Cuba was listed from 1787 as attached to the overseer's house, and in 1793 to the bookkeepers' house,[27] where she would briefly have lived and worked alongside Dorothy. That Cuba was excused manual labor or field work may have been owing to her skill with the needle or because even by 1787 she was listed as elderly and weakly. More likely, however, it was because she had borne and raised six children, though this fact was not recorded until 1794 (when she was 65), and none of her children is certainly known.[28] In 1794 and 1796 Cuba was also laconically listed as not able, though the actual record of her death is missing.

8 / Specialists: Five Slave Craftsmen

TO a degree that most planters denied, Jamaican sugar plantations were dependent even more on specialist than on laboring slaves. Because of the shortage of white artisans, black or colored slaves came to perform vital tasks that in an earlier period had been given to indentured white servants or, in other colonies such as Barbados, still generally went to the poorer free whites.

Planters attempted to disguise the indispensability of their slave artisans and craftsmen by decrying the quality of their work and restricting them as far as possible. Plantation ironwork, woodwork, and masonry were functional rather than elegant, and Jamaican furniture, for example, where it was not imported, had none of the delicate refinement found in the North American colonies. Yet the craftsmen's importance could not be entirely hidden from those who were, inevitably, among the most sophisticated slaves. This explains the real, if limited, degree of superiority enjoyed by slave craftsmen and specialists. However, the frustrating restrictions they suffered also help to explain why it was these slaves who often led the rest in the later slave plots and revolts.

Craftsmen were vital to the efficient running of an estate, but they lacked the mobility of such specialists as road wainmen and were rarely unsupervised. In choosing them, the managers were therefore even more concerned with skills than with fidelity—a factor that helped to undo the masters in western Jamaica in the Christmas Rebellion of 1831, when it was such assimilated and skilled slaves who provided the rebel leadership. However, a well-ordered estate such as Worthy Park (which, incidentally was scarcely affected by the Christmas Rebellion) chose its craftsmen slaves for confidentiality, as well as skills.

MAY, LATER ROSE PRICE (1771-1824)

Born at Worthy Park in 1771, May passed through the first three field gangs, to become wainboy at the age of 18. He must have shown an aptitude for this specialist occupation, for under Rose Price's reorganization he was made head road wainman in 1794, at the early age of 23—a position he held until his sudden death thirty years later.

Most of the long-lived slaves so far looked at in detail suffered a double decline in their later years, gradually losing whatever position of importance or prestige they had attained as the estate tailored their job to their diminishing fitness. In contrast, May, who occupied one of the most sought after and prestigious jobs at Worthy Park and even took his owner's name, died at the height of his powers.

Specialist cattlemen tended the draft oxen and mules in the pens, and mulemen were often in attendance when their animals were being used for pulling carts and wains. Yet the wainmen were expected to be able to manage mules when necessary and were regarded as experts in handling the stolid oxen. Similarly, though major repairs to the wains were carried out by carpenters, coopers, and blacksmiths (who may have made the vehicles in the first place), wainmen were expected to carry out minor repairs, as well as maintain the oxbows, yokes, cattle chains, and rudimentary harnesses made of rope. Head wainmen, provided with padlocks and keys, were responsible for all the wagonage stored in the cattle mill yard—which in 1813 consisted of six cane and three road wains with their tackle, one spare new wain and another being repaired, a "truck," three wheelbarrows, two handbarrows, two new wagon wheels, and a grindstone.[1]

Of all wainmen, the road wainmen, or wagoners, were the elite. Theirs was the critical task of getting the processed muscovado and rum down to the coast without undue waste or spoilage—a journey of up to thirty-five miles, taking at least two days. Although arduous, the job was valued for providing a licit opportunity of leaving the narrow confines of Worthy Park, though no wainmen could venture out without a ticket-of-leave signed by the overseer, specifying job, time, and distance.

Until 1794 the only route for the sugar wains was over Point Hill to Old Harbour Bay, entailing a stiff pull to 2,000 feet within six miles, followed by a serpentine twenty-mile downgrade, with overnight stops at Guanaboa Vale and Spring Garden, three miles from the wharf.[2] The opening of the New Road by Rose Price in the year that May became head road wainman lowered the summit over which Worthy Park sugar was hauled but lengthened the journey to the coast to thirty-five miles. Though the shoulder of Mount Diablo crossed by the wains was less than 1,800 feet high, this involved a climb of 650 feet in under two miles, followed by a drop of 1,000 feet in a further five miles. The wains carrying three or four hogsheads of almost a ton apiece over this stretch, would likely be pulled by eight yoke of oxen—sixteen beasts— all hitched to the front on the steep upward climb, but four yoke each, fore-and-aft, on the dangerous descent into St. Thomas-ye-Vale. The noise would be heard from afar—lowing oxen, shouting men, groaning wheels, with the explosive crack of May's long ox-whip and the periodic hoots of the conch shell warning other traffic to pull to one side.[3]

Leaving Lluidas Vale at dawn, the wains would come by evening to the Price's pen at Mickleton, just south of the present Linstead, where the road began to ease. Here men and oxen would rest overnight, and at least two oxen were unyoked and left for the return journey. At daybreak the next morning began the second and longest stage. Half of this was through the twisting gorge of the River Cobre, where the Vale of St. Thomas debouches on the southern coastal plain. At the height of the sugar crop, the line of sugar wains through this defile was almost continuous. With only two or three places to pass, jams and delays were frequent. A particular bottleneck was the famous Flat Bridge near the southern end of the gorge, where flash floods occasionally swept away wains and dozens of oxen.[4]

Once out of the Sixteen Mile Walk at Angels, the going was easy. But it was still ten miles through Spanish Town to the warehouse and dock at Port Henderson. Had they been delayed, May might have driven men and animals through the night, or else pitched camp only when darkness fell. An encampment close enough to the teeming yards of the Spanish Town slave quarter would have been popular with the up-country men, despite the danger of being caught breaking curfew or found anywhere at any time without a master's pass. In contrast, Port Henderson had no distractions, being simply a shipping point on the barren west shore of Kingston Harbour, faced by the tantalizing lights of Port Royal and Kingston itself, across the water. It is not surprising that, throughout Jamaica, road wainmen were among those who most frequently ran away.[5] However tightly controlled and scared of penalties for running away, road wainmen nevertheless made many contracts and were responsible for considerable clandestine commerce. They were also the plantation slaves' best source of information about events in the world outside.

During May's tenure, the revolutionary war in Haiti, the Second Maroon War, and the intermittent crises of the Napoleonic and second American wars occurred. It was especially vital for security that the head road wainman, above all, should be faithful and reliable. That he held his position uninterruptedly for so long, and in 1811 could choose without objection the baptismal name of Rose Price,[6] suggest that May was quite exceptional in the degree of his fidelity and assimilation. Being a kind of supercargo on the sugar wains, May was possibly also to a certain extent literate—which would have made him a rare slave indeed.

Though there was very occasionally need to send to the coast or the towns for supplies in the second half of the year, the special role of road wainman was, in general, seasonally confined to the period of the sugar crop. Some road wainmen might be assigned to help with the tasks of shifting stones, clay, lime, wood, manure, and grass, in which home wainmen were engaged out of crop. In due course their traditional out-of-crop employment was as plowmen.[7] Worthy Park's owners, like the majority of planters, however, were for a very long time reluctant to use the plow. This was only partly because soils and

225

Wielder of ambiguous authority at the summit of the slave elite: black slave driver in the field.

cane-planting methods were not ideally suited to plowing. Though they made the plea that blacks lacked the intelligence to adapt to such a skill, many planters felt that skilled plowmen might become independent through proving invaluable. They also feared that greatly increased efficiency in the out-of-crop period might release too many slaves into dangerous idleness. Rose Price in the 1790s was the first at Worthy Park regularly to take the risk of plowing, though it did not become at all common till the 1830s. It was yet another mark of the trust reposed in May that he was one of the first Worthy Park slaves listed as plowman, in 1794.[8]

Extremely hard working and apparently very fit, the black Rose Price died suddenly on May 28, 1824, probably of a heart attack, at the age of 53. Of all Worthy Park's slaves he had doubtless been among the most content. In a sense, however, he was fortunate that he died before economic conditions deteriorated and the loyalty of even the most assimilated of slaves was sorely tried by planters and managers who felt themselves increasingly under economic and political siege.[9]

ADAM, LATER WILLIAM PARKER (1774-1830)

Adam was black, and at least one of his predecessors as head carpenter was African. Craftsmen, however, by the end of slavery were almost exclusively Creoles and a high proportion were also colored—by definition among the most assimilated of slaves. Adam's career illustrates not only the normal method of training craftsmen but also the growing preference for colored slaves as craftsmen.

Adam was born at Worthy Park in 1774 and was taken out of the fields at the age of 13 to become a "Boy Carpenter, Learning." At this time the head carpenter—his teacher—was the aged African with the name so common among assimilable slaves that it became a by-word: Quashie.[10] After an apprenticeship of at least five years Adam was listed in 1793 simply as carpenter, succeeding to the position of head carpenter some time between Quashie's death (from tetanus) in 1796 and 1813.

Of all the craftsmen's jobs on a sugar estate that of carpenter involved the largest number of different tasks and skills, of which the head carpenter had to be master of all. One carpenter might specialize in the building and mending of wains and their tackle, another regularly employed in odd jobs such as making boxes, coffins, window frames, and guttering. Occasionally, the special ingenuity of the head carpenter would be called upon for unusual jobs, such as constructing a coffee barbecue or weather vane, or mending the factory coolers and the wooden parts of the mills. In a country where all bricks had to be imported, and in a locality where the stone was not ideally suited for building, the most common activity of estate carpenters was the making and mending of buildings, nearly all of which were constructed almost entirely of wood. For example, between 1787 and 1788 the Worthy Park carpenters built a new millhouse, first shaping and mortising the frame and rafter timbers received from the sawyers, then fixing the laths for the mason to plaster, and finally tacking the cedar-wood shingles in place.

During Rose Price's residence, the Worthy Park carpenters were particularly busy, extending the Great House (first built by Francis Price nearly a hundred years before) and building many new store-houses and new Negroes' houses. Thereafter, their main duties involved repairs, though occasionally they were called on to construct a new fowl house or pigsty or replace some building in the factory yard which had succumbed to the climate. Clearly, men who could fashion louvred windows, bannistered stairways, and decorated porches were quite capable of producing furniture; but from the evidence it seems that the Worthy Park carpenters only constructed the simplest tables, benches, and stools. The heavy mahogany furniture listed in the owner's, overseer's, and bookkeepers' houses had probably been brought in from Spanish Town, or even from England, long before.[11] One reason may have been the unsuitability of the wood obtainable in Lluidas Vale, because most of the best timber trees had long since been cut down.

Adam's sanctum was the carpenter's shop, where he was responsible for looking after an impressive variety of woodworking tools. From the various inventories in the plantation books it is clear that the Worthy Park carpenters were at least provided with the means of undertaking the most sophisticated tasks in that age of wood: five types of saw, seven of plane, various kinds of file and chisel, compasses, gauges, squares, and a lathe, as well as the cruder adzes and axes.[12] One indication that the carpenters had developed their skills to a pitch where they became almost invaluable lies in the price placed upon them by their owners. An ordinary carpenter was thought to be worth more than a head driver, and a head carpenter might command as much as £300 Currency—the value of four healthy male field slaves.

Adam, known from 1816 as William Parker, lived until 1830. But he was head carpenter only until 1821. After this he was listed once again simply as carpenter. This demotion may have been caused by declining health and effectiveness, for in 1822 he was called weakly and in 1824 was said to be ruptured. A more likely explanation may be, however, that the black William Parker gave way to a mulatto, Richard Douglas (alias Dick Richard or Mulatto Dick), son of Sarah Price and brother of Manuel, the head boiler and superintendent of Apprentices. William Parker died of pleurisy on December 6, 1830, but Richard Douglas continued as head carpenter until the end of slavery. This completed a succession of head carpenters that it is tempting to over-stress—in three generations changing from an African, to a black Creole, and to a colored Creole almost perfectly assimilated.

Charles, later Charles Hunt (1778-1836)

In an operation which might require as many as a thousand new hogs-heads and puncheons a year, and in which badly made barrels could cause the leakage of a quarter of the sugar and rum, skilled coopers were almost as valuable as head carpenters. The career of the colored Charles Hunter illustrates both the prestige attached to the cooper's job and the way in which ill-health could decrease a tradesman's value and thus block his social mobility.

Charles was born at Worthy Park six years before the surviving records begin. Listed as a quadroon, he was obviously the son of a mulatto slave woman (probably a domestic) and one of the white managerial staff, though there is record of neither his mother nor father. At the age of 13 he was set to work as an apprentice cooper, chosen surely for his color rather than any special skills he had already demonstrated. Unfortunately he also suffered at this early age from yaws, and the disfiguring and debilitating effects of this progressive disease probably explain why he never advanced to become head cooper in forty years at the job of making barrels.

Under the head cooper the half dozen or so coopers at Worthy Park were responsible for making not only all the sugar hogsheads, rum puncheons, and other barrels but also the wheels for the wains and shingles for roofs. Some estates did not employ nearly so many coopers, bringing in "shook," or broken-down barrels that were simply reassembled as needed. A well-organized and economical estate like Worthy Park, however, saved much money by having enough skilled slaves to make their own barrels from scratch. No plantation activity, save perhaps the "striking" of sugar (halting the evaporation process at the critical moment of crystallization) or the distillation of rum, required more craft than barrel-making. First the staves were split from cedar logs, then cunningly shaped with adzes, draw-knives, and spoke-shaves, while held in a vise.[13] Then the flat heading was shaped and fitted with pins and binding rope. Finally, with the help of the blacksmith the four riveted iron hoops were slipped on while red-hot, constricting the many joints watertight as they cooled.

Fitting the binding iron on wain wheels was rather like "hooping off" a barrel; but a wheelwright's work was regarded as easier than cooperage. So critical were the tolerances involved that an adequate hogshead-maker might be incapable of making a perfectly watertight puncheon, and apprentice coopers graduated from the one operation to the next. A practiced cooper was expected to make between three and four barrels in a working week, so that in the years when Worthy Park was producing 500 hogsheads of sugar and 300 puncheons of rum, or more, the coopers were busily employed in all seasons.

On many estates the head cooper was a white man. Where he was a slave almost invariably he was colored, and might be valued as high as £400 Currency. Even ordinary coopers, who were often themselves colored and almost never Africans, were commonly valued at between £200 and £300 Currency. Even then, with ready-made hogsheads and puncheons costing £3 each and shooks £2, an estate with a corps of skilled, hard-working, and healthy coopers could save up to £1,000 Currency a year.

It is doubtful, however, that Worthy Park's overseer regarded Charles Hunter as consistently pulling his weight. As the years went by and the agonizing ulceration gradually grew worse, his efficiency must have declined to vanishing point. Finally, in 1831, at the age of 53, he was relieved of his cooper's job as weakly from an ulcerated leg and made a watchman. In this less taxing though lowlier occupation he survived five more years, dying on January 25, 1836, from extensive ulceration.

Specialists at work in a still-house (rum distillery): in top hat, the white distiller; to the right, the black head cooper.

230

MULATTO JOHN, LATER JOHN MCDONALD (1750-1833)

As in many ancient cultures, smiths carried potent, almost mythical prestige in West Africa. They were the guardians of fire and the mysteries of working the metals without which the culture would be retrograde. Something of this aura carried over into the slave plantations of the New World, though it was greatly reinforced by the blacksmith's invaluable contribution to the plantation economy. White masters and black slaves concurred in regarding smiths highly, though it was rarely that the masters chose Africans as blacksmiths on sugar estates. If a white man was not available they preferred the most assimilated of Creoles. The combination of prestige, value, and assimilation to the master culture is subtly conveyed by the careers of the one white and two colored slaves who were successively Worthy Park's head blacksmith between 1787 and 1836.

Mulatto John had been born in the short interval of peace between the War of the Austrian Succession and the Seven Years' War, probably at Worthy Park as the son of a bookkeeper and a black female slave. When occupations were first listed in 1787 he was already a blacksmith, having long learned his skills from an unknown predecessor. He worked under the supervision of a white man called Charles Dale who was employed as head blacksmith at Worthy Park from August 23, 1787, at £40 Currency a year. Mulatto John was himself styled head blacksmith from 1794 onwards. But he almost certainly occupied this position after June 18, 1791, when Charles Dale left Worthy Park, and just before Rose Price arrived to reorganize the estate. By 1794 there was also a second or under blacksmith, in addition to the boy apprentices and menial helpers in the forge.

From early middle age Mulatto John suffered from a bone ache that may have been some form of occupational disease. Yet it was not until 1822 that he was listed as weakly, being classed an invalid two years later, at the age of 74. Unlike most elderly slaves he was not made a watchman, with the estate draining out the last dregs of usefulness. Probably in respect for his long years of skill and prestige, he was allowed to live out his years as one of the very few ever listed as superannuated unemployed. Perhaps because of this, Mulatto John, called John McDonald from 1816, lived on until April 18, 1833, to the age of 83, the oldest male slave recorded at Worthy Park.

CHARLES DALE (1790-1836)

The successor to the mulatto blacksmith John McDonald was, significantly, both a quadroon and the son of the former white head blacksmith, Charles Dale. Charles Dale the second was born to the female mulatto domestic called Phogo on May 5, 1790, more than a year before his father left Worthy Park. At the age of 6 he was in the Pickney Gang; but some time before 1813 he had become under head blacksmith, being trained as the helper and eventual successor of Mulatto

John. Young Charles Dale took over as head blacksmith in 1824, at the age of 34, occupying this position until 1836, when he went into a sudden decline and died on March 14, aged only 45.

The skill of the blacksmith was indispensable to a plantation. Working at his forge either with charcoal or coal specially imported from England in hogsheads, he spent much of his time shaping individual barrel hoops, wain tires, and horseshoes, either from scrap or imported bar iron. Like most estates Worthy Park found it cheaper to import than to make the metal parts of such basic tools as hoes, axes, and cutlasses (all which could be used for scrap when worn out). But a skilled blacksmith could save much time and money by fashioning less routine tools and replacement parts. Special needs and breakages were difficult to predict, and often it took weeks to find replacement parts in Jamaica, and up to nine months if they had to be ordered from England. Then there were the expenses of freightage and the high cost of employing someone else's blacksmith.

At Worthy Park the blacksmiths quite often made replacement parts for the machinery of mills, boiling-house, and still, as well as wain parts, special tools, brackets, hinges, hooks, and large nails.[14] Besides ironwork they were also expected to work items in copper, tin, lead, and brass and be experts in brazing and soldering. Presumably it was also the blacksmiths who were responsible for unshackling and branding the new slaves, and for fitting anklets and chains to the recalcitrants in the Vagabond Gang, though there is scarcely a hint of these unsavory aspects of their work in the Worthy Park records.[15]

With indispensability came as much prestige as was accorded to any slaves. If any male slaves could have founded minor dynasties as well as enjoying lives of comparative dignity, such colored tradesman as John McDonald and Charles Dale would be expected to be among them. Fortunately something is known of Charles Dale's family at least, and this demonstrates the reverse case: that even for such privileged and respected craftsmen as colored blacksmiths the chances of upward social mobility through assimilation, and even marriage, were minimal.

Charles Dale was succeeded as head blacksmith by a sambo called Alexander Dale, who was only 13 and an apprentice at the beginning of 1836. Alexander was Charles's son by a black woman, whom the records disclose was actually an African, later called Nancy Dale, born in 1780 and still working at Worthy Park in 1842. Charles and Nancy Dale, whether or not they were ever formally married, had three other children, all girls: Katy or Catherine (born 1811), Polly (1818), and Susan or Susannah (1821). There are records of the christening of at least three of these children, that of Katy being among the first recorded for any Worthy Park slaves.[16] This almost unique evidence of a tightly integrated bifocal family suggests a high degree of social assimilation for the Worthy Park Dales. The fact that Charles chose as his mate, or was forced to choose through lack of wide choice, a black African

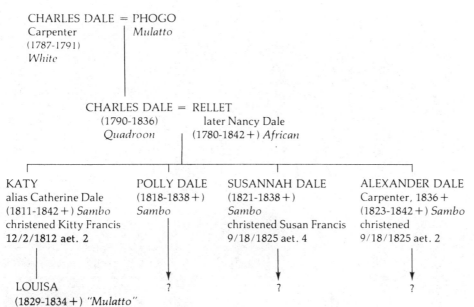

Figure 33. A Standard Nuclear Slave Family? The Family of Charles and Nancy Dale

rather than another colored Creole, did not augur well for his children's chances of bettering themselves on the socioeconomic scale. Sambos, being offspring of racial regression, colloquially called "ingraft," were not expected to improve their families' fortunes. That all four of the children of Charles and Nancy Dale were constrained to continue as workers at Worthy Park after emancipation and that three of them never rose above the status of ordinary field workers seem to bear this out.[17]

As mistresses of white men, colored slavewomen could aspire to fashion, with servants of their own.

9 / Accommodators: Five Patterns of Miscegenation

THE surest and most common route of upward mobility for slaves was that which was cynically destructive of family life and, by being open only to slave women, damaging to social cohesion in general: the progressive mating of black and colored slave women with free white men. The rigid system of color classification, the listing of mothers, and the custom of giving colored children their fathers' surnames make the tracing of kinship for the colored minority far easier than for the mass of black slaves—though the incidence of stable monogamous unions was probably even lower among coloreds than among blacks.

As has been shown earlier, the child of a union between a black and a white was styled a mulatto; of the miscegenation of mulatto and white, a quadroon; of a quadroon and white, a mestee or octoroon. In Jamaica, the child of a mestee and a white could legally pass as white. Since the mating of male Negroes with white women was unthinkable (at least on plantations),[1] and in practice all children of colored slave women by black men tended to be styled sambos, the fathers of all those listed as mulattos, quadroons, and mestees are known to have been white.[2] If the surnames chosen by the slave women for their lighter offspring match with those of whites known to have been employed on the estate at the time of conception, the presumption of paternity is very high. In the not infrequent cases where a putative father manumitted a child bearing his surname—and maybe the mother too—the presumption becomes a virtual certainty. At Worthy Park the records are sufficiently full to make such detective work frequently rewarding.

MULATTO KITTY, LATER MARY ELLIS (1795-1838+)

Of at least nine patterns of miscegenation between slave women and white craftsmen, bookkeepers, and overseers traceable in some detail, that centering on Mulatto Kitty is perhaps the most complete. Because few of the colored offspring involved were actually manumitted, the records of most remained in the Worthy Park slave books.

Kitty's mother was a black Creole field slave called Amy, who seems to have had only one other child, the black Morocco (later

Figure 34. The Classification of Jamaican Coloreds

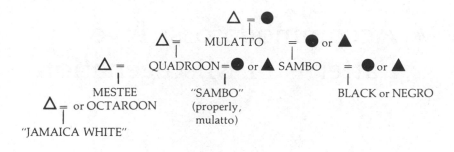

Key:

white male △

black male ▲

black female ●

William White), who was born eight years after Kitty and, still a field slave, died of scrofula in 1831, aged 28. Kitty was born on December 1, 1795. Although she was not christened Mary Ellis until April 1814,[3] she was almost certainly the daughter of Robert Ellis, employed at Worthy Park as bookkeeper from 1787, and as overseer in 1795. Ellis left Worthy Park on May 28, 1795, to become overseer at Thetford (where he remained until at least 1799),[4] but the short interval between his departure and Kitty's birth would have allowed for Kitty's conception while he was still at Worthy Park.

Kitty, like the vast majority of colored female slaves, went to work as a domestic, being employed in the overseer's house sometime before 1813. Probably she was extremely attractive as well as complaisant. As soon as she was old enough, she began to bear a succession of children, mostly the quadroon offspring of Worthy Park's successive bookkeepers and overseers. Kitty's first child, born when she was barely 15, was Kitty's Dennis, a quadroon later called Patrick King, who was probably the son of A. J. King, overseer in 1814, and bookkeeper earlier. Kitty's next three children, Elizabeth, John, and Anne, were born between 1813 and 1818. All quadroons and surnamed Pearce, they were almost certainly the offspring of Benjamin Pearce, employed at Worthy Park from 1813 to 1822, first as bookkeeper and then as overseer.

In 1819, either as the result of an indiscretion or because Benjamin Pearce had taken another woman (perhaps even a wife) to his bed, Kitty —now Mary Ellis—broke the sequence and gave birth to a sambo girl, whom she called by her own baptismal names. Yet in 1821 and again in 1829 Kitty produced further quadroon children: James, christened James Christie in 1825, and Thomas, who probably did not survive. Kitty's eighth and last recorded child was another sambo, Jane, born in August 1831, when her mother was 36 and possibly no longer attractive to the plantation's whites.

Kitty remained a domestic until the end of slavery, when she was

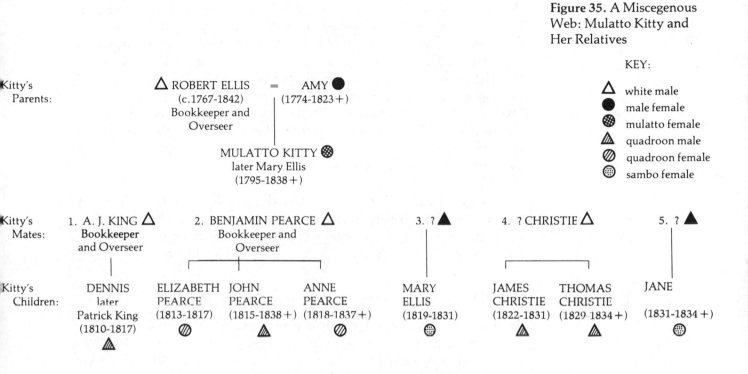

Figure 35. A Miscegenous Web: Mulatto Kitty and Her Relatives

KEY:

△ white male
● male female
◉ mulatto female
▲ quadroon male
◍ quadroon female
◉ sambo female

Kitty's Parents:

△ ROBERT ELLIS = AMY ●
(c.1767-1842) (1774-1823+)
Bookkeeper and Overseer

MULATTO KITTY ◉
later Mary Ellis
(1795-1838+)

Kitty's Mates:

1. A. J. KING △
Bookkeeper and Overseer

2. BENJAMIN PEARCE △
Bookkeeper and Overseer

3. ? ▲

4. ? CHRISTIE △

5. ? ▲

Kitty's Children:

DENNIS
later
Patrick King
(1810-1817)
▲

ELIZABETH PEARCE
(1813-1817)
◍

JOHN PEARCE
(1815-1838+)
▲

ANNE PEARCE
(1818-1837+)
◍

MARY ELLIS
(1819-1831)
◉

JAMES CHRISTIE
(1822-1831)
▲

THOMAS CHRISTIE
(1829-1834+)
▲

JANE
(1831-1834+)
◉

43. She seems to have been less ambitious for herself and her children than many colored female slaves. Perhaps the shiftless nature of Worthy Park's whites and the consequent lack of lasting attachments provided few opportunities for advancement. More likely, being the mistress of a succession of overseers she was thus de facto "mistress" of the overseer's house, and this may have been sufficient reward in itself. The fact that Kitty did not avail herself of the legal right to be excused work on the birth of her sixth living child in 1831 is a significant indication. Like Monk Lewis' beautiful slave Psyche, Mary Ellis may have begun by trading her charms with the many men of all kinds who desired her, before—like Lewis' Mary Wiggins—becoming one of those well-established "housekeepers" described by many visitors to Jamaica. As such she would have managed the household even when the master was present and dominated it while he was absent, ruling the domestics like a benevolent despot and claiming the title of "Mistress Mary" by right.[5]

Certainly, such a household, despite its sexual anarchy, would be a more comfortable environment in which to bring up children than the slave cantonments. It might even be regarded as providing greater security than the life of a colored freedman in times of stress and economic hardship such as the 1820s and 1830s. What in fact happened to Kitty's children? The first two died in 1817, aged 7 and 5. John Pearce, brought up in the overseer's house, became a carpenter by the time slavery ended, when he was 23. Anne Pearce, christened at the age of 7 in 1825, worked as a domestic under her mother's supervision between the ages of 13 and 19. On May 19, 1837, she became free by buying up her own Apprenticeship, perhaps in order to marry (as yet she had no children). The younger Mary Ellis was also a domestic, but remained in bondage until slavery ended in August 1838, when she too was 19. James (Christie) seems to have died in 1831, at the age of 9. Thomas and Jane were both young enough to be immediately freed on August 1, 1834, but presumably stayed with their mother in the overseer's house for the four further years of Apprenticeship. Thereafter the records are silent; neither Mary Ellis nor any of her children continued to work at Worthy Park after full freedom came.

Besides Eleanor Price, whose genealogy is fully outlined later, at least three other Worthy Park slave women found that miscegenation led eventually to manumission—in ways that may explain why the same did not happen to Amy, Kitty, and Kitty's children.

Sambo Sally, later Sarah Richards (1780-1836)

Sambo Sally was another domestic working in the overseer's house who had children of various colors by different fathers. Born in 1780, she was fifteen years older than Kitty, but never quite achieved Kitty's position of authority. Perhaps this was because Sally was almost certainly the daughter of Robert Richards, millwright at Worthy Park in the 1780s and a mere craftsman rather than overseer. In the overseer's house Sally was never listed as more than a humble washer. Even her color was indeterminate, being listed alternatively as sambo and mulatto—probably because her father was "Jamaica white" rather than pure white. In 1808 Sally had given birth to a boy, Sally's Francis (later Francis Foster), who was listed as a quadroon, and in 1809 to another, Sally's Romeo, who was classified black—apparent incompatibilities. Finally, in 1811 Sally gave birth to a third boy, Sally's Thomas, listed again as quadroon. This boy, who was christened Thomas James at Worthy Park on May 22, 1811, was the son of Charles James, a "white" carpenter employed at Worthy Park from 1810 to 1817.

In 1816 Thomas James, aged 5, was manumitted by his father in return for another slave, Martin, aged 10, and carried away from Worthy Park when Charles James moved on in the following year. By doing this Charles James was following a pattern already established by Robert Richards, Sally's millwright father, who had manumitted two of his other colored children in 1795.[6] Perhaps "passing white" craftsmen were more likely than overseers to acknowledge their bastards, who were valued greatly as potential helpers and successors in their craft.

Sally's eldest child, the quadroon Francis, was freed in November 1834 by buying up his own Apprenticeship, though the black Romeo died in 1828 as a slave. Sally herself was still a domestic in 1836 when she died, aged 56.

Nelly Douglas (1775-1836)

Nelly Douglas was yet another mulatto domestic who bore at least one quadroon child. This was James, later called James Brailsford, born in 1803, who, like many other colored male slaves, became a carpenter. James Brailsford's father was Thomas Brailsford, Worthy Park's overseer and attorney between 1816 and 1823, who had much earlier been a bookkeeper on the estate. When he died in 1823, Thomas Brailsford freed his son under the terms of his will, though James Brailsford was not actually released until November 26, 1824, when he was replaced by another slave, Edward.

The manumitting of colored children by testamentary deed—either paying the assessed value of the young slaves or providing replacements, and lodging security with the parish churchwardens— was one of the commonest ways in which white men freed their illegitimate offspring. Often the mothers were freed at the same time. The famous Sir Charles Price had followed the tradition on his death in 1772, manumitting through his will "a Mulatto woman named Margaret residing at Rose Hall and her two Elder children."[7] At a humbler level no less than four Worthy Park slaves benefited similarly from the will of William Pingilly, white bookkeeper from 1812 to 1823.

The process began in the previous generation. Clementina (1759-1838+) was a black Creole slave who bore both black and mulatto children. Although primarily a field slave she was occasionally employed as a domestic and after 1813, when she was 54, was permanently listed as house cook and washerwoman. In 1789 Clementina gave birth to the mulatto girl Susanna, in between her two other children, Beckford (born 1784) and Catherine (1791), both of whom were black.

Susanna, later Susanna Cummings (1789-1824+)

Susanna, called Susanna Cummings after 1816, was, like her mother, both field worker and domestic, being employed (as was Sambo Sally, too) in the comparatively menial role of washer. Between 1811 and 1823 she bore no less than four quadroon children. The first, Susanna's Joseph (later Joseph Hammel), was the child of a transient bookkeeper called Hammel. The others, William, Elizabeth, and Tom, were the children of the more permanent William Pingilly. In fact it was Joseph Hammel who gained his freedom first, apparently being manumitted in 1817 at the age of 6.[8] Susanna herself was freed by the bequest of William Pingilly on May 22, 1824, along with her three Pingilly children, aged 8 years, 5 years, and 7 months. At the same time two child slaves, Moses and Susanna, were delivered to Worthy Park as partial replacements.[9]

Mulatto Kitty, alias Mary Ellis, was a more influential domestic than Sambo Sally, Nelly Douglas, Clementina, or Susanna. Even if Kitty enjoyed sufficient prestige and comfort at Worthy Park to consider manumission even for her children an equivocal blessing, the ini-

Slaves at their leisure: (a) in a Negro yard; (b) on the way from the Negro Grounds; (c) in a mission compound; (d) at a Christmas Junkanoo.

tiative was not entirely in her hands. It is also true that the various fathers of her eight children had neither the incentive nor the opportunity to manumit their colored offspring. None of them were "poor white" craftsmen like Robert Richards or Charles James, who would have valued their sons as potential helpmates. However, unlike Thomas Brailsford and William Pingilly, none of them died before 1838 so that by a parting gesture they could offer their children the two-edged gift of legal freedom.

For a black slave woman to trade her body with a white man in return for transient rewards was perhaps as voluntary as it was casual. But once conception occurred the process was inexorable. The colored offspring of such liaisons lived in the twilight zone of the half-caste, stranded between two cultures. All were bound to attempt maximum assimilation, which for the colored females meant becoming the bedmates of whichever white men laid claim to them.

The rewards of domestic concubinage might include relative comforts, equivocal prestige, even some backstairs power for the concubine herself. For the offspring, it might lead to a choice of the best slave jobs and the chance of manumission. Yet even in the most fortunate cases these were scarcely compensations for a life of sexual anarchy and the loss of the most recognizable features of a stable family life. In less fortunate cases—where, for example, the children died, or the colored slave lost favor through sterility, ill-health, or advancing age—the results of miscegenation could be demoralizing to the point of alienation.

CHARLOTTE, LATER CHARLOTTE TOPHAM (1791-1834)

The life of the mulatto Charlotte Topham suggests a tragic contrast to the lives of the more fortunate colored domestics already considered. Born on March 8, 1791, she was the daughter of the Creole Phyllis, whose own life was in several aspects remarkable. Born in 1764, Phyllis was an able and healthy field hand when, on May 29, 1790, she ran away from Worthy Park. She was recaptured in August but while at large had conceived her first child, by an unknown white man. This may have occurred on another estate, but more likely in the sailors' stews of Kingston. Phyllis' punishment was probably mitigated on account of pregnancy, and Worthy Park's management was doubtless pleased when the baby proved both live and colored. Yet neither Phyllis nor her eldest child could expect any sort of protection or privilege from Charlotte's distant, and unascertained, father.

Phyllis, however, seems to have been a woman of character and resource, though scarcely lucky with her health. By 1813 she had risen to the rank of Second Gang driveress, having in the meanwhile borne the sambo child John Lodge in 1793, the black London in 1796, and Jugg (later Louisa Ellis) in 1805. In 1821 ill-health relegated her to the position of ordinary field laborer, but in the following year she was taken on as cook in the overseer's house, perhaps through the intercession of her mulatto daughter, who already worked there. Yet the overseer and the bookkeepers who shared his table did not relish the idea of a sickly cook, and after two years in a comparative sinecure as Great House cook Phyllis was sent back once more to the fields at the age of 61, a member of the Grasscutter Gang. She died five years later on September 3, 1830.

The causes of Phyllis' death were given as old age and catarrh, and it seems likely that she suffered from tuberculosis. Contagious and incurable, this wasting disease made even a semblance of family life a positive penalty. The eldest son of Phyllis, John Lodge, died of tuberculosis in 1814 at the age of 21, and the same affliction may have carried off her other son, London, who died in infancy. Tuberculosis also blighted the life of Charlotte and her children.

As was normal for the children of field slaves even if they were colored, Charlotte began work in the Pickney Gang as soon as she was 6. Just as routinely she became a domestic as soon as she reached adolescence, being listed as a washerwoman in 1813. By this time she was already known as Charlotte Topham, having been one of the very first group of Worthy Park slaves to be baptized—on May 23, 1811. In 1817, when she was 26, she gave birth to her first and healthiest child, Sally (later Anne Bryan). The father was evidently a black man, since the child was classified sambo. Surviving the measles epidemic of 1822, Sally lived at least until 1838. The other children were less hardy. Jane, listed alternatively as mulatto or quadroon (and thus probably sired either by a white or a light-colored man), was born in 1820. Surviving measles in 1822 she perished of lung trouble at the age of 4. Margaret, probably sambo though listed as black, was born in 1823 and died of tuberculosis, dropsy, and worms at the age of 8, in 1831. Throughout these years of travail Charlotte remained as washer in the white men's houses, progressively weakened from the aptly named "consumption," of which she finally died on June 6, 1834. In the cases of Phyllis and Charlotte, the whole brutalizing system of slavery and miscegenation especially deserved the label vulgarly pinned to the disease from which they also suffered: "the White Man's Scourge."

Slave stocks: punishment for minor infractions, day and night.

STOCKS for HANDS and FEET, with BED and HAND STOCKS (from the approved Models)

244

10 / Resisters: Five Slave Nonconformists

F OR estates like Worthy Park, which never experienced actual slave rebellion, records of running away provide the most discernible evidence of slave alienation and resistance to the plantation system. What is known of five very different runaways—two Africans, three Creoles; two women, three men—not only illustrates what happened to such slaves but also suggests reasons why they ran away in the first place.

One of the key problems is deciding to what extent the incidence of running away was related to the harshness of the system, and to what extent to the weakness of control. Here the time scale is important. In the mid-eighteenth century the treatment of recalcitrant slaves in Jamaica was notoriously savage, but since the plantation whites were not compelled to keep records of runaways or slave punishments, direct evidence is difficult to find.[1] At the same time the emphasis in the slave laws on the control of slave movements and the apprehension and return of runaways suggests that it was relatively common for slaves to run away. In the 1790s the forces of control were tightened at Worthy Park as throughout Jamaica, but this did not necessarily mean that the symptoms of unrest were actually more marked. With the majority of estates being by now firmly established, with the number of Creoles growing, yet with Africans still available to fill the more menial posts, the plantations may have been at a balance point of stability about this time. In contrast, in the 1820s more slaves ran away than ever before. This may have been owing as much to the deterioration of conditions on plantations as to the slackening of the forces of control and better opportunities for those who ran away.

In 1792 Rose Price established a Vagabond Gang at Worthy Park in order to punish slaves for insubordination, stealing, and running away. In his habitually calculating way, he may have regarded this method of weeding out the recalcitrants and placing them in chains under the actual lash as more efficient (even more humane) than having them scattered around the gangs, which would then all be placed under the generalized threat of the drivers' whips. Three years later a Jamaican Consolidated Slave Law laid down the standard treatment for runaways; but it aimed as much at tightening up on slack overseers and fixing limits for slave punishments as actually punishing runaways.

245

The 1795 law reiterated earlier provisions that no slaves were to be allowed tickets-of-leave for more than a month at any one time. Any slave missing for ten days or more, or found more than eight miles from his estate without a valid ticket, was regarded as a runaway. It was the duty of all free men to apprehend runaways and to carry them either back to their masters or to the parochial workhouse. Captors, however, were to be paid 10s., plus a mileage allowance for each captive, except for Maroon slavecatchers who, under the terms of the 1739 treaty, were paid a bounty of 40s. a head, alive or dead.[2]

Attempts were made to differentiate workhouses (based on English models, with a local committee, plus supervisor, overseer, treasurer, clerk, and surgeon) from the "houses of correction," or jails. Runaways were to be kept in jails only in those parishes which had no workhouse.[3] St. John was such a parish, with only a lock-up (at Point Hill). But most of the St. John's runaways seem to have found their way into the workhouses of Spanish Town (St. Catherine) and Kingston. Workhouse supervisors regularly listed runaways in the local newspapers, and the institutions at Spanish Town and Kingston were so busy that advertisements appeared each week. Every three months or so, unclaimed or unidentified runaways were advertised for auction.[4]

Lady (c. 1763-1792+)

Lady was the earliest persistent runaway listed in the surviving Worthy Park records. In March 1786 she was said to have been a runaway since August 11, 1785, and from the records she seems to have sustained herself in freedom throughout 1786 and 1787. In 1788, however, she was recaptured, giving birth to a girl called Diana—presumably conceived outside Worthy Park—on June 30. By 1789 Lady was back working in the fields, described as "Able but a Runaway." On September 15, 1791, she became missing once again, probably shortly after the death of her little girl.[5] This time she remained at large for only five months. On February 18, 1792, the following advertisement appeared in the local newspaper, the *St. Jago de le Veja Gazette:*

> In Spanish Town Workhouse, Feb. 16, 1792 . . . Lady, a Coromantee, to Price's Luidas estate, marks not plain, 4 feet 10½—Feb. 10.

This time the estate was not prepared to make the effort of restraining the recalcitrant. On March 13, 1792, Lady was laconically reported in the slave book as "Shipt off," probably sold at auction to some optimistic or unsuspecting planter, without returning to Worthy Park. A reason for the estate's decision, and perhaps for Lady's obduracy too, can be guessed from the newspaper advertisement itself. Lady was a Coromantee, one of those African slaves whom Jamaican planters found almost impossible to master.[6] Yet Betty, another persistent African runaway who was also "shipt off" in the same year, was not a Coromantee but a Congo. Perhaps, in fact, all Africans were equally likely at this time to make for freedom if they were not tightly controlled; and masters for their part may have been prepared to gratify the desire of such troublesome slaves as Lady and Betty to escape, to the extent of shipping them off to another estate. It was, after all, the period of the cataclysmic revolution in St. Domingue, and even if the average African knew little or nothing of the doings of the Haitian slaves, Jamaican planters were positively paranoid about the dangers of revolutionary "infection."

STRUMPET (1764-1838+)

Strumpet was another early Worthy Park runaway, but she was retained upon recapture, perhaps because she was a Creole, not an African. Although troublesome for some years, she lived on to see out slavery itself without running away again. As with the even more crudely named runaway, Whore, it is tempting to speculate whether Strumpet's name was in any way relevant to her running away. Did she run away for shame at being forced by the estate into a life of harlotry? Did she run away for greater opportunities to exercise a certain propensity for which she had been named? Or was she named as punishment for running away, after the trade she was forced to follow to sustain herself in freedom?[7]

Strumpet, aged 20, already carried her callous slave label in the earliest surviving Worthy Park list (1784). She was also called "Field, Able, Runaway" in the first roll which added descriptions (1787). As if it had been wished upon her, she ran away again between September and December 1787, the only occasion specifically recorded. Returned to work in the fields, she was listed graphically as a "skulker" in 1789, and in 1791, along with the "Runaway, Worthless" Whore, she was sent to Spring Garden, where at least they were liable to infect fewer slaves with their footloose ways.[8]

Unlike Whore, Strumpet was returned to Worthy Park later in 1791, and on February 8, 1793, she bore her only child, Nina (1793-1829). Motherhood may have provided an anodyne, which proved to be lasting, because Nina, unlike Lady's Diana, survived. Certainly no further trouble from Strumpet was recorded after 1793, when she was 29. Until she was 59 Strumpet was a healthy worker in the Great Gang, being relegated in 1823 to the Grass Gang as weakly. From 1830, the year after Nina died, until 1832, Strumpet was listed as infirm, but employed as "Orphan's Nurse, Attending her Grandchildren." Finally, from 1833 until August 1838, between the ages of 69 and 74, she was one of the very few "Invalids" listed as unemployed. By now, however, her help may have been needed with great-grandchildren, for Nina's three surviving girls were already 20, 18, and 15 in 1833. Any children born after August 1, 1828, however, could have been freed immediately on August 1, 1834.[9]

As far as can be discovered, Strumpet was never christened, retaining her slave sobriquet all her life. Almost certainly, time and famil-

*Jamaican Slave Prison.
Though sketched during the
Apprenticeship period,
these methods—treadmill,
whipping of females, chain-
gang—were commonplace
in slavery days. Print from
an abolitionist tract, 1837.*

iarity softened the harsh connotation of the name, just as they may have smoothed even the asperities of bondage.

The dual purposes of the slave laws to standardize control procedures and establish the limits of punishment became gradually more marked in the amended laws of the so-called Amelioration period. This phase began with the laws of 1787 and 1795, but change was greatly accelerated between 1823 and 1831 as emancipation really made strides in England. It therefore seems at first glance ironical that, from evidence at Worthy Park as throughout Jamaica, conditions for plantation slaves apparently deteriorated, punishment grew harsher, and unrest grew in the very last years of slavery. At Worthy Park it was in the later 1820s that the only direct evidence of cruelty was recorded, albeit from a slightly tainted source. A sensational antislavery campaigner called Benjamin M'Mahon wrote (in 1839) that when he visited Worthy Park in 1828 he discerned that the overseer and attorney, John Blair, was a veritable sadist. According to M'Mahon, if Blair "had not the satisfaction of mangling the flesh of ten or a dozen negroes before breakfast every morning his countenance would be black and threatening; but on the contrary, after indulging in his morning's amusement, he would be cheerful and pleasant." The overseer allegedly told the visitor that if slaves on an estate he managed were not seen to be wearing bloody breechcloths at crop time, word would get around that the place was "going to hell."[10] Similarly, it was during this period of the owner's absenteeism that the largest numbers of Worthy Park slaves were punished by being sentenced to the workhouse for life, and with the slavemasters ultimate weapon (once the laws had made slave murder through "justified correction" illegal)—transportation to another, perhaps foreign, colony.

SUE'S DAVID, LATER WILLIAM LORD (1811-1830+)

Sue's David was one of the three children of the Creole black, Big Sue, later called Sukey Lowe (1782-1838+), who spent her working life as a field laborer. From the records Sue seems to have caused no trouble to her masters, but when their separate entries are collated it is seen that her trio of children elicited unfavorable comments from the Worthy Park bookkeepers, especially in 1830. Driven to comment on this remarkable concurrence, the estate management would doubtless have dismissed all three as a thoroughly bad lot. Yet a later analyst can guess at sound psychological causes for the disaffection. Big Sue's children grew up in a time of unfulfillable expectations, their alienation made the more poignant by miscegenation.

Sukey Lowe's oldest child, Mary Anne, later called Sophia Gillon (1804-1832), was a mulatto, probably conceived casually by some temporary field bookkeeper. Bearing a colored child did not bring the mother the comparative ease of a domestic's job, and even the daughter could not retain a position in the white men's houses. After two years in the Great House (where she bore a quadroon child called John in 1821 when she was only 17), and several more years in the overseer's house, Mary Anne was sent back to work in the fields. In 1830, while working alongside her mother in the Great Gang, she was listed as ill-disposed. She died on February 17, 1832, of obstructed menses, aged only 28.

If prostituting themselves to white men brought neither Sue nor her daughter any lasting benefit, it must have brought special alienation and resentment for Sue's two black sons. In general, male slaves could have felt nothing but enmity for the white men who preempted the slave womenfolk, and contempt for those black and colored females who gave their favors willingly. But David and his brother in particular must have resented a family stain that brought no profit.

In the absence of African recruits, cut off by Abolition in 1808, both were destined for a life of degrading toil in the field. David entered the Pickney Gang in 1817, his brother, Hannibal, in 1821. Both caused trouble from the beginning, but particularly once they came together in the Second Gang in 1829. By inference it seems that they ran away from work as often as they could—at first like modern truants from Lluidas Vale school, bird's-nesting, fishing, stealing cane, fruit, and provisions; then, as they became adults, venturing further afield into more serious theft. In December 1830, at the age of 20, David—now called William Lord—was carried to the Slave Court at Point Hill and tried as an "Incorrigible Runaway." In such cases condemnation was almost inevitable. David was sentenced to the workhouse for life. As a final gesture the court put a price on him, so that in the curious plantocratic fashion David's owner could be compensated by the Jamaican government for what amounted to his own failure. At a time when a healthy adult male slave was normally worth £150 Currency, David was valued at a contemptuous £34.9.0.

Hannibal, alias Peter Hammel, aged 16, was listed in 1830 as an "Incorrigible Thief and Runaway"; but, suitably warned by the example made of his brother, he seems to have mended his ways. He did not run away again, and during the period of Apprenticeship was classified as a First Class field laborer, even being employed—as a humble cane-carrier—after slavery ended. His fate, though scarcely enviable, was surely preferable to that of David. Workhouse slaves were employed in gangs on the public roads or contracted out as jobbing slaves to individual planters. In either case their mortality was sometimes as high as 25 percent per year, and the alternative work on the notorious workhouse treadmills might even have been preferred.

Presumably, such slave life sentences as David's came to an end with an amnesty in August 1838. But there was little likelihood that David would ever have returned to Lluidas Vale and the life of a wage-earning peasant. If he was still alive in 1838 it is more likely that he spent the rest of his life as a piece of rarely employed jetsam in some Jamaican town, trying, with mixed success, to avoid the harsh provisions of the Police and Vagrancy Acts judiciously passed by the Jamaican Assembly in advance of emancipation.

POLYDORE (1788-1832+)

Even more than in the cases of David and Hannibal, the disaffection of Polydore can be attributed to conditions special to the last decade of slavery. Born as early as 1788, he seems to have been resigned, if not content, right up to 1830, after which he rapidly earned the unenviable label of "Incorrigible Runaway."

Polydore was the third of the four children of an African called Esther or Easter (1759-1795),[11] who quite remarkably was first made an ordinary domestic and then cook in the overseer's house, when Polydore was 4 years old. But the young slave was not to enjoy a domestic background, or even any semblance of family upbringing, for his mother died when he was 7, and he appears to have been the sole survivor of Esther's children.

Polydore then seemed destined for a life in the fields, rising through the gangs until he entered the Great Gang at 24, in 1813. In the following year he was also employed in the factory during crop time, as a boiler, thereafter alternating between factory and field according to the season. Yet any aspirations he may have had to rise to one of the senior boilermen's posts, or to become any kind of craftsman, were stunted by the superfluity of more eligible Creoles. Indeed, as time went on it became evident that because of the increasing shortage of sturdy male field workers Polydore could no longer expect to be employed solely in the light recuperative jobs traditional for boilermen out of crop. Instead, at a time when the number of freedmen and underemployed slaves on other decayed estates was increasing, Polydore and his kind were expected to toil six months in the humid inferno of the boilinghouse, followed by six months in the fields during the rainy season, digging cane holes and trenches.

Polydore's response was to run away as often, as far, and for as long as he could. Finally, on August 5, 1832, he was tried at the Slave Court and, like David and at least three other Worthy Park slaves,[12] sentenced to the workhouse for life, at the age of 43.

BRITAIN (1787-1817 +)

The African slave called Britain was probably, in conventional terms, more of a villain than most other Worthy Park runaways. His fate was correspondingly even more severe. Yet Britain, as much as anyone, was a victim of circumstances.

Born in an unknown part of Africa in 1787, Britain was one of the last new slaves brought to Worthy Park before the ending of the slave trade. His name first appeared in the records in 1814, when he was already 27. In basic respects he was one of the least fortunate of all Worthy Park slaves; he was a despised African at a time when even Creoles were competing hopelessly for the better jobs. Unlike the survivors of the African influx of the 1790s he did not enjoy the consolation of shipmates, for he came to the estate alone. His case was desperate; he did not fit. Alienated, he turned to crime and running away.

The comments on Britain in the Worthy Park slave books are brutally succinct:

1814: . . . 27, Fieldman, A Great Rogue . . .
1816: . . . 29, Fieldman, Runaway . . .
1817 (Decrease): . . . Nov. 22 tried at a Slave Court and convicted of Robbery, sentenced to be transported off the Island for life (aged) 30 years. Certificate of Value £50 . . .

No planters were anywhere permitted to disown their slaves on purely economic grounds.[13] Yet the Jamaican Assembly did allow for the transportation of the most troublesome Jamaican slaves. Cuba provided the least critical and most lucrative market. In their chauvinistic way the eighteenth-century Jamaican legislators had reckoned that to sell a slave into foreign bondage—especially Spanish—was a fate worse than execution, if less culpable. They were ignorant of the fact that slaves in Spanish colonies at that time were probably worked less hard than English slaves and also had at least a remote chance of buying their own freedom on an instalment plan (by the system of *coartación*). Ironically, however, by the time the unfortunate Britain was transported in 1817 the development of the Cuban sugar economy and the shortage of slaves had reversed the trend, so that conditions for Cuban slaves were growing progressively more severe.[14] As a newcomer, the 30-year old Britain was not likely to have lasted long.

*A Plantation Overseer.
Often coarse, licentious,
and cruel, they, too, were in
a sense victims of the
system.*

11 / Backra: Three Plantation Whites

Robert Ellis (c. 1767-1843)

Ironically it is often more difficult to individualize the master class of plantation whites than it is to trace the humble lives of individual slaves. Estates did not need to keep biographical details beyond the names and dates of employment necessary for filling in the Deficiency Law returns. Besides this, few whites either stayed long enough in one location, or emerged sufficiently far out of the obscurity of plantation life, to leave lasting traces.

At the bottom of the social scale of plantation whites were the craftsmen—poor, illiterate, and socially immobilized. At the other end were those healthy, ambitious, able (or unscrupulous) bookkeepers who rose through the ranks to become overseers, attorneys, even planters. In exceptional cases of upward mobility, their lives can be pieced together from parish registers, deeds, wills, and almanacs. Yet, far from owning the properties and slaves, or attaining the public offices and militia ranks which rated listing in the *Jamaica Almanack*, the majority of plantation whites neither made nor saved enough to record financial transactions or leave complicated wills. They were also held so firmly under contractual obligations that they enjoyed neither the leisure nor status to hold the humblest offices or rise from the militia's lowest ranks. Besides this, few plantation whites were respectable or fortunate enough to marry or to record the baptism of their children. Many, indeed, died or left Jamaica as casually and anonymously as they had come to the island, or as they migrated from estate to estate within it.

If the lives of individual plantation whites were characterized by obscurity, much is known from the records and published descriptions of their lives in general.[1] Thus, to a degree, the lives of any of the hundred or more whites employed at Worthy Park between 1783 and 1838 could be imaginatively reconstructed with equal verisimilitude. Robert Ellis is chosen, however, not quite arbitrarily. He lived and stayed long enough—was successful enough—to progress from bookkeeper to overseer. Thus he can serve as an example of both. Although his upward mobility did not continue much farther, he did leave a scattering of official records. In particular, he was typical of members of the plantations' managerial class in being, as has been suggested already, a promiscuous miscegenator.

On the analogy of the army, all whites were officers, separated by an almost unbridgeable gulf from the mass of slaves and even the NCOs of the slave elite. "What bockra man," asks the old Jamaican proverb, "im nebber 'tan good?"[2] Yet in the actual army of the colonial militia (in slavery days, virtually a white preserve), the hierarchy of rank was subtly related to civilian status. Bookkeepers, along with craftsmen and other poor whites, provided merely the "other ranks" to the officer class of officials, merchants, planters, attorneys, and overseers. This made them all the more conscious of the privileges pertaining to their race, and ever determined to extend them, accepting harsh conditions only for lack of alternatives and in the hope of improvement if they survived.

Bookkeepers were often freshly arrived in the colony, generally young, underpaid, and unmarried. Though in the later period they were rarely indentured, they were initially bound by strict contracts and permanently subject to the strictures of the Masters and Servants Laws. They could be prosecuted for withholding their services once they had signed on, yet in practice dismissed for trivial causes. Their only security was the difficulty of finding replacements at short notice, or any replacements for an estate as isolated as Worthy Park.

A bookkeeper like Robert Ellis—first employed by Worthy Park in 1787 at £40 Currency per year—typically came out from the United Kingdom between the ages of 17 and 20, after a term of apprenticeship as clerk in some countinghouse—perhaps driven by tedium and lack of prospects, or drawn by exaggerated tales of adventure, power, and an easy fortune. Life in Jamaica was certainly strange, and initially exciting, if not terrifying. The type of naive newcomer was satirized in Jamaica as "Johnny Newcombe," falling a victim to tropical fevers, rum, and loose black women while hardly off the boat.[3] Plantation life was less picturesque, yet equally harsh and novel. Armed with little more than bare literacy and some facility with figures (as well as the easy eighteenth-century assumption of the superiority of white to black), the new bookkeeper was ignorant of sugar technology, field husbandry, and slave management. Like a green subaltern he was dependent upon his senior subordinates, while likely to be tyrannized by the plantation's overseer and attorney, his captain and major.

Learning while allegedly supervising, in field, factory, or office, the bookkeeper worked daily hours as long as the slaves', and often was busiest with his accounts at weekends while the slaves were free to work their grounds. Partly for security against the slaves, and partly for fear they would not return, bookkeepers were rarely allowed off the estate. On a bad estate the six or so bookkeepers were kept almost in captivity. Besides being worked long hours and given few opportunities for leave, they were housed in ill-furnished, kennel-like barracks, served with inferior provisions, and even expected to dine separately

Johnny Creolizes and puffs sickness away.   John gets wet & plays the Devil with Quashee.   Johnny capers a la Samboese to the tune of Morgan Rattlehed.

*Often hated by the slaves,
"obishas" and bookkeepers
—especially newcomers—
were also ridiculed by more
fortunate whites.*

from the overseer. Consequently, the young white men tended to be mutinous, lazy, and drunken. Once their original contract was up, they were as likely to be dismissed capriciously as to leave in disgust.

Worthy Park was as remote from the distractions and consolations of towns as any Jamaican estate, and conditions for the inferior whites may have been eased in consequence. In the isolation of the Jamaican "outback," white men tended towards solidarity, while at the same time wise overseers realized how difficult good bookkeepers were to replace. One indication is that Worthy Park salaries, rising to £80 or £100 Currency for mere bookkeepers, were marginally higher than average.

Yet much depended on the quality and character of the overseers. As the old proverbs have it, "Obisha drink, bookkeeper drunk," and "Good owner musn' hab 'tingy obisha."[4] Roughley in 1823 characterized the good overseer as

> a man of settled, sober habits, presenting a gentlemanlike appearance, keeping a regular, well supplied, comfortable table, without profusion, (which the internal means of an estate, in small stock and provisions, generally afford, if attended to) not only for himself and the white people under him, but for the benefit of such sick and convalescent slaves as require salutary and restoring nourishment.

The wise overseer, added Roughley,

> should be attentive to the white people under him, that their rooms, linen &c are regularly kept clean, showing an example of cleanliness in his own person. He should suffer them to sit, after business hours, in his company, instead of morosely banishing them either to their own sleeping-rooms, or to a distant dark part of the house, till meal-time is announced, which induces them to take gross freedoms with the slaves in the house, and meanly assimilates their manners to such company. This, alas! is too often the case. This has sprung from the weak, envious, jealous tempers, too frequently indulged; and has been cherished as an old custom, thinking that by keeping young men in fear, and at an awful distance, it added dignity to the overseer's station.[5]

Luxury in the West Indias

Enjoying the perquisites of petty power, "many plantation whites sank into a hopeless moral torpor, eating, drinking, and fornicating themselves into an early grave."

That so many Worthy Park bookkeepers graduated to overseer may be as much evidence that the social line was not too strictly drawn as of the difficulty of recruiting overseers from outside the estate. It could also, of course, mean that in matters of quality and character there was little to choose between overseers and bookkeepers at Worthy Park, and that all fell short of Thomas Roughley's ideal. Certainly, in respect to cohabiting with slave women, all white men in Lluidas Vale —planters and craftsmen, as well as overseers and bookkeepers—were equally reprehensible, differing only in the quality of their bedmates. Such promiscuous intercourse, however, may have been less from choice than from the shortage of white women prepared to marry plantation whites or live in the Jamaican backwoods. For better or worse, white women were almost unknown in the "slave society" of Lluidas Vale, and Robert Ellis was quite normal in remaining unmarried and siring only illegitimate and colored children.

Unlike most of Worthy Park's white hirelings, Robert Ellis spent six years on the estate, and at least a quarter of his 76 years in the parish of St. John's. Discharged from Worthy Park after 3½ years' service on October 10, 1790, he was personally reengaged by Rose Price on January 21, 1793, at a salary of £80 Currency. At the beginning of 1795, aged about 28, he was appointed overseer at £200 currency a year, though he left Worthy Park only five months later to take up a similar post at neighboring Thetford.[6]

258

Robert Ellis fathered at least two colored children at Worthy Park. Richard, christened Robert Ellis on May 23, 1811,[7] was born on January 6, 1795, the son of the black field slave Sally (1775-1813). Helped by his color to become a carpenter, he died of tuberculosis in May 1834, aged 39. The second child, Kitty—whose life has already been described—was born only eleven months after Richard, in December 1795. Indeed, the potential embarrassment of having sired children by different mothers in the same year may have contributed to Robert Ellis' decision to move from Worthy Park.

The fragmentary state of Thetford's records makes it impossible to trace whether Robert Ellis continued his privileged philandering in his new post.[8] But in 1805 the parish register recorded the baptism at Prospect, St. John Parish, of two mulatto daughters of Robert Ellis and a certain Priscilla McDonald: Maryanne, aged 6, and Nancy, a baby. Rather unusually, three sponsors were listed, all inhabitants of Lluidas Vale: Susannah Price and Nancy Quier, the mistress and the daughter of Dr. John Quier (who brought up at least one of the girls), and Eugene Mahoney, one of Robert Ellis' successors as overseer at Worthy Park.[9]

As to the details of the later career of Robert Ellis, the records are tantalizingly meager, almost certainly because he did not advance beyond the rank of overseer. He remained at Thetford at least until 1798 and was one of the two elected churchwardens of St. John's in 1799, but he seems to have left the parish for the eastern parts of Jamaica before 1810. Probably moving restlessly from estate to estate, he never became a planter, or even a slaveowner. If he ever married he does not seem to have fathered any legitimate children. In a brief will dated August 1843, Robert Ellis, then of St. James Parish, bequeathed all his goods, not numerous enough to be specified, to his "reputed son," yet another Robert Ellis.[10] That even such a once-powerful man as Robert Ellis could die after 50 years of service in Jamaica with neither substantial property nor legitimate family suggests that ordinary whites, for all their vaunted superiority, could be almost as much victims of the slave system as the blacks they ruled.

Dr. John Quier (1739-1822)

By far the longest-lived and most famous of the white inhabitants of Lluidas Vale was John Quier of Shady Grove, who served as doctor for Worthy Park and other estates from 1767 to 1822. Remarkably, in such an unlettered society, he was also something of an author, though a study of his contributions to *Letters and Essays on the Smallpox* (1778), already referred to,[11] suggests that he had no genius and less originality than he is sometimes credited with.

If John Quier had any distinction it grew with age. In a period when most whites became absentees as soon as they could, and practically none spent a lifetime in a single parish, Worthy Park's doctor preferred a life of usefulness, ease, and honor in backcountry Jamaica to the competitive hurly-burly of his homeland. In the course of time he became a respected medical and social authority, a patriarch. Though by choice, temperament, and abilities he seems to have clung to his received eighteenth-century aesthetic, social, and medical ideas, his life is chiefly interesting as it demonstrates how he was, in fact, gradually conditioned and shaped by his environment. It is not an exaggeration to say that John Quier's life suggests ways in which it was the tropical world and the black majority, rather than white men and European ideas, which were the dominant forces in slave society—a conclusion that would have shocked the likes of Edward Long.

John Quier was born of modest yeoman stock, at Chard in the county of Somerset, in 1739. Educated first at the local grammar school, he managed to find his way to the medical schools of London and Leyden, where he graduated M.D. in the year of the Treaty of Paris. At a time when there was still disagreement whether medicine was an art or a science and quacks abounded,[12] John Quier was relatively fortunate in his medical training. Medicine had not yet shaken free of the dogma of the four humors, but in London and Leyden he must have been influenced by the teachings of Sydenham and Boerhaave that the patient was the center of any treatment and the pragmatic observation was superior to any scientific argument. Like Hans Sloane before him, he was well versed in practical anatomy though markedly reluctant to resort to the knife. For long to come, surgery was regarded as inferior to, as well as more dangerous than, the practice of physic.

After graduating, John Quier served some years in the army. This was doubtless a useful training for ministering to regiments of slaves, with medicines issued in insufficient quantity from a central commissary. At this time he became acquainted with Dr. Donald Monro, a member of the famous medical clan of Edinburgh and later physician of St. George's Hospital, London, with whom he was to correspond on Jamaican slave diseases. Both doctors left the army for lack of employment in a time of peace, Quier, the man without family influence in the profession, choosing to try his fortune in Jamaica. In so doing he was one of a very long line of expatriate British doctors of moderate abilities or less (a remarkable number of them Scottish), though in remaining fifty-six years in the West Indies he was probably unique.

Almost immediately after arriving in Jamaica in 1767, John Quier settled in Lluidas Vale, buying the 250-acre holding called Shady Grove and building a modest house. He never became much of a planter, the hilly estate being used chiefly for growing provisions, with just a little sugarcane and coffee for processing in nearby factories. Although attached to Worthy Park for the purpose of the Deficiency Laws (which alone made his presence worth £25 Currency a year to the owners), he ministered also to the slaves on up to a dozen plantations in St. John and neighboring parishes. With as many as 4,000 slaves under his care at a per capita fee that rose from 5s. to 6s.8d. per year (the estates providing medicines)—not to mention the whites he charged £1 Currency a visit—he came to make a very comfortable income.

Lluidas Vale suited John Quier in other ways. He found its climate and elevation much healthier for newcomers than other parts of Jamaica, though less so for those who had spent any time in the lowlands. Lluidas was also very attractive scenically. Within a year of arriving, John Quier provided what is the best early description of the valley in a letter to Donald Monro, blending in quintessentially eighteenth-century fashion genuine enthusiasm, scientific observation, and rich romanticism.[13]

As has been shown earlier, John Quier faced a daunting array of tropical diseases and ailments, which he treated with probably no more than average success, at Worthy Park and the other estates under his care. He discovered no startling new remedies either in the European pharmacopoeia or through his growing acquaintance with bush medicine and does not seem to have used with great success even the mercurial compounds and quinine which alone of his medicines, in cases of venereal disease, yaws, and malaria, possessed some curative properties. Yet John Quier has been credited with preventative and diagnostic achievements at least in combating the twin scourges of smallpox and measles. Of the former disease, a contemporary colleague said that Quier "carried the practice of Inoculation to a much greater degree, than . . . by any of the boldest empirics of Europe," and a modern commentator has claimed that he perfected a diagnosis for measles in advance of his European contemporaries.[14] Both verdicts were almost certainly exaggerated. Quier's importance as a pioneer even in these limited fields was based simply on the unrivaled scope of his practice, the opportunities he had for experiment, the time he had in which to change his mind, and the publication of some of his observations. From his longevity it also seems that he followed better than most of his white patients his own sensible health rules for living in the tropics.

As he grew older and wiser, John Quier's fame and fortune grew, though never to extravagant heights. Inevitably be became important outside his profession, being elected successively vestryman, churchwarden, and (from 1799 to 1803) member of the Assembly for St. John's, as well as appointed justice of the peace and surgeon-major in the Militia.[15] On several occasions his opinion was sought by the Assembly on such matters as childbirth and polygamy among the blacks. Long and close acquaintance with slaves had made him as expert on them as any white, and though he continued to believe that the Europeans had more to teach the Africans than vice versa, familiarity does seem gradually to have given him more respect for blacks' qualities than one has come to expect from the planter class. In 1771, only four years after his arrival in Jamaica, he had written that he tried to avoid inoculating female blacks at the time of their menstruation but had found it difficult to ascertain their periods, "as the stupidity of the negroes is so great." His opinions of the native intelligence of unassimilated Africans, and of their morality "in the present State of their Notions of Right and Wrong," remained low. Yet in 1788, when testifying to the Jamaican Assembly on the tendency to polygyny, John Quier wrote without censure of the blacks that they were "universally known to claim a Right of disposing of themselves . . . according to their Own Will and Pleasure, without any Controul from their Masters."[16]

What doubtless gave John Quier his special insight into the black character was that he himself had notoriously "gone native." Like so many Worthy Park whites he habitually cohabited with slave women, and he never married. As he became an old man his house at Shady Grove became an easygoing ménage of several generations of his lovers and children, just like the traditional *casa grande* of the Portuguese colonies.[17]

Dr. John Quier died on September 19, 1822, at Shady Grove, the parish register unusually adding a comment to the notice of his burial that he had lived 56 of his 83 years in Lluidas Vale and the sentiment that his death was "much and deservedly regretted."[18] Jamaican wills are often useful in providing insights into the private lives of white men, but that of John Quier, originally written in June 1818, but added to in March 1819, is exceptionally revealing. It also sheds light on the subsequent fate of Shady Grove, which was to become the nucleus of the present village of Lluidas Vale.[19]

John Quier's English connections must have almost faded away after more than half a century in Jamaica without a single return. Only one English beneficiary was named in his will. Samuel Brown, a clothier of Chard, his "maternal relation," was left a small parcel of land in Somerset and £200 held in the "three percent funds of Great Britain." The doctor bequeated his medical books to a colleague, James Thompson, M.D.; but the remainder of his property was distributed among the members of his extended family and household, particularly to his two surviving mistresses, three "reputed" children, and three "reputed" grandchildren.

The patriarch's "old and faithful servant" Jenny or Jane was manumitted, with the understanding that "she should continue to occupy the house and provision grounds at Shady Grove." His "friend and housekeeper," Susannah Price, was intended to be one of the chief beneficiaries, along with her daughter Catherine Quier, but since Susannah died in 1819, a codicil bequeathed her share to Catherine Ann Smith, daughter of Catherine Quier by Thomas Smith of Blue Mountain Estate.[20]

The doctor's oldest surviving child and only son, Joseph Quier, the son of a Worthy Park slave called Dolly, had been manumitted as long before as 1778.[21] Now he was bequeathed simply £20 Currency and a small holding of 13 acres, 34 rods, at "Battalos, formerly part of Pusey," purchased from Mrs. Mary Delaney. This land was to revert to John Quier Davis, one of John Quier's "reputed grandsons," who, like his brother, Peter Quier Davis, was left six of his grandfather's slaves.

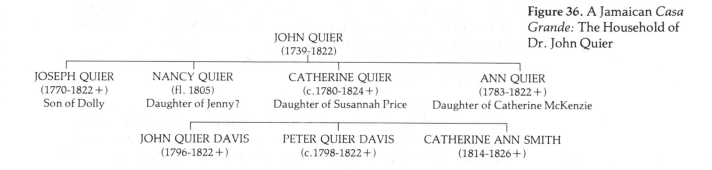

Figure 36. A Jamaican *Casa Grande:* The Household of Dr. John Quier

Since her father considered that she was already "rich . . . and fully portioned," John Quier's youngest surviving child, Ann, daughter of a free mulatto woman called Catherine McKenzie,[22] was simply confirmed in possessions that he had already provided for her: three personal slaves, and a house in Spanish Town purchased from the Honorable Charles Grant, owner of Tydixon, for £835 Currency.

In three minor bequests, John Quier left £25 Currency and (by the codicil) a female slave to Marianne Ellis, "a young privileged woman of colour who has long lived under my protection as an adopted daughter"; £10 Currency to John Quier Hammel, a "free lad of colour"; and £5 Currency a year to Patience Christian, "my female negro slave."

The most valuable of John Quier's possessions, the small estate of Shady Grove, was left in joint tenancy to Catherine Quier and Catherine Ann Smith, who also received the majority of the doctor's 65 slaves.[23] When Catherine Quier died, her share was to go to her sons, John Quier Davis and Peter Quier Davis, who, with their half-sister Catherine, were instructed "to have and to hold" the land "to themselves and their heirs in fee simple for ever not as joint tenants but as tenants in common, share and share alike"—an almost classic description of traditional Jamaican "family land" tenure.[24]

In fact both the land and slaves of Shady Grove were fairly rapidly dispersed after 1822. Catherine Quier (who, incidentally, seems to have been illiterate) married one William Turner, another "free person of colour," in 1824 and transferred all her 44 slaves to him.[25] When he died in 1826, his executor sold them. Similarly, Catherine Ann Smith's 24 slaves seem to have been swallowed up in the holding of her "guardian," Thomas Smith of Blue Mountain (one of John Quier's executors), who owned 62 in 1826, but 72 in 1832.[26]

By 1827 no Quiers were listed as slaveowners in the Register of Returns of Slaves, and Shady Grove had ceased to be listed as an estate in the *Jamaica Almanack*. The process of subdivision, sale, and transfer was complex and obscure, but between 1827 and 1850 Dr. Quier's estate was split up by John and Peter Davis, Catherine Smith, and their heirs, into lots which ranged from ten acres down to tiny house plots, giving the present village of Lluidas Vale its fascinating heterogeneity.

John Quier's house and fields have disappeared, as has the memory of the doctor himself, though the name Shady Grove lingers as a popular alternative to the village's official name.

Sir Rose Price (1768-1835)

Only member of the fifth of six generations of the Price family to own Worthy Park, Rose Price (created baronet in 1815) was quintessentially typical of his class and period. An absentee throughout the thirty-seven years of his own proprietorship, he spent only three years in Jamaica. Yet his brief period of residence resulted in an intensive reorganization that not only shaped Worthy Park's response to the economic and social disruption of slavery's last years but also conditioned Rose Price's lifelong attitudes towards the West Indies, sugar, slavery, and the blacks. Rose Price also left behind him in Jamaica two illegitimate colored children, who neatly symbolized the symbiotic, if unacknowledged, relationship between whites and blacks and their common involvement in the sugar-slave nexus and its aftermath.

Worthy Park had been founded by Rose Price's great-great-grandfather Francis (1635-1689), a penniless adventurer with Welsh antecedents, who spent more than half his life in Jamaica. It was developed as a sugar estate and its large slave population founded by Francis' son Charles (1678-1730), who probably never left the island. During the

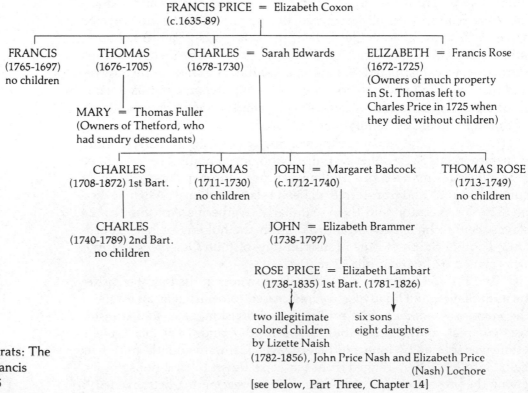

Figure 37. Plantocrats: The Descendants of Francis Price, c.1635-1835

heyday of West Indian sugar prosperity and plantocratic power, Worthy Park was jointly owned by two generations of Price cousins: a Cornish absentee and his son, both called John (1712-1740; 1738-1797), and a Jamaican grandee and his son, both called Charles and successively speakers of the House and baronets (1708-1772; 1740-1789). It was the Jamaican cousins who actually managed the estate, along with many other Price family holdings. Rose Price was the only surviving son of the second John Price, destined on his father's death in 1797 to become the sole owner of Worthy Park because his Jamaican uncle, the second Sir Charles Price, died childless.[27]

Rose Price enjoyed the somewhat exaggerated privileges and opportunities granted to the sole heir of a nouveau riche. Throughout his life he took for granted social privileges which were fortuitous. In modern parlance, he was spoiled. His father had been educated as a gentleman and had good political connections through his famous Jamaican uncle and cousin, the two Sir Charles Prices. But it was only the continuing high price of sugar and the accidents of mortality which reduced the number of those with a share in Worthy Park's income—from four to three in 1730, two in 1749, and one in 1789—that enabled him to aspire to the rank of country squire. In 1774, when Rose Price was six, his father was appointed high sheriff of Cornwall, and the family's social position seemed secure.

Brought up in John Price's townhouse in Penzance and country cottage of Chi-owne (or Chun), Rose Price was educated first at the local grammar school and then at Harrow before being entered as a gentleman commoner at Magdalen College, Oxford, in 1786. Having the leisure and wealth to be both litterateur and patron, John Price and his wife kept a modest salon, and it was here that Rose Price met Peter Pindar (1738-1819), the West Country satirist, quack doctor, and old Jamaican hand, and the artist John Opie (1760-1825), nicknamed "The Cornish Wonder." Another protégé of John Price was the brilliant scholar the Reverend John Vinnicombe, tutor and constant companion of Rose Price from 1786 to 1795.[28]

Rose Price's early life was varied and interesting, but protected. He was cocooned by wealth from the harsh proletarian realities of a tin-mining county already largely industrialized, shielded by the presence of his clerical mentor from the less gentle aspects of a public school and university education, and enjoyed a European Grand Tour uninterrupted by the outbreak of the French Revolution. Remotest of all was the source of the family wealth. Jamaica, which even his father had visited but once, before Rose Price was born, was known to the young man only from books, travelers' tales, and the half-yearly letters and accounts sent by Sir Charles Price or one of his agents. Unlike many absentee planters, the Penzance Prices did not affect black servants, and the only blacks whom Rose Price is likely to have seen were the sleek and liveried menials in other houses. Even the material to be gleaned from books would almost certainly have been limited to the outdated and sensational descriptions in Hans Sloane's *Jamaica* (1707) and the comfortable negrophobics in Edward Long's *History of Jamaica* (1774).[29]

As Rose Price was completing his education, however, events brought his Jamaican patrimony into close focus. In 1787, Sir Charles Price the younger arrived in England, in flight from the wreck of his Jamaican affairs. Two years later he died, leaving Worthy Park in John Price's unencumbered possession. At the same time, revolution threatened to spread from France to the colonies, and public attention was drawn to the slave trade and plantations by the report of the first government slavery inquiry.[30] The regular attorney's reports ordered since Sir Charles Price left Jamaica and the first returns under the Jamaican Act of 1787 disclosed that Worthy Park (like many West Indian estates) was suffering from a serious slump. Accordingly, John Price decided that his son—at almost exactly the same age as he himself had sailed to Jamaica just after the Seven Years' War—should go out to survey and, if necessary, reorganize the estate.

After much discussion and preparation, particularly in making arrangements for greatly extended credit, Rose Price and John Vinnicombe set sail, late in 1791 or early in 1792. Doubtless the pair had armed themselves with the 1789 Report of the slavery inquiry and William Beckford's two recent tomes on Jamaican planting and the blacks.[31] They were in fact embarked on an adventure in which only the energy, self-confidence, and certitude of youth were proof against their ignorance. In many ways the impact of Jamaica must have been similar to that on a later absentee, Matthew Gregory Lewis, who first visited his estate, Cornwall, in St. Elizabeth, in 1815, though Monk Lewis was older, did little reorganization, and planned to stay three months, not three years.[32]

Since his father lived at Penzance, Rose Price probably set out from Falmouth, in one of the regular West Indies packet boats. After raising Madeira and calling first perhaps at Barbados, Antigua, or Tortola, they reached Jamaica after from three to eight weeks, according to winds and the route taken. In 1792 the captain would have given a particularly wide berth to French Hispaniola, already in the throes of slave rebellion. Jamaica, in contrast, was peaceful though nervous. Coasting the southern shore and entering the wide expanse of Kingston Harbour, Rose Price, like Lewis, would have been excited by the novelty of the "dark purple mountains, the shores covered with mangroves of the liveliest green down to the very edge of the water, and the light-coloured houses with their lattices and piazzas."[33] Coming ashore to the ovenlike heat, the stench and noise of a large but featureless town, he was doubtless struck, like most first visitors, with the unexpected impression that this was overwhelmingly a *black* country. Even though it was quickly established that social hierarchies were comfortably similar to those of rural Cornwall, and that as planter Rose Price's squirearchical status was transferable and reinforced, it was bound to be sometime before the strangeness of finding class equated with race wore off.

At the quayside Rose Price would have met his father's attorney and Worthy Park's overseer, whose task it was to introduce the newcomer to the estate and its affairs, before handing them over. There too, deferential but curious, were likely to be the first Worthy Park slaves—coachman and wainman—the LP brand on whose shoulders must have given Rose Price the sudden realization that these were not just his father's workers like the laborers at Chi-owne but also his property, his *slaves*.[34]

Setting out as soon as possible for the country, probably in a pair of two-wheeled, two-horse gigs, and followed by their baggage at the more leisurely pace of an ox-wain, Rose Price and John Vinnicombe would have stopped briefly in Spanish Town. Here the new planter would have presented his formal compliments and letters of introduction to the lieutenant-governor of Jamaica and the custos of St. Catherine (by whom he was soon rewarded with the post of justice of the peace), while the cleric presented his credentials from the bishop of London to the top-ranking local ecclesiastic, the rector of St. Catherine's.[35] Then, probably with mounting excitement, they would have continued inland, through the Rio Cobre gorge and the wide green valley of St. Thomas, and over the blue shoulder of Mount Diablo. At the end of a long day they would have enjoyed their first sight of the beautiful Vale of Lluidas, where (as John Quier had enthused some twenty-three years earlier), "which ever way the eye is turned, it is regaled with an endless variety of pleasing prospects: below the plain delights it with the regularity of art; if directed upwards, it is never tired with viewing the romantic scenes which arise from so agreeable an assemblage of mountains, capped with clouds, shaggy woods crowned with perpetual verdues, steep precipices and hanging rocks.[36]

Rose Price's welcome at Worthy Park, by slaves who were greeting a member of their owner's family for the first time in many years, was probably as effusive, if as insincere and transient, as that given Monk Lewis by his slaves in 1815. Lewis, in the best and most plausible such account ever written, described the miniature "John Canoe" parade at his arrival, with shouting, drumming, dancing, and with every inhabitant (not to mention hogs, dogs, and fowls) pressing forward to see the master and pledge their fidelity with such sentiments as "So long since none come see me. Massa; good Massa, come at last."[37] For a few days all would have been gaiety, as an extra holiday was celebrated and small presents such as bells, buckles, and badges distributed.

For Rose Price it would have been a time of discovery and wonder, as aspects of sugar production only read of in books took on reality, and slaves who had simply been picturesque names in a ledger and then a clamoring sea of black faces, assumed individual identities as persons, however strange. In particular the lusty young man of 23, familiar with tales and whispers of the planter's unofficial droits de seigneur, must have had eyes for the most attractive of his father's female slaves, Worthy Park's equivalents of Cornwall's Psyche and Mary Wiggins.[38]

The period of euphoria and mutual goodwill must have been short at Worthy Park in 1792. It soon became clear that Rose Price was in Jamaica not for a courtesy visit but for a term of years, with strenuous plans for reorganization, and that he was a young man impatient of slackers, inefficiency, and unasked for advice. Unlike Monk Lewis, he lacked the warmth, humanity, or maturity to get close to his slaves. He did not even enjoy the effortless sense of superiority which had enabled Sir Charles Price to practice noblesse oblige. Moreover, his metropolitan sensibility, his somewhat defensive pride of lineage, and his disgruntlement that the Jamaican legislators had done little to rescue his family fortunes in the previous decade tended to isolate him from Jamaican whites of all sorts, almost as much as from the slaves. Apart from John Vinnicombe, his only close white associates seem to have been Dr. Quier of Shady Grove and Peter Douglas of Point Hill, neither of whom had been born in Jamaica.

Enough has been written already of the technical changes introduced by Rose Price: the increases in cultivation and production through opening up new fields, manuring, ratooning, introducing new machinery and bookkeeping methods, streamlining communications between fields, mills, and factory, building the New Road.[39] What has not been fully calculated is their effect on slaves and master. Most changes meant harder work for the slaves, closer supervision, and less free time, even if these were offset by rather better food, clothing, and medical treatment. More radical, the influx of new Africans meant an exacerbation of social divisions and tensions, as well as a serious increase in the incidence of disease. Creoles jealously guarded their superiority over new arrivals, but this depended on the master's concurrence, and it is likely that Rose Price as a newcomer himself was unaware of such subtle distinction between mere slaves. Shades of color, even degrees of what white men called "civility," were easier to distinguish. Yet for those Creoles forced to work alongside the new Africans in the fields, the situation was particularly onerous.

Traditionally, slaves much preferred a master living in the Great House to a plantation run by an attorney and overseer for an absentee. Though it contrasted sadly with their own condition, slaves even took pride in the style which their masters affected, as if such conspicuous consumption lent them reflected validity. A resident master certainly could act as arbiter against the slaves' immediate oppressors,[40] and an extravagant household could mean an easy, well-fed life for the domestic retinue. Rose Price lived in considerable style in the Worthy Park Great House from 1792 to 1795, but this was no more than he was accustomed to in Cornwall. From his scrupulous character it is unlikely that within three years he grew careless over the standards of household economy or protocol expected. Only those masters who gradually admitted defeat in the constant battle to keep food and stores from disappearing into the slave quarters, and to keep the domestics in the right place at the right time, were ever likely to grow close to their ordinary slaves.

As the practical difficulties of slave husbandry materialized (made worse by the outbreak of a 20-year war in 1793), Rose Price became ever more aloof from his workers at Worthy Park. If this were possible while he was a resident planter, it was all the easier once he was 4,000 ocean miles away, linked only by ledger entries and a capricious postal system, progressively disenchanted by sugar's failure, and looking for scapegoats. From the evidence of a book written many years later,[41] he seems to have adopted and maintained a view of the black similar to that of Edward Long, another writer whose authority was said to be buttressed by personal experience but who spent much of his life in England. Far from acknowledging the demoralizing effects of a system which equated blackness with servitude and judged a slave solely on fidelity and usefulness without providing any of the incentives or pride which came from ownership, Rose Price was quite ready to characterize the black as "naturally" unreliable, dishonest, untruthful, reluctant to work or learn. By a curious circular logic, alleged characteristics which—if they existed at all—stemmed from slavery were cited as evidence that those who possessed them were "natural slaves."[42]

If pressed, Rose Price, like many of his peers, would doubtless have maintained that the black was a perennial child who should be treated with strict paternalism. If so, this was self-deluding. Rose Price did indeed treat his own children with a Victorian strictness, but the treatment of his slaves was paternalism without a trace of love—even of that affection which a stockman might come to feel for the animals in his care. In Rose Price's dealings with his slaves, justice had no relation to mercy, and reasonable treatment was based not on charity but on a cold calculation of its value and of the counterproductivity of overt cruelty.

After 1797 mastery for Rose Price was only a concomitant of profit. Earlier, while his father was alive and he himself was living in Jamaica, mastery alone had been his chief reward, containing within it consolations for the isolation which it brought. Chief among these consolations were the far from innocent bodies of the female slaves he fancied. With or without the connivance of John Vinnicombe, Rose Price eventually took as his mistress a slave named Lizette, later Lizette Nash, or Naish. Predictably, she was not to remain a slave for long. She was a quadroon—probably like Mary Wiggins, neither brown nor "yellow" but what Monk Lewis called "ash-dove." She was also disgracefully young, seemingly no more than 13 when she bore the first of Rose Price's two Jamaican children.

Lizette, born in 1782, was the oldest child of a Worthy Park mulatto slave called Nelly or Eleanor Price, almost certainly fathered by an unrecorded white bookkeeper called Nash or Naish. Nelly/Eleanor, along with two other quadroon children, Kitty and Bessy, had already been manumitted in March 1789 by Peter Douglas of Point Hill, the children's father, for a payment of £200 Currency. Eleanor Price lived as Peter Douglas' wife from about 1784 until he died in 1821, taking Douglas as a middle name in 1817 and as a surname after Peter Douglas' death. The couple had no less than ten children, all of whom received equal shares under their father's will.[43]

Lizette was hired out to Peter Douglas in 1793 and manumitted on March 1, · 1794. The official document stated that John Price of Penzance, through his attorney Rose Price, in return for five shillings paid by John Vinnicombe, "hath Manumized released Enfranchized and Forever Set Free a Quadroon Woman Slave named Lizette of and from all Manner of Slavery Servitude Whatsoever on the Issue of her Body to be begotten." In the statutory manner, a bond for 100 Currency, to bring in £5 Currency a year to guarantee the ex-slave's upkeep, was lodged with the churchwardens of St. John's, John Quier and Samuel Queenborough. The witness to the whole transaction was Robert Ellis, head bookkeeper at Worthy Park.[44]

Lizette Nash was not pregnant when she was freed but became impregnated immediately afterwards, for her first child, Elizabeth Price Nash (later Lochore), was born on January 1, 1795, ten months to the day after the manumission document was completed. As with Ann Boleyn, it is interesting to speculate whether virginity was not used as a bargaining counter. Certainly Rose Price treated Lizette with reasonable generosity, first paying for her upkeep in the household of Peter Douglas, and then enabling her to become a modest landowner and slaveholder. She survived her lover by 21 years, to describe herself in her 1865 will as a "Gentlewoman."[45]

Lizette Nash and Rose Price had a second child, John Price Nash, born early in 1796. But by the time the boy was born the father had returned to England. Concerned about his own father's declining health, the development of the war, and the campaign to end the slave trade, Rose Price sailed with John Vinnicombe in one of the summer sugar convoys of 1795. Doubtless bored with Jamaica he yet had reason for satisfaction with progress at Worthy Park and for the fact that he had survived more than three years in the tropics in perfect health. A miniature painted shortly after his return from Jamaica shows him to have been a handsome young man, with a shrewd and lively face and silky black hair worn in the fashionable romantic style. With a guaranteed £6,000 a year after his father died in 1797, and often far more, he was clearly very eligible.

Within two years of his return from Jamaica and one year of John Price's death, Rose Price married Elizabeth Lambart, the beautiful 16-year-old daughter of an aristocratic but impoverished Irish family. This lady, whose full-length portrait by John Opie still graces the hallway of one of her descendants, bore Rose Price fourteen children before she died in 1826, at the age of 44. She also brought the connections which made him socially one of the most successful, as well as one of the last, of the great absentee sugar barons. Living in splendid style at Trengwainton House near Penzance, which he substantially rebuilt, Rose Price also spent much time with his titled relations, particularly the Earl Talbot of Ingestre Hall, Staffordshire. In 1814 Rose Price emulated his father in becoming high sheriff of Cornwall, and in the following year was created baronet.[46] Unlike the first Price baronetcy, held only by the two Sir Charles Prices, this creation still endures.

Significantly, Sir Rose Price chose for his title his Cornish estate, Trengwainton, not Worthy Park, the source of his wealth. Like most absentees he tried to turn his back on the West Indies, sugar, and slavery. But this proved impossible. As sugar prices fell so did Rose Price's income, and, as emancipation sentiment gradually spread, he found himself an object of increasing oppobrium. Successful exploitation is blithely ignored or rationalized; failure is doubly intolerable.

Sir Rose Price continued to peruse scrupulously the duplicate Worthy Park records he ordered sent regularly to England, but he grew progressively embittered and recriminatory over falling production, declining population, and mounting debts. He corresponded frequently on improved methods of technology, but increasingly preferred to maintain his English life-style and search out alternative investments, rather than pour good money after bad. As he grew older his temper did not improve, and his well-nurtured sense of propriety grew even sharper. Between 1818 and 1824 he was involved in bitter controversies over the salt duties, a theological controversy with a local Baptist minister, and an absurd and discreditable prosecution under the archaic Game Acts of Queen Anne's reign.[47] In 1826 he also suffered the double blow of the death of his wife and eldest son, which was followed a few years later by the disaffection of his second son and one of his daughters.

In addition, during the later 1820s and early 1830s, as the spirit of what Rose Price and his fellow Tories regarded as radical reform gained ground in England, the Jamaican question became more and more insistent, like a putrefying wound. Finally, in 1832 Rose Price turned to print. *Pledges on Colonial Slavery*, privately printed in Penzance, extravagantly defended slavery against those whom the author saw as the system's enemies. At the same time realizing that emancipation was probably inevitable, the embattled Rose Price argued strongly for apprenticeship for ex-slaves and generous compensation for slaveowners.

Both these limited objectives were achieved in principle in the parliamentary debates of 1833. But Sir Rose Price did not live to see them fail in practice to solve the planters' labor problems or to rescue their fortunes. He died on September 29, 1834, only a few weeks after the first Emancipation Act came into effect. One of the last and most stereotypical of his kind, he had also founded a divided dynasty—on both sides of legitimacy's blanket—that was to move away in every direction from slavery's stain and shame. Yet even this ultimate escape continued to be a function of economic and racial privilege.

Part Three

The Sons of Slavery

Jamaican mixed cane cutting gang around 1890, almost as driven, enduring, and anonymous as actual slaves.

12 / The Transition to Free Wage Labor, 1834-1846

THE fortunate survival of early wage records as well as slave ledgers among the papers of Worthy Park Estate provides a unique opportunity to analyze one of the crucial socio-economic transitions in West Indian history. Taking into account the degree to which Worthy Park can be said to have been typical, and its district analogous to Jamaica as a whole, such an analysis can be used to suggest conclusions of a validity general to Jamaica. As long as the conditions and circumstances special to Jamaica are considered, it could also be used to shed light on the rest of the British Caribbean and on other areas making a similar transition from slavery to "free" wage labor.[1]

With 3,000 acres (450 in canes) and 500 slaves, Worthy Park was one of the 100 largest of 859 Jamaican sugar estates in 1804, one of 23 in St. John Parish, and of 5 in the Lluidas Vale district. In St. John's and Jamaica alike in 1804, sugar plantations accounted for some 65 percent of the arable land under cultivation, and a similar proportion of the slave population.[2] By 1848 Worthy Park remained among the 508 surviving Jamaican sugar estates (the number tumbled to 330 by 1854), the 9 of St. John's, and the 2 in Lluidas Vale.[3] As with all surviving estates, Worthy Park's trimmed work force could be drawn not only from the ex-slaves from decayed estates but from a population at last beginning to expand naturally.[4] Both in St. John's and Jamaica as a whole only some 25 percent of the working population now found employment on sugar estates, a figure that probably fell to 15 percent by 1854. Worthy Park, which had commanded 20 percent of the population of Lluidas Vale in 1804, called on no more than 10 percent of the population in 1848, at a time when alternative employment in the locality had been reduced by more than half. At the same time, however, the working population of Lluidas Vale, St. John's, and Jamaica as a whole shared aspirations—and similarly limited opportunities—to move into the independent cultivation of the 40-50 percent of once cultivated land now classed as "ruinate," and the far greater acreage of potentially cultivable land which had never been cultivated during slavery days.

This chapter concentrates on four important general sets of questions, the first two proving susceptible to fairly precise answers, the second two leading to conclusions more speculative in nature. First, it considers how the switch to free wage labor changed the work force and the society formed by the slaves, and whether this was a sudden or gradual change. Second, it asks whether free wage labor was more efficient than that of slavery, comparing the labor costs and productivity of the two systems. Third, it speculates whether the changes observed were the result of a calculating policy on the part of the master class, and how they were affected by the will of the ex-slaves, by purely mechanical developments in the system, and by the operation of external forces. Finally, this chapter considers whether the dominant pattern or theme emerging from the events and conditions of 1834-1846 is one of change, or continuity.

Certainly (to hint at the final conclusion while tackling the first general question), in the layout of weekly employment in Figures 38, 39, and 40, there are some patterns which are still traceable today, and others more usually associated with slavery days. There are also features that would surprise both a modern employer and a pre-1834 slaveowner. The graphs of weekly employment and wage bills illustrate the plunge in employment during the Christmas and August holidays which are still familiar on sugar plantations, along with the preceding surge and subsequent slow build-up. Rather more surprising is the minor slump between March and April, in the middle of the crop season. Although based on figures from only two years this was probably a perennial feature, explicable not by the coincidence of bad weather but by the customary switchover from the harvesting of plant canes, which took fifteen months to mature, to ratoons, which took only a year.[5]

The employment and wages graphs illustrate a comparative lack of seasonal variation that is closer to slavery than to modern patterns. This comparative continuity of employment is even more apparent in the wages paid week by week than in the numbers employed, both because the higher paid workers were more continuously employed and because the larger gangs contained more people working less than a full week. Yet in both graphs it would be difficult for a stranger to identify the five-month crop period which is so distinct from the longer *tempo moto*, "or off-season," in modern sugar operations. Largely because of the overlap of operations, between 1842 and 1846 slightly more workers were employed and more wages paid in the period when the factory was running down or actually closed than in the peak (or peaks) of the crop. The continuity of employment could be made even more obvious if the graphs included the salaries paid consistently throughout the year to overseer and bookkeepers, as well as wages paid by the day and task. In any case there is a vivid contrast with the fivefold multiplication of employment and wages during crop time of recent Jamaican practice.[6]

Three important conclusions follow from this observation. It has often been noted why periodicity of employment was alien to the

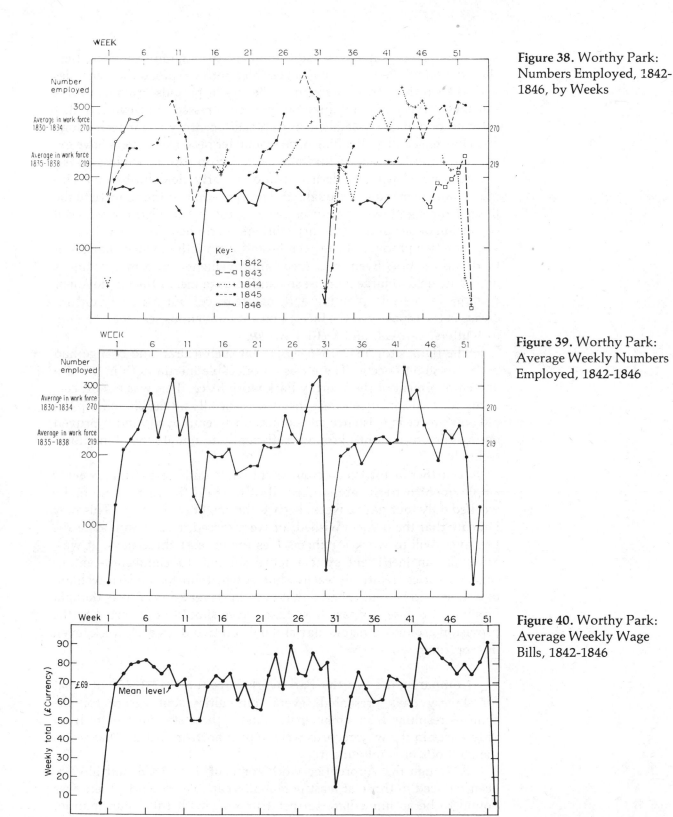

Figure 38. Worthy Park: Numbers Employed, 1842-1846, by Weeks

Figure 39. Worthy Park: Average Weekly Numbers Employed, 1842-1846

Figure 40. Worthy Park: Average Weekly Wage Bills, 1842-1846

277

system of slavery. If slaves had to be kept throughout the year, they should be employed as evenly as possible, both to spread their energies and to keep them from dangerous idleness in periods of comparative slackness. What has not previously been stressed, however, is that extreme periodicity was alien to eighteenth-century sugar technology and cane husbandry. Reading back from later practice, writers have exaggerated the "five-month fury of the sugar crop" during slavery days.[7]

Compared with modern operations, early field husbandry was much more demanding throughout the year, while at the same time the limited throughflow capacity of early factories curtailed the seasonal expansion of demand for factory workers. Periodicity of labor demand was largely a product of nineteenth- and twentieth-century changes in field and factory. Even with great improvements in farm techniques and cane yields a large increase in cane acreage meant the employment of more laborers in planting and maintenance; but a twentyfold increase in the capacity of the factory meant a ravenous seasonal demand for cutters, carriers, and factory workers.

The figures for 1842-1846 show that such a dramatic change had not yet begun to occur. There was a noticeable inertia both in the size and employment of the Worthy Park work force. This was almost certainly for two concurrent reasons: it was socially advisable to keep the old work force in existence and continuously employed, and it proved impossible on economic grounds sufficiently to update the plantation's technology.

A further factor becomes apparent when daily rather than weekly employment patterns are studied. By the 1840s the factory normally worked only four days a week, even at the height of the crop. This may indicate that the owners wished, or were forced, to accommodate the ex-slaves' will to work for themselves for at least three days. It was, however, an inefficient system more suitable to eighteenth-century sugar factories, relatively easily shut down, than to modern technology. It should be remembered that even in slavery days it was thought feasible, and wise, to pass laws that slaves should be diverted to the provision grounds, first one day and then on two days each week, even in crop time.

Comparing the Worthy Park work force for 1842-1846 with that for slavery days presented several difficulties; but except for the changes resulting from emancipation itself, these stemmed more from differences in the way records were kept than from actual changes in the methods of employment.

Although the Apprentice work force of 1834-1838 had already been reduced to those at least potentially capable of work, there was bound to be an immediate further trimming with full emancipation. Unlike the slave lists, which included in work categories many who were temporarily or even permanently unemployable simply because the estate was responsible for them, the Worthy Park wage books included only those who actually worked. Besides this, far more details were provided of work done after 1838 than was found necessary when drawing up the slave records. This did not imply great changes in actual employment, but rather a need to know more precisely what had been done, in order to assess wages.

The precise differentiation of tasks, however, blurs the distinction between gangs, and not entirely because such divisions were less important than during slavery days. For example, cane-cutters continued to form a definite class; but since demands for cane were flexible even during crop time, the same people might cut cane and perform other tasks in the same week, or the whole cane-cutting group might be switched to the same tasks as others who were never employed in harvesting cane. Also, switchings between factory and field, and between specific craftsmen's tasks—as from trash-carrier and cooper to cane-carrier and fencer—were probably no more frequent than in slavery days; but the greater detail surviving gives such changes undue prominence.

Other difficulties occurred because of variations in the method of payment. The vast majority of Worthy Park's workers, including field headmen, were paid by daily rates. Distillers and some craft apprentices, however, were usually paid by the month or over less regular periods, so that they appeared only at intervals in the weekly records. For some reason the six female domestics were paid separately and, like the salaried managerial staff, did not appear in the weekly wage records at all.[8] Also, a fluctuating number of employees were paid not by daily wages or salaries but by tasks. These workers included messengers sent to Kingston or the post office at Ewarton, certain craftsmen such as hedgers and ditchers, and the "Immigrants"—the handful of white laborers unsuccessfully imported in 1842—who as far as was possible were kept distinct from the mass of ex-slaves. A final difficulty was that the headmen, except for the field superintendents, were not distinquished as a class, though it was quite easy to identify the head boiler-man, head carpenter, head cattleman, and head watchman by the wages paid.

In all, complete wage records still existed for 117 of the 214 weeks between January 1, 1842, and February 14, 1846, providing individual names, daily tasks, and the daily wages paid. With this material alone, three major analytical tasks were made possible, and many important conclusions emerged concerning continuities and changes.

First, continuities could be traced individually. By taking the last Apprentice list of names of 1838 it was possible to discover which of the Apprentices were still employed in 1842, whether they continued to be employed until 1846, whether they continued in the same jobs, and to what extent their employment was, and remained, continuous in any one year.

Second, it was possible to make a complete reconstruction of the Worthy Park work force for the crucial years 1842-1846, showing numbers of both sexes employed from week to week, the classes of employment, and the jobs done. This material could then be compared in general with what had already been discovered about the slave and Apprentice work forces for 1783-1838.

Third, a great deal of analysis was possible concerning the wages paid. Above all, by looking at the periodicity of employment and the fluctuating totals of wage bills against sugar production and prices, it was possible to work out the profitability of the system of wage labor as then practiced, to compare it with that of slavery, and to suggest why and in what ways it changed from 1842 to 1846.

Unfortunately, the nature of the wage records did not allow for the deduction of demographic material to match and compare with that trove gathered from the slave period and analyzed in Part One above, save for the calculation of the sex ratio of the workers employed and an estimate of the effect of changes observed. Nor did it prove feasible to perform the same kind of individualization with the 117 wage lists of 1842-1846 as has been undertaken earlier for the 34 slave and Apprentice lists of 1783-1838. Such an exhaustive task would require many years of research. Instead, it was decided to concentrate on individualizing the 1842 work force, or more specifically those 338 workers employed at Worthy Park during seven carefully selected weeks in that year—three during harvesting periods and four outside, including the August holiday week. Once these workers had been indexed it was possible to trace with fair accuracy and detail employment patterns not only within 1842 but also forwards into certain weeks of 1844, 1845, and 1846 and backwards into the last days of slavery and Apprenticeship.[9] This is illustrated in Tables 53 to 58.

Tables 59 to 66 relate to the calculation of productivity, costs, and profits during the period 1839-1848, and provide a comparison with the years 1830-1838. Wherever feasible, like was compared with like. This was easiest in determining Worthy Park's gross revenue, and it also proved easy to compare productivity.[10] Comparing production costs, and particularly the cost of the labor component, was much more difficult. The total cost of wages for 1839-1847 could be known with some precision from the almost complete breakdown for 1839 and the weekly totals for 1842-1846 in the extant records, and from the supplementary evidence presented by George and Thomas Price to the Graham Commission in 1848. But how could these costs accurately be compared with the costs of buying and maintaining slaves? And what of other plantation costs?

The chief method of comparing costs used might be termed overlapping extrapolation: taking the known costs of each system of employment and applying them to the other, in order to see whether there was an actual rise or fall. This method had the advantage of discounting any radical changes in the composition of the work force, though care had to be taken to discover whether there were any significant general inflationary or deflationary trends over the period studied, and to take these into account if necessary.

Two rough indications of cost accounting from the earlier period were that it was said in 1790 that in Jamaica it cost on the average £5 a year to maintain, and £10 a year to hire, a single slave. This might have indicated an average anuual cost of £15 per laboring slave but for several snags. The £5 included clothing as well as food and was an average for unproductive as well as for healthy laboring slaves. Hired slaves were provided with food and tools by the person hiring, but not clothing. It was not clear how much of the £10 was profit for the owner, or whether it could be said to include a realistic sum for capital depreciation on the slave's original or replacement cost. All in all, it seemed likely that the cost of nonhired slaves was closer to the jobber's average of £10 a year than to £15, once depreciation was added to maintenance cost and the profit ignored.[11]

If it were allowed that hiring costs were a direct indicator of slave labor costs, the discovery in the Worthy Park papers of a set of hiring rates for 1837, broken down by classes, was especially fortunate. These rates were applied to the known work forces not only for 1830-1838 but also for 1842-1846, to make the first extrapolated comparison. Rather surprisingly, this magnified the difference between actual wages paid in 1842-1846 and the costs calculated for 1830-1838, by suggesting that the wage bill for 1842-1846 at 1837 rates would have been lower than for either 1830-1834 or 1834-1838.

The findings obtained by projecting the 1837 hiring rates forward were reinforced by the second extrapolation: the projection of actual wage rates paid in 1842-1846 back to the period 1830-1838.

Although there seems to have been an overall inflation of as much as 25 percent in Jamaica between 1830 and 1846, the calculations given here suggest that the system of free wage labor as practiced at Worthy Park between 1842 and 1846 was almost twice as expensive as the cost of labor in the last days of slavery. This could only have been justified economically by commensurate improvements in the average productivity of the workers, or by cost economies elsewhere.

In fact there were great savings in nonlabor costs at Worthy Park in the period 1839-1847 as compared with the days of slavery and Apprenticeship. Managerial staff was trimmed, and because the owners were resident no commission had to be paid to a local attorney. Freight and insurance rates and the commission paid on sales were also greatly reduced. These reductions, and the increased cost of labor, meant that the labor component in the cost of production rose from about 30 percent towards the end of slavery days to over 60 percent. This represented about 13s.9d. per hundredweight of sugar, of the approximately 25s. per hundredweight which a Jamaican committee in 1847 calculated was the average cost of production in the island.[12] With the London price of sugar declining towards the average cost of production, and with the price actually received by the estates probably falling below it in nearly all cases in 1845, the question of the cost of the existing system of labor had become critical.

Returning to the patterns disclosed in the employment tables and estimating their significance, it is clear that though the switchover to paying wages represented a revolution in the financial organization of the estate, the changes in factory, field, and labor husbandry were made far more gradually. Some practice in the payment of wages had already been gained during the Apprenticeship period, when wages were paid at official rates for hours worked in excess of the weekly maximum of 40. At the same time, the work force had been considerably stream-lined. With a run of reasonably productive years in the later 1830s, when sugar prices appeared to be on the increase again, a continuation of much the same system seemed to have been called for after emancipation, except that wages would now be paid for all hours worked.

In 1842 the Worthy Park work force was still essentially the same as it had been four and more years earlier, in organization and even in personnel. At first glance there did seem to be certain differences disclosed by a comparison between the components of the 1842 work force and those of the slave and Apprentice work force for 1783-1838, even when the unproductive were removed from the earlier pattern. Closer examination, however, showed these to be owing more to changes in labels and disparities in knowledge of the two work forces than to any substantial reorganization of Worthy Park's labor system. Moreover, it was clear that there was an even greater similarity disclosed by a comparison between the 1842 work force and that for the period immediately before emancipation, rather than for 1783-1838 in general.

Similarly, as to personnel, at first sight there seemed to have been a considerable flight from Worthy Park by the ex-slaves upon their full emancipation. Of the 233 Apprentices still on the estate on July 31, 1838, only 83 could be certainly traced in 1842, and 94 in all—40.4 percent—between 1842 and 1846. But when the individuals were looked at more carefully, particularly once males were separated from females, the picture changed dramatically.

Of the 70 male workers of 1838 with two names, at least 51 were still working at Worthy Park in 1842, and no less than 60 were detected in the ten lists examined for 1842-1846. Of the mere 10 whose names did not recur, 3 were over 55 in 1842, almost too old for useful plantation work, and, on the average, death might have accounted for all 7 of the others. Among the 18 males with only one name in 1838, only 3—Duncan, Guy, and Italy—were still found in 1842. But 7 of the remainder were over 58, and the other 8 may have died, or else have acquired new names and gone on working at Worthy Park. All in all, at least 79 percent, and perhaps as many as 95 percent, of all the eligible male "old hands" continued to work at Worthy Park in the 1840s.[13]

The figures for the women workers were less remarkable, but still impressive once the same factors, and others peculiar to females, were taken into account. Of the 145 female Apprentices of July 31, 1838, 121 had two names and 24 one. Of the former, only 28 at most could be traced in 1842, and 30 for the entire period 1842-1846. Of the latter, only one, Damsel, was found in the 1840s' lists—though she became the last survivor of all the single-name slaves, the only one to be listed in 1846. Even when the 19 female slaves with double names and the 11 with single names who were listed as "invalid" in 1838 or were over 55 in 1842, and an additional 8 who might on the average be presumed to have died in the interim, were deleted, 77 females—well over half—remained unaccounted for.

The increase in the proportion of males in the Worthy Park labor force while the total remained more or less static implied that slightly more women dropped out than men. But several additional factors make it clear that this proportion was far less than the apparent 53.1 percent. As with the men, many of the 10 single-name female Apprentices under 55 in 1842 may have continued working at Worthy Park after changing their names. Besides this, a considerable number of females changed their names for other reasons: most commonly by adopting the surname of a new husband or marital partner, or, to avoid confusion through duplication, by taking the name of a deceased person or even through simple whim—for which there is definite evidence in the records.[14]

These tendencies made the figures for the continuity of females' employment at Worthy Park after emancipation even less calculable than for males, but it seemed likely that at least 75 percent of Worthy Park's eligible female ex-Apprentices worked on the estate at least part of the time during the early 1840s. Taking the Apprentice work force as a whole, the percentage was almost certainly close to 90, though the number of *regular* workers was probably nearer to 80 percent in the case of the men, and considerably less in the case of the women.[15]

Although it is usually said that it was during the years immediately after emancipation, when all produce prices were relatively high, that the most rapid migration from the estates occurred, it was evident that as late as 1842 the old hands remained the core of the Worthy Park work force, at least as far as the men were concerned. Not only did nearly all the males remain in employment, they also monopolized the most essential and prestigious jobs. Of the posts open to males in 1842 counted as elite in the earlier slave analysis, old hands occupied twenty-one out of twenty-three, despite the fact that the total number of males employed had risen by 18 percent, and the newcomers actually outnumbered the ex-Apprentices.

The old hands remained faithful to Worthy Park at least four years after they were free to leave; but their fidelity may have been purchased by the improvement in their lot which virtually all the male old hands enjoyed. Craftsmen remained craftsmen, but probably with more practical independence as the tyranny of the bookkeepers was loosened. Many men listed in 1838 simply as laborers—albeit "first

Jamaican Market around
1840, little changed from
slavery days. Lithograph
from a daguerreotype by
Duperly showing Falmouth,
Trelawny.

class"—became craftsmen, while others graduated from the tedium of
field labor to employment as wainmen, fence-makers, or woodcutters.
Even those few still constrained to work in the fields almost invariably
carried cane rather than cutting it, or plowed land rather than having to
dig cane holes with mattocks as in the bad old days. Seven of Worthy
Park's eight plowmen in 1842 were old hands.

No doubt most men worked better under such promising conditions, and the owners of Worthy Park might have believed that encouraging their long-term workers would have a beneficial effect upon pro-

ductivity and profits. But if they were disappointed—if productivity did not at least stay level and profits, for whatever reason, declined—a policy of encouragement would have seemed an encouragement to inefficiency, acceptable only in times of dire labor shortage. Moreover, it is a commonplace of labor employment that conditions cannot be continuously improved for all workers and production maintained, without fundamental reorganization.

A further examination of the entire work force at Worthy Park in 1842 and afterwards—particularly of the degree to which employment was continuous throughout the year, and of the scale of dropping out as the 1840s progressed and economic conditions deteriorated—disclosed that the employers' policy was not simply one of inducing old hands to stay on, and that even the old hands were not so secure as at first seemed.

The switching of jobs with the change in seasons noticeable in 1842 indicated a willingness on the part of the management to retain valuable workers and a desire of many workers to remain even in a less well paying job for the sake of continuous employment. There was, however, a high correlation between those continuously employed and those in the more prestigious and lucrative jobs, as well as between the continuously employed and those who had been longest at Worthy Park. This situation boded ill for any later needs for ordinary laborers. Wages were never high; but with more continuous employment the yearly totals paid on the average to individuals were higher than in subsequent years, when employment was more sporadic even if daily wage rates were fractionally higher.

There was also plentiful evidence that differentials in wages were used as inducements. In place of the tenuous attractions of promotions towards easier and more senior jobs in slavery days, a very wide range of pay scales was used at Worthy Park in the 1840s. So varied were the payments that it would be easy to conclude at first glance that all workers were paid by the task rather than at daily rates. A few were, but the majority received different daily rates according to sex and seniority and also, presumably, proven efficiency, reliability, and fidelity. Over the whole period 1842-1846, wages ranged from 9d. a day for young female laborers, to 4s.6d. a day for senior boilermen. But there were six different rates at one time for field laborers alone, and in most occupations with only three or four workers, each received a different daily rate.

Increased wages did not necessarily relate to increased authority. Field headmen, with 2s. a day (for the one field headwoman it was 1s. 6d.), were paid less than half as much as under boilermen. The real authority wielded by the field headmen may have been a substitute for higher wages, but the status of those in such authority was certainly not reinforced with money. The new hierarchy of wage scales and methods of payment may have been as important a change as the introduction of wages themselves, even if it could be shown to have stemmed from the different monetary valuations placed on slaves according to their skills. A worker earning 4s.6d. a day clearly had a different life-style and regarded himself superior to one earning a third or a sixth as much. Those valued craftsmen who could command task rates were clearly in a superior class yet, though still inferior to those favored employees paid monthly salaries: bookkeepers, distillers (in 1842 and 1844 at least), and even, for a time, the head cattleman, lord of the range.

The most notable change in the composition of the 1842 work

force was the decrease once more in the proportion of women. Even if the half-dozen domestics paid separately were added, the overall proportion of males rose from just under 40 percent in 1838 to over 60 percent, a return to the ratio of the earliest days of slavery. Women had always been restricted from most of the relatively prestigious and skilled jobs. But now, though women continued to constitute 70 percent of the first, or cane-cutting, gang, men occupied a far higher proportion of other laboring jobs, especially those requiring a degree of specialization. Women, besides occupying the most menial and lowest-paid jobs (being paid as little as half as much as men for equivalent tasks), were on the average also far less continuously employed than men. Clearly, the management preferred male employees. Women continued to be employed in large numbers only of necessity, and despite their comparative unreliability. The lack of reliability, in turn, was probably partly a response to being treated as of inferior value.

These trends surely had important social effects. Altogether, with the increase in the proportion of males employed from 40 to 60 percent and the employment of the reduced proportion of women on the average of no more than 200 days in the year—not to mention the decline in the number of plantations which meant that the population in general toiled less at plantation work—there must have been at least a 50 percent decline in the time and energy expended by Jamaican women in estate labor in the decade after 1834. The improvement effected on the birthrate and the chances of rearing more healthy children, aided also by the increase in the number of marriages and other stable monogamous relationships, could not be calculated accurately. But the 1844 census data did indicate a rapid shift towards a stable population. Even a minimal increase in the birthrate while general health conditions remained static would have provided the population with a natural increase, even in the last days of slavery.[16] Indications were that in the two decades after 1834 the Jamaican crude birthrate increased to almost double the slavery figure, so that almost instantly after emancipation the Jamaican population was able to sustain itself and expand. But for a slow decline in the birthrate after 1860, and the continuation of appalling health conditions (especially as related to infant mortality) coupled with much emigration, the Jamaican population would have risen much faster than it did in the later nineteenth century. Only in the second quarter of the twentieth century, with a birthrate still 50 percent higher than in slavery days, dramatic improvements in health conditions, and a reverse in the flow of migration, did Jamaica's population really begin to soar.[17]

Another significant change noticeable in the 1842 wage lists, though minor in scale and not lasting, was the presence of ten white immigrants. Taking advantage of the harsh economic situation in Europe, the employers were obviously attempting to revert to the old era of the white indentured servant. Coupled with the widespread flight of the old white staff, the establishment of a white proletariat would have had radical social repercussions. Although kept at separate jobs and paid by task, Worthy Park's white laborers received an average of only 9s.11½d. a week in February and March 1842, which placed them some way down the estate's wage hierarchy. However, they did not last long. By the week of June 6-11, 1842, only three were still listed. The most pathetic was Mary Geraghty, paid 6s.3d. for six days' cleaning the cane-yard in place of her husband and brother-in-law, who were in the process of drinking themselves to death.[18] Mary herself was not recorded again, though two of the immigrants were found periodically listed as task laborers—no longer distinguished in the wage bills—as late as April 1844.

Later, Jamaican estates, including Worthy Park, imported indentured "coolies" from India on the plea of a labor shortage. In fact, the presence of European and Asian laborers in Jamaica did not necessarily signify an actual shortage of labor, but more likely the search for reliable, and if possible cheap, laborers tied to the estates by enforceable contracts. Certainly, positive evidence exists in the Worthy Park records that the owners tried to retain their original laborers first, either by binding them or by offering inducements. Like most Jamaican estates, Worthy Park attempted from 1838 to lighten its wage bill and to capitalize on the desire of many of its ex-slaves to stay on in their houses and plots, by charging resident laborers rent. In 1839, £342, nearly 15 percent of wages, were deducted at source for rent. In the following year, Worthy Park's owners tried to have the best of both worlds by also charging £2,570—more than they paid in wages—for the provision grounds belonging to the estate which were worked by the laborers "on the side," or by others. The intention was to make it financially impossible for those who wished to use the cottages not to work for the estate, or for those who worked for the estate to cultivate much land independently as well.

These tactics failed signally. By 1842 the total of rent collected—all for houses—was under £50, and within a few more years it was nothing at all. In effect Worthy Park was then offering rent-free cottages and land to its regular workers. But even this did not effectively tie cottagers to the estate (like most English farm laborers at the time) until it was backed up by a fairly ruthless policy of evictions. This policy mainly came later in the century, but it failed to increase the number of workers tied to the estate, while at the same time antagonizing many potential, if occasional, workers.

As long as land was available elsewhere, and money could be made from peasant farming, there was bound to be a shortage of cheap labor. Besides, since the peaks of crops tended to be concurrent, the agricultural needs of peasant farmers tended to compete directly with those of the estates. It was notable that at Worthy Park it was the field workers whose work was most sporadic. Of the 112 who appeared only once in the seven lists in 1842, no less than 93, or 83 percent, were field laborers, though the field workers made up only 56 percent of the total work force. Paradoxically, those who were most industrious (at their own work) might be those who were nost unreliable from the estate's point of view; those who had been given most (in the way of workable land) were most likely to be labelled "disloyal." As George Price complained in a chilling phrase in 1848, not even the most benign employer could guarantee to "put his hand on the laborer" exactly when he needed him. The 1842-1846 employment graph (Figure 39) provided an excellent example of this. Before both Christmas and the August holiday there were surges of employment as the "benign" employer encouraged the desire of workers for holiday money, even to the extent of "making work." Yet after Christmas, as the crop began, and after the first week in August, when it was best to plant, the work force built up far more gradually than the planter would have wished.

By 1845 it was necessary for Worthy Park's owners to send one William Graham into St. Anne Parish during the August holiday, for 4s., to look for laborers. Such recruits as were rounded up, like the gangs of "jobbing" (hired) slaves of an earlier period, were kept distinct from the regular workers, as a Strangers' Gang. Such a group was found at Worthy Park as early as June 1842, but it consisted solely of 10 women and 7 men. By July 1845 there were two large gangs of strangers at Worthy Park, totaling nearly 100—no longer designated Strangers' Gangs since they now outnumbered the old field hands.

By this time, Worthy Park's labor recruitment and organization had undergone substantial changes. The period of transition from cohesion and continuity of employment to a pool of free wage labor was well under way. Yet these changes were accompanied and shaped by other changes. Between 1843 and 1847 the Prices spent at least £ 30,000 on capital improvements: installing a Boulton and Watt steam engine in the mill, railways in the fields, and a cableway across the Great Gully and up the hillside on the way towards Ewarton. For the first time plows were used systematically. Year by year the labor force was increased, to install the new machinery and to raise the capabilities of the fields towards the increased capacity of the factory, which George Price claimed was 700 tons a year.

Not only were the new laborers largely strangers, they were also employed more casually, or, rather, more commonly employed only when they were strictly needed. In slavery days efforts were made to have the slaves working as many days as possible, with the factory running almost continuously in crop time despite the laws which by the end of slavery decreed that one-and-a-half days each week be devoted to provision grounds. In the 1840s the Worthy Park factory rarely ran more than four days a week, a pattern already common throughout Jamaica and found elsewhere in the British West Indies. Though this may have been because the owners were forced to accept the laborers' wish for at least three days for themselves, it was still the factory owners who decided when the factory would operate, and to an increasing degree only those workers strictly needed were employed on extra days. By the later 1840s even the craftsmen, for whom alternative employment had once been found when the factory was closed down, now tended to be laid off, not only in the off-season but in the dead periods of the week too.

In the very last wage list of the series studied, that for the week of February 9-14, 1846, there was much evidence of the rationalization of the Worthy Park work force to suit the demands of four days' operations in the factory and the major improvements still being made to the fields and plant. The cane-cutters and carriers together formed a distinct cadre, though divided into separate groups for different cane-prices. But for the rest the old system of gangs had almost disappeared. The total number employed, 288, was not noticeably greater, but the number of groups had multiplied as they were tailored to suit the complex needs of that particular season, week, or set of days. No one was employed longer than was strictly necessary. For factory laborers and cane-cutters this meant a four-day week, though some carriers and other field laborers worked five days. Even field headmen were employed only for the same length of time as their group. Masons and mortarers were needed for four days, but their lime-carriers for five. Some carpenters and blacksmiths were needed for six days, and cattlemen and watchmen for every day and night, of the week. Even the head boilerman was only employed for four days, and his assistants a mere two days. The distiller was paid for six days' work, but this journeyman treatment was quite a comedown from earlier years, when the distiller was one of the few workers paid a monthly salary (£2.10.0 a month or £30 a year, in 1842).

It was also clear that by 1846 the number of old hands at Worthy Park had quite markedly declined from 1842. Only 44 of the 233 Apprentices of 1838 were to be found for certain in the last wage list for February 9-14, 1846, 34 men and a mere 10 women out of a total of 288 workers. If the degree of continuity in the work force down to 1842 was remarkably high, this sudden trend in the opposite direction was equally remarkable.

The difficulties of identifying women discussed earlier apply again here with increasing force. But even the decrease in male old hands is far greater than could be attributed to death or advancing age. The surviving old hands continued to occupy posts that were relatively well paid and responsible and that offered the best prospects for continuous employment; they stayed because they valued such employment, or they gravitated towards those jobs because they elected to stay. The owners may still have valued and protected them to a degree for the sake of cohesion and continuity. Yet, though the remaining male old hands still held more than their proportional share of the elite and preferential jobs, they were now in a minority even there. By 1846 they occupied only one of the five superintendents' positions, 6 of the 15 factory craftsmen's posts, and 6 of the 25 nonfactory craftsmen's jobs, a total of 13 out of 35, compared with 21 out of 23 only four years earlier.

What has still to be decided is whether the Worthy Park rationalization was the result of a calculated policy of reorganization on the part of the estate's owners, or whether it was forced on them by economic circumstances or by a failure of workers to work when required. Two of the owners, George and Thomas Price, went out to Jamaica in 1842 to manage the estate in person, and when they gave detailed evidence to the Parliamentary Commission in 1848, the Price brothers certainly claimed that they—even more than the workers —were the victims of an economic decline. They did not blame themselves save for being too optimistic about sugar prices and the reliability of Jamaican laborers; and they claimed credit both for their attempts at mechanization and for their readiness to double Worthy Park's wage bill against the general tide of retrenchment. The Prices claimed to have paid almost £5,000 in wages in 1846, and £6,000 in 1847.[19] But these sums were shared among such a transient labor force that what they represented in individual annual averages was doubtless pitiful. Moreover, the boost was bound to be temporary, being brought about by an expansion aimed at increasing productivity, and thus eventually reducing work force and wage bills alike.

The Prices' calculations for a viable operation were based on the maintenance of a sugar price that was at least 20 percent above the cost of production, of which wages should constitute no more than 50 percent at the most. This modest assessment compared closely with slavery days, when the labor component was rarely more than a third of total costs, which in turn were often less than half of revenue.[20] In the early 1840s, while efforts were still being made to induce continuous employment, sugar prices were such that wages constituted 50 percent, not of costs but of *revenue*. During the period of reorganization, the Prices did not have much difficulty in recruiting gangs at 2s.6d. per day per worker, especially out of the harvesting season when peasant farmers had few commitments of their own. But 1846 and 1847 brought bitter disillusion. Far from doubling production and trebling productivity, the expensive changes were followed by an actual fall in production between 1845 and 1847, so that production per field worker was considerably lower than during slavery and Apprenticeship. To compound the trouble, the sugar price declined by 30 percent between 1846 and 1848, so that the wages paid at Worthy Park reached the impossible proportions of double the estate's total revenue.

Like most planter witnesses in 1848, the Prices complained that the laborers would not work when wanted, whatever the wages. Yet the planters' main threnody was that the essential villian was the wholesale sugar price. In this there was much justification; but the situation had become so critical that if raising the price were to be the only solution, only a magical doubling of prices would serve. With Parliament prepared to go no further than to delay the final repeal of protection for six years, all that could be hoped for sugar prices was a slight recovery through increased consumption outrunning any increase in production.

291

By any system of accountancy the only remaining ways in which the bankruptcy of sugar estates could be staved off were increased productivity and the drastic trimming of wage bills by abandoning all inducements to continuous employment. Because Jamaica was even less suitable for modernization than other British colonies, new technology was introduced extremely slowly. At the same time, the collapse of so many estates, coupled with an accelerating population increase, a fall in peasant produce prices, and the consequent shrinkage of the fund of cash in circulation, produced an increasingly competitive pool of rural labor susceptible to casual employment.

Although it was the age of imperial laissez-faire as far as protection and the provision of financial aid to the colonies were concerned, the situation was exacerbated by government policies. These included the cynical increase in labor competition through the importation of coolies, and forcing would-be peasants off their land and into the rural proletariat by means of policies of dear Crown Land and squatter eviction, on the principles advocated most notably by E. G. Wakefield.

The combined result of all these developments was the gradual shift to Jamaica's version of sugar equilibrium: the land used wastefully, outdated factories barely ticking over, most of the workers employed four days a week, five months in the year, at a daily rate of wages that did not increase for a hundred years and was preferable only to its alternative, starvation.

Against all the odds, George Price (incidentally, an implacable opponent of the tyrannical Governor Edward Eyre) retained a reputation for being a fair employer in the 1850s; that is, he paid at least the going rate of wages and did not resort to the convenient provisions of the Masters and Servants Laws except in extreme cases. Yet as a planter he failed. Subsequent owners of Worthy Park—first absentees, then a new generation of "improving" residents whose Jamaican roots did not go back to slavery days—had no qualms over evicting squatters or taking laborers to court who illegally withheld their labor once they had started work. These plantocratic actions were regarded as painful duties owed to the estate's parlous economy.[21] They only became outdated by the combination of economic success and the political organization of the workers after World War II.

As early as June 1832, William Taylor, a Jamaican overseer giving evidence before the Inquiry into the Christmas Rebellion, stated the opinion that no ex-slave would continue working on a sugar plantation a moment after slavery ended, given viable alternatives.[22] Presuming that this expert prediction was fulfilled, and citing the planters' complaints of labor shortages to the Graham Commission in 1848, many writers have spoken of a general flight of the ex-slaves from plantations immediately after emancipation. Closer study of the years after 1834, however, suggests a more gradual change, and a rather more complex causal pattern.

On most sugar plantations the slaves had already had practice as part-time peasants through cultivating the provision grounds, from which they had been able to sell surplus produce for years through the connivance, indifference, or ignorance of the masters. On one estate at least, the work force did not suddenly change in 1838, despite the abrupt escalation in costs because of the wage bill. The changes made immediately were probably no more radical than during the transition from slavery to Apprenticeship four years earlier.

At Worthy Park the personnel changed no more rapidly than the methods. The old cohesion of the plantation's population was not lost until 1846, when the transition began to the modern system of employing the minimum number of workers, and only when needed, for minimal wages. This naturally increased the ex-slaves' preference for peasant cultivation, making them more than ever determined to work for wages only when they had to.

The immediate reason for the changes in the later 1840s was the impossibility of the owners continuing to pay what amounted to salaries for a resident population, in the face of a sugar price tumbling towards, and below, the old cost of production, with no compensatory rise in productivity. Without exaggerating the case, it seems arguable that it was the external sugar market rather than the ending of formal slavery in itself which precipitated the breakup of the old society, with a concurrent transition to a more modern, or "industrial," phase of "wage slavery."

Once triggered, however, the change was maintained. Carefully avoiding the suggestion that a defense of chattel slavery is being proposed, it is still clear that the wage labor system substituted was in many ways even more degrading and exploitative. A greatly increased labor cost coupled with declining sugar prices made a resident population impractical. It also necessitated technical changes which exacerbated the tendency of sugar production towards a seasonal periodicity of labor demand—eventually to the degree that five times the labor force was needed during the five-month crop period than during the remaining *tempo moto*. This seasonal period of extremely high labor intensity, in conjunction with the monopolistic control of wage-paying labor held by sugar estates, and a population growth that tightened the competition for employment, forced down wages and working conditions to ever lower levels of exploitation.

The exploitation of the wage labor force was made easier by its very impersonality. At the same time, the white owners, cushioned by a managerial class now largely colored rather than white, felt themselves less rather than more integrated into the socioeconomic system. Alienation was at least as general as in the days of formal slavery. Moreover, not only was the new system virtually that of wage slavery but its effects, by somewhat loose extrapolation, have actually conditioned modern views of formal slavery—on the part of black laborers, owners and managers, and black radical ideologues alike.

	1842		1843		1844	
Week	Wage bill (£ Currency)	Number employed	Wage bill (£ Currency)	Number employed	Wage bill (£ Currency)	Number employed
1	64				10	46
2	60	185				
3	65	187				
4	54	184				
5	66					
6	59					
7	79	197				
8	75					
9	81					
10	41	155			75	228
11	72					
12	47	121				
13	20	54				
14	54	182				
15	73	182			69	214
16	67	183			68	203
17	61	168			79	239
18	61	174				
19	70	181				
20	53	165				
21	64	161				
22	72	192				
23	82	182				
24	60	178			50	207
25					74	222
26	73				76	231
27	73	186			75	249
28	59	176				
29	64					280
30	77					
31	8	25			23	43
32	50	161			36	146
33	55	166			61	215
34					63	204
35					53	168
36	46	162			71	215
37	61	167				
38	49	164			98	285
39	53	159			90	295
40	60	172			80	268
41	50					
42					93	329
43					91	304
44					84	301
45			61	171	101	309
46			63	158		
47			75	194		
48			70	186	59	222
49			76	197	58	211
50			80	207	57	214
51			90	234	58	59
52			5	16	6	20

TABLE 51. Worthy Park: Wage Bills and Labor Force, by Weeks, 1842-1846

Source: Worthy Park records (as yet uncalendared).

Notes: Totals in wage bills rounded to nearest pound. Blanks in table indicate missing data.

Free Wage Labor

1845		1846		Averages 1842-1846		
Wage bill (£ Currency)	Number employed	Wage bill (£ Currency)	Number employed	Wage bills (£ Currency)	Number employed	Wages per capita (Currency)
46	166	60	176	45	129	7s.
63	201	86	251	70	208	6s.9d.
66	208	93	264	75	223	6s.9d.
77	241	109	283	80	236	6s.9½d.
74	242	103	282	81	262	6s.2½d.
		104	288	82	288	5s.8½d.
77	250			78	224	6s.11d.
				75		
76	309			79	309	5s.1½d.
90	279			69	229	6s.0½d.
71	259			72	259	5s.6½d.
53	160			50	141	7s.1d.
79	187			50	120	8s.4d.
82	228			68	205	6s.8d.
				74	198	7s.5½d.
77	207			71	198	7s.2d.
86	221			75	209	7s.2d.
				61	174	
				70	181	
60	204			57	185	6s.2d.
47	208			56	185	6s.0½d.
76	235			74	214	6s.11d.
88	241			85	212	8s.
90	252			67	213	6s.3½d.
105	292			90	257	7s.
				75	231	6s.6d.
				74	218	6s.9½d.
112	350			86	263	6s.6½d.
102	323			77	301	5s.1½d.
85	313			81	313	5s.2d.
14	42			15	37	8s.1½d.
28	73			38	127	6s.
75	219			63	200	6s.3½d.
88	216			76	210	7s.3d.
81	244			67	216	6s.2½d.
				60	189	6s.4d.
				61		
				74	225	6s.7d.
				72	227	6s.4d.
66	221			69	220	6s.3½d.
65	223			58	223	5s.2½d.
				93	329	5s.8d.
80	258			86	281	6s.1½d.
91	290			88	295	6s.
86	257			83	246	6s.10d.
97	282			80	220	7s.4d.
				75	194	7s.8½d.
112	302			80	237	6s.8½d.
91	274			75	227	6s.7d.
106	309			81	243	6s.8d.
126	304			91	199	9s.1½d.
				6	18	6s.8d.
		Total wages		£ 3,628		
		Av. per week		69	216	6s.4½d.

TABLE 52. Worthy Park: The Last Apprentice Work Force, 1838, with Continuities, 1842-1846

Source: Worthy Park records.

[a] Categories numbered as in Fig. 26, with more precise employment where known.

[b] X = employed; blank = unemployed.

Surname (for those christened)	Christian name (and baptism date where known)	Slave name (where known)	African or Creole	Color (black, mulatto quadroon, sambo)	Birth date
		Males			
ANDERSON	James (1822)		C	B	1794
ASHLEY	Joseph	Newland's Joe	C	B	1826
ASHLEY	Richard	Richard	C	B	1827
ASHLEY	Robert	Cato	C	B	1783
ASHLEY	Robert II	Sukey's Adam	C	B	1812
BENNETT	Charles	Scipio	C	B	1786
BLYTHE	Robert	Manuel	C	B	1800
BOSWELL	Robert	Frederick	C	B	1796
BOURKE	James	George	C	B	1824
BOURKE	Thomas		C	B	1784
BOWDEN	Thomas	Plato	C	B	1804
BROWN	Harrison		C	B	1798
BROWN	Robert (1835)	Yorky	C	B	1814
BURRELL	Robert		C	B	1818
BYFIELD	George	Rosamond's Robert	C	B	1809
BYFIELD	Thomas	Ned	C	B	1819
DALE	Alexander (1825)		C	B	1824
DAVIS	James	Jamie, Temmie	C	B	1790
DAVIS	William		C	B	1812
DAWKINS	William L. (1835)	Wakefield	C	B	1799
DOUBT	Isaac	Phoebe's Blackwood	C	B	1812
DOUGLAS	Anthony (1825)		C	B	1808
DOUGLAS	James		C	B	1784
DUNCAN	John		C	B	1821
DEFFELL	William	Cupid	C	B	1803
GAYNOR	John L. (1813)	Ready's Cudjoe	C	B	1810
GAYNOR	John	Strafford	C	B	1772
GAYNOR	Richard	Douglass	C	B	1812
GORDON	Charles	Park	C	B	1806
GRANT	George	Jane Quier's Joe	C	M	1826
GREY	Jemmy	Jemmy	C	B	1825
HAMMEL	Peter	Hannibal	C	B	1814
HAMMEL	Thomas	Scotland	C	B	1805
HARRISON	Charles	Charles	C	B	1829
HASLAM	James	Isaac	C	B	1825
HOWELL	Thomas	Duppy	C	B	1795
HUNTER	George		C	M	1819
KING	Henry	Mars	C	B	1799
KING	Thomas	Teckford	C	B	1803
McDERMOTT	John	John	C	M	1815
McDERMOTT	William	William	C	M	1815
McKENZIE	Charles	Britain	C	B	1813
McLEOD	William (1835)	Cherry	C	B	1816
MAHONEY	Edward	Caesar	C	B	1816
MAHONEY	Sam	Rodney	C	B	1787
MAHONEY	William (1820)	Wilkin	C	B	1819
MARSHALL	George	Jacob	C	B	1800
MORRIS	William		C	B	1810
NEATLY	Robert	Bob	C	B	1813
NEWLAND	George		C	M	1816
PARKER	John	Jack	C	B	1815

Employment, 1838[a]	Employed in 1842[b]	Number of times in 7 lists	Employed 1843-1846	Employment, 1842[a] (or 1843-1846)	Employed, February, 1846	Employment, 1846[a]
				Males		
3 Hosp. attend.			X			
11	X	6		10 Weeding	X	13 Mortarer
11	X	7		7 Cattleman		
5 Sawyer	X	4		13 Fencer		
9	X	5		8 Ratcatcher		
7 Hogman	X	5		13 Fencer		
1 Headman	X	6		5 Carpenter	X	5 Carpenter
9	X	6		4 Boilerman	X	4 Boilerman
11	X	4		7 Wainman (H)	X	5 Blacksmith
9	X	5		13 Woodcutter	X	13 Mortarer
4 Boilerman						
9	X	6		1 Woodcutter		
10	X	2		9 Canecarrier		
9	X	4		4 Boilerman	X	4 Boilerman
9	X	5		7 Plowman	X	7 Wainman (road)
10	X	5		7 Plowman		
4 App. blacksmith	X	1S		5 Blacksmith		
1 Hd. cooper	X	5		4 Cooper		
5 Carpenter	X	6		5 Carpenter		
5 Mason	X	2		5 Lime kiln		
9						
9			X	4 Cooper	X	10 Weeder
4 Cooper	X	6		13 Fencer	X	4 Cooper
2 Domestic			X	7 Cattleman		
9			X	7 Wainman (home)		
9	X	3		9 Cane-carrier		
Unemployed						
9	X	6		6 Trashman	X	6 Truckman
9	X	7		1 Superintendent	X	1 Superintendent
11	X	5		13 Woodcutter		
11	X	6		7 Wainman (home)	X	13 Wood-carrier
9	X	6		9 Cane-carrier		
7 Cattleman	X	7		7 Cattleman	X	7 Cattleman
11	X	2		10 Weeder	X	7 Cattleman
11	X	10	X	10	X	13 Lime carrier
4 Cooper	X	5		4 Cooper		
10	X	1		5 App. carpenter	X	13 Mortarer
5 Carpenter						
4 Cooper			X	5 Carpenter	X	5 Carpenter
2 Domestic	X	4		5 Mason	X	5 Mason
2 Domestic						
9	X	5		7 Muleman		
10	X	4		7 Plowman	X	7 Wainman (R)
9	X	4		4 Boilerman	X	4 Boilerman
9						
10	X	5		7 Plowman	X	9 Cane-carrier
9	X	5		7 Plowman	X	13 Fencer
9						
9	X	5		7 Plowman	X	7 Wainman (R)
4 Cooper	X	4		5 Mason	X	13 Mortarer
9	X	5		9 Cane-carrier	X	4 Boilerman

TABLE 52. (*continued*)

Surname (for those christened)	Christian name (and baptism date where known)	Slave name (where known)	African or Creole	Color (black, mulatto quadroon, sambo)	Birth date
		Males			
PARKER	William (1813)		C	B	1811
PEARCE	John	John (Pearce)	C	Q	1815
PEARCE	John	John	C	B	1816
POORMAN	James		C	B	1815
PRICE	Charles		C	B	1820
PRICE	Jasper D. (1825)		C	B	1821
PRICE	John		C	B	1815
RICHARDS	Alexander	Marshall	C	B	1800
SADLER	George F.	Hob	C	B	1814
SADLER	Henry	Sabrai's Harry	C	B	1811
SMITH	William (1835)	Edline	C	B	1801
THOMAS	Henry	Kingston	C	B	1791
THOMAS	James	James	C	B	1821
THOMAS	William	Toby	C	B	1812
VINNICOMBE	John	Duncan	C	B	1775
WILLIAMSON	Joe (1835)		C	B	1821
WINTER	Thomas	Winter	C	B	1784
WRIGHT	George	Quaw	C	B	1823
WRIGHT	Thomas (1835)	Homer	C	B	1817
		BECKFORD	C	B	1825
		BURKE	A	B	1774
		DUNCAN	C	B	1820
		FOREST	A	B	1769
		GUY	C	B	1820
		HECTOR	C	B	1807
		ITALY (Livvie's)	C	B	1813
		JOSEPH	C	B	1822
		KENT	C	B	1807
		NELSON	C	B	1817
		OXFORD (Present's)	C	B	1809
		PRINCE	C	B	1805
		RAPHAEL	C	B	1808
		REBUS	A	B	1781
		REUBEN	A	B	1768
		RHINO	A	B	1768
		STONE	A	B	1780
		YORK	A	B	1784

Employment, 1838[a]	Employed in 1842[b]	Number of times in 7 lists	Employed 1843–1846	Employment, 1842[a] (or 1843–1846)	Employed, February, 1846	Employment, 1846[a]
				Males		
9	X	3		4 Boilerman		
5 App. carpenter						
5 Carpenter	X	6		5 Carpenter		
10	X	2		10 Weeder	X	13 Mortarer
10			X	5 Carpenter	X	5 Carpenter
10						
9	X	6		7 Plowman	X	7 Wainman (R)
9	X	6		7 Wainman (H)	X	13 Lime-carrier
4 Cooper	X	3		4 Cooper		
9	X	5		4 Boilerman		
9	X	4		7 Wainman (H)	X	13 Fencer
5 Carpenter	X	6		13 Fencer	X	5 Carpenter
10			X	10 Weeder		
9	X	5		6 Stoker	X	6 Stoker
Unemployed						
10	X	3		10 Weeder		
5 Carpenter			X	13 Woodcutter		
11	X	2		7 Carter	X	6 Mill feeder
9	X	3		4 Boilerman	X	4 Boilerman
11						
14 Watchman						
10	X	7		7 Cattleman		
Unemployed						
10	X	5		7 Wainman (H)		
9						
10	X	6		7 Cattleman		
11						
14 Watchman						
9						
9						
14 Watchman						
7 Cattleman						
14 Watchman						
Unemployed						
Unemployed						
14 Watchman						
14 Watchman						

TABLE 52. (*continued*)

Surname (for those christened)	Christian name (and baptism date where known)	Slave name (where known)	African or Creole	Color (black, mulatto quadroon, sambo)	Birth date
		Females			
ASHLEY	Letitia		C	B	1822
BANKS	Kitty	Edie	C	B	1764
BENNET	Johanna	Juno	C	B	1774
BENNET	Letitia	Letitia	C	B	1826
BENNET	Rebecca	Lucinda's Strawberry	C	B	1812
BLACK	Amelia	Queen	C	B	1801
BLACK	Jane T.	Virtue's Peggy	C	B	1802
BLAKE	Jane (1835)	Rainbow's Juba	C	B	1811
BLYTHE	Bessy	Bess	C	B	1823
BLYTHE	Elizabeth	Grace	C	S	1802
BOURKE	Amelia	Catalina	C	B	1815
BOURKE	Katy Ann	Coquette	C	B	1818
BOURKE	Louisa	Rosey	C	B	1813
BOURKE	Polly M.	Polly	C	B	1827
BRAILSFORD	Charlotte	Jenny's Charlotte	C	B	1802
BROWN	Cecilia	Princess	C	B	1821
BRYAN	Anne	Sally	C	S	1816
BURRELL	Eleanor		C	B	1804
BURRELL	Kitty		?	?	1764
BYFIELD	Amelia (1835)	Rosamond	A	B	1780
BYFIELD	Juliana	Flora	C	B	1796
BYFIELD	Lusty Ann	Costina, Curtina	C	B	1802
BYFIELD	Mary Ann	Moll	C	B	1800
BYFIELD	Rosey Ann	Rubina	C	B	1805
CHAMBERS	Mary Ann		C	B	1826
CLEGG	Johanna G.	Antonia	C	B	1797
DALE	Catherine	Nanny's Katy	C	S	1811
DALE	Nancy	Rellet	A	B	1780
DALE	Polly		C	S	1818
DALE	Susannah (1825)		C	S	1821
DAVIS	Ann E.	Diligence	C	B	1814
DAVIS	Eleanor	Eleanor	C	B	1808
DAVIS	Johanna	Virtue	A	B	1774
DAVIS	Susannah	Countess	C	B	1775
DAWKINS	Charlotte	Charlotte	C	B	1794
DOUGLAS	Eliza (1835)	Eliza	C	B	1814
DOUGLAS	Clarinda (1835)	Sybil	C	B	1792
EDWARDS	Christian	Ready	A	B	1780
ELLIS	Cecilia	Sally	C	B	1766
ELLIS	Louisa	Jugg	C	B	1805
ELLIS	Maria (1825)		C	S	1819
ELLIS	Mary	Mulatto Kitty	C	M	1795
ELLIS	Nancy	Ariadne's Bappa	C	B	1791
FRANCIS	Ann (1835)	Violet's Beneba	C	B	1808
GAYNOR	Eleanor D.	Eleanor	C	B	1816
GAYNOR	Jane	Lilly	C	B	1815
GAYNOR	Polly R.		C	B	1807
GODLY	Jessy		?	?	1807
GORDON	Jessy	Nancy Ellis's Phoebe	C	B	1826
GREEN	Johanna	Phoebe	C	B	1785
HAMMEL	Bessy	Bessy	C	B	1824

Employment, 1838[a]	Employed in 1842[b]	Number of times in 7 lists	Employed 1843-1846	Employment, 1842[a] (or 1843-1846)	Employed, February, 1846	Employment, 1846[a]
				Females		
11						
Unemployed	X			10 Weeder	X	10 Weeder
13 Tallywoman						
11						
9						
9						
9						
9						
12			X	13 Cleaning		
9	X	5		10 Cane-cutter		
9						
9						
9						
11						
10	X	6		10 Weeder		
11	X	5		10 Weeder		
9						
Unemployed						
Unemployed						
Unemployed	X	4		10 Weeder	X	10 Weeder
Exempt						
9						
9						
9						
11						
10						
2 Washer	X	3		10 Weeder		
Unemployed	X?6			6 Cleaner		
10						
2 Domestic						
9	X	6		9 Cane-cutter	X	9 Cane-cutter
9						
Unemployed						
Unemployed						
9						
10	X	6		10 Weeder	X	10 Weeder
9						
3 Nurse						
Unemployed						
9						
10						
2 Domestic						
Unemployed						
9						
9						
9						
9						
11						
12						
Unemployed						
11	X	6		10 Weeder	X	10 Weeder

TABLE 52. (*continued*)

Surname (for those christened)	Christian name (and baptism date where known)	Slave name (where known)	African or Creole	Color (black, mulatto quadroon, sambo)	Birth date
		Females			
HAMMEL	Letitia	Clara	C	B	1816
HAMMEL	Louiza I		C	B	1811
HAMMEL	Louiza II	Louiza	C	B	1817
HANSON	Adeline	Rainbow's Bessy	C	B	1808
HARRISON	Justaphena	Jessy	C	B	1816
HIBBARD	Margaret (1835)	Lucretia	C	B	1808
HORNSBY	Sarah	Marina	C	B	1818
HORNSBY	Susannah (1835)	Balinda's Sabina	C	B	1809
HOWELL	Mary		C	B	1800
JOHNSON	Sarah	Sophia	C	B	1817
JOHNSON	Susannah		C	?	1818
LEE	Johanna	Gracey	C	B	1807
LEE	Mary Ann	Margaritta	C	B	1819
LEWIS	Clarissa		C	?	1818
LEWIS	Frances	Fanny	C	B	1816
LOWE	Sukey (1835)	Big Sue	C	B	1782
McBEAN	Jane	Jenny	C	B	1812
McDONALD	Susannah (1825)		C	S	1817
McKENZIE	Racey (1835)	Racey	A	B	1768
MAHONEY	Thomasina		C	B	1821
MAHONEY	Valentina	Valentine	C	B	1809
MABLETOFF	Molly	Rachael's Molly	C	M	1812
MARSHALL	Lusty Ann (1835)	Juba	A	B	1772
MARTIN	Bessy	Little Bessy	C	B	1759
MORGAN	Christian		?	?	1763
MORGAN	Sally	Monimia	C	B	1796
MORRIS	Nancy (1825)		C	B	1788
NELSON	Lavinia	Hagar	C	B	1800
NEWMAN	Elizabeth	Catherine	C	B	1791
PARKER	Amelia	Big Amelia	C	B	1784
PARKER	Catherine		C	B	1779
PEARCE	Maria	Maria	C	?	1771
PINGILLY	Jane		C	B	1806
PINNOCK	Eliza (1835)	Behaviour	C	B	1779
POORMAN	Louiza (1835)	Patty	C	B	1814
PRICE	Bessy Ann (1825)	Psyche	C	B	1819
PRICE	Caroline (1825)		C	B	1817
PRICE	Christina	Baddy	C	B	1796
PRICE	Diana	Rixella	A	B	1780
PRICE	Mary	Mary	C	B	1813
PRICE	Molly	Molly	C	B	1823
PRICE	Venus	Venus	C	B	1822
QUIER	Jane	Caroline	C	S	1798
REID	Anthena	Famma	C	B	1805
REID	Elizabeth	Eve	C	B	1808
REID	Mary	Molly	C	B	1776
REID	Rosanna	Grace	C	B	1804
RICHARDS	Sarah	Sambo Sally	C	M	1780
RUSSELL	Christina	Hope	C	B	1816
RUSSELL	Sarah	Diana	C	B	1788
SADLER	Eleanor	Penny	C	B	?

Employment, 1838[a]	Employed in 1842[b]	Number of times in 7 lists	Employed 1843-1846	Employment, 1842[a] (or 1843-1846)	Employed, February, 1846	Employment, 1846[a]
				Females		
9						
9	X	2		9 Cane-cutter		
9	X	4		9 Cane-cutter	X	9 Cane-cutter
9						
9	X	5		9 Cane-cutter	X	9 Cane-cutter
9						
9						
9						
9	X	1		9 Cane-carrier	X	10 Weeding
10						
9						
10						
10	X	6		6 Panwoman		
9						
13 Grass cutter	X	4		9 Cane-carrier	X	10 Weeding
10						
10						
Unemployed						
11	X	5		6 Panwoman		
9						
9	X	3		9 Cane-carrier		
Unemployed						
Unemployed						
Unemployed						
9	X	1		6 Feeder		
1 Superintendent	X	6		1 Superintendent	X	Superintendent
9	X	6		9 Cane-cutter	X	9 Cane-cutter
10						
Unemployed						
2 Domestic						
Unemployed						
9						
Unemployed						
9						
10						
9						
2 Domestic						
13 Grass cutter						
9						
11						
11	X	6		10 Weeder		
9						
9						
9						
Unemployed						
9						
2 Washer						
9						
10						
1 Superintendent						

TABLE 52. (*continued*)

Surname (for those christened)	Christian name (and baptism date where known)	Slave name (where known)	African or Creole	Color (black, mulatto, quadroon, sambo)	Birth date
		Females			
SERVICE	Lusty Ann (1835)	Whanica	C	B	1774
SERVICE	Susanna Ann (1835)	Patty	C	B	1807
SEWELL	Matilda	Matilda	C	B	1821
SEWELL	Pinkey	Penny	C	B	1774
TAYLOR	Margaret	Juliet	C	B	1807
TAYLOR	Mary	Olive	C	B	1774
THOMAS	Elizabeth	Amelia's Agnes	C	B	1812
THOMAS	Julia	Juliet	C	B	1827
THOMAS	Julia(n)		?	?	1796
THOMAS	Letitia	Whanica's Fidelia	C	B	1808
THOMAS	Maria	Margaret	C	B	1806
THOMPSON	Eleanor		C	B	1789
TULLOCH	Bessy Ann (1835)	Nancy	C	B	1802
WALKER	Sally	Olive	C	B	1815
WALLACE	Amelia	Amelia	C	B	1822
WILLIAMS	Charlotte (1825)		C	B	1817
WILLIAMS	Mary	Bathsheba	C	B	1801
WILLIAMS	Mary Ann I	Rapid	C	B	1815
WILLIAMS	Mary Ann II (1835)	Clarence	C	B	1817
		ANN	A	B	1754
		ANN II	C	B	1822
		BEATRICE	C	B	1790
		BECKY	C	B	1823
		BELINDA	C	B	1780
		CANDICE	A	B	1788
		CHARLOTTE	C	B	1827
		CLARINDA	C	B	1822
		CLEMENTINA	C	B	1759
		CHRETIA	A	B	1772
		DAMSEL	C	B	1803
		DORINDA	C	B	1808
		FEMINA	C	B	1814
		GAMESOME	A	B	1774
		JANE	C	B	1827
		JUNO (Queen's)	C	B	1811
		LIVVIE	C	B	1789
		PRINCESS (Ribbon's)	C	B	1811
		RAPINA (Redame's)	C	B	1808
		RAVEFACE	A	B	1768
		RIDDLE	A	B	1781
		ROSEMARY	A	B	1774
		STRUMPET	C	B	1764
		VIOLET	C	B	1787

Employment, 1838[a]	Employed in 1842[b]	Number of times in 7 lists	Employed 1843-1846	Employment, 1842[a] (or 1843-1846)	Employed, February, 1846	Employment, 1846[a]
				Females		
13 Field Cook						
9						
11						
Unemployed						
9						
Unemployed						
9	X	6		9 Cane-cutter		
11						
Unemployed						
9	X	1		10 Weeder		
9						
13 Grass cutter	X	?2		9 Cane-carrier	X	9 Planting
9						
9						
11	X	6		10 Weeding		
9						
9	X	4		9 Cane-cutter		
9	X	5		9 Cane-cutter		
10				6 Stoker		
Unemployed						
11						
9						
11						
13 Grass cutter						
Unemployed						
11						
11						
Unemployed						
Unemployed						
10	X	2		10 Weeding	X	10 Weeder
9						
9						
13 Grass cutter						
2 Domestic						
9						
13 Grass cutter						
13 Grass cutter						
9						
Unemployed						
Unemployed						
Unemployed						
Unemployed						
13 Grass cutter						

TABLE 53. Worthy Park: Patterns of Employment in Seven Selected Weeks of 1842

Source: Worthy Park records.

	Week beginning								
	2/21			3/7			4/18		
	Males	Females	Total	Males	Females	Total	Males	Females	Total
Superintendents and headmen	5	1	6	5	1	6	5	1	6
Domestics	0	6	6	0	6	6	0	6	6
Factory craftsmen	18	0	18	6	0	6	11	0	11
Other craftsmen	6	0	6	7	0	7	6	0	6
Factory laborers	11	16	27	10	9	19	6	12	18
Stock workers	35	0	35	23	0	23	29	0	29
Nonfactory, non-field workers	0	0	0	1	0	1	0	0	0
Field laborers I (cutting & carrying)	21	32	53				13	37	50
Field laborers II (planting & weeding)	6	25	31	23	41	64	10	22	32
Field laborers III (woodcutting, etc.)	13	1	14	20	0	20	31	3	34
Watchmen	7	0	7	7	0	7	7	0	7
Totals	122	81	203	102	57	159	118	81	199

TABLE 54. Worthy Park: The 1842 Work Force and Labor Continuity

Source: Worthy Park records.

1842 work force and period

Week	Work period	Males	Females	Totals	% Males
February 21-26	Crop time	122	81	203	60.1
March 7-12	Intercrop	102	57	159	65.0
April 18-23	Crop time	118	81	199	59.3
June 6-11	Crop time	112	75	187	60.0
August 1-6	Holiday	18	7	25	72.0
August 8-13	Maintenance	106	61	167	63.5
September 26- October 1	Planting	88	85	173	50.9
Averages		103	74	177	58.2

Continuities within 1842 (based on 7 wage lists)

	Males	Females	Totals	% Males	% of total	Continuities, 1844-1846			Apprentices of 1838 listed in 1842		
						1844	1845	1846	Males	Females	Total
On 1 list	65	47	112	58.0	33.3	13	15	13	2	3	5
On 2 lists	26	23	49	53.1	14.4	16	17	9	4	4	8
On 3 lists	16	21	37	43.2	10.9	12	14	11	5	4	9
On 4 lists	24	13	37	64.9	10.9	21	19	17	7	3	10
On 5 lists	31	18	49	63.3	14.4	32	25	21	17	6	23
On 6 lists	28	16	44	63.6	13.1	25	24	24	12	10	22
On 7 lists	10	0	10	100.0	3.0	5	5	3	5	1	6
Total	200	138	338	69.2	100.0	127	119	98	52	31	83

	Week beginning																
6/6			8/1			8/8			9/26			Averages without week of 8/1					
Males	Females	Total	Males	Females	Total	Males	Females	Total	Males	Females	Total	Males	Females	Total			
5	1	6	1	0	1	5	1	6	5	1	6	5	1	6
0	6	6	0	6	6	0	6	6	0	6	6	0	6	6
16	0	16	1	0	1	14	0	14	0	0	0	11	0	11
5	0	5	0	0	0	4	0	4	8	0	8	6	0	6
11	14	25	0	0	0	0	0	0	0	0	0	6	9	15
25	0	25	9	0	9	19	0	19	18	0	18	25	0	25
1	0	1	0	0	0	2	0	2	1	0	1	1	0	1
14	41	55	1	1	2	} 42	53	95 }	3	0	3 }	} 25	55	80
13	13	26	0	0	0				39	63	102			
14	0	14	2	0	2	13	1	14	9	12	21	17	3	20
8	0	8	4	0	4	7	0	7	8	0	8	7	0	7
112	75	187	18	7	25	106	61	167	88	85	173	103	74	177

Continuities, 1842-1846 (based on 10 wage lists)

	Males	Females	Totals	% Males
On 1 list	44	37	81	54.3
2 lists	22	19	41	53.7
3 lists	27	19	46	58.7
4 lists	7	10	17	41.2
5 lists	20	15	35	57.1
6 lists	23	14	37	62.2
7 lists	25	14	39	64.1
8 lists	16	7	23	69.5
9 lists	12	3	15	80.0
10 lists	3	0	3	100.0
Total	199	138	337	59.2

TABLE 55. Worthy Park: Continuity of Labor in 1842

Source: Worthy Park records.

Category	Listed 5 or more times	Listed once	Average in category	Those listed 5 or more times, as % of category
Superintendents	2	0	2	100.0
Craftsmen (factory)				
Boilermen	4	1		
Potters	2	0		
Distillers	1	0		
Coopers	2	1		
Total	9	2	13	79.2
Craftsmen (nonfactory)				
Carpenters	6	4		
Sawyers	0	1		
Blacksmiths	0	1		
Total	6	6	7	85.7
Stockmen				
Cattlemen	6	2		
Mulemen	4	0		
Home wainmen	9	1		
Road wainmen	6	1		
Total	25	4	26	96.2
Miscellaneous				
Fence-makers	6	0		
Woodcutters	2	2		
Ratcatcher	1	0		
Total	9	2	11	81.8
Factory Laborers	15	4	15	100.0
Field Laborers	30	93	90	33.3
Watchmen	7	1	7	100.0
Grand Total	101	112	171	59.1

TABLE 57. Worthy Park: Wages and Continuity of Work, 1842-1846, Selected Weeks

Source: Worthy Park records.

	Number of days employed for wages						
Week	One	Two	Three	Four	Five	Six	Seven
Feb. 21-26, 1842	6	2	22	115	19	1	14
April 18-23, 1842	6	8	8	131	3	0	8
April 15-20, 1844	10	5	8	30	134	0	21
April 20-25, 1845	10	5	4	53	109	10	8
Feb. 9-14, 1846	3	9	1	170	36	20	15

TABLE 56. Worthy Park
Work Force: Three April
Crop Periods Compared,
1842, 1844, 1845

Source: Worthy Park records.

[a]As in Fig. 26.

	Category[a]	Crop period									Averages, 1842-1845		
		April 18-23, 1842			April 15-20, 1844			April 20-25, 1845					
		Male	Female	Total	Male	Female	Total	Male	Female	Total	Male	Female	Total
1	Superintendents and headmen	5	1	6	5	1	6	6	1	7	5	1	6
2	Domestics	0	6	6	0	6	6	0	6	6	0	6	6
4	Factory craftsmen	10	0	10	14	0	0	15	0	15	13	0	13
5	Nonfactory craftsmen	6	0	6	12	0	12	10	0	10	9	0	9
6	Factory laborers	6	12	18	5	9	14	15	16	31	9	12	21
7	Stockmen	29	0	29	24	0	24	25	0	25	27	0	27
8	Nonfactory, nonfield	0	0	0	0	0	0	0	0	0	4	0	4
9	Cane-cutters and carriers (First Gang)	13	37	50	25	39	64	19	40	59	18	39	57
10	Weeders, planters, etc. (Second Gang)	10	22	32	19	16	35	10	5	15	13	14	27
11	Woodcutters (Third Gang)	8	0	8	12	3	15	12	0	12	11	1	12
12	Inferior field workers (Grass-cutters)	4	2	6	3	1	4	4	7	11	4	3	7
13	Misc. field workers	9	1	10	0	0	0	8	1	9	5	1	6
14	Watchmen	8	0	8	20	1	21	8	0	8	12	0	12
	Immigrants	10	0	10	0	0	0	0	0	0	3	0	3
	Total	118	81	199	139	76	215	132	76	208	133	77	210

Employed on weekly tasks	Paid wages monthly	Total employed	Man-days worked	Average days worked	Total wage bill (£ Currency)	Average per worker (Currency)	Average daily rates (Currency)
17	2	198	853	4.31	74	7s.6½d.	1s.9d.
15	4	183	781	4.27	59	6s.6d.	1s.6½d.
6	0	214	1005	4.70	69	6s.5d.	1s.4½d.
9	0	208	941	4.52	77	7s.5¼d.	1s.7d.
13	0	267	1161	4.35	104	7s.9¼d.	1s.8½d.

TABLE 58. The Worthy Park Work Force in February 1846

Source: Worthy Park records.

Separate gangs	Males	Females	Employment	Days worked	Wage rate (daily unless spec.)
			Field Workers		
	4	1	Superintendents	4-5	1s.6d.-2s.
	7	31	Cane-cutting, 2 days; planting, 1 day; turning trash, 1 day	4	1s.3d.-2s.3d.
(i)		14	Cane carrying	4	1s.3d.-2s.3d.
		6	Cane loading	5	1s.9d.
(ii)		10	Weeding, trashing, cleaning ratoons, and planting	4	1s.3d.
(iii)		10	Weeding, trashing plant canes	4	1s.6d.
(iv)	10	20	Cleaning plant canes	4	1s.6d.
(v)	14	20	Weeding, trashing, turning trash	5	1s.6d.
	6		Bamboo cutting, trench lining, trenching	4-5	1s.3d.-2s.
	7		Fencemaking	4	1s.-1s.6d.
	3		Cane carrying	5	1s.3d.-1s.9d.
	1	1	Wood carrying	5	1s.6d.-1s.9d.
	2		Turning trash	1	1s.6d.
	3		Cane-cutting and carrying, gutter digging	2-5	1s.6d.-2s.6d.
			Factory Specialists		
	7		Boilermen (inc. head boiler)	2-4	3s.9d.-4s.6d.
	2		Potters	4	1s.
	2		Distillers	6	1s.-2s.6d.
	4		Coopers	4	6s.
	5		Mill feeders	4	1s.-3s.3d.
	3		Truckmen	4	2s.6d.-3s.3d.
	1		Liquor pumper	4	2s.5d.
	7	2	Stokers, cleaners, panworkers	4	1s.6d.-2s.6d.
	1	5	Trash carriers	4	1s.6d.-2s.3d.
			Other Craftsmen		
	20		Carpenters	1-6	1s.-3s.
	3		Blacksmiths	4-6	1s.-1s.6d.
	2		Masons	4	2s.
	3		Lime carriers	5	1s.3d.-1s.9d.
	12		Mortar mixers	4	1s.2d.-1s.6d.
			Other Specialists		
	7		Cattlemen	7	1s.-1s.3d.
	6		Road wainmen	One trip	9s.6d.-10s.6d.trip
	7		Watchmen	7 days & nights	5s.-6s. week
			Miscellaneous and Taskwork		
	2		Messengers	2	1s.6d.-1s.9d. + expenses (4s.)
	2		Woodcutters		2s. per cord
	1		Adzers of shingles		2s.7d. per 100
	1		Excavators at works	4	2s.6d.
	1		Water carriers	6	1s.3d.
	1	1	Unspecified		3s.-5s. week

	Category[a]	1830-1834	1834-1838	1842	1842-1846
1	Heads and drivers	12	8	6	8
2	Domestics	16	10	6	6
3	Hospital	4	3		
4	Factory craftsmen	8	7	11	10
5	Other craftsmen	11	9	6	15
6	Factory laborers			15	20
7	Stockmen			25	15
8	Nonfactory, nonfield	4	4	1	2
9	First Gang	57	83	80	
10	Second Gang	53	32		130
11	Third Gang	38	26	20	
12	Fourth Gang	35	24		
13	Misc. field	14	5		
14	Watchmen	16	10	7	10
	Unknown	3	1		
	Total workers	271	219	177	216

TABLE 59. Worthy Park: Comparative Numbers in Employment Categories, 1830-1846

Source: Worthy Park records.

[a]As in Fig. 26.

	Category[d]	Hiring rates, 1837	Approx. wages, 1839	Approx. average wages, 1842-1846
		Labor costs (£ Currency p.a.)		
1	Heads and Drivers	12	21	20
2	Domestics	7	9	10
3	Hospital	5	0	0
4	Factory craftsmen	16-25	12-30	10-50
5	Other craftsmen			
6	Factory laborers	9	12	15
7	Stockmen	12	12	15
8	Nonfactory, nonfield	10	12	15
9	First Gang	12		
10	Second Gang	9	8-15	15-20
11	Third Gang	7		
12	Fourth Gang	4		
13	Misc. Field	9	6-12	10-20
14	Watchmen	4	8	10
	Unknown or other	10	0	0

TABLE 60. Worthy Park: Individual Labor Costs, by Categories, 1837-1846, Selected Years

Source: Worthy Park records

[a]As in Fig. 26.

TABLE 61. Worthy Park: Projected Wage Bills, by Categories, at 1837 Hiring Rates (£ Currency)

Source: Worthy Park records.

[a]As in Fig. 26.

	Category[a]	1830-1834	1835-1838	1842	1842-1846
1	Heads and drivers	144	96	72	96
2	Domestics	112	70	42	42
3	Hospital	20	15	0	0
4	Factory craftsmen	146	130	220	200
5	Other craftsmen	176	144	120	300
6	Factory laborers	0	0	135	180
7	Stockmen	48	48	300	180
8	Nonfactory, nonfield	0	0	10	20
9	First Gang	684	996	880	1300
10	Second Gang	477	288		
11	Third Gang	266	182		
12	Fourth Gang	140	96	140	
13	Misc. field	126	45		
14	Watchmen	64	40	28	40
	Others or unknown	30	10	0	0
	Total annual wage bill (£ Currency)	2,443	2,180	1,937	1,258
	Average annual wages per worker (£ Currency)	9.01	9.96	10.94	10.92

TABLE 62. Worthy Park: Projected Wage Bills, by Categories, at Actual Rates for 1842-1846 (£ Currency)

Source: Worthy Park records.

[a]As in Fig. 26.

		Projected wage bills	
	Category[a]	1830-1834	1834-1848
1	Heads and drivers	240	160
2	Domestics	160	100
3	Hospital	40	30
4	Factory craftsmen	240	210
5	Other craftsmen	330	270
7	Stockmen	60	60
9	First Gang	998	1,458
10	Second Gang	928	560
11	Third Gang	570	390
12	Fourth Gang	525	360
13	Miscellaneous field	210	75
14	Watchmen	160	160
	Others	36	12
	Total annual projected wage bill (£ Currency)	4,497	3,845
	Annual average per worker (£ Currency)	16.59	17.56

TABLE 63. Worthy Park: Projected Labor Cost, 1830-1838, in £ Currency (at £ 5 per Capita per Year, plus Depreciation of 7 Percent on Average £ 50 Cost)

Source: Worthy Park records.

Period	Total wage bill (£ Currency)	Annual average per worker (£ Currency)
1830-1834	4,375	8.75
1834-1838	3,500	8.75

	Total annual wage bill (£ Currency)	Weekly average total (£ Currency)	Average number of workers	Annual average per worker (£, shillings, & pence Currency)	Weekly average per worker (shillings & pence)
1842-1846	3,588	69	216	16.11.5	6.4½
1844	3,576	69	215	16.12.7	6.4¾
1845	4,013	77	230	17. 9.0	6.8½
1846	4,982	96	250	19.18.7	7.10
1847	6,576	126	300	21.18.5	8.5¼

TABLE 64. Worthy Park: Actual Wage Bills Paid, 1842-1847

Sources: Evidence of George Price, March 1, 1848; *British Sessional Papers, Reports* (*1848*), XXIX, No. 4879.

Category (as listed)	Number employed	Wage rate (Jamaica Currency)	Totals for year (£, shillings, & pence, Currency)
Superintendents	4-6	£1.15.0 month	151.12. 1
Tradesmen	8-11	10s. week or tasks	244.24 1½
Distillers (inc. stillhouse laborers)	6-46	varied with skill	213. 3. 6½
Domestics	5-6	10s. to £1 month	140 9. 2
Cattle keepers	6-7	8s. 9d. - 11s. 8d. week (7 days)	191.19. 6
Stock providers	25-60	5s. week	105. 8. 4
Small stockkeepers	3	5s. week	30. 8. 4
Mulemen	6-11	1s. 3d. day	13. 8. 4
Messengers	1-2	1s. 3d. day	14. 6. 5½
Field laborers	95-400	about 6s. week	913. 0. 0[b]
Fence & Pen Gang	c. 25	daily piece work	64.10. 7
Road repairers	3-12	weekly task work	92. 5.10
Watchmen	2-5	2s. 3d.-4s.4d. week	92.17. 2¼
Total[a]			2,288. 3. 5¾

TABLE 65. Worthy Park: Total Annual Wages Paid, by Categories, 1839

Source: Worthy Park records.

[a]Missing two months' field laborers' wages—about £180.
[b]Only wages paid until October 26.

TABLE 66. Worthy Park:
Production, Revenue, Pro-
ductivity, Costs, Profits,
1830-1848

Source: Worthy Park records.

ª 1848 sugar produce unknown.

	Sugar produced (hhds.)	Jamaican sugar production (thou. tons)	% of Worthy Park production of Jamaican total	Average London sugar price (shillings per cwt.)	Worthy Park gross revenue (£thou. Stg.)
1830	555	69.0	0.61	26	14.43
1831	471	69.8	.51	24	11.30
1832	589	71.6	.60	28	16.51
1833	484	67.9	.53	30	14.52
1834	490	62.8	.59	29	14.21
Av. 1830-1834	518	68.2	.57	27	14.19
1835	427	57.4	.55	33	14.09
1836	407	52.7	.58	41	16.69
1837	370	45.2	.61	35	12.95
1838	406	52.7	.58	34	13.80
Av. 1835-1838	403	52.0	.58	35	14.38
1839	350	39.4	.69	39	13.65
1840	150	26.5	.43	49	7.35
1841	263	27.6	.71	40	10.52
1842	299	40.2	.81	37	11.06
1843	232	33.3	.52	34	7.89
Av. 1839-1843	239	33.4	.63	40	10.11
1844	261	27.6	.75	34	8.87
1845	309	37.1	.63	33	10.20
1846	303	28.6	.79	34	10.30
1847	267	37.6	.53	28	7.48
1848	ª	31.4		24	
Av. 1844-1848	285	32.5	.68	31	9.21

Total estate population (1830-1838)	Total workers	Sugar produced per worker (hhds.)	Revenue per worker (£Stg.)	Estate's gross costs (£thou. Stg.)	Estate's profits (£thou. Stg.)	Profit per member of population, 1830-1838 (£Stg.)	Profit per worker (£Stg.)
522	323	1.72	44.6				
517	275	1.71	41.1				
494	262	2.25	63.0				
483	246	1.97	59.0				
467	250	1.96	56.8				
497	271	1.91	52.3	10.15	4.04	8.1	14.9
417	239	1.78	58.8				
c.407	234	1.74	71.3				
c.361	208	1.78	62.3				
c.338	194	2.09	71.1				
c.381	219	1.84	65.9	9.00	5.38	14.7	24.6
	175	1.36	57.8	8.25	1.86		10.6
	225	1.27	41.0	12.25	-3.04		-13.5

315

13 / Continuities: Worthy Park's Modern Workers

BY 1973 the Worthy Park work force was in a critical state of flux and imbalance, but it still exhibited many traditional characteristics. It was, indeed, drawn from a population largely descended from Worthy Park's old workers. This population had increased tenfold since 1838, but the concomitant expansion of Worthy Park's operations had more than kept pace, so that the dominance of the surrounding area and its population by the estate was one of the most obvious continuities with the nineteenth century, or even with the days of formal slavery.

Dominance and continuities were amply borne out by an analysis of the work force employed by Worthy Park between 1963 and 1973, despite the complication that the records of the field and pen laborers employed by Worthy Park Farms, Ltd., were kept separately from those of the workers for Worthy Park Factory, Ltd., and used a slightly different method.[1]

The separation between field and factory operations at Worthy Park, as on all Jamaican sugar estates, was brought about almost accidentally by the exigencies of Jamaican tax laws and subsidy arrangements that made it convenient for sugar estates to sell cane to their own factories as if the estates, too, were independent cane farmers. At first glance it seemed to offer a natural separation suitable for ideological analysis, dividing the industrial proletariat factory workers from the rural proletariat and would-be peasant field laborers. However, the distinction was by no means so clear as it seemed at first, and it is unlikely that even a comprehensive program of individual interviews would disclose relationships between types of work and differences of background, outlook, or aspirations such as would fulfil the predictions or satisfy the theories of a doctrinaire Marxist. Some workers switched from field to factory employment and back; any might be—or wish to be—peasants rather than proletarians in the technical senses; most were deeply conservative in the "peasant" manner; some were radical, but regardless of employment or role. The "factory-in-a-field" of sugar production would seem to offer insuperable difficulties for Marxian analysis, if not to make nonsense of it.[2]

Above all, in Jamaica a common sentiment seems to unite those working in the "industrial" and "rural" sectors into which sugar estate operations could, artificially, be divided: the desire to escape the system's bonds. It may be that it is the field worker who most commonly wishes for a small holding productive enough to obviate the need to labor for wages, and the factory worker—in a manner acknowledged as a feature of "modernization"—more commonly aspires to alternative employment in the country's burgeoning towns and less traditional, as well as more lucrative, industries. Yet, it is a characteristic of Jamaican rural life that successful sugar factory workers tend to to be among the most prosperous smallholders as well; and it is a fact of life in Jamaican towns that the slums are crowded with refugees from what is regarded as the ill-paid degradation of field labor on sugar estates. Both the preference for peasant proprietorship over wage labor and the flight to the towns suggest a continuing alienation from the plantation system on the part of all workers. Yet neither trend appears to be even potentially revolutionary, or easily adaptable by radical leaders to revolutionary purposes.

Despite the differences between them, the personnel records of Worthy Park Farms and Worthy Park Factory provided material to illustrate four significant patterns: the sexes and ages of all workers; the continuing low standards of education among farm laborers; the limited catchment area from which the estate's workers were drawn; and finally, through a comparative study of surnames, the continuity of families in employment since the slavery period.

In some ways the work force had remained similar in composition since the early nineteenth century. As was true even in slavery days, virtually no females were employed in and around the factory. Though after slavery ended the number of females employed in the farming operation was progressively trimmed to a bare minimum, in 1963 some 30 percent of the field labor force still consisted of women. This proportion was much the same as in 1900, but lower than the figures of over 40 percent in the 1840s and over 60 percent in 1834. Women were no longer found in the modern equivalent of the First Gang, for cane was exclusively cut by men, and mechanization had almost entirely removed the need for tying and carrying cane or even the digging of cane holes. Except for traditionally feminine roles such as that of field cook, women were now chiefly employed in lieu of sufficient men willing to undertake the drudgery of the worst-paid jobs: planting, weeding, and fertilizing cane and picking fruit.

Just as women were employed instead of, rather than in preference to, men, so the constraints of labor shortage could be traced in the patterns of workers' ages. As late as 1963, Worthy Park Farms employees demonstrated a nineteenth-century pattern, with very few employed under the age of 20 or over the age of 55, and the majority in the range of optimal maturity and health. Already, however, there was evidence of the need to take on immature youths and to retain old men for the

317

Figure 41. Age Distribution: Worthy Park Farms, 1963, Worthy Park Factory, 1973, and Data

Source: Worthy Park records.

[a]That is, those in 1963-1973 file recorded as starting employment in 1963 or earlier.
[b]Those employed any time in 1973.

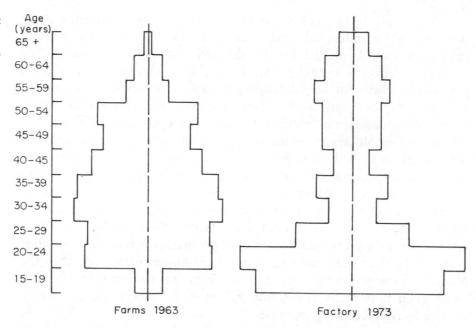

Farms 1963   Factory 1973

Age Cohorts	Worthy Park Farms (1963)[a]		Worthy Park Factory (1973)[b]	
	Numbers	% of total	Numbers	% of total
65+	5	0.90	6	2.99
60-64	17	3.09	11	5.47
55-59	25	4.56	15	7.46
50-54	56	10.19	12	5.97
45-49	49	8.90	12	5.97
40-44	64	11.64	8	3.98
35-39	83	15.08	15	7.46
30-34	88	16.00	10	4.98
25-29	72	13.08	24	11.94
20-24	73	13.28	48	23.88
15-19	18	3.28	40	19.90
Total	550	100.00	201	100.00

lack of enough healthy young men prepared to undertake or persevere with field labor. The average age of Worthy Park's field workers in 1963 was 37.01 years, roughly that of the years of "age imbalance" at the very end of slavery.[3] By 1973 the average age may have been well over 40 years, despite the willingness to recruit more laborers straight out of school.

For Worthy Park Factory, these problems had been magnified, as the age pyramid for 1973 amply demonstrates. Because of the paucity of men between 25 and 45, by 1973 the factory work force consisted largely of older men and boys just out of school. The average age was 33.1 years, considerably less than for the field workers; but this was simply because there were many more boys at work in the factory. In fact, only 12.44 percent of the factory workers tabulated were in their 30s, compared with 31.08 percent of field workers. The mature young men were mainly employed outside of Lluidas Vale in such better paying operations as the bauxite factory at Ewarton, simply because they were the group whose strength and skills were the most salable. Even the youngsters, given a chance, denied to previous generations, of working in the factory from the age of 16, seemed to work no more than a year or two on the average, moving on just as soon as they acquired rudimentary industrial skills. Those remaining were the ageing guard of old reliables, tied by long habit, lack of transferable skills, or, in fortunate cases, small holdings in Lluidas Vale.

Even in 1973, the two-thirds of the Worthy Park work force who worked in the fields showed less of an age imbalance than those who worked in the factory. The chief reason for this may be traced in the dismal record of educational attainment illustrated in Table 68.

That only 173, or 16.6 percent, of the 1,041 who worked for Worthy Park Farms, Ltd., between 1963 and 1973 claimed any sort of education at all is a startling indictment of the Jamaican rural school system, and fuel for the contention that sugar estate field labor is the only resort of the illiterate. The facts that the majority of those with education above Grade 3 were the younger recruits and that with even these limited qualifications a youngster could aspire to rather more prestigious and lucrative employment elsewhere partly explain why the field work force was steadily ageing. Even the steady changeover to mechanization seemed unable to reverse the trend, because it was brought about more by the shortage of labor than by a desire to upgrade the quality of work offered.

Unfortunately, the absence of education data for Worthy Park Factory, Ltd., made precision impossible; but it was certain that the average educational level was far higher for factory workers than for field laborers. That 44 percent of factory workers were aged under 25 in 1973, and thus would have been of school age after compulsory schooling began to be enforced in rural Jamaica, compared with only about 20 percent of field laborers, alone indicated that at least bare literacy and skill with numbers were the norms in Worthy Park's factory. Moreover, the proportion of those formally apprenticed for three years to learn factory skills was far higher than the pitiful 1 percent of farm laborers who claimed a Worthy Park apprenticeship as their chief educational qualification.

That education and acquiring mechanical proficiencies were seen as means to escape from sugar estate employment may explain why Jamaican governments committed to encouraging sugar production had been decidedly ambivalent towards rural education, concentrating most expenditure and effort on education in urban areas. For their part, sugar estate employers had been even less inclined to support the local schools, claiming with some justice to see in the very form of education a tendency to train young people away from traditional values, which included a willingness to become farm laborers as well as to value the rural life.

Lluidas Vale's school—all too typical of those throughout rural Jamaica—was desperately overcrowded in 1973, even though the attendance record was poor. As well as being complicated by the policy to inculcate standard English (almost a second language to that Jamaican Creole spoken by all countrymen on normal occasions), the education offered was in every sense elementary, concentrating on the rudiments of the three R's. Technical education—either agricultural or industrial—was nonexistent locally, and though there was a technical school within a dozen miles, at Dinthill near Linstead, only a scattering of Lluidas Vale children ever managed to reach it. Even the Youth Camp established in Lluidas Vale in 1972, with its excellent 18-month course of practical training for underprivileged boys, was not open to local youngsters—even less privileged than most—on the plea that it would tend to disrupt the separation carefully maintained between camp and village.

If Lluidas Vale's youngsters were given little opportunity for technical education, no compensating efforts were made to suggest that the inevitable alternatives could be either dignified or worthwhile. Instead, a vague assumption permeated the teaching that education in bare literacy would magically raise the standards of life for the new generation. In practice this meant that the more successful aspired to leave the familiar ground of their village for the anonymous and asocial shanties of Spanish Town and Kingston, while the remainder resentfully resigned themselves to perpetuate their parents' and ancestors' roles. It seemed, in sum, that the devaluation of the laboring and rural life, whether as wage laborer or self-employed peasant, was as much a product of the educational system as of the "folk memory of slavery" which radicals, and most educators, assumed.

Although modernization was rapidly changing the nature of the population from which Worthy Park drew its work force, studies of the labor catchment area and the workers' surnames demonstrated that in 1973 the estate's employees were still overwhelmingly local and also descended from generations of earlier Worthy Park workers. Dependence upon the estate, though strong, was not total. Indications were that the locational ties were at least as much those of landownership as of the availability of wage labor.

Some transient laborers working at Worthy Park only during crop time may have given the nearby village as their permanent address; but it was still a remarkable fact that 45 percent of Worthy Park's field workers employed between 1963 and 1973, and 40 percent of factory workers over the same period, lived in Lluidas Vale Village itself while they worked. In all, 48 percent of all workers lived within two miles of Worthy Park's fields or factory, 72 percent within what was regarded as fairly easy walking distance, and no less than 88 percent within the outside radius of the area in which it was possible both to live and to work. Beyond a radius of ten miles, proximity to Worthy Park was no longer relevant. The density of workers drawn to Worthy Park from an area between ten and twenty miles distant was no greater than that in the area between twenty miles and the farthest bounds of Jamaica.

This pattern of radial concentration around sugar estates was fairly general throughout Jamaica, and perhaps the entire West Indies. One unfortunate effect was generally obvious. Throughout Jamaica it was possible to sense proximity to a sugar estate by a deterioration in the housing and living conditions. Beyond a certain distance, the majority of the houses were those of independent smallholders, small, but neat and in good repair, with animals in the yard, and surrounded by land ingeniously and industriously cultivated. Within the malign circle of dependence and influence, however, there were, first, the dilapidated houses and slovenly yards of those who could be neither wholly dependent on small holding nor fully employed; then, in the inner ring, there was almost invariably the estate-oriented village, crowded with those with no choice between wage labor and beggary, and those transients immigrating for seasonal work. Lluidas Vale and its village were no worse, but little better, than a dozen equivalents elsewhere in Jamaica.

In general it was the true villagers who were most dependent and depressed. Rent payers living on small house lots, with no land to work for themselves, were bound to seek wage labor just for subsistence. Many were living on lots owned by Worthy Park, paying nominal rents of $4 Jamaican Currency a year. But these persons were not necessarily more tied than others who lived in the Shady Grove sector of the village, or were subtenants on Worthy Park lots of absentees living in Kingston or England, who were forced to pay up to $4 Jamaican Currency *a week* and thus driven into wage labor by their greater need for cash for rent. In fact, faced with a shrinking pool of willing wage laborers, Worthy Park would have liked to evict absentee profiteers, abolish rents altogether, and actually build more cottages for rent-free occupation, had it been legally possible to tie such tenements to estate work. It was not the direct influence of the estate which increased tensions so much as the pressure of a growing population upon limited space, coupled with the disaffection from agricultural labor, particularly among the young with as yet uneroded aspirations.

Not all villagers, and not all those who worked for the estate, were utterly dependent, however. A surprising number of house lots in the southwest quarter of Lluidas Vale Village were linked to small holdings, and their owners were more like urban peasants than true villagers. Other village dwellers owned, rented, or even squatted on, parcels of bush in the surrounding hills. They worked these lots out of season or the estate's working hours, and their womenfolk and children did so at other times. A few minor potentates with responsible jobs at Worthy Park—mainly in the factory and garage—were employers themselves,

13. Northern St. John's District: Worthy Park Farms and Factory Labor Catchment

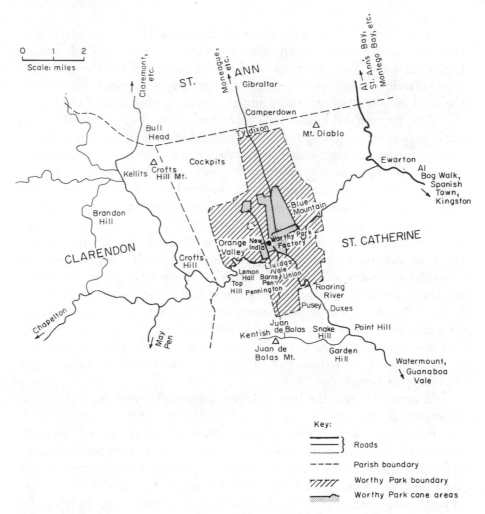

Key:

—— } Roads

- - - - Parish boundary

////// Worthy Park boundary

∙∙∙∙∙∙ Worthy Park cane areas

paying old men, boys, or neighboring smallholders to work their land, which they owned or rented and might seldom visit, producing provisions for market or cane for the Worthy Park factory.

The localization of Worthy Park's work force was chiefly enforced by the tradition of working land as well as working for wages, just as the curious mixture of peasant and proletarian activity conditioned all aspects of social organization. These influences were best observed in the regions beyond Lluidas Vale Village, where nearly all those who worked at Worthy Park lived on or near a piece of "family," "buy," or rental land. In the first case, a system of complex joint ownership, made even more complicated by extended and often fairly casual family relationships, ensured that work as well as produce and wages were shared as equitably as possible by all family members. However, in a period of rapid population growth, such sharing often led to the overextension of the available resources. With individually owned buy land the situation was simpler, and astute owners were able to prosper, and even expand, by virtue of controlling the total produce and by being able to restrict expenditure to a bare minimum. The social effects of the possession of buy land included also a tendency to restrict family

322

size, with superfluous hands (and mouths) being encouraged to migrate, in a manner familiar to Europe during the age of expansion, when (or where) primogeniture was the rule. Some favored workers even rented cane lands from Worthy Park, though since the lands offered for rental were in the hilly areas to the southeast of the property, regarded as uneconomic for estate production, it was not surprising that only those who rented them in addition to other lands found them really worthwhile. Those who lived on them as well found them insufficient to sustain a family without more or less continuous wage labor for the estate. This may have been an intentional effect. Renters who did not live on their land were compelled, or induced, in a different way. For them, the possession of the land was regarded by the estate as a well-earned—though reversible—reward for faithful service.

As for the comparative distribution between Worthy Park's factory and field workers in the immediate locality, no distinctive patterns emerged, save that the inhabitants of the settlements of New India (mostly the descendants of the Indian "coolies" brought to Worthy Park between 1845 and 1917) and Pennington, two miles south of Lluidas Vale, tended to work in the factory rather than the fields, groves, and pen. Elsewhere, factory and farms workers alike came in roughly their due proportions, very largely from those areas to which the ex-slaves migrated after 1838.

Of 581 field and 233 factory workers employed between 1963 and 1973 not living on Worthy Park Estate land or in Lluidas Vale Village, 178 and 72, or 30.7 percent in all, lived in the fertile climbing valley of scattered holdings towards the southeast, linked by the dusty artery of the road (and bus route) to Kingston, by way of Point Hill, Guanaboa Vale, and Spanish Town. A further 94 and 24, or 14.5 percent, came from the valleys and ridges to the southwest, served by the motor road from Lluidas Vale into Clarendon. A third group of 64 and 30, 11.5 percent, came from the precipitous cockpits to the north, close to the road crossing the shoulder of Mount Diablo into St. Ann's. As to the reverse slopes of Lluidas Vale, a sprinkling of workers came from along the well-traveled Ewarton road, and a few from Croft's Hill and Kellits. But in general there were remarkably few workers entering the valley from the densely populated areas of Clarendon and what was once St. Thomas-ye-Vale, which were filled after slavery ended with people from estates in those parishes rather than from Lluidas Vale.

One anomaly occurred in the catchment pattern: the migration of 53 field workers from the district called Madras in St. Ann's, twenty-five miles to the north. Each year since about 1955, up to 30 male workers had come to Worthy Park for the sugar crop, living in a tumble-down barracks in the Swansea sector. They originally came because of the poverty and lack of wage employment in their own district and were encouraged to return through the very definite esteem they had earned for themselves from the Worthy Park management. For the estate, such a "strangers' gang" possessed the advantages of high morale through group solidarity and a voluntary commitment, and a reliability stemming from the fact that any private plots these workers owned or might have worked were out of practical range. Besides this, a body of men seeking only seasonal employment was especially welcome.

With complex family patterns and often casual naming habits, absolute precision cannot be ascribed to surname analysis. Yet it did not need an expert in statistical probability theory to show that the continuance of family names in the Worthy Park employment records denoted a remarkable lack of movement in and out of the Lluidas Vale area since slavery days.

In 1838 there were 95 different surnames in use at Worthy Park, accounting for 188 of the working population of 229. Of these names 59 still survived in the work force of Worthy Park Farms, Ltd., between 1963 and 1973, accounting for no less than 485 individuals out of a roll of 1,164 with 343 different surnames. This meant that the 17.3 percent of the surnames which dated from the earliest list accounted for 41.7 percent of the modern workers.

As was shown in the previous chapter, the 1840s saw a substantial reorganization and augmentation of the Worthy Park work force; and 118 new surnames were added as the total of identified workers rose to 417. These came not only from strangers brought into Lluidas Vale but also from the newly employed ex-slaves from neighboring decayed estates (such as the 14 workers surnamed Fuller who presumably came from Thetford, once owned by the Fuller family), and those 40 or so single-name slaves at Worthy Park who had since been christened and chose new names. Of the 118 new surnames of the 1840s, 52 were still extant in 1963-1973, accounting for 276 persons. Altogether, the 111 surnames surviving from the period 1838-1846 accounted for 761, or 65.4 percent, of the 1,164 persons employed by Worthy Park Farms, Ltd., in the period 1963-1973. On the average, each old surname was shared by 6.86 persons.[4] The remaining 231 modern surnames were shared by only 403 persons, an average of 1.74 persons per name.

A separate analysis of the employees of Worthy Park Factory, Ltd., in 1973, suggested an even greater degree of continuity. There, 31 of the 1838 and 60 of the 1838-1846 surnames survived (including 3 not found among those working for Worthy Park Farms) among only 117 different surnames. The original 60 surnames accounted for 130 persons of 204 employed. Thus, in the factory not only did those with old surnames predominate, with 63.7 percent of the work force (compared with 65.5 percent of the farms workers), but, in contrast to the field work force, even the old surnames themselves were not outnumbered by the new.

In countries where the naming process is standard—with marriage before childbirth the general rule, children normally taking the surname of both parents, and the level of illegitimacy both low and ascertainable—such data as used here would allow not only a fairly exact computation of in and out migration from the sample area but also some useful conclusions about family patterns. In rural Jamaica, however, the analysis is clouded because unions, though usually monogamous, occur in an almost infinite variety between formal marriages and transient unions without cohabitation. In the entire population of Jamaica the incidence of illegitimacy, in the strictest sense, is over 75 percent. Although children normally take their putative father's name, this is not invariably so. Women also may or may not assume the surname of the man with whom they live. Thus Jamaican surnames, while they can convincingly illustrate continuities in general, give no accurate indication of patterns of union, and absolutely none of family composition.

Only a painstaking series of individual studies could achieve such an analysis. This is beyond the scope of the present enterprise. Something in this line is attempted, if unsystematically, in the second of the genealogies which follow, and in the concluding chapter of the book dealing with the modern inhabitants of Lluidas Vale as discovered through oral interviews. However, these sections, like the rest of the book, do have a wider relevance to the general questions raised by the statistics presented here. They attempt to trace the incidence and effects of continuities in general—not only of the continuance of families in the same district but also the persistence and perpetuation of methods, customs, and attitudes among all "the Sons of Slavery."

Occupation	Male	Female	Total	Period	Pay ($Jamaican)[a]
Worthy Park Factory, Ltd.					
Managing director	1	0	1	1 year	7,000/year
Factory manager	1	0	1	1 year	6,400/year
Chief engineer	1	0	1	1 year	6,200/year
Asst. engineer	1	0	1	1 year	3,600/year
Chemist	1	0	1	1 year	2,288/year
Timekeepers	4	0	4	1 week	20-28
Scale clerks	2	0	2	1 week	16
Storekeeper	1	0	1	1 week	28
Store clerks	2	0	2	1 week	24
Security guards	3	0	3	1 week	20-28
Watchmen and guards	5	0	5	7 days	11
Factory (operators & assistants)	87	0	87	7 days	10-30
Foreman mechanics	5	0	5	1 week	29-38
Foreman mechanic	1	0	1	7 days	35
Asst. mechanic	16	0	16	7 days	10-20
Mechanic helpers	7	0	7	7 days	10-13
Reporting chemists	1	0	1	7 days	12
Bench chemist & sample boys	14	0	14	1 week	10-15
Painters	5	0	5	Task	10-12
Plumbers	2	0	2	1 week	10-24
Machinist (chief)	2	0	2	1 week	36-37
Machinist (asst.)	4	0	4	7 days	10-13
Welder (chief)	1	0	1	1 week	36
Welder (asst.)	4	0	4	7 days	10-21
Electrician	1	0	1	1 week	36
Electrician's helpers	1	0	1	7 days	10
Carpenters	8	0	8	7 days	12-28
Masons	7	0	7	7 days	10-27
Tractor drivers	2	0	2	7 days	14-25
Tractor drivers' sidemen	4	0	4	7 days	10
Sugar boiler	7	0	7	1 week	21-33
Sugar curers	8	0	8	Task	12-15
Laborers	16	0	16	7 days	10
General stores	3	0	3	7 days	10-13
Total	228	0	228		
Worthy Park Farms, Ltd.					
Cane Cultivation & Harvesting					
Managing director	1	0	1	1 year	6,000/year
Farms manager	1	0	1	1 year	5,000/year
Agronomist	1	0	1	1 year	3,000/year
Cane overseer	1	0	1	1 year	2,500/year
Cane superintendent	1	0	1	1 year	2,200/year
Chief clerk	1	0	1	1 week	50
Timekeeper	1	0	1	1 week	32
Clerks	3	0	3	1 week	17-22
Headmen	6	2	8	7 days	11-22
Cane-cutters	110	0	110	Task	12-30
Cane-cutters & carriers	29	0	29		
Laborers, misc.					
Planters, sprayers, weeders	37	48	85	6 days	6-10
Trenchers, grass diggers	4	0	4	Task	17-22
Applying fertilizer	0	19	19	Task	7
Total	196	69	265		

TABLE 67. Worthy Park Factory, Ltd., Worthy Park Farms, Ltd., and Worthy Park Administration, Wage Bill, April 4, 1971

Source: Private correspondence, G. M. Clarke, Esq.

[a]All salaries per week unless otherwise noted.
[b]Rangers, office maid, messenger, etc.

Occupation	Male	Female	Total	Period	Pay ($Jamaican)[a]
			Garage		
Superintendent	1	0	1	1 year	3,000/year
Foreman	1	0	1	1 week	40
Mechanics	3	0	3	1 week	14-22
Mechanics' asst. & helpers	6	0	6	7 days	10-14
Tractor drivers	9	0	9	7 days	15-27
Tractor drivers	5	0	5	Task	27-48
Tractor sidemen	12	0	12	Task & 7 days	10-17
Truck drivers	5	0	5	1 week	18-25
Truck sidemen	6	0	6	6 days	10-12
Car drivers	4	0	4	1 week	16
Car drivers	1	0	1	6 days	12
Welder & asst.	3	0	3	7 days	10-21
Tireman & asst.	2	0	2	7 days	10-18
Carpenters, asst. & helpers	4	0	4	6 days	10-15
Gas station operator	1	0	1	1 week	15
Scrappers	4	0	4	Task	18
Headmen	2	0	2	6 days	13
Laborers, misc.	12	0	12	7 days	10
Watchmen	2	0	2	7 days	11
Total	83	0	83		

Administration (split between factory and farms)

Occupation	Male	Female	Total	Period	Pay
Office manager	1	0	1	1 year	4,800/year
Company secretary	0	1	1	1 year	3,400/year
Accountant	1	0	1	1 year	3,000/year
Liaison officer	1	0	1	1 year	2,600/year
Cashier	0	1	1	1 week	32
Typist	0	1	1	1 week	24
Clerks	4	4	8	1 week	14-32
Laborers, misc.[b]	9	1	10	6 days	10-13
Total	16	8	24		

Education level reached	Numbers listed
Secondary school	1
Grade 9 primary school	7[a]
Grade 8	0
Grade 7	1
Grade 6	49
Grade 5	26
Grade 4	27
Grade 3	11
Grade 2	3
Grade 1	7
"Elementary" or "primary"	31
Worthy Park apprenticeship	10
None, or none listed	868
Total	1041

TABLE 68. Worthy Park Farms, 1963-1973; Entries under "Education/Qualifications" in Personnel Records

Source: Worthy Park records.

[a]Includes one with 2 Jamaican Schools Examination Certificates.

TABLE 69. Worthy Park
Farms and Factory: Labor
Catchment Area, 1963-
1973

Source: Worthy Park records.

Radius (miles)	Direc- tion	Stated residence	Farms	Factory	Total	Laborers within a different radii	% of total known	Density of laborers (per sq. mile)
		Worthy Park	8	5	13			
		New India	4	14	18			
		Blue Mountain	1	0	1			
0-2	S	Lluidas Vale	488	222	710			
	S	Union	0	10	10			
	S	Barn's Pen	0	4	4			
	SW	Orange Valley	0	3	3	Within 2 miles, 759	48	60.40
2-5	S	Pennington	6	33	39			
	S	Juan de Bolas		2	2			
	SE	Roaring River	24	9	33			
	SE	Pusey	5	9	14			
	SE	Duxes	19	15	34			
	SW	Lemon Hall	70	8	78			
	SW	Top Hill	12	14	26			
	W	Crofts Hill	36	13	49			
	N	Tydixon	54	20	74			
	N	Camperdown	10	10	20	Between 2 & 5 miles, 369	'24	4.92
5-10	SE	Point Hill	127	30	157			
	SE	Snake Hill	0	4	4			
	SE	Garden Hill	0	3	3			
	S	Kentish	22	2	24			
	SE	Watermount	3	2	5			
	E	Kellits	10	6	16			
	NE	Bull Head	1	5	6			
	E	Ewarton	50	2	52	Between 5 & 10 miles, 267	16	1.13
10-20	SE	Gibraltar	1	1	2			
	NE	Brandon Hill	1	3	4			
	N	Clover Hill	0	8	8			
	N	Claremont	3	0	3			
	W	Linstead	10	0	10			
	SW	Bog Walk	3	4	7	Between 10 & 20 miles, 31	2	0.03
20	N	Madras, St. Ann	53	0	53			
	SE	Kingston	7	7	14			
	SE	Kingston	7	7	14			
	SE	Spanish Town	4	0	4			
	NW	Alexandria	4	0	4			
	W	Jericho, Hanover	0	4	4			
		49 other P.O.s	46	19	65	Over 20 miles, 144	10	.04
		Totals known	1,082	491	1,573			
		Unknown residence	34	63	97			
		Grand totals	1,116	554	1,670			

Surname initial	1838		1842-1846		Worthy Park Farms, Ltd., 1963-1973	
	Number of surnames	Persons in each initial group	Additional surnames	Persons in each initial group	Number of surnames	Persons in each initial group
A	2	6	3	4	8	29
B	12	33	9	20	42	157
C	2	2	7	13	27	74
D	7	19	3	6	19	66
E	2	6	1	2	10	26
F	1	1	8	24	13	44
G	6	12	9	15	17	86
H	8	16	12	26	24	70
I	—	—	1	1	1	1
J	1	2	4	8	9	53
K	1	2	3	5	7	11
L	3	5	6	14	18	63
M	11	20	14	26	31	100
N	4	4	4	6	12	23
O	—	—	1	1	5	19
P	6	21	4	8	19	44
Q	1	1	1	1	1	1
R	3	8	11	22	20	73
S	4	7	7	10	23	70
T	4	12	3	4	7	43
V	1	1	—	—	2	2
W	6	10	6	12	28	109
Y	—	—	1	1	—	—
Totals	95	188	118	229	343	1,164

TABLE 70. Worthy Park Work Forces, 1838, 1842-1846, and 1963-1973: Analysis of Surnames

Source: Worthy Park records.

Worthy Park Farms, Ltd., 1963-1973

Surname initial	Worthy Park Factory, Ltd. 1973		Surnames surviving from 1838	Persons in each initial group	Surnames surviving from 1842-1846 (not including 1838)	Persons in each initial group	New surnames 1963-1973	Persons in each initial group
	Number of surnames	Persons in each initial group						
A	5	12	2	14	—	—	6	15
B	16	31	7	62	4	42	31	53
C	9	15	1	8	5	32	21	34
D	5	7	4	46	2	3	13	17
E	4	7	2	15	1	3	7	8
F	2	2	1	18	3	4	9	22
G	7	11	4	52	3	24	10	10
H	5	10	4	21	4	27	16	22
I	2	2	—	—	—	—	1	1
J	3	7	1	19	3	26	5	8
K	5	6	1	3	—	—	4	8
L	5	6	2	16	2	22	14	25
M	14	20	10	37	4	16	10	32
N	2	2	3	10	1	1	8	12
O	2	4	—	—	1	4	4	15
P	6	7	4	23	2	2	13	19
Q	—	—	—	—	—	—	1	1
R	5	16	3	27	9	33	8	13
S	9	14	2	21	4	16	17	33
T	6	10	3	37	2	7	2	3
V	—	—	—	—	—	—	2	2
W	5	15	5	56	2	14	21	39
Y	—	—	—	—	—	—	—	—
Totals	117	204	59	485	52	276	223	392

Table 70 (*continued*)   Worthy Park Factory, Ltd., 1973

Surname initial	Surnames surviving from 1838	Persons in each initial group	Surnames surviving from 1842 to 1846 (not including 1838)	Persons in each initial group	New surnames 1973	Persons in each initial group
A	2	8	1	1	2	3
B	6	14	3	7	7	10
C	1	2	2	6	6	7
D	3	5	1	1	1	1
E	—	—	1	1	3	6
F	—	—	—	—	2	2
G	3	5	2	4	2	2
H	1	2	2	6	2	2
I	—	—	—	—	2	2
J	—	—	2	6	1	1
K	—	—	1	1	4	5
L	1	1	2	3	2	2
M	3	4	2	3	9	13
N	1	1	—	—	1	1
O	—	—	1	2	1	2
P	1	1	1	1	4	5
Q	—	—	—	—	—	—
R	1	6	4	10	—	—
S	1	2	2	4	6	8
T	4	8	—	—	2	2
V	—	—	—	—	—	—
W	3	11	2	4	—	—
Y	—	—	—	—	—	—
Totals	31	70	29	60	57	74

14 / The Rope Unraveled and Respliced: The Evidence of Genealogy

SLAVE society, like a multicolored rope, involved three major strands: white masters, black slaves, and a colored "middle class." The biographies given earlier suggest that despite subtle variations within each and some sexual intercourse among all, the strands were distinct. Yet, while slavery lasted all three were intertwined: "symbiotically inter-related by interdependence and emulation, and by a perverse admixture of fear, hatred, sex, grudging respect, and occasional affection."[1] What happened then when emancipation and the related decline of the colonial sugar economy occurred, and what has lasted to the present? How was the rope unraveled, if indeed it was unraveled at all?

Some commentators have characterized modern West Indian society as consisting essentially of a lower class descended from the mass of the laboring slaves, and a middle class descended from domestic slaves. For Jamaica this seems a useful working hypothesis, but only so far as it goes. What, for example, happened to the upper class of slavery days, what connections can be traced between the modern and the original master class on sugar plantations, and what of the latecomers to West Indian society?

To discover the fate of the descendants of Worthy Park's slave society it was at first planned to trace three genealogies: those of the descendants of a typical black slave couple, of the children of a colored domestic slave, and of the Price family which owned the estate throughout the slavery period.

Of these genealogies, that of the Prices proved easiest to follow up, though ultimately the least rewarding in the present context. Landed aristocrats, almost by definition, are most concerned with lineage, and in this case it was merely a question of fleshing out the entry under "Price of Trengwainton" in *Burke's Peerage, Bronetage and Knightage*,[2] with the help of the many contemporary descendants of the obscure Cromwellian lieutenant who founded the estate and dynasty in 1670. The exercise was fascinating, but the mass of biographical material gathered proved more suitable as the possible nucleus of a different book.

Even before George Price gave up the struggle to salvage the wreck of his father's Jamaican estate in 1865, the Price family had moved resolutely away from the shame and disappointment of West Indian sugar. If legacies of pioneer colonialism and slave mastery remained, they resided in a habit of authority, a sense of privilege, and, while the Empire lasted, of imperial mission. The family history of the Prices of Worthy Park and Trengwainton could indeed be written as an epitome of British imperialism, but not just as part of the history of slave society.

Sir Rose Price, who died within a few weeks of the Emancipation of 1834, bequeathed little wealth to his many children. But his daughters married new capital or old titles, and his sons and grandsons, as soldiers, sailors, or senior civil servants, served the Empire during its Victorian heyday and afterglow. Some lived lives like those of heroes in the boys' novels of G. A. Henty, fighting in wars and skirmishes from China to Gallipoli; others married heiresses or invested wisely, settling down to the lives of country squires. One was killed and (along with a Chinaman and a Kanaka) eaten by aborigines in an early exploration of Australia; another was the hunting companion of General Custer and narrowly missed the Massacre of the Little Big Horn; a third held the record for shooting wild bison in northern India. One of these later Prices was a colonial governor and, perhaps significantly, two were prison overseers. The most controversial was Sir Rose Price's fourth son, John, savagely murdered by convicts in 1857 while he was Superintendent of Penal Settlements for New South Wales. With or without justice, John Price was the model for the brutal Maurice Frere in Marcus Clarke's novel *For the Term of His Natural Life*.[3]

To find the most plausible continuities, it proved more fruitful to look at the old Jamaican sugar planters' structural rather than strictly genetic heirs. Almost uniquely, Worthy Park remained firmly in family hands, with the modern owners, the Clarkes, exhibiting many of the characteristics of their seventeenth-, eighteenth-, and nineteenth-century forerunners. However, though they had many connections by marriage with the old Jamaican plantocracy, they were not an old Jamaican family. The modern dynasty was founded by Henry Clarke, an Englishman who went to Jamaica as a practically penniless teenager in the desperate 1840s, at much the same time as the groups of even less fortunate Irish and German peasants and the first of the Jamaican East Indians and Chinese.[4]

Curiously, in his character and attitudes Henry Clarke seems to have held much in common with George Price, the last of Worthy Park's original owners to live in Jamaica. Both came to serve in the Legislative Council, where they showed implacable opposition to arbitrary government, whether by Governor or Colonial Office. They also shared a genuine, if paternalistic, respect for the ordinary black Jamaican countryman, whom Price found at least as loyal, sober, and cleanly as working-class Englishmen and whom Clarke claimed was just as hard working where his case was not hopeless. "The Negro in temper is very like the Irishman," wrote George Price provocatively for an English audience, "and therefore very superior to an Englishman in that respect."[5] George Price and Henry Clarke were able and humane men, who stood out for what they saw as the common weal rather than for the narrow plantocratic interest. But it should be remembered that both lived during the age of planting's failure, one seeing the loss of his family's plantation, the other never quite becoming a landed planter on his own account. Neither, it might be argued, was hardened or corrupted by complete involvement in the profit nexus of the sugar plantation system in its most exploitative forms, in slavery days and in the twentieth century.

Henry Clarke started as a schoolteacher in western Jamaica, became an Anglican parson, founded the Westmorland Building Society, and served as a plantation manager as well as member of the Legislative Council. Lord Olivier, the Fabian who was a member of the 1898 West India Commission and later governor of Jamaica, when describing Henry Clarke's outspoken condemnation of social conditions in Jamaica at the time of the Royal Commission in 1898, called him "one of the most sincere, courageous, and hard-working men he ever knew."[6] Four of Henry Clarke's five sons went into plantation work. Beginning as humble bookkeepers, all progressed to be estate overseers and attorneys, and two became genuine planters. The most successful was Frederick Lister Clarke, who became the sole owner of Worthy Park in 1918, where fifty-two years later, at the time of the tercentenary of the estate, his grandsons and their cousins were beginning to take over from his sons.

Percipient visitors to the Worthy Park celebrations in November 1970 could have learned more in a day about contemporary plantation society than from any book, and the well-read would have been fascinated by the juxtaposition of modern trends with relics from the age of Bryan Edwards and Edward Long.

The centerpiece of the celebrations was a public fete and speechfest at the Worthy Park cricket ground. Under the euphoric influence of food and drink, speaker after speaker congratulated the Clarkes on three hundred years of progress, glossing over for an afternoon the centuries of slavery and the fact that the Clarkes had owned Worthy Park for only the last sixth, and most successful part, of the period being celebrated. Not a single representative of the Price family was present at the feast.

It was a truly *Jamaican* occasion, with the temporary shelter reserved for the feasting of the elite crammed with planters, plutocrats, prelates, and politicians, half of whom, it seemed, were led in turn to the podium to add their praise or blessing. The highlight was the spectacular descent in a helicopter of the governor-general, Sir Clifford Campbell, a black man, who spoke briefly of the continuing importance of the sugar industry and the need for countrymen to continue to give their labor to the cause. These sentiments were enthusiastically received by the planters, one of whom remarked that Sir Clifford was "a good sport"—the ultimate planters' accolade. Meanwhile the mass of the villagers, dressed in their Sunday best, continued to enjoy the sideshows of the fete, totally ignoring the speeches. The only exceptions were a handful of elderly blacks, who stood at the fence of the dignitaries' kraal and gaped at the strange behavior within. Most of these ancients were patiently waiting for their own part in the celebrations: the presentation of "long service" awards.

After the speeches and presentations (a setting of crockery inscribed *Worthy Park 1670-1970* for all those who had worked at least a year, a Timex watch for those who had served fifty years, an engraved silver salver for managers and directors) almost unlimited free food and drink were distributed, and dancing began once the sun went down. While the ordinary folk re-enacted the festivities of slavery days, the elite departed, either back to town or to their own celebration at the house of the managing director. There a curious social ritual special to such occasions was performed. Cocktails were shared by all the Worthy Park senior staff, who included blacks and browns as well as whites; but at the approach of supper the darker-hued dutifully took their leave. This was based upon the polite fiction that supper was a family affair, though on such an occasion the "family" might include the Anglican parson and his wife, visiting scholars, and Canadians from the nearby ALCAN bauxite works—all, not coincidentally, white.

For the younger set of whites at Worthy Park such a setting was far too staid. At their own parties there were more likely to be loud music and gambling for high stakes, empty champagne bottles thrown over shoulders, and hunting forays after peacocks with the pistols which most of the men carried in their belts. On the night of the tercentenary a group of young white men conspired to desert their womenfolk and return to the cricket ground, looking for "sport." The escapade fizzled out when the disgruntled women banded together and went to join them. For the white men, heated with rum, any adventure which began when they whirled up into a dance the most attractive of the young black girls or East Indian "squaws" (the young whites' own disgraceful term) was quite legitimate. But when the white women began dancing with the boldest of the blacks the atmosphere quite suddenly changed.

The day and night of the tercentenary passed off unblemished by serious argument or scandal. With the return of the humdrum round, reality replaced euphoria. A more leisurely survey of attitudes and relationships disclosed irremediable rifts and tensions. For a start, the plantation whites, invariably educated abroad, spoke two or three virtually different languages, depending on the hearers: polished standard English to foreign visitors, upper-class Jamaican to each other, the broadest Creole dialect when dealing with the workers. Most expressed pride in Worthy Park and affection for the scenic beauties of Lluidas Vale but irrationally decried the blacks for not sharing in these essentially proprietary and sophisticated sentiments. Excessively indulgent to their own children, they were paternalistic to their servants and workers, but in a fashion in which true affection, respect, or even understanding, were almost absent.

With considerable justice the whites complained of innumerable instances where generosity and kindness were reciprocated by thanklessness, unreliability, and downright larceny. Invariably these were attributed to allegedly typical traits in the blacks, rather than blamed on a social system equating class with race. Most whites had their favorite blacks, but usually these turned out to be old nannies or other faithful retainers, often idealized in retrospect. The more common reality was servants turned sullen, dismissed, or moving on as soon as mutual trust had gone or the "missus" became too sharp about the volume of customary perquisites disappearing out of the kitchen.

Plantation whites still knew little and cared less about conditions in the village outside the gates. The ignorance of Frederick Clarke in 1929 when asked to fill in a questionnaire about the diet of his laborers would still have applied forty-five years later.[7] It generally took an outsider with an anthropological bent to show an interest in the fascinating rituals which enlivened and dignified village life—such as the Nine Nights wake at a villager's death. The Worthy Park ladies performed social work in the way of help at the clinic or organizing children's parties, but resolutely on their own ground. Even then they were usually disappointed and resentful at the lack of response or thanks. For example, in 1973 four of the ladies joined the parson and his wife in offering an adult literacy class in the Anglican church hall. With all six teachers having a university degree, it must have been the best qualified group (on paper) in all Jamaica. But the teachers quite often outnumbered the adult illiterates coming forward to be taught, and the class soon fell into abeyance. Such failures make the brilliant success of the anthropologist Edith Clarke (a genteel cousin of Worthy Park's owners) in researching an estate village similar to Lluidas Vale all the more remarkable.[8]

Ignorance and indifference bred fear and fed upon it. Mutual hatred and latent violence lay not far below the surface of plantation relationships—in the 1970s as in slavery days. The older men, the generation of Frederick Clarke's sons and their black contemporaries, had learned to dissemble. The young, products of a more desperate, less tolerant age, were far more volatile. A session of steady work accompanied by jocular repartee quite suddenly flared into crisis when one of the four white undermanagers cuffed a cane-cutter for insolence and refusal to work. A long drawn-out dispute over grazing rights on the margins of estate roads turned suddenly ugly when another young white man dragged a black independent cultivator's donkey to its death behind his Land Rover. Behind these incidents lay a story almost Grecian in its starkness: the murder of the mother of two of the young whites by her black chauffeur, who saved himself from the gallows by the plea that the lady was his lover.

Miscegenous relationships between whites and nonwhites were quite as taboo in Jamaica in the 1970s as they had been two centuries earlier. Yet the presence even at Worthy Park parties of persons who in an earlier age would have been termed "Jamaica Whites" demonstrated that such relationships were far more common than generally acknowledged. And the great variety of skin shades among the middle reaches of modern Jamaica society illustrated that miscegenation between coloreds and blacks was extremely common and between coloreds themselves was the rule rather than the exception.

To understand better the complex role that miscegenation had played in shaping postslavery society in Jamaica, an attempt was made to trace the descendants of the two children whom the quadroon ex-slave Lizette Nash bore to Worthy Park's owner, Rose Price, in 1795 and 1796. The two genealogies provided a fascinating contrast, but since Elizabeth Price Nash and her descendants rejected Jamaica along with the triple stigma of illegitimate, black, and slave origins, and John Price Nash and his descendants remained just as firmly Jamaican, the descent of Elizabeth Price Nash is merely sketched, while that of her brother is given a whole chapter to itself.

In his own way Rose Prise did his duty by his two Jamaican children. It was, however, an unwritten and unequal contract: an education, aid in finding employment, and a small annuity in return for a tacit agreement to remain unembarrassingly invisible.

The father kept in touch with Peter Douglas, in whose sprawling household the children were brought up, learning to read and write if little more. Around 1810, as they approached the dangerous age of puberty, Rose Price—like the father in Richard Hughes's *High Wind in Jamaica*—sought to save the children from what he saw as the enervation, superstitions, and temptations of a tropical environment. Torn from their mother and the easygoing company of ten uncles and aunts (all darker than they), they were shipped off to a strange and chilly "homeland," and there separated.

It is not known where Elizabeth Nash's education was "finished," but it was probably at some cut-price girls' boarding school in northern England or lowland Scotland. Around 1815 she became, like Jane Eyre, governess in the household of a landed gentleman, in this case James Dennistoun of Colgraine, near Glasgow—though, unlike the Brontë heroine, it was she and not her employer's wife who was the West Indian. A miniature dating from this period depicted a handsome, almost beautiful girl, with the rounded features, liquid eyes, and dusky skin of the traditional *belle creole*, and an air almost of languor, which the Scottish climate, age, and matriarchy gradually sharpened.[9]

For such a transplanted exotic, prospects of a suitable marriage must often have seemed remote. Yet chance, and perhaps a discerning employer, played their parts. Since 1812 James Dennistoun had also employed a young graduate of the Divinity School of the University of Glasgow, Alexander Lochore, the son of a Glasgow shoemaker, as tutor to his two growing boys—much as John Price of Penzance had employed John Vinnicombe as tutor to his only son.[10]

Romance bloomed between dominie and governess—the Scottish granite warmed by the tropical sun. By 1823 an understanding had been reached, and only the question of a living for the would-be minister remained. In January 1825, the couple were married, a few months after Alexander Lochore had at last been called to the kirk of Drymen (just north of Glasgow) and ordained.

It was a match of which Elizabeth's father, though a staunch Anglican, doubtless approved. Alexander Lochore, again like John Vinnicombe, came from humble origins and was a brilliant scholar, but knew his place. A kirk was the summit and circumference of his ambition, and he stayed at modest Drymen throughout the fifty-three years of his ministry. Though acquaintances remarked that apparently the minister's wife had no close relatives, for none ever visited her, Elizabeth Price Nash Lochore from her marriage to her death in 1885 enjoyed an annuity of £25, secured by an outright bequest of £325 in Sir Rose Price's will when he died in 1834.[11]

Genetically as well as temperamentally the Alexander Lochores were a splendid match. Between the ages of 30 and 43 Elizabeth dutifully bore eight sturdy children, four of each sex, who not only survived into adult life but lived to an average age of 78. All grew tall and handsome, though their mother's trace of African blood, as much as their father's lowland Scots, saved them and their descendants from the somewhat foppish good looks of some of the Prices. Only one, the third son, Alexander, carried a direct hint of African ancestry, in a slightly swarthy skin and crinkly hair; and he never married.

Setting the children up in life was even more of a problem for the Lochores of Drymen than for the Prices of Trengwainton, for the fledglings of the manse were given nothing but good health, good looks, and a sound Scottish education. The solutions, however, were similar, if on a different social plane: marry off the nubile daughters to the wealthiest and worthiest men available; place those who did not find a husband in respectable employ; encourage the young men (if not the women too) to treat the whole world as their oyster. If the likes of the Prices refertilized the landed aristocracy and provided the officer class for an expansive empire, the offspring of a thousand manses such as Drymen not only provided a constant reinforcement for the Scottish middle class but also added to the flow of dynamic settlers who made imperialism work.

The most notable descendants of Elizabeth Price Nash and

Alexander Lochore were Scottish shopkeepers and ministers and New Zealand farmers—the latter a numerous clan stemming from one of the three sons of Alexander and Elizabeth Lochore who followed the hopes of gold from Ballarat and Bendigo in 1851, to Otago in 1857, and Westland in 1865. Socially and geographically the two branches grew far apart, but both were even farther removed from the Jamaican element in their origins. Undoubtedly, though, it would be the bluff antipodeans rather than the solid bourgeois of Stirling or Perth who would more easily come to terms with the curious facts of their background. One of the New Zealand descendants, George Weenink, whose mother was another Elizabeth Lochore, recounted that when he returned to the homeland for the first time in 1935 his Scottish cousins seemed to his "colonial eyes" to be "extremely well off," and "though extremely kind, somewhat high-falutin'."

The visitor from New Zealand heard with fascination and at first hand of the Reverend Alexander Lochore and his wife Elizabeth (after whom his own mother had been named), though all his cousins concentrated on the Scottish and not the Jamaican side. "Only *one*," he recalled in a letter, "mentioned the illegitimacy of E.P. and none referred to Negro blood. I myself take the view that as we have no choice of ancestors, it is hypocrisy to pretend that we are descended from a parcel of Saints (what an uninteresting Pedigree that would be!)."[12]

It was an eager ambition of this New Zealand Lochore to meet his Price and Nash cousins in England and Jamaica. But it has to be admitted that the strands connecting Prices and Lochores with Jamaican slavery, and even with each other, are now tenuous indeed and have no great place in the present book. However, for the families that have never left Jamaica—for any Jamaican family—the links and memories are still difficult to ignore or forget and should be stressed. The next two chapters contrast the status and attitudes of the Jamaican descendants of Lizette Nash with the fate of the only black slave couple from Worthy Park whose genealogy could be traced with certainty, Nelson and Biddy.

These families, one colored, one black, descended from house and field slaves, respectively, can stand for types and illustrate general trends. They also shed some oblique light on the nature of slavery itself. Yet they leave underrepresented the mass of the descendants of the ordinary black slaves—that great majority of the inhabitants of Lluidas Vale district who have never left, or been able to leave, the orbit of Worthy Park Estate. It was also surely in the folk memory of this all-important section of the modern population that fresh material relevant to the understanding of slavery remained to be recovered. Their precise genealogies proved almost impossible to trace; yet roles and attitudes have a genealogy of their own, as closely related to the general environment and its history as to family connections. Accordingly, the concluding chapter of this book has a double purpose: seeking to sum up the legacies of slavery through the lives and perceptions of a representative cross section of slavery's truest sons, while at the same time trying to recover from the oral tradition facts about slavery and slave society not yet found in books.

Legatees. The new colored middle class aspired, with limited expectations, to the style of their white prede-cessors.

340

15 / From House Slave to Middle Class: The Descendants of John Price Nash

JAMAICAN families, for the most part, show neither the obsessive interest in family history of the Prices nor the detailed knowledge demonstrated by at least one descendant of the Lochores. For one thing families in Jamaica tend to be loosely knit by formal ties, so that Jamaican genealogical tables, were they fully traceable, would be analogous to tropical undergrowth when compared with the typical English middle- or upper-class "family trees." Besides (whether result or cause of this entangling), it is almost a rule among black and colored families alike that direct knowledge of forebears—kept records, mementoes, anecdotes, even names—does not extend back beyond the third generation, or about seventy-five years.[1] Thus, quite apart from any conscious or unconscious dissociation from slavery, there generally exists a gap of several generations between the most attenuated family memories and the records of slave ancestors. This is further complicated by the fact that the patchy parochial records were reorganized on a colonywide basis only in 1871.

To close the gap is relatively easier for those who are middle class in the Jamaican context, and are descended from colored slaves like the Price Nashes, than for the proletarian descendants of ordinary black slaves. Almost by definition, middle-class Jamaicans are more scrupulous than the majority about formal marriage ties, and thus their family memories are more easily corroborated and extended through official records of births, marriages, and deaths. Colored slaves also appeared more commonly in the manumission records and were the earliest of the nonwhites to be baptized, married, or have their burials recorded in the parish registers. Moreover, in most middle-class families there would be at least one outstanding person, whose career could be traced in almanacs, newspapers, and official correspondence, as well as in the statistical returns. Such a man was John Price Nash (1796-1870), whose career epitomized the limited degree of upward mobility open to the colored Jamaican in the decade before, and the three decades after, emancipation.

Just as his sister was usefully educated to be a governess, John Price Nash was trained in Britain to be a superior mechanic, probably as an apprentice in a factory in the English Midlands. After more than ten years in the "homeland," he returned to Jamaica in 1823, at the age of 27, modestly styling himself as "millwright" rather than "engineer." No portrait exists of him, but being son, grandson, and great-grandson of white men, he was almost certainly sufficiently European in appearance to have passed as a swarthy white in England. In Jamaica, however, as an octoroon he was still regarded as a "mulatto" or "free person of colour," denied the full exercise of "the privileges and immunities of his majesty's white subjects of this island."[2]

As recently as 1796 free coloreds born as slaves had been treated throughout their lives almost as slaves before the courts. Even those like John Price Nash who were born of freed mothers could not litigate or give evidence against whites in the courts, serve on juries, inherit more than £2,000, become sugar planters or hold many slaves, vote in elections, serve in the Assembly or vestries, hold any "offices of trust" even as lowly as constables, or be granted commissions in the militia, even for the mulatto and black regiments.

Nash, however, profited from the steady improvement in the status of the Jamaican free coloreds in slavery's last years, the tacit assumption of which was that free coloreds would likely be treated as whites the more they behaved like them or slavishly followed their lead. From 1813 the colored freedman could be granted a "privilege certificate" removing many of his legal disabilities, but only on the attestation of custos, justice of the peace, or churchwarden in open vestry. After 1819 these privilege certificates were normally granted at the same time as manumission, and in the year that John Price Nash returned to Jamaica other disabilities concerning eligibility for service and the holding of property were lifted, under pressure from Westminster. It was not until 1830, however, that all restrictions were removed, so that all freedmen were legally equal, regardless of color; and even then there continued to be covert discrimination in the form of property qualifications, flexibly interpreted.[3]

By 1830 John Price Nash had made considerable progress, however. On his return he had resettled in St. John's with his mother, in the community of his colored uncles, aunts, and cousins, the Douglases and Quiers. As the best educated of a fairly disorganized family, he increasingly served them as agent, executor, and attorney. At the same time, he was trying to establish himself as a planter. In 1823 he was listed as owning only 3 slaves, given to him by Sir Rose Price from Worthy Park, London and Cato, aged 28, and Joseph, 32. By 1826 he had acquired 5 more slaves by bequest from Ann Quier and was listed with 22 more as executor of Ann Quier's will. He acquired 3 by becoming guardian of Catherine Douglas in 1827, and 5 on his marriage to Anne Maria Howell in 1828. In addition, he clearly controlled the slaves belonging to his mother, Lizette Nash, and perhaps also those of his grandmother, Eleanor Price Douglas. The triennial slave registrations correctly divided the ownership, but the annual *Jamaica Almanack* gradually accorded all the slaves to John Price Nash. For example, the last slave registration in 1832 listed him as having only 9 slaves, with Lizette Nash 14, and Eleanor Price Douglas 12; but the *Almanack* for 1830 had given John Price Nash 20, Lizette Nash none, and Eleanor Price Douglas 7. On the eve of final emancipation in 1837, John Price Nash was listed in the *Almanack* as possessing 30 Apprentices, with neither his mother nor grandmother having any at all.[4]

In the same 1837 edition of the *Almanack*, John Price Nash appeared as one of the four assessors of Apprentice work loads for St. John's. Although, unlike his three fellow assessors who were said to be "Planters," he was described simply as "Millwright," Nash, with his effective labor force of 20-30 slaves and Apprentices, had for years worked a small estate he called Overton.[5] The place name is no longer to be found in Jamaica, but it seems to have applied to the southern half of the old Douglas plantation of Point Hill, which Nash definitely owned rather later and where he had his house.[6] At first this large rambling property straddling the road from Lluidas to Guanaboa Vale, some six miles long by half a mile wide, along with more than 100 slaves, had been shared by the ten Douglas children. But it had never prospered, and even in the days of Peter Douglas the works were tumble-down and the slaves mainly let out for jobbing.[7] As the Douglases departed or died, John Price Nash took over more and more responsibility, until by the 1850s he was virtually owner of the whole of Point Hill Estate.[8]

What cleared out the Douglases was probably the emancipation of the slaves, followed by the depression of the 1840s. This double blow also seems, in time, to have dashed the hopes of John Price Nash to become a planter like his father. Much of the flavor of the period, and virtually all we know of Nash's opinions and family relationships, are contained in the letter which he wrote to his sister, Elizabeth, at the very end of 1840, when he was 44 and she had been married to the Reverend Alexander Lochore and installed at Drymen for nineteen years.

Overton December 31st. 1840

My Dear Sister,

It is some long time now since I last wrote you, in which time, I have received your letters of May 6th. & 27th. Dec. I am happy to hear yourself, your Lord, and the Children are well. The yellow fever is still raging, and Carrying of Numbers. Thanks be to God, we have been spared from so dreadful an affliction up to now. I notice what you say respecting Mr. Salmon, should he come into the district I am in, I will pay every attention for past favours. But I fear this will not be the case, as by the Arrivals of this month, I notice the Isabella has arrived at Falmouth, a very great Distance from me, and no doubt, he will be employed down there, on some Estate or other, if he intends being a planter, or in the Town as a Book Clerk; however should I meet with him, I shall do as you desire. The articles you have sent under his care, as soon as they come to hand shall be distributed as you have written.

I feel obliged to you, for the hint respecting my Son's Education, he at present is at day school in Town. As soon as I can make it convenient, I intend sending him to England, but not before he can take care of himself, which is very necessary. I am just now labouring under heavy pecuniary difficulties, and God only knows how it will terminate, if for the better, I will send him next year to you. It is contemplated that we will soon have Schools established in Jamaica as equal to those in England, this may be as regards *education* but not as to *Manners*, and *Moral principles* which are much required amongst societys of this Country. My eldest Daughter is growing very fast, but is backward in her Education. However I hope the time will arrive that I may send all of them to you, for a few Years.

I cannot express to you, the joy of My Dear Mother on the receipt of your last letters, as also the Children on hearing you had sent them something, which they will soon get. The old lady is quite well and strong. My Grand Mother is also well and strong, is astonishing to see her going over hills & dales, walking, in her advanced age. She cannot be less than 90 or upwards, she looks well, and is still handsome, she must have been a splendid personage when young, she also keeps her health well.

I forget if I did inform you of our Uncle Robert Ross Douglas' death, he died some time ago. He has left a family, his wife, has turned out a very bad woman much to our disgrace. There is only four of the old Lady's children alive, out of eleven; they are all well.[9]

I assure you we begin to experience the fruits of our slaves being taken from us: numbers will be beggars by it. We cannot get money fast enough to give to the labourers, as to House Servants, it is impossible to meet with one honest, to remain with you—they are full of importunance and villany. The planters & many have thrown up their cultivation in consequence. I think I shall be obliged to throw up mine also. We plant, but when to reap, except to pay double the price of labour, your crop may rot for what they care. The country is so fine they can live almost without working.

I must conclude by wishing you, and all your family, a happy and a prosperous New Year. Make our united love to the Children and accept the same from us, and a tender of our joint regards to your better half, and believe me ever to remain,

my Dear Sister,
Your Affectionate Brother,
John Price Nash.[10]

Though John Price Nash was unequivocally a colored man, there is nothing in his letter which suggests that he was not a member of the white plantocracy, with all the traditional attitudes and prejudices. Absenteeism, or at least an education in the metropolis in sound *"Manners"* and *"Moral principles,"* is taken to be the norm; the ending of slavery (or rather, "our slaves being taken from us") is deprecated; the ex-slaves are castigated for refusing to work with a will, or cheaply enough, for their former masters. It might be held that this letter indicates no more than that the division between masters and workers was, or had become, essentially a socioeconomic, or class, rather than a racial, matter. This is more likely to have been true for a person like John Price Nash, known to be of mixed blood, than for someone fortunate enough to be white, as well as a master. He, after all, did not reject but clearly admired his mother, who was twice as black as he, or even that "splendid personage," his grandmother, who was half black, half white. The pure racism was more likely on the side of Elizabeth Price Nash Lochore, who papered over her Jamaican origins and never welcomed her colored relatives to Drymen manse.

Nonetheless, whether socioeconomically or racially inspired, John Price Nash was unequivocally devoted to a set of manners and attitudes—a concept of class—that until recently had been exclusively white. He tried to succeed on traditional terms rather than seeking radical changes, and in this respect he seems to have been consistent to the end of his life, despite many disappointments.

As he feared he would have to, Nash seems to have "thrown up [his] cultivation" in the mid-1840s, and Point Hill Plantation fell into the decay from which it has never emerged. Instead, he offered his technical skills to those few estates, such as Worthy Park, which still needed them. During the installation of new machinery at Worthy Park in the later 1840s he certainly worked alongside his half-brothers, George and Thomas Price, though whether or not the relationship was ever acknowledged cannot be told.

With the collapse of 1847-48, John Price Nash, as an employee, was in even more desperate straits than the Prices. Late in 1847, he was reduced to applying, along with other "colored mechanics," for jobs that were being advertized in Sierra Leone. "I shall be fifty five in 1848,"[11] he wrote in reply to queries from the Colonial Secretary of Jamaica:

> My family consists of a Boy two girls & a wife. My son will accompany me, the remaining part of my family will follow afterwards.
> 2. I was taught the Millwright and Engineer professions in England, on my return to the Island I have been engaged in a mixed description of work Viz. Carpenters, Mason, Smith, Mill & Engine all of which I superintend and am now doing so on Worthy Park Estate in Saint John.
> 3. I have had several apprentices, and I feel myself competent to teach any number that may be placed under my care.
> 4. I avail myself of all improvements and adopt them when necessary. But as regards to Machinery in this Country, I very often have to adapt my own invention to suit the emergency required.
> 5. My income is at present small, I lately enjoyed £600 pr Ann. I will leave for £800 pr Ann. The period of our engagement will depend on our general health, which if enjoyed will be for life if otherwise for three, five or Seven years. If this is required I will give testimonial of my general habits & acquirements.[12]

Nothing came of the application, probably because £800 a year (plus £150 for his son) was too much to pay for the risk of sending out a family man in his 50s to the notorious "graveyard" of West Africa. Instead, Nash turned to supporting his family from his garden plot, while looking around for whatever employment remained, either on estates or in local government service.

Despite the difficulties of making a comfortable living in Jamaica, John Price Nash rose steadily up the social scale—at least on the parochial level. As early as 1833 he had become a vestryman, along with his uncle, John Quier Douglas, and in the same year he was one of the first colored men to become an officer in the Jamaica militia, being commissioned as ensign in the St. Dorothy & St. John Regiment of the Middlesex Division of Foot. Thereafter, his promotion was uninterrupted: lieutenant in April 1838, captain in May 1840, and between 1843 and 1865, lieutenant colonel and commanding officer.[13] Traditionally, militia rank was an index of a man's social standing, but, ironically, his steady promotion was concurrent with a steady decline in the social prestige of the militia, both as the need for a military defense force declined and as the few whites who remained in Jamaica showed less enthusiasm for serving as brother officers (or even subordinates) to aspiring colored men. Even in the 1840s the militia had ceased to meet regularly, and by the 1860s it was completely moribund, eventually being succeeded by the Jamaica Volunteers about the time that "Colonel" John Price Nash died.

In a similar fashion, he became one of the most prominent men in his parish, but at a time when St. John's was becoming one of the poorest parishes in poor Jamaica, being, like neighboring St. Dorothy's, eventually swallowed up by St. Catherine's in the consolidation of 1867. In 1857, John Price Nash was elected one of the two churchwardens for St. John's, and in 1859 and 1860 was appointed one of the two assessors of property for the Census of 1861, at a modest stipend of £12 Currency a year. From 1862 until his death, he held the picturesque office of poundkeeper for Upper St. John, to which was added the function of collector of petty debts in 1868.[14] The poundkeeper's job brought only £12 a year in salary, to which were added fees of 3s. a day for looking after stray cattle, 2s. for asses, and commission on the debts collected; but this paltry income may well have been all that kept him from penury in old age.

Even in his declining years, John Price Nash must have been the most important man in the hilltop village of Point Hill. On a contemporary map "Mr. Nash's House" was singularly identified, next to the knob of land he gave to the government for building the police barracks.[15] Yet it is probably significant that, unlike his half-brother George Price of Worthy Park, John Price Nash was never appointed a JP, let alone elected member of the Assembly, or chosen to be custos and member of the Executive Council. In that postemancipation era, a colored man who played by the rules could aspire to the middle slopes of the social pyramid, but race and lineage, even more than territorial holdings and abilities, still determined who should dominate the upper reaches.

Searches in the Jamaica Island Record Office disclosed the skeletal information of the birth registrations of John Price and Anne Nash's three children, William Hutcheson, Lizette Forbes, and Joannah Forbes, between 1829 and 1832, and of eight children born to William Hutcheson Nash and his wife Caroline (Thomas) between 1859 and 1873. But there the traces faded out. In contrast to slavery days, modern records are easiest to trace through the male line, since surnames remain the same. With females, married names have to be known before searches can be made, that is, if marriages actually occurred. No husbands or children could be traced for either of John Price Nash's two daughters; and except for John Price Nash II, who died young, all of William Hutcheson Nash's children were girls.[16]

A visit to Point Hill early in 1973 disclosed the indistinct ruins of a works or great house on a piece of land still known locally as Nash's, but in the place where "Mr. Nash's House" stood in 1858 was a modern bungalow, whose tenants were strangers to the district. However, an elderly neighbor remembered tales of several "white ladies" called Nash who lived in Point Hill around the turn of the century, none of whom married, though one or two had "brown" children. The informant knew none of the Nashes personally, but believed that one of the brown children had married "one Pantry," and was still living somewhere in Kingston.

A distinct impression was conveyed—later corroborated—of a large, impoverished family cursed by a lack of sons, with daughters condemned by the lack of dowries or suitably light-skinned partners either to spinsterhood or a reversion to the custom, common among the poorer classes in Jamaica, of informal, often temporary, liaisons, with the typical household consisting of mother and children living alone. From the point of view of John Price Nash—and doubtless his mother and grandmother too—this would have been a regression, serologically as well as socially, with the children almost bound to be darker than their mothers, as well as denied the benefits of legitimacy or a normal family.

Telephone calls to the many Nashes listed in the Jamaica Directory drew blanks, but an inquiry placed in the Daily Gleaner with the help of the columnist "Thomas Wright" (Morris Cargill) immediately opened the trail again. Almost in the next post came letters from Mrs. Beulah Myers, daughter of W. H. Nash's sixth daughter, with the family names Lizette Eleanor Price Nash (1865-1919), and from G. C. Pantry, whose mother, Iona, born in 1905, was the Pantry thought to be living in Kingston, and who was daughter of W. H. Nash's youngest child, Caroline Rosamund Nash (1873-1946).

Coincidentally, as registrar-general, G. C. Pantry was the best man in Jamaica to help with any genealogical research, being the senior official in charge of all records of births, marriages, and deaths. Even with his help, the Nash family tree still looked more like a pollarded willow than a spreading oak. Far more illuminating was the joint interview, lasting a long evening, which he set up and presided over, between, on the one side, three researchers, and on the other, the Pantry family and their cousin, Mrs. Myers.[17]

Mr. Pantry's house turned out to be such as would be expected from someone who had "made good," rather than inheriting wealth, style, or a love of the traditional: a typical upper-middle-income bungalow, set in the first large suburban area developed in Kingston, in the mid-1950s. Nothing in evidence was much older than the house itself. Though protected by the inevitable vociferous dogs and the burglar-bars which are the most unfortunate of class indicators in Jamaica today, the house was roomy rather than sumptuous, the furniture functional plastic and metal rather than the traditional Jamaican mahogany, or even fake antique. The pictures on the walls were neither the eighteenth-century prints or maps found in many upper-class homes nor the religious or sentimental cutouts which brighten many Jamaican shacks, but rather that type of safe, bland mass-production that has become a common denominator for such homes throughout the western world. Few books were in evidence, though the ubiquitous eye of the dead TV glowered as if deprived of an accustomed dominance. For the benefit of the visitors, refreshments included imported cocktail dainties, Scotch, and wine, as well as the "wine" of the country, Appleton rum, and the delicious Jamaican "party patties"—served with plate and fork, rather than to be eaten with the fingers as in upper- and lower-class gatherings alike.

For an outsider, the most interesting obvious characteristic of this family was the wide variety of skin shades and features inevitable in any family in which all parents are colored.[18] More subtle, and difficult to assess, were the ways in which these external differences affected personae.

Mrs. Beulah Myers would almost have filled the description of a Jamaica White, with complexion of a brown so light as to be almost pink, and with silvery, straight hair. Proudly, she produced a 100-year-old sepia photograph of her mother when young, which—even discounting the photographer's art—depicted a delicately beautiful young lady, indistinguishable from a European. Although she claimed to have paid very little attention to family trees, Mrs. Myers remembered her mother telling her she was descended from Sir Rose Price "of Worthy Park and Rose Hall." Of all those gathered, she was proudest of the connection with the old plantocracy, and at the same time the most conservative. Yet though eloquent about the past and the contemporary decline of standards, her knowledge was extremely faulty.

Self-confident and ebullient, Mrs. Myers spoke standard English with an upper-class Jamaican accent. Although in her mid-70s, she was proud of the fact that she was still "gainfully employed," working for the Jamaican Legion, "giving praise to God every day" for keeping her in such good health. She was greatly respected in the family for her spirit, her self-made success in a long and busy life, and for the selfless way she had supported her mother and aunts in penurious old age.

Although a first cousin, Mrs. Iona Pantry could hardly have been more different from Mrs. Myers. Her complexion, in Jamaican parlance, was "cool dark," her features distinctly negroid. In the fashion common in her class, she wore a black wig simulating European-type hair. Soft-voiced and retiring, Mrs. Pantry also spoke standard English, but more slowly and less confidently than her cousin. She showed little knowledge of, and least interest in, the distant past or the family's antecedents, and was even reticent about her own early days. The only claims she made were that all her early life she had labored to make sure that her children had a better chance than herself, especially in education, and that she was satisfied she had done her best for them in difficult financial circumstances.

Mrs. Pantry's pride was overly modest, for her children proved a remarkable, if diversified, trio. G. C. (or "Gee"), the registrar-general, was the oldest and, being used to making decisions and giving commands, the most assured and decisive—though still with that style of qualification and reserve to be expected in a successful civil servant. Dark brown in complexion and with kinky hair (though seemingly more East Indian than African in features), his appearance and manner were quite different from those of his sister, Vita (Lewis). Her complexion was light, her hair straightish and stylishly upswept in "Eliza Doolittle" fashion, her chic trouser-suit in rather sharp contrast to the conservatively sensible clothes of her brothers. As suited a lecturer at the College of Arts, Science and Technology and one of the first Arts graduates of the University College of the West Indies, Mrs. Lewis spoke fluently and precisely in standard English, articulately expressing views about history and society in general.

The middle member of the trio in age, Fitz, or "Skipper," was in appearance midway between his sister and brother, having a reddish complexion, rather European features, and tight, curly hair. In contrast to both, his manner, though not subdued, was laconic, humorous, less assertive; and though he could speak correct English, his accent and idiom easily lapsed into broad Jamaican. These characteristics reflected the facts that he had worked more with his hands, and spent more of his life in the country, than either Vita or Gee. He had even worked for some years as a mechanic in the garage at Worthy Park, proud of his seniority over mere field laborers, but apparently unaware of the irony that he was great-great-great-grandson of the estate's former owner.

In fact, all three of Mrs. Pantry's surviving children had been brought up in the country, rather surprisingly at Point Hill in John Price Nash's old house, which was only demolished around 1950. The children had gone first to Point Hill primary school just before World

War II, moving to better schools in Kingston later. Because of straitened circumstances, only the youngest, Vita, had been able to go on to higher education, the boys being regarded as fortunate to be well placed in the civil service and an engineering apprenticeship, respectively. All three spoke with nostalgia of their country childhood—of fruits in the orchard, the swimming hole in the river, donkey rides to church—though none had plans to move back there before retirement. The Jamaican countryside, with its poor schools and primitive influences, was no place to bring up a family, and Point Hill was too far removed from work, friends, and the amenities of Town.

Without prompting, none of the Pantrys—even the Arts graduate—had a very precise notion of the Jamaican past, let alone of their family's role in it. Yet when, apparently for the first time ever, family memories were pooled, a picture began to emerge, like the uncovering of a fractured mosaic. When the researchers corroborated and extended the family's memories with their own discoveries, interest expanded almost with a sense of revelation. The connection with the Price family was of particular interest. This was not entirely through a sudden access, or reinforcement, of snobbery, though there was an element of that. Rather, it reflected family pride that they had an association with persons and events in the past which were regarded as worthy of historical research. This provided a sense of authenticity, of which their previous ignorance and indifference had been the reverse.

All remembered the ruins of the sugar mill some 300 yards behind the Point Hill house, and the nearby Congo Ground where slave "duppies" (ghosts) were said to lurk. The two old ladies remembered William Hutcheson Nash, who died about 1910, as a blind and chair-ridden old man, who had been a wheelwright in his prime; but of John Price Nash no memories or anecdotes remained. All had heard vaguely of the Price connection, but this authentic tradition was no stronger than the obviously spurious story that the family was related to the founder of the firm which made Nash cars in the United States.

Beulah and Iona chiefly remembered their mothers and aunts, impoverished spinsters who made up in character what they lacked in wealth. "Aunt Addy," for example, was a prim, religious lady, who sat in her own pew at church (Church of England, of course) wearing veil and gloves. She was strict and meticulous, especially with children, pedantic about ladylike behavior and speech. Like her sisters, she was as poor as the proverbial church mouse, somehow making a living from needlework and handicrafts. Aunt Mary was much more tolerant and sympathetic, which was attributed to the fact that she had traveled. "Goddy," Iona Pantry's mother, was remembered as the scholar of the family, the proud possessor of "a whole box of books," including Shakespeare and Thomas Hardy. Her bookishness was thought to have been inherited from her father, to be passed on in the present generation to Vita, the English lecturer at C.A.S.T.

As the evening wore on, and the conversation mellowed with the

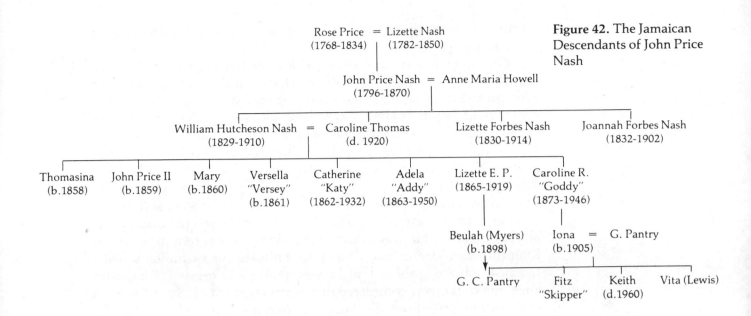

Figure 42. The Jamaican Descendants of John Price Nash

refreshments, the family talked with increasing freedom of class, color, social roles, plantations, and their feelings about the slave and imperial past, the present, and the future.

Despite the geniality of the occasion, there were even more of the contradictions and inconsistencies than might have been expected from such a spontaneous discussion, reflecting deep ambivalences in the individuals themselves. Though skeptical about formal politics, all claimed to be democratic, progressive, and modern. Yet these values (rather to their own surprise) proved to be relative and quite distinctly varied—from Beulah's innate toryism, to Vita's rather lukewarm social democracy. Their attitudes towards the past varied between nostalgia, condemnation, and indifference; yet out of discussion emerged a common uncertainty about the future and a distaste for radical solutions that suggested a fundamental affinity for the status quo, and even for traditional values.

All claimed to be egalitarians, or at least to believe in equal opportunities for all; yet the underlying assumption seemed to be that equality was fine as long as it was their class, or, more precisely, their family, which benefited most. All agreed that class divisions were inevitable, claiming that in modern Jamaica they were based more on money than on color. At the same time they admitted that the majority of blacks were still proletarians (and vice versa), and that whites were still dominant out of all proportion to their numbers. They vigorously denied that it was the colored middle class which had taken over the leading role in society, pointing out that black people could, and did, become rich and occupy top posts in government. But the vigor of their denial, and the accompanying attacks on Cuban and Haitian solutions, left a sense that dominance by the colored middle class seemed a more natural turn of events than either an excessive leveling or an adoption of Black Power principles.

One of the Pantrys quoted as an ideal the Jamaican motto "Out of Many, One People," but all admitted that prejudices still existed and even provided unconscious evidence that they were not entirely innocent of prejudice themselves. Gee (whose wife was darker than himself) claimed that there were more people than cared to admit it who saw benefit only in marrying someone lighter than themselves; and that many still referred to European characteristics such as straight hair, pointed nose, and thin lips, as "good" features. Vita, the most sociable of the three younger Pantrys, had to admit that there were still one or two places in Jamaica where colored persons like herself felt uncomfortable. A cause célèbre was discussed involving a restaurant in suburban Kingston where the manager had been pilloried for excluding a black Jamaican on the grounds that he was improperly dressed. Vita, who knew the restaurant, considered that the manager (a foreigner) was, in fact, racially prejudiced; Gee suggested that it was more likely that the manager was afraid of antagonizing his wealthier clients; while Skipper unequivocally agreed with the manager's action, since the expelled black had apparently been wearing a dashiki—African dress. When questioned, all three agreed there were many places where they could not go for the reverse reasons, such as downtown bars frequented by working-class blacks, but claimed that this was for purely class, not color, reasons. Similarly, one of them admitted that at mass political gatherings they felt "stifled" and "strange."

As to slavery, Vita, the best-read, was the most vocal, and all deferred to her opinion that it was an evil, dehumanizing, indefensible institution. However—not just in deference to their guests—the Pantrys also agreed that the blame for slavery should not be laid squarely on the white man alone, but also on the Africans who enslaved their brothers and sisters, and on the blacks who were corrupted by the system. From a recent reading of Orlando Patterson's novel *Live the Long Day*, Vita cited the black drivers who persecuted their fellows for the sake of power and an easier life. Skipper responded, to general agreement, by drawing a parallel with modern union leaders who, he claimed, played upon the natural tensions between employers and employed, and the natural human tendencies to work as little for as much reward as possible, in order to further their own position and political ends.

Rather curiously, the notion that slavery and exploitation were perpetuated in the sugar plantation system, a commonplace of radical rhetoric, seemed novel to some in the family group. Yet when the proposition was elaborated by the visitors, with some help from Vita, there was common agreement. Skipper in particular drew many parallels between his own experience while working on plantations and what was described as the slavery system, but without conveying any sense of resentment. Sugar work was surely hard and oppressive, but it was a fact of life. Someone had to toil, and someone else direct. Rewards were fittingly in proportion to the parts played in the operation. All seemed to regard the sugar plantation system as inevitable, and had no truck with radical solutions for nationalizing the factories and reallocating the land to smallholders, let alone abolishing the sugar economy altogether.

The Pantrys felt no jealousy or antagonism towards the Clarkes (the present owners of Worthy Park), rather the reverse. Vita remembered with pleasure a visit to Worthy Park a full sixteen years before while working on the investigations which led to the Sugar Industry Pension Scheme, when she was entertained and charmed by "Mr. George." What particularly impressed her were the homegrown beef at lunch and the fact that even then George Clarke was talking about the need for someone (preferably a Jamaican) to write the plantation's history. The Pantrys' impressions of the Clarkes were of people who regarded themselves as Jamaicans first and foremost, were fair and open to their workers, loved their land, and did not ostentatiously flaunt their wealth. Resentment was reserved for those "foreigners" (including Syrians, Jews, and Chinese) who, they felt, exploited the country and its people, with the help of crooked politicians and union leaders, and such misleading slogans as "Black Power."

The future of Jamaica, the land they loved, seemed jeopardized by political strife and economic decline. Both seemed conspiracies, though there was ambivalence and confusion as to where to place the blame. All talked nervously of galloping inflation and of its potential effects when persons actually began to starve. Although the situation was mainly attributed to a conspiracy by greedy capitalists, Mrs. Myers also railed at the "outrageous" demands for higher wages being made by housemaids and garden boys. When it was mentioned that her plea sounded very much like the current complaints of the planters over the wage demands they were being faced with, she candidly agreed. The trouble with "those people" (that is, the black laborers, whether domestic or agricultural) was, she averred, that they no longer either knew their place or wanted to work.

Members of a middle class who also happen to be colored are doubly in a kind of no-man's-land. Economically and socially, while they aspire, with limited hope, towards the upper class of wealth, prestige, and power, they fear submergence in the dark tide of the majority. Clearly, the Pantrys all felt more sympathy with the old landed families such as the Clarkes and Prices than with "upstarts," of whatever color. When pressed, they even agreed that they felt more akin to the old plantocracy than to ordinary working-class Jamaicans, laughing when it was suggested that this was only natural, since they were themselves descended from the Prices. At that euphoric end of a memorable evening, no one thought to point out that, genetically, far more of their ancestors were black and slave, than white and free, or to recall and quote on their behalf the words of Derek Walcott:

> Something inside is laid wide like a wound,
>
> some open passage that has cleft the brain,
> some deep, amnesiac blow. We left
> somewhere a life we never found,
>
> customs and gods that are not born again,
> some crib, some grill of light
> clanged shut on us in bondage, and withheld
>
> us from that world below us and beyond,
> and in its swaddling cerements we're still bound.[19]

16 / From Field Slave to Peasant-Proletarian: The Descendants of Biddy and Nelson

SOME of the difficulties of tracing authentic lines of descent for specific plantation slaves can be illustrated by the story of Daniel R.[1] As has been shown, the systematic listings of births and the names of slaves' mothers after about 1800 has enabled the piecing together of at least matrilineal relationships among the slaves and Apprentices at Worthy Park, in some cases as far back as the 1750s. Surname analysis has further suggested that a high proportion of the descendants of the slaves remained in the locality of Lluidas Vale. The problem, then, was to link up present families with the slaves over a gap of 135 years, in a community for which the "three generation rule" of genealogical memory was the very best that could be hoped for, and where, in cases of extreme dislocation and deprivation, some people did not even know the names of their grandparents.

Clearly, the oldest members of the community were likeliest to have the most extended memories. Since the connection with Worthy Park was of paramount interest to the research, it was decided to look first for links among those with the longest record of service to the estate—in particular, the twenty-five employees given rewards for more than fifty years' service, at the tercentenary celebrations in 1970. The field manager himself suggested that the best candidate was likely to be Daniel R., still vigorously working as field headman in his mid-70s, after sixty years of service, whose father had been headman before him, and whose mother was said to be 100 years old.

As field headman, the researchers were already familiar with Daniel R., but only as a name in the records. In fact, since they discovered that a white bookkeeper of the same uncommon surname had resided at Worthy Park in the 1780s, and it was well known that elite workmen were often the colored bastards of plantation whites, they had suggested to the field manager that perhaps Daniel R., the hereditary headman, was descended from the eighteenth-century bookkeeper. The manager, when he next saw Daniel, jokingly remarked on the possibility—finding it humorous because of the headman's unequivocal blackness. Daniel, however, was not surprised at the suggestion. "Dat explain," he replied proudly, "why me hair so good."

Subsequently it was found that Daniel R.'s descent from his book-

355

keeper namesake was virtually impossible. The bookkeeper had left Worthy Park by 1790, whereas the first laborer of that surname did not appear in the estate's lists before 1846, coming in on the Strangers' Gang. Nonetheless, when interviewed in 1973, Daniel R. told the researcher, as a matter of fact, that he was descended from "one white 'busha from slavery days." The credibility of Daniel's sense of genealogy immediately evaporated, and it was not fully restored by later interviews with his sister and aged mother.

Almost inevitably, the only person for whom it proved possible in the limited time available to trace a certain direct connection with Worthy Park slaves turned out to be exceptional in several respects. Isaac "Dozer" Brown was elderly, poor, and black; but unlike most of his neighbors he had never worked for Worthy Park, had traveled quite widely, and was relatively well educated. Born in Lluidas Vale in 1895, in a house rented from Worthy Park, he was—again unusually—an only child. It was this that gave him better than average opportunities for pursuing an education and learning a trade. A good student at the village primary school, he might have become a teacher, but instead was apprenticed to a cobbler in Linstead in 1913—his parents actually paying a small premium for his first two years of training.

After completing his indentures, Isaac was footloose in Cuba for five years, working his way as a cobbler and picking up just enough Spanish to get by. Later in his career, when money was even thinner than usual or prospects beckoned, he spent two years (1931-32) as a banana-boat "tally-man" in Kingston, and three years as a contract laborer on agricultural projects in the United States (1943-1946). But as long as he could make ends meet there, he always preferred to live in Lluidas Vale, where in 1925 he married a girl called Iris Walker, with roots in the locality as deep as his own.[2]

For some years the Browns lived cramped in the home of Iris' mother and grandmother. But in 1930, after Isaac's mother died, they moved in to share his father's wattle-and-thatch hut, set on a corner of the half-acre plot of family land which had been bought in 1847 by Isaac's maternal great-grandparents from the old Shady Grove estate of Dr. John Quier for £3.4.0.[3] Isaac inherited this property entirely in 1946 after his final return to Lluidas Vale from the United States, eventually starting to build a more substantial concrete house in 1972, with the help of money sent by his son. Here, however, he lived alone, since his wife preferred to live in Kingston, where she ran a small dressmaking establishment.

Once firmly established in Lluidas Vale and fully independent, Isaac Brown gradually became one of the most respected village elders, combining the jobs of poundkeeper and cemetery tender with his cobbling. He was also valued for his expertise in framing a business letter, his knowledge of the byways of government and legal bureaucracy, and his contacts with local officials. He had always had an unusual degree of interest in his family's genealogy (in its widest ramifications

Part peasants, part proletarians. A family of Granny Sue Blair's generation and their house, around 1890.

almost a genealogy of the village), which stemmed not only from his natural bookishness but from the hours he had spent as a solitary boy in the company of an aged cousin, Granny Sue Blair. This grand old lady, who was born a slave around 1817 and lived to be 98, was a mine of fact and anecdote and regarded as the standard authority on local history, custom, and lore—a mantle which Isaac Brown himself had unconciously assumed when he in turn grew old.

Isaac Brown's exhaustive knowledge of kith and kin spread a net over the entire village and district, and back for several generations. Yet, since he was unfamiliar with the concept of a family tree, and the relationships themselves were often tangled and obscure, it was only after several visits that the web was teased into an orderly, simplified pattern, with rough birth and death dates derived from Isaac's recollection of persons' ages when they died. Predictably, the links were strongest through the female lines, returning to a matriarchal figure, Caroline Dawkins, who was born at Worthy Park about 1817 and died a few years before Isaac's birth. Many others of those recalled were clearly also born as slaves. Several, including Caroline Dawkins, were said to have worked at Worthy Park all their lives, as, indeed, had most of their descendants.

Figure 43. Isaac Brown's
Forebears, by His Own
Account

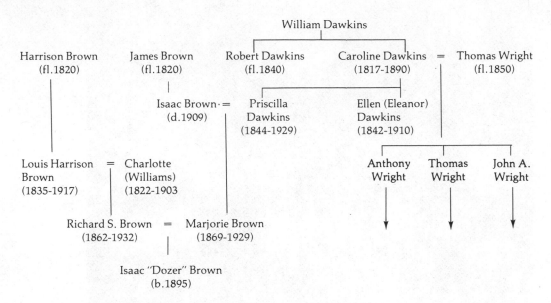

Having constructed a sketchy family tree for Isaac Brown, corroboration and extension were then sought from the Worthy Park records, the Register of Returns of Slaves in the Jamaica Archives, and the St. John Parish Register of christenings, marriages, and burials, in the Island Record Office. Besides this, there was the tattered deed by which Isaac's family land had been conveyed in 1847 to Robert and Caroline Dawkins, whom Isaac thought were brother and sister.

Of the six earliest names which occurred in Isaac Brown's sketch genealogy, William and Robert Dawkins, Harrison Brown, and Thomas Wright were found in the pre-1838 Worthy Park records, but not James Brown or Caroline Dawkins. Subsequent detective work, however, rediscovered them both as slaves. The father of Isaac Brown (1844-1909) was actually James Haslam, earlier called Isaac, the boy taking the surname of his mother, Cecilia Brown, and his father's earlier first name.[4] Caroline Dawkins (whose name, like that of James Haslam, did appear in the 1842-1846 wage lists) had in fact been Caroline Price, and was the wife, not sister, of Robert Dawkins.[5] Caroline and Robert had two daughters, Isaac's grandmother Priscilla and Ellen (Eleanor), before Robert died in 1847. Thereafter Caroline married, or lived with, Thomas Wright, whom Isaac had thought was her only mate, and bore him three sons.

From the slave records it was possible to discover that William Dawkins' slave name was Wakefield, Cecilia Brown's Princess, Robert Dawkins' Nelson, Thomas Wright's Homer, and Caroline Price's Biddy, as well as the fact that James Haslam had once been Isaac. It was also

Figure 44. The Revised
Family Tree of Isaac Brown

Note: Names in capital letters were
slave names

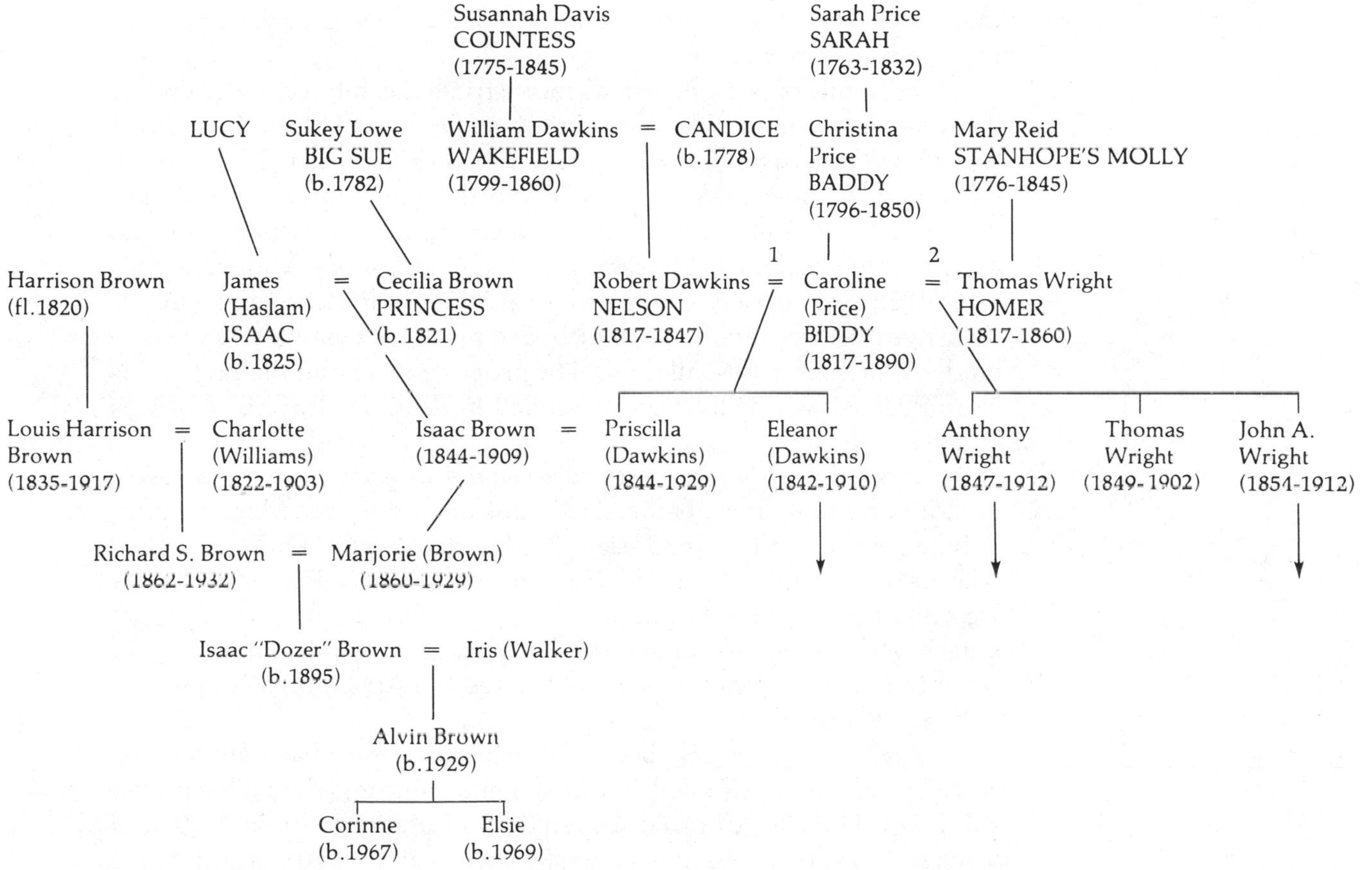

Susannah Davis
COUNTESS
(1775-1845)

Sarah Price
SARAH
(1763-1832)

LUCY   Sukey Lowe   William Dawkins = CANDICE   Christina   Mary Reid
        BIG SUE   WAKEFIELD   (b.1778)   Price   STANHOPE'S MOLLY
        (b.1782)   (1799-1860)   BADDY   (1776-1845)
                                                      (1796-1850)

Harrison Brown   James   = Cecilia Brown   Robert Dawkins = Caroline   = Thomas Wright
(fl.1820)   (Haslam)   PRINCESS   NELSON   (Price)   HOMER
                  ISAAC   (b.1821)   (1817-1847)   BIDDY   (1817-1860)
                  (b.1825)   (1817-1890)
                                                              1   2

Louis Harrison = Charlotte   Isaac Brown = Priscilla   Eleanor   Anthony   Thomas   John A.
Brown   (Williams)   (1844-1909)   (Dawkins)   (Dawkins)   Wright   Wright   Wright
(1835-1917)   (1822-1903)   (1844-1929) (1842-1910) (1847-1912) (1849-1902) (1854-1912)

Richard S. Brown = Marjorie (Brown)
(1862-1932)   (1860-1929)

Isaac "Dozer" Brown = Iris (Walker)
(b.1895)

Alvin Brown
(b.1929)

Corinne   Elsie
(b.1967)   (b.1969)

possible to trace the mothers of all six: Countess, Big Sue, Candice, Stanhope's Molly, Baddy, and Lucy, and even Baddy's mother, Sarah. In the cases of Biddy, Baddy, and Sarah, corroboration was redoubled by the coincidence of the baptismal surname Price, disclosed in registration returns and parish records alike.

Isaac Brown's recollections proved to be inaccurate in minor details, yet still largely provable in general outline. For example, he had the birth dates of the three sons of Caroline and Thomas Wright out by a decade, but in the correct sequence. Corroboration from the parish records resolved the problem of an apparent case of polyandry: that Caroline Price-Dawkins-Wright seemed to have had overlapping children by two husbands. In fact, her two daughters by Robert Dawkins and three sons by Thomas Wright appeared almost magically from the records, born in neat sequence between 1842 and 1854, while she was herself aged between 25 and 37.

Perhaps the most useful aspect of joining up testimonies such as

Isaac Brown's with slave records is that it permits the identification of couples not recorded in the matrilineally oriented slave lists. For example, his memory that Robert Dawkins' father was William Dawkins was coupled with the information from the slave records that Robert's mother was Candice, to provide knowledge of a union previously unrecorded, and long forgotten.

The family of Isaac Brown as reconstructed exhibited a wonderful, if rather depressing, uniformity. Every single one of those in a direct line who was born before 1838 and identified originally by Isaac Brown turned out to have been attached to Worthy Park, rather than to any other estate. In contrast to Isaac's own comparative independence, no less than eleven of the thirteen included in his genealogy who were born after 1838 were closely connected with Worthy Park at least part of their lives, as workers, tenants of house plots, or tenants of workable land, or, in many cases, all three. The proportion among the fifty of his close relatives whose lives were recalled in detail by Isaac Brown was equally high.

Eventually, 15 slaves were rediscovered in Isaac Brown's ancestry and, among those born before 1838, not one nonslave. More remarkably, each one of the 15 had been listed in the Worthy Park and island records as "Black" or "Negro." Isaac Brown's son and granddaughters were lighter than himself because of the strong admixture of miscegenous blood in his wife's family line, but if Isaac himself had any trace of white ancestry the genes must have entered the stream through persons not yet identified.

However, if uniformly black, Isaac Brown's traced ancestors were, with one exception, Creole-born, with Jamaican roots dating back over 200 years. The sole African discovered was Candice, born in 1778, and brought to Worthy Park from a unspecified region of Africa some time between 1796 and 1807. As might be expected, nearly all of these slaves were ordinary field laborers. Of the 13 whose slave employment was known, 11 toiled in the Worthy Park fields throughout their prime. The only exceptions were Wakefield (William Dawkins), who was a mason, and Baddy (Christina Price), a domestic, although, unlike most colored craftsmen and house slaves, their children reverted to field labor.

In the modest improvement that many of the Worthy Park "old hands" enjoyed after slavery ended, Harrison Brown graduated from gang laborer to woodcutter in the 1840s, and Homer (Thomas Wright), from digging and cutting to boilerman in the factory. Yet this upward job mobility was not general among Isaac Brown's forebears or long sustained by any. Isaac's recollections of their livelihood and life-style presented a uniform picture of struggle, dependence, socioeconomic inertia, or regression. Isaac's great-grandmother Caroline, for example, though a matriarch in the family with control over a valuable plot of family land, worked as a laborer at Worthy Park until she was old—her circumstances markedly deteriorating as she became a widow for the second time, and the number depending on the family land grew.

Of Caroline's five children, four also worked all their lives for Worthy Park. The two Dawkins girls lived on the family plot, while working as field laborers, and their children and grandchildren in turn lived there when they could. When space became too constricted, other house plots were invariably rented from Worthy Park, the tenants thereby being more than ever constrained to work for the estate, when called upon, at the going rates of wages. The three Wright boys were expected to fend for themselves and made valiant efforts to become economically independent. Thomas and Anthony lived together, first on a small area of buy land in Lluidas Vale, and then at Croft's Hill, where Thomas generally worked the land while Anthony commuted daily to his work as blacksmith in the forge at Worthy Park. The third brother, John Wright, followed a more common pattern, not only working all his life at Worthy Park but living on a rented house plot in the village, while cultivating on the side a small parcel of provision ground at Coffee Walk, also rented from the estate.

On the other side of Isaac Brown's family occurred at least one example of defeated enterprise that must have been just as common. In the first generation of freedom, Harrison Brown was largely successful in shaking loose from the bonds of permanent wage labor by becoming an independent cultivator on a plot of land acquired at Long Grass, Point Hill, and by making extra income from woodcutting and charcoal burning. At his most prosperous he must have aspired to the economic status of his Point Hill neighbor and contemporary, John Price Nash, while Nash's fortunes were on the ebb. Yet if John Price Nash could not bequeath prosperity to his son, Harrison Brown could offer even less to Louis Harrison Brown. Although the Point Hill land continued in the family, each child's share was minimal, and Louis was forced to move back into Lluidas Vale. Most of his life he worked at Worthy Park, while trying to sustain his burgeoning family on a small piece of rental land. His three sons and four daughters had even less choice, tied as they were to the land and to the estate. Only two girls managed to escape, by marrying men in the neighboring parish.

It is from this generation, roughly 1875 to 1914, that most of the tales of excessive rent and evictions for nonpayment of rent in Lluidas Vale dated, the days of Busha Scarlett and the Calders. Isaac Brown's own parents suffered from eviction during that period. In 1911, rather than pay more rent than they could easily afford, or work for Worthy Park under the estate's own terms, they took their modest goods and chattels and crowded into Caroline Dawkins' plot in Shady Grove.

They were fortunate in having family land to resort to. From the mid-nineteenth century, the pressure of a growing population on local resources, combined with a permanently depressed peasant economy, conspired to force most Jamaican countrymen into wage labor on disadvantageous terms. In the first half of the twentieth century, pressures became so severe and competition for work among the "free" laborers so intense that a policy of evictions aimed at strengthening the hand of the estates, rather than simply raising additional revenue, was hardly necessary any longer. The one moderating factor was the greatly improved chances of out-migration: to the Jamaican towns, especially Kingston, to Cuba, Panama, the United States, and Great Britain—anywhere, in fact, away from the harsh economic realities of rural life. After World War II, out-migration eventually led first to a shortage of labor employable on the estate's own terms and then to an absolute shortage, with massive internal migration into urban areas after overseas migration was curtailed.

Isaac Brown's own wanderings in his earlier days, though common enough for urbanized Jamaicans, were then the exception rather than the rule for backcountry Lluidas Vale. But in his son's generation, the pattern was almost general, so that overseas visitors to Jamaica could enjoy the phenomenon of meeting, in the deepest rural areas, countrymen who could swap anecdotes of Brixton, Birmingham, Toronto, or the Bronx. Alvin Brown himself, born in 1929, an only son like his father, was actually sent to school in Kingston, where he learned a useful trade as machinist and fitter at the Technical College. After nine years of working at Kingston Industrial Works and applying for visas, he eventually went to work in the United States in 1970, sending for his wife and two children once he was firmly established.

Because Isaac Brown now lived alone on the family plot, and because, with no one to trim the yard, the undergrowth which so easily springs up in Jamaica had not been kept at bay, his Shady Grove home seemed in 1973 far more rural than the teeming yards in the estate-owned Thetford section of village. Though no more than 200 yards from the main road, the plot was almost impossible to find without a guide, being approached by a branching footpath leading off the un-surfaced, unmarked side road locally known as Ackee Lane. With no signs or fences, the boundaries of the plot, running from one large tree or stone to another, seemed much more a question of customary acceptance than formal demarcation. Almost hidden among the fruit trees and undergrowth were the tumble-down relics of the wattle houses built by Isaac's parents in 1911 and 1927 with the ready help of neighbors on an unpaid "partner" basis.[6] Close by, guarded by the traditional "red devil" croton bushes, were the graves of Isaac's parents, his grandmother Priscilla Dawkins, and doubtless other family members. Also, half-buried in the ground and still used for storing water was a rare Spanish earthenware jar inherited from Caroline Dawkins and probably far older than Shady Grove itself.

Isaac Brown's home consisted of a single-room concrete cube, with separate but adjacent kitchen-cum-pantry of wattle-and-daub, and an earth privy discreetly hidden in the bushes out back. Plans to extend the house to include a living room, kitchen, bathroom, and porch had been postponed until money became less scarce. As with most homes in Lluidas Vale, the house had neither electricity nor running water, relying on kerosene lanterns and the standpipe out on the main road. Yet Isaac professed himself quite comfortable in his simple house, which seemed quite large enough now that his wife was away. Besides, he no longer had to cook, as he ate all his meals in the home of a hospitable neighboring cousin. Quite unselfconsciously he entertained the young lady interviewing him in his single room, which was crowded with an ancient hand-carved double bed, a table, armchair, and stool. Under the bed were two trunks containing papers and clothes, and hanging on the wall four decent, but well-worn, suits.

Despite his age and arthritis which had slowed him down, and his quite evident poverty, Isaac Brown proved a lively, humorous, and strangely contented man. Though of serious and gentlemanly demeanor at home, he obviously gained great satisfaction not just in the researchers' interest but in the fact that his interviewer was an attractive young lady from Kingston. One day when they were talking together on the public road, Isaac was slyly asked by one of his fellow ancients who his "nice daughter" (that is, girl friend) was. "My *grand* daughter," he replied with subtle emphasis, adding with a chuckle, "I may be old, but I ain't cold."

After much prodding, Isaac revealed the origin of his nickname, "Dozer," which dated from his early youth. One night he was visiting a certain young lady long after nightfall ("without any intentions," he insisted), when her boy friend suddenly appeared. Rather than fleeing out the back door, Isaac affected to be snoozing away in the chair. "You can't doze here," warned the angry suitor. Thereafter, every evidence of what Isaac maintained was merely his natural, pure friendliness towards the ladykind, was commonly misrepresented and referred to as "dozing."

In his reminiscences, Isaac Brown was tirelessly helpful. Despite an occasional absentmindedness concerning material things, his memory was phenomenal, either summoned up by intense, closed-eye thought, or apparently coaxed out by a polishing motion of the hand across his smooth bald head. Several mornings he sent word that he had recalled further details in the night, "as in a dream."

Although he had little knowledge of and no fixed views about the Empire or the larger implications of Jamaican independence, or much real sympathy for Jamaican politics (subjects which clearly seemed irrelevant to him), Isaac Brown was deeply interested in and knowledgeable on local affairs and attitudes. In these respects, he was a true villager and countryman. But he also held much in common with elderly persons and peasants everywhere, in that he was far from radical and viewed the past—at least that within the compass of his own awareness—not with distaste or recrimination, but almost with nostalgia.

Isaac Brown's view of slavery was possibly rose-tinted by his fond memory of Granny Sue Blair, and by Sue's own perhaps romanticized recollections. A brown lady, who wore the elegant wide skirt, bodice, and kerchief of a bygone era, Sue Blair spent all her working life in the white men's houses at Worthy Park, where her slave mother had been a domestic before her. Sue was quite proud of the fact that she had had a white lover, Busha Barrow, who had been, as she put it, "the first to break my seal," and was the father of her light brown child, Becky Barrow, born about 1871. At the time of the Christmas "John Canoe" and the August 1 emancipation celebrations, Granny Sue would become quite excited, taking charge and showing the youngsters in Shady Grove how the dances were done in slavery days.

It was the Christmas and August holidays and the village dances held nearly every Friday night that Isaac Brown remembered most warmly from his childhood. In those long lost days, when Kingston was like a foreign country, the whole community would congregate to perform set dances such as the quadrille, under a grass tent, to a village band of fiddles, fifes, flutes, tambourines, drums, and guitar. The local white folks would often come to watch, and on very special occasions, the Worthy Park "busha" would send down a steer to be slaughtered and roasted. Such, imagined Isaac Brown, must have been the celebrations in slavery days, which did much to make up for the hardship and cruelty during the rest of the year.

Isaac Brown considered that modern Jamaican "reggae," a type of song and dance beat, was very likely a natural development from the traditional dances; but he greatly deplored the substitution of jukeboxes and "sound systems" for the old village bands. He also blamed modern politicians for abolishing the celebration of emancipation on August 1 and substituting an Independence Day for which there was much less popular enthusiasm. Isaac attributed this change to Alexander Bustamante, "when he began his business in Lluidas Vale" around 1938.[7] Apparently, when urging a strike against the Clarkes, the labor leader had told the Worthy Park sugar workers that they were free now and should give up all relics of slavery, including the celebration of its demise. Isaac Brown could understand "Busta's" point—that conditions in the sugar plantations in 1938 were little different from slavery—but he could not see that the politicians of themselves had brought about many fundamental changes since. Their chief motive, he believed, was to set themselves up in place of the planters as the leaders the people needed, or even to take the place of the old slave heroes.

Isaac Brown acknowledged that material conditions had always been bad in Lluidas Vale, but maintained that in 1973 they were worse than they had ever been. Besides, where once conditions had been moderated by a strong sense of community, they were now compounded by a communal malaise, especially among the young people. Much more money was spent on education, but it was his impression that truancy was rife and that even more children came out of school illiterate than in his own early days. Overcrowding was certainly worse, with up to six houses crammed in a "yard," and sometimes ten persons forced to share a single room, with an inevitable deterioration of morals and manners. Food was probably worse than it used to be, since the cost of foodstuffs had run way ahead of any increase in income.

Rather than the usual scapegoats of economic oppression and the demoralization of hopeless poverty, Isaac Brown blamed the breakdown of parental control, a general devaluation of agricultural work, and sheer idleness for the children's lack of progress in school, their "rudeness," and their disinclination to work in Lluidas Vale, either for the estate or for themselves. When asked what was chiefly lacking in Lluidas Vale, he said first "money," then "money and land," and finally "land and the will to work it." In the old days, he said, no one came near starvation whether they worked for wages or not. For all had some ground which they cultivated, and cooks were extremely ingenious in making tasty dishes out of scraps and plants growing wild in the bush (some of which were *bunga*, or African, in origin); and when things came to the worst, everyone would share what little they had.

Though he admitted that the management could be hard when it knew that people were forced to take what work, wages, and terms were offered, Isaac Brown was remarkably fair to the owners of Worthy Park. There was, he knew, considerable resentment of them among the villagers, but this was as much the envy of the idle and unskilled as of those truly dispossessed. He believed that no Jamaican government could take over the estate, for family owner-management was bound to be more efficient than any impersonal government operation could be. Besides, government would almost certainly have to charge more in rents than Worthy Park ever charged in effect. A case in point was the government's low cost housing scheme which none of the villagers wanted, finding it far cheaper to remain and build their own houses on Worthy Park rental land, even if it were sublet at ten times what was paid to the estate.

Asked about racial matters, Isaac Brown (who called himself "dark," rather than the more fashionable "black") said that among the ordinary people in Lluidas Vale there now seemed absolutely no discrimination concerning skin color or other physical features in making choices of sexual partners, though he agreed that this might well be because virtually all were black.

Concerning Black Power, Isaac Brown was at first dismissive, claiming that it was a slogan he only heard bandied by ignorant people in the village. The country blacks, he maintained, would still be downtrodden and poor if all the rulers, and all the wealthy, were blacks. That, indeed, would be worse than the old system of dominance by the whites. But when it was argued by the interviewer that Black Power could mean true democracy and the establishment of racial equality—with all blacks having absolutely equal chances, economically, socially, and politically, and black aesthetic values given their due respect—Isaac said, "If it really means that, I am along with it." He then pointed out that one of the troubles was that black people were often prejudiced against their own kind. What they needed was more pride and self-respect, as well as better opportunities.

Redressing the balance was all very well, he went on, but persecuting the whites would not be a cure. To dispossess them immediately would be foolish, since it was they who had the best resources of education and expertise, as well as money. Blacks at present, he claimed, could not control themselves, let alone others. Take away the whites and the whole island would flop. In any case, he added with an ironic grin, to discriminate against whites would surely be undemocratic.

Isaac Brown agreed that sugar plantation work was tantamount to "slavery without the whip," but could not visualize an alternative. Laborers would always have to be found, and maybe there were natural "hewers of wood and drawers of water." More likely, however, it was the ambition of most men, like himself, to be independent—to work for themselves, to feel they owned something, at least to feel they belonged. He felt himself to be triply fortunate. He had been given a skill which he had been able to trade out on his own terms; he had inherited land where he could live rent-free and from which he could make a little income; and he had developed an independence of mind which allowed him to be friendly to all men, by being beholden to none.

In traditional Jamaican style, Isaac Brown drove home his point with a proverb: "Hirin' out hab no ratoon." Having nothing to sell but your labor was just like slavery. Selling your labor was simply a way of raising money, to help along existence from hand to mouth. There was no personal involvement, no real inducement, no investment, material or spiritual. In contrast, even with his modest parcel of family land, Isaac Brown could proudly say, "What my forefathers planted in the land, I reap; what I plant, my descendants will reap."

17 / Coda and Conclusion: The Seamless Cloth

Driber 'tan mi side, but let mi talk to mi 'busha;
Whan 'busha gan, is mi an' yu deyah;
Howdy 'busha, tenke Massa.[1]

Emancipation song, remembered by Miriam R., aged 100

IN the search for the Invisible Man, the sugar plantation slave, one of the most obvious difficulties is posed by the lack of personal testimonies. That explains the excitement in 1966 which greeted Miguel Barnet's brilliant editing of the autobiography of the centenarian Cuban ex-slave, Esteban Montejo, which substantially modified commonly held views of West Indian slavery.[2] To this was later added the remarkable reconstruction of "The World the Slaves Made" by Eugene Genovese in *Roll, Jordan, Roll*, based largely on the nineteen volumes of first-hand testimonies of American ex-slaves gathered in the 1930s.[3] Formal slavery in Jamaica ended fifty years earlier than in Cuba, and thirty years before it ended in the United States. Thus direct reminiscences of Jamaican slave life and culture were no longer possible. But was there not a chance that the oral tradition could provide indirect illumination?

In 1973 some fifty interviews concerning slavery were carried out in the Lluidas Vale district, of which the sessions with Isaac Brown were merely the most extensive. The exercise had four main purposes. It began with an attempt to trace the actual descendants of Worthy Park slaves. But besides the interest in genealogies, it was hoped to recover specific facts about slavery, as well as to establish what were the perceptions of the slaves' descendants of slavery and their attitudes towards it. Much valuable material was garnered, though the enterprise predictably suffered even more from the fading of the traditions and the overlaying of extraneous influences than in the cases of the ancient American ex-slaves and the Cuban Esteban Montejo. In the end what was learned of continuities proved much more extensive and valuable than the traces of formal slavery recovered. For that matter, there was far more in the testimonies of the American ex-slaves which related to black culture in postemancipation times than in slavery, and Montejo's exceptional direct testimony shed more light on the culture of Cubans of African descent who combined peasant cultivation with plantation wage labor than on slavery itself.

Out of a local population of many thousands who was chosen for interview? As already explained, the search for informants began with the Worthy Park lists; but very quickly the net was thrown wider until

Continuities. Draft oxen were used well into the twentieth century; cane cutting methods remained unchanged even longer.

it brought in a representative cross section of the entire district of Lluidas Vale. At the same time, Jan Vansina's classic description of the "good informant" was borne in mind, a person who "still lives the customary life, who recites traditions without too much hesitation, who understands their content but is not too brilliant—for if he were, one would suspect him of introducing distortions—and who is old enough to have acquired some degree of personal experience of his cultural environment. In short, a good informant is the common man who has reached a position which enables him to be conversant with traditions."[4]

These criteria excluded the young, who rejected the customary life, devalued its traditions, and were, indeed, being educated (as far as education went) towards a different cultural environment. Yet among the mature and rooted, the question of relative literacy remained. There seemed to be a positive correlation between literacy and the eloquence of oral testimony, as in the case of Isaac Brown. This very eloquence may have been suspect, however. Those with a relatively good education might have been expected to reinforce their testimony from knowledge received in school or from books. Yet, to a heartening degree, most of those interviewed distinguished quite clearly between facts on slavery in general received from books and teachers, and local oral traditions. Their education seemed to give them not only greater knowledge but also greater discrimination.

On the other hand, it might have been presumed that illiterate informants—cut off from books and in some cases even from radio and the cinema—would have provided a simpler, yet more authentic, testimony. In fact, many of their testimonies were not only simple but also ignorant and riddled with unacknowledged or unrecognized borrowing. In this respect it is revealing to quote a summary of all the perceptions of "slavery" retailed by Robert C., a semiliterate smallholder, born at outlying Juan de Bolas in 1911:

1. Slaves were under the absolute control of a master. They were given no pay, but *kept.*

2. The masters were all white men. They were called "backra" because they kept the slaves' backs raw with whipping.[5]

3. Slaves ran away when they could, particularly into a local "cockpit" called Barn's Pen, where their "duppies" [ghosts] could still be seen—a benign type which loved to gather round fire, appearing either like fireflies, or as ghostly flames.

4. The name Lluidas was originally Spanish, like the old name for Spanish Town [Santiago de la Vega].[6] St. Ann's Bay was once a Spanish seaport for Lluidas Vale.[7] The old Jamaican coin called a "quattie" was originally Spanish.[8]

5. The slaves were freed by Queen Victoria on August 1.[9] This day was celebrated annually until Jamaican Independence.

6. The Jamaican Creole dialect was basically African.[10]

7. Africa was once a rich country. White men plundered it with the aid of "Black Judases."

Such testimony has some real value, if mainly negative. But in general it was the intelligent elderly with an antiquarian bent, like Isaac Brown, or the very elderly illiterate, like the centenarian Miriam R. (mother of the Worthy Park field headman, Daniel R., mentioned earlier), who provided the most convincing, consistent, and original details. One partial exception was Reuben B. of Long Hill, scarcely older, but far more perceptive, than Robert C. At first he professed ignorance, having had no schooling. But when encouraged, he "remembered" authentic details unlikely to have been taught in local schools: that the Worthy Park slaves were kept in barracklike huts; that the superannuated slaves were still provided for by their masters, but skimpily; that the mothers of six children were excused manual work.[11] He also gave the opinion that since slaves were bought and sold it was simply the fact that the owners had money that made them masters. Only when pressed did Reuben acknowledge, almost with surprise, that masters were exclusively white and slaves exclusively black.

Because their memories were longer, because they reached back closer to the era sought after, and because they were least cluttered and confused by modernizing tendencies, the most valuable informants were all middle-aged, elderly, or ancient. Of the fifty persons interviewed, the ten (including Isaac Brown) who stood out as exceptional informants averaged 68 years of age, nearly all with memories stretching back before World War I and with clear recollections of persons who had been born in slavery. Though, like the great majority of the local countryfolk, all but one were black rather than brown, their backgrounds and testimonies exhibited almost as wide a range as the district offered. In fact, as in the case of Isaac Brown, each testimony was subtly conditioned by the informant's special circumstances.

The two oldest were, like Isaac Brown, inhabitants of Lluidas Vale Village, though, unlike Isaac, both were illiterate, had been closely connected with Worthy Park all their working lives, and still lived on plots rented from the estate. In other respects, the 100-year-old Miriam R. was remarkably different from her near neighbor, Emanuel B., an ex-laborer of 89 whose grandfather had been a slave on Thetford Estate.

Miriam, the widow and mother of Worthy Park headmen, was, like most of her family, proud of her long association with the estate, though she looked back with nostalgia to a time when she lived on family land, and spoke of conditions in her youth that were little better than slavery. Emanuel, on the other hand, felt that his family had always been in thrall to the estate. As a young man he would have moved away, but was constrained by his mother's poverty and dependence on Worthy Park. After more than seventy years' work for the estate he had made no progress, still living in the same shack his family

371

had rented for three generations. Now that he could work no longer, either for the estate or himself, he had even less security than formerly. His tiny pension, grudgingly awarded by Worthy Park, left nothing to spare for paying rent. As an old "Thetford" man, Emanuel felt especially resentful. He maintained that after emancipation the land of Thetford Estate had been left "to mind the slaves till God come," but had been seized and rented out by "Scarlett and Clarke."[12] The least the present owners could do, he considered, was to give tenure to those who had lived there for generations.

Similar differences were detectable among three rather younger informants. Reuben B. was an illiterate aged 63, scraping a marginal existence by combining seasonal wage labor with the farming of a small plot at Long Hill rented from his occasional employers. Unemployable elsewhere through his illiteracy and lack of nonfarming skills, his tenure dependent upon his seasonal availability, he could expect neither full-time work nor an eventual pension. Despite these bleak prospects, his philosophy was fatalistic and his attitude towards Worthy Park uncritical, though these viewpoints may have stemmed from his vulnerability as much as from the torpor of hopelessness.

Nehemiah B. (a cousin of Isaac Brown), literate, aged 71, was considerably more independent than Reuben both in status and attitude, having during a hard-working life at Worthy Park managed to acquire an acre or two of his own at Duxes, just outside the estate's boundaries. Though a stoic plodder by some standards, he yet believed that land such as his own was the reward for fortitude and hard work as much as fate. He also held that it was the nature of all estates like Worthy Park to concede nothing unless forced to.

The most independent of the trio, in every respect, was Doris D., a dark brown lady aged 62, living on the ruins of the old coffee plantation house at Juan de Bolas, six miles from Worthy Park. A literate and highly articulate independent cultivator, Doris was, almost uniquely, equally proud of her two lines of descent, both of which, she considered, had contributed to her independence. On one side (the "yellow") she was descended from William Queenborough, the last owner-occupier of Juan de Bolas Estate, who had left Jamaica in the 1820s. On his departure, her story went, he had offered his colored mistress, Mary, all the land she wanted. To his amazement, Mary had asked for only five acres—all that she could manage and less than would make her neighbors jealous. On the other side (the "black"), Doris was proudly descended from a line of squatters who, when slavery ended, had industriously developed the virgin valleys beyond the reach of estates such as Worthy Park, until, in the course of time, the land had become their own. In this they were following a tradition established by the almost legendary Juan de Bolas himself, in the years before the English ever penetrated into the Jamaican interior.

The remaining four chief informants also provided valuable contrasting testimonies. John T., literate, aged 56, uniquely combined

14. Lluidas Vale District: Location of Chief Informants

shopkeeping in rented premises, the working of a rented small holding, and occasional wage labor—a combination which provided him with comparative prosperity but was painfully dependent on his continuing energy, good health, and good standing. Daniel G., illiterate, aged 65, was a desperately poor but proudly independent smallholder of Cockcrow, a huddle of huts perched on the spectacular Clarendon shoulder of the local hills, the inhabitants of which looked as much to the ancient decayed estate of Lemon Hall as to Worthy Park for links with slavery. Daniel had inherited a tradition of absolute independence from his grandfather, but found this an impossible ideal. He worked seasonally at Worthy Park, but only because he had no choice.

Even more reluctant to work for wages was Carleton T., an illiterate aged 53, farming with three other families a private enclave of twenty-two acres within Worthy Park land, beside Canoe Pond in what was once Tydixon Estate. Tracing ancestors outside Lluidas Vale, he was as alienated from Worthy Park as from slavery itself. Indeed, wage labor for the esate was, for him veritable slavery, "only de chains take off." On the other hand, Wilfrid W., an illiterate field laborer and watchman aged 58, had always been as hopelessly tied to Worthy Park as any slave. Born in the barrack hamlet of New India on the estate itself, he had never left Lluidas Vale. Yet his antecedents were not chiefly Negro and slave. His grandmother, who died around 1926, said to be aged 105, came to Jamaica from India in 1845.

During the interviews questions were asked concerning personal antecedents dating back to slavery days, received facts and anecdotes related to slavery, and generalized impressions of slavery. At the same time a record was kept of incidental information possibly relevant to slavery, including folklore, folkways, proverbs, riddles, songs, dialect vocabulary, and anecdotes relating to family, relationships, work, and tenures.

The attempt to trace precise lineage—by which it was optimistically hoped to join most of the Worthy Park slaves in an interlocking network with the modern inhabitants of Lluidas Vale—led to disappointment in nearly every case. At best the information was inaccurate; at worst there was ignorance or even indifference. Isaac Brown's impressive knowledge of genealogy proved exceptional, and so hazy was information about great-grandparents and beyond that the three generation rule of genealogical ignorance applied in nearly every case. Under these conditions it was only possible to suggest, rather than to prove, the direct connection between modern families in Lluidas Vale and the Worthy Park slave community.

The attempt to recover nongenealogical data from the slavery period came up against similar problems. A considerable dossier was eventually compiled, but the material was patchy and jumbled because the ordinary informant had great difficulty in relating what he or she knew of the past to a specific period. Not surprisingly, few countryfolk had any notion of the concepts (or conceits) in which "sound" historians are schooled: objective truth, proportion, developmental perspective, dates. Nonliterate cultures in general rarely have any more sophisticated concept of time than that determined by the seasons in each year, the generations of important persons, occasional phenomenal events. These characteristics were bound to apply with increased force wherever change had been minimal, or where the past had tended to be devalued by being discredited.

Unfortunately there were no pinpoint corroborations possible in Lluidas Vale of the type provided for historians in other cultures by phenomenal events such as eclipses and natural disasters, except for the most recent years. At first hearing, anecdotes about "Charles Price rats"—said to have been trapped, smoked, and eaten by the slaves—seemed to provide a precise link with the distant past, since the slave-owning magnate after whom they were named died in 1772. Yet the label, applied to any large rat, is common usage throughout Jamaica, and its origin is now obscure. Moreover, the necessity of having to use such animals to supplement diet may have been more recent than many would care to admit.[13] A similar apparent link with the eighteenth century was the phrase "Lick-Batty Gutter" (Whip-Bottom Trench) used by several informants to describe the Worthy Park aqueduct and said to refer to the savage driving of the slaves who built it (in the 1750s).[14] The plausibility of the link was weakened, though, by the concurrence of the obviously spurious etymology of the word "backra," attested to by a similar number of informants—that a white was likely to make a black's *back raw* from whipping.[15]

References to external events dating back beyond present lifetimes were, in fact, remarkably absent in the Lluidas Vale testimonies. The earliest specific reference was to "Missis Queen's Bogue's War" (the Boer War, 1899-1902) by Emanuel B., born in 1884.[16] At least this provided further, if still negative, evidence to suggest that Lluidas Vale had been isolated and introspective until modern times. Famines, rebellions, wars from historical times apparently had left no traces. For that matter even the experience of the Middle Passage of the slaves from Africa, said by Stanley Elkins to have been "almost too protracted and stupefying to be called mere 'shock,'" had left absolutely no trace in the folk memory.[17]

For the historian, the most satisfying corroborations were those provided by archeology and by estate and island records. In 1970 an oral tradition about the exact location of Thetford's windmill was borne out by some hacking and digging at the indicated site, and by a close examination of the Hakewill view of Lluidas Vale in 1793 in the Encumbered Estates records.[18] In 1973 another local tradition was vindicated over professional skepticism. Doris D. and her family at Juan de Bolas, an area where coffee had not been grown commercially in living memory, maintained that the ruins of Queenborough's old coffee factory were to be found in the valley below their house. An expedition with cutlasses indeed revealed ruins; but a preliminary exploration of their layout, coupled with the evidence from the island records that Queenborough had been a sugar producer in 1800, convinced the explorers that this was not a coffee but a sugar factory. Subsequent, more systematic uncovering, measurements, and comparison with plans of authentic coffee factories convinced the explorers that the oral tradition, after all, had been correct. Further corroboration was provided by island records, which showed that Juan de Bolas Estate switched from sugar to coffee production around 1810.

One way in which it was hoped that the oral tradition might prove useful lay in identifying the exact sites of slave cantonments later plowed over, such as the five slave communities of Lluidas Vale of which no superficial traces remained. A similar experiment, using an aged Worthy Park retainer to identify the ancient boundaries of the separate estates that existed in Lluidas Vale in slavery days, did not encourage optimism: boundary markers and lines were confidently pointed out which bore no possible relation to authentic old maps. However, the identification of ancestral homes and burial places might be expected to be nearer the consciousness of local blacks than such owner-oriented matters as property demarcation. Indeed, the local tradition that the Thetford slave quarters were close by the factory was corroborated by a reading of an old map rediscovered later in the Institute of Jamaica, though no digging was undertaken such as that so usefully carried out by Barry Higman at Montpelier Estate in St. James.[19]

At least 250 specific items and anecdotes relating to the past were gathered which were not likely to have been mentioned in local school history classes, read in the more accessible modern books, or heard on the radio. Instead, they provided echoes across the years, from nineteenth-century social commentators such as E. B. Underhill, W. G. Sewell, James Phillippo, or even the eighteenth-century writers on slavery, Edwards, Beckford, Long, Leslie, and Sloane.

Perhaps predictably, these survivals were far richer in the areas of everyday living and the folk and slave culture, such as food, clothing, housing, entertainment, and beliefs, than in elements relating specifically to the servile condition, such as work and punishments. However, many informants did retail stories of whippings and runaways, though some associated the use of the whip in plantation labor with their parents' rather than their great-grandparents' era, and others seemed to confuse punishments for running away with the much later custom of JPs sentencing laborers taken to court by their planter employers for refusing to work. A more remarkable concurrence was the anecdote, told by three unrelated old persons, that slave mothers were driven so hard that they carried their infants on their backs as they worked, slinging their breasts over their shoulders to suckle them.[20]

Nothing in the testimony of ordinary people referred to the mysteries of management, and there was curiously little concerning Christian religion or European customs. Possibly the two most remarkable survivals were Miriam R.'s imperfect memory of the name of the cloth used for slaves' clothing, "haxenbugs" (osnaburg cloth), and Emanuel B.'s amazing recollection that the original inhabitants of Lluidas Vale were "lickle brown men" whom the first English drove out with their guns.[21] Yet these two oldest inhabitants of Lluidas Vale alone provided a mine of unsorted details. They recalled the food eaten by their predecessors, such as the salt herring or shad and cornmeal issued by the masters, the cane-piece rats and "cunny rabbits" ("Injin cunny" to Emanuel B., the Indian coney or agouti, a common food among the Arawak Indians) used by the slaves to supplement their protein, and the distinctively West African dishes, *fu-fu* and *sham-sham*. Then there was the clothing issued or made up by the people themselves, such as the linen trousers, smocks, and broad felt hats of the men, and the voluminous skirts, petticoats, and head kerchiefs of the women; the huts with their wattle-and-daub walls, grass roofs, earth floors, gourds, hammocks, and crocus-sack beds; the double-ended, goatskin-covered *tambu* drums and bamboo flutes used for dancing; the punishments such as chains, the "driber" whip, the cat-o-seven-tails ("seven blows in one"), the treadmill at Linstead, and the fierce dogs used to track down runaways; and finally, such miscellaneous items as cockfighting, clandestine sugar-making with wooden hand-mills, digging with hoes, and the importing of building bricks as ballast in the sugar ships.

Such jumbled detail required much chronological sorting; but this was easy compared with the interpretation of more extended and less factual anecdotes, particularly those relating to legend, belief, and the spiritual life. For example, in the Lluidas Vale testimonies much could be made of the persistent belief in duppies, particularly slave duppies. Despite Christianity, belief in spirits among Jamaican countryfolk of all ages was almost as widespread as one would expect it to be in modern rural West Africa. These Jamaican spirits consisted not only of people's ghosts but also of such terrific manifestations as the "Merrymaids" (mermaids) and the "Rolling (Roaring) Calf." Often they were associated with specific places: burial sites, rivers, trees, and areas of bush.

At least five of the Lluidas Vale informants (as the Nashes had earlier) related the duppies directly to slavery. Besides Robert C., who talked of the runaways' duppies in Barn's Pen, Emily R., daughter of the aged Miriam R., mentioned that slave duppies were often seen where gourd trees or "dragon's blood" (croton) bushes marked old slave burial grounds. Hubert O., an illiterate nonagenarian of Cockcrow, remembered being told as a child not to venture into the bush during holiday celebrations, for the slave duppies were dancing there and might take him as one of their own. Carleton T. of Canoe Pond told of an empty metal cup thrown down by a duppy poltergeist which was thereafter always kept full of water, and of ghostly whiplashes heard proceeding from Thetford to Cocoree on August 1.

Emanuel B., as in all his testimony, was objective and circumstantial. He recalled that in days when August 1 was still celebrated, no one would dare walk by the "breeze mill" at Thetford, for singing and drumming were said to be heard there, coming from the site of the old slave quarters. Emanuel gave his opinion that the old slaves were not Christians but heathens, and that the custom of burying kinfolk in the house yards was African in origin. His slave-born grandfather was buried next to the house on the family land at Rolling River, but Emanuel had buried his parents in the churchyard, for fear of "spoiling the land," that is, deterring potential purchasers.

Few of the inhabitants of Lluidas Vale were as dispassionate, or as perceptive, as Emanuel B. They believed in duppies as unquestioningly as they took part in the Nine Nights ritual of the "Set Up" when someone died, or believed that the newborn were not fully human until they had survived nine days.[22] Traces of animistic religion were clearly retained, relating the spirits of the living to those of the dead and the yet-to-be-born, and relating all human spirits to those residing in what Christianity teaches is the inanimate world. When pressed, some informants connected these beliefs to slavery days, or even to Africa, but not in any systematic way.

Just as it was the details of everyday private life which were more commonly recalled than the details of work, so it was the group memory of those celebrations which enlivened the humdrum annual round that was most vivid of all. The most common of all anecdotes, retailed by more than a dozen persons, concerned the August celebrations. Ostensibly these commemorated emancipation, but it is worth noting that they surplanted the traditional "crop-over" saturnalias of slavery days—brief interludes of legitimate catharsis, involving feasting, singing, dancing, satire, and role-reversal—and that these may have had West African equivalents. Several informants, such as Isaac Brown, also recalled complex "set dances" from the days of their youth, which almost certainly dated back to slavery days, or even earlier.

Associated with the August festivities was also the so-called "Tenke Massa" (Thankyou Master) song, recollected by many informants as far back as 1880, though it clearly derived from one heard by "Monk" Lewis in 1816.[23] Unhappily, the "Tenke Massa" song was the only similar song to be recovered from Lluidas Vale, though found in many subtle variations. The following six chief versions allowed for fascinating speculative analysis, especially when it was realized that in Jamaican dialect "Massa" ambiguously means both God and the temporal master. Of the six, perhaps the most significant was the last. Sung by the aged Miriam R. in an eerie, oracular falsetto, it seemed to encapsulate not only the relationships between workers, drivers, overseers, and masters but also the ways in which these were changed, and yet not changed, by the ending of formal slavery.

1. (Miriam R., 100)	If you kick mi, mi kick yu back;
	Tenk yu Massa.
	If yu buck mi, mi buck yu back;
	Tenk yu Massa.
	If yu lick mi, mi lick yu back;
	Tenk yu Massa.
2. (Cecil B., 80)	Massa, yu buck mi now an'
	mi buck yu back;
	Massa, yu kick mi now an'
	mi kick yu back;
	Massa, yu beat mi now an'
	mi beat yu back.
3. (Charlotte B., 75)	Tenke Massa;
	Yu luv mi, mi luv yu;
	Tenke Massa.
4. (Arthur B., 75)	Howdy Massa;
	Yu kick mi, mi kick yu back;
	Tenke Queenie.

5. (Nehemiah B., 70) King give mi mi freedom;
Tenke Massa.

6. (Miriam R., 100) Driber 'tan mi side,
but let mi talk to mi 'busha;
Whan 'busha gan, is mi an' yu deyah;
Howdy 'busha, tenke Massa.

What, then, to make of this brief excursion into the oral tradition in Lluidas Vale, and how to sum up the search for the Invisible Man? In general, the amount recovered of genealogical information and of facts directly related to formal slavery was disappointing. Yet in the realms of attitude, ethos, myth, a very great deal was learned, whether or not it could be related to objective realities. "Whatever neger say," runs an old Jamaican proverb, "if a no so, a nearly so."[24] Moreover, the very paucity of material on formal slavery, or, rather, the failure of the folk memory clearly to distinguish the era of formal slavery from other periods, proved to have an unexpected significance.

At first it was believed that ignorance of personal antecedents stemmed solely from dissociation from a slave past generally regarded as discreditable, a reluctance to resurrect the family on the principle of the Jamaican proverb, "Fowl 'cratch up too much dutty [dirt] him run de risk a findin' him gramma 'keleton."[25] However, it proved to be a far more complex matter. Some genealogical ignorance could be attributed simply to influences common to all similar peasant societies where the family was less important than the community, where tenures were not invariably dependent upon lineal inheritance, and where there was not a strong tradition of genealogical storytelling of the type found in the Old Testament or equatorial Africa. To this could be added influences more special to the West Indies, with its syncretic, or creolizing, processes and its slave background: the diffusing effects of the introduction of bilateral for unilateral kinship, the often anarchic state of individual families, the existence of irregular or complex tenures such as squatters' rights and commonage, and the further decay of the local storytelling tradition under the influence of modernization. Even beyond this, there were subtle differences in attitudes towards the family past, largely depending on relationships to the plantation system, old and new.

Many informants were fascinated, indeed proud, to hear of family links discovered from written records, penetrating the two- or three-generation veil, and dating back to slavery days, even to Africa. Daniel G. and other members of the community of Cockcrow, for example, conveyed the sense that a precise knowledge of slave and African ancestors would provide (as information about their European forebears did for the Nashes) an authenticity denied them by their ignorance and lowly state. Several informants later begged for a family tree such as those drawn up in detail only for Isaac Brown, the Nashes, and the Prices.

There was', however, often a reluctance to associate with slavery and Africa where no family links were involved, because enslavement was vaguely felt to be part of a grim, even discreditable, past, and therefore not worthy of recall. This resulted in part from the common human tendency to remember only the happy days; but it went deeper. The private lives of the slaves, their blackness, their African-ness, had always been ignored, devalued, by the dominant culture. They were still depreciated, covert.

This depreciation, expressed in many Jamaican proverbs relating to slavery, and in the dialect usage of African names only for unfavorable characteristics, could take the form of dissociating from slavery and Africa and preferring European, white, and Christian cultural norms.[26] One common example was the tendency to refer, even in conversation with other black folks, only to white ancestors, though they represented a tiny proportion of the genetic mix. Another was the tendency, bred by generations of doctrine in most types of Christian church, to see no positive virtues in African religion, even to deny that it persisted. *Obi* in particular suffered, with only its negative, sinister, and medicinal qualities emphasized.[27]

In this tendency to distort (or to perpetuate distortion) there seemed to be elements of that mythologizing idealization which B. K. Malinowski characterized as a society creating a self-justifying "charter" out of imaginary, or preferred, rather than authentic roots.[28] There was also an element of what Peter J. Wilson has called the quest for *respectability*, the drive towards stratification, running counter to the quest for *reputation*, the drive towards equality.[29] It was clear that with a certain type of informant distortions were introduced, either consciously or unconsciously, as a form of self-justification or wish fulfillment. In this category came Daniel R.'s acceptance of the myth of a white bookkeeper ancestor.

Daniel R. was, in fact, the most extreme example encountered of a type of black as old as the plantation system itself. A hereditary servitor, he owed his position of subordinate authority to slavish fidelity to the plantation ethos and its stratification. His was the classic "quashee personality," in the senses that subscription to the dominant' norms and stereotyping in return for status in due course led inevitably to unquestioning belief in the norms and fulfillment of the stereotype.[30] Such quashees led the way, imposing the dominant culture more effectively than the white man ever could alone. Yet beneath the quashee elite, all plantation blacks were permanently affected. For the sake of an easier life they took on the stereotype image of themselves as lazy, larcenous, alternately sullen and manic, craven and childlike, but in time it became second nature to them.

To varying degrees, elements of these types of distortion were still apparent in most blacks living close to Worthy Park. Even those inhabitants of Lluidas Vale who vocally resented the estate's dominance, and worked for wages only when they had to, did not hesitate to receive the largesse periodically handed out as an act of noblesse oblige, or to participate (if with mixed enthusiasm) in official estate celebrations such as the tercentenary of 1970. Praedial larceny, or any theft from the estate, was not commonly condemned or even considered a crime at all. It was regarded as more proper for a person caught red-handed to beg the manager for mercy than to be carried to the police station and the criminal courts. The owner-managers were still regarded as the fount of justice as well as of bounty. The fact that they were white seemed part of the natural order of things.

Such self-perpetuating attitudes were far less common among those who owed nothing to Worthy Park Estate, such as Isaac Brown or the proud, impoverished stoics of Cockcrow. In the terms used by Peter J. Wilson, respectability meant less to them than their own criteria of reputation. When actually out of range of estate and village they might even have been more attracted to an African past than to the European, white, Christian culture, were it not for the gradual syncretic, or creolizing, process brought about by the passage of time.

It was determined that the most plausible informants were the elderly, the least modernized, and those locationally rooted, but that the nature of all testimony depended upon personal attitudes. These depended, in turn, as much upon individual characteristics as upon factual knowledge, eloquence, or even intelligence. Particularly noteworthy were differences in ages, roles in family and community, employment histories, land and house tenures, types of education, psychological traits. Above all, testimonies were affected by the almost ubiquitous presence of Worthy Park Estate. It was impossible to assess an informant's view of slavery without taking into account his or her relationship to the nearby estate, which dominated Lluidas Vale, provided a connective theme and point of reference in most lives, and had been in continuous operation for 300 years. Those informants with the most independent character tended to have the most objective view; but there was a correlation between, on the one hand, independence and objectivity, and, on the other, the propinquity to and dependence (psychological as well as material) upon the estate.

Perhaps the most significant characteristic of all testimonies was the tendency to *meld* the past, with little historical differentiation. This is a well-known feature of oral traditions in general, but it occurred to a far greater degree with the people of Lluidas Vale than would be expected with a similar population in another country where plantations were not the economic norm. For example, Emanuel B.'s excellent testimony included, with minimal differentiation, elements of "slavery" derived from his own long lifetime and those of his parents, items such as the treadmill at Linstead that clearly dated after 1834, genuine slave anecdotes, "African" survivals, and even, incredibly—in his reference to the aboriginal Arawaks—what seemed an authentic "memory" of the precolonial period in Jamaica. In Lluidas Vale the overwhelming senses were of community and of a historical continuum. Actual slavery had left far fewer traces than the culture of peasant and plantation society since 1838, which was not surprising; but it had left scarcely more traces than those of the African past.

What then were slavery and slave society in the popular view? Slavery was felt to be something from the "bad old past," productive of cruelty, hardship, and alienation. Yet slavery, as commonly understood, related not solely to the formal institution which ended in 1838 but also to the socioeconomic effects of the plantation system in general. Wilfred W. and others in New India considered that slavery included the system of indentures by which their forebears came as coolies to Jamaica as late as 1917. Miriam R. identified as slavery the constraints by which children were herded in the Pickney Gang and punished with whipping in the days of her youth. And Carleton T. regarded the conditions under which laborers were forced to work for the estate in 1973 as slavery with only the chains removed.

Perhaps, after all, it was only for the historian that slavery was a formal phase. For ordinary people, particularly the "sons of slavery," myth had surplanted fact. Even as the historian wavered between preconceptions that suggested either a Hobbesian or Panglossian view of formal slavery, so countervailing myths affected popular views of slavery and slave society. While this book was being written it seemed that in Jamaica it was political awareness and official mythology, as much as mere modernization, education, and the influence of the media, which were currently helping to reshape the past. Political parties or ideological groups surplanted in the popular consciousness a view of the past, right or wrong, that overlaid and changed feelings genuinely held. Slavery had come to stand generically for the socioeconomic evils of the bad old days, but with a decidedly political slant. The official heroes of Jamaica were not primarily those who resisted and overturned formal slavery, nor were they Africans; they were, rather, nineteenth- and early twentieth-century protopolitical figures such as George William Gordon, Paul Bogle, and Marcus Garvey, and the modern political leaders Alexander Bustamante and Norman Manley.[31] Significantly, the celebration of Jamaican Independence (1962) had taken the place of the traditional August celebrations, a change which some of the older country people genuinely regretted.[32]

The young were increasingly alienated from the plantation system, as from agricultural work in general, the countryside, and all traditional ways. In contrast, amid the disorienting clamor and clutter of modernity, the elderly—like many of similar age and background throughout the world—did retain, perhaps perversely, some feelings of nostalgia. In particular they tended to hearken back to the greater sense of community, the closer family links, the familiar local culture of their younger days. They might even have felt ambivalently about the days of formal slavery, long past and shadowy, when at least the social groups were more tightly knit than ever since, and the old culture was felt to be in a purer form.

In this atmosphere of contrapuntal mythologization, it seemed probable that it was already too late for oral testimony to be used either to add much worthwhile specific information about formal slavery, or to make an accurate judgment whether formal slavery was better or worse than the picture derived from written sources. In both respects, the Worthy Park slave books after all seemed to promise better results. Yet the historian was not driven back empty-handed from the oral tradition to his own traditional methods, trusting only what was written down. The life-style and world view of those few who still carried the oral tradition could do as much as the slavery records to help reconstruct, or visualize, the Invisible Man.

In more senses than was previously recognized, slave and modern countryman were one and the same. First, the minute study of the slave community and the individual slaves which concerned the first two-thirds of this book demonstrated how complex and stratified plantation slave society was and how much it had developed before slavery ended. Above all it was discovered that the distinction between African and Creole slaves was almost as important as that between slave and free, and between black and white. The period when African slaves and influences dominated was long past when the existing Worthy Park records began, yet for that matter so was the period when the determinant force in the plantation society was the will of the master class, rather than the exigencies of sugar production. Creole slaves predominated while slavery was still at its height, and it was the Creole environment which did as much as the sugar system to determine the form and style of slave society.

Well before slavery ended, the plantation black was a bifurcated individual, no longer divided between Africa and the New World so much as between proletarian and peasant. The plantation system forced the blacks into one set of socioeconomic norms: slaving at a peculiarly intensive, alienating form of labor, stratified for the purposes of the estate into a hierarchy fixed solely by economic value, and yet for the sake of petty privilege or ease constrained to adopt, superficially, the scale of values of the dominant class, including the white man's degrading image of the black. But in their private, and largely secret, lives, the slaves constructed another style and set of values. In their family life, their work in the Negro grounds, their worship and festivities, they made a world of their own beyond the control, and comprehension, of the master class. African influences were strong, but they faded as they were adapted to local conditions and mingled with selected influences from Europe and elsewhere. Before the slaves were formally freed, a distinctive Creole family pattern had emerged, neither African nor standard European, along with a form of agriculture peculiarly suited to the Jamaican hills, and syncretic forms of worship, music, dance, and play.

Even after 140 years of nominal freedom, changes in the socioeconomic system were outweighed by continuities. Moreover, those changes that had occurred were in few respects improvements. For a generation, sugar declined and the hopes for a system of peasant proprietorship were high. But then sugar revived, in a more capital-intensive and exploitative form. The social elements in slave society were reshuffled, but quickly re-formed. Those with mobility escaped the initial collapse. Owners and those in the middle ranks tended to move away; but others quickly refilled the ranks when needed, replicating the traditional roles. For the ordinary black workers the switch to wage labor gave only a temporary illusion of choice; as population expanded the labor force competed against itself to the benefit of the employers. Similarly, the gradual decline in the employment of women as laborers was in the interests of efficiency, not humanitarianism.

The plantation worker remained a bifurcated individual; indeed, the splitting of his roles approached the level of schizophrenic alienation. The old cohesion of plantation society was swept away and was not refashioned in the villages and hills. In place of slavery the ex-slave hoped for the life of an independent peasant; instead, he remained part peasant, part proletarian, with decreasing security in either role. The comment of Karl Marx in 1844 on the fate of the European worker in the period of capital intensification could have applied to the slave; but it applied with even more poignancy to the slaves' descendants:

> In what does the alienation of labour consist? First, that the work is external to the worker, that it is not a part of his nature, that consequently he does not fulfil himself in his work but denies himself, has a feeling of misery, not of well-being. . . . The worker therefore feels himself at home only during his leisure, whereas at work he feels homeless.[33]

Marx's solution to the dilemma was, of course, the revolution, though his disciples have never been entirely sure whether he expected this to come through a proletarian upheaval or from the decay of the capitalist system from within. As to the first, the Jamaican countryman was far from being a revolutionary—probably because his aspirations were those of a peasant rather than a proletarian. His hope of an ample return from peasant cultivation declined steadily and his role as wage laborer became increasingly inevitable, yet he seemed even less likely to bring down the sugar system by revolutionary means than his slave predecessors were to achieve a successful rebellion. On the other hand, there were signs—in the intrinsic weakness of the sugar system and the ideological opposition to it on the part of socialist politicians—that after all the ancient malefactor was doomed.

Bringing down the sugar plantation system would not magically undo the socioeconomic and psychological deformations of 300 years. Only when the victim is recognized as hero, his dignity restored, his aspirations fulfilled, will the ordinary black countryman, son of slavery, Invisible Man, come into his own.

Appendixes
Notes

Appendix A / The Slave Data and Its Deficiencies

D ESPITE notable deficiencies, the Worthy Park data for 1783-1838 are among the widest-ranging and most complete sets of such material still in existence. Their compilation and survival result from an almost miraculous combination of circumstances. The estate's owners were concerned to know more about their slaves for reasons of economic efficiency; this concern coincided with the interest of the Jamaican legislature that all "settlements" should make regular returns to the parish vestries for the purposes of control and taxation, at first annually but eventually each quarter. To this was later added the decision of the imperial government that a register of all slaves be kept, to prevent illegal transfers and to check whether the slave population was increasing or declining following the ending of the slave trade. Perhaps the most remarkable fact is that so many of the Worthy Park slave books survived the ravages of time and neglect. Most were redis-covered in a loft by two boys playing hide-and-seek in 1919, and one more book—mysteriously abducted from Worthy Park at an earlier date—turned up in the Library of Congress in Washington.[1]

As the result of a recent Jamaican legislative act, Worthy Park began keeping duplicates of the returns to the St. John's vestry in 1783.[2] Each return recorded the total number of slaves, together with the number of "Increases" since the last return through birth, purchase, and transfer and the "Decreases" through death, sale, transfer, manumission, running away, and transportation. In order to comply with the Jamaican Deficiency Laws, which taxed owners who kept less than a certain proportion of whites on their estates, the returns also included the names of all whites living at Worthy Park.

To implement the vestry returns, the estate began to keep lists of the names of individual slaves in 1784, and further invaluable informa-tion was gradually added as the demand arose. In 1787 the bookkeepers began entering the occupation of each slave and notes—mainly relating to health—under a heading, "Condition." The zeal with which this was carried out clearly increased as a result of the provisions of the compre-hensive Slave Act of 1792, which required estate doctors to make re-turns of all causes of death, and owners to reward overseers with £3

Currency for each child born in excess of the number of slaves who died.[3] The same Act exempted from manual labor all female slaves with six or more children living and, besides listing these from 1793, Worthy Park's management took the opportunity in 1794 to make a painstaking analysis of all childbearing on the estate. Even more valuable, from 1794 the ages and colors of all slaves were entered. Finally, from 1817, as a consequence of the Jamaican Registration Act of that year, the Worthy Park ledgers recorded whether each slave was an African or a Creole.

One unfortunate lacuna was the absence of any of the records of punishments ordered to be kept on each estate during the amelioration period. More serious problems resulted, though, from the discontinuity of the records; the different dates at which categories began, and the actual gaps. Worthy Park's own records are missing for the years 1796-1811, 1817-1821, and 1824-1830. However, the individual data for 1817-1832 could be corroborated and supplemented by the Register of Returns of Slaves kept in the Jamaican Archives at Spanish Town. This consisted of a full nominal list for all Jamaican estates in 1817, and the names of all slaves who had come into the population by Increase, or left by Decrease, by the date of the triennial returns in 1820, 1823, 1826, 1829, and 1832.[4] There remained, however, the complete gap in the wartime years between 1796 and 1811, for which even the summary estate slave totals given in the *Jamaica Almanack* for other years were missing.

However, a heartening number of the deficiencies in the Worthy Park records could be remedied. For a start, by identifying each member of the slave population on separate file and computer cards when he or she first appeared in the lists, and then adding the entries for subsequent years, a great deal of corroboration was possible, as well as the reconstruction of many complete life patterns. In all, 1,377 different slaves and Apprentices have been identified at Worthy Park between 1783 and 1838, for whom there were no less than 10,540 entries. As many as 189 of the 1,377 appeared in only one year of the records, but there were 776 with entries in five or more years, 405 in more than ten, and 35 in more than twenty. Nine, strangely enough all females, were listed in twenty-seven years, and the joint record-holders, whose names also appeared in a partial list for a twenty-eighth year, were Amelia, alias Big Amelia, later Amelia Parker, born in 1784 and excused work after her sixth child in 1818, and the unfortunately named Strumpet, born in 1764, who lived at least to the age of 78. In addition to the 1,377 unfree, there were altogether 183 different whites listed at Worthy Park, in nine lists between 1783 and 1823.

Another useful check was provided by the tabulation of numbers of individuals recorded for the first time in each year of the lists. These numbers, naturally, were large after time gaps in the lists, but in other years consisted of very few more than those known to have been born or purchased. In solving the problem of the composition of the 1831-

	First entries	Total entered	Last entries	Known departures (death, manumission, sundry)
1783	7	7	7	7
1784	330	331	8	6
1785	8	317	12	4
1786	4	301	22	0
1787	49	334	8	3
1788	15	343	15	13
1789	10	341	13	14
1790	18	342	5	5
1791	31	377	30	7
1792	25	16	17	1
1793	197	541	34	17
1794	32	530	77	58
1795	15	21	18	1
1796	19	469	237	23
1811	9	14	11	9
1812	26	35	16	15
1813	259	490	28	10
1814	31	458	17	12
1815	18	24	18	16
1816	30	507	44	9
1817	20	64	53	28
1820	1	6	0	0
1821	56	504	18	12
1822	16	512	25	20
1823	10	489	11	8
1824	12	502	168	23
1830	82	414	88	23
1831	7	333	28	24
1832	12	311	19	14
1833	5	301	19	17
1834	1	293	30	25
1835	0	263	9	5
1836	1	260	19	11
1837	7	251	21	14
1838	1	233	219	2
				19[a]
Total	1,377		1,377	475

TABLE 71. Worthy Park, 1783-1838: Individuals' First and Last Entries in Records, with Annual Totals Entered and Known Departures

Source: Worthy Park records.
[a]Sundry (not entered by year).

1834 population (which might have included a large number of new slaves transferred in that period), this tabulation, along with individual corroboration, allowed the deduction that it consisted essentially of the original Worthy Park slaves.[5]

Although the color of slaves was not consistently given, there were very few slaves who could not be identified in this respect, either by cross-reference or by parentage. In respect of slaves' ages, a much greater degree of final certainty was possible, amounting to almost 90 percent identification. Ages listed showed the tendency to round figures usual in such unsophisticated compilations, especially among the older slaves. But if we exclude the single anomaly that the computer, with the unconscious humor of its kind, repeatedly came up with a mythical slave who was 999 years old, there were remarkably few wide discrepancies. With the multiplication of entries and cross-checking, it was possible to ascribe a birth date with a high degree of certainty in no less than 1,179 cases, dating back as far as 1709. In all, there were 21 of the Worthy Park slaves listed after 1783 who were born in or before 1730 and thus were possibly listed in Colonel Charles Price's inventory of that year. The four most likely candidates were two specifically listed as Creoles, Creole Quashy and Creole Cuba (born in 1729 and 1724 respectively), and two slaves almost uniquely named after their fathers —who can also be identified on the 1730 list—Counsellor's Cuba (born 1729), and Washer's Juba (born 1724).

Next to the absolute completeness of information as to sexes, and the relative completeness of the birth data, the most pleasing discovery was that in no less than 1,187 cases it was possible to discover whether a slave had been born in Africa or Jamaica. Despite the fact that in only five of the lists was the side of the Atlantic on which a slave was born indicated for every individual, this high degree of certainty was possible both by cross-tabulation and by including all those slaves born at Worthy Park as Creoles.

Death data were by no means so complete. Dates of death were ascribable in only 474 cases (though in 376 of these both death and birth dates were known). When a slave died at Worthy Park who had already been listed, the death seems to have been invariably recorded, in the Decrease list if not also in the Condition column of the total roll, usually with the actual day given. However, slaves who were born and died within the period between lists may not all have been recorded, though some were. Some slaves, moreover, just disappeared from the surviving lists without explanation. In programming, "Unknown Deaths" included those on the Decrease lists recorded as sold, transferred, manumitted, permanently run away, or transported. They also included all of the 219 still alive on August 1, 1838, when the records ended. Others dropped out during the periods for which there were gaps in the records. Corroboration with the Jamaican Register of Returns of Slaves allowed for the filling in of information for the periods 1817-1821 and 1824-1830; but for the period 1796-1811 it was not possible to know for certain which of the slaves who had disappeared had actually died. A reasonable guess, based on other periods, would be about nine-tenths.

Perhaps the least satisfactory of the data considered was that relating to the colored segment of the population. For most years it was possible to give the number of those listed as "Mulatto," "Sambo," "Quadroon," or "Mestee." But it was not certain whether this was a truly comprehensive total of all colored slaves. Did the bookkeepers go on appearances, on genetic facts, or use some other criteria? In Jamaica it was remotely possible for persons to "pass as white" on appearances alone. Equally, he or she could pass as black if it suited the recorder, or it did not matter. It would be pleasant to believe that black racial pride played a part in the overlisting of "Negroes"; but such feelings, if they existed, clearly would not have moved the white men making the lists.

More likely is the supposition that bookkeepers tended to list in one of the categories of colored only those known to have been the product of true miscegenous liaisons (that is, in which one of the partners was serologically pure), and to ignore most of the offspring of partners who were both the offspring of previous miscegenation. If this tendency were general it would greatly complicate the study of the West Indian colored population by overstating the numbers of blacks by an ever-widening margin. After slavery ended, however, the category "Brown" (not found in the slavery records) was increasingly used.

The deficiencies and problems candidly considered above should not be exaggerated. They refer mainly to the whole run of data for the 1,377 slaves. In many separate years the material was so much more complete that far greater assurance was possible in evaluation; and this study was as much concerned with Worthy Park at different points in time as over a more extended period. It should merely be pointed out how much stress has been laid on the relative completeness of the available material for different years when assessing the value of findings. It was indeed the lacunae and failings in the material for the overall period of fifty-six years which presented the first serious methodological problem. With deficient data it was often quite possible to make plausible projections. Deaths, for example, could have been extrapolated from life expectancy patterns and the predictable number of non-death Decreases. Using many such projections it might have been possible to make the Life Tables given in Chapter 3 more plausible. After deliberation, however, it was decided to avoid projections wherever possible, especially in the tables. However tenuously hypotheses have been presented in the conclusions, the tabulation of statistics has been restricted wherever possible to the actually known or precisely calculable. Nonetheless, it is hoped that the data presented are sufficiently full for a wide range of projections to be made by more competent demographers if they wish to do so.

One final apparent anomaly remains to be explained. Comparison between the annual official totals of slaves at Worthy Park (given in the Prologue) and those tabulated in Chapters 2-5 discloses marked discrepancies. In certain years the numbers available for tabulation fell short of the known totals; yet in just as many years they actually exceeded them. There were several reasons for these discrepancies not necessarily including the fallibility of the researchers. The estate bookkeeping was at times haphazard, especially in the earliest years before the system of official returns was finally established. In a very few cases names were missing through the ravages of damp or insects on the books. It may also have been that in some years slaves resident at Spring Garden and Mickleton were "given in" as Worthy Park slaves, though not recorded in the rolls of the plantation at Lluidas Vale. More important, when making certain tabulations, only those slaves were recorded for whom *all* relevant information was known. Deficiencies which were often insignificant in separate categories therefore cumulatively multiplied the number of exclusions. The most extreme case was found in the demographic tabulations by sex, age, and place of birth for the years 1784-1791, when 32.7 percent of the slaves were not accounted for. In fact, some information was available for nearly all the slaves excluded even in those years.

On the credit side, details were known and material tabulated for more slaves than Worthy Park officially recorded in at least fourteen years. This was not because the estate cheated on its tax returns (it seems that very few estates did this, both because of the penalties and the fact that they were compensated for slaves lost through war, permanent running away, imprisonment, transportation, or even murder), but because the extra slaves had died or left the estate in the intervals between the official giving-in dates. This can be borne out by identifying the years in which mortality is known to have been extreme. Besides this, slaves obviously not recorded in one year were frequently picked up in another. Overall, though perhaps the 1,377 slaves of whom something was known may have been 10 percent short of the grand total of those at Worthy Park for the fifty-six years between 1783 and 1838, it was almost certainly within 5 percent of the full total of the forty-two years for which most details are known, including the period 1831-1834 when far fewer slaves were specifically listed than the totals given in. Moreover, it was clear that the omissions were almost entirely random, and therefore did not invalidate overall findings. The only clear exception was the Apprenticeship years, when there were no children under 6. But this omission was obvious and easily taken into account.

In looking at the tables in Part One at least one caveat is called for. Careful study of the numbers entered in each of the twenty categories for all twenty-seven years for which data existed shows why the data for the sample years 1787, 1793, 1796, 1813, 1821, 1831, 1835 are more valuable in some respects than that for the entire period 1787-1838. The figures in the overall tables, even when they are averaged out, relate to *entries*. They are therefore subject to the gaps in the material, as well as to changes in the estate's methods of job allocation and labeling. The long gap in the records for 1796-1813 is particularly frustrating.

Certain aspects of the tables of occupational mobility are also disappointing. The idea is sound enough. The tables show every individual movement from one category to another that is known. If this material were complete, and the credibility of the various categories absolutely established, the tables would indicate better than any other method not only the socioeconomic hierarchy of the estate but also its dynamics. However, the tabulations simply record *listings*, so that the gaps in the series mean that, at best, they merely indicate average mobility (if there was such a thing), rather than giving a precise picture of the total mobility of each slave included. Moreover, though the tables provide a useful general picture of the amount of occupational movement and its directions, they cannot give individual job histories. No man is average, and a far more vivid view of the types of mobility, where mobility existed at all, is given in the sample career biographies in Part Two.

Appendix B / The Computer Programs

FROM the outset of this project it was presumed that the bulk of the computer analysis would be made using the Statistical Package for the Social Sciences available on the IMB 360/75 computer at the University of Waterloo, Ontario. This package was chosen over several others available because of the comparative simplicity of the input and because it provides excellent labeling features for tabular output as well as automatic file documentation. This latter feature proved invaluable, as the project eventually spread over several years and the data were modified and added to on many occasions.

Much of the data analysis involved the identification of trends over the period from 1783 to 1838. For this reason a case or record was defined to be the set of observations available on an individual slave from a given calendar year. Thus a slave could have one or more records, depending on the number of years he or she was included in the Worthy Park records. Some data elements did not change from year to year, whereas others did. Information which remained fixed for a given individual, such as sex, African/Creole, color, and date of birth, was duplicated on each one of that individual's records. Information which varied referred chiefly to occupation and health condition, and variables derived from these. This made it possible to determine relationships between the yearly variables and the "fixed" variables, and to produce statistics either by year or by individual from a single data file.

Most of the file creation and editing were performed by programs written especially for the task in hand, in either the FORTRAN G or WATFIV language and run at the University of Waterloo or at Computel Systems, Ltd., in Ottawa. The same two languages were also used in the generation of special tables for which the S.P.S.S. system was not suitable.

The data are presently stored on two magnetic tapes, one containing the original 11,055 records on 1,377 individuals, and the second containing a revised set of 8,797 records covering the period from 1817 to 1838. This second tape, which was used primarily for calculations of mortality and population cohorts in this period, had data added wherever gaps appeared in an individual's sequence of yearly records. Both tapes are preserved in the Tape Library in the Computer Center at the University of Waterloo.

A Doctor's Views on Childbirth, Infant Mortality, and the General Health of His Slave Charges, 1788

"THE Examination of John Quier of the Parish of Saint John, Practitioner in Physic and Surgery.

"Saith:—

That he studied surgery in London, and Physic at Leyden, and served His Majesty as an Assistant Surgeon in the Military Hospitals in the former War in Germany; that he has practised in this Island for upwards of twenty one years; that for the greater part of that time he has had from four to five thousand Slaves constantly under his Care, in the Parishes of Saint John and Saint Thomas in the Vale, and of late years in the Parish of Clarendon.

"Saith:—

That the local Circumstances attending difference of Situation in this Island occasion so great a Diversity in the Diseases to which the Inhabitants of different parts of this Country are subject that very few Observations thereon will be found to be universally true. That he has not in general observed any very great Mortality amongst the Negro Infants, soon after their Birth, in that part of the Country where he practises, nor any peculiar Disease to which they are more subject, than any other Children would be under the same Circumstances, namely: 1st. The known Want of Cleanliness arising from the obstinate Attachment of Negro Women to their Old Customs, particularly to one so evidently mischievous in a warm Climate, as that of not shifting the Childs Clothes for the first three days after its Birth, and sometimes from the Deficiency of Linen, and other Necessaries proper for a new born Infant; 2ndly. The Nature of their Habitations, sometimes suffocating with Heat and Smoke, at others, when the Fire subsides, especially by Night, admitting the cold damp Air through innumerable Crevices and Holes of the Walls which are seldom kept in proper repair, which sudden Transition from Heat to Cold, by occasioning Peripneumonic Fevers, he thinks to be the most general Cause of the death of new born Negro Infants, in that part of the Country where he practises. And lastly, the injudicious Custom of Suckling a new born Child for the first week after its Birth, or longer, with the Milk of a Woman who often has a Child at her Breast a year Old or perhaps older.

"Saith:—

That in his Opinion, difficult Labours happen as frequently amongst Negro Women here as amongst the Females of the Labouring Poor in England; but that he has not observed that a greater proportion of the Infants of the former perish in the Delivery than of the latter; that he does not conceive the Tetanus or Locked Jaw to be a disease common to Infants in the part where he practises; that he apprehends there may be reason to suppose that a Symptom which generally attends approaching Death, from whatever Cause it may proceed, in Children vizt. a Paralysis of the Muscle of the Lower Jaw, has been frequently mistaken by People unacquainted with Medicine, for the Tetanus, as he has often observed the same name to be given in common discourse to both those Aflictions though of so very different a Nature.

"Saith:—

That the Negroe women, whether Slaves or Free, do not in his Opinion, breed so frequently as the Women among the labouring Poor in Great Britain; that he ascribes this chiefly to the promiscuous Intercourse which the greater number of Negroe women indulge themselves in, with the other Sex; that he believes the Abortions which he thinks to be rather frequent amongst them, to be ascribable to the same Cause; that he has not met with any Cases of Abortion which he could fairly impute to ill Usage or excessive Labour; that moderate Labour is beneficial to pregnant Women as being the best Means of preserving general Health.

"Saith:—

That the Custom of carrying young Children into the Field in the Manner, and with the Precautions, it is now practised is by no Means hurtful to the Infants; that he believes a greater number of Children under the Age of ten years dies here than in England; that there are some Disorders to which Children are more liable than Adults; that the Yaws, a Disease originally African, occasions numbers of them to perish; that Worm Complaints are more frequent here, than in England, and that the same Epidemic Diseases which are incident to Children in Europe, vizt. the Small Pox, Measles, and Whooping Cough, are equally common to Negro Children here, and in a severer Degree, moreover, that from the frequent shifting of the Connexion between the Sexes, many Children are lost through Neglect, and the want of Maternal Affection, which these Mothers seldom retain for their Offspring, by a former Husband.

"Saith:—

That in his Opinion, any Attempt to restrain this Licentious Intercourse, between the Sexes, amongst the Slaves in this Island in the present State of their Notions of Right and Wrong, by introducing the Marriage Ceremony amongst them, would be utterly impracticable, and perhaps of dangerous Consequence, as these People are universally known to claim a Right of disposing of themselves in this Respect, according to their Own Will and Pleasure without any Controul from their Masters.

"Saith:—

That a greater Proportion of those called New Negroes die than of those that are seasoned to the Country; that in his Opinion this is often occasioned in those recently imported, by the bad Habit of Body those People have contracted from long Confinement, bad Food and improper Treatment in the Voyage; that within these last twenty years the treatment of new Negroes in this Island, has been greatly altered for the better; that those People are now in general treated with great Humanity and Tenderness; both before and after they are become seasoned to the Country, and that he does not conceive the greater Mortality amongst them commonly to arise from Want of Food or severe Labour.

Signed/Jno. Quier"[1]

Appendix D / Medicine at Worthy Park in 1824

List of Medicines required for Worthy Park Estate, 1824:

Cantharides	1 lb.
Blistering Plasters	2 lbs.
Powder of Rhubarb	1 doz. 4 oz. bottles
Jalap	2 lbs.
Bark	12 lbs.
Snake Root	8 oz.
Cerute	6 lbs.
Basilicon	6 lbs.
Marsh Mallow Ointment	4 lbs.
Mercurial Ointment	2 lbs.
Adhesive Strapping	10 yds.
Adhesive Plaster	1 lb.
Sulphur	1 lb.
Cream Tartae	3 lbs.
Red Precipitate	8 oz.
Calomel	4 oz.
Scammony	4 oz.
Antimony Powder	4 oz.
Corrosive Sublimate	3 oz.
White Vitriol	1 lb.
Dover's Powder	12 oz.
Tincture of Foxglove	2 oz.
Powder of Foxglove	2 oz.
Opium	4 oz.
Spirits of Lavender	2 lbs.
Nitrous Ether	2 lbs.
Vitriolic Ether	1 lb.
Aniseed Oil	2 oz.
Tincture of Steel	1 lb.
Oil of Vitriol	1 lb.
Aloes	4 oz.
Lunar Caustic	1 oz.

Olive Oil	12 pints
Flowers Benzoin	1 oz.
Furdar Emetic	2 oz.
Ipecacuanha	12 oz.
Jeubinthine [?]	3 lbs.
Eye Ointment	2 lbs.
Magnesium Salts (Henry's)	6 bottles
Epsom Salts	50 lbs.
Spirits of Hartshorn	3 lbs.
Squil Vinegar	4 lbs.
Powder Squils	2 oz.
Guinea Ammonia	2 lbs.

1 gum lancet
4 lancets and case
4 glystic pipes
6 penis syringes
10 lbs. tow
2 lbs. lint
12 bougies and case
3 dozen phials
3 new pill boxes
1 Wedgewood mortar
1 tin saucepan
1 Mudge's Inhaler[1]

Notes

Prologue

1. Noel Deerr, *The History of Sugar*, 2 vols. (London, Chapman & Hall, 1949-50).

2. Douglas G. Hall, *Five of the Leewards, 1834-1870* (Barbados, Caribbean Universities Press, 1971), pp. 59-95.

3. The Tharp estates, the papers for which are lodged in the County Record Office, Cambridge, England, cry out for a comprehensive scholarly treatment. Barry Higman, *Slave Population and Economy in Jamaica, 1807-1834* (Cambridge, Cambridge University Press, 1976), and Michael Craton, "Jamaican Slave Mortality: Fresh Light from Worthy Park, Longville and the Tharp Estates," *Journal of Caribbean History*, 3 (November 1971), 1-27, merely touch the hems of the material.

4. Ward Barrett, "Caribbean Sugar Production Standards in the Seventeenth and Eighteenth Centuries," in J. Parker, ed., *Merchants and Scholars* (Minneapolis, University of Minnesota Press, 1967), pp. 147-170.

5. Richard S. Dunn, *Sugar and Slaves; The Rise of the Planter Class in the English West Indies, 1624-1713* (Chapel Hill, University of North Carolina Press, 1972), pp. 84-116. This is an extended version of an article published in the *William and Mary Quarterly* in 1969.

6. Derived by Richard S. Dunn from the *New Map of the Island of Barbadoes* published by Richard Ford around 1674. A second edition of the map is reproduced in Jeanette D. Black, ed., *The Blathwayt Atlas* (Providence, Brown University Press, 1970), and in Richard S. Dunn, "The Barbados Census of 1680: Profile of the Richest Colony in English America," *William and Mary Quarterly*, 26 (1969), 18.

7. In 1683 it was estimated that there were 358 "sugarworks" in Barbados; Richard B. Sheridan, *The Development of the Plantations to 1750* (Barbados, Caribbean Universities Press, 1970), p. 29.

8. There were said to have been 409 windmills and 76 cattle mills in 1710, and 427 and 19 in 1768; ibid.

9. Richard S. Dunn, *Sugar and Slaves*, pp. 117-148. The average size of the 133 sugar estates in Antigua in 1829 was 376 acres, but there were only 27 over 500 acres and only 6 over 750 acres; D. G. Hall, *Leewards*, pp. 185-203.

10. By the early eighteenth century Barbadians were beginning to claim that their soils were overworked and exhausted, which may have been partially true but does not explain the relative recovery of Barbados after slavery ended. At that time Jamaicans, faced by unassailable competition, were themselves complaining of soil exhaustion. Planters' complaints and reasoning should always be treated with skepticism.

11. The 1684 total of sugar plantations was based, like that for Barbados in 1674, on a study of a map, *A New and Exact Mapp of the Island of Jamaica* by Charles Bochart and Humphrey Knollis (1684); Richard S. Dunn, *Sugar and Slaves*, p. 169. Dunn also counted 299 Jamaican cotton or provision farms, 73 cattle pens, 40 indigo plantations, and 32 cocoa "walks," a total of 690 "plantations," though there were only 467 planters listed. Forty-seven planters owned three or more plantations and 10, six or more.

12. Based on a partial study of will inventories in the Jamaican Archives; Richard S. Dunn, *Sugar and Slaves*, pp. 170-171, 264-265.

13. J. Harry Bennett, "Carey Helyar, Merchant and Planter of Seventeenth Century Jamaica," *William and Mary Quarterly*, 21 (July 1964), 53-76; Richard S. Dunn, *Sugar and Slaves*, pp. 84, 154, 212-223.

14. Island Record Office, Jamaica, Deeds, 1/115, October 3, 1673 (henceforth I.R.O.).

15. R. M. Bent and E. L. Bent-Golding, *A Complete Geography of Jamaica* (London, Collins, 1966).

16. Though filed on March 13, it was not registered in the "plat book" of the parish of St. John until November 28, 1670, the date the present owners of Worthy Park selected as the anniversary—largely because it was out of crop time.

17. For a time it was probably the largest, though after Francis Price's death it was reduced to 1,300 acres by the creation of Thetford Estate; Michael Craton and James Walvin, *A Jamaican Plantation: The History of Worthy Park, 1670-1970* (London, W. H. Allen, and Toronto, University of Toronto Press, 1970), pp. 47-49.

18. "The Account of the Familes both whites and Negroes in the Parish of St. John's, Jamaica," London, Public Record Office, C.O. 1/45/109 (henceforth P.R.O.).

19. Though Bryan Edwards talked of their desirability as late as 1793, the 16 servants along with 280 slaves on the Liguanea estate of Philip Pinnock in 1753 mentioned by Pitman and Sheridan were clearly exceptional, since Pinnock imported skilled craftsmen specifically to construct one of Jamaica's most imposing Great Houses; Frank W. Pitman, "The Settlement and Financing of British West India Plantations in the Eighteenth Century," in *Essays Presented to Charles McLean Andrews by His Students* (New Haven, Yale University Press, 1931), pp. 261-270; Richard B. Sheridan, *Plantations*, pp. 45-46.

20. Craton and Walvin, *A Jamaican Plantation*, p. 38.

21. Ibid., pp. 71-94; Michael Craton, "The Real Sir Charles Price," *Jamaica Journal*, 4 (December 1970), 10-14.

22. See Map 5, published by Charles Leslie in 1740. Although Leslie purported to show only "Sugar Works," his information was already well out of date when his book was published and bears a suspicious similarity to that given in Hans Sloane's book,

published in 1707. For example, no sugar works were shown in Lluidas Vale where it is known there were 3 by 1740, and the total shown for St. John Parish is only 14, though there were said to be 21 as early as 1730. Nonetheless, unless Leslie was hopelessly inaccurate, his total of 187 sugar works for the 1730s would seem to make the 246 shown by Bochart and Knollis for 1684 extremely optimistic. As far as it is possible to relate Leslie's map to the parish boundaries of 1774-1793, shown in Map 7, the following is a breakdown of all the plantations shown:

Parishes and counties	Sugar works	Cotton & provisions	Cattle pens & hog crawles	Cacao walks & Indigo works
St. John	14	18	5	—
St. Catherine	10	8	2	—
St. Dorothy	9	9	1	—
St. Thomas-ye-Vale	28	2	4	—
Clarendon	16	11	4	2
Vere	5	5	1	27
St. Mary	11	28	4	1
St. Ann	1	31	1	—
MIDDLESEX totals	94	112	22	30
Kingston & St. Andrew	25	12	1	—
Port Royal	1	2	—	—
St. David	21	9	2	—
St. Thomas/East	17	—	—	—
Portland	—	6	—	—
St. George	—	25	—	—
SURREY totals	64	54	3	0
St. Elizabeth	21	42	8	—
Westmorland	5	5	3	—
Hanover	2	22	—	—
St. James	1	18	—	—
Trelawny	—	—	—	—
CORNWALL totals	29	87	11	0
JAMAICA totals	187	253	36	30
Total plantations	506			

23. Richard S. Dunn, *Sugar and Slaves*, p. 171.

24. The growth of the population and economy of St. John Parish follows: 1680, 751 slaves and 90 servants with perhaps 15 sugar plantations (P.R.O., C.O. 1/45/109); 1734, 5,242 slaves; 1740, 5,875; 1745, 5,728; 1761, 5,888; 1768, 5,455 and 21 sugar estates (Edward Long, *The History of Jamaica*, 3 vols. [London, 1774], II); 1787, 5,880 and 21 (Bryan Edwards, *The History, Civil and Commercial, of the British West Indies*, 2 vols. [London, 1793], I, 229); 1823, 6,295 slaves (G. W. Bridges, *The Annals of Jamaica*, 2 vols. [London, 1828], II, 561-567); 1829, 6,075 and 21 estates with more than 86 slaves each (*Jamaica Almanack, 1829*, pp. 10-13); 1833, 5,985 slaves (R. M. Martin, *The British Colonies: Their History, Extent, Condition and Resources*, 6 vols. [London, 1851-1857], II, 188-191).

25. The actual population was 257 slaves in 1731, but unusually high proportions were old men and women (52) and boys and girls (57); Craton and Walvin, *A Jamaican Plantation*, p. 69n30.

26. Ibid., pp. 95-124.

27. The aqueduct was shared with Murmuring Brook, much later part of Thetford, but this estate was in the Juan de Bolas foothills and never really prospered.

28. *An Inquiry concerning the Trade, Commerce and Policy of Jamaica*, anonymous pamphlet (London, 1759). At the same time there were said to be 360 "polinks" (provision grounds), 110 cotton works, 180 cattle pens (to raise 250 head apiece), 60 pimento walks, and 30 ginger plantations—a grand total of 1,190 agricultural holdings of all kinds and sizes.

29. Craton and Walvin, *A Jamaican Plantation*, pp. 88-89.

30. I.R.O., Deeds, 277/159; 350/77; 153/2; 227/170. Spring Garden was acquired in 1776, but the Prices may have had a coastal pen much earlier because Francis Price's holdings included a "Flamingo Savanna" in St. Dorothy, which cannot be identified; Craton and Walvin, *A Jamaican Plantation*, pp. 30, 62, 70.

31. Long's statistics were based upon tax rolls in which slave totals were notoriously understated, perhaps by 15%. There were also certain implausibilities in the figures for two parishes later subdivided, St. James (1770) and St. Elizabeth (1825), particularly the latter, the populations of which (combined with Manchester after the division) were reported to have jumped from 10,110 in 1768 (and 13,280 in 1789 according to Bryan Edwards) to 35,766 in 1823 (St. Elizabeth, 18,350, Manchester, 17,416; Bridges, *Annals*, II, 561-567), long after the slave trade had ended and when the total slave population of Jamaica was actually declining. Long's slave total for 1768 should perhaps be revised from 166,924 to about 190,000.

32. Presuming 56% of his stated total slave population lived on sugar estates. Besides 680 sugar estates in 1774, Long reckoned there were 600 "polinks and provision places," 500 "breeding pens," 150 coffee, 110 cotton, and 30 ginger plantations, 100 pimento walks, and 8 indigo works—an almost incredible increase over the figures given for 1759.

33. The capital value of such an estate (the chief base for Edwards' calculations) was said to total £41,480 Jamaica Curr. or £30,000 Stg., made up of £14,100 Curr. for land, £7,000 for buildings and plant, £17,500 for slaves, and £2,880 for animal stock. For a discussion, see Michael Craton, *Sinews of Empire: A Short History of British Slavery* (New York, Doubleday, and London, Temple Smith, 1974), pp. 132-140.

34. Craton and Walvin, *A Jamaican Plantation*, pp. 95-124. It is interesting to compare Worthy Park with Edward Long's own estate, Sevens, in Clarendon. This estate, with 304 slaves, produced an average of 280 hogsheads a year from 1,826 acres between 1772 and 1779:

	Acres		Acres
Crop canes	480	Guinea grass pasture	36
Nursery canes	54	Common pasture	200
Fallow cane land	259	Woodland	285
Plantain walk	60	Works and buildings	15
Ground provisions	30	Let to tenants	120
Negro provision		Waste (Rocky River	
grounds	150	courses, gullies)	137
Total acreage			1706

Source: Pitt Papers, P.R.O., 30/8/153, 40.

35. Although tabulating 710 for 1789, Edwards wrote that there were 767 in 1793. This comes in a table in which he sets out to enumerate all estates which had collapsed, and been founded, since Edward Long wrote. It is difficult to resolve. Besides sugar estates, Edwards claimed that in 1793 there were 607 coffee estates, no less than 1,047 grazing pens, and innumerable small holdings; *British West Indies*, I, 311-315.

36. To the 210,894 enumerated in Table 4 Edwards estimated that a further seventh should be added for those slaves belonging to owners with less than 6 slaves who were usually not taxed. Such small parcels would, however, not normally be engaged in sugar production. Out of 210,894, 128,798 is actually 61.1%; ibid.

37. However, he calculated 140,000 out of 250,000 or 56%—in line with the higher figure of 767 estates for 1793. He reckoned that 21,000 slaves lived on coffee plantations, 31,000 on pens, and 58,000 in small holdings or in towns; *British West Indies*, I, 311-315.

38. Evidence given before the Parliamentary Inquiry of 1788 by the *Jamaica Almanack, 1787*, though it was noted that the figure was "rather beyond probability." See *British Sessional Papers, Commons, Accounts and Papers, 1789*, LXXXIV, pt. III, p. 51 (henceforth *B.S.P.*).

39. See Table 7 for the pattern of linkage in Trelawny. Thetford and Swansea both had auxiliary pens towards the coast as well as large acreages of "crawles" in the surrounding foothills. Edward Long's 1788 account of Sevens does not directly mention related holdings, but there was a Long's Wharf at Old Harbour and a Longville Crawle in adjacent St. John Parish (Sevens was also called Longville).

40. Elsewhere I have argued for 75% with an average of 240 slaves per unit based on the higher figures of 767 estates and 56% of the slaves; "Jamaican Slavery," in *Race and Slavery in the Western Hemisphere: Quantitative Studies*, edited by Stanley L. Engerman and Eugene D. Genovese (copyright (c) 1975 by The Center for Advanced Study in the Behavioral Sciences, Stanford, California), pp. 251-52. Reprinted by permission of Princeton University Press. Either is equally likely to be correct.

41. Craton and Walvin, *A Jamaican Plantation*, pp. 79-82, 155-182. The most famous of the casualties of the Price "disaster" was Sir Charles's sybaritic retreat in St. Mary's, The Decoy, which has since disappeared without certain trace.

42. Richard Hill before the Parliamentary Inquiry of 1856. His figures, however, are a little suspect. Like Bryan Edwards, he was arguing a traumatic decline, in this case as a result of the loss of protection after slavery ended, from a total of 859 estates in 1804 (646 in 1834 and 644 as late as 1844, to 330 in 1854). See Table 10.

43. Craton and Walvin, *A Jamaican Plantation*, pp. 175-178.

44. Ibid., pp. 173-174.

45. Craton and Walvin, *A Jamaican Plantation* (p. 131) says £13,472. This was actually the total known to have been paid by Rose Price on the evidence of deeds of sale, but for only 196 slaves. The 225 slaves he is known to have purchased from all sources in 1792-1793 would have cost him £15,300 Currency at £68 each.

46. Ibid., pp. 208-233.

47. The process apparently was never satisfactorily completed. Lloyd's and Aylmer's, as well as Juan de Bolas, quite rapidly changed hands. In standard fashion,

Samuel Queenborough's bequests were divided among legitimate but distant relatives in England, and numerous colored bastards in Jamaica; I.R.O., Wills, 91/194 (1814-1815). Queenborough's substantial coffee mill was rediscovered in dense underbrush on a steep tributary of the Murmuring Brook in March 1973.

48. I.R.O., Wills, 100/57 (1821-22).

49. I.R.O., Wills, 103/7 (1822-23).

50. Craton and Walvin, *A Jamaican Plantation*, pp. 208-233.

51. Lord Shrewsbury happened to be related by marriage to Rose Price, but the connection was a tenuous one, and there is no certain evidence of devious collusion.

52. S. G. Checkland, *The Gladstones* (Cambridge, Cambridge University Press, 1972). It is interesting to compare the history of Thomas Gladstone's Guiana plantations, which also failed in the long run, with those in Jamaica.

53. The Worthy Park Great House, built originally by Francis Price around 1680, lasted rather longer. Though not lived in after about 1830, and tumbled down from mid-century, it was not finally broken up until the 1940s, to form the foundation of a tennis court.

54. London (George Allen & Unwin, 1957). Although Lluidas Vale Village is remarkably similar to "Sugartown" in the book, Miss Clarke spent no time specifically researching there—perhaps for the very reason that she is a first cousin of Worthy Park's owners.

55. Craton and Walvin, *A Jamaican Plantation*, pp. 240-264.

56. Eric Williams, in his magisterial *Columbus to Castro*, provides some figures for the development of Cuban plantations in the nineteenth century that compare very usefully with Jamaica. A plantation producing just over 1,000 tons of sugar a year around 1859 used 3,300 acres of land, but needed only about 150 slaves in order to make a return of 18% on capital. By that time, however, the largest Cuban plantation, Santa Susana, stretched over 11,000 acres, of which 1,700 were in cane, employing 866 slaves, and producing 2,700 tons of sugar a year. Although described as a "monster plantation" (comparing closely with Worthy Park in 1975 in some respects), it was still not comparable with later *centrales*. In the 1890s, for example, the American-owned Soledad plantation had 5,000 acres in canes, out of a total of 12,000, with 23 miles of private railway, and employing 1,200 men in crop time. Central Constancia, probably the largest sugar plantation in the world at that time, produced 19,500 tons of sugar in 1890, roughly the total output of Jamaica then; *Columbus to Castro: The History of the Caribbean, 1492-1969* (London, Deutsch, 1969), pp. 362-365.

57. I.R.O., Deeds, 963/250, 14/16; Craton and Walvin, *A Jamaican Plantation*, pp. 246-250.

58. Ibid., pp. 259-285.

59. C. R. D. Shannon's report from the Research Department, Jamaican Sugar Manufacturers' Association, 1968.

Part One Chapter 1
1. Hans Sloane, *A Voyage to the Islands Madera, Barbados, Nieves, St. Christophers and Jamaica . . .* , 2 vols. (London, 1707, 1725); Thomas Roughley, *The Jamaica*

Planter's Guide . . . (London, 1823); Bryan Edwards, *The History, Civil and Commercial, of the British Colonies in the West Indies,* 2 vols. (London, 1793); William Beckford, *A Descriptive Account of the Island of Jamaica . . .* , 2 vols. (London, 1790); Edward Long, *The History of Jamaica,* 3 vols. (London, 1774).

2. Sloane, *Jamaica,* Introduction, p. xlvi.

3. I.R.O., Wills, 18/76.

4. Michael Craton, *Sinews of Empire: A Short History of British Slavery* (New York, Doubleday, and London, Temple Smith, 1974), pp. 122-126.

5. Sloane, *Jamaica,* Introduction, p. lii.

6. Michael Craton, "Jamaican Slave Mortality: Fresh Light from Worthy Park, Longville and the Tharp Estates," *Journal of Caribbean History,* 3 (November 1971), p. 24.

7. Philip Curtin, *The Atlantic Slave Trade: A Census* (Madison, University of Wisconsin Press, 1969), p. 160. The proportions (rounded) were: Gold Coast, 34%; Bight of Benin, 20%; Bight of Biafra, 16%; Central Africa, 9%; Windward Coast, 8%; Sierra Leone, 7%; Senegambia, 6%.

8. "They are not only the best and most faithful of our slaves, but are really all born Heroes. . . . There never was a raskal or coward of the nation, intrepid to the last degree, not a man of them but will stand to be cut to pieces without a sigh or groan, greatful and obedient to a kind master, but implacably revengeful when ill-treated. My Father, who had studied the genius and temper of all kinds of negroes 45 years with a very nice observation, would say, Noe man deserved a Corramante that would not treat him like a Friend rather than a Slave." Christopher Codrington (Barbados) to Board of Trade, December 30, 1801, *Calendar of State Papers, Colonial, America & West Indies* (1701), p. 721.

9. Sloane, *Jamaica,* Introduction, p. lii.

10. Ibid., p. xlviii.

11. Ibid., p. lii.

12. "The *Negros* are of several sorts, from the several places of *Guinea,* which are reckoned the best Slaves, those from the *East-Indies* or *Madagascins,* are reckoned good enough, but too choice in their Diet, being accustomed in thier own Countries to Fresh Meat &c, and do not well here, but very often die." Ibid., p. xlvii.

13. Ibid., pp. xlix, lii.

14. Ibid., p. xlviii.

15. Ibid., p. xlix.

16. The rebellions that broke out on the plantation of Edmund Duck in the St. John's Red Hills in April 1678, that which spread to the plantation of Madame Guy in March 1686, and that which was led by the Coromantine Tacky during much of 1760.

17. Sloane, *Jamaica,* Introduction, p. lvii.

18. Edward Long, *History of Jamaica*, II, vii, 76n.

Chapter 2

1. This was the conclusion drawn in 1789 from the first statistical analysis made of slave cargoes (1765-1785) for the great Inquiry into the Slave Trade. Earlier estimates were localized, or pure guesswork. *B.S.P., Commons, Accounts & Papers, 1789*, XXVI, IV, 15.

2. Craton and Walvin, *A Jamaican Plantation: The History of Worthy Park, 1670-1970* (London, W. H. Allen, and Toronto, University of Toronto Press, 1970), pp. 131, 172.

3. The work of the Colonial Registrar of Slaves, R. G. Amyot, was presented to the Parliamentary Inquiry of 1832; *B.S.P., Commons, Reports, 1831-2*, XX, 565-577.

Chapter 3

1. For the most comprehensive discussion of the parameters of this equation, see the "cliometric" R. W. Fogel and S. L. Engerman, *Time on the Cross*, vol. I: *The Economics of American Negro Slavery* (Boston, Little, Brown, 1974).

2. Michael Craton, "Jamaican Slave Mortality," Fresh Light from Worthy Park, Longville and the Tharp Estates, *Journal of Caribbean History*, 3 (November 1971), 12-14.

3. Buxton claimed that the slave population of the British West Indies had absolutely declined by over 100,000 in the previous 23 years; Charles Buxton, ed., *Memoirs of Sir Thomas Fowell Buxton, Bart.*, new ed. (London, John Murray, 1877), pp. 122-126.

4. *B.S.P., Commons, Reports 1831-2*, XX, 565-577.

5. Evidence of Dr. John Quier, November 12, 1788, *Journal of the Assembly of Jamaica, 1788*, VIII, 434; given as Appendix C below.

6. George W. Roberts, "A Life Table for a West Indian Slave Population," *Population Studies*, 5 (March 1952), 238-243.

7. E.g., in his work on Montpelier Estate, Barry Higman, while acknowledging that at least some infants who died in their first week were recorded at Montpelier, suggests both high infant mortality and considerable underrecording in the first nine days of life, citing Robert Renny and others for the deaths at "between 25 and 50% of all live births" in that period; B. W. Higman, "Household Structure and Fertility on Jamaican Slave Plantations: A Nineteenth Century Example," *Population Studies*, 27 (November 1973), 545; Robert Renny, *A History of Jamaica* (London, 1807), p. 207. See also Chap. 4, n. 14 below.

8. The "pyramid" cohort date yield only 214 females for 1794, of whom 36 Creoles and 78 Africans were aged 15-49. However, since the tabulated total (451) was some 15% short of the true total population (530)—with females representing 48%— this does indicate a total of about 252 females. In the 1794 pyramid, 53.3% were in the fertile age range, suggesting about 134 out of a total of 252, or 128 out of the 240 counted in 1795. Of course, some of the women interviewed at the behest of Rose Price would have been elderly, with grown children. Some 19.2%, or 46, would have been 50 or over in 1795.

9. In 1789, 1; 1794, 3; 1796, 2; 1813, 4; 1816, 5; 1821, 6; 1822, 7; 1823, 7; 1828, 8; 1830, 5; 1831, 4; 1832, 5; 1833, 5; 1834, 5; 1835, 5; 1836, 3.

10. This was predicated on infant mortality being a quarter (25%) of total mortality, of whom about half (12.5% of the total) died in the first year. If this was understated by 50%, overall mortality was understated by about 8%.

11. George W. Roberts, "Life Table," pp. 242-243.

12. Carlo M. Cipolla, "Four Centuries of Italian Demographic Development," in D. V. Glass and D. E. C. Eversley, eds., *Population in History* (London, Arnold, 1965), pp. 570-587.

13. Michael Craton, "Jamaican Slave Mortality," p. 26.

14. The same was true of the general Jamaica population after emancipation, especially in the towns, during the dreadful cholera epidemics of the 1850s and 1860s.

15. Alexander M. Tulloch and Henry Marshall, *Statistical Reports on the Sickness, Mortality & Invaliding among the Troops in the West Indies* (London, War Office, 1839), quoted in George W. Roberts, *The Population of Jamaica* (Cambridge, Cambridge University Press, 1957), pp. 165-167.

16. *B.S.P., Commons, Accounts & Papers, 1831-2*, XLV, 33. The areas studied besides London, Leeds, and Essex were Rutland, Chester, Norwich, Carlisle, Bolton, Bury, Preston, Wigan, Bradford, Stockport, Macclesfield, Holbeck, and Beeston. There is also useful information on burials in Manchester for 1821-1830; ibid., p. 37.

17. The rate disclosed in 1795 was about 23%; 123% of 23.16 per thousand is 28.48 per thousand.

18. Particularly the material from the Barham-owned estates, Mesopotamia in Westmorland, and Island in St. Elizabeth, between 1756 and 1838, currently being worked on by Richard S. Dunn. The following valuable breakdown of the fecundity of the female slaves on Island Estate in 1808 and 1811 is possibly unique:

Tabulation 1: Classification of Females
in 1808 and 1811

Condition	1808	1811
Left off breeding	28	30
Barren	17	13
Breeding	18	13
Likely to breed	15	22
Children	21	20
Total females listed	99	98
Total Slaves	197	197

Tabulation 2: Breakdown of Females by Ages and
Conditions in 1808 [incomplete]

Condition	Ages	Number	Condition	Ages	Number
Invalid	75-80	2	Likely to breed	30-35	1
Left off breeding	65-70	3		25-30	2
	55-60	7		23	1
	45-50	3		21	1
	40-45	3		19	3
	35	1		16	1
	32	1		14	3
Barren	65-70	1		13	2
	45-50	2		12	1
	35-40	4	Under 12 years		
	30-35	4	Healthy		9
	30	3	Weakly		1
	25	2	Yaws		2
Breeding	35-40	7	Broke Back		1
	30-35	5	Infants		
	25-30	5	Healthy		6
	23	1	Yaws		1
			Total females listed		89

19. Michael Craton, "Jamaican Slave Mortality," p. 25.

20. Stanley M. Elkins, *Slavery: A Problem in American Institutional and Intellectual Life*, 2nd ed. (Chicago, University of Chicago Press, 1968), pp. 104-119.
The most remarkable reconsideration of the psychological and physiological effects of life in concentration camps is Terrence Des Pres, *The Survivor: An Analysis of Life in the Death Camps* (New York, Oxford University Press, 1976). Among much other relevant evidence, Des Pres cites the testimony of Weinstock on Buchenwald: " . . . one hundred per cent of the female prisoners ceased to menstruate at the very beginning of their term of captivity; the function did not reappear until months after their liberation." Eugene Weinstock, *Beyond the Last Path* (New York, Boni and Gaer, 1947), p. 235; Des Pres, *The Survivor*, p. 189.

21. Stanley L. Engerman, "Some Economic and Demographic Comparisons of Slavery in the United States and the British West Indies," *Economic History Review*, 29 (May 1976), 270-274.

22. Evidence of Sir M. Clare, *B.S.P., Lords, Reports, 1831-2*, XXVII, 51, 82. See also Thomas Roughley, *The Jamaica Planter's Guide* (London, 1823), p. 118; Dr. Collins, *Practical Rules for the Management and Medical Treatment of Negro Slaves in the Sugar Colonies* (London, 1803), p. 170; and Gilbert Francklyn, *Observations Occasioned by the Attempts Made in England to Effect the Abolition of the Slave Trade* (London, 1789), p. 52.

23. *An Account of the Native Africans in the Neighbourhood of Sierra Leone* (London, 1803).

24. Including Worthy Park's own doctor. For John Quier's opinion on the relationship between "promiscuity" and both low fertility and ill-health, see the evidence given to the Jamaican House of Assembly in 1788 in Appendix C below.

Chapter 4

1. Not excluding Michael Craton, *Sinews of Empire: A Short History of British Slavery* (New York, Doubleday, and London, Temple Smith, 1974), pp. 192-194. The ideas in this chapter largely stem from remarks concerning the dubious benefits of European medicine practiced in West Africa, made by Philip D. Curtin while commenting on a paper on West Indian slave doctors by Richard B. Sheridan at the conference on comparative slavery at Rochester, N.Y., in March 1972. Curtin's own article, "Epidemiology and the Slave Trade," *Political Science Quarterly*, 83 (June 1968), 190-216, was the pioneer work on this subject. See also Richard H. Shyrock, "Medical Practice in the Old South," *South Atlantic Quarterly*, 29 (April 1930), reprinted in *Medicine in America: Historical Essays* (Baltimore, The Johns Hopkins Press, 1966), pp. 49-70.

2. For an analysis of the mortality in West Africa, mainly white, which shaped European views, see K. G. Davies, "The Living and the Dead: White Mortality in West Africa, 1684-1732," in *Race and Slavery in the Western Hemisphere: Quantitative Studies*, edited by Stanley L. Engerman and Eugene D. Genovese (copyright (c) 1975 by The Center for Advanced Study in the Behavioral Sciences, Stanford, California), pp. 83-98.

3. Hans Sloane's strictures against black doctors (1707) could indeed be turned by modern commentators against such white practitioners as Sloane himself: "There are many such *Indian* and Black Doctors, who pretend, and are supposed to understand, and cure several Distempers, but what I could see of their practice . . . they do not perform what they pretend, unless in the vertues of some few Simples. Their ignorance of Anatomy, Diseases, Method, &c. renders even that knowledge of the vertues of Herbs, not only useless, but even sometimes hurtful to those who imploy them."; *A Voyage to the Islands Madera, Barbados, Nieves, St. Christophers and Jamaica,* 2 vols. (London, 1707, 1725), I, cxli.

4. Jamaican Act of 32 George III, c. XXIII, clauses 33-35.

5. Another example is George W. Roberts, *The Population of Jamaica* (Cambridge, Cambridge University Press, 1957), pp. 165-175. Roberts, however, does not prove his contention, he asserts it, substituting figures for a later period of the worst known infant mortality (the 1890s), on the assumption that slavery must have been as bad, or worse.

6. Michael Craton, "Jamaican Slave Mortality: Fresh Light from Worthy Park, Longville and the Tharp Estates," *Journal of Caribbean History*, 3 (November 1971), 1-27. The percentage of Africans at Worthy Park actually rose steeply in 1792 itself because of the influx of over 200 new Africans. It was 45.7% in 1791 and 60.3% in 1793.

7. The British Guiana data is cited in G. W. Roberts, *Population of Jamaica*, p. 175. The St. Catherine's data is derived from Jamaica, I.R.O., St. Catherine's Copy Register, Causes of Death, vol. I. There is a list of death causes in Edward Brathwaite, *The Development of Creole Society in Jamaica, 1770-1820* (Oxford, Clarendon Press, 1971), pp. 286-288, but since these refer to the deaths of soldiers in the military hospital, it is not comparable. See also B. W. Higman, *Slave Population and Economy in Jamaica, 1807-1834* (Cambridge, Cambridge University Press, 1976), pp. 112-114.

8. In allocating causes of death for St. Catherine, the total sample of 472 was made up as follows: Old Age, Debility—"Old Age," 17; Dysentery, Flux—"Putrid

Fever," 40, "Flux," 4; Dropsy—"Dropsy," 16; Pulmonary Diseases—"Consumption,"
25, "Pleurisy," 2; Fevers (inc. Measles, Smallpox)—"Fever," 159, "Fever and Worms,"
4, "Nervous Fever," 2, "Smallpox," 21, "Spotted Fever," 1, "Putrid Sore Throat," 1;
Yaws, Ulcers—"Decayed," 28, "Sore Leg," 1; Inflammations, etc.—"Swelling," 1,
"Gout," 9, "Schirrous Liver," 1, "Gout in Stomach," 2, "Bilious Fever," 5, "Bellyache,"
2, "Swollen Liver," 1, "Gravel," 1, "Obstruction," 1; Accidents—"Accident," 2, "Murdered," 2, "A Fall," 3; Convulsions—"Fits," 26, "Convulsions," 3, "Palsy," 1; Lockjaw—"Lockjaw," 4; Syphilis—"Sores & Ill Habits," 5; Others and Unknown—"Unknown," 28, Not stated, 7, "Infancy," 1, "Childbirth," 6, "Rheumatism," 1, "Surfeit,"
1, "Mortification," 1, "Apoplexy," 3, "Teething," 1, "Suspicious," 2, "Suddenly," 7,
"Hystericks & Broken Hearted," 2, "Hanged" (for forgery), 1, "Insobriety," 4, "Cancer," 1, "Want," 1. In these St. Catherine's diagnoses "Decay" might well be a synonym
for the "Debility" used in British Guiana. "Putrid Fever" may well be a synonym for
"Flux." The incidence of fever was disastrously high among the members of the white
army garrison. The two victims of bellyache were both planters. Some of those listed
with convulsions may well have suffered from worms. Leprosy (like venereal disease)
was probably not specifically diagnosed for social reasons. A high proportion of the
population of St. Catherine's was white, colored, and free, though persons were not invariably identified by race or status in the Register.

9. Between 1817 and 1836 the average annual mortality for white troops stationed in Jamaica was 121.3 per thousand, of whom 101.9 died from fevers; total
figures for black troops were 30.0 per thousand (fevers 8.7). The comparable figures for
the Windwards and Leewards station were 78.5 per thousand for white troops (fevers,
36.9), and 40.0 (fevers, 7.1) for black troops. G. W. Roberts, *Population of Jamaica*,
pp. 165-172, quoting Tulloch and Marshall.

10. B. W. Higman, *Slave Population*, pp. 58, 78.

11. As late as 1851, the annual mortality rate in New Orleans was 81 per thousand, three times as high as contemporary rates in London, New York, and Philadel-
phia. The rate for Jamaica as a whole in the last decades of slavery was about 35 per
thousand, compared with the 1792-1838 average for Worthy Park of 40%.

12. B. W. Higman, *Slave Population*, pp. 99-138.

13. For contemporary views on dirt eating, see Thomas Dancer, *The Medical
Assistant: or Jamaica Practice of Physic . . .* (Kingston, Jamaica, Aikman, 1801) p. 171;
James Thompson, *A Treatise on the Diseases of Negroes as they occur in the Island of
Jamaica* (Kingston, Jamaica, Aikman, 1820), pp. 24, 32; James Stewart, *A View of the
Past and Present State of the Island of Jamaica* (Edinburgh, Oliver & Boyd, 1823), p.
307. Some modern commentators have suggested a connection between dirt eating and
the deficiency disease beri-beri; Shyrock, "Old South," p. 50.

14. In his report to a committee of the Jamaican House of Assembly in 1788, Dr.
Quier was reported as saying, "That he has not in general observed any very great
Mortality amongst the Negro Infants, soon after their Birth, in that part of the Country
where he practises, nor any peculiar Disease to which they are more subject, than any
other Children would be under the same Circumstances. . . . That in his Opinion,
difficult Labours happen as frequently amongst Negro Women here as amongst the
Females of the Labouring Poor in England; but that he has not observed that a greater
proportion of the Infants of the former perish in the Delivery than of the latter; that he
does not conceive the Tetanus or Locked Jaw to be a disease common to Infants in the
part where he practises; that he apprehends there may be a reason to suppose that a
Symptom which generally attends approaching Death, from whatever Cause it may

proceed, in Children vizt. a Paralysis of the Muscle of the Lower Jaw, has been frequently mistaken by People unacquainted with Medicine, for the Tetanus, as he has often observed the same name to be given in common discourse to both those Afflictions though of so very different a Nature." Report of the Assembly on the Slave Issues, enclosed in Lt. Gov. Clarke's No. 92 of the 20th. of November, 1788, London, P.R.O., C.O. 137/88.

Relative to the common belief that many slave infants died of the tetanus before they reached the age of nine days it is worth pointing out both that tetanus is rarely fatal in less than two weeks and also that slave mothers probably regarded the killing of an ailing infant less than nine days old as abortion, not infanticide, since the humanizing spirit was believed to be acquired after the ninth day. For tetanus, see also Edward Long, *The History of Jamaica*, 3 vols. (London, 1774), III, 713; Thomas Dancer, *Medical Assistant*, p. 269.

15. At Braco Estate, Trelawny, e.g., there was an average of 68 slaves "In the Hothouse, in Yaws house with sores, Pregnant, lying in & attendants" in June 1796, out of a population of 402; Braco Slave Book, April 1795-December 1797, Braco, Trelawny.

16. Modern Worthy Park offers an illuminating parallel. When the Sugar Industry Labour Welfare Board clinic was set up on the estate in 1951, the doctor was called upon to treat no less than 331 cases of yaws and 250 of syphilis, but only 28 of gonorrhea. In a comparatively short time yaws and syphilis were contained, but the cases of gonorrhea treated multiplied to hundreds. Such is progress. Michael Craton and James Walvin, *A Jamaican Plantation: The History of Worthy Park, 1670-1970* (London, W. H. Allen, and Toronto, University of Toronto Press, 1970), p. 308. That gonorrhea was in fact common among the Worthy Park slaves, at least around 1824, is suggested by the purchase by the estate of the six penis syringes included in the list of medicines and equipment given in Appendix D below.

17. Thomas Trapham, *A Discourse on the State of Health in the Island of Jamaica* (London, Boulter, 1679), passim. The equating of black slaves with animals by a plantation doctor immediately brings to mind a parallel between slave and veterinary medicine. If planters and their doctors regarded slaves as little more than valuable animals, it is not surprising that slave medicine was little better than "horse doctor cures." Veterinary science—probably because the treatment of animals has been required to remain cheap, and animal doctors are even less regarded as colleagues by MBs and MDs than they once were—has made comparatively far less progress than medicine for humans. E.g., horses are still poulticed, blistered, and cauterized, much like eighteenth-century slaves.

18. Quoted in Elizabeth Donnan, *Documents Illustrative of the History of the Slave Trade to America*, 4 vols. (Washington, Carnegie Institute, 1930-1931), I, 410.

19. The miners of quicksilver at Almadén in Spain, the Japanese of Minimata who ate mercury-poisoned fish, and the thousands of Iraquis who ate mercury-dusted seed grain, were alike found to be suffering from locomotor ataxia and other manifestations thought to be classic symptoms of tertiary syphilis. It would be instructive to discover how often locomotor ataxia and the other symptoms occurred in persons with syphilis before they were treated with mercurials.

20. It was not long since surgery had been entirely in the hands of barbers. Readers of Samuel Pepys' diaries will recall with what trepidation Pepys submitted to surgery for the stone, and his gratitude to the Almighty for allowing him to survive what was technically a very simple operation. In Pepys' case the "miracle" was almost certainly that the surgeon used a brand new knife. Until the days of Lister, deaths from appendi-

citis were far more common among those operated on than those with whom nature was allowed to takes its course.

21. Douglas Guthrie, *A History of Medicine*, rev. ed. (London, Nelson, 1958), pp. 216-231.

22. Hans Sloane, *Jamaica*, I, passim. This work was not published until 1707, 18 years after Sloane's sojourn in Jamaica as physician to his kinsman, Governor Albemarle.

23. J. Quier, J. Hume, and others, *Letters and Essays on the Smallpox* (London, Murray, 1778). The letters, dating from 1769 to 1776, were addressed to Dr. Donald Munro of London, a member of the famous Edinburgh medical clan of that name.

24. Heinz Georke, "The Life and Scientific Works of Dr. John Quier, Practitioner of Physic and Surgery, Jamaica, 1738-1822," *West India Medical Journal*, vol. 5, pp. 22-27.

25. Guthrie, *History of Medicine*, p. 89.

26. Cotton Mather, who promoted inoculation in Boston in 1721, wrote to a fellow member of the Royal Society in London in 1716 that he had heard of variolation from one of his own slaves, a "Guramantee" fittingly named Onesimus; Frederick C. Kalgan, "The Rise of Scientific Activity in Colonial New England," *Yale Journal of Biology and Medicine*, 22 (December 1949), 130.

27. See Dr. Quier's evidence to the Jamaican Assembly in 1788, Appendix C below.

28. This argument is developed in Michael Craton, "Jamaican Slave Mortality"; *Sinews of Empire*, pp. 194-199; "Jamaican Slavery" in Engerman and Genovese, *Race and Slavery*.

29. The mortality of the slaves on the Middle Passage was probably about 20% per voyage on the average at the beginning of the eighteenth century, and just about 15% by the end of the century. This represented an annual rate of nearly double these figures, since voyages averaged only about six months. These rates of 300-400 per thousand per year were probably equaled among the slaves from the time of their capture until the time of shipment; Michael Craton, *Sinews of Empire*, pp. 96-98.

30. The annual rate among white troops stationed in Jamaica of 121.3 deaths per thousand, though the second highest in the world, was made to seem quite moderate by the West African figures. As late as 1823-1826, the death rate for British troops stationed in Sierra Leone was 483 per thousand, and for the Gold Coast, 668 per thousand. In the slave trade, between 20 and 25% of all white crewmen died on each round trip, which averaged about a year, in the 1780s, compared with less than 3% on ships sailing simply between England and the West Indies. G. W. Roberts, *Population of Jamaica*, p. 167; K. G. Davies, "The Living and the Dead"; Craton, *Sinews of Empire*, p. 97.

31. See, e.g., Elsa Goveia, *Slave Society in the British Leeward Islands at the End of the Eighteenth Century* (New Haven, Yale University Press, 1965), pp. 183-188.

Chapter 5
1. In Tables 42 and 43 and Figure 23, gross revenue is sugar at average London price exclusive of duty (hhd. = 16 cwt.) with 25% added for rum. Commission was rated at 2.5% of gross sales, freight at 5-15% according to peace or war, and insurance

5-25% similarly. Provisions were assesed at £4 per slave at the beginning of the period covered, £5 at end, with inflation up to three times during war; other supplies were roughly equal. Salaries remained fairly stationary, except when the owner was away and an attorney was paid 2.5% on sales. The cost of new slaves, mostly paid in 3 years, is here spread out. In fact, much of it accounted for the rise in interest, which may be rather understated here. Rose Price increased his mortgages steeply in a manner irrelevant to Worthy Park by providing for his huge brood of children on his death. Doubtless his own accountancy would therefore have given a much lower profit figure. Similarly, like all planters, he grossly exaggerated the true capital value of his estate, in order to bring down his apparent returns and also to raise his credit rating. In his will he valued his entire property at Worthy Park at £133,823.17.1 (I.R.O., Inventories, 151/210-3), though it was sold 28 years later for £8,550. For a discussion of this point, see Michael Craton, *Sinews of Empire: A Short History of British Slavery* (New York, Doubleday, and London, Temple Smith, 1974), pp. 134-136.

2. *B.S.P., 1848,* XXIII, Select Committee on Sugar and Coffee Planting, evidence of Thomas Price, pp. 53-54.

3. R. W. Fogel and S. L. Engerman, *Time on the Cross,* vol. I: *The Economics of American Negro Slavery* (Boston, Little, Brown, 1974), pp. 144-157. The authors, however, base their percentage figure on the rearing costs of a cohort, some of whom died. Yet they calculated that the 1800 annual income in the United States was only about a fifth of the prime-age price of a slave at that time.

4. Bryan Edwards, *The History, Civil and Commercial, of the British Colonies in the West Indies,* 2 vols. (London, 1793), I, 262.

5. See Pt. Three, Chap. 12 below.

6. This clear monopolization of certain specialist and elite jobs by men runs absolutely counter to the situation predicated (from very little actual research) by Orlando Patterson: "The slave man's sexual difference was in no way recognised in his work situation by the all-powerful outgroups." *The Sociology of Slavery: An Analysis of the Origins, Development and Structure of Negro Slave Society in Jamaica* (London, McGibbon & Kee, 1967), p. 167.

7. Michael Craton, *Sinews of Empire,* pp. 75-78.

8. For the fate of the free blacks and coloreds, see the essays in L. Cohn and J. P. Greene, eds., *Neither Slave nor Free* (Baltimore, The Johns Hopkins Press, 1972); Mavis Christine Campbell, *The Dynamics of Change in a Slave Society: A Sociopolitical History of the Free Coloreds of Jamaica, 1800-1865* (Rutherford, N.J., Fairleigh Dickinson University Press, 1976).

9. Thomas Roughley, *The Jamaica Planter's Guide* (London, 1823), p. 96.

10. E.g., Robert Moore, "Slave Rebellions in Guyana," *Transactions of the Third Conference of Caribbean Historians* (Georgetown, Guyana, April 1971).

11. For further discussion, see the biography of Strumpet (1764-1838+), Pt. Two, Chap. 10 below.

12. See Chap. 1, Table 14 above.

13. Ibid.

14. Besides the 14 Akan day-names, the following apparent African names or corruptions thereof occur in the Worthy Park lists: Old Assey, Asso, Badda, Baddoo, Baddy, Becca, Nanny Cobidia, Custina, Didna, Famma, Fima, Foshiba, Foshuba, Bappa, Pastora, Jugg (2), Jutah, Jabritt, Kally, Libra, Lievvie (3), Manna, Mintape, Monimia (2), Mopsey, Morrato, Tabia, Pela, Phogo, Prim, Rappo, Rompe, Sabrah, Satuba, Sewie, Succuba, Symbria, Mimba, Babba, Raveface, Whanica, Bossoes, Dupp (2), Ketto, Momiet, Momus, Nearcow, Pasco, Prade, Prial, Sambo, Shoudan, Tombo (2), Tompipes, Yaw (2).

15. These names were Ebo Katy (1764-1834, first recorded 1813), Ebo Mary (1792-1830; 1813), Ebo Nancy (1795-1830+; 1813), Ebo Peggy (1795-1830+; 1813), Ebo Sarah (1787-1830+; 1813), Congo Betty (fl. 1784-1792; 1784), Congo Scotland (1729-1796+), Congo Tom (1771-1824+; 1813), Congo William (1770-1833; 1813), Coromantu Peggy (1788-1824; 1813), Coromantu Reason (d. 1794; 1793), Coromantu Cubba (1724-1796+; 1784), Chamba Lettice (1791-1823+; 1813), Chamba Mary (1792-1824+; 1813), Moco Nell (1787-1794+; 1813) Moco Sukey (1759-1830+; 1784), Bonny Yabba (d. 1788; 1784). The table below is a breakdown of the 1778 list from York Estate, Trelawny, which uniquely gave the tribal origins of all the 241 Africans who made up 49.4% of the population, as well as valuable information on ages, conditions, and valuation, with details of Creoles, too. The data is taken from the Gale-Morant Papers, University Library, Exeter, Devon, England.

16. See Frederic G. Cassidy, *Jamaica Talk: Three Hundred Years of the English Language in Jamaica* (London, Macmillan, 1961); "Multiple Etymologies in Jamaican Creole," *American Speech*, 41 (1966), 211-215. See also Robert A. Hall, Jr., *Pidgin and Creole Languages* (Ithaca, Cornell University Press, 1965); J. L. Dillard, *Black English* (New York, Random House, 1972); and the excellent discussion in Peter H. Wood, *Black Majority: Negroes in South Carolina* (New York, Knopf, 1974), pp. 167-191.

17. Peter H. Wood, *Black Majority*, pp. 181-186.

18. This implied equalization alone may account for the engaging inventiveness shown by modern black West Indians in naming their children. Reading West Indian school registers out loud is a rare pleasure for an Englishman surfeited with dull Michaels, Peters, and Marys.

19. I.R.O., St. John's Parish Register, 1759-1825, Baptisms; see also Pt. Two, Chapter 8, n.6 below.

20. "An Act for providing Curates for the several Parishes of this Island and for promoting Religious Instruction amongst the Slaves," December 19, 1816. In 1824 it was reported in Britain that one Jamaican parson who had been in the habit of baptizing an average of 100 persons a year between 1800 and 1816 had baptized 24,000 in six months since the passing of the 1823 Act; *Edinburgh Review*, 40 (March 1824), 232-33, quoted by Robert W. Smith, "Slavery and Christianity in the British West Indies," *Church History*, 1 (1955), 171-186.

21. The first three Worthy Park slaves baptized were John Morris, the "Black Doctor" (a black, in fact), Charles Dale, "Under Smith" (quadroon), Dick Gardner, carpenter (mulatto).

22. Sidney W. Mintz, "The Question of Caribbean Peasantries; A Comment," *Caribbean Studies*, 1 (1961), 31-34.

23. Sidney W. Mintz and Douglas G. Hall, "The Origin of the Jamaican Internal Marketing System," Yale University Publications in Anthropology, vol. 57, (New Haven, Yale University Press, 1960), pp. 1-26.

Tribal labels	Adult males (aged 18-73)	Av. age	Av. value (£Curr.)	Adult females (aged 16-63)	Av. age	Av. value (£Curr.)	"Boys" (aged 14-23)	Av. age	Av. value (£Curr.)	"Girls" (aged 14-16)	Age	Value (£Curr.)	Total males	Total females	Grand Total	Av. age	Av. value (£Curr.)
Eboe	11	29.8	80	22	35.6	44	18	16.7	65	0	—	—	29	22	51	27.7	59
Coromantee	25	30.8	78	13	44.8	38	2	19.5	67	1	14.0	60	27	14	41	34.2	64
Papa	18	28.3	46	21	24.2	67	0	—	—	0	—	—	18	21	39	26.1	57
Congo	27	34.2	58	7	42.3	43	0	—	—	0	—	—	27	7	34	37.8	64
Moco	9	24.7	47	6	41.8	56	4	16.5	74	0	—	—	13	6	19	26.1	42
Portage	16	27.6	62	0	—	0	1	23.0	30	0	—	—	17	0	17	27.4	60
Chamba	7	28.7	61	9	23.6	60	0	—	—	0	—	—	7	9	16	25.8	61
Fantee	4	21.8	76	1	22.0	75	5	17.0	59	1	16.0	70	9	2	11	19.1	68
Nago	3	19.0	72	4	31.0	54	0	—	—	0	—	—	3	4	7	25.9	61
Mundingo	1	38.0	150	1	35.0	50	0	—	—	0	—	—	1	1	2	36.5	100
Ashantee	2	22.0	55	0	—	0	0	—	—	0	—	—	2	0	2	22.0	55
Duccosia	1	63.0	5	0	—	—	0	—	—	0	—	—	1	0	1	63.0	5
Alio	0	—	—	1	39.0	25	0	—	—	0	—	—	0	1	1	39.0	25
Totals Africans	124	29.7	63	85	33.6	52	30	17.1	64	2	15.0	65	154	87	241	29.3	59
Creoles	44		121	78		66	69		68	53		36			248		62

24. William Beckford, *A Descriptive Account of the Island of Jamaica . . .*, 2 vols. (London, Egerton, 1789), II, 151-187.

25. Richard Ligon, *A True & Exact History of the Island of Barbados . . .* (London, 1657), pp. 47-53; Hans Sloane, *A Voyage to the Islands Madera, Barbados, Nieves, St. Christophers and Jamaica*, 2 vols. (London, 1707, 1725), I, xlvii-lvi.

26. "Household Structure and Fertility on Jamaican Slave Plantations: A Nineteenth-Century Example," *Population Studies*, 27 (November 1973), 527-550; "The Slave Family and Household in the British West Indies, 1800-1834," *Journal of Interdisciplinary History*, 6 (Autumn 1975), 261-287.

27. M. G. Smith, *West Indian Family Structure* (Seattle, University of Washington Press, 1962), p. 12; Sidney M. Greenfield, *English Rustics in Black Skin* (New Haven, Yale University Press, 1966), p. 45; Orlando Patterson, *Sociology of Slavery*, p. 167; Elsa Goveia, *Slave Society in the British Leeward Islands at the End of the Eighteenth Century* (New Haven, Yale University Press, 1965), pp. 235-236.

28. This precept, adopted by the British, was at least as ancient as the Spanish slave law, the *Siete Partidas*.

29. The Act of 32 Geo. III, c. xxxiii, sec. 3 decreed that "the merchant or factor by whom sales are conducted must, on clearing the vessel, and paying the duties, make oath, under like penalty [£500], that he has done his utmost to classify and sell together mothers and their children, and brothers and sisters." Such provisions were extended to all sales, and made obligatory rather than simply testimonial, by later acts.

30. 32 Geo. III, c. xxxiii, sec. 36.

31. Barry Higman, "Slave Family Structure," pp. 14-16.

32. Jamaica Archives, St. John's Parish Register, 1759-1825; I.R.O., Index of Marriages, St. John, 1759-1850. Many of the slave marriages recorded in Jamaica during the last phase of slavery were performed by sectarian missionaries, especially Methodists. However, the memoirs of the Methodist missionary John Riland attest that the sectarians were scarcely more active in St. John in this respect than were Anglicans. Of approximately 2,500 slave weddings performed in Jamaica between 1821 and 1825 (of which 601 were in Kingston and no less than 1,085 in St. Thomas-in-the-East) only 3 were performed in St. John, where only one had been recorded before 1821; Rev. John Riland, *Memoirs of a West-India Planter* (London, Hamilton & Adams, 1837), pp. 118-119.

33. Matthew Gregory ("Monk") Lewis, *A Journal of a West India Proprietor* (London, Murray, 1834 ed.).

34. Michael Craton, *Sinews of Empire*, pp. 256-280.

35. Rose Price, *Pledges on Colonial Slavery, to Candidates for Seats in Parliament, Rightly Considered* (Penzance, Vigurs, 1832).

Part Two Introduction

1. Frederic Mauro, *Le Portugal et L'Atlantique au XVIIe siècle, 1570-1670. Étude économique* (Paris, 1960), cited in C. R. Boxer, *The Portuguese Seaborne Empire, 1415-1825* (London, Hutchinson, 1969), pp. 103-104.

2. Oloudah Equiano, *Interesting Narrative of the Life of Oloudah Equiano or Gustavus Vassa, written by himself* (London, 1789), pp. 32-34.

3. Eugene D. Genovese, *Roll, Jordan, Roll: The World the Slaves Made* (New York, Pantheon, 1974).

4. Henry Bleby, *The Death Struggles of Slavery* (London, 1868), pp. 122-127.

5. At a rough count, 37 Africans (26 males, 11 females), 216 Creoles (85 males, 131 females) and 37 whites (32 males, 5 females).

Chapter 6
1. In 1771-1780, 2.1%; 1781-1790, 29.7%; 1791-1807, 40.1%; P. D. Curtin, *The Atlantic Slave Trade, A Census* (Madison, University of Wisconsin Press, 1969), Table 43, p. 150. In 1798, 69 of the 150 Liverpool slaveships sailed to Angola, compared with 10 out of 88 in 1752 and one in 1771; Gomer Williams, *History of the Privateers . . . with an Account of the Liverpool Slave Trade* (London, 1897), pp. 675-685.

2. C. B. Wadström, *An Essay on Colonization*, 2 vols. (London, 1794), I, 125-126.

3. Oloudah Equiano, *Interesting Narrative of the Life of Oloudah Equiano . . .* (London, 1789), pp. 40-42.

4. Michael Craton, *Sinews of Empire: A Short History of British Slavery* (New York, Doubleday, and London, Temple Smith, 1974), pp. 96-98.

5. Lindo had five slaveships from Angola advertised in the *Royal Gazette*, in 1793. The *Benjamin* and the *Ann Delicia* seem to have been the most likely, from their dates of arrival; *Joseph*, *Fancy*, and *Commerce* arrived together (in convoy?) in August; altogether the five vessels brought 1,148 Congoes into Kingston in 1793.

6. Forty-three unnamed slaves for £2,555 Currency, I.R.O., Deeds, 406/102; 63 unnamed slaves for £3,610 Currency, I.R.O., Deeds, 407/198. Evidence that the 85 slaves bought earlier were partially seasoned lies both in their price, £7,024 Currency and in the fact that they were already named when bought—every name beginning with the initial letter R. Their average age on arrival may have been as low as 18.7 years (males 18.0, females 19.9); I.R.O., Deeds, 402/92; Worthy Park slave books.

7. That the Worthy Park slaves were so branded is borne out by the following notice of a recaptured runaway in the *St. Jago de la Vega Gazette:* "In Spanish Town Workhouse, Jan. 12, 1792 . . . Betty, a Creole, to Price's Lluida's estate, LP twice in both shoulders, 5 feet 5." In fact Betty may have been an African since in the Worthy Park records she was listed as Congo Betty.

8. This at least was a common practice in the Lesser Antilles, as described by Sir William Young, *A Tour through . . . Barbados, St. Vincent, Antigua, Tobago and Granada* (London, Stockdale, 1801), p. 51.

9. Boston (aged 44); Boy (27, with elephantiasis); Dicky (45), Falmouth (35, consumptive); Fletcher (47, distempered); Germany (55); Julius (59); London (70); Mingo (45, weakly); Congo Scotland (65); Tim (d. 1793); Titus (49, almost blind); Withywood Tom (60); Wakefields (59, one eye); Wolfe (39, sore leg); Worcester (49); Whydaw (43).

10. Library of Congress, Worthy Park Plantation Book, 1791-1811, p. 27.

11. Captain Phillips of the slave ship *Hannibal* (1693), quoted in Elizabeth Donnan, *Documents Illustrative of the History of the Slave Trade to America*, 4 vols. (Washington, D.C., Carnegie Institute, 1930-1931), I, 410.

12. Fox, aged 21, ate poison on June 23, 1794. Boston (not to be confused with the watchman of the same name) committed suicide in the same manner on June 23, 1796, two years later to the day.

13. Michael Craton and James Walvin, *A Jamaican Plantation: The History of Worthy Park, 1670-1970* (London, W. H. Allen, and Toronto, University of Toronto Press, 1970), p. 131.

14. I.R.O., Deeds, 402/92.

15. Craton and Walvin, *A Jamaican Plantation*, pp. 171-174.

16. Thomas Roughley, *The Jamaica Planter's Guide* (London, 1823), pp. 103-104.

17. Average age of 18 males, 39.2 years; 24 females 44.7; 14 Africans 63.3; 38 Creoles, 31.7.

18. And was perhaps impregnated in Jamaica rather than in Africa. Her first child, Rachael, was at least once listed as a sambo (1813). Since Raveface was unequivocally black, this implies that Rachael's father was at least partly colored and presumably Creole.

19. Roughley, *Planter's Guide*, p. 100.

20. Ibid.

21. For Christmas, Easter, and crop-over festivals, see Anon., *Marly, or the life of a Planter in Jamaica* (Glasgow, 1828), pp. 46-48. For the secret yam festival, see the report of certain slaves tried for conspiracy in 1824 who were said to have engaged in it, P.R.O., CO 137/157; Orlando Patterson, *The Sociology of Slavery . . .* (London, McGibbon and Kee, 1967), pp. 242-246.

22. "We find that negroes in general are strongly attached to their countrymen but above all to such of their companions as came in the same ship with them from Africa. This is a striking circumstance: the term *shipmate* is understood among them as signifying a relationship of the most enduring nature."; Bryan Edwards, *The History, Civil and Commercial, of the British Colonies in the West Indies*, 3 vols. 2nd ed. (London, 1801), II, p. 156.

23. So critical was the role of head boiler—simple mistakes in processing could ruin a whole batch of sugar—that estates preferred a white man for the post. At Worthy Park this was so in the 1790s, but by the time Register was in the factory both the head and under head boilers were black—as was the case on most small estates far earlier. Although they could be occupied by either whites or blacks, head boilermen's posts were naturally the focus of considerable social tension, as well as of the aspirations of the slaves most ambitious for assimilation.

24. Craton and Walvin, *A Jamaican Plantation*, pp. 108-111.

25. Every one of the slaves specifically listed as factory workers at Worthy Park was African born, though there were many years when factory workers were not distinguished from field laborers.

26. Register was one of the first Worthy Park's Africans to take a Christian name. Unfortunately his baptism is not recorded in the St. John Parish register under the Worthy Park listings (which begin in 1811). Either he was baptized elsewhere in Lluidas Vale or, more likely, during the period 1825-1836 for which there is a lamentable gap in the parish records.

27. P. D. Curtin, *Atlantic Slave Trade*, pp. 184-185, 246. At least one of the "R" slaves of 1792 was a Coromantine, the female Coromantu Reason, who died in 1794.

28. Craton and Walvin, *A Jamaican Plantation*, p. 173.

Chapter 7
1. The great-great-great grandmother of Isaac "Dozer" Brown; see Pt. Three, Chap. 15 below.

2. Only the 13th listed, and the 8th black; I.R.O., St. John's Parish Register 1759-1825, Baptisms, Dec. 2, 1813. Since "Mulatto Dick" was later called Richard Douglas, his father may have been Peter Douglas of Point Hill, long associated with Worthy Park; see below Pt. Three, Chap. 14.

3. There was also a female superintendent, Nancy Morris (b. 1788), appointed driveress around 1830, who, unlike Robert Blythe, continued in her superintending role for at least eight years after slavery ended.

4. Thomas Roughley, *The Jamaica Planter's Guide* (London, 1823) pp. 79-80.

5. See, e.g., Rose Price's own words (1832); Michael Craton and James Walvin, *A Jamaican Plantation: The History of Worthy Park, 1670-1970* (London, W. H. Allen, and Toronto, University of Toronto Press, 1970), pp. 191-195.

6. James Kelly, *A Voyage to Jamaica* (Belfast, 1828), p. 19; Orlando Patterson, *The Sociology of Slavery* . . . (London, McGibbon and Kee, 1967), p. 63.

7. "It is reckoned in Jamaica on a moderate computation that not less than 10,000 of such as are called Head Negroes . . . possess from two to four wives." Bryan Edwards, *The History, Civil and Commercial, of the British Colonies in the West Indies*, 2 vols. (London, 1793), II, iv.

8. "Household Structure and Fertility on Jamaican Slave Plantations: A Nineteenth Century Example," *Population Studies*, 27 (November 1973), p. 539.

9. It might be argued that the headmen if they were indeed chosen as being "of well-earned and reputed good character" might themselves have spearheaded the movement towards respectable monogamy. On the other hand, the tendency towards polygyny—or, rather, to equate power, wealth, potency, and paternity—may well have been one of the "petty vices" condoned by Thomas Roughley. The evidence is equivocal. None of the Worthy Park slave headmen were certainly married, though Grace, named Elizabeth Newland in 1816, became Elizabeth Blythe in 1836 and may have been Robert Blythe's wife.

10. Craton and Walvin, *A Jamaican Plantation*, pp. 165-169.

11. In 1793 the total of slaves listed around the Worthy Park Great House was an astounding 58, 24 being males. Yet 30 or even less were true domestics and at least 17 were new Africans suitable only for the simplest tasks in the grounds. In 1796 the total number of domestics fell to 15, roughly what it had been in 1789.

12. Edward Long, *The History of Jamaica*, 3 vols. (London, 1774), II, 282.

13. And who had died, in a fall from a horse, in 1807. It would be interesting to know if Duncan had heard of his namesake's demise.

14. Alternatively, they may have been husband and wife. James Vinnicombe, not listed in 1838, may possibly have been the 18-year-old cattleman simply called Duncan, who was still employed under that name in 1842. In 1843 there was no Duncan employed, but there was a cattleman called James Vinnicombe.

15. That is, if a slave took or ate anything belonging to his master, or to any master, the master had no proper cause for complaint. H. P. Jacobs, "Dialect, Magic and Religion," in Morris Cargill, ed., *Ian Fleming Introduces Jamaica* (London, Deutsch, 1965), pp. 86-87.

16. Thomas Roughley, *Planter's Guide*, p. 96. It is worth noting the Worthy Park's African head watchman in 1813, Forest (1769-1838+), was listed as a runaway in 1814, though on his return he was reinstated. Another watchman who ran away was Mingo (b. 1787) who, suffering from elephantiasis and a ruptured back, was a watchman at 25. Once he ran away in 1817 he was apparently never recaptured, though he remained on the Worthy Park lists until 1830.

17. There is some confusion about this. In at least one early year she was listed as African, presumably as she had been bought; yet she was described as Creole consistently from 1813 onwards.

18. I.R.O., Deeds, 353/140.

19. Both died in 1822.

20. Thomas Roughley, *Planter's Guide*, p. 95. For medicines actually supplied to Worthy Park in 1824, see Appendix D below.

21. I.R.O., St. John's Parish Register, 1835, Baptisms. Whanica's only surviving son, Yorky, was christened Robert Brown in the previous week, Jan. 25, 1835.

22. I.R.O., St. John's Parish Register, 1759-1825, Baptisms.

23. I.R.O., Wills, 18/76, Charles Price, Jan. 14, 1730.

24. Another such slave was Washer's Jubba (1724-1796+) in old age employed as "doctor's midwife," who was probably the girl Jibba listed in 1730, and daughter of the senior male slave Whasus.

25. Craton and Walvin, *A Jamaican Plantation*, pp. 71-94, 155-169.

26. *B.S.P. House of Commons, Accounts and Papers*, 1789, XXVI, Appendix: Michael Craton, "The Real Sir Charles Price," *Jamaica Journal*, 4 (December 1970), 10-14.

27. Probably the same building, since Rose Price, living in the Great House, was his own overseer, 1791-1794. Even when the owner was an absentee, the bookkeepers lived in a barracklike wing of the overseer's house—both of which still existed in 1977, as the field manager's house and "lock-up" stores.

28. Very likely one was Counsellor (1759-1796+), field worker and home wainman, named after his grandfather.

Chapter 8

1. "Inventory of Sundries on Worthy Park Estate taken this 11th May 1813," Jamaica Archives, Worthy Park Plantation Book, No. 4, 1811-1817.

2. Michael Craton and James Walvin, *A Jamaican Plantation: The History of Worthy Park, 1670-1970* (London, W. H. Allen, and Toronto, University of Toronto Press, 1970), pp. 59-64.

3. For a contemporary description, see Matthew Gregory Lewis, *A Journal of a West India Proprietor* (London, Murray, 1834 ed.), pp. 359-366.

4. For the dangers of traveling by the Rio Cobre gorge in rainy weather, see Phillip Wright, ed., *Lady Nugent's Journal* (Kingston, Institute of Jamaica, 1966), pp. 109-110, 151-152.

5. Two examples were Fergus (1762-1824+), wainman from 1789 to 1814, made watchman after he ran away in 1822, Edline, alias William Smith (1801-1846 1), who ran away once, when he was 19.

6. He was christened at Swansea Estate on May 23, 1811, along with seven other Worthy Park slaves, his fellow blacks Dennis Mahoney (aged 44), James Doubt (57), John Morris (25, later "Black Doctor"), Charlotte Topham (20), the mulatto Robert Ellis (16, son of the overseer), and the quadroons Lucy Montgomery (2) and Thomas James (an infant). Before this, only two Worthy Park christenings were recorded, both in 1809; I.R.O., St. John's Parish Register, 1759-1825, Baptisms.

7. E.g., the 8 plowmen employed in 1842 (no less than 7 of whom were old hands) were also wainmen.

8. The very first was John Cudjoe (1749-1826), a Creole, first listed in 1784, who actually combined the job of plowman with that of head sawyer.

9. This is the argument put forward as a possible cause of the phenomenon of the 1832 rebellion in Michael Craton, "Jamaican Slavery," in *Race and Slavery in the Western Hemisphere: Quantitative Studies*, edited by Stanley L. Engerman and Eugene D. Genovese (copyright (c) 1975 by The Center for Advanced Study in the Behavioral Sciences, Stanford, California), pp. 249-284. Reprinted by permission of Princeton University Press.

10. Far from exhibiting the attributes of lying, laziness, and lack of judgment which Orlando Patterson characterizes as the "Quashee personality," the Worthy Park Quashies demonstrated qualities of skill, adaptability, and leadership. Of the 7 slaves called Quashie listed in the surviving Worthy Park records, Quashie (1729-1796) was head carpenter, Guy Quashie (1734-1796+) head driver, and Juba's Quashie (c.1750-1789) head wainman. The second slave simply called Quashie (1793-1830+) was an ordinary wainsman suffering from yaws, Girl's Quashie (George Bright) born in 1808 died in 1817, and Rebecca's Quashie, born in 1811 did not survive his first year. A slave called Quashie Jaffee was listed only in 1784. That contemporary whites contemtuously labeled a certain type of Negro Quashie (a contempt that lingers in present-day Jamaica in the epithet "Quashie" or "Quashie-fool" for "ignorant peasant") may in fact have been a defensive ploy that implied that even the most confidential slaves were

barely worthy of trust. Quashie, incidentally, is the Akan day-name for children born on Sunday—the female variant is Quasheba; Orlando Patterson, *The Sociology of Slavery* . . . (London, McGibbon and Kee, 1967), pp. 174-181.

11. See the description of the Worthy Park Great House in 1731; Craton and Walvin, *A Jamaican Plantation*, pp. 55-56.

12. Two detailed consignments of carpenter's tools made in 1788 and 1789 are listed in Jamaica Archives, Worthy Park Plantation Book, No. 2, 1787-1791. This volume also provides the inventory of the carpenter's shop in 1791: "7 hand saws, 1 tenon saw, 1 dovetail saw, 1 cross-cut saw, 4 whip saws, 5 trying planes, 5 jack planes, 3 smoothing planes, 1 tooth plane, 1 flister plane, 1 rabbit plane, 12 padmoulding planes, 3 adzes, 1 cooper's adze, 8 axes, 4 hand axes, 1 broad axe, 13 socket chisels, 4 other chisels, 1 turning lathe, 10 gauges, 2 calipers, 1 compass, 1 pair of compasses, 1 bench vice, 1 screw clamp, 2 hold-fasts, 1 hand hammer, 15 augers, 1 rasp and file, 1 pair of pincers, 1 oil stone, 3 screw kegs."

13. The inventory of tools in the cooper's shop in 1791 gives some idea of the methods used: "4 adzes, 4 axes, 2 pair compasses, 2 drawing knives, 2 crows, 2 spoke shaves, 1 hand saw, 1 vice, 1 break iron, 1 bung borer, 4 jointers, 2 cold chisels, 1 bawlker, 1 punch"; Jamaica Archives, Worthy Park Plantation Book, No. 2, 1787-1791.

14. The following is a list of some of the miscellaneous work done by the blacksmith at Harmony Hill, Trelawny, in 1797: "3 large iron wedges, 8 cart bolts repaired, 2 washers and linch pins, hook and eye hinges"; Harmony Hall, Journal and Accounts 1796-1800, Jamaica Archives, Gifts and Deposits, 7/56, I.

15. There are ambivalent references to "stocks" in the Worthy Park records and many to "cattle chains" but no direct evidence that these were used to imprison or enchain the slaves. The following inventory of items in the blacksmith's shop in 1791 gives a good idea of the degree of the smith's sophistication: "1 bellows, 1 anvil, 2 working hammers, 6 small hammers, 4 screw plates, 3 small plates, 1 iron square, 1 brace, 6 soldering irons, 1 small ladle, 1 set shoeing tools, 1 drill bow, 1 vice stake, 1 set tools for making horse shoes, 3 chisels, 1 set tools for wain tyres, 1 set pins for holeing iron, 1 set nail tools, 12 pair tongs, 1 set hammers, 1 sleeve vice"; "An Inventory of Sundries . . . about the works on Worthy Park Estate," Jamaica Archives, Worthy Park Plantation Book, No. 2., 1787-1791. The Worthy Park records disclose that one exception to the rule that there was no interchange between estates was the exchange of blacksmith's tools and materials. On July 20, 1785, certain tools were returned or loaned to the Thetford blacksmith, Read Best Parson. In April and June 1786, Read Best Parson was lent two hogsheads of coal imported in the *Betsy*. On August 13, 1787, the following were received from Thetford as "Under Blacksmith's Tools": "1 hand mill, 1 bench iron, 1 vice, 1 sledge hammer, 1 pair stocks, 2 rubbers, 1 punch, 2 solder irons"; Jamaica Archives, Worthy Park Plantation Book, No. 1, 1783-1787.

16. Kitty Frances Dale was among the 6 slaves in the third group of slaves baptized at Worthy Park, on Dec. 2, 1813. Susan Frances Dale and Alexander Dale were baptized together with 13 others on Sept. 18, 1825; I.R.O., St. John's Parish Register, 1759-1825, Baptisms. A Susannah McDonald, sambo aged 8, was baptized at the same time; this may have been a daughter of John McDonald, though he was already aged 63 when she was born.

17. According to the Jamaica Archives, Register of Returns of Slaves for 1829 and 1832, Katy Dale did at least aim towards improved mobility for her children, bearing at least two mulatto children by an unknown white father; Louisa in 1829, and an unnamed child in 1832.

Chapter 9

1. Even with the most painstaking research, Edward Brathwaite was unable to find as many as a dozen actual marriages of white women and colored men in the period 1781-1813. Of 14 mixed marriages recorded altogether, in no cases was there more than a single degree of color between the partners; Edward Brathwaite, *The Development of Creole Society in Jamaica, 1770-1820* (Oxford, Clarendon Press, 1971), pp. 188-189. Sexual intercourse between white women and black men was probably even less common in Jamaica than it was in England.

2. Jamaican color classifications were much simpler than those said to be used in Latin American colonies, where 128 color variants were identified; Marvin Harris, *Patterns of Race in the Americas* (New York, Walker, 1964), pp. 54-62. The Spaniards doubtless had a special name for the offspring of a quadroon with a black, and when pressed a Jamaican would probably acknowledge such a person as a mulatto; in fact all children fathered of colored women by black men tended to be classified sambo or even black. To trace interbreeding among people of color (which of course was far commoner in the Spanish colonies than in Jamaica since the processes of miscegenation were centuries older), Jamaicans had to rely almost entirely on appearance. The suggestion by Edward Long that it might be useful to adopt at least the Spanish classification *El tente en el aire* (literally "suspended") for those who showed neither "progress" (lightening) nor "regression" (darkening) came to nothing; Edward Long, *The History of Jamaica*, 3 vols. (London, 1774), II, 261.

3. Mary Ann Ellis, along with 4 other Worthy Park slaves, was christened at Dr. Quier's Shady Grove, April 2, 1814; I.R.O. St. John's Parish Register, 1759-1825, Baptisms.

4. Jamaica Archives, Thetford Slave Book, 1798-1808, 4/23. Robert Ellis was one of the two churchwardens in St. John's Parish in 1799; *Jamaica Almanack, 1800*.

5. M. G. Lewis, *A Journal of a West India Proprietor* (London, Murray, 1834 ed.) pp. 63, 70, 77-78, 179, 203; Orlando Patterson, *The Sociology of Slavery . . .* (London, McGibbon and Kee, 1967), p. 589.

6. These were the quadroons Valentina (b. Oct. 28, 1789) and Henry (b. July 14, 1792), children of Jenny, alias Joanney (1778-1813+) a mulatto, who were manumitted on Feb. 24, 1795; Jamaica Archives, Manumissions, 21. The witness to the transaction was Robert Ellis, then Worthy Park's overseer. The young slave Harard was brought in as partial replacement for the two slaves freed.

7. I.R.O., Wills, 40/152; Michael Craton and James Walvin, *A Jamaican Plantation: The History of Worthy Park, 1670-1970* (London, W. H. Allen, and Toronto, University of Toronto Press, 1970), p. 94, n.65.

8. Manumission recorded in Worthy Park records for June 26, 1817, but not traced in Jamaica manumission records.

9. Manumissions and replacements likewise recorded in Jamaica Archives, Worthy Park Slave Book, 1821-1824, but not traced elsewhere in the Archives. William Pingilly had been employed at neighboring Thetford as early as 1798, and there were quadroon slaves born there to one Elizabeth Pingilly in 1825, 1830, and 1831; Jamaica Archives, Thetford Slave Book, 1798-1808, and 1822-1832.

Chapter 10

1. See, e.g., Bryan Edwards' description of the suppression of the 1760 rebellion, *The History, Civil and Commercial, of the British West Indies*, 2nd ed., 3 vols. (London, 1801), III, 75-80.

2. Consolidated Slave Law of 1795, clauses xxix-xxxii.

3. Ibid., clause lxi.

4. For a study of Jamaican runaways based almost entirely on an analysis of advertisements in newspapers, see P. A. Bishop, "Runaway Slaves in Jamaica, 1704-1807," unpub. M.A. thesis, University of the West Indies, Mona, Jamaica, 1970.

5. Diana is not recorded again in the Worthy Park records after her birth; she was therefore almost certainly dead before 1791.

6. For qualities of the Coromantees (Coromantines), see Bryan Edwards' admiring account, *British West Indies*, 2nd ed., III, pp. 75-85.

7. Of other degradingly named slaves, Trash (1787-1796+) and Villain (1767-1793+) were both runaways, the latter (who was also subject to fits) being "shipped off the island being a notorious runaway" on March 27, 1793. Noisome was so named at birth, since he died at the age of three months, on April 1, 1785. Trouble (1808-1824+) was an unemployed cripple.

8. Another persistent runaway who was sent to Spring Garden was Creole Cuba's Cuffee, who was listed as having run away at least 6 times in four years: May 30, 1787; June 24, 1788; in 1789; March 1, 1790; May 24 and August 27, 1791. Finally he was shipped off to Spring Garden on October 27, 1791.

9. Though the 1833 Emancipation Act provided for orphans under 6 to remain in bondage for their own protection.

10. Benjamin M'Mahon, *Jamaica Plantership* (London, 1839), pp. 59-63; Michael Craton and James Walvin, *A Jamaican Plantation: The History of Worthy Park, 1670-1970* (London, W. H. Allen, and Toronto, University of Toronto Press, 1970), pp. 201-202.

11. The others were Margery (1783-1784), Fox (1785), and James (1794-1796).

12. The 1832 Register of Returns of Slaves also records George, Will Parker, and Washington as being sentenced to the workhouse for life. These were Price's George (b. 1809), field slave sentenced in 1830, valued at £42.10.0; Jenny's Parker, alias William Hyde Parker (b. 1809), stockman sentenced July 20, 1830, valued at £40.8.4; and Washington (b. 1803), field slave who had once worked around the Great House (in 1822), called 'Incorrigible Thief and Runaway," sentenced Dec. 4, 1830, valued at £46.13.4.

13. "Compare the 1730 Bermudian" Act for Extirpating all free Negroes, Indians, Mulattoes Such as have been Slaves (and freed or to be freed) so as they do not remain in these islands; Bermuda Archives, Hamilton.

14. For slave conditions in Cuba related to sugar production, see Eric Williams, *From Columbus to Castro: The History of the Caribbean, 1492-1969* (London, Deutsch, 1970), pp. 278-279, 310-312, 361-372.

Chapter 11
1. E.g., William Beckford, *A Descriptive Account of the Island of Jamaica*, 2 vols. (London, 1789), II, 14-17, 376-380; J. B. Moreton, *Manners and Customs of the West India Islands* (London, 1790), pp. 79-80; Thomas Roughley, *The Jamaica Planter's*

Guide (London, 1823), pp. 39-74; J. Stewart, *An Account of Jamaica and its Inhabitants* (London, 1808), pp. 190-195.

2. I.e., "What white man never did well?" Izatt Anderson and Frank Cundall, eds., *Jamaica Proverbs and Sayings*, 2nd ed. (Kingston, 1927), pp. 20, 83. "Bockra," like "backra" or "buckra," is Creole for white man.

3. In 1807 Robert Renny recorded a chilling introduction to Jamaica chanted by four black female fruit sellers riding in a canoe in Kingston Harbour on spying a newly arrived white man: "New-come buckra,/ He get sick,/ He tak fever,/ He die,/ He die . . ."; Robert Renny, *A History of Jamaica* (London, 1807), p. 138.

4. I.e., "If an overseer drinks at all, he can expect his underling bookkeepers to drink to excess"; "An owner expecting success should not employ a stingy [meanly avaricious] overseer"; Anderson and Cundall, *Proverbs*, nos. 164a, 1022, pp. 25, 91.

5. Thomas Roughley, *Planter's Guide*, pp. 49-50.

6. Jamaica Archives, Worthy Park Plantation Book Nos. 1-3, 1783-1811.

7. May 23, 1811, at Worthy Park; I.R.O., St. John's Parish Register, 1759-1825, Baptisms.

8. The Thetford "slave books" in the Worthy Park papers in the Jamaica Archives cover only the periods 1798-1807 and 1822-1832.

9. Aug. 21, 1805; I.R.O., St. John's Parish Register, 1759-1825, Baptisms. It was probably this Maryanne Ellis rather than Kitty (Mary Ann Ellis) who was the "Marianne" Ellis remembered with a £25 bequest in the 1821 will of Dr. John Quier as one "whom I have looked upon as adopted daughter"—even though Kitty had been christened at Shady Grove in 1814; I.R.O., Wills, 103/7. Eugene Mahoney (who died in 1813) was Worthy Park overseer (and attorney) at least in 1811-1812.

10. I.R.O., Wills, 122, 2/167, dated Aug. 1, 1843.

11. Pt. One, Chap. 4 above.

12. For this and other details of eighteenth-century medicine, see Douglas Guthrie, *A History of Medicine*, rev. ed. (London, Nelson, 1958), pp. 216-231.

13. J. Quier, J. Hume et al., *Letters and Essays on the Smallpox . . .* (London, Murray, 1778), p. xxvii; Craton and Walvin, *A Jamaican Plantation: The History of Worthy Park, 1670-1970* (London, W. H. Allen, and Toronto, University of Toronto Press, 1970), pp. 1-5.

14. Thomas Dancer, *The Medical Assistant: or Jamaica practice of physic . . .* (Kingston, Jamaica, Aikman, 1801), p. 153; Heinze Goerke, "The Life and Scientific Works of Dr. John Quier, Practitioner of Physic and Surgery, Jamaica, 1738-1822," *West India Medical Journal*, vol. 5, pp. 22-27.

15. *Jamaica Almanacks*, 1781-1782.

16. Quier et al., *Letters and Essays*, p. 13; *Journal of the Assembly of Jamaica*, Nov. 12, 1788, VIII, 434; Edward Brathwaite, *The Development of Creole Society in Jamaica, 1770-1820* (Oxford, Clarendon Press, 1971), p. 185; Appendix C below.

17. See particularly, Gilberto Freyre, *The Masters and the Slaves* (1946) (New York, Knopf, Borzoi ed., 1956), pp. 255-357.

18. I.R.O., St. John's Parish Register, 1759-1825, Burials, 1822.

19. I.R.O., Wills, 103/7.

20. This is presumed from the fact that Thomas Smith was later listed as Catherine Ann Smith's guardian; *Jamaica Almanacks*, 1824-1826; Jamaica Archives, Register of Returns of Slaves, 1826.

21. A mulatto boy named Joseph, son of the Negro slave Dolly, was manumitted by John Price of Penzance through his attorney, Malcolm Laing, on the payment of £ 65 by John Quier in 1778; Jamaica Archives, Manumissions, 12/218.

22. Ann's age and mother's name are determined by the entry for her baptism on May 2, 1784, as a quadroon aged 8 months; I.R.O., St. John's Parish Register, 1759-1825, Baptisms.

23. The number of Dr. Quier's slaves recorded in the *Jamaica Almanacks* actually fluctuated from 63 to 73. The Givings-In for the March quarter of 1823 given in the *Almanack* for 1824 listed the following, as well as 73 for "Quier, John (deceased)": Quier, Ann (estate, executor, J. P. Nash), 20; Quier, Catherine A., 44; Smith, Catherine A., 24; Davis, John Q., 7; Davis, Peter Q., 10. Jamaica Archives, Register of Returns of Slaves, 1824 (generally more accurate than Givings-In), gave the following totals, respectively: 22, 43, 24, 7, and 0.

24. John Quier Davis and Peter Quier Davis could well have been sons of Nathaniel William Davis, white bookkeeper employed at Worthy Park in the late 1780s and early 1790s.

25. "William Turner and Catherine Quier, both of colour, of this parish"; I.R.O., St. John's Parish Register, 1759-1825, Marriages.

26. Jamaica Archives, Register of Returns of Slaves, 1826, 1832. Neither Thomas nor Catherine Ann Smith was listed as a slaveowner in the 1820 registration.

27. Craton and Walvin, *A Jamaican Plantation*, pp. 26-94, 155-165. The genealogical information on the early Prices in Burke and Debrett is inaccurate, though not quite so fictional as that in Burke's *Extinct Baronetage*.

28. Craton and Walvin, *A Jamaican Plantation*, pp. 164-165, 180-181.

29. Hans Sloane, *A Voyage to the Islands Madera, Barbados, Nieves, S. Christophers, and Jamaica with the Natural History of the last of those Islands*, 2 vols. (London, 1707, 1725).

30. "Inquiry into the Slave Trade and the State of the Sugar Colonies," *B.S.P., Commons, Accounts and Papers, 1789.*

31. *Remarks on the situation of the Negroes in Jamaica* (London, 1788); *A Descriptive Account of Jamaica.*

32. M. G. Lewis, *A Journal of a West India Proprietor* (London, Murray, 1834 ed.).

33. Ibid., p. 58.

34. Ibid., p. 62.

35. In 1792 the lieutenant-governor of Jamaica was Major-General Adam Williamson.

36. John Quier et al., *Letters and Essays*, p. xxvii.

37. M. G. Lewis, *Journal of a West India Proprietor*, p. 62.

38. "Mary Wiggins and an old Cotton-tree are the most picturesque objects that I have seen for these twenty years."; ibid., p. 70. Lewis called Mary Wiggins a mulatto, but from his description she was probably an octoroon or mestee. Psyche, the heroine of a novel by H. de Lisser, was considerably darker; ibid., pp. 63, 77-78, 202.

39. See Prologue above; Craton and Walvin, *A Jamaican Plantation*, pp. 169-174.

40. Monk Lewis, e.g., became unpopular with his neighboring planters and the more tyrannical of his own white staff by listening to slave complaints from nearby estates; *Journal of a West India Proprietor*, pp. 140-145.

41. *Pledges on Colonial Slavery, to Candidates for Seats in Parliament, Rightly Considered* (Penzance, Vigurs, 1832).

42. The Negro, wrote Rose Price in his *Pledges*, "is destined by Providence in a state of slavery, *of some sort or other*, till the curse of Adam is removed from the face of the earth, and from the brow of man in God's appointed time. The freedom of black men is attended by difficulties (by the laws of nations and of God himself) *which never impeded the freedom of white men*. Nature presents every reason for the white men's freedom as a *fellow labourer on earth*; and every reason for the black men's bondage, as such, *to cause the earth to produce its abundance*." P. 32.

43. Jamaica Archives, Manumissions 18/25, entered March 12, 1789. It is interesting to speculate whether the mulatto slave Nelly—clearly the daughter of a white man and a black woman—in choosing the surname Price was indicating that she was actually daughter, as well as property, of one of the Prices. Similarly, it is conceivable that Eleanor Price was at least half-sister of the mulatto Susannah Price who became mistress of Dr. John Quier. If true, this would provide a genetic link to explain the closeness of Prices, Quiers, and Douglases. There was also a Catherine Price, mulatto aged 34, christened at Swansea on Nov. 25, 1809; I.R.O., St. John's Parish Register, 1759-1825, Baptisms.

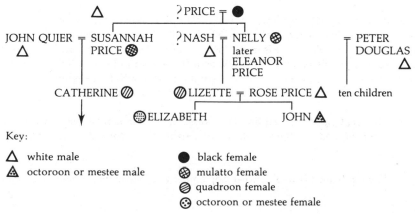

Key:

△ white male

▲ octoroon or mestee male

● black female

⊗ mulatto female

⊘ quadroon female

⊙ octoroon or mestee female

I.R.O., Wills 100/57, entered December 20, 1821. The 10 children were to share all movable property and to hold Point Hill Plantation as "tenants in common" until it was convenient to sell or dispose of it. To Eleanor Price were given specific bequests and £ 20 Currency per year. Lizette Nash received £70 Currency. The executors, guardians, and trustees were John Douglas of Kingston, William Douglas of St. George's, James Grant and John Quier of St. John's. In fact, Peter Douglas' slaves seem to have been apportioned before he died. In the 1817 return he is not credited with any, but Eleanor Douglas Price is listed as having 7; John Quier Douglas, 13; Robert Ross Douglas, 18; Edmund Jordon Douglas, 19; Sholto Douglas, 15; Catherine Douglas, 15; Eliza Douglas, 14; Louisa Douglas, 13; Mary Douglas, 14; and Lizette Price Nash, 4; Jamaica Archives, Register of Returns of Slaves, 1817-1838, vol. 19, pp. 203-207. By 1823 this total of 132 had fallen to 94, with Sholto Douglas, Louisa Douglas, and Mary Douglas no longer listed. Of the huge Douglas household the following were baptized together at Point Hill on June 20, 1796: Eleanor Price, Elizabeth Price, Catherine Douglas, Elizabeth Douglas, John Quier Douglas, Sholto Douglas, Archibald Douglas, Robert Douglas, Louisa Douglas. Edmund Jordan Douglas and Charlotte Simpson Douglas were baptized on March 31, 1799. Elizabeth Price Nash was not baptized until April 2, 1814, at Dr. Quier's Shady Grove, at the age of 19. An Eliza Douglas, "free child," was baptized at Point Hill on July 8, 1816; I.R.O., St. John's Parish Register, 1759-1825, Baptisms.

44. Jamaica Archives, Manumissions 21/March 1, 1794.

45. I.R.O., Wills, 130/64, entered October 26, 1865. After debts were paid, everything was left to John Price Nash who, with George N. Howell, was also executor.

46. Craton and Walvin, *A Jamaican Plantation*, pp. 183-186. At Trengwainton (an estate of 775 acres) Rose Price maintained his own pack of hounds, coach with bewigged postilions, brewery, and the first icehouse seen in the district. Legend has it that he was created baronet for refusing, as sheriff, facilities for Catholics publicly to debate their enfranchisement.

47. British Museum, Boase Papers, Add. MSS. 29281 ff. 133, 207, 218, 226; Craton and Walvin, *A Jamaican Plantation*, pp. 183-185, 204.

Part Three Chapter 12
1. This was the topic of the Seventh Caribbean Historians' Conference held at Mona, Jamaica, in April 1975, at which a version of this chapter was given as a paper; *Transactions of the Seventh Caribbean Historians' Conference* (Kingston, 1976).

2. P.R.O., London, C.O. 137/330, cited in Douglas G. Hall, *Free Jamaica, 1838-1865* (New Haven, Yale University Press, 1959), p. 82.

3. Figures for 1848 calculated by D. G. Hall, ibid. Noel Deerr, *History of Sugar*, 2 vols. (London, Chapman & Hall, 1949-50), I, 174-177 says that there were 513 sugar estates in 1848. The 1854 figure is from P.R.O., C.O. 137/330. The 9 St. John's estates in 1848 were probably Worthy Park, Swansea (these two in Lluidas Vale), Lloyd's & Aylmer's, Cedar Mount, Lemon Hall, Watermount, Spring Vale, Belmont, and Mountain River, of which at least 3 were moribund, and defunct by 1854.

4. Michael Craton, "Jamaican Slave Mortality: Fresh Light from Worthy Park, Longville and the Tharp Estates," *Journal of Caribbean History*, 3 (November 1971), 1-27.

5. Thus the cane planted between September and November would be ready be-

tween January and March, 15 months after planting, while ratoons would be cut annually between April and June.

6. This applied at least until the later 1950s. As late as 1968, the number employed at Worthy Park varied from 236 in the first week in the year, to 848 at the peak of the crop in June, though the average throughout the year was 569; Craton and Walvin, *A Jamaican Plantation: The History of Worthy Park, 1670-1970* (London, W. H. Allen, and Toronto, University of Toronto Press, 1970), pp. 310-313.

7. Not excluding the authors of *A Jamaican Plantation*, pp. 97, 105.

8. It is likely that domestics were paid directly by the overseer and bookkeepers. The separation is retained even today. Indeed, the modern treatment of domestics on plantations, a mixture of noblesse oblige and paternalism, coupled with resigned complaints of ingratitude, sloth, and dishonesty, provides one of the most obvious links with the past.

9. However carefully chosen, the sample of only seven weeks in any one year must give a partial view of a free wage labor force. Statistical calculations, though, make it seem likely that the 338 workers identified were at least 85% of all those employed during the whole of 1842. Similarly, a high proportion of those survivors of the slave and Apprentice years who worked for any length of time between 1842 and 1846 were traced, though in this case there was a considerable disparity between the number of men and the number of women positively identified, for reasons given below.

10. Revenue was determined simply by multiplying production by prices received, productivity by dividing production by the number of workers employed.

11. The jobbers' £10 charge was based entirely on depreciation, clothing costs, and profit. With a low actual depreciation, profits were very high, though death rates of 20% per year in jobbing gangs were not unknown. Actual decrease on slave estates was something like 2%, which indicates a depreciation in usefulness of less than 5%. Thus a depreciation of £3-5 a year (3-5% of £50-100) was added to a maintenance cost of £5-7.

12. To be precise, 22s. 7½d.; Sir Charles Grey to Colonial Office, Feb. 17, 1848, P.R.O., C.O. 137/295, cited in Hall, *Free Jamaica*, pp. 85-87.

13. That is, certainly 63 out of a total depleted by death and old age to 72, with perhaps another 5 still working under a new name.

14. As many as 49 of the females who had authentic single Christian names as slaves had completely different Christian names once they acquired two names. Six were known in the records by two surnames, presumably their married and maiden names, though in three cases both names were changed: Jane Gaynor (later Christian Hanson), Jane Pingilly (King), Bessy Ann Price (Davis), Molly Price (Mary Davis), Matilda Sewell (Diane Marshall), Elizabeth Thompson (Hanson). Three apparent survivors who seem too old or invalid to be genuine, whose names may have been assumed by others, were Kitty Banks, Nancy Dale, and Eleanor Thompson. Another possible source of confusion may be the frequency of the names Elizabeth, Ann, Mary, Margaret, and their diminutives. In addition, up to 6 old female hands may be unrecorded, since domestics were listed in 1838, but not in 1842-1846.

15. It is rather remarkable that none of the male old hands at Worthy Park employed in the 1840s had been born in Africa and, for certain, only two of the women.

One, Amelia (or Milly Ann) Byfield, formerly Rosamond, was still employed in February 1846, probably the last African to work at Worthy Park.

16. The crude death rate in Jamaica in the last years of slavery was probably no more than 30 per thousand, but the crude birthrate on sugar plantations was little if any more than 20 per thousand. By 1860, however, the Jamaican crude birthrate, by the calculations of G. W. Roberts, was as high as 40 per thousand; G. W. Roberts, *The Population of Jamaica* (Cambridge, Cambridge University Press, 1957), p. 43.

17. In 1891, 639,491; 1911, 831,383; 1921, 858,118; 1943, 1,237,063; 1960, 1,606,546.

18. George Price, *Jamaica and the Colonial Office* (London, 1855), p. 5. *A Jamaican Plantation*, p. 218, stated that there were only two immigrants at Worthy Park. This was an error resulting from incomplete research in the wage records. Nearly all the white immigrants, some 1,300, came to Jamaica in 1841.

19. *B.S.P., Reports (1848)*, XXIX, March 1, 1848, responses, nos. 4963-4964.

20. Pt. One, Chap. 5 above.

21. For the attitude of Frederick Lister Clarke (1883-1932) in this respect, see *A Jamaican Plantation*, pp. 265-268.

22. *B.S.P, Reports (1832)*, "Report of Select Committee on Slavery"; Session of June 6, 1832, XLVI.

Chapter 13

1. The personnel records kept since 1963 by Worthy Park Farms and Worthy Park Factory differ in minor but significant respects. Although a similar individual file card was used by both operations, different entry and filing methods were used. The cards for Farms employees invariably provided entries under "Name," "Age," "Address," "Education or Qualifications," and "Date First Employed," and frequently included comments on sickness, injury, absenteeism, or other complaints, under "General Remarks." Besides this, all those employed by Worthy Park Farms since 1963 were filed together with those who had since ceased employment, whereas Worthy Park Factory workers employed in the current year were filed separately from those employed since 1963 not currently working. Since personnel cards were kept quite distinct from wage records, and the latter were not open for inspection, it was, unfortunately, not possible to analyze either the continuity of labor in any one year or wage patterns on an individual basis for either operation. The patchy manner in which entries were made for "Trade Union Affiliation" also made it impossible accurately to measure the relative strength of each union. The casualness of the estate's bookkeeping in this respect, however, suggested that no trade union was really strong at Worthy Park, supporting the contention that all three trade unions were fatally weakened by their close relationships to different political parties, by competition with each other, and by the sugar estate's recognition of these facts.

2. For a fuller discussion of this problem, see Michael Craton, "Searching for the Invisible Man; Some of the Problems of Writing on Slave Society in the British West Indies," *Historical Reflections/Réflexions Historiques*, 1 (September 1974).

3. Pt. One, Chap. 2 above.

4. The most common were Gordon, 44; Brown, 33; Williams, 31; and Douglas, 31. There were still 14 Prices.

Chapter 14
1. Michael Craton, *Sinews of Empire: A Short History of British Slavery* (New York, Doubleday, and London, Temple Smith, 1974), p. 158.

2. See also *Who Was Who, 1897-1916* (London, A. & C. Black, 1920), under "Sir Rose Lambart Price, 3rd. Bt." and "Captain Henry Talbot Price"; Major Sir Rose Lambart Price, Bt., F.R.G.S., *The Two Americas* (London, Sampson Low, 1877); and *A Summer in the Rockies* (London, Sampson Low, 1898).

3. First published in 1865, and since reprinted many times. An extremely adverse, and often inaccurate, account of John Price was given in John Vincent Barry, *The Life and Death of John Price; A Study in the Exercise of Naked Power* (Melbourne, Melbourne University Press, 1964). That Marcus Clarke had John Price in mind when creating Maurice Frere is, however, fairly clear. Barry's book included fascinating extracts from the unpublished biographical sketch of Price entitled "The Demon," written by Henry Beresford Garrett, a convicted bushranger, in the 1880s, from personal acquaintance both in Tasmania and Norfolk Island.

4. Craton and Walvin, *A Jamaican Plantation: The History of Worthy Park, 1670-1970* (London, W. H. Allen, and Toronto, University of Toronto Press, 1970), pp. 260-261.

5. George Price, *Jamaica and the Colonial Office* (London, 1869), pp. 2-6.

6. Sydney Olivier, *The Myth of Governor Eyre* (London, Hogarth, 1933), pp. 128-130.

7. Craton and Walvin, *A Jamaican Plantation*, pp. 265-268.

8. Edith Clarke, *My Mother Who Fathered Me* (London, Allen & Unwin, 1957).

9. Described from memory by George Weenink from a picture seen in the home of a Scottish descendant in 1936, but not traced since.

10. Alexander Lochore's papers are preserved in the Archives of Glasgow University, P/Cn. 41, but unfortunately the only trace of Elizabeth Lochore's background is the death duty receipt for the bequest of £325 made by Sir Rose Price to his illegitimate daughter in 1834.

11. Ibid. The death duties were levied under the Act of 55 Geo. III, c.184 (1815). Elizabeth Lochore's bequest paid the maximum duty of 10% because she was listed as "Stranger" (i.e., "any Person in any other Degree of Collateral Consanguinity, or to Strangers in Blood to the Deceased"). For acknowledged children the rate was only 1%; if the donor had died before April 5, 1805, nothing.

12. George Weenink to Michael Craton, July 21, 1972.

Chapter 15
1. This "three-generation rule" may in fact be general for all societies in which genealogy is not formally studied.

2. Edward Long, *History of Jamaica*, 3 vols. (London, 1774), II, 261. The legal use of the word "mulatto" as a synonym for "colored" was rather confusing, since mulatto was also in common usage precisely to define the half-breed offspring of a white and a black.

3. For the development of the Jamaican Free Coloreds, see Mavis C. Campbell, *The Dynamics of Change in a Slave Society: A Sociopolitical History of the Free Coloreds of Jamaica, 1800-1865* (Rutherford, N.J., Fairleigh Dickinson University Press, 1976); Sheila Duncker, "The Free Coloured and their Fight for Civil Rights in Jamaica, 1800-1830," unpub. M.A. thesis, University of London; Douglas Hall, "Jamaica" in David W. Cohen and Jack P. Greene, eds., *Neither Slave nor Free: The Freedom of African Descent in the Slave Societies of the New World* (Baltimore, The Johns Hopkins University Press, 1972), pp. 193-213.

4. Jamaica Archives, Register of Returns of Slaves, 1817-1832; *Jamaica Almanacks* for 1816-1838.

5. *Jamaica Almanacks* for 1826-1837. The name Overton, when first seen in John Price Nash's handwriting, was confused with Ewarton. It is possible to guess that John Price Nash spent his years of apprenticeship in Britain at Overton-on-Dee, near Wrexham, where there were indeed mines and mills.

6. Institute of Jamaica, Map, St. Catherine, 827, dated July 15, 1858. On this map, only the southern portion of Point Hill Plantation, bordered by the Lluidas Vale-Guanaboa Vale road was listed as belonging to the "Heirs of J. P. Nash."

7. Library of Congress, Worthy Park Plantation Book, 1791-1811.

8. This was clear from the 1858 map, which related to a dispute between John Price Nash, "the representative of Point Hill," and a neighbor, James Robinson, who claimed that Nash had cut down "certain Santa Maria trees" on his side of the boundary line. The map, drawn up to establish lines more precisely, was produced by the famous surveyor, Thomas Harrison, "for the information of J. P. Nash Esquire."

9. The "old Lady" referred to here was Eleanor Price Douglas, the relict of Peter Douglas, who had borne Lizette Nash, and then John Quier, Robert Ross, Edmund Jordan, Sholto, Catherine, Eliza, Louisa, Mary, Archibald, and Charlotte Simpson to Peter Douglas. By 1840, Charlotte, Archibald, Sholto, Louisa, Mary, and Robert were certainly dead, leaving Lizette and three among John, Edmund, Catherine, and Eliza Douglas still living, probably in Spanish Town or Kingston.

10. Copy of letter provided by George Weenink, of Westland, New Zealand.

11. This age is something of a puzzle. If John Price Nash was indeed 55 in 1848, he had been born in 1793, and thus in slavery, since his mother, Lizette Nash, was not manumitted until March 1794. In fact, according to the Worthy Park slave records, Lizette was born in 1782 and could hardly have borne a child at the age of 11 years. Besides, no manumission record exists for John Price Nash, either with his mother in 1794 or at any time; so it seems certain that he was born after his mother's manumission and also after his sister's birth on January 1, 1795—though before the end of 1796, since Rose Price left Jamaica in 1795. In sum, he seems to have been 52 not 55 in 1848. But why should a job applicant in his 50s exaggerate his age?

12. John Price Nash to Robert Russell, colonial secretary of Jamaica, dated Spanish Town, December 13, 1847, P.R.O, London, C.O. 137/297.

13. *Jamaica Almanacks* for 1833-1870.

14. Ibid., 1869.

15. Institute of Jamaica, Map, St. Catherine, 827.

16. I.R.O., Birth Registrations, St. John's, 1/305 (William Hutcheson Nash, born 1829); 1/373 (Lizette Forbes Nash and Joannah Forbes Nash, 1830, 1832); 9/305 (Thomasina A. M. Nash and John P. Nash II, 1859, 1860); 14/176 (Mary J. Nash, Versella L. S. Nash, Catherine E. Nash, 1861-1863?); *Jamaican Law VI of 1871*, 1/179 (Adela W. Nash, Lizette E. P. Nash, 1863, 1865); 3/352 (Caroline R. Nash, 1873).

17. The interview, held in March 1973, was conducted by the author, with help from Garry Greenland and Sharon Chacko. The session was completely informal. Each of the three interviewers wrote their own notes independently immediately afterwards, and these were collated for the present account.

18. Only in such one-sided liaisons as were usual in slavery, with "pure" whites on one side, were children anything like uniform in color—being no darker than the darker partner. Similarly, in a pairing with one pure black partner, the offspring would be bound to be darker than the lighter partner. The pairing of two colored persons, of course, made mockery of the attempt to classify persons strictly by color, since offspring could theoretically vary in one family between the shades of the darkest and lightest ancestors. This variation occurred in the Nash family at least in the 1860s, since in their birth registrations two of William Hutcheson Nash's last three children were listed as "Coloured," and one as "Brown"—as well as being labeled "Legitimate." These categories, however, were only required by the Act of 1871, and the shade categories of the earlier children, and of W. H. Nash and his two sisters, cannot be known through this source.

19. Derek Walcott, "Laventville," *The Castaway, and Other Poems* (London, Jonathan Cape Ltd., 1969), p. 35. These lines are reprinted with the permission of Jonathan Cape and of Farrar, Straus & Giroux, Inc., from *The Gulf* by Derek Walcott, Copyright © 1963, 1964, 1965, 1969, 1970 by Derek Walcott.

Chapter 16

1. Except for Isaac Brown and his immediate family, initials are used for surnames from here on, in the interests of anonymity.

2. Iris Walker was almost certainly descended from the mulatto slave Susanna Cummings and the white bookkeeper-overseer William Pingilly whose relations were described in the biographical section of Part Two, and thus, through Susanna, from the black slave Clementina, born at Worthy Park in 1759. Iris' maternal grandmother was one Elizabeth Pengelly, or Pingilly (c.1850-1929), who was almost certainly a grandchild of Susanna and William—though the direct link is missing.

3. The land was actually purchased from James and Emelia Anderson, who were probably the original purchasers from the Quier estate. Witness to the 1847 deed was one Charles Davis, who was very probably a grandson of Catherine Quier, and son of either John Quier Davis or Peter Quier Davis. Isaac Brown well remembered John Davis (c.1840-1925), a "brown man with straight hair," who was a son of Charles Davis, and owned a shop, now defunct, situated at the point where the old road to Shady Grove and Barn's Pen joined the main road through Lluidas Vale Village.

4. There was in fact a real person called James Brown, a legendary figure who

fathered innumerable "outside" children. It is just possible that James Haslam renamed himself Brown some time later in life, but a calculation based on the age of James Brown's known children, one of whom was born in 1889, makes it seem more likely that James Brown was actually the brother of the first Isaac Brown, rather than his father, and that Isaac "Dozer" Brown was confused by the facts that his great-grandmother's surname was Brown and his great-grandfather's first name James.

5. The actual sequence of discovery was: (1) failure to find a slave called Caroline Dawkins; (2) a guess, based on the 1847 deed, that Robert and Caroline were husband and wife; (3) the discovery of a Caroline Price, alias Biddy, daughter of Baddy, of the right birthdate; (4) corroboration, not directly through the marriage record, which was missing, but through the Index of Marriages for St. John's, which showed that the entries for Robert Dawkins and Caroline Price were not only at the same date (1839) but on the selfsame page.

6. That is, with everyone giving their time in the evenings and at weekends, on the understanding that the help will be reciprocated later, with the only direct reward being the traditional "wetting the roof" and party on completion. This is still the most common method of house-building in rural Jamaica, just as cooperation of this kind is much more common, and more taken for granted, than in "developed" countries. A system called "Partner" is also the most common method of saving in rural Jamaica. By this, a sum (often a substantial proportion of an individual's total income) is contributed to a pool by every participant every week, with each individual drawing the weekly total in rotation—the interval determined by the number of partners involved.

7. Bustamante did begin his labor agitation in 1938, but at Frome in Westmorland. Isaac Brown was probably referring to some disturbances that occurred at Worthy Park in 1944; Craton and Walvin, *A Jamaican Plantation: The History of Worthy Park, 1670-1970* (London, W.H. Allen, and Toronto, University of Toronto Press, 1970), pp. 303-307.

Chapter 17
1. Driver, stand by my side, but let me talk to my overseer; When the overseer is gone, it is me and you there; How do, overseer, thankyou Master.

2. Interviews by Barnet started in 1963 were first published as *Biografiá de un Cimarrón* (Havana, 1966); translated as *The Autobiography of a Runaway Slave* (London, Bodley Head, 1968). In 1968, Andrew Salkey obtained an equally remarkable interview with Esteban Montejo, then allegedly aged 108, published in *Havana Journal* (London, Penguin, 1969), pp. 166-185.

3. George P. Rawick, *Sundown to Sunup: The Making of the Black Community; The American Slave: A Composite Autobiography* (Westport, Conn., Greenwood Press, 1972-1974). Eugene D. Genovese, *Roll, Jordan, Roll: The World the Slaves Made* (New York, Pantheon, 1974), pp. 676-678.

4. *Oral Traditon: A Study in Historical Methodology* (London, Penguin, 1973), p. 192. This book was first published as *De la Tradition Orale: Essai de Méthode Historique* in the Annales du Musée Royal de l'Afrique Centrale, 1961, and first published in English by Routledge & Kegan Paul, 1965.

5. The term "backra" is almost certainly from the West African *mbakara*, "he who surrounds, or governs"; Frederic G. Cassidy, *Jamaica Talk: Three Hundred Years of the English Language in Jamaica*, 2nd ed. (London, Macmillan for the Institute of Jamaica, 1971), pp. 155-156.

6. The origin of the name Lluidas is certainly obscure. It first appeared around 1670 as "Luidas," without the Welsh-sounding double letter "l." There is a faint chance that it may be Spanish, though a corruption of "Lloyd's" seems more plausible.

7. St. Ann's Bay was the site of the first Jamaican "capital," Sevilla la Nueva (1510-1524), but it was not used as a port for Lluidas Vale sugar until the early twentieth century.

8. There was no such coin. A "quattie" was "three cents," or 1½d., that is, a *quarter* of 6d., a common silver coin of the British period; Martha Beckwith, *Black Roadways: A Study of Jamaican Folk Life* (Chapel Hill, University of North Carolina Press, 1929), p. 49.

9. Ths clearly applies to "Full Freedom" on August 1, 1838, since Victoria did not become queen until 1837. The first Emancipation Act came into effect on August 1, 1834, in the reign of William IV.

10. It is not. Africanisms—vocabulary and constructions—comprise the second largest component of Jamaican Creole, but amount to less than 10%; Cassidy, *Jamaica Talk*, pp. 394-397.

11. This, of course, was a fact, following the Act of 1787.

12. At the time of emancipation, Thetford belonged technically to the Trustees of Greenwich Hospital in London, but being long decayed it was heavily squatted on by the freed slaves. It reverted to the Crown for the persistent nonpayment of quit rents under the Jamaican Land Law of 1867, from which time it was surveyed and attempts made to evict squatters in order to establish clear title to the property. It was purchased from the Jamaican government by the Talbots in 1881, for £1,300, after which further evictions were made. John Scarlett was the Talbots' overseer. The Clarkes bought Thetford, along with the rest of Worthy Park, in 1918, though apparently the last Thetford evictions had occurred during the regime of their predecessors, the Calders (1899-1918); Craton and Walvin, *A Jamaican Plantation: The History of Worthy Park, 1670-1970* (London, W. H. Allen, and Toronto, University of Toronto Press, 1970), pp. 234-258.

13. Many countryfolk recall that "Charles Price rats" were once smoked and eaten, being "about as large as a new-born piglet." This may refer to the agouti, still found in remote parts of Lluidas Vale in 1973. Some commentators have speculated that Sir Charles Price introduced the cane-piece rat, *mus sacchivorus*, into Jamaica; others, that the Charles Price rat is the mongoose, introduced into Jamaica long after the time of Sir Charles Price; Craton and Walvin, *A Jamaican Plantation*, p. 93.

14. Ibid., pp. 86-89.

15. The whole question of local variation in dialect usage, and the ways in which even excellent books like Cassidy's *Jamaica Talk* can be normative, needs further study. For example, two Lluidas Vale informants testified to the uses of *Bunga-men* for Africans (adj. *bungu*) without any of the disparaging connotations ascribed by Cassidy to this—as to almost all generic African labels, including the common modern usage "quashie-fool" for "ignorant peasant"; Cassidy, *Jamaica Talk*, pp. 157-159.

16. Emanuel B.'s idiosyncratic variants also included "sayboll" for "sinkhole," and "Mamming Brook" for "Murmuring Brook." He also retailed a nonsense jingle that he alleged was African, simply because he did not understand its English: Talala Hey/Talala Hey/Talala Hey-la/Sy-mon Petre ha wan harss fe charm dem! (Simon Peter has a horse to charm them with.)

17. Stanley M. Elkins, *Slavery: A Problem in American Institutional and Intellectual Life* (Chicago, University of Chicago Press, 1959), p. 100.

18. London, P.R.O., C.O. 441/4/4.

19. *Jamaica Journal* (Summer 1974).

20. Compare the account given by Hans Sloane, quoted in Pt. One, Chap. 1 above.

21. Emanuel B. "recalled" that the plantation whites kept an armory of guns in "the courthouse" at Spanish Town, and carried out sweeps against the little brown men, with the help of dogs. This seems to be a fascinating amalgam of several factual elements: the use of the militia against the Maroons in the eighteenth century; the sporadic fighting against the mestizos left by the Spanish, which was over by 1660; and even the conflict between the Spanish settlers and the indigenous Arawaks, which was probably over by 1550.

22. During the research period in Lluidas Vale in 1973, a Set Up occurred in the Thetford section of Lluidas Vale Village, conforming closely to the accounts given in Martha Beckwith, *Black Roadways*, pp. 70-87, and Edith Clarke, *My Mother Who Fathered Me* (London, Allen & Unwin, 1957), pp. 217-227.

23. Oh me good friend, Mr. Wilberforce, make we free!
God Almighty thank ye! God Almighty thank ye!
God Almighty, make we free!
Buckra in this country no make we free!
What negro for to do? What negro for to do?
Take force by force! Take force by force!
　　Matthew Gregory Lewis, *A Journal of a West India Proprietor* (London, John Murray, 1834 ed.), p. 228.

24. Martha Beckwith, *Jamaica Proverbs* (New York, 1925, reprinted by Negro Universities Press, 1970), no. 865. This editor, however, provided a very dubious explanation, for some reason equating "neger" with "obeah-man."

25. Frank Cundall, *Jamaica Negro Proverbs and Sayings* (Kingston, 1910), reprinted as *Jamaica Proverbs* (Irish University Press, 1972), no. 350.

26. Cassidy, *Jamaica Talk*, pp. 157-159.

27. As late as 1929, Martha Beckwith tended towards a description of "Obeah" that was little different from that found in eighteenth-century plantocratic writers; *Black Roadways*, pp. 104-141. Orlando Patterson, in *Sociology of Slavery: An Analysis of the Origins, Development and Structure of Negro Slave Society in Jamaica* (London, McGibbon and Kee, 1967), pp. 185-189, mainly follows Beckwith, attributing the spiritual elements in Jamaican Negro religion to "Myalism," which is clearly of Christian derivation. In comparison, see Edward Brathwaite, *The Development of Creole Society in Jamaica, 1770-1820* (Oxford, Clarendon Press, 1971), pp. 218-220: "In African and Caribbean folk practice, where religion had not been externalized and institutionalized as in Europe, the obeah-man was doctor, philosopher, and priest."

28. B. K. Malinowski, *Magic, Science and Religion, and Other Essays* (New York, Doubleday, 1954).

29. Peter J. Wilson, *Crab Antics* (New Haven, Yale University Press, 1973).

30. The attitude is perhaps encapsulated in the quotation given by Lilian A., aged 76: "To reap Eternity we must labor full time for the Lord"—applying it as much to the earthly master as to God. The same ambivalence is detectable in the very word "Massa" —used either for the plantation boss or the Creator. For a rather limited view of the quashee personality, see Orlando Patterson, *Sociology of Slavery*, pp. 174-181, 285. This shows many similarities to the description of the American "Sambo" in Stanley M. Elkins, *Slavery*, pp. 131-132, 192, 227-228. Patterson's quashie concept is viewed critically in both Michael Craton, *Sinews of Empire, A Short History of British Slavery* (New York, Doubleday, and London, Temple Smith, 1974), p. 236, and "Searching for the Invisible Man: Some of the Problems of Writing on Slave Society in the British West Indies," *Historical Reflections/Réflexions Historiques* (September 1974). In particular, it is pointed out that the true quashie (who carried the Akan day-name for those born on Sundays or possessing certain special qualities) were usually favored, able, well assimilated slaves—more akin to the traditional American Uncle Toms.

31. Contrast the public statues in Port-au-Prince, Haiti; heroes of the revolution against slavery and imperialism such as Toussaint and Christophe, but also a magnificent representation of *Le Marron Inconnu* (The Unknown Maroon). Political campaigning in Jamaica provides a treasury of cultural ambivalence. In 1973, for example, Michael Manley campaigned successfully on a combination of radical rhetoric, Negritude, and the Judaeo-Christian connotation of his nickname "Joshua," sensibly playing down the reflected charisma which came from being the son of one of the official heroes of Jamaica.

"What independence they give we ma'am? You think we got independence?" asked one old lady of the lady researcher, Sharon Chacko. Perhaps, however, she was merely echoing a similar skepticism that might have been heard in the old days about the nominal freedom celebrated on August 1.

33. Karl Marx, *Economic and Political MSS* (1844). This version is quoted in John Fowles, *The French Lieutenant's* Woman (London, Cape, 1970), p. 84.

Appendix A
1. Craton and Walvin, *A Jamaican Plantation: The History of Worthy Park, 1670-1970* (London, W. H. Allen, and Toronto, University of Toronto Press, 1970), pp. vii-xi.

2. Act of 23 George III.

3. Act of 32 George III, cap. 23, xxxv.

4. Jamaica Archives, Register of Returns of Slaves, 1817-1832.

5. *A Jamaican Plantation*, pp. 187, 196. In 1815 Russell and Derry Pens were also acquired, and at least some of their slaves may have been incorporated into the Worthy Park population, which rose from 514 in 1814 to 527 in 1816, at a time when few plantations were even maintaining their numbers by natural increase.

Appendix C
1. From Jamaica, House of Assembly, "Report of the Assembly on the Slave Issues," enclosed in Lt. Gov. Clarke's No. 92 of November 20, 1788, P.R.O., C.O. 137/88.

Appendix D
1. Jamaica Archives, 4/23; Worthy Park Plantation Book, vol. 5, 1821-1824.